PIGS AND HUMANS
10,000 YEARS OF INTERACTION

Pigs and Humans

10,000 Years of Interaction

Edited by

UMBERTO ALBARELLA, KEITH DOBNEY,
ANTON ERVYNCK & PETER ROWLEY-CONWY

Bioarchaeology of Pig Domestication Research Project,
Department of Archaeology,
University of Durham

OXFORD
UNIVERSITY PRESS

OXFORD
UNIVERSITY PRESS

Great Clarendon Street, Oxford OX2 6DP

Oxford University Press is a department of the University of Oxford.
It furthers the University's objective of excellence in research, scholarship,
and education by publishing worldwide in

Oxford New York

Auckland Cape Town Dar es Salaam Hong Kong Karachi
Kuala Lumpur Madrid Melbourne Mexico City Nairobi
New Delhi Shanghai Taipei Toronto

With offices in

Argentina Austria Brazil Chile Czech Republic France Greece
Guatemala Hungary Italy Japan Poland Portugal Singapore
South Korea Switzerland Thailand Turkey Ukraine Vietnam

Oxford is a registered trade mark of Oxford University Press
in the UK and in certain other countries

Published in the United States
by Oxford University Press Inc., New York

British Library Cataloguing in Publication Data

Data available

Library of Congress Cataloging in Publication Data

Data available

Typeset by SPI Publisher Services, Pondicherry, India
Printed in Great Britain
on acid-free paper by
Biddles Ltd., King's Lynn, Norfolk

ISBN 978–0–19–920704–6

1 3 5 7 9 10 8 6 4 2

Foreword

The long 10,000 year relationship between humans and pigs has been both multifaceted and complex. From pets to pariahs, pigs have served as sources of sustenance and status, as well as symbols of both the sacred and the profane. There is no other domestic animal that has intersected with so many different aspects of human existence. There is no other animal domesticate that is as interesting or as challenging to the archaeo- or ethno-zoologist.

From the very beginning, pigs have been a contrarian domesticate, the only omnivore among the major livestock species. The pathway to pig domestication was likely quite different than for other domesticates. Pig domestication was probably preceded by a getting-to-know-you period in which bolder, less wary boars were drawn to human settlements to scavenge on human refuse. Tracking the progression from this initial commensal relationship into a domestic partnership between humans and pigs is one the more challenging and rewarding areas of archaeozoological inquiry. Not only does it necessitate the development of fine tuned markers capable of teasing out the subtle shifts in the human/pig dynamic, it also requires a rethinking of the very meaning of 'domestication' as a general concept.

The geographic range of wild boar is broader than that of the progenitors of other livestock species (from western Europe to the Far East) and, thus, presents a special challenge to those interested in identifying the site of initial pig domestication. In fact, it now seems that the search for domestic origins in pigs can begin almost anywhere within this wide geographic zone, with genetic data pointing to multiple different centres of origin in which different people navigated a broad range of different relationships with resident pig populations.

The diverse range of possible swine management regimes from free-range (in the broadest sense) to sty-bound carries a number of different economic, social, and ecological implications which add further challenges, and opportunities, to the study of the history of human–pig interactions. The undiscriminating and highly adaptable diet of pigs has made them not only a beach-head species for humans colonizing new territories, but also chief sanitation officers for human communities throughout the ages. The use of pigs in human adaptation to new and built environments is, then, another exciting avenue for study.

The dietary habits of pigs have also contributed to their being labelled as unclean, even taboo animals by many peoples around the world. In fact, perhaps the greatest pig paradox of all is why both Jews and Muslims, living in one of the earliest centres of pig domestication, developed strict dietary prohibitions against them. A related question is why, despite their high birth rates and impressive *per capita* yield of high-fat-content meat, pigs never assumed a major role in any ancient Near Eastern subsistence economies. This is especially true in later urban societies where pigs seem to have resided outside the larger economy as the special province of the urban poor. It is an area of research that continues to draw researchers from diverse fields of archaeology, anthropology, psychology, economics, history, and religious studies.

In other global contexts, however, pigs have been a highly prized prestige item—an important element in cementing clan and community in New Guinea society, a sacrificial animal of Hawaiian chiefs, a primary source of wealth and economic prestige in Europe. And here too we see a growing number of researchers focusing on human–pig interactions as a way of gaining new insight into the history of human interaction with their environment and each other.

This book brings together leading researchers exploring the multifaceted pig paradox from a number of disciplines and cutting edge methodological approaches. It contains the latest word on *Sus* evolution—from both morphological and molecular perspectives. It presents new considerations of the initial pig domestication and a wide array of studies examining different management regimes developed around the world (both past and present). It presents new considerations of the role of pigs in ritual and art. This volume, then, provides the reader with a sampling of the many exciting avenues of investigation open to those interested in exploring the long history of human interaction with this fascinating animal. In so doing it highlights some of the most exciting current work in the study of human/animal interactions and points the way to productive and rewarding new research in the future.

Melinda A. Zeder

Archaeobiology Program
National Museum of Natural History
Smithsonian Institution
Washington, DC

Acknowledgements

This book was conceived during research carried out as part of the University of Durham's 'Bioarchaeology of Pig Domestication' project, which in turn was generously supported by fellowship and research grants from the Wellcome Trust and the Arts and Humanities Research Council. We also owe a large debt of gratitude to our many collaborating colleagues around the world who have provided so much invaluable data, insight and expertise into this complex but intriguing subject. We especially thank the University of Durham for its support during the project itself, Jeff Veitch for help with improving the quality of some of the illustrations and photographs, and colleagues at the Flemish Heritage Institute (especially An Lentacker) for valuable input into the editing of this volume. This book would not have been possible without the various contributions and enthusiasm of all the participants of the Walworth Castle workshop, and to them we also offer our heartfelt thanks. Finally, we would like to thank all the staff of the Walworth Castle hotel for providing such relaxing surroundings for the workshop, and to the villagers of Walworth itself who made us so welcome and who helped us celebrate this unique domestic animal.

More specific thanks and acknowledgements for selected chapters are as follows:

Chapter 1: Special thanks to K. Fletcher and Donna Baylis of Wildside Photography <*http://www.wildsidephotography.ca*> for allowing us to use their copyrighted image (no. 22133) of a pair of Sulawesi warty pigs (*Sus celebensis*) photographed at a saltlick in lowland rainforest, Suaka Margasatwa Nantu nature reserve, Sulawesi.

Chapter 2: This study was supported by a Wellcome Trust Bioarchaeology Research Fellowship (Keith Dobney: grant reference 060888) a research grant from the Arts and Humanities Research Board (Peter Rowley-Conwy and Umberto Albarella: award reference no. B/RG/AN1759/APN10977) a Smithsonian Institution Short-term Visitors award (Keith Dobney) and a Leverhulme Trust grant (Greger Larson). We are especially grateful to the Smithsonian Museum of Natural History and to the many other institutions and individuals who provided access to material and collections, and for allowing us to sample them for DNA analysis. These include: Alain Ducos, Productions Animales—UMR INRA Cytogénétique, École Nationale Vétérinaire de Toulouse, France; Chris Gerrard, Department of Archaeology,

University of Durham, UK; Elizabeth Maclean, Ossabaw Hog Farm North
Carolina, USA; Marco Masseti, University of Florence, Italy; Paolo Agnelli,
Museum of Natural History, University of Florence, Italy; Field Museum,
University of Chicago, IL, USA (B. Stanley); Filippo Manconi, Tempio Pau-
sania, Italy; Institute for Forest Ecology and Forest Inventory, Eberswalde,
Germany (Goretzki and Manfred Ahrens); Institute of Portuguese Archae-
ology, Lisbon, Portugal (Simon Davis); Jonathan Lee, Northern Australia
Quarantine Strategy, Australia; Laboratoire d'Anatomie Comparée, Paris,
France (Jean-Denis Vigne); Natural History Museum Berlin, Germany
(Peter Giere); Oliver Brown, Department of Archaeology, University of Syd-
ney, Australia; Pig Biodiversity Consortium <*http://www.projects.roslin.ac.uk/
pigbiodiv/*>; Ross Fraser, President of the Rare Breeds Conservation Society of
New Zealand, 58 Wills Rd, West Plains, RD4, Invercargill 9521, New Zealand;
Roslin Institute, Edinburgh, Scotland; South Australia Museum, North Ter-
race, Adelaide, SA5000, Australia (Terry Bertozzi and Steve Donnellan); Sue
Bulmer, Bulmer & Associates, 10 Tansley Ave, Epsom, Auckland, New Zealand; Smithsonian Museum of Natural History, Washington, DC, USA; University of Hildesheim, Germany (Horst Kierdorf); Oxford University Museum
of Natural History, UK (Malgosia Nowak-Kemp); Professor Richard Redding,
University of Michigan Museum of Anthropology, USA; and finally the
Zoological Institute in Yerevan, Armenia (Ninna Manaserian).

Chapter 4: This study was supported by a Wellcome Trust Bioarchaeology
Research Fellowship (Keith Dobney: grant reference 060888), a research
grant from the Arts and Humanities Research Board (Peter Rowley-Conwy
and Umberto Albarella: award reference no. B/RG/AN1759/APN10977),
and by the Flemish Heritage Institute, Belgium. Many colleagues and institutions provided access to material and information regarding the archaeological and recent samples. Within the context of the paper, especially
mentioned are Kim Aaris-Sørensen and Knud Rosenlund, Zoological Museum, Copenhagen, Denmark; Mikiko Abe, Department of Anatomy, Graduate School of Medicine, Osaka City University, Osaka, Japan; Tomoko
Anezaki, Gunma Museum of Natural History, Gunma, Japan, Adrian Bala-
sescu, Anne Tresset, and Jean-Denis Vigne, Musée d'Histoire Naturelle, Paris,
France; Gennady Baryshnikov, Institute of Zoology, St Petersburg, Russia;
Janet Bell, Salisbury and South Wiltshire Museum, UK; Norbert Benecke,
Deutsches Archäologisches Institut, Berlin, Germany; Hans-Jürgen Döhle,
Landesmuseum für Vorgeschichte, Halle, Germany; Lena Drenzel, Historical
Museum, Stockholm, Sweden; Peter Giere, Natural History Museum Berlin,
Germany; Susanne Hanik, Brandenburgisches Landesamt für Denkmalpflege
und Archäologisches Landesmuseum, Wünsdorf, Germany; Hitomi Hongo,

Graduate University for Advanced Studies, Japan; Yuan Jing, Institute of Archaeology, Chinese Academy of Social Sciences, Beijing, China; Horst Kierdorf, University of Hildesheim, Germany; Roel Lauwerier, Rijksdienst voor het Oudheidkundig Bodemonderzoek, Amersfoort, Netherlands; Akira Matsui and Masakatsu Fujita, Nara Archaeological Research Center, Japan; Augusta McMahon, University of Cambridge, UK; Richard Meadow and Viva Fisher, Peabody Museum, Harvard University, Cambridge, MA, USA; Nanna Noe-Nygaard, University of Copenhagen, Denmark; Marc Nussbaumer, Naturhistorisches Museum Burgergemeinde Bern, Switzerland; Inger Österholm, Gotland University College, Sweden; Jörg Schibler, University of Basel, Switzerland; Bill Stanley and Bill Simpson, Field Museum of Natural History, Chicago, USA; Jan Storå, University of Stockholm, Sweden; Jacqueline Studer, Natural History Museum Geneva, Switzerland; Kyomi Yamazaki, Iwaki Junior College, Japan; Melinda Zeder, Smithsonian Institution, Washington, DC, USA; Field Museum of Natural History, Chicago, USA; Smithsonian Institution, Washington, DC, USA; Museum of Comparative Zoology, Harvard University, Cambridge, MA, USA; Institute of Zoology, St Petersburg, Russia; Natural History Museums of Paris, France and Geneva and Bern, Switzerland, and Berlin, Germany; University of Hildesheim, Germany; University of Istanbul, Turkey; Institute of Archaeology, Beijing, China.

From Japan, the most important suppliers of study material were Atsuhiro Isakoda and the Iwaki City Board of Education; Hajime Komiya and the Chiba Museum; Masato Nishino and the Chiba Prefecture Archaeological Center, the Archaeological Institute of Kashihara, Nara Prefecture; Fukuoka Prefecture Board of Education; Kanagawa Archaeological Center; Miyagi Prefecture Board of Education; Nagasaki Prefecture Board of Education; Nara Cultural Institute, Nabunken; Okayama Prefecture Board of Education; Osaka Prefecture Archaeological Center; Tamagawa Cultural Research Center; Wakasa Museum of History and Folklore, Obama.

Chapter 5: Many people over the years have helped the author in various ways, in particular by providing unpublished data, especially Liora Kolska Horwitz, Simon Davis, Sebastian Payne, Emmanuelle Vila, Allan S. Gilbert, and Melinda Zeder. Arlene Rosen kindly supplied the typescript of her forthcoming publication on environmental change in the Middle East.

Chapter 6: The following individuals and institutions have generously made the archaeological pig remains available for our study (individual names in alphabetical order): Katsuhiko Amitani, Tsuruga Junior College; Tetsuya Inui; Teruhisa Kenmotsu, Yokosuka Archaeological Circle; Hajime Komiya, Chiba Prefecture Archaeological Research Center; Kazuhiko Kobayashi, Korekawa Archaeological Museum; Akira Matsui, Nabunken–Nara

Cultural Property Research Center; Hiroshi Miyazaki, Tokyo Metropolitan Government; Manzo Maeda; Toyohiro Nishimoto, National Museum of Japanese History; Hiroto Takamiya, Faculty of Cultural Studies, Sapporo University; Hajime Tanida, Graduate School of Biosphere Science, Hiroshima University; Hajime Taru, Kanagawa Prefectural Museum of Natural History; Wakasa History and Folklore Museum, Fukui Prefecture; Chiba Prefecture Archaeological Research Center; Chiba Municipal Board of Education; Mobara Municipal Board of Education; Narita Municipal Board of Education; Kanagawa Archaeology Fundation; So-Nan Cultural Research Center; Kanagawa Archaeological Foundation, Tamagawa Cultural Institute; Fukushima Archaeological Research Center; Hashikami Town Research Center; Shichinohe Town Board of Education; Ethnology and Archaeology Research Department, Keio University; Iwate Prefectural Museum; Rikuzen-Takada City Museum; Tohoku Historical Museum; Iwaki City Board of Education; Iwaki Educational and Cultural Foundation; Ohshima Town Board of Education; Miyake Village Board of Education; Niijima-Mura Museum; Hachijo Town Board of Education; Yokosuka City Museum; Kushiro City Archaeological Research Center; Furano City Board of Education; Hokkaido Archaeological Research Center; Chitose City Board of Education; Tomakomai City Archaeological Research Center; Date City Board of Education; Abuta Town Board of Education; Assabu Town Board of Education; Otobe Town Board of Education; Hakodate City Board of Education; Historical Museum of Hokkaido. This study was partly supported by Grants-in-Aid for Scientific Research (B) (1) 15405017 (Primary Investigator H. Hongo) and (C) (2) 11610421 (Primary Investigator K. Yamazaki) from the Japan Society for the Promotion of Science.

Chapter 7: Kim Aaris-Sørensen, Zoological Museum, Copenhagen, Denmark; Nanna Noe-Nygaard, Institute of Historical Geology and Palaeontology, University of Copenhagen, Denmark; Lena Drenzel, Statens Historiska Museum, Stockholm, Sweden; Inger Österholm and Göran Burenhult, Gotland University College, Visby, Sweden; and Leif Jonsson, University of Göteborg, Sweden are thanked for access to the material in their care, and for many stimulating discussions.

Chapter 8: Appreciation and gratitude go to the following friends and colleagues for their suggestions and assistance: Oliver Brown, Department of Archaeology, University of Sydney, Australia; Miguel A. Carretero, Centro de Investigação em Biodiversidade e Recursos Genéticos (CIBIO) Vairão, Porto, Portugal; Claudio Ciofi, Department of Ecology and Evolutionary Biology, Yale University, New Haven, CT, USA; Caroline Grigson, Institute of Archaeology, University College London, UK; Sebastian Payne, English

Heritage, London, UK; Joris Peters, Institut für Paläeoanatomie und Geschichte der Tiermedizin Ludwig-Maximillian University, Munich, Germany; Peter Rowley-Conwy, Department of Archaeology, University of Durham, UK; Adamantios Sampson, University of the Aegean, Rhodes, Greece; Katerina Trantalidou, Ephorate of Paleoanthropology and Speleology, Athens, Greece. Special thanks are due to Colin P. Groves, School of Archaeology and Anthropology, Australian National University, Canberra, Australia, for his help in the taxonomic identification of the wild pigs of Komodo.

Chapter 9: The study was supported by the Flemish Heritage Institute, Belgium, and by a Wellcome Trust Bioarchaeology Research Fellowship (Keith Dobney: grant reference 060888). Mark Van Strydonck and Mathieu Boudin of the Royal Institute for Cultural Heritage, Brussels, Belgium are acknowledged for previous work on stable isotopes from Flemish archaeological sites.

Chapter 10: Elwira Szuma and her colleagues at the Mammal Research Institute in Bialowieza, Poland, Per-Ola Andersson of the wild game butchery in Sjunkaröd, Sweden, and Søren Andersen, together with the staff at the Conservation Department, Mosegård Museum, Denmark, deserve thanks for making recent and archaeological samples accessible for study. Christina Lindh and colleagues at the Department of Oral Radiology, Center for Oral Health Sciences, Malmö University, Sweden, are acknowledged for facilitated access to equipment and assistance. Funding to examine the Ringkloster mandibles was obtained through a grant from the European Commission's programme 'Transnational Access to Major Research Infrastructures' to COBICE (Copenhagen Biosystematics Center), Denmark.

Chapter 11: T. Dayan and I. Hershkovitz are thanked for their invaluable guidance, D. Wool for statistical advice, T. Shariv of the Tel Aviv University Zoological Museum and R. Rabinovitch of the Department of Evolution, Systematics, and Ecology, the Hebrew University of Jerusalem, Israel, for their help with the reference collections under their care, and the reviewers for their useful comments. This research was supported by the Israeli Antiquities Authority. The author is a Rami Levin fellow.

Chapter 12: Acknowledgements go to Prof. Yoram Yom-Tov and Ms Tzila Shariv of the Tel Aviv University Zoological Museum who facilitated access to the osteological collection of Tel Aviv University, Israel, and to the late Prof. Eitan Tchernov who facilitated access to the Comparative Mammalian Collection of the Hebrew University of Jerusalem, Israel.

Chapter 13: The work presented in this paper was made possible by the financial support of the UK Arts and Humanities Research Board (now 'Council') (Umberto Albarella and Peter Rowley-Conwy: award ref. B/RG/AN1759/APN10977) and the Wellcome Trust Bioarchaeology Fellowship (Keith Dobney: award ref. 060888). The staff of the Multi-Imaging Centre in Cambridge where the scanning electron microscopy work was undertaken are also acknowledged for their help. Thanks also go to all colleagues who allowed us access to the archaeological material discussed in this paper.

Chapter 15: This chapter presents research results of the Belgian Programme on Interuniversity Poles of Attraction (IUAP 05/09) initiated by the Belgian Federal Science Policy Office. The text also presents the results of the Concerted Action of the Flemish Government (GOA 02/2) and the Fund for Scientific Research—Flanders (Belgium) (FWO, G.0245.02). Scientific responsibility is assumed by its authors. Anton Ervynck, Flemish Heritage Institute, is acknowledged for his help during the analysis of the LEH; Keith Dobney, University of Durham, kindly made available the data to calculate the index of different sites. The English was corrected by Sheila Hamilton-Dyer, Southampton, UK.

Chapter 16: The work presented in this chapter was made possible by the financial support of the UK Arts and Humanities Research Board (Umberto Albarella and Peter Rowley-Conwy: award ref. B/RG/AN1759/APN10977) and by the kindness of the pig herders who made their time available for the interviews. Remy Ricci in particular provided us with a great range of information about Corsican pig breeding and introduced us to other breeders. Many thanks also go to Giancarlo Spada, Antonello Sechi, and François de Lanfranchi for their invaluable help in contacting pig breeders, and Marina Ciaraldi for help in formulating the questionnaire. Simon Davis, Paul Halstead, and Marina Ciaraldi also kindly provided valuable comments on a first draft.

Chapter 18: The data on pigs analysed were published previously (Sillitoe P. 2003. *Managing Animals in New Guinea: Preying the Game in the Highlands.* London: Routledge). The publishers are acknowledged for permission to use them again here. Thanks go to every household in the Was valley that has cooperated in surveys at intervals enquiring into the composition of their pig herds. In particular, Wenja Neleb and Maenget Saendaep are acknowledged for their assistance throughout this work. The valuable advice and criticism of Robin Hide is also highly appreciated.

Chapter 19: Jan-Waalke Meyer is acknowledged for comments and encouragements, and Lise Willcox for the translation of this chapter.

Chapter 20: The following institutions are acknowledged for offering free copyright permission for the reproduction of illustrations and, where appropriate, for the supply of images: Bodleian Library, University of Oxford, UK (Figs 20.1 and 20.2); Historische Museum, Frankfurt am Main, Germany (Fig. 20.3); Bishop Tunstall's Chapel, Durham Castle, University of Durham, UK (Fig. 20.6). Copyright permission was granted for reproduction, and, where appropriate, images were supplied by the Rijksmuseum, Amsterdam, Netherlands (Fig. 20.4) and the Rothschild Collection, National Trust, UK (Fig. 20.5). Thanks also go to Anwen Caffell who willingly proofread this chapter.

Contents

List of Figures

List of Tables

Authors

Umberto Albarella Department of Archaeology, University of Sheffield, Northgate House, West Street, Sheffield S1 4ET, UK <*u.albarella@sheffield.ac.uk*>

Leif Andersson Department of Medical Biochemistry and Microbiology, Uppsala University, Uppsala Biomedical Center, Box 597, SE-751 24 Uppsala, Sweden <*leif.andersson@imbim.uu.se*>

Tomoko Anezaki Gunma Museum of Natural History, 1674–1 Kamikuroiwa, Tomioka City, Gunma Prefecture 370-2345, Japan <*anezaki@gmnh.pref.gunma.jp*>

Richard Carter Centre for Continuing Education, Room EH133, Sussex Institute, University of Sussex, Falmer, Brighton, BN1 9QQ, UK <*r.j.carter@ sussex.ac.uk*>

Anne-Sophie Dalix HISOMA, Maison de l'Orient et de la Méditerranée, 7 rue Raulin, F-69007 Lyon, France <*Anne-Sophie.Dalix@mom.fr*>

Goggy Davidowitz Department of Ecology and Evolutionary Biology, University of Arizona, Tucson, Arizona 85721, USA <*goggy@email.arizona.edu*>

Bea De Cupere IUAP 05/09, Royal Belgian Institute of Natural Sciences, Department of Anthropology and Prehistory, Vautierstraat 29, B-1000 Brussels, Belgium <*Bea.DeCupere@naturalsciences.be*>

Keith Dobney Department of Archaeology, University of Durham, South Road, Durham DH1 3LE, UK <*k.m.dobney@durham.ac.uk*>

Anton Ervynck Flemish Heritage Institute, Koning Albert II-laan 19, box 5, B-1210 Brussels, Belgium <*Anton.Ervynck@pandora.be*>

Caroline Grigson University College London, Institute of Archaeology, 31 Gordon Square, London WC1H 0PY, UK <*CGrigson@compuserve.com*>

Colin Groves School of Archaeology and Anthropology, Building 14, Australian National University, Canberra, ACT 0200, Australia <*colin.groves@anu.edu.au*>

Annat Haber Department of Zoology, Tel-Aviv University, Tel-Aviv 69978, Israel <*h_annat@yahoo.com*>

Hitomi Hongo   School of Advanced Science, Graduate University of Advanced Studies, Shonan Village, Hayama, Kanagawa 240–0193, Japan <*hongou_hitomi@soken.ac.jp*>

Liora Kolska Horwitz   Department of Evolution, Systematics and Ecology, The Hebrew University, Jerusalem 91904, Israel <*lix100@excite.com*>

Horst Kierdorf   Department of Biology, University of Hildesheim, Marienburger Platz 22, D-31141 Hildesheim, Germany <*kierdorf@rz.uni-hildesheim.de*>

Uwe Kierdorf   Institute of General and Systematic Zoology, University of Giessen, Heinrich-Buff-Ring 26–32, D-35392 Giessen, Germany <*kierdorf@lindlar.de*>

Greger Larson   Henry Wellcome Ancient Biomolecules Centre, University of Oxford, Department of Zoology, South Parks Road OX1 3PS, UK <*greger.larson @zoology.oxford.ac.uk*>

An Lentacker   Flemish Heritage Institute, Koning Albert II-laan 19, box 5, B-1210 Brussels, Belgium <*an.lentacker@ename974.org*>

Ola Magnell   Historical Osteology, Department of Archaeology and Ancient History, Lund University, Sandgatan 1, 223 50 Lund, Sweden <*ola.magnell@spray.se*>

Ingrid Mainland   Department of Archaeological Sciences, University of Bradford, West Yorkshire, BD7 1DP, UK <*i.l.mainland@ bradford.ac.uk*>

Filippo Manconi   Via Daniele Manin 25, Tempio Pausania (SS), Italy <*fmanconi@tiscalinet.it*>

Marco Masseti   Dipartimento di Biologia Animale e Genetica 'Leo Pardi', Laboratori di Antropologia, Università di Firenze, Via del Proconsolo 12,50122 Firenze, Italy <*marco.masseti@unifi.it*>

Gundula Müldner   Department of Archaeology, University of Reading, Whiteknights, PO Box 227, Reading RG6 6AB, UK <*g.h.mueldner@reading.ac.uk*>

Sarah Phillips   Department of Archaeology, University of Durham, South Road, Durham DH1 3LE, UK <*sjfsphillips@googlemail.com*>

Daniel Pillonel   Laboratoire de Dendrochronologie, Service et Musée Cantonal d'Archéologie, Laténium, 2016 Hauterive, Switzerland <*Daniel.Pillonel@ne.ch*>

Mike Richards Department of Human Evolution, Max Planck Institute for Evolutionary Anthropology, Deutscher Platz 6, D-04103 Leipzig, Germany <*Richards@eva.mpg.de*> and Department of Archaeology, University of Durham, South Road, Durham DH1 3LE, UK <*michael.richards@durham.ac.uk*>

Peter Rowley-Conwy Department of Archaeology, University of Durham, South Road, Durham DH1 3LE, UK <*p.a.rowley-conwy@durham.ac.uk*>

Paul Sillitoe Department of Anthropology, University of Durham, 43 Old Elvet Road, Durham DH1 3HN, UK <*paul.sillitoe@durham.ac.uk*>

Jacqueline Studer Muséum d'Histoire naturelle, CP 6434, 1211 Genève 6, Switzerland <*jacqueline.studer@mhn.ville-ge.ch*>

Hiroki Sugawara Historical Museum of Jomon Village Okumatsushima, 81-18 Sato, Miyato, Higashimatsushima City, Miyagi Prefecture 981–0412, Japan <*h-sugawara@city.higashimatsushima.miyagi.jp*>

Osamu Takahashi Chitose Salmon Aquarium/ Museum, 312, 2-chome, Hanazono, Chitose City, Hokkaido 066–0028, Japan <*sake@ city.chitose.hokkaido.jp*>

Sofie Vanpoucke Katholieke Universiteit Leuven, Department of Archaeology, Erasmushuis, Blijde-Inkomststraat 21, B-3000 Leuven, Belgium <*Sofie.VanPoucke@naturalsciences.be*>

Jean-Denis Vigne CNRS—Muséum national d'Histoire naturelle, Dept Ecology and Biodiversity Management, USM 303, Case postale N° 56 (Bâtiment d'Anatomie comparée), 55 rue Buffon, F-75231 Paris cedex 05, France <*vigne@mnhn.fr*>

Emmanuelle Vila Archéorient, Maison de l'Orient et de la Méditerranée, 7 rue Raulin, F-69007 Lyon, France <*emmanuelle.vila@mom.fr*>

Marc Waelkens Katholieke Universiteit Leuven, Department of Archaeology, Erasmushuis, Blijde-Inkomststraat 21, B-3000 Leuven, Belgium <*Marc.Waelkens@arts.kuleuven.ac.be*>

Tom Wilkie Department of Archaeological Sciences, University of Bradford, West Yorkshire, BD7 1DP, UK <*tomwilkie@hotmail.com*>

Kyomi Yamazaki Iwaki Junior College, 37 Suganezawa, Kamata, Taira, Iwaki-City, Fukushima 970–8568, Japan<*yamazaki@tonichi-kokusai-u.ac.jp*>

Introduction

Umberto Albarella, Keith Dobney,
Anton Ervynck & Peter Rowley-Conwy

In terms of human–animal relationships, pigs are perhaps one of the most iconic but also paradoxical domestic animals. On the one hand, they are praised for their fecundity, their intelligence, and their ability to eat almost anything, but on the other hand, they are unfairly derided for their apparent slovenliness, unclean ways, and gluttonous behaviour. In complete contrast, their ancestor (the wild boar) is perceived as a noble beast of the forest whose courage and ferocity has been famed and feared throughout human history.

The relationship of wild boar and pig with humans has been a long and varied one. Archaeological evidence clearly shows that wild boar were important prey animals for early hunter-gatherers across wide areas of Eurasia for millennia. During the early Holocene, however, this simple predator–prey relation evolved into something much more complex as wild boar, along with several other mammal species, became key players in one of the most dramatic episodes in human history: the shift from hunting and gathering to agriculture, involving the domestication of plants and animals. From that moment, wild boar turned into pigs and became much more than mere components of human subsistence strategies. They were key entities in the complex cultural development of some human societies around the world and played an important role in the history of human dispersal. Interestingly, the consumption of pork also became (and still remains) perhaps the most celebrated, and widespread, case of dietary proscription.

In terms of their relationships with humans, pigs are victims of their own success. Even more than wolves, they are highly adaptable and generalized omnivores, which means that they have a range of possible relationships with humans that is perhaps wider and more complex than for most other animal species. In fact, the biology and behaviour of pigs present a number of special challenges to their study, in addition to offering opportunities to further understand aspects of human history.

The concept of this book grew out of an international workshop, entitled 'Pigs and Humans', held over the weekend of 26–28 September 2003, at Walworth Castle, County Durham, UK. It explored various research themes including evolution and taxonomy; domestication and husbandry; new methodologies; ethnography; and ritual and art. The various invited contributions to this book explore this somewhat diverse spectrum in more detail, each grounded firmly within the disciplines of zoology, anthropology, and archaeology. All present new evidence and/or data as a series of specific case studies or syntheses from around the world, and all attempt to enhance our current understanding of many of the issues regarding humans' complex and ever-changing relationship with wild boar and domestic pigs.

THE HISTORY OF PIGS AND HUMANS

A major focus of the research presented here is the study of the actual fossil remains of *Sus* (used here as a general term for both wild boar and domestic pig) and what they reveal about both the animals and humans in the past. Terms such as archaeozoology and zooarchaeology are present throughout the book, and although it might at first appear to be inconsistent usage of terminology, these separate terms very deliberately reflect the range of emphasis, from zoological (archaeozoology being the biological study of animal remains from archaeological sites) to anthropological (zooarchaeology being the study of past human behaviour through excavated animal remains). Within these subdisciplines, current research themes are highlighted and new approaches in addressing and understanding them are explored.

Few reviews of the history of pig domestication and husbandry exist, and to our knowledge the only wide-ranging zooarchaeological work available is represented by the unpublished dissertation of the late Berrin Kuşatman (1991). The only multi-authored book that is in any way comparable to the one presented here is *Pigs for the Ancestors*, edited by Sarah Nelson (1998*a*), which, like this book, presents the study of pig history in a multidisciplinary setting. A plethora of specific archaeological and historical works of course also exist (e.g. Flannery 1983; Epstein & Bichard 1984; Rowley-Conwy 1999*b*; Smith 2000; Wiseman 2000; Ervynck *et al.* 2001; Albarella & Serjeantson 2002; Magnell 2004) but more general studies which try to detect broad trends through the integration of different sources of evidence are harder to come by. The ethnographic record is richer, but biased towards New Guinea (Rappaport 1968; Rubel & Rosman 1978; Sillitoe this volume) and only recently the history of pigs has been popularized in a scientifically sound way (Watson 2005).

A fundamental problem is differentiating between the fossil remains of the various wild *Sus* species that exist throughout the world, a particular issue in Island South East Asia where a number of separate species are sympatric. Superimposed upon this, is the complication of establishing whether domestic pigs or wild boar (or both) are present on archaeological sites. The picture is often particularly diffuse because in most of the world domestic pigs live in areas also populated by wild boar, and inevitably interbreeding occurs, bringing 'wild' blood into domestic populations. In addition, domestic pigs are often kept in free-range conditions and can escape to breed with local wild boar. Where the latter were absent, escaped domestic pigs sometimes created entirely feral populations.

Perhaps the most contentious and longstanding issue in the field of archaeozoology/zooarchaeology is the search for the geographic origins of domestication and an understanding of the processes involved. Until recently, perhaps a greater interest has been shown in the evolution of other domestic animals, such as caprines, bovines, and equids. There are probably two main reasons for this: one is that, until recently, there was a widespread view that pigs were domesticated later than sheep and goats (Bökönyi 1976; Clutton-Brock 1999). As a consequence, pigs were not regarded as directly relevant to the beginning of the so-called Neolithic farming revolution. The second reason is that pigs do not provide any secondary products such as milk and wool, or have additional uses such as transport or power, as do some of the other common farmyard animals. This has probably led to the view that they were of lesser importance and has created the perception that, in a human context, pigs merely existed as meat providers.

It is perhaps not surprising that the pig has been somewhat overlooked, as several issues make the study of the history of the pig–human relationship a daunting task:

- The first is related to the huge geographic scale of the phenomenon. Wild pigs were distributed over a vast area (most of Eurasia), wider than that of any other ancestor of a domestic animal (except for the wolf), and they came into contact with humans in a great variety of environmental, economic, and social contexts.

- The temporal scale is also very long and encompasses many millennia, so pigs have been hunted by humans probably as long as we have encountered them, and recent evidence suggests that pig husbandry may be as ancient as 10,000 years.

- In addition, pig history can, and probably should, be investigated by using a multidisciplinary approach, which takes into account the potential of disciplines as disparate as zoology, palaeontology, genetics, ethnography, archaeology, and history. Each of these subjects can provide an important contribution, but all will be insufficient if taken in isolation. This is precisely why researchers with different expertise and backgrounds have been invited to contribute to this volume.

The earliest studied archaeological assemblages of animal bones that included *Sus* came from Danish shell middens, Swiss lake dwellings, and Italian *terramare* settlements. Winge (in Madsen *et al.* 1900: 188) believed that prehistoric European domestic pigs were descendants of the wild boar of Europe, northern Asia, and North Africa, '*Sus scrofa ferus*'. Modern domestic pigs in South East Asia were apparently more similar to the local wild boar, which he believed might be a different species, '*Sus vittatus*'. Beyond this, however, Winge did not seek the geographical origins of pig domestication. Various other ideas were soon purported. Pira (1909: 373), working on Swedish material, argued for local domestication because the earliest domestic pigs appeared closest to local wild boar in both size and morphology. However, by now archaeologists were finding ever-earlier evidence for agriculture in the Near East, with pigs as part of the 'package'. So a growing view through the mid to late 20th century was that pigs were domesticated in the Near East and brought to Europe by immigrant farmers (e.g. Childe 1958; Flannery 1983). Dissenters, like the geographer Sauer (1952), preferred a South East Asian origin for domestic pigs, whereas others (Higgs & Jarman 1969) in the late 1960s argued the case for the existence of 'intermediate' or 'semi-domestic' pigs under extensive control; a trend towards closer relations, which for pigs could potentially occur anywhere in their vast geographic range across Eurasia, not just in the previously recognized domestication centres or 'hearths' (e.g. Jarman 1976; Zvelebil 1995).

However, the dominant view—held by most researchers until very recently—still argued for a limited geographical origin for pig domestication in the Near and (probably) Far East. In Japan, one of the longest-running debates within archaeology is whether *Sus* was merely hunted, semi-managed, or domesticated by Middle and Late Jomon hunter-gatherers (see Hongo *et al.* this volume). New techniques and approaches (e.g. statistical, biomolecular, palaeopathological), many of which are described in this volume, are now helping us to take major interpretative leaps forward in our understanding of many of these questions. For example, DNA studies have now all but refuted the central or twin 'hearth' theory of pig domestication (see Larson *et al.* 2005 and this volume).

Archaeozoological and ethnographic studies of pigs have also helped us refine the somewhat traditional (and often very ethnocentric) views of the processes involved in the early domestication of certain species. These often simplistic ideas of a largely human-driven process, beginning with hunted wild animals and ending in fully managed domestic ones, are now being challenged and replaced by a more evolutionarily-based approach. These paint a more complex (and realistic) picture of the possible range of relationships that existed (and indeed still exist) between humans and animals, one that involves the animals more in the interaction and also takes into account the differences in biology and behaviour of individual taxa. In the case of wild boar, it is clear that they share more in common with wolves (for example in terms of their behaviour and omnivorous diet) than they do with domesticated artiodactyls such as the bovines and caprines. A similar scenario has, therefore, been suggested for the early interaction with humans of both wild boar and wolves, one in which humans initially played little direct role (e.g. see Ervynck *et al.* 2001).

Once domesticated, relationships between humans and pigs became ever more diverse and complex throughout the Holocene. Husbandry regimes became gradually more intensive and specialized, resulting in the sty-reared, the urban, and the exclusively indoor-reared animals so familiar to the agro-industry of today and a far cry from the noble beast of the forest of former times. To assume, however, that urban and sty pigs are a recent western phenomenon would be wrong. For example, it is clear that from the beginnings of civilization in the Near East, pigs played a significant role in provisioning some of the inhabitants of the earliest cities (e.g. Zeder 1998*b*), certainly between the 5th and 2nd millennium BC. Unusual pathological conditions associated with the teeth of pigs excavated from 2nd millennium BC deposits at Chagar Bazar, Northern Syria, strongly hint that pigs were being fed household scraps and kept within the confines of the city, perhaps in sties adjacent to houses (Albarella *et al.* 2006). Similarly, findings of naturally shed deciduous pig teeth clearly point to the fact that pigs were roaming the bustling streets of the Sumerian city of Tell Abu Salabikh, Southern Iraq, during the 3rd millennium BC (see Grigson this volume).

In the Near East, large-scale pig-keeping would have been severely constrained by both ecological and maintenance factors. The animals' high water requirements, poorly suited to semi-arid regions where shade is limited, and an inability to utilize cellulose-rich pasture plants, meant that pigs would have been best kept close to or within settlements (see Grigson this volume). Some zooarchaeological data even suggest that a possible socio-economic differentiation for swine-keeping occurred at some sites (Mudar 1982; Weiss *et al.* 1993). By the 3rd millennium BC, the importance of pigs in these urban centres declines, and caprines (sheep and goats) become the dominant domestic mammal in both the zooarchaeological and earliest textual records. Why was this? Since urban pig-keeping would confer an element of autonomy to individuals, households, or groups in terms of their own food supply, pig-keeping may have become undesirable in the eyes of the temple and urban authorities who, as we can tell from the many cuneiform tablet archives, clearly retained broad control over food production and urban provisioning (Zeder 1998*b*; Dobney *et al.* 2003).

Is it then a coincidence that the Near East is where the most famous food proscription associated with any mammal appears? Much has been written about the origins of pork avoidance for both the Jewish and Muslim faiths, and many theories as to why it occurred abound: disease vectors including nematodes, disgust for the unclean habits of the pig, ethnic identity and/or demarcation (Harris 1974; Diener & Robkin 1978; Simoons 1994). Could it be that its origins lie in the need for simple political control? Pigs may have been such an important and reliable autonomous resource in times when weaker political integration and control were the norm, that this symbol of autonomy was quickly proscribed when centralized power was established (Zeder 1991).

Although much of our understanding about many of these issues stems from studies of the archaeological remains, research into extant wild boar populations throughout Eurasia, as well as modern ethnographic studies of the so-called 'pig cultures' of the Far East and Oceania, have all been important in highlighting the range of complex relationships that could have existed between pigs and humans in the past (e.g. Rosman & Rubel 1989; Sillitoe this volume).

THE PROBLEMS OF METHODOLOGY

Methodologically, the study of pig remains from archaeological and palaeontological sites presents several challenges, such as the previously mentioned difficulties in distinguishing domestic and wild forms, the dearth of adult animals in the archaeological record, and the general fragmentary nature of the evidence. However, there are ways in which these problems can be tackled, as can be seen in a number of examples in this volume. These contributions form an alternative to the quite strong element of conservatism that has characterized attempts to assess morphological characters of archaeological pigs and wild boars in some of the earlier works. By carrying on simply using measurements of third molars (M_3) and withers heights (useful as they may be), and strictly adhering to criteria for the separation of wild boars and domestic pigs which are rarely applicable to archaeological material (such as the shape of the lachrymal bone), researchers have often missed the opportunity to fully exploit the potential of available bone assemblages.

Most reports of vertebrate faunal assemblages almost inevitably end with the statement that not enough data were available to assess pig size or shape. Equally often, pig remains are attributed to the domestic and/or wild form without a proper justification for such identifications. This approach may have been justifiable 30 years ago or so, but not today. Payne & Bull (1988) showed how it is possible to overcome the problem of assessing morphology in pigs, in spite of the great proportion of juveniles. However, almost two decades after publication, their proposed new methodology has not been taken on board as widely as one might have expected or hoped.

Better use can be made not only of newly excavated collections of pig remains but also of material already studied, when still available for analysis. In particular, improved techniques for the analysis of size and shape of the animals (biometry) (Davidowitz & Kolska Horwitz this volume); the detection of kill-off patterns (Haber this volume); and the histology, chemistry, and biochemistry (Kierdorf & Kierdorf, Andersson and Larson *et al.* this volume) of bones and teeth can substantially improve our ability to make the most of the evidence available.

The interpretation of the history of pig husbandry requires confronting the issues related to the wide geographic and temporal scales mentioned above. The question of geographic scale is important because one of the problems hampering interpretation of the evidence from particular sites can be an overly narrow geographic remit, which does not allow an appreciation of potential patterns of variation in widely different environmental and cultural contexts. However, any approach that deals with large geographic scale inevitably leads to a loss of resolution with regard to specific local issues. Local issues can help in reconstructing the large-scale narrative, while, at the same time, this provides the opportunity to understand the evidence of a particular site or specific area in its more general context. This is why this book presents geographic reviews that operate at different scales, ranging from the small regional context to an almost global coverage.

If the worldwide geographic approach allows broad patterns of variability in different pig populations and human societies to be discerned, the large temporal scale achieves the same diachronic objective. Archaeologists have often looked at the phenomenon of pig domestication as if it were restricted in time (the Mesolithic–Neolithic transition) and space (the Middle East), but this has generated an unnecessary interpretative straightjacket for our understanding of this complex phenomenon. In fact, modern and historical practices can be illuminating for our understanding of phenomena that occurred in early prehistory and therefore constant communication between specialists of different time periods is essential. Generally, if we want coherent patterns to emerge, it is important that many geographically and chronologically different data sets are compared with each other, as exemplified by all chapters presented in Part B of this book. Of course, inter-site comparison inevitably brings its own problems, but these can be addressed, especially once a sound methodology based on long-term observations and analysis has been developed.

Particularly if seen as an integrated whole, the evidence and the ideas presented in this book should provide substantial advances in our knowledge of the pig–human relationship and its history. The contributions also highlight possible avenues for further investigation. One research area of particular potential seems to be diet, since pigs are versatile in their feeding habits and therefore prone to significant variation. The detection of such variation can provide a key insight into the systems of management applied to domestic pigs, and is especially important because it affects growth, size and morphology. A combined analysis of tooth microwear (Wilkie *et al.* this volume), tooth development (Vanpoucke *et al.* and Dobney *et al.* this volume), biometry, stable isotopes, and dental pathology (Ervynck *et al.* this volume) should provide an important contribution to the clarification of many issues regarding various aspects of pig variability. In general, bone chemistry represents a potential source of information that has so far not been explored sufficiently. Brothwell (2001), for example, has recently highlighted the importance of iodine deficiency in retarding growth in animals, a factor that has been neglected in archaeological interpretations, but which now has a good chance of being tackled with the improvement of the techniques of the chemical analysis of bone.

Genetics are rapidly providing new information, but in many respects this new field is still in its infancy and many further advances can be expected. The work by Larson *et al.* (2005 and this volume) has proved that wild boars possess a clear phylogenetic structure across Eurasia. This allows inferences to be made on the geographic origins of populations of domestic pigs on the basis of their mitochondrial DNA (mtDNA) sequences. However, although powerful, this research only documents the maternal lineages and does not provide fine geographic detail (i.e. all European wild boar populations, with the exception of those living on the Italian peninsula, are characterized by just two mtDNA haplotypes). Methods and techniques for DNA extraction in modern, historical and ancient material will most probably improve in the future and this should eventually open up the possibility to target nuclear DNA, providing further, and more refined, genetic information.

The morphometric analyses reported in this volume (Rowley-Conwy & Dobney, and Davidowitz & Kolska Horwitz) only represent the tip of an iceberg of possibilities in the processing and analysis of metrical data. There are certainly endless further opportunities to look at various different types of analysis of linear measurements; some may prove inconclusive, but there is always the possibility of identifying a morphometric pattern that allows some distinction of populations. A potential future development, until recently not sufficiently explored, is the study of geometric morphotypes in pigs. Preliminary work using this technique has been explored by Bignon *et al.* (2005), Warman (2005), and Cucchi *et al.* (2006), and it is possible that this technique may in the future provide an even greater potential for distinguishing populations than any analysis of linear measurements, however sophisticated.

THE PROBLEMS OF INTERPRETATION

Whatever analyses are selected, a key question with which one will inevitably and invariably always be confronted concerns the multiplicity of relations between humans and animals. In pigs this may range from random predation to the factory farms sadly common in our modern world. Scholars have often described past relations between humans and animals simply in terms of a dichotomy between hunting and husbandry. Such an approach cannot entirely be discounted as superficial, because the archaeological evidence in particular can often provide only enough information for an extremely simplified view of the past. Indeed, taking into account that the past can at best be described with the limited tools available, it must not be forgotten that what we are able to explain is merely an approximation of that past. In addition, we must try to find ways to better understand the complex factors affecting the functioning of past societies, and not just be content with the interpretative models constructed by previous research.

That the relationship between pigs and humans cannot easily be categorized also emerges clearly from several contributions to this book (e.g. Rowley Conwy & Dobney, Masseti, Albarella *et al.*). If we start at the predation end of the spectrum of potential interactions, we can observe that even wild boar populations are affected to a variable degree by human activities, and in general by the creation of human-made environments. The size and morphology of wild pigs may vary according to hunting pressure as well as habitat modification caused by encroaching human settlements. In some cases wild boars live in very close contact with human populations, and sometimes they are even partly managed. A recent phenomenon is the trend for wild boars to settle in urban environments, as amply reported in the media (e.g. Möllers 2004 and Hongo *et al.* this volume). In this instance the fine line between wild and domestic can be well appreciated. The wild boars not only seem to mirror the urban domestic pigs of medieval times, but also the first *Sus* exploring the oldest permanent human settlements, during those early days of developing agriculture.

In modern times, we know that separate domestic and wild populations can and do coexist in the same area, and that crosses are likely to occur. Certainly such situations must also have occurred in the past. Redding & Rosenberg (1998) have suggested that management patterns observed in contemporary New Guinea may be applicable to the interpretation of the evidence from sites of potential early pig domestication in Anatolia. In some New Guinea Highland cultures (Rosman & Rubel 1989), all male pigs born in the village are castrated and reproduction relies on females straying into the forest where they mate with wild pigs (which in the case of New Guinea are most certainly 'feral').

Even where full domestication (however it is defined) was achieved, control of pig herds could have been very loose. Pigs can be largely self-sufficient in their dietary requirements, without losing their domestic status because of this. Free-range pigs, living totally independently at certain times of the year, still today represent the traditional system of pig-keeping in Sardinia and Corsica (Albarella *et al.* this volume) and may also have been commonplace in prehistoric times. Of course, similar systems of pig management are not necessarily associated with similar economic patterns in human societies. In Saxon and Early Medieval England, free-ranging pigs were taken to pasture as part of a communal management system (Wiseman 2000), whereas in Sardinia and Corsica the organization is entirely based on the enterprise of the individual swineherd, though economic relations between different breeders do occur (i.e. loaning of sires, sale and purchase of animals, etc.). It would be interesting to discover what kind of relations there might have been between free-range pig husbandry and the organization of society in prehistoric times, whether, for instance, it was more similar to medieval England or modern Corsica, or something altogether different. To address these questions an integration of different sources of archaeological and other evidence will certainly be required.

Systems of free-range husbandry could easily lead to a complete loss of control over the pigs, which would eventually revert to a fully independent life. When all ties with the swineherds are cut, pigs become feral and may even acquire some phenotypic characters more typical of wild boar, although certain morphological signatures of their original domestic status may survive (Rowley-Conwy & Dobney this volume). Individual pigs kept free-ranging are rarely lost; therefore pigs usually only become feral either as a consequence of deliberate human action (e.g. introductions to islands where they could represent a source of meat through hunting), or because of a change in economic circumstances. Economic conditions could potentially make pig-keeping not worth bothering with, either because other resources become more viable, or as a result of the abandonment of human settlements in areas suitable for pigs. Feral pigs can even become pests to be hunted, as is today the case in certain parts of Australia (Lee & Seymour 2003). This shows that the process of evolution from predation to domestication is not necessarily unidirectional. A return to hunting practices as a consequence of the 'feralization' of domestic animals has also been reported for other species, such as reindeer (Ingold 1974), and may well have occurred numerous times in the past.

Several factors such as the depletion of the environment, the reduction of forest cover (ideal pasture for pigs), and the need to increase the meat output per individual animal, can bring about the need to move from free-range systems of pig husbandry to closer forms of control (Ervynck *et al.* this volume). It may perhaps be unrealistic to think of intensive stock-breeding in prehistory, but changes in animal management certainly occurred, and an increasing separation between wild and domestic populations can be identified in the archaeological record. Work in progress shows that this phenomenon certainly occurred in parts of Europe such as Portugal, Italy, Switzerland, and Greece (Albarella *et al.* 2005; Albarella *et al.* in press *b*).

Many varieties of human–pig interaction, alternative to the two extremes of hunting and intensive stock-breeding, certainly exist. Many changes from one form of exploitation to another have been recorded in human history, but these should certainly not be seen as an inevitable progressive sequence. In some societies pig hunting may well have remained the most viable system to procure a protein supply. The great number of possible forms of interaction between pigs and humans indicates that the classification of swine as either wild or domestic can only help to describe these animals in very crude terms. Nevertheless, this does not mean that such a distinction is invalid, as most human societies interacting with pigs will have no hesitation in perceiving them as belonging to either one category or the other. Even pigs that cross regularly with wild boars are regarded as domestic by their owners, because they maintain some form of mutual interaction with human groups, even if this may only be represented by occasional feeding or shelter. Conversely, feral pigs (which biologically may be regarded as domestic) are, from an anthropological and archaeological viewpoint, wild, because they live totally independently from humans. Inevitably, some grey areas between different forms of interaction exist, but this problem is inherent to the complexity of both the natural world and human cultural diversity, and should not stop us from trying to study and understand it.

PIGS AND HUMANS: 10,000 YEARS OF INTERACTION

The history of animal domestication and husbandry goes hand in hand with the history of people in the last 10,000 years, and it is key to understanding our origins, heritage, and attitude towards the natural world. In this history, pigs have played a significant role, and zoologists, anthropologists, archaeologists, and historians should therefore afford this animal the attention proportionate to its importance, something that has not always occurred. As previously stated, there are reasons for this (partial) neglect, and the research presented in this book not only contributes to filling this gap in our knowledge, but also highlights how future research can compensate for such an oversight. Many lessons are still to be learnt, and the invited contributions to this volume constitute an important step towards this goal.

Pigs are fascinating creatures that have enriched our history, and continue to contribute to making the biological diversity of the world interesting and stimulating. Sadly, many wild pig species and populations are today threatened, traditional practices of pig husbandry are disappearing, and most domestic pigs are now kept in poor, confined conditions, deprived of their most basic biological needs. Research into the relationship between pigs and humans can hopefully contribute to raising awareness of the importance that these animals have had for our own history, and will hopefully persuade our society to treat them with the respect and compassion they surely deserve.

Part A

Evolution and Taxonomy

1

Current views on taxonomy and zoogeography of the genus *Sus*

Colin Groves

There has never been any dispute that the family Suidae, being even-toed ungulates, belong to the Artiodactyla but their position within this order has undergone some revision over the past 10 years. The standard taxonomic arrangement is that of Simpson (1945) (Table 1.1). Though Simpson's taxonomic philosophy was explicitly not based on phylogeny, his classification of the Artiodactyla has nonetheless been interpreted as reflecting the general outlines of artiodactyl evolution. This general schema is shown in Fig. 1.1, which is based largely on Thenius (1979), except that Thenius went against the general view by aligning the Tragulidae with the Cervidae.

Since the 1970s, there has been a growing consensus that taxonomy should reflect phylogeny as far as possible, and in this context the revolution in the understanding of artiodactyl evolution that took place during the 1990s (summarized by Waddell *et al.* 1999) has left the taxonomy of the Artiodactyla in some disarray, particularly because it is now clear that the Cetacea (whales and dolphins) are nested deep within it, as a sister-group to the hippos. The new phylogenetic understanding is shown in Fig. 1.2, and a new classification is proposed in Table 1.2. Some comments on this new classification follow:

- Waddell *et al.* (1999), in combining the Cetacea with the Artiodactyla, call the combined order Cetartiodactyla. Helgen (2003), however, has argued that, since the Cetacea are actually nested within the artiodactyls, rather than being their sister-group, it is appropriate to continue to use the name Artiodactyla for the order. The pigs therefore continue to be artiodactyls, not cetartiodactyls.

Table 1.1. 'Traditional' classification of the Artiodactyla (Simpson 1945).

Order Artiodactyla
        Suborder Suiformes
                Infraorder Suina
                                Family Suidae
                                Family Tayassuidae
                Infraorder Ancodonta
                                Family Hippopotamidae
        Suborder Tylopoda
                                Family Camelidae
        Suborder Ruminantia
                Infraorder Tragulina
                                Family Tragulidae
                Infraorder Pecora
                        Superfamily Cervoidea
                                Family Cervidae
                      Superfamily Giraffoidea
                                Family Giraffidae
                      Superfamily Bovoidea
                                Family Bovidae
                                Family Antilocapridae

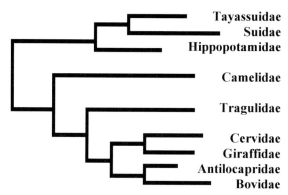

Fig. 1.1. Outline of artiodactyl phylogeny as accepted prior to the 1990s (see text)

- The new names introduced by Waddell *et al.* (1999) are given no taxonomic rank, and I have given them ranks here. But under the Whippomorpha I have left the two subdivisions, Ancodonta and Cetacea, unranked rather than introduce parvorders and the like.

- In Fig. 1.2 I have followed the phylogeny of Hassanin & Douzery (2003), but I have not given names and ranks to all their clades.

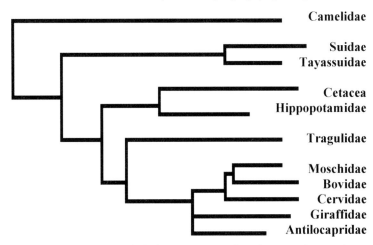

Fig. 1.2. Outline of artiodactyl phylogeny as revised in the 1990s (see text)

Table 1.2. New classification of the Artiodactyla (after Waddell *et al.* 1999).

Order Artiodactyla
  – Tylopoda
                                         Family Camelidae
  – Artiofabula
  Suborder Suina
                        Family Suidae
                        Family Tayassuidae
  Suborder Cetruminantia
    Infraorder Whippomorpha
      – Ancodonta
                        Family Hippopotamidae
      – Cetacea
    Infraorder Ruminantia
      Superfamily Traguloidea
                        Family Tragulidae
      Superfamily Cervoidea
                        Family Moschidae
                        Family Bovidae
                        Family Cervidae
                        Family Giraffidae
                        Family Antilocapridae

THE CLOSEST RELATIVES OF THE PIGS

Even given the turmoil into which the taxonomy of the Artiodactyla has been thrown, still no one disputes that the closest living relatives of the pigs are the peccaries (family Tayassuidae). The two families share the striking specializa-tion of a terminal snout disk, but differ in that the Tayassuidae lack the outer lateral toes on the hindfeet, and possess a glandular area on the dorsum. The maxillary canines of Tayassuidae point downwards and are not sexually dimorphic, whereas those of the Suidae are strongly sexually dimorphic and, in the males, point upwards. As analysed by Herring (1972), the peccary canine is a simple defensive weapon, whereas that of male pigs has been elaborated into a display organ, and the two types are associated with different jaw musculatures and correlated with different forms of social organization.

Peccaries flourished in the New World, to which today they are confined, but they survived in the Old World into the Neogene. Actually, peccaries nearly became our ancestors. *Hesperopithecus haroldcooki* Osborn, 1924 was described as a Miocene protohuman from Nebraska, USA. Three years later, more material of the species was uncovered, and it turned out to be a peccary.

The three living species were placed in two genera, *Tayassu* and *Catagonus*, by Grubb & Groves (1993), but Grubb (1993*a*), after a brief review of the literature, placed each in a different genus, as follows:

- *Catagonus wagneri*, Chacoan peccary
- *Pecari tajacu*, collared peccary
- *Tayassu pecari*, white-lipped peccary.

Note that, since the '*Tayassu*' is an Anglo-Germanic attempt to render the sound of '*tajaçu*', the scientific names of the collared and white-lipped pec-caries are essentially a reversal of each other. This is the sort of thing that gets zoological nomenclature a bad name, but given the general advantages of the Linnaean system it is just something we will have to live with.

THE OTHER PIGS

The family Suidae (Fig. 1.3) is divided into three subfamilies (Grubb 1993*a*): Babyrousinae, Phacochoerinae, and Suinae. The subfamily Babyrousinae has a single genus, *Babyrousa*, known as the babirusa, literally 'pig deer' (Indonesian *babi* = pig, *rusa* = deer). Until recently this genus was regarded as monotypic but this classification has now undergone a radical revision, as new views of what constitutes a species have gained ground.

Until the 1990s, the so-called *biological species concept* (BSC) held sway. Under this concept, if two closely related taxa overlap in distribution they are to be regarded as distinct species because they must be, by definition, repro-ductively isolated. This is the key criterion for recognizing species under the

Fig. 1.3. Members of the Suidae (after Porter 1993: Plate 1): (a) wild boar, different subspecies (*Sus scrofa*), (b) pygmy hog (*Sus salvanius*), (c) bearded pig (*Sus barbatus*), (d) Javan warty pig (*Sus verrucosus*), (e) babirusa (*Babyrousa babyrussa*), (f) giant forest hog (*Hylochoerus meinertzhageni*), (g) warthog (*Phacochoerus aethiopicus*), (h) red river hog (*Potamochoerus porcus*), and (i) bushpig (*Potamochoerus larvatus*)

BSC. So far so good, but the converse tended to be assumed as well: that everything that is not sympatric is conspecific, in other words that if they do not overlap in distribution they are not reproductively isolated. This, of course, does not follow logically. In fact, the BSC is silent when it comes to allopatry; if two taxa do not overlap in distribution, there is simply no way in which we can judge whether they are reproductively isolated or not. This is one of several reasons why many taxonomists now prefer the *phylogenetic species concept* (PSC), which defines species as having fixed heritable differences from their relatives; they are genetically isolated rather than reproductively isolated. We can go further and note that there may even be some interbreeding between different species, yet they nonetheless retain fixed differences between them. In other words, the process (the existence or not of interbreeding) is not in itself a criterion of species difference, it is the pattern (what effect any such interbreeding may have) that is important. And so it is that Meijaard & Groves (2002) proposed that the genus *Babyrousa* actually has three species:

- *Babyrousa babyrussa*, from south Sulawesi and the Sula islands and Buru
- *Babyrousa togeanensis*, from the Togean islands
- *Babyrousa celebensis*, from the northern peninsula of Sulawesi.

They are distinguished by size, skull shape; the size and shape of the males' canines; and the length, texture, density, and colour of body hair.

When we look at the distribution of *B. babyrussa*, an anomaly arises. Babirusa are not found on Peleng, the large island that intervenes between Sulawesi and the Sula islands; moreover, no mammals except bats are common to Sulawesi and Sula, and almost no mammals at all (except bats) live on Buru. It is thus on the whole very likely that babirusa were introduced to Sula and Buru. Presumably the mediaeval rajahs, the pre-Islamic rulers of the central Indonesian polities, transported them around as gifts to each other; certainly, the Balinese were impressed by tusks emerging from the cheeks, and depicted demons called Raksasas in just such a manner, as for example on the ceiling of the Hall of Justice and Floating Pavilion in Klungkung.

The subfamily Phacochoerinae also contains a single genus, *Phacochoerus*, which was traditionally awarded a single species until Grubb (1993*b*) showed clearly and convincingly that there are actually two: the common warthog (*P. africanus*), widespread from Senegal to Somalia and south to Namibian and Kwazulu-Natal, and the desert warthog (*P. aethiopicus*), now restricted to Somalia and northern Kenya but, until about 1860, found also in the Eastern Cape, South Africa.

The subfamily Suinae contains three genera: *Hylochoerus, Potamochoerus,* and *Sus.* The giant forest hog (*Hylochoerus meinertzhageni*) is known by three apparently highly distinctive subspecies (Grubb 1993*b*), possibly candidates for species status. The species (if a single species it truly is) is named for Colonel Richard Meinertzhagen (1887–1967), who 'discovered' it in 1904, while hunting big game in the Aberdares in Kenya. The distribution of the giant forest hog, unlike that of the babirusa, is explicable by normal biogeographic processes.

The second genus of the Suinae is *Potamochoerus*, which has two species, the bizarrely beautiful red river hog (*Potamochoerus porcus*), from gallery forests and rainforests in Central and West Africa, and the Bushpig (*P. larvatus*), from East and South Africa. Another biogeographical anomaly is the fact that bushpig occur on Madagascar, although no other mammal species is common to both Madagascar and the African mainland, except some bats.

THE GENUS *SUS*

The pigs which have been domesticated, and their relatives, all belong to the genus *Sus*. Groves (1981) recognized five species, but it is probably much more complicated than that. At least the species listed in Table 1.3 can be distinguished. The two 'groups' are informal only. They differ in two main ways:

- The male's lower canine is triangular in cross-section. In the *scrofa* group, the inferior surface is narrower than the posterior, but in the *verrucosus* group the inferior surface is wider. The evolutionary polarity of these two character states is unclear. Moreover, *Sus philippensis* has an exaggerated form of the 'verrucose' canine, the diameter of the inferior surface being usually more than 150% of the diameter of the posterior surface, whereas

Table 1.3. Species of domesticated pigs and their relatives.

Sus scrofa group	
Sus scrofa	Wild boar
Sus salvanius	Pygmy hog
Sus verrucosus group	
Sus verrucosus	Javan warty pig
Sus bucculentus	Indochina warty (?) pig
Sus celebensis	Sulawesi warty pig
Sus barbatus	Bearded pig
Sus ahoenobarbus	Palawan pig
Sus cebifrons	Visayan pig
Sus philippensis	Philippine pig

Sus bucculentus has a narrower inferior surface than most, and so is somewhat intermediate between the two 'groups'.

- All pigs have a long face and a deep preorbital fossa. In the *scrofa* group the fossa is shallow and poorly outlined, and the face is shorter; in the *verrucosus* group the fossa is very deep and sharply defined beneath an overhanging shelf, and the face is grossly elongated.

SUS SCROFA, OR IS IT MORE THAN ONE SPECIES?

The common Eurasian wild pig, known in sexist terminology as wild boar, is generally reckoned as consisting of a single species, *Sus scrofa*. Groves (1981) recognized 16.5 subspecies, the extra half being an anomaly from Sri Lanka. These are very briefly listed and discussed below.

1. *Sus scrofa scrofa*. This is the common wild pig of western and central Europe, from France to Belarus, and possibly Albania. There is variation in size across the range, northern individuals (north-eastern Germany) being larger in size than southern ones (Italy and northern Spain).

2. *Sus scrofa meridionalis*. This is a small-sized, thin-coated, almost maneless subspecies from Corsica, Sardinia, and Andalusia. There is no indication that the Corsico-Sardinian pig wild pigs were derived from imports that had ever been seriously domesticated (Groves 1989); most probably, they were imported by very early settlers in a wild or rudimentarily tame condition.

3. *Sus scrofa algira*. From the Maghreb, closely related to *Sus scrofa scrofa*.

4. *Sus scrofa attila*. A huge, yellowish pig with a long mane found from eastern Europe into Kazakhstan, to the northern flanks of the Caucasus, and to Iraq. Its range appears to meet that of *Sus scrofa scrofa* along quite a well-defined boundary from central Belarus to Transsylvania; *scrofa* is found in the Tatra, *attila* in the Carpathians. The chromosome number is different: as in most Eurasian wild pigs, *S. s. attila* has 38 chromosomes, whereas *S. s. scrofa* usually has 36 (very occasionally 37 or 38), as a result of the translocation of a small chromosome on to a larger one.

5. *Sus scrofa lybicus*. A small, pale, virtually maneless pig from south of the Caucasus through the Levant to the Nile delta, and west through Turkey to the Balkans.

6. *Sus scrofa nigripes*. A light-coloured pig with black legs, from the flanks of the Tianshan mountains. Like *Sus scrofa scrofa*, it has 36 chromosomes, not the 38 that are usual for the species, but the translocation is different.

7. *Sus scrofa sibiricus.* A small pig from Mongolia and Transbaikalia.

8. *Sus scrofa ussuricus.* This is the largest subspecies of *Sus scrofa* (boars often over 300 kg), with a low-crowned skull; it has almost no mane, but thick pelage which is yellowish-grey in winter but black in summer when the long, light hair tips have worn off. It lives in the Russian Far East, Korea, and north-eastern China.

9. *Sus scrofa leucomystax.* A smallish, short-legged yellow-brown pig, with virtually no mane, from the main islands of Japan (not Hokkaido). There is a neat cline of diminishing size from north to south.

10. *Sus scrofa riukiuanus.* A small pig from the Ryukyu islands.

11. *Sus scrofa taevanus.* The small black wild pig from Taiwan.

12. *Sus scrofa moupinensis.* This is a fairly small, short-maned pig with a broad, high-crowned skull, from most of China and Vietnam. I have severe doubts whether this is all one subspecies; specimens seem, for example, to be darker in the north, brindled yellow in the south; larger in the north, smaller in the south, larger again in Vietnam. The recent rediscovery and cataloguing of the huge Heude collection (Braun *et al.* 2001), which contains a large number of wild pig skulls, will help to disentangle this complex situation.

13. *Sus scrofa davidi.* A small, light brown pig, with a long thick mane, from the arid zone from eastern Iran to Gujarat, and perhaps north to Tadjikistan.

14. *Sus scrofa cristatus.* Another long-maned form, differing from *S. s. davidi* by being brindled black, and by its high-crowned skull. From the Himalayas south to central India, and in South East Asia to the Isthmus of Kra.

15. *Sus scrofa affinis.* In my 1981 monograph I distinguished this southern Indian and Sri Lankan pig from *S. s. cristatus* solely by its smaller size. I am more than dubious about it. Phenotypic plasticity in size characterizes pigs, and variability, especially in Sri Lanka, is very great.

16. *Sus scrofa* subspecies? Under this category I placed a single very small skull from 'Bopata' or 'Bopeta', Central Province, Sri Lanka. This could be Bopitiya, at 7°10′N, 80°43′E, 923 m. a.s.l., although there is a town called Bopetta in the Province of Sabaragamuwa at 7°04′N, 80°15′E, 123 m. a.s.l. These localities are in the wet zone, whereas other skulls I saw from Sri Lanka were apparently from the dry zone. Again, I would now hesitate to hypothesize a separate taxon on such incomplete evidence.

17. *Sus scrofa vittatus.* The peninsular Malaysian and West Indonesian wild pig: the peninsula and offshore islands, Sumatra, the Riau-Lingga archipelago, Java and along the Nusatenggara chain as far as Komodo. (In this

case, they probably just swam to cross the deep sea channels. But why not from Komodo to Flores, though?) A small, low-crowned, short-faced pig with very sparse pelage. There is a huge range of size and colour throughout this region, but it is so sporadically distributed, with intermediates between the extremes, that it is impossible to divide it up.

So are they all one species? I now tend to doubt it. Sharp boundaries exist, even though there may be evidence of hybridization along them: between *scrofa* and *attila*, between *davidi* and *cristatus*, and between *cristatus* and *vittatus*, to name just the three most obvious. Isolates, or near-isolates, like *nigripes*, *leucomystax*, and *riukiuanus*, are other candidates. Since my 1981 revision, more material (especially from China and neighbouring countries) has come to light, and a new revision should look for the diagnosable (absolutely distinct) entities.

DOMESTIC PIGS, ONE SOURCE OR MORE?

The view that domestic pigs, even if we restrict ourselves to those that come from the *Sus scrofa* group, have more than one wild origin has a respectable history, going back at least to 1860 (reviewed in Groves 1981: 59–60). As indicated in the previous section, there is a distinction between the western and northern wild pigs, which are low-skulled, and eastern and southern ones, which are high-skulled. Within the latter there is a distinction between the excessively short, high-skulled *vittatus*, with its short face and, especially, short nasal bones, and the less extreme *moupinensis/cristatus* type. When I looked at skulls of feral pigs and 'primitive' domestic breeds, I found that they too slotted into this dichotomy: to the *vittatus* type belonged skulls from South East Asia, the Admiralty islands, Espiritu Santo (Vanuatu), and the Andamans, and to the *moupinensis* type belonged skulls from Europe and from Togo, as well as from Tinian and Saipan in the Marianas (Groves 1981: 61–2). The *moupinensis* affinities of the western pigs would seem to make sense, given that most European breeds have a Chinese origin, in whole or in part, dating from the 19th century: the remaining European pure-bred native breeds are now rare.

Work on DNA has now corroborated, added to and refined these conclusions. I will try to summarize the findings on wild/domestic affinities to date, without anticipating new work to be reported in this volume (see Larson *et al.*, this volume). From the very beginning, separate European and Chinese clades were identified. Using the restriction endonuclease method, Watanabe *et al.*

(1985, 1986) and Chen & Leibenguth (1995) distinguished mtDNA types A (European) and B (Asian). As would be predicted knowing their history, some European breeds had the one type, some had the other. Not all findings were so straightforward: Lan & Shi (1993) confirmed type B in the Sichuan wild pig but, unexpectedly, type A in Vietnamese.

Since the mid-1990s, although direct sequencing has taken over from restriction endonuclease, the overall conclusions have been the same, but with some noteworthy refinements. Giuffra *et al.* (2000) and Okomura *et al.* (2001) found three mtDNA clades: two European (one containing wild pigs from Poland and Israel, plus European native breeds, and the other including just Italian wild pigs), and one Asian (Ryukyu and mainland Japanese wild pigs, plus Chinese and Chinese-derived breeds). Kim *et al.* (2002) confirmed the essential European vs East Asian split, and that some European breeds belonged to one clade, some to the other.

The position of some of the East Asian wild pigs has received special attention in more recent papers. Watanobe *et al.* (2001) determined that *Sus scrofa riukiuanus* forms a subclade separate from other Asian pigs (*S. s. leucomystax* and *?ussuricus* plus domestic breeds). The same team (Watanobe *et al.* 2002) later sequenced archaeological samples of domestic pigs from the Ryukyus, showing that none of them appeared to be derivable from *S. s. riukiuanus*.

Hongo *et al.* (2002) obtained mtDNA from two series of skulls from Vietnam, which they divided into two quite distinct groups, Large and Small; unfortunately, the exact origin and status of these two groups was unknown, but they considered the Large type to be probably from the wild, whereas the Small type could be 'either primitive breed of domestic pigs or a small wild boar'. Intriguingly, all but one of the Large type formed a clade with *Sus scrofa riukiuanus* (the remaining one assorted with a Korean wild pig), but all but one of the Small type was part of the East Asian domestic clade (the remaining one was similar to *Sus scrofa taevanus*, which in turn was related to *S. s. leucomystax*).

As to the question of what, precisely, these two types of Vietnamese pigs may be: the Heude collection, in the Institute of Zoology, Beijing (Braun *et al.* 2001), includes a number of skulls from 'Indochina', none of them unfortunately localized in detail but all known to be from the wild. All are large. I strongly suspect that Hongo *et al.*'s Large type are wild pigs, and their Small type are a northern Vietnamese domestic breed. I have not been able to study them in detail so far but, contrary to my expectations, they appear to be different from any Chinese wild pig skulls.

Finally, we have a little more information on the affinities of European wild pigs to each other and to domestic breeds. According to Hongo *et al.* (2002), European native breeds are close to Turkish rather than to Western European wild pigs. This seems to make sense: domestic pigs have 38, sometimes 40, chromosomes, so an origin from wild stock with 2n = 36, such as *Sus scrofa scrofa*, would be unlikely. Alves *et al.* (2003) found that Iberian native breeds are not unlike Spanish wild pigs, though they did not specify from what part of Spain their wild sample had come (recall that, according to Groves 1981, northern and far-southern Spanish wild pigs are distinctly different).

In no published work so far has *Sus scrofa vittatus* featured. Its inclusion is necessary to test the proposal that some Pacific pigs derive from it, rather than from Chinese *S. s. moupinensis* (Groves 1981).

THE OTHER PIGS

The pygmy hog, *Sus salvanius*, is today an endangered species, confined as far as is known to the Manas National Park on the Asaam/Bhutan border. It seems unlikely that anyone has thought to domesticate it, though Mohr (1960) did propose that the famous Vietnamese pot-bellied pig breed might be derived from it.

The South East Asian pigs of the 'verrucose' group are all handsomely equipped with pendulous warts in adult males: three warts (on the snout, below the eyes, and on the jaw angles) in the true warty pig, only two in the others; and many of them have bushy beards or jaw tufts in addition. They were all placed by Groves (1981) in three species: *Sus verrucosus, barbatus*, and *celebensis*. All the wild pigs of the Philippines were included in *Sus barbatus*; this was greatly over-lumped, even by the standards of those days. A special study on the Philippine pigs (Groves 1997) separated *Sus philippensis* and *Sus cebifrons* as separate species, but continued to recognize the Palawan wild pig as a subspecies of *Sus barbatus*; even this now seems questionable. A preliminary application of the PSC suggested to Groves (2001) that the following species can be recognized in South East Asia:

- *Sus verrucosus*, the warty pig of Java, Madura and Bawean, which now seems vulnerable to extinction.

- *Sus bucculentus*, an Indochinese pig, still known for certain by only three specimens. It is distinct from Indochinese *Sus scrofa*, but probably less strongly differentiated than I once thought, and it is necessary to examine large series of specimens from the region in order to discriminate them and delineate their ranges of variation and distribution.

- *Sus barbatus*, the Bearded Pig of Borneo, Sumatra, Bangka, the Riau archipelago, and the Malay peninsula.

- *Sus ahoenobarbus*, the Palawan pig. This pig was regarded by Groves (1981, 1997) as a subspecies of the bearded pig, which it closely resembles externally, but it is much smaller, and DNA evidence suggests that they are not in fact very closely related.

- *Sus philippensis*, the common (or formerly common) wild pig of Luzon, Mindanao, Balabac, Samar, Leyte, Bohol, and Catanduanes. It was placed as a subspecies of *Sus barbatus* by Groves (1981); as explained above, the male has differently shaped lower canines, and there are cranial and external differences.

- *Sus oliveri*, from Mindoro, originally described by Groves (1997) as a subspecies of *Sus philippensis*.

- *Sus cebifrons*, the Visayan pig, endemic to the Visayas, a group of islands in the central Philippines separated from each other by shallow seas, but from the other Philippine islands by deep water. The species is now extinct on Cebu, but still exists in very small numbers on Negros, Panay, and Masbate. Pigs from the three remaining populations are being bred successfully in captivity under a conservation program; experience shows that the three are rather different from each other externally, but there are problems with taking this any further in taxonomy: (1) the species was originally described from Cebu, on the basis of skulls only, and the external features of the topotypical population are unknown, so cannot be compared with those of the three extant populations; and (2) among the three surviving populations, the skull is known only for the Negros population, *Sus cebifrons negrinus*. None of the Negros skulls is precisely like the type (a male), or the only other known skull (a female), from Cebu; but we have to wait, hovering expectantly and ghoulishly, until Panay and Masbate specimens die and can have their skulls examined, until we can rule out the possibility than one of them may be *Sus cebifrons cebifrons*. If, and only if, they are different, then we can think about setting them apart taxonomically.

AND FINALLY: THE PICK OF THE LITTER

The pride of the bunch is the Sulawesi warty pig (*Sus celebensis*—see Fig. 1.4), a very small species with two pairs of warts and a fetching toupee in young adult males (until it abrades with age). And the species has a truly bizarre distribution: Sulawesi and offshore islands, including Peleng and Salayar, Halmaheira, Timor, Roti and Lendu, Flores, and Simuleue. Three bits of information seem to give away the secret of this odd geography: (1) there are domestic pigs on Timor and Roti that are clearly derived from it, even though they may

Fig. 1.4. Sulawesi warty pigs (*Sus celebensis*) photographed at a salt lick in lowland rainforest, Suaka Margasatwa Nantu nature reserve, Sulawesi (copyright K. Fletcher and Donna Baylis of Wildside Photography, reproduced here with their kind permission)

sometimes be piebald rather than the usual black; (2) the language of Simuleue is related to those of south Sulawesi, especially Bugis; and (3) the Papuan pig has characters of both *Sus celebensis* and *Sus* (cf. *scrofa*) *vittatus*.

On Flores, *Sus celebensis* occurs alongside *scrofa*-like pigs; there is no indication which of these might occur wild, which domestic (though the skulls of the *scrofa* type have domestic-like features). Both of these kinds were named as separate species in the 19th century; ironically, both were dubbed (quite independently!) *Sus floresianus*! Three skulls collected in the early 20th century on Komodo, an offshore island west of Flores, separated from it by shallow sea, are pure *Sus* (cf. *scrofa*) *vittatus*. Yet photos taken in the 1990s of wild pigs on Komodo, shown to me by Dr Marco Masetti, seem more like hybrids. On Timor, too, there are two species of pigs; again, we do not know whether the *scrofa* type is wild as well as domestic, but we do know that *Sus celebensis* is both. From Halmaheira I have seen a skin and skull of *Sus celebensis*, with no indication that it was anything but wild. Yet apparent hybrids are known from Morotai, Ternate, and Bacan, shallow-water islands off Halmaheira.

Putting this all together, I proposed (Groves 1981) that *Sus celebensis* was a domestic species in parts of Island South East Asia, and in this form was distributed around the archipelago by seafaring peoples such as the Bugis. But when domestic pigs derived from *Sus scrofa* were introduced (or indigenously domesticated, as I suggested above), they displaced *Sus celebensis* in most places, leaving it only in outlying areas, in some of which it hybridized with the newcomers. And it was these hybrids that were taken to New Guinea, where they form the basis of the native domestic and feral pig.

CONCLUSION

Clearly, lots of pigs have been of interest to lots of people at many different times throughout history. Presumably this explains the odd distributions of some species, which are unprecedented among mammals (with one exception: bats).

2

Current views on *Sus* phylogeography and pig domestication as seen through modern mtDNA studies

Greger Larson, Umberto Albarella, Keith Dobney
& Peter Rowley-Conwy

INTRODUCTION

The history of pig domestication is also the history of the beginnings of Eurasian agricultural civilization. Wild boar were an important hunted resource for many millennia before the domestication process significantly altered this relationship between pigs and humans. The end result of this process (involving not just pigs but all other farm animals and pets) has led not only to the development of a staggering number of breeds and variations of what were once solely wild animals, but also to the intensification of the relationship between human beings and domestic animals, to the point of near total dependence of each upon the other. By investigating when, where, and how many times pigs (and other animals) were domesticated, we not only gain an insight into the process of domestication, itself, but also (by extension) a deeper understanding of human history, evolutionary biology, biogeography, and a host of other disciplines.

The beginnings of pig management and domestication probably began sometime between the 10th to 8th millennium BP. In western Eurasia, the earliest archaeological evidence for pig domestication comes from a number of sites in Eastern and central Anatolia: Çayönü Tepesi (Ervynck *et al.* 2001), Hallan Çemi (Redding & Rosenberg 1998; Redding 2005), and Gürcütepe (Peters *et al.* 2005). At Çayönü Tepesi, a unique 2,000-year stratigraphic sequence, spanning the 9th to 7th millennia BP, has provided perhaps one of the best opportunities to observe the actual process of domestication for pigs. Thus, biometrical and age-at-death data led Ervynck *et al.* (2001) to postulate several shifts in the intensity of pig–human relationships, not necessarily directly driven by humans in its initial stages. Active involvement of humans in this process, it was argued, took place much later.

However the process is specifically defined, the evidence from Çayönü Tepesi clearly reflects an intensification of the relationship between people and pigs over two millennia, and points to eastern Turkey as a centre of early pig domestication. Unfortunately, most early archaeological sites do not possess such long, continuous, or reliably dated occupation sequences, which has made the identification of other centres of animal domestication difficult at best. Uncertainties regarding the dating of sites in China, for example (Yuan & Flad 2002), have recently undermined original claims of very early pig domestication in East Asia, although recent molecular studies (discussed later) at least support claims of independent pig domestication somewhere there, even if they cannot corroborate the timing.

The often equivocal nature of the zooarchaeological record from Neolithic sites in Europe has prompted some to argue for independent pig domestication occurring within Europe (Bökönyi 1974), whereas others have cited the lack of intermediate forms between larger wild boar and smaller domestic pigs found at these sites as evidence for the introduction of domesticated varieties from elsewhere (Rowley-Conwy 2003), most probably the Near East.

Once domesticated, pigs were dispersed widely around the globe by humans. Modern domestic and feral pigs are found not only across the historical natural range of wild boar in Eurasia, but also across the continents of Australia and North and South America, regions their wild counterparts never reached unassisted. Given the expansive range of both wild and domestic *Sus*, and the cultural importance of pigs across the globe, the possibility of independent pig domestication outside Anatolia and China remained real, and recent advances in techniques and approaches, particularly in the field of genetics, are now allowing us to explore some of these outstanding questions in more detail.

GENETICS AND PIG DOMESTICATION: PREVIOUS STUDIES

Molecular studies investigating pig domestication have tended to focus on the control region of the mitochondrial genome. Several factors, including the mitochondria's maternal inheritance pattern, its lack of recombination, and its relatively rapid evolution (as compared to the nuclear genome) have made the control region the ideal locus for examining recent biological events such as domestication.

The main conclusion of the several previous genetic studies (Giuffra *et al.* 2000; Kijas & Andersson 2001) has been the identification of a significant genetic split between domestic pigs derived from Europe and those derived from Asia (not including those European breeds which have been historically hybridized with Asian breeds to create 'improved' breeds; see Jones 1998). Various molecular clock analyses have also produced a wide range of dates to mark the divergence between western and eastern Eurasian pigs, the results of which all significantly predate the earliest accepted archaeological dates for pig domestication (Giuffra *et al.* 2000; Kijas & Andersson 2001). Though molecular clock analyses have been criticized (and the results are fraught with uncertainty; see Ho & Larson 2006), the data suggest that pigs were independently domesticated at least once in western Eurasia and at least once in eastern Eurasia.

The studies mentioned also revealed a divergent clade consisting solely of Italian wild boar, which suggested that Italy may have acted as a refugium during the height of the last glaciation (Giuffra *et al.* 2000; Kijas & Andersson 2001). A similar study (Alves *et al.* 2003) of modern wild and domestic Iberian pigs found significant introgression of Asian haplotypes into Spanish and Portuguese domestic breeds, but found no evidence to suggest that Spain and Portugal had similarly acted as refugia for wild boar during the last glaciation.

Because none of the studies referenced above sequenced either definitive indigenous modern wild boar, or ancient *Sus* from the Near East or Anatolia, their data could not be used to comment on the important archaeological question (discussed below) of whether modern domestic pigs in Europe are the product of an independent and indigenous domestication event or events, or whether they derive from pigs domesticated from wild boar indigenous to the Near East or Anatolia. In order to address this question, more domestic and wild samples from these regions were needed to establish whether domestic pigs from Europe were genetically similar to pigs from Turkey. If they were, then the most likely conclusion would be that pigs domesticated in Turkey were transported into Europe and that European wild boar were never independently domesticated. If European pigs and Turkish pigs were genetically dissimilar, then the opposite conclusion was more probable and the number of independent domestication 'events' would climb to three.

PHYLOGEOGRAPHY

To establish both the number of times and the regions where wild boar were domesticated, the most obvious approach is a phylogeographic one. The first step requires the establishment of the strength of the correlation between the geographic origins of a wild progenitor with each individual's genetic signature. The stronger the phylogeographic signal (i.e. the tighter the correlation between geography and genetics), the more readily domestic animals can then be tied to locations where their genetic haplotypes occur in the wild. As the phylogeographic signal weakens, however, the possible geographic range over which domestication took place increases, thus reducing the specificity of possible centres of domestication and reducing certainty regarding the number of times the process took place.

Though a strong phylogeographic correlation is ideal, establishing it for wild progenitors of other modern domestic animals has proved difficult. The primary reason for this is the relatively recent extinction of several wild progenitors, including the ancestors of the modern-day horse (Jansen *et al.* 2002), cow (Troy *et al.* 2001), and dromedary (Stanley *et al.* 1994). Even in cases such as dogs, where (like pigs) the wild ancestors are not extinct (and the natural range of wolves is similar to that of wild boar) a single haplotype was shown to exist in wolves from Turkey, Sweden, and Portugal. Another haplotype was found in Saudi Arabia, Mongolia, and China (Savolainen *et al.* 2002). The lack of correlation between a specific geographic locale and a cluster of closely related haplotypes has meant that the establishment of the number and location of domestication 'events' has required the use of more subtle statistical and phylogenetic methods.

Despite these difficulties, the general pattern that has emerged through molecular studies into domestication has been the consistent conclusion that domestication has taken place in a range of geographic locations involving numerous wild haplotypes (Bruford *et al.* 2003).

THE GENETICS OF WILD BOAR AND PIG DOMESTICATION

In order to more fully ascertain the strength of the phylogeographic signal in wild boar, a recent study (Larson *et al.* 2005) analysed an alignment of 663 base pairs of the control region of mitochondrial DNA (mtDNA) from 686 wild and domestic pigs from around the world. A consensus tree (Fig. 2.1), built using a Bayesian Monte Carlo–Markov chain method, provided a structure from which several conclusions could be drawn. First, the shape of the tree reveals that the origins of *Sus* are located in Island South East Asia (ISEA), more specifically on the Malaysian peninsula and the islands of Sumatra, Borneo, and Java. Wild boar then initially spread from ISEA into the Indian subcontinent, as far north as Nepal and western Pakistan. A second radiation took place into continental East Asia before extending west into North Africa and Western Europe.

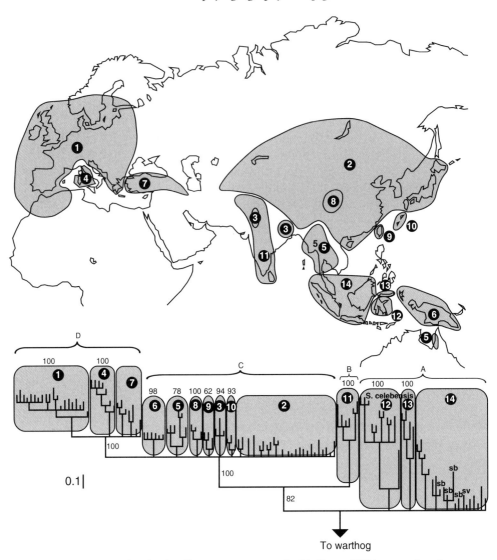

Fig. 2.1. A Bayesian (MCMC) consensus tree of 122 *Sus* mtDNA control region haplotypes rooted by a common warthog (*Phacochoerus aethiopicus*). A total of fourteen clusters (labelled 1–14 on the tree and on the map) are contained within four major clades on the tree (A, B, C, D). Pigs from Sulawesi are *Sus celebensis*. All other tips on the tree represent wild *Sus scrofa* unless indicated by the following two-letter codes: sb, *Sus barbatus*; sv, *Sus verrucosus*. Regions 1–6 represent suggested centres of domestication (figure adapted from Larson *et al.* 2005)

The tree also reveals a remarkably strong phylogeographic signal. More than 98% of the samples fall into one of fourteen distinct regions across the natural range of wild boar, each of which possesses a specific set of haplotypes unique to that region. The six wild boar that violate the correlation are likely the result of human-mediated introgression and/or dispersal, and are discussed below. Far from being problematic, these pigs provide an important opportunity to better understand domestication and human dispersal by investigating why they fall out of place. More importantly, the strong phylogeographic signal allows the identification of 'centres' of domestication by associating the geographic region associated with each wild genetic signature genetic signatures obtained from different breeds and regionally distinct domestic pigs. Larson *et al.* (2005) proposed multiple centres of domestication, four of which were identified for the first time.

Mainland Europe

Two new conclusions regarding the independent domestication of wild boar in Europe can be drawn (see Fig. 2.1, no. 1):

- In contrast to cattle (Troy *et al.* 2001), European wild boar must have been independently domesticated.
- Because wild boar from Turkey, Iran, and Armenia all possess unique haplotypes unrelated to those found in Europe, the implication is that if pigs originally domesticated in Turkey were transported into Europe by Neolithic farmers (or any time thereafter), those pigs have left virtually no descendants in modern European farmyards.

The lone exception is a single feral pig from Corsica that, though it should possess a standard European haplotype, instead clusters within the group of pigs that includes all of the Turkish, Iranian, and Armenian specimens. This pig may, therefore, represent one of the last feral or domestic pigs in Europe whose ancestors were transported into Europe from Turkey during the Neolithic invasion and suggests that the domestication of European wild boar may have been the result of a transfer of ideas.

Interestingly, a single 'wild' specimen from Armenia possesses the most common domestic European haplotype. Though all other Armenian pigs cluster with wild boar from Turkey and Iran, the presence of this specimen strongly implies that European domestic pigs have at some time in the past been moved east and become feral in Armenia. These two exceptions demonstrate not only the long and complicated history of domestication and human-mediated dispersal of domestic pigs, but also the ability of genetics to begin to tease apart that history.

East Asia

This region had also been previously identified as a centre of pig domestication by the earlier studies cited above. The phylogenetic tree in Fig. 2.1 (no. 2) shows numerous Chinese breeds all clustering closely with (and in some cases even being identical to) several native wild boar from East Asia. The same tree also reveals a monophyletic clade (no. 8) consisting of Chinese wild boar from central China, which thus far does not include any domestic pigs. This implies that, though East Asian domestics may have been derived from several lineages of wild boar, there are also distinct wild populations that have never contributed DNA to modern domestic stocks. Network analysis (Larson *et al.* 2005: fig. 3) also reveals that although wild boar from Japan are closely related to Asian domestic pigs, they were probably never themselves domesticated, since no modern Japanese domestic pigs sampled to date posses the Japanese wild boar haplotype.

Two pigs, one from the southern tip of Malaysia and a second from Pulo Babi, Sumatra, also possess East Asian haplotypes despite being surrounded in the tree by wild boar whose genetic signatures place them in the most basal cluster. A high percentage of modern habitants in these regions are immigrants from China and thus these pigs may be feral pigs derived from domestics originally derived from China (K. Helgen pers. comm.; Groves 1981).

India

Several wild boar from Kashmir and Bengal on the Indian subcontinent form their own monophyletic clade. A single domestic pig, also from Bengal, shares the identical haplotype with one of the wild boar, thus implying that wild boar from India have either been independently domesticated, or have contributed maternal DNA to domesticates brought in from other places. This finding supports previous tentative claims of independent pig domestication in India (Groves 1981), though this result has yet to corroborated by zooarchaeological data.

The three regions discussed above all contain both wild and domestic pigs that share the same haplotypes and, as such, allow us to draw the straightforward conclusion that these must have all been separate centres of pig domestication. The final regions (discussed below) are two further purported centres, based upon close genetic affiliation, although the geographic origins and heritage of the domestic pigs cited here are not identical to the wild boar with which they share a genetic heritage.

Italy and Sardinia

The distinct clade of central Italian wild boar (originally identified by Giuffra *et al.* 2000; Kijas & Andersson 2001) was also identified by Larson *et al.* (2005), with the addition of further specimens of wild boar from the Maremma region of north-west Italy, the traditional remaining enclave of indigenous Italian wild boar. Two (out of 15) pigs from Sardinia, identified as feral, also fell into this clade, suggesting several plausible hypotheses. *Sus* is so far absent in the zooarchaeological record from Sardinia before the 7th millennium BC (Vigne 1988), implying that domestic and feral pigs found there today must have been transported to the island by people. Indigenous Italian wild boar may have been independently domesticated in Italy before being taken to Sardinia (a claim supported by a recent zooarchaeological survey of Italian *Sus* by Albarella *et al.* in press *b*), or perhaps the island was seeded with native Italian wild boar by early hunters/settlers, a practice known to have occurred in the prehistoric Mediterranean (e.g. Vigne & Buitenhuis 1999). The future DNA sequencing of both ancient Sardinian pigs and additional native domestic pig breeds from Italy will certainly help clarify the picture further.

Not only have indigenous Italian pigs (of as yet undetermined status) been moved to Sardina, but European domestic pigs have also been moved into Italy. A recently collected specimen, identified as an Italian wild boar, possesses the most common domestic haplotype found in Europe, not one of the distinctive haplotypes associated with the Maremma wild boar. The most likely explanation for this is that it derives from a European wild boar, known to have been introduced into the region for centuries, most recently following World War II (Apollonia *et al.* 1988).

South-East Asia

From Fig. 2.1 it is evident that recent wild boar from Burma and Thailand group together to form a monophyletic clade more similar to other clades found in East Asia than to the cluster of clades located in ISEA. Though no domestic pigs from either of these two countries were sampled, a handful of feral pigs from Cape York in Australia share a close genetic affiliation with this clade. The genetic signatures of several of the feral pigs sampled from Cape York place those pigs into the general East Asian cluster, but more than ten pigs shared the same haplotype within the Burma/Thailand clade, suggesting that native wild boar from Burma and Thailand were domesticated and then moved to Australia. Although other evidence for the transfer of pig-specific parasites (i.e. a nematode and tick: Heise-Pavlov & Heise-Pavlov 2003) from

South East Asia to Australia supports this conclusion, historical records indicating a similar importation of pigs during historic times are not known.

Possible additional centres

Though the strength of the phylogeographic signal allows for the specific identification of five independent centres of domestication, a number of important questions remain. The vast majority of all domestic pig stocks worldwide are derived from either mainland European or East Asian stock. The four additional regions discussed above (as well as Eastern and central Turkey, identified through zooarchaeological data) have all played host to some degree of indigenous domestication (or at least some degree of interaction/movement between people and indigenous wild boar), though why pigs from those regions have not contributed DNA to modern breeds is unclear. It is also possible that, with supplementary sampling of wild boar and domestic pigs in regions not covered by this study, additional centres of domestication will be identified.

The most obvious candidate is ISEA, where domestic pigs and tamed wild boar are a significant component of the indigenous cultures. Thus far, the only pig outside ISEA that possesses an ISEA-like haplotype (and may thus indicate indigenous domestication and subsequent movement) derives from Sri Lanka. However, a specimen from Sri Lanka, morphologically similar to *Sus barbatus* was identified (and subsequently lost) and named *Sus zeylonensis* (Blyth 1851). It is therefore possible that the Sri Lankan pig with an ISEA haplotype sequenced in this study may have been mis-provenanced, and is actually a bearded pig from Borneo (K. Helgen pers. comm.).

Recently published sequence data deriving from several domestic pigs from Sarawak, Borneo (Fig. 2.2), suggests that local wild boar (all of which fall into the cluster labelled 14 on Fig. 2.1) may have been independently domesticated. Additionally, a feral pig from Flores shares a close genetic affiliation with *Sus celebensis* samples, indicating that wild boar indigenous to Sulawesi may also have been domesticated and then transported to adjacent islands. If this evidence is supported by ongoing sample collection, the total number of domestication centres will likely climb even higher (Larson *et al.* 2007).

CONCLUSION

A number of important conclusions can be drawn from the results discussed above. First, humans have been hunting, domesticating, and moving wild

Fig. 2.2. Domestic pigs from Sarawak, Borneo from which hairs were sampled for mtDNA analyses (samples and photographs courtesy of Dr Phil Piper)

boar across the natural range of the species for millennia. Though these activities would be expected to reduce the correlation between geography and genetic haplotype, wild boar have retained a remarkably strong phylo-geographic signal. Why this should be remains as yet unanswered.

Perhaps less surprising is the finding that multiple regions (combing those identified through genetics and archaeology) have played host to some degree of pig domestication. Over the past decade, each new published result from genetic studies that has incorporated domestic animals from previously unsampled regions has increased the number of new centres of domestication. This has been especially true for goats (Sultana *et al.* 2003; Joshi *et al.* 2004) and cows (Mannen *et al.* 2004; Lai *et al.* 2006) and is now also the case for pigs (Larson *et al.* 2005) where a multitude of new haplotypes were found when samples from previously excluded regions were added to existing data sets.

These collective results imply that perhaps the question should no longer be 'where did domestication occur?', but rather 'where did domestication *not* take place?'. First, however, a better understanding of how DNA from wild animals from different regions has become incorporated into domestic stock is required. A scenario in which domestication is the result of a transfer of either the idea, or of actual domestic animals which are then hybridized with native wild boar, has very different ramifications about the nature of domes-tication, compared to a scenario in which the process took place wholly independently in disparate regions by unrelated cultures.

Other caveats to these perhaps too simplistic conclusions should also be borne in mind. First, we are only dealing here (through mtDNA) with maternal lineages. Further exploration of male lineages (through studies of the Y chromosome) may show a different—perhaps conflicting—story, as has recently been the case for cattle (Hanotte *et al.* 2000) and even humans (Haak *et al.* 2005). Second, care needs to be taken in precisely what is meant by the term 'independent domestication'. In reality, the various possible scenarios for these processes or events are likely far more complex than the genetics can ever reveal. For example, if a few male domestic pigs were brought into a new region by colonizing agriculturalists, and local wild female boar were captured, tamed and bred with them, the mtDNA would appear to show separate domestication of indigenous wild boar. As ever, the archaeological context, and integration of all other associated evidence (beyond genetics), will be most important in unravelling the finer (and ultimately more informative) story.

More problematic still is the use of modern extant wild boar mtDNA to reconstruct the past. Comparative specimens are only as useful as the infor-mation supplied with them, and it is clear that for both museum collections and recent tissue sampling from living populations, used in this and other studies, certain assumptions have been made about the status and genetic affinities of specimens, based largely on phenotypic variables, oral history, or even just geographic location. If a specimen labelled 'wild' is in fact derived from feral populations or even hybrids between wild and domestic individuals (a distinct possibility in many regions), then statements about indigenous domestication or not become rather circular. In these cases larger samples are needed to ensure that geographically specific 'wild' haplotypes stand up to scrutiny by being repeated in numerous specimens.

More empirical evidence inevitably leads not only to answers, but also to modifications of previously held assumptions, and of course, to more questions. Phylogeography has significantly altered our understanding of the history of pigs (and domestic animals as a whole). However, large geographic and phylogenetic gaps remain in the collective data set and filling them will no doubt lead to yet more surprising, but ultimately rewarding, conclusions.

3

The molecular basis for phenotypic changes during pig domestication

Leif Andersson

INTRODUCTION

Pig domestication was initiated some 10,000 years ago. Thus, within a fairly short period of time, from an evolutionary perspective, a remarkable change in phenotype has taken place. Until recently (the last few hundred years), the selection intensity was weak but selection on traits such as behaviour and disease resistance must have occurred early. Docile animals resistant to stress were likely to be kept by the early farmers. Less obviously, coat colour is a trait that also was altered early during domestication. New coat colour variants occur by spontaneous mutations, but in nature there is a strong purifying selection eliminating such mutations because they provide less efficient camouflage or fail to attract mates. In contrast, such mutations have accumulated in domestic animals—why? One reason is of course relaxed purifying selection, but this is not the only reason. A less efficient camouflage of the domestic stock could be advantageous for the farmer and maybe it was used to distinguish improved domestic forms from their wild counterparts. Today, coat colour is often used as a breed-specific marker. For instance, a Large White pig should be white and a Piétrain pig should be spotted. Furthermore, there is strong selection for white colour in some breeds because of consumer demand for pork meat without any pigmented spots in the remaining skin.

Charles Darwin was the first to realize that the phenotypic change in domestic animals resulting from selective breeding is an excellent model for phenotypic evolution due to natural selection (Darwin 1859). In fact, he became a pigeon breeder himself and used domestic animals as a proof-of-principle for his revolutionary theory on natural selection as a driving force for evolution. The first chapter of *The Origin of Species* (Darwin 1859) concerns observations on domestic animals, and nine years later he published two volumes on *The Variation of Animals and Plants under Domestication* (Darwin 1868). In the latter book he describes the phenotypic changes that have occurred in the pig and other domestic animals as a consequence of domestication. As a result of the development of molecular tools in the form of well-developed genetic maps and large number of genetic markers we are now in position to start unravelling the molecular basis for phenotypic changes in the pig and other domestic animals. Complete genome sequences have already been determined for a number of organisms (e.g. >100 prokaryotes, *Drosophila*, human, mouse, rat, dog, horse, and domestic fowl) but this has not yet been accomplished for the pig. However, an international consortium has now raised the necessary funds to achieve this milestone for pig biology (Swine Genome Consortium n. d.).

THE GENETICS OF PHENOTYPIC DIFFERENCES BETWEEN WILD AND DOMESTIC PIGS

Surprisingly little is yet known about the genes and mutations that distinguish a domestic pig from a wild boar. The reason for this is that the great majority of phenotypic traits in pigs (and all other organisms) have a complex genetic background where the phenotype is determined by a number of genes together with environmental effects. Thus, each gene explains only a small fraction of the phenotypic variation. However, we pioneered this field when in the late 1980s we generated an intercross between European wild boar and Large White domestic pigs. The aim was to generate a resource for establishing the first genetic map of the pig and for mapping some of the genes that cause phenotypic differences between wild and domestic pigs. The basic principle of such an intercross is outlined in Fig. 3.1.

We started by mating two wild boar males with eight Large White females which generated the F_1 generation. For each chromosome pair the F_1 animals carry one chromosome derived from each founder line and are thus expected to be heterozygous at all major loci, causing phenotypic differences between the wild boar and Large White domestic pigs. Thus, the F_1 animals are expected to be homogenous in their heterozygosity at major trait loci. In contrast, the F_2 generation is very heterogeneous, since Mendelian segregation generates all possible genotypes. This is illustrated in Fig. 3.1 by the segregation at the locus controlling Dominant white colour in the pig. The Large White founders were homozygous for the dominant allele (*I*) for white colour and the wild boars were homozygous for the wild type allele (*i*). All F_1 animals were white and heterozygous *I/i*, whereas a classical Mendelian 3:1 segregation for white and coloured piglets was observed in the F_2 generation. Another important reason for

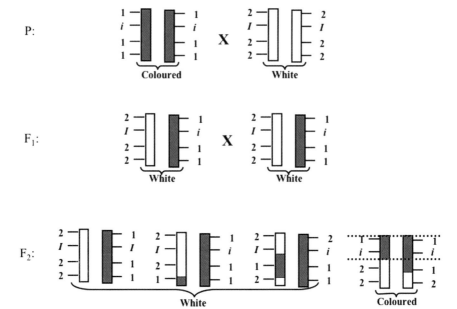

Fig. 3.1. Schematic illustration of the segregation of alleles in an F_2 intercross between wild boar and domestic pigs. *I* and *i* refer to the alleles for dominant white colour and for wild type colour, respectively. 1 and 2 refer to alleles at marker loci used to trace the segregation of chromosome segments inherited from the two founder lines. The dotted lines mark the region that can harbour the gene for Dominant white colour based on the data presented in the figure. P, parental generation; F_1, first intercross generation; F_2, second intercross generation

the great genetic diversity in the F_2 generation is the genetic recombination (crossing-over) that occurs during meioses in the gametes generated by the F_1 animals (Fig. 3.1). This means that every F_2 animal receives a unique combination of alleles derived from the two founder populations.

Genetic markers are used to trace the inheritance of individual chromosome segments through the pedigree. The criteria for a genetic marker are that it shows a simple mode of inheritance and that it can be easily analysed in the laboratory. Microsatellites (short tandem repeats showing length differences between alleles) or single nucleotide polymorphisms (SNPs) are the most commonly used markers today. A genetic marker is specific for one position in the genome, and a set of a few hundred genetic markers is sufficient to trace the inheritance of all chromosome segments in the pig genome. Thus, by collecting extensive records on phenotypic traits (coat colour, morphology, growth, fat deposition, etc.) and scoring the entire pedigree for hundreds of genetic markers it is possible by statistical analysis to define regions harboring one or more genes affecting a certain trait. This is illustrated in Fig. 3.1; the chromosomal region between the dotted lines (in the rightmost F_2 animal) is the only one that could harbor the Dominant white locus according to the coat colour of the progeny and our genetic model for the inheritance of white colour in the pig.

MUTATIONS UNDERLYING COAT COLOUR VARIATION IN THE PIG

One of the most striking observations in our F_2 generation was the variation in coat colour. Our genetic analysis showed that the variation could essentially be explained by two major coat colour loci, Dominant white (I) and Extension (E), as illustrated in Fig. 3.2. The Dominant white locus is epistatic to Extension, which means that animals carrying the Dominant white allele inherited from the domestic pig are white irrespective of the genotype at the Extension locus. Thus, a classical 12:3:1 segregation ratio of white, wild coloured, and spotted animals was observed in the F_2 generation (Fig. 3.2). Segregation analysis revealed that the Dominant white locus is located on pig chromosome 8 (Johansson *et al.* 1992) and that the Extension locus is on chromosome 16 (Mariani *et al.* 1996).

P:	Wild coloured	X	White
	i/i, E⁺/E⁺		*I/I, eᵖ/eᵖ*
F_1:	White	X	White
	I/i, E⁺/eᵖ		*I/i, E⁺/eᵖ*
F_2:	White	Wild coloured	Black spotted
	I/–, –	*i/i, E⁺/–*	*i/i, eᵖ/eᵖ*
	12/16	3/16	1/16

Fig. 3.2. Segregation at the *Dominant white (I)* and *Extension (E)* coat colour loci in an intercross between the European wild boar and Large White domestic pigs. The *I* and *eᵖ* alleles inherited from the domestic pigs cause dominant white colour and black spotting, respectively, whereas the *i* and *E⁺* alleles are inherited from the wild boar. The genotypes for each class are given in italics below the coat colour. The expression *I/–* means that the animals are either heterozygous (*I/i*) or homozygous (*I/I*) for the dominant allele. P, parental generation; F_1, first intercross generation; F_2, second intercross generation. The expected Mendelian segregation ratio for the three coat colour classes in the F_2 generation is given at the bottom

Comparative genomics strongly suggested the *KIT* gene as a positional candidate gene for Dominant white colour in the pigs since previous studies had revealed that mutations in this gene cause Dominant white spotting in mice (Mouse Genome Informatics n.d.) and the Piebald trait in humans (OMIM n.d. *a*). *KIT* encodes a tyrosine kinase receptor with a crucial role for the migration and survival of stem cells derived from the neural crest during development. The KIT receptor is located in the cell membrane and binds a growth factor, the so-called KIT ligand. The binding of the ligand leads to an intracellular signalling that is essential for the survival of the cell. KIT is expressed in melanocytes, haematopoietic cells, and germ cells. *KIT* mutations may therefore cause pigmentation disorders, anaemia, and sterility.

Dominant white colour in the pig has a simple monogenic inheritance, but the underlying molecular basis is more complicated than first expected. We have shown in a series of papers that Dominant white colour is caused by two different *KIT* mutations and there exist a considerable genetic heterogeneity at the *KIT* locus in white commercial pig breeds (Johansson Moller *et al.* 1996; Marklund *et al.* 1998; Giuffra *et al.* 2002; Pielberg *et al.* 2002, 2003). One of the mutations is a large tandem duplication of 450 kilobase pairs that encompass the entire coding sequence of *KIT*. Our interpretation is that the duplication does not include all the regulatory regions that are required for normal gene expression. Thus, we assume that the duplication acts as a regulatory mutation, i.e. the coding sequence is intact but the gene regulation is altered. The presence of the duplication alone is associated with a partial white phenotype. We have also identified a second mutation, which is a splice site mutation that occurs at the first nucleotide in intron 17 that leads to the skipping of exon 17 in the mature *KIT* transcript. This mutation eliminates 41 amino acids from the tyrosine kinase domain and we have postulated that this mutant form has normal ligand binding but abolished tyrosine kinase activity. Based on mouse data, we expect that a single *KIT* copy with this splice mutation would be lethal in the homozygous condition because of the lack of any KIT signalling. However, most pigs carrying this mutation also carry the *KIT* duplication which ensures sufficient KIT signalling to avoid severe negative effects on haematopoiesis and fertility. A third *KIT* mutation is most likely associated with the *Belt* allele causing a white belt across the shoulders and forelegs in (for instance) Hampshire pigs. We have shown that the *Belt* mutation also maps to the *KIT* locus but it is associated neither with a duplication nor with the splice mutation. It is most likely caused by a regulatory mutation since we did not find any mutation in the *KIT* coding sequence (Giuffra *et al.* 1999).

Another striking observation is the considerable genetic heterogeneity at the *KIT* locus in white commercial pig breeds. The reason for this is that the presence of two nearly identical copies of a large DNA segment is genetically unstable and unequal crossing-over may generate new haplotypes carrying one or three copies (Pielberg *et al.* 2002, 2003). The haplotypes present in white lines may contain one, two, or three *KIT* copies and the splice mutation is present on none, one, or two of these copies (Fig. 3.3). An interesting consequence of this is that we would expect white feral pigs to lose their white colour because of this genetic instability at the *KIT* locus and strong selection against white colour, since it gives poor camouflage and poor protection against sunlight. Our results explain why pig breeders have not been able to eliminate coat colour heterogeneity in white lines, despite the fact that they have selected for white colour for more than a hundred years.

Comparative genomics strongly suggested that the Extension locus in pigs, defined by classical segregation analysis of coat colour variants, corresponded to the gene for melanocortin receptor 1 (*MC1R*). We were able to confirm this by sequencing the *MC1R* gene from a variety of pig populations including the founders of our wild boar intercross (Mariani *et al.* 1996; Kijas *et al.* 1998, 2001). MC1R is expressed in the melanocyte and MC1R signalling leads to a switch from production of red pheomelanin to production of black eumelanin. The MC1R ligand is the melanocyte stimulating hormone (MSH) peptide that is produced by proteolytic cleavage from the polyprotein proopiomelanocortin (POMC). Furthermore, the agouti protein is an MSH antagonist that blocks MC1R signalling. Consequently, complete loss of function of MC1R and POMC leads to red pigmentation whereas a loss of agouti expression leads to black pigmentation (Jackson 1994). Mutations leading to a constitutively active

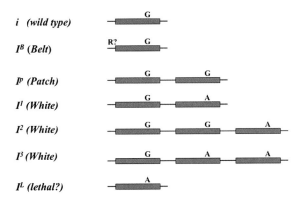

Fig. 3.3. Haplotypes identified at the *KIT/Dominant white* locus in pigs. The presence of a *KIT* duplication or triplication and a splice mutation at the first nucleotide in intron 17 is associated with dominant white colour; G and A refer to the wild type and the mutation at this splice site, respectively. R? indicates the postulated regulatory mutation causing the Belt phenotype. 'lethal?' indicates that lethality in the homozygous condition has been predicted for this allele but not yet proved

MC1R (i.e. a receptor that does not need ligand binding for its activity) causes dominant black colour irrespective of the genotype at the *POMC* and *Agouti* loci. *MC1R* mutations have already been associated with coat colour or plumage colour variants in a number of birds and mammals. For instance, some coat colour variants in mice (Robbins *et al.* 1993); red hair and fair skin in humans (OMIM n.d. b); chestnut colour in horse (Marklund *et al.* 1996); black and red colour in cattle (Klungland *et al.* 1995); and black plumage in the domestic chicken (Kerje *et al.* 2003) are all associated with *MC1R* mutations.

Sequence analysis of *MC1R* from a variety of pigs with different coat colour phenotypes have revealed six different alleles, as summarized in Fig. 3.4 (Kijas *et al.* 1998, 2001). The alleles found in European and Japanese wild boars encode identical proteins but differ by a single synonymous nucleotide substitution. Two missense mutations are associated with the recessive red colour in Duroc pigs, and we have suggested on the basis of the degree of conservation across species that the Ala243Thr mutation is the causative one. Two different forms of alleles for Dominant black colour was revealed, one present in Chinese Meishan pigs and in Large Black pigs from the UK and the other found in Hampshire pigs. The most interesting allele is the one denoted E^P causing black spots either on a red or white background (Fig. 3.5). Why the apparent activity of the MC1 receptor could differ so dramatically between the red/white areas and the black spots was an enigma. The explanation is that this allele is associated with two *MC1R* mutations: (1) the same Asp124Asn mutation as associated with dominant black colour in Hampshire pigs and (2) an insertion of two C nucleotides at codon 22 (Fig. 3.4). The insertion of

Allele	Coat coluor	Popu- lation	Codon 17	22	95	102	121	122	124	164	243
MC1R*1 (E^+)	Wild type	EWB	GCG Ala	CGG Arg	GTG Val	CTG Leu	AAT Asn	GTC Val	GAC Asp	GCG Ala	GCG Ala
MC1R*5 (E^+)	Wild type	JWB	--- -	--- -	--- -	--- -	--C -	--- -	--- -	--- -	--- -
MC1R*2 (E^{D1})	Black	MS, LB	--A -	--- -	A-- Met	-C- Pro	--C -	--- -	--- -	--- -	--A -
MC1R*3 (E^{D2})	Black	H	--- -	--- -	--- -	--- -	--- -	--- -	A-- Asn	--- -	--- -
MC1R*6 (E^P)	Black spots	L, LW,P	--- -	+CC FS	--- -	--- -	--- -	--- -	A-- Asn	--- -	--- -
MC1R*4 (e)	Red	D	--- -	--- -	--- -	--- -	--- -	--- -	--- -	-T- Val	A-- Thr

Fig. 3.4. Summary of pig *MC1R/Extension* alleles and their effect on coat colour. EWB, European wild boar; JWB, Japanese wild boar; MS, Meishan; LB, Large Black; H, Hampshire; L, Landrace; LW, Large White; P, Piétrain; D, Duroc; FS, frame shift

Fig. 3.5. Striking phenotypic similarity between the coat colour pattern for a domestic pig illustrated in a 14th century English medieval manuscript (the *Luttrell Psalter*) (left) and one of the coat colour pattern observed among the F_2 progeny in a wild boar/domestic pig intercross (right); the latter is a photo by Mats Gerentz, SLU, Sweden

two nucleotides leads to a frameshift and a premature stop codon. This means that no functional MC1 receptor should be produced from this allele consistent with the lack of black pigment in the red/white areas. However, the insertion of the two base pairs was found to be somatically unstable and back mutations may restore the reading frame (Kijas *et al.* 2001). When this happens the dominant black mutation comes into action again which leads to the formation of black spots. Thus, this allele gives a very characteristic coat colour pattern. Interestingly, a domestic pig with a strikingly similar coat colour pattern is illustrated in an 14th century English medieval manuscript, the Luttrell Psalter (Fig. 3.5), suggesting that this *MC1R* allele may have been present already in medieval domestic pigs. Furthermore, spotted pigs occur in Papua New Guinea and in Polynesia. It would be straightforward to test if these pigs have inherited the gene for black spots from European domestic pigs or if the phenotype is caused by another mutation. It is very likely that this allele for black spots has a European origin since it differs by only two mutations from the European wild boar sequence but by seven substitutions from the *MC1R* sequence found in black Chinese Meishan pigs (Fig. 3.4).

The *KIT* and *MC1R* genes are clearly some of the best available genetic markers that can be used to distinguish domestic pigs and wild boars. The great majority of Western domestic pigs differ from the wild boar at *KIT* and/or *MC1R*. In fact these loci have been used to reveal wild boar/domestic pig hybrids in Sweden (Andersson unpublished) and Finland (Gongora *et al.* 2003).

PIG PHYLOGENY

The observation that the *MC1R* alleles carried by black Chinese Meishan pigs and Large Black pigs from the UK were identical and differed by five nucleotide substitutions (among *c.*1000 nucleotides) from the *MC1R* sequence

found in the European wild boar (Fig. 3.4) gave us some important hints
about pig phylogeny and the history of pig domestication. First, it strongly
suggested that European and Asian domestic pigs originate from genetically
distinct wild boar populations. Secondly, it showed that Asian germplasm has
contributed to the development of some European pig breeds. Therefore we
decided to generate sequence data for mitochondrial DNA from wild boar
and domestic pig populations from Europe and Asia (Fig. 3.6) (Giuffra *et al.*
2000; Kijas & Andersson 2001). The results revealed three distinct mtDNA
lineages. European lineage 1 (E1) included European domestic pigs and most
European wild boars whereas European lineage 2 (E2) only included some
wild boars from Italy. The Asian lineage (A) contained Asian domestic pigs
and Asian wild boars. There was a 1.2% sequence difference between the
Asian and European mtDNA lineages (Kijas & Andersson 2001). By comparing this figure with the estimated rate of sequence divergence for mammalian
mtDNA sequences we came to the conclusion that Asian and European wild
boars diverged from a common ancestor *c.*900,000 years before the present
(BP). The fact that pig domestication took place *c.*10,000 years BP leads to the
inevitable conclusion that Asian and European domestic pigs must have
originated from genetically distinct wild boar populations. We also observed
that many modern domestic pig breeds from Europe, such as the Large White,
Landrace, and Piétrain, must be considered as hybrids between European and
Asian domestic pigs since they carry both Asian and European mtDNA types.
This result was fully consistent with written records from the 18th and 19th
century indicating that Asian domestic pigs were introgressed into European
domestic pigs during this period (Jones 1998). The molecular data revealed
that Asian domestic pigs have had a considerable impact on the development
of modern domestic pig breeds in Europe and North America.

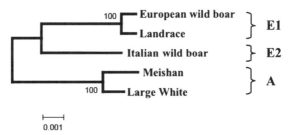

Fig. 3.6. Phylogenetic tree of the near complete mtDNA genome (*c.*16 kb) showing the
existence of three distinct lineages of mtDNA sequences, one Asian (A) and two European
(E1 and E2). The neighbour-joining tree was constructed using the MEGA software
(Kumar *et al.* 2001). Bootstrap support for the given branch order based on 1000 replicates
is shown at branch nodes and a scale bar for the nucleotide distances is given at the bottom

MUTATIONS INFLUENCING MULTIFACTORIAL TRAITS IN DOMESTIC PIGS

Traits like growth, fertility, and disease resistance generally show a multifactorial inheritance, which means that the phenotype is determined by an unknown number of genes in combination with environmental factors. Most phenotypic differences between the wild boar and domestic pigs have such a complex genetic background. It is much more difficult to map and identify genes underlying a multifactorial trait than finding a gene for a monogenic trait like coat colour. In our intercross between the European wild boar and Large White domestic pigs we measured a large number of traits on the F_2 animals including growth, fat deposition, muscularity, weight of internal organs, length of the small intestine, meat quality, immunological traits, and incidence of osteochondrosis. For all these traits, we have been able to identify one or several chromosome regions harboring genes affecting the phenotype (Edfors-Lilja *et al.* 1993, 1995, 1998; Andersson *et al.* 1994; Andersson-Eklund *et al.* 1998, 2000; Knott *et al.* 1998). Curiously, Charles Darwin describes in his book *The Variation of Animals and Plants under Domestication* (1868) that one of the phenotypic changes during pig domestication is an increased length of the small intestine and we were able to localize a locus explaining part of the difference in intestinal length between the wild boar and domestic pigs (Andersson *et al.* 1994).

In one case we have gone all the way from mapping a gene for a multifactorial trait to the identification of the mutation underlying a phenotypic difference between the wild boar and domestic pigs (Van Laere *et al.* 2003). This success story started with the identification of a locus on the tip of the short arm of pig chromosome 2 that had a large impact on muscle growth, fat deposition, and the size of the heart (Jeon *et al.* 1999). The allele derived from the domestic pig increased muscle growth and the size of the heart, and decreased fat deposition. Thus, it made the pig leaner. It is very likely that this allele has been favoured by the strong selection for lean growth in many domestic pig populations in the last 50 years. This locus was independently identified by Michel Georges and colleagues (University of Liège) using an intercross between Piétrain and Large White pigs (Nezer *et al.* 1999). A particularly interesting observation in both studies was that this locus showed paternal expression, which means that only the allele from the father is expressed and the maternal allele is silent. The great majority of mammalian genes are expressed from both the paternal and maternal chromosome, but a small number of genes (less than 100 have been identified so far) show either paternal or maternal expression (see Beechey *et al.* 2005).

   The observation of paternal expression immediately led to the identification
of *IGF2*, encoding insulin-like growth factor II, as an obvious positional candidate gene because *IGF2* is one of the few paternally expressed genes in the actual
chromosome region and it is a well-known growth factor. In collaboration with
the Liège group and researchers at the Roslin Institute in Edinburgh we carried
out segregation analysis in order to put together a collection of chromosomes
that either carried the allele for high muscle growth (denoted *Q*) or normal
muscle growth (denoted *q*). We then re-sequenced the entire *IGF2* gene and the
neighbouring insulin gene, in total 28,600 base pairs from 15 chromosomes
associated with the *Q* or *q* alleles. The analysis demonstrated that a single
nucleotide substitution in the middle of intron 3 must be the mutation causing
this phenotypic effect (Van Laere *et al.* 2003). A sequence comparison with seven
other mammalian species revealed that the mutation occurs in a non-coding
region that is as well conserved as a coding sequence. Furthermore, the mutation
occurs in a segment of 16 base pairs that is completely conserved among the

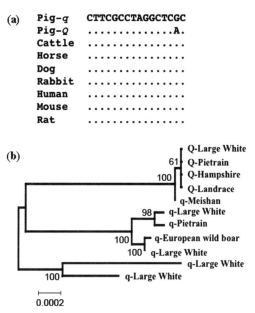

Fig. 3.7. A single nucleotide substitution in intron 3 of the *IGF2* gene in pigs has a
major effect on muscle growth, fat deposition, and the size of the heart. (a) Alignment
of a part of *IGF2* intron 3 among eight mammalian species showing the mutated site
(*IGF2*-intron3-nt3072). (b) Neighbour-joining phylogenetic tree of *IGF2* sequences
from domestic pigs and wild boars carrying the wild type allele (*q*) or the mutation
(*Q*). Bootstrap support for the given branch order based on 1000 replicates is shown
at branch nodes and a scale bar for the nucleotide distances is given at the bottom

eight species, strongly suggesting that it is functionally important (Fig. 3.7a). Thus, most humans have the same nucleotide as the wild boar at the mutated site. Functional studies revealed that this DNA segment binds a nuclear factor that most likely regulates *IGF2* expression, and the mutation abolishes the binding of this factor to DNA. In fact, *IGF2* expression was shown to be three times higher for the *Q* allele than for the *q* allele in skeletal muscle and heart, but *IGF2* expression was unaltered in liver or fetal tissue, showing that the mutation has a tissue-specific and developmental stage-specific effect. The finding has revealed a new mechanism regulating muscle growth in mammals. The conservation of this mutated site suggests that animals carrying this mutation have a selective disadvantage in the wild, despite the fact that pigs carrying this mutation appear perfectly healthy. The mutation does, however, lead to defective gene regulation so the animal may be less able to adjust muscle mass and fat deposition depending on environmental conditions. Thus, wild animals carrying the mutation may be less able to survive periods of starvation and resist cold periods, because they have less subcutaneous fat.

A phylogenetic analysis showed that the *IGF2* sequence from the mutated *Q* haplotype differs considerably from the sequence in the European wild boar and in European domestic pigs not carrying the mutation, but is nearly identical to the wild type sequence found in Chinese Meishan pigs except at the mutated site (Fig. 3.7b). Our interpretation is that the mutation arose on an Asian haplotype. It is still unclear if this happened in Asia or in Europe after the introgression of Asian germ plasm that took place about 200 years ago. The finding confirms our prediction that the introgression of genetic material from Asia has contributed to the selection response that have been obtained in modern domestic pigs in Europe and North America (Giuffra *et al.* 2000).

The *IGF2* mutation has gone through a 'selective sweep' and replaced the wild type allele in many pig breeds strongly selected for lean growth (more muscle, less fat). Furthermore we observed exactly the same allele in different breeds like Large White, Landrace, Hampshire, and Piétrain showing that there must be some gene flow between breeds. The mutation increases muscle content by 3–4%, corresponding to 3–4 kg more meat for a pig slaughtered at 100 kg. Thus, this mutation has had a major impact on the pig industry and is one important reason why pigs are much leaner today than they were at the beginning of the last century when humans preferred pork with a high fat content.

CONCLUSION

With the further development of resources such as the complete pig genome sequence and improved technology for genome research, many more examples of genes explaining phenotypic differences between the wild boar and domestic pigs will be revealed. This also means that we may be able to use DNA analysis of archeological samples to reconstruct the evolutionary history of the domestic pig and date when different phenotypic changes have occurred.

Part B

The History of Pig Domestication and Husbandry

4

The transition from wild boar to domestic pig in Eurasia, illustrated by a tooth developmental defect and biometrical data

*Keith Dobney, Anton Ervynck, Umberto Albarella &
Peter Rowley-Conwy*

INTRODUCTION

A growing body of evidence strongly suggests that the evolution from wild boar (*Sus scrofa*) to domestic pig (*Sus scrofa* f. domestica) was a gradual phenomenon, spanning many generations and centuries, or even millennia (Albarella *et al.* 2006). Certainly for Çayönü Tepesi, one of the important sites where early pig domestication has been claimed, this picture is corroborated by a recent review of the zooarchaeological material (Ervynck *et al.* 2001). Within the context of this recent study, it has been demonstrated that, in addition to the commonly used criteria for recognizing change in peoples' relationship with certain animals in the archaeological record (see Davis 1987: 133), the analysis of pathological conditions, in this case linear enamel hypoplasia (LEH), also has much potential. As a result of a currently ongoing research project on pig domestication and evolution throughout Eurasia, a vast data set on LEH has been collected, covering both modern wild boar populations and archaeological assemblages (from palaeolithic to medieval times). On the basis of the subset for central and northern Europe, it has been demonstrated that the analysis of LEH provides insight into changes in the relationship between *Sus* and humans, during Mesolithic and Neolithic times (Dobney *et al.* 2004, see further).

The aim of the present paper is to establish whether the patterns established for central and northern Europe can be extrapolated to other areas of the world. In order to evaluate this, teeth from recent wild boar populations and early archaeological sites, collected from south-west Asia, China, and Japan, have been included in the analysis. This material was selected because these are regions where claims for the early domestication of pigs have been made (e.g. Stampfli 1966 in manuscript, cited by Lawrence 1980 and published as Stampfli 1983; Bellwood 1996; Nelson 1998*a*; Yuan & Flad 2002; Nishimoto T. 2003). Before the analysis of the material will be presented, some background information on LEH is provided.

LINEAR ENAMEL HYPOPLASIA

Mammal teeth can provide many clues to an individual's living conditions, and certain developmental defects of teeth have been used as a retrospective way of studying physiological stress in mammal populations. Linear enamel hypoplasia (LEH) is a deficiency in enamel thickness occurring during tooth crown formation, typically visible on a tooth's surface as one or more grooves or lines (Colyer 1936; Fig. 4.1). The condition is generally caused by developmental stress (Sarnat & Moss 1985), the causes of which can be varied in nature, but nutritional deficiencies are certainly an important factor. Within anthropological studies of archaeological and recent material, the analysis of

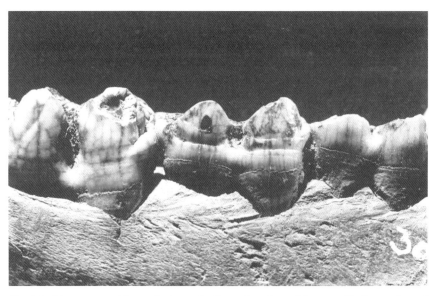

Fig. 4.1. Linear enamel hypoplasia on the lingual surface of the mandibular molars of a medieval European domestic pig (Ename, Belgium, *c*.1000 AD) (courtesy of the Flemish Heritage Institute)

LEH has successfully been used to assess the general health status of human populations (Goodman *et al.* 1988).

The methodology for recording LEH on pig molars from the lower jaw has been published by Dobney & Ervynck (1998), and revised by Dobney *et al.* (2002). Subsequently, it has been proved, using archaeological material, that LEH is not a rare or randomly occurring event in domestic pigs. In fact, it was possible to construct a chronology of physiological stress events, which explained why, generally, LEH is always present at the same heights on the molar crowns. It was proposed that birth and weaning are the direct causal agents of two discrete peaks in the height distribution of LEH on the first permanent molar (M_1), and a period of undernutrition encountered during the first winter of the animals' life is thought to be the main causal factor for the occurrence of the single distinct LEH peak noted on the M_2. A broad peak on the M_3 is similarly interpreted, i.e. as reflecting the animals' second winter. This chronology could be consistently applied to five archaeological collections (Dobney & Ervynck 2000), and this pattern has been further corroborated by studies on additional archaeological assemblages (Dobney *et al.* 2002). Finally, it was shown that the link established between the patterns of LEH and the developmental physiology of the domestic pig allows inferences to be made about former environmental conditions and husbandry practices (Ervynck & Dobney 1999).

The recent survey for Central and Northern Europe made clear that LEH does occur in recent and ancient north-west European wild boar populations (and that the occurrence of the condition can be explained by the same events within the animals' life as suggested for archaeological domestic pig populations), but with a frequency that is consistently low. This is a remarkable observation given the pronounced differences in the living conditions of these two diachronically well-separated groups, mainly linked with the increasing human pressure on recent populations of wild animals. Early domestic populations generally showed high LEH frequencies, although considerable variation existed between the samples. It was suggested that these high frequencies are, in general, the result of human interference, and the variation could be related to differences in early husbandry (Dobney *et al.* 2004).

MATERIAL AND METHODS

Linear enamel hypoplasia was recorded from the permanent mandibular molars of museum specimens collected from recent wild boar populations in south-west Asia, Europe (France, Germany, Switzerland, and Poland), China,

Table 4.1. Collections of recent wild boar mandibles studied.

Country	Collection	No. of M_1	No. of M_2	No. of M_3
Iran, Iraq, Syria, Eastern Turkey	Field Museum of Natural History, Chicago; Smithsonian Institution, Washington, DC; Museum of Comparative Zoology, Harvard University; Natural History Museums of Geneva and Berlin	47	39	29
Germany	Natural History Museums of Berne, Berlin; University of Hildesheim; Smithsonian Institution, Washington, DC	64	62	55
France	Natural History Museums of Paris, Geneva, Berne, Berlin	53	51	37
Switzerland	Natural History Museums of Geneva, Berne, Berlin	56	55	31
Poland	Natural History Museum of Berlin	76	72	50
China	Field Museum of Natural History, Chicago; Smithsonian Institution, Washington, DC; Museum of Comparative Zoology, Harvard University; Natural History Museum of Berlin; Institute of Zoology, St Petersburg	39	39	31
Japan (except Ryuku islands)	Nara Cultural Institute (Nabunken), Japan; Smithsonian Institution, Washington, DC; Natural History Museum of Berlin	28	28	22
Ryuku islands	Nara Cultural Institute (Nabunken), Japan	31	32	24
Indonesia	Smithsonian Institution, Washington, DC; Natural History Museums of Berne and Paris	55	55	50

and Japan (Table 4.1). Archaeological material was analysed from selected sites from the same regions (see Table 4.2), disregarding isolated teeth. A full account of the recording methodology can be found in Dobney & Ervynck (1998) and Dobney *et al.* (2002). Basically, the occurrence of individual LEH events has been observed and measured on all separate cusps of the permanent mandibular molars (M_1, M_2, and M_3). Subsequently, the frequency of LEH within the populations studied was evaluated using an index defined as:

$$\text{index}_{\text{(population A)}} = \text{average}[F_{\text{(tooth } x, \text{ cusp } y)\text{(population A)}} /$$
$$F_{\text{(tooth } x, \text{ cusp } y)\text{(allpopulations)}}]$$

where *F* is the number of LEH lines observed divide by the number of specimens observed, calculated per population, for each individual tooth cusp, when number of specimens > 0 (Ervynck & Dobney 1999). This calculation enables the comparison of the relative frequency of LEH (averaged over all tooth cusps) for a population against that calculated for all populations together (which by definition equals 1). The standard deviation of the calculated average describes the variation between teeth and cusps within a population. It should be stressed that the index values obtained are relative to each other, implying that a population's average value and standard deviation will change following the inclusion of additional samples in the data set, or their removal from it. However, the relative position of the data points to each other (lower or higher) will not change.

In previous studies on LEH in wild boar and archaeological pig populations, it has been stated that a comparison of the index values is meaningless when the aetiology of LEH differs markedly between the populations studied. Possible differences in aetiology can be tested by establishing the chronology of LEH relative to that of tooth development. In the cases of a Neolithic site from England and four medieval sites from Belgium, it has indeed been demonstrated that the chronology of LEH was broadly the same (Dobney & Ervynck 2000), a result further corroborated by the analysis of an Early Medieval stratified site from England and a Late Medieval assemblage from Belgium (Dobney *et al.* 2002). A survey of 29 Mesolithic and Neolithic sites from Europe, and the analysis of European wild boar material, further confirmed the consistency of the underlying chronology of LEH (and thus most probably also of the aetiology) (Dobney *et al.* 2004). In contrast, at the Eastern Anatolian site of Çayönü, the relative chronology of LEH showed certain aspects similar to those recorded at other sites, but others that did not correspond with observations from other populations (Ervynck *et al.* 2001), although the data set for this site was rather limited. Small sample sizes also hampered the evaluation of the chronology for the other south-west Asian archaeological assemblages discussed in this paper, and for the wild boar material from China and Japan. However, the analysis of the chronology for the Chinese and Japanese archaeological sites (combined by country in Figs 4.2 and 4.3) revealed patterns that are broadly the same as the ones previously published (i.e. Dobney & Ervynck 2000; Dobney *et al.* 2002; Dobney *et al.* 2004), taking into account that data from sites with very different chronology and geography have been combined. Therefore, for the following analyses, the assumption is that the underlying aetiology of LEH is comparable throughout.

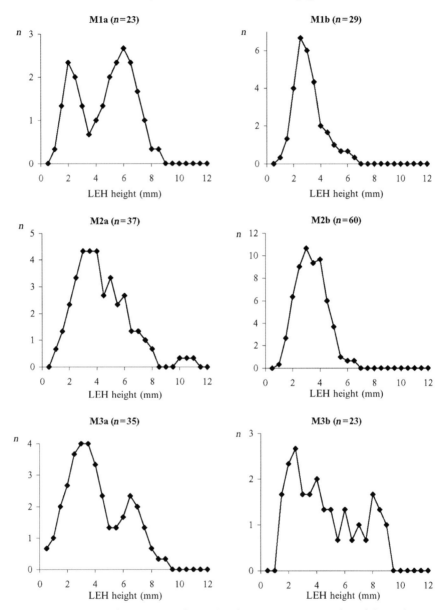

Fig. 4.2. Frequency distribution of LEH heights per cusp, per molar of the archaeo-logical pigs from China (all sites combined, n = running mean)

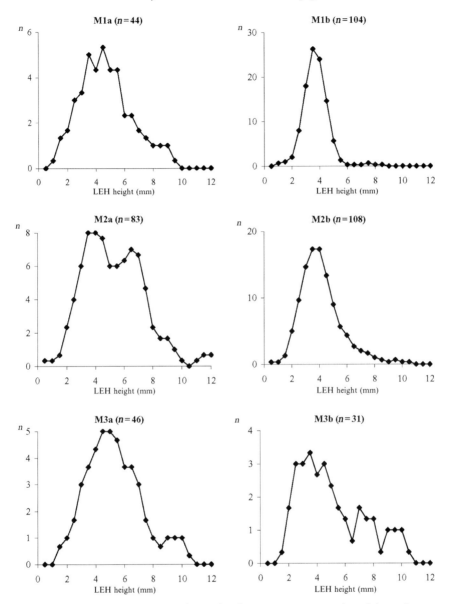

Fig. 4.3. Frequency distribution of LEH heights per cusp, per molar of the archaeological pigs from Japan (all sites combined, n = running mean)

RESULTS

Figure 4.4 summarizes the LEH index values for the selected wild boar populations and archaeological assemblages from the Eurasian data set (total number of teeth observed = 5188). It should be noted that, in comparison to Dobney *et al.* (2004), the data set for Neolithic Sweden is slightly different, owing to the recent acquisition of new data. Furthermore, in the case of Japan, data from sites of contemporaneous date have been combined (see further). From the overview, it is clear that the variation between the average values per sample is considerable (ranging from 0.2 to 1.9) and that the standard deviations in some cases reach high values (even up to 0.9). However, the number of teeth differs widely between samples, ranging from 18 (for the Mesolithic of Switzerland) up to 1045 (for the Neolithic of Switzerland). For the purposes of this paper, first the data from recent wild boar will be discussed, followed by an analysis of the archaeological data set by region.

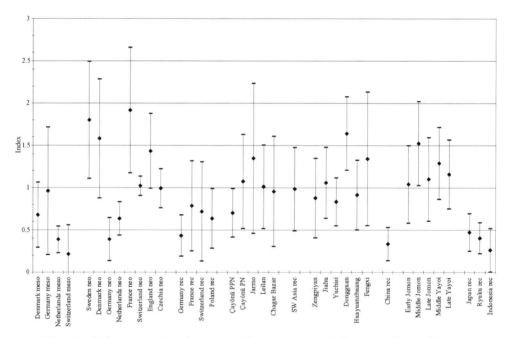

Fig. 4.4. Index comparing the average frequency of LEH between all populations studied. The error bars are calculated as the mean plus or minus the standard deviation (meso, Mesolithic wild boar; neo, Neolithic domestic pig, possibly including wild boar; rec, recent wild boar; for sample sizes see Tables 4.1 and 4.2)

Wild boar

Compared to most archaeological assemblages, the recent wild boar samples almost always show low mean index values (Fig. 4.4). The European Meso-lithic samples (which must also be wild boar) show index values that are similarly low, a pattern possibly explained by natural selection (as discussed in Dobney *et al.* 2004). When the recent wild boar data are plotted separately (Fig. 4.5, total number of teeth observed = 1211), it can be seen that the south-west Asian population (consisting of specimens from Turkey, Syria, Iraq, and Iran) is characterized by a rather high frequency of LEH, compared to Europe and East Asia. The East Asian data set comprises specimens from China, Japan, and Indonesia, the Japanese population being further divided into two subspecies—*Sus scrofa leucomastyx* from the main islands, and *Sus scrofa ryukuensis* from the Ryuku archipelago. This subdivision is justified by the extreme size variation between both subspecies, the result of long-term island isolation of the Ryuku animals (Groves 1981), and by their morpho-logical differences (Endo *et al.* 1994, 1998*a*, 1998*b*). Despite the vast geo-graphic separation of the populations studied, and the different climatic conditions they experience, the East Asian wild boar populations show

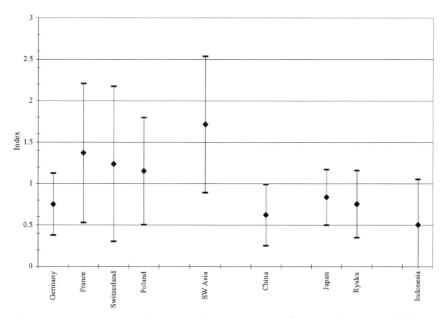

Fig. 4.5. Index comparing the average frequency of LEH between the recent wild boar populations studied (for sample sizes see Table 4.1)

consistently low LEH index values. Although there is some variation between the modern European samples, they tend to reach higher values than the East Asian ones, but lower than the modern south-west Asian sample.

As to the suitability of recent wild boar as an appropriate comparison for ancient material, it could be questioned whether the recent wild boar from mainland Japan, curated at the Nara Institute, represent a valuable population. This material was sourced from animals managed by humans, and probably regularly fed or even penned (Matsui, Hongo, and Anezaki pers. comm.). However, a recent evaluation of LEH in another wild boar skeletal collection, curated at the Department of Anatomy, Graduate School of Medicine, Osaka City University and representing a truly 'wild' population hunted some 40 years ago, demonstrated the same low LEH frequency (data not presented here).

South-west Asia

Sufficient archaeological pig material was available only from four sites from south-west Asia: the Neolithic settlements of Çayönü Tepesi (eastern Anatolia, Turkey) and Jarmo (northern Iraq), and the early urban centres of Leilan and Chagar Bazar (northern Syria). With the exception of Çayönü, sample numbers are low, a pattern that reflects the generally low frequency of the pig in many sites in the Levant and Mesopotamia during prehistoric times. Early eastern Anatolian sites are characterized by higher pig frequencies, but recently excavated material, for example from Hallan Çemi (Redding, pers. comm.), could not yet be included in this study. Since the animal remains from Çayönü cover a large time period, the sample has been subdivided in two chronological groups, the Pre-Pottery Neolithic (10200–8000 uncal. BP) and the Pottery Neolithic (8000–7500 uncal. BP) (see Ervynck *et al.* 2001). The Jarmo assemblage is contemporaneous to the material from Pre-Pottery Neolithic Çayönü, whereas the finds from Leilan are slightly younger than those from Pottery Neolithic Çayönü. The bones from Chagar Bazar represent much younger prehistoric material (Table 4.2).

As already reported in a previous analysis (Ervynck *et al.* 2001), the frequency of LEH is higher in the Pottery Neolithic of Çayönü than in the Pre-Pottery phase (Fig. 4.6, total number of teeth observed from archaeological sites = 450). The index for Jarmo shows a large standard deviation due to limited sample size, but is much higher than the value for the partly contemporary PPN sample from Çayönü. The assemblages from Leilan and Chagar Bazar show comparable index values to Jarmo and Pottery Neolithic Çayönü. Since data for pre-Neolithic wild boar are not available, the archaeological samples could only be compared with recent wild boar specimens,

Table 4.2. Collections of archaeological domestic pig mandibles studied.

Country	Location	Period	Dating	Collection	No. of M$_1$	No. of M$_2$	No. of M$_3$	References
Turkey	Çayönü	Pre-Pottery to Pottery Neolithic	10200–7500 uncal. BP	University of Istanbul	98	73	67	Ervynck et al. (2001)
Iraq	Jarmo	Late PPNB	7600–6400 cal. BP	Field Museum of Natural History, Chicago	23	16	9	Stampfli (1983)
Syria	Leilan	Ubeid 4	5000–4500 cal. BC	Smithsonian Institution, Washington, DC	41	30	22	Zeder (1999)
Syria Europe	Chagar Bazar See Dobney et al. (2004), Table 2	Middle Bronze Age See Dobney et al. (2004), Table 2	c.1850–1650 cal. BC See Dobney et al. (2004), Table 2	Site depot, Syria See Dobney et al. (2004), Table 2	1089	775	666	McMahon et al. (2001) See Dobney et al. (2004) Table 2
China	Zengpiyan cave	Neolithic	10,550–5600 cal. BC	Institute of Archaeology, Beijing	19	14	16	Institute of Archaeology et al. (2003)
China	Jiahu	Neolithic	7000–6200 cal. BC	Institute of Archaeology, Beijing	31	28	21	Henan Provincial Institute of Cultural Relics and Archaeology (1999)
China	Yuchisi	Neolithic	2800–2600 cal. BC	Institute of Archaeology, Beijing	37	40	28	Institute of Archaeology et al. (2001)
China	Dongguan	Neolithic	2400–2000 cal. BC	Institute of Archaeology, Beijing	23	17	12	Dept of Archaeology, National Museum of Chinese History et al. (2001)
China	Huayuanzhuang	Bronze Age	1520–1380 cal. BC	Institute of Archaeology, Beijing	29	26	18	Yuan & Tang (2000)
China	Fengxi	Bronze Age	1050–750 cal. BC	Institute of Archaeology, Beijing	9	4	5	Fenghao Archaeology Team (2000)
Japan	Torihama	Early Jomon	5500 uncal. BP	Wakasa Museum of History and Folklore, Obama	84	72	39	Inaba (1983), Shigehara et al. (1991), Anezaki (2002)
Japan	Haneo	Early Jomon	6900–6100 cal. BP	Tamagawa Cultural Research Centre	11	9	7	Toizumi et al. (2003), Anezaki et al. in press
Japan	Kusakari	Middle Jomon	–	Chiba Prefecture Archaeological Centre	17	12	14	Nogari (1990)

(Continued)

Table 4.2. (*Continued*)

Country	Location	Period	Dating	Collection	No. of M_1	No. of M_2	No. of M_3	References
Japan	Ariyoshikita	Middle Jomon	5000–4600 BP	Chiba Prefecture Archaeological Centre	9	4	3	Nishino (1999)
Japan	Satohama	Late Jomon	2970–2870 uncal. BP	Miyagi Prefecture, Board of Education	3	1	0	Board of Education, Miyagi Prefecture (1986*b*), Tohoku History Museum (1986, 1987)
Japan	Tagara	Late Jomon	3500–3000 uncal. BP 2820–3010 uncal. BP (^{14}C)	Miyagi Prefecture, Board of Education	33	24	18	Board of Education, Miyagi Prefecture (1986*a*)
Japan	Aikoshima	Late Jomon	4500–3190 uncal. BP (14C)	Iwaki City Board of Education	0	1	0	Yamazaki (1997)
Japan	Kokanza	Late Jomon	c.3600–3200 uncal. BP	Chiba Prefecture Archaeological Centre	2	1	1	Ono & Nogari (1982)
Japan	Ikego	Middle Yayoi	2500–1700 uncal. BP	Kanagawa Archaeological Centre	20	17	8	Nishimoto & Anezaki (1999*a–c*)
Japan	Higashinara	Middle Yayoi	BC 250–1st century AD	Osaka Prefecture Archaeological Centre	5	6	4	Abe (1981)
Japan	Shinpo	Middle Yayoi	400–250 uncal. BC	Kobe City Archaealogical Centre	19	14	13	Matsui & Maruyama (2003)
Japan	Kamei	Middle Yayoi	BC 250–1st century AD	Osaka Prefecture Archaeological Centre	19	19	9	Matsui (1986)
Japan	Tsuboi	Early–Middle Yayoi	BC 3rd–4th century?	Archaeological Institute of Kashihara, Nara Prefecture	15	16	11	Matsui & Miyaji (2000)
Japan	Kadota	Late Yayoi	300–200 AD	Okayama Prefecture Board of Education	21	15	17	Kaneko (1983)
Japan	Gebayashi Nishida	Late Yayoi	300–200 AD	Fukuoka Prefecture Board of Education	4	4	3	Nishimoto & Anezaki (1998)
Japan	Harunotsuji	Middle–Late Yayoi	BC 4th–3rd century AD?	Nagasaki Prefecture Board of Education	1	2	2	Matsui (1995)

Abbreviations: neo, Neolithic; PPNB, Pre-Pottery Neolithic B.

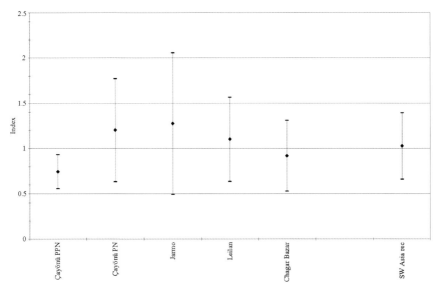

Fig. 4.6. Index comparing the average frequency of LEH between all populations studied from south-west Asia (PPN, Pre-Pottery Neolithic; PN, Pottery Neolithic; rec, recent wild boar; for sample sizes see Tables 4.1 and 4.2)

taking into account that these show a rather high frequency of LEH compared to other Eurasian wild boar populations (see Fig. 4.5).

Europe

The data from Europe (Fig. 4.7, total number of teeth observed from arch-aeological sites = 2530) mostly show higher index values and higher variation for Neolithic sites compared to Mesolithic and modern wild boar. Exceptions among the Neolithic sites have been attributed to possible differences in the extent of human interference with the *Sus* populations. Examples could be low-intensity husbandry strategies, or the continuation of hunting subsist-ence strategies into the Neolithic (taking into account that a significant number of wild boar could be present within the *Sus* population) (Dobney *et al.* 2004). Moreover, most sites within the data set do not span long occupation sequences, which make it rather difficult to observe trends through time. Intriguingly, in the rare case of the diachronic assemblages from Zürich-Mozartstrasse (Switzerland), it is clear that LEH frequency gradually increased through time (Fig. 4.8).

The chronology and nature of pig exploitation in Scandinavia has recently also been debated, on the basis of age at death profiles and biometry (Benecke

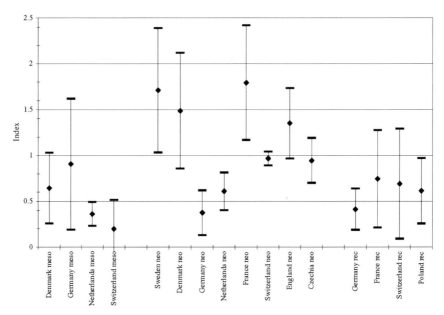

Fig. 4.7. Index comparing the average frequency of LEH between all populations studied from Europe (meso, Mesolithic wild boar; neo, Neolithic domestic pig, possibly including wild boar; rec, recent wild boar; for sample sizes see Tables 4.1 and 4.2)

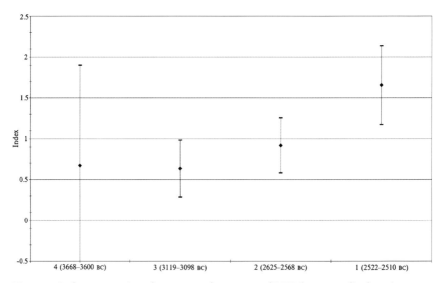

Fig. 4.8. Index comparing the average frequency of LEH between diachronic strata from Zürich-Mozartstrasse (sample sizes: $n = 43$ for phase 4, $n = 136$ for phase 3, $n = 82$ for phase 2, $n = 90$ for phase 1)

1994; Rowley-Conwy & Storå 1997). The analysis of LEH from some of the key sites from Scandinavia significantly contributes to this discussion but this analysis is presented elsewhere (see Rowley-Conwy and Dobney this volume).

China

Sus remains from six archaeological sites from China have been analysed for LEH. The sites represent different locations within the north-eastern and central parts of the country, and vary widely in chronology, spanning the period from the Early Neolithic to the Bronze Age. In general, the material from Zengpiyan (Guangxi province, 10550–5600 cal. BC), Jiahu (Henan province, 7000–6200 cal. BC), Yuchisi (Anhui province, 2800–2600 cal. BC), Dongguan (Shanxi province, 2400–2000 cal. BC), Huayuanzhuang (Henan province, 1520–1380 cal. BC) and Fengxi (Shaanxi province, 1050–750 cal. BC) is not numerous (total number of teeth observed from archaeological sites = 377) but shows LEH index values markedly higher than that for recent Chinese wild boar (Fig. 4.9). This observation, however, must be regarded with caution since both the recent and the archaeological specimens were collected from a wide area within China. Amongst the archaeological samples,

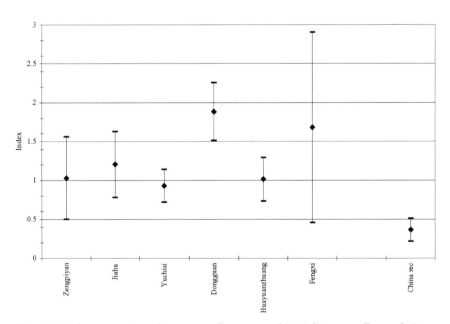

Fig. 4.9. Index comparing the average frequency of LEH between all populations studied from China (rec, recent wild boar; for sample sizes see Tables 4.1 and 4.2)

the Fengxi material shows a very large standard deviation, without doubt the result of small sample size (see Table 4.2), and the pigs from Dongguan are characterized by the highest LEH frequency.

Japan

A total of 16 archaeological assemblages from Japan have been analysed (see Table 4.2). Because some of these are very limited in terms of sample size, further grouping by cultural period has been applied, despite the fact that the sites are located in different geographic areas. In this way, the data have been broadly grouped into the Jomon 'hunter-gatherer' culture and the subsequent Yayoi agricultural society. The oldest period can be subdivided into Early Jomon (Torihama and Haneo), Middle Jomon (Kusakari and Ariyoshikita), and Late Jomon cultural phases (Satohama, Tagara, Aikoshima, and Kokanza). The Yayoi period is represented by Middle Yayoi (Ikego, Higashi-nara, Shinpo, and Kamei) and Late Yayoi sites (Tsuboi, Kadota, Shimobaya-shi, and Harunotsuji).

The archaeological data show much higher LEH frequencies than the modern Japanese wild boar populations (Fig. 4.10, total number of teeth

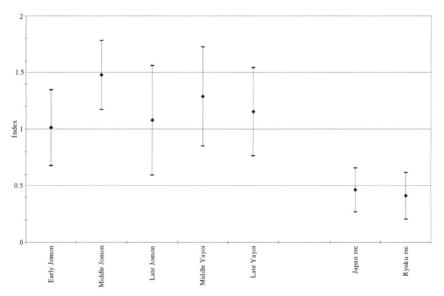

Fig. 4.10. Index comparing the average frequency of LEH between all populations studied from Japan (rec, recent wild boar; for sample sizes see Tables 4.1 and 4.2; for grouping of the sites see text)

observed from archaeological sites = 620), but the index values for the Jomon and Yayoi cultural phases seem to be broadly similar. Whether the differences between the average values (such as for the Middle Jomon period) are meaningful remains to be proven.

DISCUSSION

It is obvious from the results presented above that there are clear patterns to be observed within the data set (see Fig. 4.4). All Neolithic assemblages (and even the Japanese Jomon sites) tend to show LEH index values that are higher than those for recent wild boar, except when the archaeological data are compared with those for south-west Asian wild boar, which show a high average index value—certainly higher than that of the other wild boar samples (see Fig. 4.5). Theoretically, it is to be expected that the LEH frequency in wild boar should be consistently low, a pattern explained by Darwinian selection if LEH susceptibility has a genetic basis (Dobney *et al.* 2004). Then, high LEH frequencies in individuals would reflect reduced fitness (certainly when there is a link between LEH and undernourishment), limiting their reproductive contribution to succeeding generations, and thus resulting in the reduced occurrence of LEH within the population. Within this evolutionary framework, however, the high frequency of LEH in south-west Asian wild boar remains unclear. An 'island effect' could be invoked, if wild boar population numbers were decimated, with many groups living in geographically isolated, reduced territories. However, this was certainly not the case during the period that the museum specimens were collected (see Harrison 1968; Harrison & Bates 1991). Alternatively, it could be the case that LEH is a purely phenotypic phenomenon, which would imply that the high frequencies are explained by unfavourable living conditions of the populations, perhaps caused by natural or anthropogenic environmental stress. Again, however, this is unlikely for the populations in question, during the time the specimens were sampled.

Within the south-west Asian data set, information is lacking about pre-Neolithic wild boar populations, such as that which could be found in palaeolithic or palaeontological assemblages. However, the oldest *Sus* material from Çayönü (Pre-Pottery Neolithic A to Early Pre-Pottery Neolithic B) could represent such a population, a statement corroborated by a limited number of biometrical data from the M_3 (Fig. 4.11, after Ervynck *et al.* 2001), showing tooth lengths even longer than those for recent wild boar from Turkey. A diachronic comparison of the M_3 lengths for Çayönü illustrates the gradual

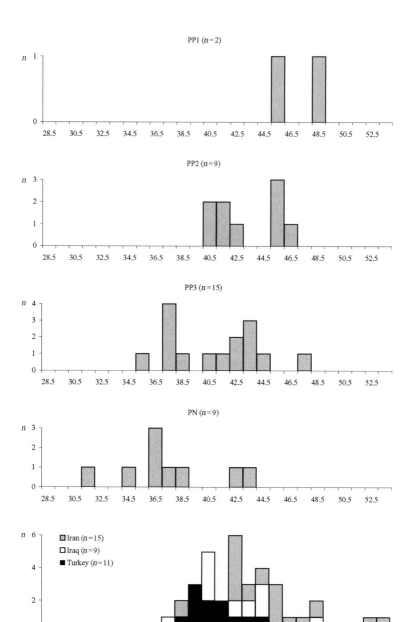

Fig. 4.11. Frequency distribution of the length (mm) of the M_3 of *Sus* per chronological phase of Çayönü Tepesi, compared to the data available from recent specimens (after Ervynck *et al.* 2001, but with adjusted data set for the modern populations). Black indicates material from Turkey, collected by Payne and Bull (Payne & Bull 1988) and Hongo (Hongo and Meadow 1998: Table 4) and specimens recorded for this study (Table 4.1); white indicates material collected from Iraq (Table 4.1); grey indicates material collected from Iran (Table 4.1)

shift to shorter teeth within the *Sus* population, throughout the Pre-Pottery and Pottery Neolithic. The *Sus* bones from the latter period (*c.*8000– 7500 uncal. BP) most probably come from domesticated animals, as suggested by the tooth lengths shorter than recent Turkish wild boar (Fig. 4.11). This biometrical trend is paralleled by an increase in the LEH frequencies, comparing the Pre-Pottery and Pottery Neolithic populations of Çayönü (see Fig. 4.6). This increase has been interpreted as the result of increased physiological stress levels in the *Sus* populations that were experiencing increasing human interference (Ervynck *et al.* 2001). If high LEH index values genuinely reflect growing human intervention, then this would suggest that the *Sus* assemblage from Jarmo certainly was no longer a primarily wild population. This is potentially interesting, considering the Jarmo material is contemporaneous to the youngest material from Pre-Pottery Neolithic Çayönü. However, the difference in LEH frequency within both contemporaneous samples from Çayönü and Jarmo could also have been related to the different geographic and climatic characteristics of the environments of the sites, located respectively in the Anatolian inland plains, and in the hills and piedmont at the foot of the mountains of the Fertile Crescent (zones B2 and C1 in Hours *et al.* 1994). The two remaining south-west Asian sites are located in the Syro-Iraqi zone of the Fertile Crescent (zone C2 in Hours *et al.* 1994). They represent urban centres in northern Mesopotamia, in which pigs most probably lived as fully domestic animals (see e.g. Zeder 1999). The LEH frequencies for both most recent sites (Leilan and Chagar Bazar) fall within the range of those for Jarmo and Pottery Neolithic Çayönü, but further research on more urban assemblages from the region will be needed in order to explain this pattern. It is known that pigs were economically important at these sites (Zeder 1999), but the details of the husbandry regimes which were practised are not yet well known.

The data set for central and north-western Europe includes Mesolithic wild boar, which show LEH index values as low (or even lower) as modern European wild boar (see Fig. 4.7). Moreover, according to previous hypotheses (Dobney *et al.* 2004), the effect of 'neolithization' can clearly be observed, although two assemblages, i.e. representing German and Dutch Early Neolithic sites with index values as low as the Mesolithic sites, do not follow this pattern. However, the detailed diachronic analysis of the Zürich-Mozartstrasse site (see Fig. 4.8) suggests that both the decrease in importance of wild boar hunting, and the increase of the domestic pig herds (or the intensification of pig husbandry), may have been gradual phenomena at many sites. In addition, it must be remembered that morphological changes also occurred within the domestic pig populations (see Fig. 4.12 for Zürich-Mozartstrasse), further complicating the picture. In general, however, the

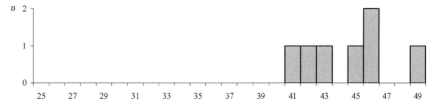

Mozartstrasse 4 (3668–3600 bc, $n = 7$)

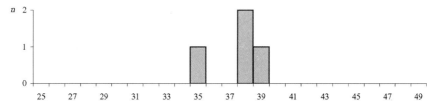

Mozartstrasse 3 (3119–3098 bc, $n = 4$)

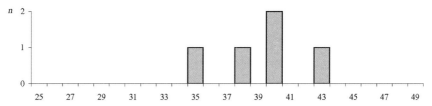

Mozartstrasse 2 (2625–2568 bc, $n = 5$)

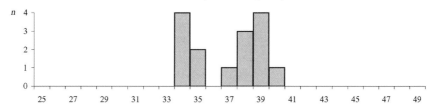

Mozartstrasse 1 (2522–2510 bc, $n = 15$)

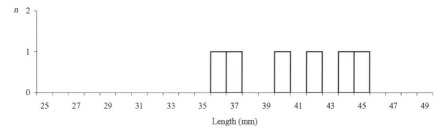

Recent wild boar ($n = 6$)

Length (mm)

Fig. 4.12. Frequency distribution of the length (mm) of the M_3 of *Sus* from the strata at Zürich-Mozartstrasse (after Dobney *et al.* 2004)

difference between wild and domestic animals remains the most striking result from the European data set.

The Chinese data, although based upon a limited number of sites, cover a large time span (10550–750 cal. BC). The oldest (and perhaps most famous) site, Zengpiyan, reputedly dating back to 10550–5600 cal BC, has been linked with an early Asian pig domestication event, merely on the basis of the age profile of the *Sus* population (Nelson 1998*b*). However, uncertainties about dating, stratigraphy, and cultural context have cast doubt upon this interpretation (Yuan & Flad 2002; Institute of Archaeology *et al.* 2003: 681). Therefore, the *Sus* remains from Zengpiyan could either represent an early prehistoric wild boar population with unusually high levels of physiological stress, or a very early domestic pig population (or possibly a combination of the two). If, however, the uncertainties about dating prove to be valid, and these animals are not from the very early phases of human occupation as originally thought, their high LEH index value may simply reflect the pattern seen elsewhere in later domesticated animals under human control.

The fact that the Chinese prehistoric wild boar (if indeed this is what they represent) shows a markedly higher LEH frequency compared to their recent counterparts (see Fig. 4.9) is in contrast to the European pattern. Intriguingly, the Zengpiyan index value is similar to that from the younger sites of Jiahu, Yuchisi, and Huayuanzhuang. Certainly, the date of the latter site suggests that an important part of the *Sus* remains must represent domestic animals (see Yuan & Flad 2002), but whether this implies that the Zengpiyan *Sus* populations also experienced some level of human intervention (in contrast to the most recent interpretation), remains to be further explored. The same is true for the Jiahu and Yuchisi samples, and it also remains unclear why the Dongguan LEH index value is so elevated. As already demonstrated by Yuan (2001), diachronic biometric comparison of the Chinese sites illustrates a gradual decrease of the length of the M_3 over several millennia (Fig. 4.13), and probably confirms the domestic status of the Huayuanzhuang pigs. The gradual trend is similar to that noted for prehistoric Çayönü (see Fig. 4.11) although it covers a much longer time period. In the case of the Anatolian site, the gradual morphological change in the dentition has been interpreted as evidence for a slow and long-term local domestication process. This interpretation can possibly be extrapolated to the Chinese data set, implying a similarly gradual, separate East Asian domestication process (perhaps already beginning at some point in the early occupation phases of Zengpiyan, although this cannot be proved without a re-evaluation of the site).

The culture to which the oldest Japanese sites belong, i.e. the Jomon, covers most of the country's prehistory (*c.*12000–2500 BP) and many aspects of its subsistence strategy still remain unclear (see Imamura 1996; Hudson 1999;

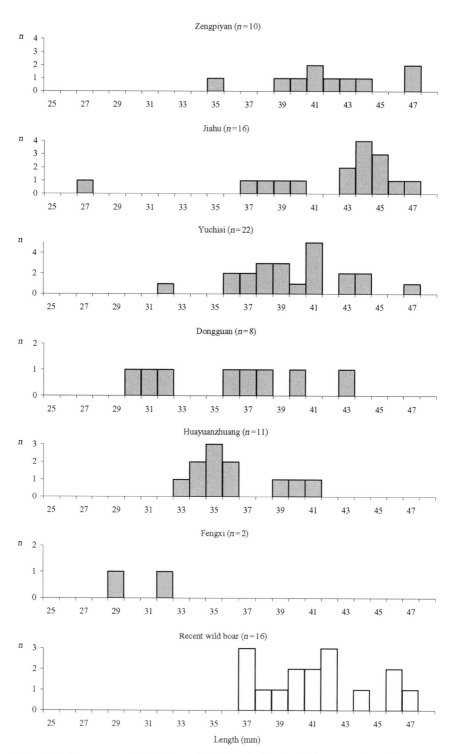

Fig. 4.13. Frequency distribution of the length (mm) of the M$_3$ of *Sus* from the archaeological sites in China, compared to the data available from recent specimens (for provenance see Table 4.1)

Yoneda *et al.* 2004). *Sus* were certainly a significant component of the Jomon food economy (together with cervids), as evidenced by their numerous remains in many sites of that period (Nishimoto T. 1991), but whether they ever experienced some degree of human management (as proposed by Nishimoto T. 2003) is still open to much debate. Many archaeologists disregard a possible close relationship between man and pigs during Jomon times and stress that domestic pig only arrived on the Japanese islands with the Yayoi people, during the last centuries BC (as demonstrated by Naora 1935, 1937*a*, 1937*b*, 1938*a*, 1938*b*; Nishimoto T. 1994). In any case, in terms of LEH frequencies, the Jomon assemblages all show high index values compared to the wild boar populations studied (see Fig. 4.14). Either these high Japanese values are peculiar for wild boar (ancient or recent), or, following the line of reasoning for the European material, they might suggest some form of human interference in the Jomon *Sus* populations. Hongo & Meadow (1998: 89), in discussing the changes in *Sus* during the long occupation of Çayönü, have outlined that many intermediate forms may have occurred in the relationship between humans and *Sus*, characterized by a true influence upon the wild populations but not reaching the full extent of domestication. The authors cite ethnographic and historical cases from India, South East Asia (including Japan), and Oceania that could perhaps also be used to explain the changes in *Sus* during the Jomon period. However, many more data are needed to substantiate this interpretation. It could well be that regional differences in habitat and therefore food availability may be a major factor influencing the LEH index values, particularly for the Late Jomon sites used here. These Jomon sites are primarily from the north of Honshu in areas of broad-leaf forest, where optimal conditions for wild boar exist. The Early Jomon sites used in this study (including Torihama) are in coastal regions. Also, the warmer climate (with less snow) during the Early Jomon period (Ota *et al.* 1982) might be a reason why the LEH index value for the pigs from Torihama and Haneo are similarly low compared to those from Late Jomon north Japan.

Is it possible that the higher LEH index value for the Middle Jomon period is the result of better living conditions for pigs at this time? Coincidentally, the Middle Jomon period is also the time when 'Jomon culture reached its climax' (Imamura 1996: 93). It is during this period, at sites around the Tokyo bay region, that pigs were buried together with humans and dogs (Nishimoto T. 2003). At the same sites, there is also tentative evidence for morphological changes occurring in the skeletons of pigs (Nishimoto T. 2003). Remarkably enough, Middle Jomon pigs also seem to have been characterized by a size increase. Analysis of the biometry of third molars (M_3), for example, shows an increase in length during the Middle Jomon period (see Fig 4.15, also noted by Anezaki 2003, and Hongo and Anezaki, pers. comm., for a different

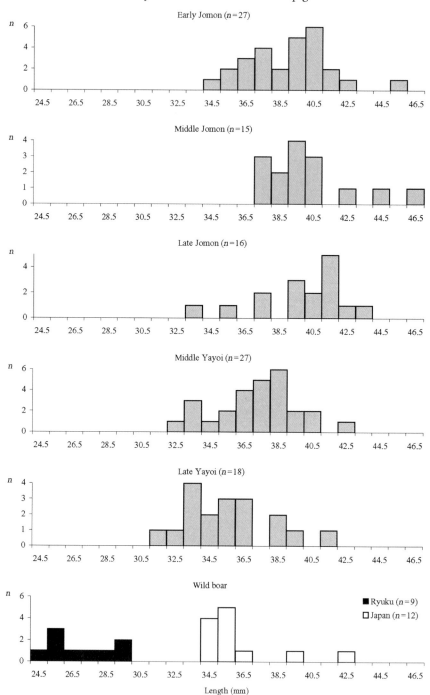

Fig. 4.14. Frequency distribution of the length (mm) of the M_3 of *Sus* from the archaeological sites in Japan (grouped per chronological phase), compared to the data available from recent specimens (for provenance see Table 4.1)

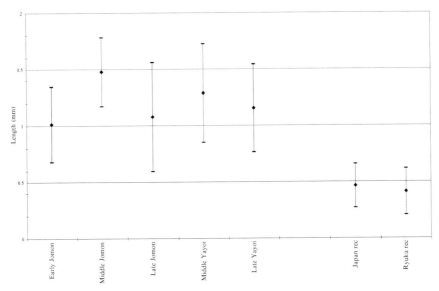

Fig. 4.15. Summary of the frequency distributions of the length (mm) of the M₃ of *Sus* from the archaeological sites in Japan (grouped per chronological phase), compared to the data available from recent specimens (for provenance see Table 4.1). The error bars are calculated as the mean plus or minus the standard deviation (for sample sizes see Fig. 4.14)

Jomon data set), followed by a steady decrease into and through the Yayoi period. However, whether the size change in the Jomon period is related to a shift in direct human interference with *Sus* populations cannot be proven.

CONCLUSION

In this broad survey of *Sus* material from four selected geographic regions, LEH frequencies tend to be higher in all archaeological sites, compared to their recent wild counterparts. It is likely that the effects of human interference (intensifying over time) were detrimental to the *Sus* populations, resulting in increased levels of physiological stress in the animals. Moreover, these high index values seem to be maintained throughout prehistory, a pattern continued even into historic times (see Ervynck & Dobney 1999; Dobney *et al.* 2002; Dobney *et al.* unpublished data). The explanation could be that, as a result of human influence, the populations under domestication did not easily reach a new equilibrium in terms of selection. In addition, or alternatively, living conditions under different husbandry regimes were most probably less than optimal. Although the wild boar populations in most areas continued to show low LEH frequencies (despite increased human disturbance), physiological stress appears to have remained an important factor in domesticated pig's lives. This trend, together with the observed gradual and slow decrease in tooth length, suggests a long drawn-out domestication process.

5

Culture, ecology, and pigs from the 5th to the 3rd millennium BC around the Fertile Crescent

Caroline Grigson

INTRODUCTION

By the 5th millennium BC people in the Middle East were dependent for their meat on four domestic ungulates: sheep, goats, cattle, and pigs, all considerably smaller than their wild ancestors (Bökönyi 1977; Uerpmann 1979; Flannery, K.V. 1983; Laffer 1983; Meadow 1983; Stampfli 1983; Grigson 1989; Ducos 1993; Horwitz & Tchernov 1998; Vigne & Buitenhuis 1999; Peters *et al.* 2000; Ervynck *et al.* 2001; and many others). It is uncertain whether equids had been domesticated at this date, but their remains are so few in most sites of the 5th, 4th, and 3rd millennia that they can be discounted in any discussion relating to the domestic economy. On the small number of sites where their remains are plentiful they are thought to be derived from wild onagers or wild asses (Uerpmann 1986). In these three millennia the numerical proportion of pig remains compared with those of other domestic artiodactyls varies from site to site. In view of the later pig prohibitions of Islam and Judaism it is of particular interest to know, for the prehistory of the area, when and where pigs were present or absent, and if absent whether this can already be accounted for by any developing social or cultural attitude, in the millennia before the establishment of these religions, or whether it must be explained by simpler economic or environmental factors.

CHRONOLOGY

All dates in the present work are based on uncalibrated radiocarbon years BC, simply because even when radiocarbon dates for the sites are available (which is by no means always the case), many have not been published in calibrated form. The period studied in the present work starts with the later pottery cultures of the 5th millennium BC which are usually designated as Early Chalcolithic (Late Halaf, Amuq E, and Ubaid 2 and 3) although in the southern Levant most authorities refer to the contemporary Wadi Rabah culture as the Late Neolithic.

The 4th millennium is the period of the Chalcolithic (or Late Chalcolithic), typically the Ghassoul-Beersheva culture of the southern Levant and the Uruk and Late Ubaid periods in Mesopotamia, northern Syria, and south-eastern Turkey.

Although in some areas the 3rd millennium may include a very late Chalcolithic, by and large its cultures belong to the Early Bronze Age (EBA), equivalent in Mesopotamia to the Early Dynastic (ED), and in northern Iraq, northern Syria and southeastern Turkey to Ninevite 5, followed later in the 3rd millennium by the Akkadian.

THE DATA STUDIED

The relative importance of pigs in the domestic economy of the sites studied has been calculated on the basis of the percentage of their remains (using NISP counts, numbers of individual specimens) to that of the total of the domestic artiodactyls (sheep, goats, cattle, and pigs). Sites with very small numbers of identified artiodactyl bones have been omitted, and in some cases my figures have been calculated back from percentages of the total number of identified bones. The most obvious variation as far as pigs are concerned is their absence or near absence in some sites and their presence in significant numbers at others. On sites where numbers are reported I have taken a level of 7% of pig bones as significant, with 2% or less considered insignificant and perhaps representing occasional wild pigs, the odd importation of joints of pork, or intrusions, with 2–7% as of doubtful significance. Although archaeozoological reports have gradually become more numerate over the years, some still lack proper quantification. However, one can often discover which of the domesticates were present in significant numbers, either from the excavator's observations in the field, or from general statements made in reports.

On all sites, from the 5th millennium onwards, where the measurements have been recorded and analysed, domestic pigs are indicated, with just the very occasional wild boar. One or two sites in which the few *Sus* remains present are thought to represent wild boar have been omitted for this reason, as have the few sites in which wild animals were in the majority. The assemblages studied are listed in Tables 5.1–5.3, together with sample sizes and the percentages of pig bones.

Table 5.1. Percentages of pig bones in 5th millennium sites from the study area.

Site	Figure	Period	Date (mill. BC)	Total domestic species	% Pig	References
Abu Zureiq	5.1	Wadi Rabah	5th	142	22.5	Horwitz (2002c)
Amuq E	5.1	Ubaid related	5th	n.s.	present	Stampfli (1983)
Arjoune trenches V & VII	5.1		5th	1448	21.3	Grigson (2003)
Arpachiyar	5.1		5th	n.s.	c.25	Watson (1980)
Banahilk	5.1		5th	777	15.7	Laffer (1983)
Cavi Tarlasi	5.1	Halaf	5th	3306	26.8	Schäffer & Boessneck (1998)
Chaga Sefid	5.1		5th	n.s.	0.0	Wheeler Pires-Ferreira (1975/7)
Eridu XIII	5.1		5th	n.s.	0.0	Flannery & Wright (1966)
Girikihaciyan	5.1		5th	1953	18.5	McArdle (1975–77)
Hagoshrim layer 4	5.1	Wadi Rabah	5th	3619	24.5	Haber & Dayan (2004)
Hagoshrim layer 5	5.1	Jericho IX	5th	1899	15.4	Haber & Dayan (2004)
Kuran, late Ubaid	5.1	Late Ubaid	5th late	183	0.0	Zeder (1998a)
Mashnaqa	5.1	Late Ubaid Ubaid 4	5th late	1285	6.5	Zeder (1998a)
Nahal Zehora I	5.1	Wadi Rabah	5th	80.5	35.4	Davis (in press)
Nahal Zehora II	5.1	Wadi Rabah	5th	121	26.0	Davis (in press)
Neve Yam	5.1	Pott Neo	5th	75	26.7	Horwitz (1988), (2002a)
Nineveh 2C	5.1		5th	n.s.	present	Thompson & Mallowan (1933)
Qatif Y3	5.1	Pott Neo	c. 4000	261	33.3	Grigson (1984a)
Ras el Amiya	5.1		5th	120	0.0	Flannery & Cornwall (1969)
Ras Shamra IVA3	5.1	Late Halaf	5th?	48	37.5	Poulain (1978)

(*Continued*)

Table 5.1. (*Continued*)

Site	Figure	Period	Date (mill. BC)	Total domestic species	% Pig	References
Sabz—Khazineh	5.1	Khazineh	5th	95	0.0	Hole *et al.* (1969)
Sabz—Mehmeh	5.1	Mehmeh	5th	120	0.8	Hole *et al.* (1969)
Siahbid	5.1		5th	513	6.2	Bökönyi (1977)
Tabaqat al-Buma	5.1	Wadi Rabah	5th	242	9.1	Banning *et al.* (1994)
Tel Aswad (Balikh)	5.1		5th	n.s.	present	Mallowan (1946)
Tel Dan	5.1	Wadi Rabah	5th	42	28.6	Horwitz (1987)
Tel Eli (=Tel Ali)	5.1	Wadi Rabah	5th	115	41.7	Jarman (1974)
Tel Te'o	5.1	Pott Neo	5th	327	28.7	Horwitz (2001)
Teleilat Ghassul 1975–95	5.1	Pott Neo+E Chalco	5th	1059	8.6	Bourke (1997a, 1997b)
Teleilat Ghassul 1995+97	5.1	Pott Neo+E Chalco	5th	515	7.2	Mairs (2000)
Tell Kurdu	5.1	Amuq E	5th	6314	20.1	Loyet (2000)
Tell Mefesh	5.1		5/4th	n.s.	0.0	Mallowan (1946)
Tell Turlu	5.1	Halaf	?early 5th	108	27.8	Ducos (1991)
Tell Ziyadeh	5.1		5th	1073	4.7	Zeder pers. comm.
Yarim Tepe II	5.1		5th	n.s.	present	Merpert & Munchaev (1973)
Ziqim	5.1	Pott Neo	5th	84	6.0	Horwitz (2002*b*)

Abbreviations: Chalco, Chalcolithic; Pott Neo, Pottery Neolithic; n.s., not stated.

Table 5.2. Percentages of pig bones in 4th millennium sites from the study area.

Site	Figure	Period	Date (mill. BC)	Total domestic species	% Pig	References
Abu Hamid	5.2, 5.3	Chalco	4th	437	25.9	Desse (1988)
Abu Matar	5.2, 5.3	Chalco	4th	165	0.0	Grigson unpubl.
Abu Matar	5.2, 5.3	Chalco	4th	245	0.0	Josien (1955)
Apamea—Chalco.	5.2	Chalco	4th	205	24.4	Gautier (1977)
Arjoune trench VI	5.2	Chalco	4th	344	25.6	Grigson (2003)
Arslantepe	5.2	Late Chalco	4th	3271	16.8	Bökönyi (1983)
Bir-es-Safadi	5.2, 5.3	Chalco	4th	516	0.0	Ducos (1968a)
Bir-es-Safadi	5.2, 5.3	Chalco	4th	3483	0.1	Grigson unpubl.
Choga Maran 1978	5.2	Chalco	4th	147	1.4	Davis (1984)
Dehsavar	5.2	Chalco	4th	580	0.5	Bökönyi (1977)
El Kowm 2 Caracol	5.2	Uruk	4th	1518	0.0	Vila (1998b)[a]
Farukhabad—Bayat	5.2	Bayat	4th	331	0.0	Redding (1981)
Farukhabad—Jemdet Nasr	5.2	Jemdet Nasr	4th	795	0.0	Redding (1981)
Farukhabad—Uruk	5.2	Uruk	4th	529	0.0	Redding (1981)
Gat Govrin	5.2, 5.3	Chalco	4th	191	19.9	Ducos (1968a)
Gilat	5.2, 5.3	Chalco	4th	6516	14.1	Grigson (2006)
Godin Tepe	5.2	Chalco	4th	161	1.2	Gilbert pers. comm.
Grar	5.2, 5.3	Chalco	4th	1185	16.4	Grigson (1995a)
Habuba Kabira	5.2	Uruk	4th	2219	1.0	von den Driesch (1993)
Hacinebi	5.2	Uruk	4th	601	9.8	Bigelow (2000)
Hacinebi	5.2	All pre-Uruk	4th	1221	31.2	Bigelow (2000)
Hassek Hoyuk	5.2	Late Uruk	4th	2875	37.6	Stahl (1989); Boessneck (1992)
Hayaz Hoyuk	5.2	Chalco	4th	401	12.2	Buitenhuis (1985)
Horvat Beter	5.2, 5.3	Chalco	4th	173	0.0	Angress (1959)
Horvat Beter 1982	5.2, 5.3	Chalco	4th	222	0.0	Grigson (1993)
Horvat Hor	5.2, 5.3	Chalco	4th	100	0.0	Horwitz (1990)
Jawa	5.2	Chalco	4th	2423	0.0	Kohler (1981)
Jebel Aruda	5.2	late Chalco	4th late	1014	0.2	Buitenhuis (1988)
Kuran	5.2	3800	4th	141	0.7	Zeder (1998)

(Continued)

Table 5.2. (*Continued*)

Site	Figure	Period	Date (mill. BC)	Total domestic species	% Pig	References
Kurban Hoyuk	5.2	Ubaid+L Chalco	4th	104	48.1	Wattenmaker & Stein (1986)
Megiddo Tombs	5.2, 5.3	Chalco.	4th	n.s.	present	Bate (1938)
Metzer	5.2, 5.3	Chalco.	4th	358	48.6	Ducos (1968a)
Munhatta I	5.2, 5.3	Chalco	4th	332	27.1	Ducos (1968a)
Nineveh 3 & 4	5.2		4th	n.s.	present	Thompson & Mallowan (1933)
Pella 1992	5.2, 5.3	Chalco	4th	373	27.1	Mairs (1994)
Pella 1994/95	5.2, 5.3	Chalco	4th	621	22.5	Mairs (1998)
Qatif Y2	5.2, 5.3	Chalco	4th	791	0.9	Grigson (1984b)
Sabz—Bayat	5.2	Bayat	4th	131	3.0	Hole et al. (1969)
Sarafabad	5.2	Uruk	4th	1170	1.4	Wright et al. (1980)
Shiqmim—93	5.2, 5.3	Chalco	4th	1504	0.0	Whitcher et al. (1998)
Shiqmim—all	5.2, 5.3	Chalco	4th	3782	0.1	Grigson (1987, in press)
						Whitcher et al. (1998)
Shoham North Cave 4	5.2, 5.3	Chalco	4th	391	15.1	Horwitz (2007)
Tel Aviv—Jabotinsky St	5.2, 5.3	Chalco	4th	588	10.9	Ducos (1968a)
Tel Eli (=Tel Ali)	5.2, 5.3	Chalco	4th	105	48.6	Jarman (1974)
Tel Eli (=Tel Ali)	5.2, 5.3	Chalco	4th	126	lots	Lev-Tov (2000)
Tel Te'o	5.2, 5.3	Chalco	4th	161	29.8	Horwitz (2001)
Tel Tsaf	5.2, 5.3	Chalco	4th	113	17.7	Hellwing (1988/9)
Teleilat Ghassul 1975–95	5.2, 5.3	Classic Chalco	4th	1464	8.0	Bourke (1997a, 1997b)
Teleilat Ghassul 1994	5.2, 5.3	Chalco	4th	266	10.9	Mairs (1995)
Teleilat Ghassul 1995+97	5.2, 5.3	M+L+VL Chalco	4th	3313	9.4	Mairs (2000)
Tell Afis	5.2	Chalco	4th	523	12.6	Wilkens (2000)
Tell Rubeidheh	5.2	Chalco	4th	1130	0.0	Payne (1988)
Tell Umm Qseir	5.2	Late Uruk	4th	142	7.0	Zeder (1994, 1998a)
Uruk (Warka) III & IV	5.2	Uruk	4th	75	1.0	Boessneck et al. (1984)
Wadi Gazze D	5.2, 5.3	Chalco	4th	61	36.0	Ducos (1968a)

Abbreviations: Chalco, Chalcolithic; n.s., not stated.
[a] Total including ?some gazelle.

Table 5.3. Percentages of pig bones in 3rd millennium sites from the study area.

Site	Figure	Period	Date (mill. BC)	Total domestic species	% Pig	References
Abu Salabikh	5.4		3rd	n.s.	'lots'	Clutton-Brock & Burleigh (1978)
Ai	5.4, 5.5	EBA	3rd	867	0.2	Hesse (1990)
Apamea—EBA	5.4	EBA	3rd	82	29.3	Gautier (1977)
Arad	5.4, 5.5	EBA	3rd	1721	0.0	Lernau (1978); Davis (1976)
Arslantepe	5.4	EBA	3rd	3571	1.7	Bartosiewicz (1998)
Arslantepe	5.4	EBA all	3rd	8006	0.9	Bökönyi (1983)
Arslantepe	5.4	EB1a	3rd	3743	0.6	Bökönyi (1983)
Atiqeh (Uch Tepe)	5.4		3rd	357	21.0	Boessneck (1987)
Azor Area A	5.4, 5.5	EB1a	3rd	225	51.6	Horwitz (1999)
Bab edh-Dhra	5.4, 5.5	EBA	3rd	183	0.5	Finnegan (1979)
Choga Maran 1978	5.4	EBA	3rd	116	6.5	Davis (1984)
En Besor	5.4, 5.5	EB1b	3rd	24	0.0	Horwitz et al. (2002)
En Shadud	5.4, 5.5	EBA	3rd	72	31.9	Horwitz (1985)
Gamla	5.4, 5.5	EBA	3rd	109	18.0	Horwitz & Tchernov (1989)
Godin Tepe	5.4	EBA	3rd	5897	1.2	Gilbert pers. comm.
Grittille Höyük	5.4, 5.6	EBA	3rd	766	17.9	Wattenmaker & Stein (1984, 1986)
Habuba Kabira	5.4, 5.6	EBA	3rd	1747	0.3	von den Driesch (1993)
Halif (Nahal Tillah) 1976–83	5.4, 5.5	EBA III	3rd	5151	c.0.4	Zeder (1990)
Halif (Nahal Tillah) 1994	5.4, 5.5	EBA	3rd	252	4.0	Grigson (1997)
Hassek Höyük	5.4, 5.6	EBA	3rd	19909	47.5	Boessneck (1992)
Hassek Höyük	5.4, 5.6	EBA	3rd	12789	52.0	Stahl (1989)
Hayaz Höyük	5.4, 5.6	EB1	3rd	325	8.9	Buitenhuis (1985)
Hirbet-ez Zeraqon	5.4, 5.5	EBA	3rd	8883	0.7	Dechert (1995)
Jericho	5.4, 5.5	EBA	3rd	441	2.0	Clutton-Brock (1979)
Kashkashok IV	5.4, 5.6	late Leilan	3rd	151	29.8	Zeder (1998)
Khirbet-el-Umbashi	5.4, 5.5	EBA early	3rd early	7787	0.0	Vila (1997)
Korucutepe	5.4		3rd	725	7.4	Boessneck & von den Driesch (1975)
Kurban Höyük	5.4, 5.6	EBA	3rd	902	14.1	Wattenmaker & Stein (1986)

(*Continued*)

Table 5.3. (*Continued*)

Site	Figure	Period	Date (mill. BC)	Total domestic species	% Pig	References
Kutan	5.4	EBA	3rd	n.s.	c. 33	Vila (1998a, in press b)
Leilan	5.4, 5.6		3rd	1029	23.9	Zeder (1998a, 2003)
Lidar Höyük	5.4, 5.6	EBA	3rd	2791	11.9	Kussinger (1988)
Megiddo Tombs	5.4, 5.5	EBA	3rd	n.s.	present	Bate (1938)
Me'ona	5.4, 5.5	EB1	3rd	105	2.9	Horwitz (1996)
Mulla Matar	5.4, 5.6	EBA	3rd	n.s.	c. 4	Vila (1998a, in press a)
Nineveh 5	5.4	Ninevite 5	3rd	n.s.	present	Thompson & Mallowan (1933)
Numeira	5.4, 5.5	EBIII	3rd	22	0.0	Finnegan (1979)
Pella 1992	5.4, 5.5	EBA	3rd	492	6.3	Mairs (1994)
Pella 1994–5	5.4, 5.5	EBA	3rd	625	6.6	Mairs (1998)
Refaim Valley	5.4, 5.5	EBA	3rd	274	15.3	Horwitz (1989a, 1989b)
Sakheri-Sughir	5.4	EDI	3rd	181	3.3	Bökönyi & Flannery (1969)
Selenkahiye 1967	5.4, 5.6	EBA	3rd	922	0.0	Ducos (1968b)[a]
Selenkahiye 1967–75	5.4, 5.6	EBA+MBA	3rd+2nd	8887	0.8	Ijzereef (1977/8)[b]
Shoham North Cave 2	5.4, 5.5	EB1	3rd	90	30.0	Horwitz (2007)
Tall Abu al-Kharaz	5.4, 5.5	EBA	3rd	1068	3.2	Fischer (1997)
Taur Ikhbeineh	5.4, 5.5	EBIa	3rd	98	7.1	Horwitz et al. (2002)
Tel Aphek	5.4, 5.5	EBA	3rd	256	9.0	Hellwing & Gophna (1984)
Tel Aphek+Tel Dalit	5.4, 5.5	EBA	3rd	1048	2.6	Hellwing & Gophna (1984)
Tel Dalit	5.4, 5.5	EBA IB	3rd	197	0.5	Horwitz & Tchernov (1996)
Tel Dalit	5.4, 5.5	EBA II	3rd	768	0.4	Horwitz & Tchernov (1996)
Tel Dan	5.4, 5.5	EBA	3rd	253	4.0	Hesse (1990)
Tel Dan	5.4, 5.5	EBA	3rd	165	5.5	Wapnish & Hesse (1991)
Tel Gat (=Erani)	5.4, 5.5	EBA	3rd	725	9.8	Ducos (1968a)
Tel Te'o	5.4, 5.5	EBA	3rd	24	37.5	Horwitz (2001)
Tel Yarmouth	5.4, 5.5	EBA	3rd	1175	0.0	Davis (1988)
Tell Abqa'	5.4		3rd	109	42.2	Amberger (1987)
Tell Afis	5.4	EBA	3rd	398	4.0	Wilkens (2000)
Tell al-Hiba 1970–1 Area A	5.4	ED3	3rd	138	8.7	Mudar (1982)
Tell al-Hiba 1970–1 Area C	5.4	ED3	3rd	889	20.4	Mudar (1982)
Tell Asmar (Eshnunna)	5.4		3rd	174	37.4	Hilzheimer (1941)
Tell Atij	5.4, 5.6	Ninevite V	3rd	865	20.0	Zeder (2003, pers. comm.)

Site		Period		Total	%	Reference
Tell Bderi	5.4, 5.6	EBA	3rd	825	0.2	Becker (1988)
Tell Bderi	5.4, 5.6	EBA 2500	3rd	161	1.2	Zeder (1998a)
Tell Brak 1994–6	5.4, 5.6	Ninevite V	3rd	166	10.8	Dobney et al. (2003)
Tell Brak 1994–6	5.4, 5.6	later 3rd	3rd	341	43.7	Dobney et al. (2003)
Tell Brak Area FS level 5	5.4, 5.6	mid? 3rd	3rd	160	20	Weber (2001)
Tell Brak Area FS levels 1–2	5.4, 5.6	post Akkad	3rd	178	27.5	Weber (2001)
Tell Brak Area FS levels 3–4	5.4, 5.6	Akkadian	3rd	332	24.4	Weber (2001)
Tell Chuera I 1976, 1982–3	5.4, 5.6	ED	3rd	433	0.0	Vila (1998a); Boessneck (1988b)
Tell Chuera I, Steinbau 1	5.4, 5.6	EBA	3rd	1980	0.0	Vila (1995)
Tell el-Hayyat	5.4, 5.5	EBA	3rd	2244	32.3	Metzger (1983)
Tell es-Sakan EB I	5.4, 5.5	EBI	3rd	102	24.5	de Miroschedji et al. (2001)
Tell es-Sakan EB III	5.4, 5.5	EB III	3rd	597	1.7	de Miroschedji et al. (2001)
Tell Gudeda II	5.4, 5.6	NinV/ Akkadian	3rd	564	1.2	Zeder (2003, pers. comm.)
Tell Halawa Tell A	5.4, 5.6	EBA	3rd	10763	0.0	Boessneck & von den Driesch (1989)
Tell Halawa Tell B	5.4, 5.6	EBA	3rd	254	0.0	Boessneck & Kokabi (1981)
Tell Iktanu	5.4, 5.5	EBA	3rd	n.s.	0.0	Prag pers. comm.
Tell Karrana 3	5.4	EBA	3rd	723	19.5	Boessneck et al. (1993)
Tell Mishrifé (Qatna)	5.4	EBA	3rd	229	13.1	Vila (pers.comm.); Vila & Dalix (2004)
Tell Raqa'i	5.4, 5.6	Ninevite V	3rd	2127	11.8	Zeder (2003, pers. comm.)
Tell Razuk (Uch Tepe)	5.4		3rd	546	17.0	Boessneck (1987)
Tell Shiuk Fawqani	5.4		3rd	358	26.5	Vila (2005)
Tell Sweyhat	5.4, 5.6	EBA	3rd	1636	0.4	Buitenhuis (1983)
Tell Sweyhat 1989, 1991, 1993	5.4, 5.6	EBA	3rd	3390	0.0	Weber (1997)
Tell Taya	5.4		3rd	335	29.5	Bökönyi (1973)
Tell Ziyadeh	5.4, 5.6		3rd	55	38.2	Zeder (2003, pers. comm.)
Titris Hoyuk	5.4, 5.6	EBA	3rd	608	1.0	Greenfield (2002)
Ur Royal Cemetery	5.4		3rd	n.s.	'lots'	Pocock (1934)
Uruk (Warka) 1956–67	5.4	ED	3rd	366	1.4	Boessneck et al. (1984)
Uruk (Warka) 1989	5.4		3rd	285	33.0	Boessneck (1993)
Yiftahel	5.4, 5.5	EBA	3rd	93	3.2	Horwitz (1997)

Abbreviations: EB, Early Bronze Age; n.s.: not stated
[a] Total including gazelle and ?deer. [b] Total including gazelle.

ENVIRONMENT

The area of the Middle East we are concerned with is the land in and around the Fertile Crescent (Figs 5.1–5.6). It consists of a semi-circle of fairly low-lying Irano-Turanian steppe, ringed with wooded mountains to the west, north, and east, and encircling desert and semi-desert. The semi-desert and desert are separated from the steppe at about the 200 mm isohyet, and the steppe from the woodland at approximately 350–400 mm (Zohary 1962, 1973). Although topography and large-scale land forms have not changed very much during the Holocene, aridification coupled with overgrazing has resulted in the devastation of luxuriant woodland and the desertification of productive steppe land, leading to widespread erosion and alluviation.

Within the desert and semi-desert there are moister micro-ecological areas produced by localized conditions, such as permanent oases fed by springs; the galleria woodlands along the Euphrates, the Tigris, and their tributaries; permanent marshland in the delta where these rivers enter the Persian Gulf; and, well to the north of this, areas that are sometimes seasonally flooded.

The cultivation of wheat and barley is possible, without irrigation, within the so-called limit of dry farming, and impossible without irrigation beyond it, except in moist micro-ecological areas. Estimates of the limit of dry farming vary enormously from one authority to another: 200 mm of annual rainfall (Oates 1973), 250–300 mm (Arnon 1972), 300 mm (Adams 1962), and 300–400 mm (Zohary 1962) have all been quoted. Probably the critical factor is not so much total annual rainfall as reliable rainfall at particular phases of the growing cycle of wheat and barley.

Although in broad palaeo-climatic terms there has been little change in the climate of the Middle East since the end of the Pleistocene, those changes that have occurred have been of great significance for human settlement, particularly in the marginal areas where even a small reduction in rainfall can produce wide latitudinal shifts in isohyets, and so make farming impossible unless compensated for by irrigation (Butzer 1978; Préhistoire du Levant 1981; Bintliff & Van Zeist 1982; Rosen 2006). Two of the wettest phases of the Early Holocene occurred during the 5th millennium uncal. BC, but were separated by a short-lived cool-dry episode known as the *8.2 KY event*. After this, rainfall fluctuated, though it was usually adequate to permit flood-water farming. However, with the onset of severe drought conditions towards the end of the third millennium, even that became impossible (Rosen 2006). These fluctuations must have meant that the isohyet delimiting dry farming moved back and forth, but there is no evidence to suggest that in broad terms its 'average' position was very different from today.

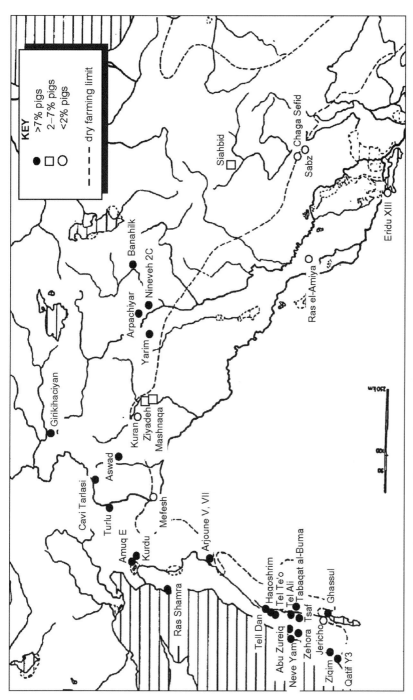

Fig. 5.1. Distribution of sites with and without pigs in the 5th millennium BC

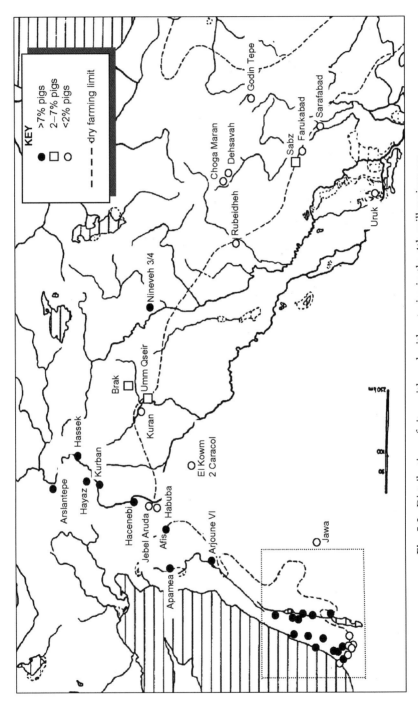

Fig. 5.2. Distribution of sites with and without pigs in the 4th millennium BC. The area indicated by the dotted line is shown on a larger scale in Fig. 5.3

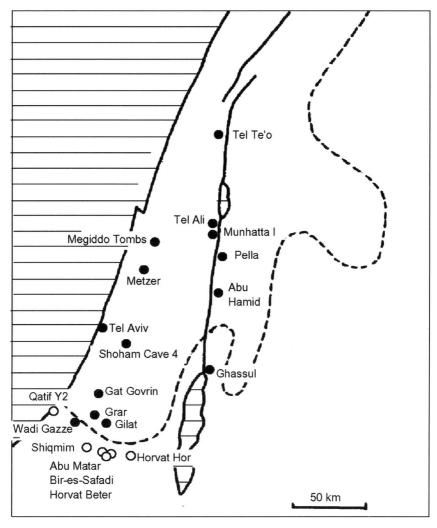

Fig. 5.3. Distribution of sites of the southern Levant with and without pigs in the 4th millennium BC

My attempts to plot the positions of the modern 200 mm and 300 mm isohyets on maps of the Middle East had to be abandoned because estimates of their positions vary so widely. This is largely because rainfall itself is extremely variable from year to year, so that any figure for mean annual precipitation will vary according to which years were used as a basis for its calculation, and different authorities use different time periods for their

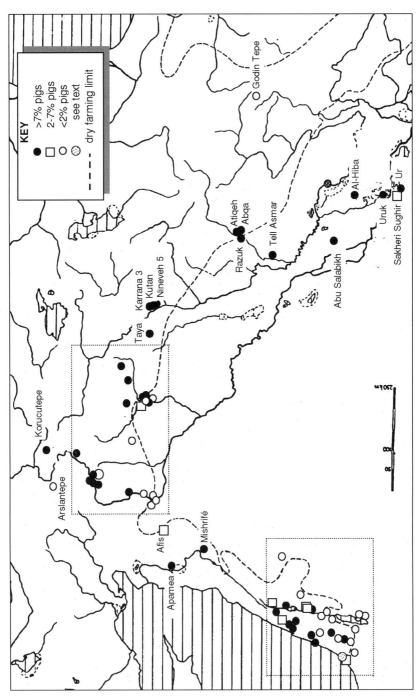

Fig. 5.4. Distribution of sites with and without pigs in the 3rd millennium BC.
The two areas indicated by dotted lines are shown on a larger scale in Figs. 5.5 and 5.6

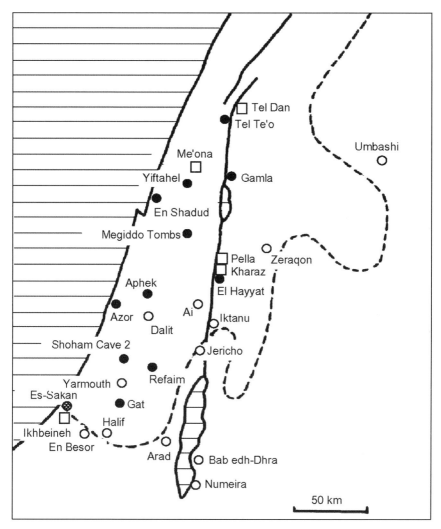

Fig. 5.5. Distribution of sites in the southern Levant with and without pigs in the 3rd millennium BC

calculations. I have therefore made use of the map prepared by Aurenche *et al.* (1981), which indicates the limits of dry farming on the basis of present land use and vegetation. In many areas, but by no means all, this line coincides with some estimates of the 300 mm isohyet.

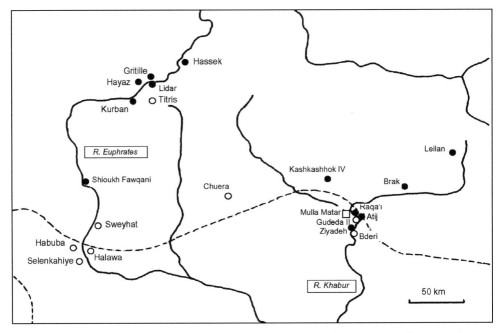

Fig. 5.6. Distribution of sites with and without pigs in the Upper Euphrates and Khabur basins in the 3rd millennium BC

ENVIRONMENTAL REQUIREMENTS OF PIGS

In order to understand how the environment might affect the distribution of pigs it is necessary to know what their environmental tolerances are. Domestic pigs are not a new species created by humans, they are a natural species, and there is no reason to think that their basic biology has been changed by domestication *per se* (Grigson 1982). Even highly domesticated British pigs can revert to wild behaviour patterns within a single generation (Stolba & Wood-Gush 1989), making it likely that the environmental as well as the behavioural characteristics of wild and domestic pigs are much the same. Domestic pigs die quickly when exposed to temperatures in excess of 36 °C unless they can compensate for their inability to sweat by wallowing in water or mud (Mount 1968). Hone & O'Grady (1980) found that at temperatures of 30 °C or more, feral pigs in Australia have to drink every day and they quickly die of exposure if not shaded from the sun when the temperature exceeds 35 °C. Even when water and mud are available in hot climates pigs will seek the shade of trees, bushes, or tall reeds during the heat of the day emerging only in the early morning and evening to forage for food (Diener & Robkin 1978). The temperature in summer sunshine in the Middle East often exceeds 35 °C. Thus, although wild pigs in the Middle East are more common in woodland in areas of moderate and high rainfall (Hatt 1959; Harrison 1968; Harrington 1977), they are also found in moist micro-environments in dry areas where there is lush vegetation watered by springs or by exotic rivers that derive their water from wetter areas, like the marshes of southern Mesopotamia and the Ghor marshes at the southern end of the Dead Sea. Wild pigs sometimes invade open country searching for food (Tristram 1865; Hart 1891; Hatt 1959; Harrison 1968), but they soon return to shaded areas.

PIGS IN HUMAN SOCIETIES

The role that domestic pigs probably played in early human societies has been discussed in a large number of publications, far too many to discuss in detail (see for example Hesse 1990; Zeder 1995). However, some of the potential advantages and implications of pig-keeping can be briefly outlined here. Pigs provide fat-rich protein, though little else. They breed very fast, which means that most can be slaughtered at a very young age without endangering herd security, so they have a potential role in risk management, since even in lean years they can be relied upon to replenish their numbers in a shorter time than sheep, goats, and especially cattle. They are thus an easily renewable resource. One of their most important attributes, still relied on in many parts of the world and formerly almost universal, is that, as urban scavengers, they are able to feed on rotting food waste that would otherwise pose a distinct bacteriological threat to humans. This conversion of food waste into edible animal protein can be an important source of human nutrition (Miller R. 1990).The role of pigs in Papua New Guinea is frequently cited in discussions of their domestication (e.g. by Redding & Rosenberg 1998), although their relationship to people so far away from the Middle East and Europe must surely have been very different. Nevertheless, these discussions have drawn attention to the possibility that pigs were sometimes used for feasting, since large numbers could be killed on particular occasions without seriously damaging herd security.

One major advantage of pigs is that, provided there is enough food available in the form of vegetable and animal waste, they do not need to be driven to pasture. They can forage around settlements, although in Europe and perhaps also in the Middle East they also used to be taken to woodland for acorn pannage in the autumn. However, pigs cannot be driven far and therefore are not part of nomadic systems of animal husbandry. Indeed, their presence argues against nomadism (Grigson 1982, 1995*b*), except in semi-nomadic dual systems where many of the sheep, goats, and cattle might have been taken further afield in search of grazing and to protect crops grown around the settlement, while pigs remained at home. Despite these advantages, at some stage the consumption of pigs became taboo in the Middle East, a subject of even more discussion. Many reasons have been advanced for this, though many potential objections to pork can equally be applied to beef.

Of course, it can be argued that the presence of pig remains on an archaeological site does not mean that the animals were actually raised in the vicinity. They could have been brought there on the hoof, or as carcasses or joints, from further afield where conditions were more suitable for pig breeding, and be acquired by purchase or barter. However, there is as yet no evidence for any animals being taken long distances for consumption, and it is particularly unlikely for pigs since they cannot be driven. Carcasses, or parts of carcasses, are also unlikely to be transported in the heat of the Middle East, except possibly as dried meat. However, when body part analyses have been carried out, they suggest dismemberment at or near the site where the bones were found. Age profiles invariably show a predominance of piglets, which also argues for local production.

RESULTS

The 5th and 4th millennia

In the 5th millennium (see Fig. 5.1) the distribution of sites with and without pigs is clearly demarcated by the present limit of dry farming. Within the limit almost all sites have at least 7% of pigs, the only exception being Siahbid in the Kermanshar Valley in Iran with only 6.2% (Bökönyi 1977), a difference which is insignificant. Beyond the limit none of the sites has a significant proportion of pigs.

The same is true in the 4th millennium (see Fig. 5.2) although two small sites in the Kermanshar valley in the mountainous part of western Iran, Choga Maran and Dehsavar (Bökönyi 1977), have very few. It is thought that the climate of western Iran in the 5th millennium was drier than today and that humidity gradually increased through the 4th millennium, reaching modern levels during the early 3rd millennium (Van Zeist & Bottema 1982). Between 1937 and 1957 Kermanshar had a mean annual rainfall of 373 mm

(Ganji 1968), so it has perhaps always been marginal for pig-keeping. Another, possibly more likely explanation is that transhumance, which is usually a feature of life in areas of high relief, was practised there. Pigs cannot be easily driven, nor are they suited to rocky mountainsides.

The pattern of distribution of sites with and without pigs in the southern Levant can be seen in greater detail in Fig. 5.3, which shows the distribution of Chalcolithic sites in the 4th millennium. The two apparent exceptions are Qatif Y2 on the Mediterranean coast and Teleilat Ghassul near the northern end of the Dead Sea. Chalcolithic Qatif Y2 had less than 1% of pigs (Grigson 1984*b*, 1995*b*), but interestingly the adjacent Late Pottery site of Qatif Y3 (Grigson 1984*a*, 1995*b*) dated to about 4000 BC had 33% pigs. Two factors might explain the difference; one is that the sea level rose between the Neolithic and the Chalcolithic, bringing the shoreline close to Y2, whereas it was several kilometres distant at the time of Y3. Y2 as a maritime site contained many marine fish bones and an unusually wide variety of animals, including hippopotamus, freshwater turtle (*Trionyx*), and porpoise, whereas the fauna at Y3 consisted almost entirely of domestic sheep, goats, cattle, and pigs. A second possible explanation is that a very slight variation shift in the limit of dry farming made pig-keeping impossible. The northern Negev would have been very marginal for pig-keeping and even a slight increase in aridity would have precluded it.

Turning to the Jordan valley, pig remains were numerous at Teleilat Ghassul near where the river Jordan enters the northern end of the Dead Sea, varying from 8 to 11% (Bourke 1997*a*, 1997*b*; Mairs 1995, 2000). Pig-keeping would be impossible in the present extreme aridity of the area, but palaeoclimatological evidence from the Dead Sea (Neev & Emery 1967) suggest a moist phase in the late 4th millennium in the area, and, more importantly, palaeobotanical and pedological analysis shows that in the Chalcolithic there was slow-moving water close to the site itself, with sedges, reed-mace, and alder trees (Webley 1969). Clearly the vegetation at Ghassul was sufficient for pig-keeping, and may have been similar to that of the Ghor to the south of the Dead Sea where wild pigs still survive (Harlan 1982; Mendelssohn & Yom-Tov 1999*a*; Tchernov pers. comm.; Goren pers. comm.).

Thus it seems that in the 5th and 4th millennia there was a close correlation between environmental conditions and the distribution of sites in whose economy pigs played a small, but significant, role. In so far as the cultural affinities of the various sites listed can be determined from the literature, within and beyond broad categories like 'Pottery Neolithic' or 'Chalcolithic', there are no variations in pig numbers that can be attributed to cultural rather than environmental factors.

The 3rd millennium

In the 3rd millennium some of the sites fit the general pattern established in the preceding millennia, with the presence or absence of significant numbers of pigs being correlated with the presumed limit of dry farming (see Fig. 5.4). However, there are numerous complications.

In examining the contribution of the four main domestic animals to the economy of the southern Levant (see Fig. 5.5) in the early 1990s, but translating numbers of bones of each species found into relative meat weights, I found that cattle were far more important in the economy of the southern Levant than sheep and goats, which in turn were much more important than pigs (Grigson 1995*b*). Nevertheless, from the Pottery Neolithic to the Early Bronze Age pigs were fairly well represented in the area as a whole, with the exception of the sites on the desert margins and the southern end of the Jordan valley, being most numerous in the northern Jordan valley. As we have seen, with very few exceptions the presence of significant numbers of pigs in the 5th and 4th millennia is closely related to rainfall and in many places there is a decline in the average number of pigs from the 4th to the 3rd millennium. In the 3rd millennium the correlation still holds good for all the sites beyond or close to the limit of dry farming, as suggested by Horwitz & Tchernov (1989), but within the rest of the area, although some sites have, as expected, fairly high proportions of pigs, a few have hardly any or even none at all. Clearly, the situation is more complex than a simple south–north relationship.

In view of the increasing aridity towards the end of the 3rd millennium one might expect a decline in pig numbers in the southern Levant. It is possible that, given a greater degree of precision in assigning sites to different sub-phases, one might be able to follow a process of decline through the Early Bronze Age, but so far that has only proved possible in one site: Tell es-Sakan (de Miroschedji *et al.* 2001), situated near the mouth of the Nahal Besor close to the limit of dry farming. In EB I, when the site was Egyptian, pigs constituted 24.5% of the artiodactyl assemblage and only 1.7% in EB III when it became a Canaanite town. Nearby Taur Ikhbeineh had 7.1% pigs in EB Ia and Ib (Horwitz *et al.* 2002), perhaps an intermediate step in the decline.

But in other sites in the southern Levant the situation is much less clear. For example at Tel Yarmouth Davis (1988) found no pigs at all in EBII and EBIII, whereas in an EBIV site in the Refaim valley near Jerusalem Horwitz (1989*a*, 1989*b*) found 15% of pigs. Of three sites close to each other near the east bank of the Jordan, Pella had about 6% (Mairs 1994) and Tell el-Hayyat had 32%

(Metzger 1983) of pig bones, whereas Tall abu al-Kharaz, situated between them, had only 3.2% (Fischer P.M. 1997). At Tel Aphek (EBI and EBII) and Tel Dalit (EBIb), two sites similar in many respects and indeed treated as one in the original archaeozoological report, Hellwing & Gophna (1984) found a low percentage of pig remains, but subsequently Horwitz *et al.* (1996) have shown that Tel Dalit contained less than 1% of pigs, so those identified by Hellwing must have come from Tel Aphek, constituting about 9% of the domestic artiodactyls there. These variations need to be explained; perhaps they were due to differences in local microclimates, or variations in the success of floodwater irrigation (Rosen 1997), or to as yet unexplored economic and social differences between the sites. Most probably a combination of all four explanations must be taken into account.

Although there is some evidence that the 4th millennium and the Early Bronze Age in the southern Levant were slightly damper than today, so that the limit of dry farming would have moved a little to the south and east, it is also well established that there was significant deterioration in climatic conditions there, and many other areas, towards to end of the 3rd millennium (Goldberg & Rosen 1987; Weiss *et al.* 1993; Rosen 1997; Weiss 1997; Rosen 2006), which led to the collapse of many settlements during EBIV and the adoption of a more pastoral, more mobile way of life (Prag 1985; Dever 1989, 1992, 1995; Esse 1991), though not full nomadism (Grigson 1995*b*). However, so far there is little faunal evidence to support or refute this, and Braemer & Échallier (1995) have argued that the deterioration in the 3rd millennium was due to overgrazing rather than climate change.

The situation along the upper Euphrates (see Figs 5.4 and 5.6) fits the pattern very well. Miller N.F. (1997) and Weber (1997) writing in the same volume, compared the results of the archaeobotanical and archaeozoological analyses from the more recent excavations at 3rd millennium Tell Sweyhat (just within the modern limit of dry farming), with those from other 3rd and 4th millennium sites further up the Euphrates, and found a rough positive correlation between increasing annual rainfall and a higher proportion of grains of wheat to barley and of the numbers of pigs to other domesticates. However, according to one more recently published archaeozoological report, Titris Höyük is an exception. The site is situated on a small tributary of the Euphrates, not far from several other 3rd millennium sites closer to the Euphrates. Although all those sites have large numbers of pigs, Titris has only 1% (Greenfield 2002). Clearly an explanation is needed. Miller N.F. (1997) argued that major deforestation occurred on the upper Euphrates between the early and the mid 3rd millennium and that the proportion of barley to wheat also increased over time, at least at the nearby site of Kurban. Titris Höyük is dated to the second half of the 3rd millennium, so perhaps what we are seeing there is an effect of environmental deterioration. The more northern site of Arslantepe saw a reduction in the proportion of pigs from 16.8% in the late 4th millennium to 2% or less in the Early Bronze Age (Bökönyi 1983; Bartosiewicz 1998), and both sites were abandoned at about 2000 BC (see below). The reduction in pigs at Arslantepe was already marked in its earliest EBA phase (EBIA) and Frangipane & Siracusano (1998) have argued that this was because of the importance of the site as a major regional centre, rather than environmental degradation.

The large 3rd millennium tell sites in the upper Khabur basin (Figs 5.4 and 5.6) have plenty of pigs, and so do three smaller Ninevite 5 sites near one another on the banks of the middle Khabur river: Tel Atij, Tell Raqa'i, and Tell Ziyadeh. However, two other small sites very close by, Tell Gudeda (Zeder 2003, pers. comm.) and Tell Bderi (Becker C. 1988; Zeder 1998*a*), have only 0–1% each, and a sixth site nearby, Mullar Matar (Vila in press *b*), has roughly 4%. Massive storage facilities have been identified in the middle Khabur sites, such as Ziyadeh, Atij, Raqa'i, and Bderi; although probably used to store grain, they may also have been used for wool and other products. Such facilities imply surplus production, at least in good years, but whether the products stored there were used for export down the Khabur to the Euphrates, and then further south, or whether they were stores to house reserves against lean harvests, is arguable (Hole 1999). Certainly the position of the sites right on the limit of dry farming suggests the latter, especially if desiccation was becoming an increasing problem, which seems to have been the case. The two scenarios are not mutually exclusive; in good years surpluses could presumably have been exported.

It has been postulated that the sites on the upper and middle Khabur were undergoing a period of economic distress, due to widespread and increasing desiccation at the end of the Early Bronze Age, which resulted in the sudden abandonment of many sites, most spectacularly Tell Leilan and Tell Brak at or soon after 2000 BC (2200 cal. BC) (Weiss *et al.* 1993; Weiss 1997). As we have seen further north near the upper Euphrates, Titris Höyük and Arslantepe appear to have been abandoned at the same time (Weiss 1997). In such a scenario, knowing their limited environmental tolerances, one would expect the number of pigs to have diminished, as indeed they appear to do, at least in Tell Atij and Tell Raqa'i, which are the only sites with large enough samples in different sub-phases of the Early Bronze Age to test this suggestion. In both there is a marked decline in pig numbers with time, as noted by Zeder (2003). Figure 5.7 shows the data set out in a histogram, based on information kindly supplied by Melinda Zeder.

Three sites in the upper Khabur basin—Kashkashhok IV, Leilan, and Tell Brak—have high proportions of pigs in the 3rd millennium. All are situated

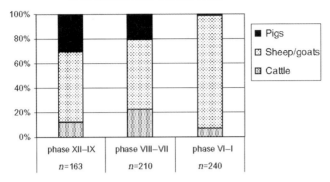

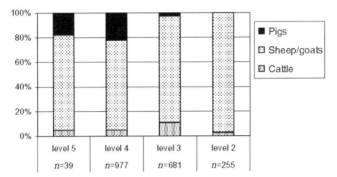

Fig. 5.7. Diachronic changes in the proportion of pigs in two sites on the Middle Khabur. Although forming a substantial proportion of the assemblage of domestic artiodactyls in the middle of the 3rd millennium, towards to end of the period they disappear almost completely (Zeder, pers. comm.; see also Zeder 2003)

above, though not far above, the limit of dry farming. However, at Tell Brak the situation is contradictory. In the 4th millennium, Dobney *et al.* (2003) have shown that there were very few pigs, as one might expect for a site near to the limit of dry farming, but in the 3rd millennium the proportion rises to 10.8% of the domestic artiodactyls in the Ninevite V period and to 43.7% in the later Bronze Age. Although pigs declined in number shortly before the site's abandonment in the early 2nd millennium there were still 26.4% of pigs (Fig. 5.8). I suspect that the explanation, at least for Leilan and Tell Brak, is that, unlike the small Ninevite V tells on the Middle Khabur, these were very large urban sites in which pigs were not only provided with shade from buildings, but also sustained by scavenging urban rubbish, so providing

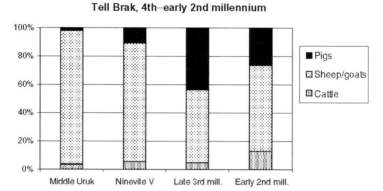

Fig. 5.8. Diachronic changes in the proportion of pigs at Tell Brak in the Upper Khabur basin. In contrast to the situation in the Middle Khabur sites, pigs increase from the 4th to the late 3rd millennium, with a slight decrease shortly before the abandonment of the site in the early 2nd millennium. It is suggested that the high proportion of pigs is related to urban conditions (data from Dobney *et al.* 2003)

food for the inhabitants as well as removing refuse. Interestingly, at Leilan, among the animal remains from what is thought to have been the workers' residential area, the proportion of pigs was about 50%, compared with about 33% in the more elite upper town. In addition, the animals consumed in the upper town included a higher proportion of very young piglets than in the lower town (Zeder 2003).

As we have seen, sites further east and south in Mesopotamia in the 5th and 4th millennia all lack pigs, which is not surprising in view of the very low rainfall of the area, which is well outside even the most optimistic estimate of the limit of dry farming. However, in the 3rd millennium (see Fig. 5.4) despite the disgracefully small number of bone reports compared with the large number of excavations, one can see that the situation became more complicated. The earliest site is the small Early Dynastic I village of Sakheri Sughir in the enclave of Ur (Wright 1969), and this has very few pigs. The next site is Uruk (Warka) where the Early Dynastic levels excavated in 1989 had 33% of pig bones (Boessneck 1993). All the remaining reports are on Early Dynastic III sites and all show high proportions of pigs. There is little doubt that this is correlated with the existence of large-scale irrigation agriculture (Postgate 1992) and urban conditions, providing swampy ground and shade as well as sustenance in the form of food waste and general urban refuse. At Abu Salabikh, where Clutton-Brock & Burleigh (1978) reported a high proportion of pig bones, water-sieved samples from later excavations by Nicholas Post-gate produced the first direct evidence for pigs as urban scavengers. Samples from the city streets included abundant rubbish, in the form of sherds, fragments of animal bone, charcoal, and burnt seeds, together with several shed milk teeth of pigs, indicating that pigs were living in the streets (Payne pers. comm).

Why should the situation in the cities differ from that at the village of Sakheri Sughir in the EDI period, by which time irrigation had already been developed? The answer may be related to settlement patterns. Adams (1981) suggests that the initial distribution of small communities around Mesopotamian cities reflected localized exploitation of the land and that later most of the producing population were persuaded or compelled to live in towns. This shift from an extensive agricultural system to one that was primarily intensive (though presumably still with an extensive element) may have been one of the factors influencing economic change in Sumer (Wright 1969). It would be logical to see sheep, goats, and cattle as elements in an extensive system, grazing, and moving seasonally across the arid steppes, with pigs concentrated at localized centres of intensive cultivation made possible by elaborate irrigation. Thus the difference in pig numbers between Sakeri Sughir and the city sites may reflect intensification over time, or the dichotomy between village and urban economies, or a combination of the two.

At Tell al-Hiba in southern Mesopotamia, as long ago as 1982, Mudar (1982) found a spatial difference in the distribution of pig bones. In Area A, a temple precinct, pigs comprised 8.7% of the domestic artiodactyls, whereas in Area C, an area thought on architectural evidence to have been either residential or bureaucratic, pigs reached 20.4%. Mudar's conclusion, based on the proportion of pigs as well as the presence of a few bones of wild animals, was that Area C was more likely to have been a residential area. At Uruk (Warka) where, as we have seen, pork was a substantial part of the diet, a later excavation yielded apparently contradictory information. The ED I–III levels excavated in 1956–67 had very few pig bones, but a high proportion of these animal remains came from sacrificial sheep and goats (Boessneck *et al.* 1984). That pigs were not afforded this special role adds emphasis to the notion of their 'ordinariness'. Similarly, although the management of sheep, goats, and cattle is elaborately documented by Mesopotamian scribes, pigs are rarely listed and artistic depictions, though not unknown, are rare (Postgate 1992). It is notable that as such ordinary animals, pigs are scarcely ever mentioned in early documents and rarely feature in animal sacrifices. Our picture of the streets and open spaces of early Mesopotamian cities should include pigs scavenging urban rubbish in much the same way as they did in towns all over Europe in the Middle Ages, and do to this day in parts of India and many other countries (Grigson 1982).

CONCLUSION

The geographical distribution of sites with and without domestic pigs from the 5th to the 3rd millennium BC in the Middle East was almost entirely dependent on rainfall, significant numbers of pigs having been found only in areas moist enough to support at least dry farming. Where pigs appear in the dry region beyond the 300 mm isohyet, it is only in micro-ecological areas where moist, shady conditions existed or were created by people, that is, where elaborate irrigation has been introduced, as in Mesopotamia in the 3rd millennium. However, indications are emerging of a relationship between social stratification and the consumption of pork, which may be relevant. Pigs must have been the meat suppliers of the ordinary people, owned perhaps on an individual basis, unlike sheep, goats, and cattle, which were kept in large herds and whose movements and management were closely controlled by the ruling elites. These were already powerful in the 3rd millennium cities, at least in Mesopotamia and north-eastern Syria. Another factor which may have contributed to pig prohibitions in later periods in the Middle East, when nomadism became more fully developed, was some tension between 'the Desert and the Sown'. However, we will only be certain that we are dealing with cultural prohibitions when we find sites that have suitable ecological conditions but no pigs.

6

Hunting or management?
The status of *Sus* in the Jomon
period in Japan

Hitomi Hongo, Tomoko Anezaki, Kyomi Yamazaki,
Osamu Takahashi & Hiroki Sugawara

INTRODUCTION

This study focuses on Japanese *Sus* and their relationships with humans during the Jomon period. Since pig (*Sus scrofa* f. domestica) is the only domestic ungulate species of which the wild progenitor (*Sus scrofa*) naturally inhabits Japan, the relationship of *Sus* and humans, including possible local domestication in the Japanese archipelago, is one of the major issues in archaeozoological studies in Japan.

There are two subspecies of wild boar in Japan, Ryukyu wild boar (*S. scrofa riukiuanus*) and Japanese wild boar (*S. scrofa leucomystax*). Today the former subspecies inhabits the Amami-Ohshima, Tokunoshima, Okinawa, Ishigaki, and Iriomote islands of the Ryukyu archipelago and the latter the main islands of the Japanese archipelago (Honshu, Shikoku, and Kyushu, but not Hokkaido). Our study deals with the latter subspecies, the Japanese wild boar. The primary aim is to examine and compile data on the regional and temporal variation of the size of the Japanese wild boar during the Jomon period, and of kill-off patterns. This, we think, is necessary for discussing whether or not a domestication process was underway during the Jomon period. Information on the variation within the wild boar population during the Jomon period also helps to evaluate the domestic or wild status of *Sus* remains from the later Yayoi Period (*c.*2700–1700 BP).

SUBSISTENCE DURING THE JOMON PERIOD
AND ISSUES OF PIG DOMESTICATION

The Jomon period lasted about 10,000 years, from 13000 to 2500 cal. BP, and, based on pottery types and styles, is divided into six phases: Incipient, Earliest, Early, Middle, Late, and Final. The subsistence economy during the Jomon period was primarily based on hunting and gathering, but it has been argued that some form of incipient plant cultivation was already practiced at least from the Early Jomon period, possibly even from the Incipient Jomon period on (e.g. Matsumoto 1979; Kasahara 1981; Umemoto & Moriwaki 1983; Habu 2001). Also, an increasing degree of sedentism is observed in central and eastern Japan from the Middle Jomon period on. Pottery was used from the beginning of the Jomon period. Jomon culture is also characterized by exquisite wood craftsmanship, as represented by lacquer ware found at some waterlogged sites. The period is also known for the formation of large shell middens along the seashore, which suggests an intensive exploitation of marine resources. Because of the acidity of the soil, however, preservation of faunal remains is generally poor, except at these shell middens and waterlogged sites. This bias, namely the lack of samples from inland sites, of course affects our study of Jomon *Sus* populations.

As shown in Fig. 6.1, wild boar (*Sus scrofa*) and deer (*Cervus nippon*) are the two major land mammal species exploited in Jomon Japan. Other species found at Jomon sites include the Japanese macaque (*Macaca fuscata*), raccoon dog (*Nyctereutes procyonoides*), river otter (*Lutra lutra*), bear (*Ursus thibetanus*), and other small mammals. Dog (*Canis lupus* f. familiaris) is the only clearly domestic species during the Jomon period.

It is generally considered that domestic pigs were imported together with rice cultivation and metallurgy from the Chinese mainland, probably through the Korean peninsula, during the Yayoi period (*c.*2500–1700 cal. BP) (Naora 1937*a*, 1937*b*, 1938*a*, 1938*b*; Nishimoto T. 1989, 1991*a*). Possible cases of local domestication of wild boar during the Jomon period have been discussed since the early 1900s (see e.g. Naora 1938*b*; Kato 1980; Ono 1984; Nishimoto T. 2003). Some archaeologists suggest that 'semi-domestication' or management of wild boar had already begun by the Middle Jomon period, and that the process of domestication intensified in the Late and Final Jomon period. Supporting evidence raised by the advocates of the existence of domestic pigs during the Jomon period includes:

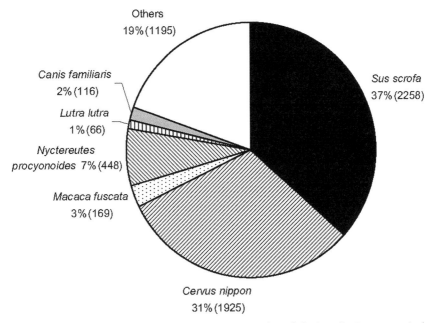

Fig. 6.1. Relative proportion of land mammals exploited during the Jomon period: combined MNI data from 60 Jomon sites from the Incipient Jomon phase to the Final Jomon phase, located in Honshu and Kyushu (based on Nishimoto 1991*b*)

- *Sus* remains found on Jomon sites from islands that lie outside of the natural distribution of wild boar, such as Izu, Sado, and Hokkaido. The Izu islands are a group of small islands located 30–200 km off the Izu peninsula south-west of Tokyo, where *Sus* remains are found from archaeological sites as early as the Earliest Jomon period (Naora 1938*b*; Kaneko 1987; Yamazaki *et al.* 2005). Hokkaido is the second-largest and northernmost island of the Japanese archipelago, and is separated from Honshu by the Tsugaru strait. The shortest distance between Hokkaido and Honshu is about 30 km. The fauna in Hokkaido is distinct from that in Honshu. It is generally accepted that wild boar were never distributed north of the Blakiston Line, a zoogeographical boundary between Hokkaido and Honshu (Inukai 1960; Kawamura 1991; Nishimoto 1985). The island of Sado is located in the Japan Sea, off the coast of the Niigata Prefecture.

- Figurines and pottery decorated with images of 'pigs' are abundant, especially from the Middle Jomon period.

- *Sus* burials at Jomon sites suggest a close relationship between *Sus* and humans. For example, a 'pig' burial associated with human burials was recently found at the Shimo Ota shell midden in Chiba Prefecture (Sugaya & Toizumi 1998; Nishimoto *et al.* 2003).

Recent genetic analysis using mtDNA of *Sus* samples excavated from Late–Final Jomon and Yayoi sites in western Japan showed a close phylogenetic relationship of some of the archaeological *Sus* specimens with the recent East Asian domestic pigs (Morii *et al.* 2002). This genetic evidence supports the introduction of domestic pigs from the Chinese Continent to western Japan as early as the Late Jomon period, and has contributed to the ongoing debate about the origin of domestic pigs in Japan.

SAMPLES

In this paper, the focus is mainly on the *Sus* remains from Jomon sites in the central and north-eastern parts of the Japanese archipelago (see Table 6.1).

Table 6.1. Archaeological sites used for the study of *Sus* remains.

Site Name	Region	Prefecture	Period
Inakuraishi	Hokkaido	Hokkaido	Late Jomon
Irie	Hokkaido	Hokkaido	Late Jomon
Bibi 4	Hokkaido	Hokkaido	Late Jomon
Kiusu 4	Hokkaido	Hokkaido	Late Jomon
Kashiwabara 5	Hokkaido	Hokkaido	Late Jomon
Mitsuya	Hokkaido	Hokkaido	Late/Final Jomon
Nusamai	Hokkaido	Hokkaido	Final Jomon
Misawa Higashi 5	Hokkaido	Hokkaido	Final Jomon
Mamachi	Hokkaido	Hokkaido	Final Jomon
Mutogawa	Hokkaido	Hokkaido	Final Jomon
Usu Moshiri	Hokkaido	Hokkaido	Final Jomon
Usu Zenkoji 2	Hokkaido	Hokkaido	Final Jomon
Hakuza	Tohoku	Aomori	Early Jomon
Hatanai	Tohoku	Aomori	Early Jomon
Futatsumori	Tohoku	Aomori	Early/Middle Jomon
Komatsu	Tohoku	Iwate	Earliest
Nakazawa hama	Tohoku	Iwate	Middle Jomon
Futsukaichi	Tohoku	Iwate	Early/Middle Jomon
Miyano	Tohoku	Iwate	Middle Jomon

(Continued)

Table 6.1. (*Continued*)

Nei	Tohoku	Iwate	Late Jomon
Satohama Hatanaka	Tohoku	Miyagi	Middle Jomon
Satohama Daigakoi (Kazakoshi)	Tohoku	Miyagi	Late Jomon
Tagara	Tohoku	Miyagi	Late/Final Jomon
Satohama Daigakoi	Tohoku	Miyagi	Late/Final Jomon
Satohama Nishihata	Tohoku	Miyagi	Final Jomon
Kogenji	Tohoku	Fukushima	Early Jomon
Ohata	Tohoku	Fukushima	Middle/Late Jomon
Aikoshima	Tohoku	Fukushima	Late/Final Jomon
Usuiso	Tohoku	Fukushima	Late/Final Jomon
Terawaki	Tohoku	Fukushima	Late/Final Jomon
Yoshii Shiroyama (#1)	Kanto	Kanagawa	Earliest and Middle Jomon
Kayama	Kanto	Kanagawa	Earliest/Middle Jomon
Nojima	Kanto	Kanagawa	Early Jomon
Haneo	Kanto	Kanagawa	Early Jomon
Denfukuji	Kanto	Kanagawa	Middle Jomon
Shoumyouji	Kanto	Kanagawa	Late Jomon
Kousaka A	Kanto	Kanagawa	Late Jomon
Ikego	Kanto	Kanagawa	Yayoi, Kodai
Shimo-ota	Kanto	Chiba	Middle, Late Jomon
Tonodai	Kanto	Chiba	Late Jomon
Uchino Daiichi	Kanto	Chiba	Late/Final Jomon
Takeshi	Kanto	Chiba	Late/Final Jomon
Sanbu ubayama	Kanto	Chiba	Final Jomon
Shimotakabora A	Izu (Oshima Is.)	Tokyo	Earliest Jomon
Shimotakabora B	Izu (Oshima Is.)	Tokyo	Late/Final Jomon
Teppoubaya	Izu (Oshima Is.)	Tokyo	Early/Middle Jomon
Kurawa	Izu (Hachijyojima Is.)	Tokyo	Early/Middle Jomon
Tobune	Izu (Niijima Is.)	Tokyo	Late/Finale Jomon
Tomochi	Izu (Miyakejima Is.)	Tokyo	Late/Final Jomon
Kokomanokoshi	Izu (Miyakejima Is.)	Tokyo	Yayoi
Torihama Shell mound	Hokuriku	Fukui	Early Jomon

Kill-off patterns and the biometry used in order to investigate changes in the human–*Sus* relationship through time, during the Jomon period. The archaeological *Sus* samples used in our study come from three different regions in the Japanese archipelago (Fig. 6.2). The first group of archaeological *Sus* samples comes from Hokkaido, Tohoku, and Hokuriku in north-east and north central Japan. The second group consists of the specimens from sites in the Kanto region in central Japan, including those from the Izu islands. The third consists of specimens from Yayoi and Kofun period sites in the Kanto region. In addition, the size of modern wild boar from central and western Japan is examined to investigate the degree of geographical variation in wild boar populations.

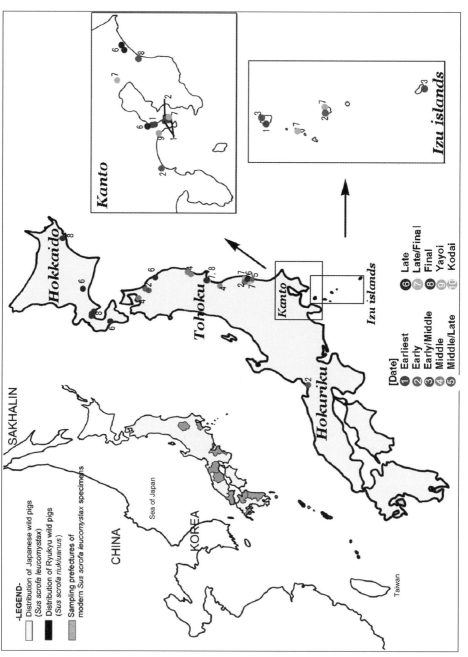

Fig. 6.2. Location of the sites where *Sus* samples were taken

AGE PROFILE BASED ON EPIPHYSEAL FUSION

Figure 6.3 shows survivorship curves for *Sus* samples from the Tohoku region (north-eastern Japan), from the Kanto and Hokuriku regions (central and western Japan) and from Izu and Hokkaido, based on the state of epiphyseal fusion of postcranial elements. The charts indicate the survival rate at each age stage, where age stage I corresponds to infantile–juvenile (until about 12 months), II corresponds to subadult (about 24 months), and III to adult (36 months). Survival rate at age stage I is generally quite high in all regions, at more than 80%. Survival rate at age stage II is still high at 70–80%, with the exception of the Early Jomon period in the Kanto region where only 50% survived this age stage. In Kanto and Hokuriku, survival rate of *Sus* at age stage III is 30–40%, suggesting that kill-off took place mainly during the subadult stage (roughly between 24 and 36 months). In the Tohoku region in the north, however, a later kill-off schedule is observed compared to the Kanto region, with 60–70% of *Sus* surviving to full adult age. Both in Kanto and Tohoku, kill-off patterns changed little over the period of about 5000 years from the Early to the Final Jomon, except for the Izu specimens in the Late-Final phase which show much higher survival rate into the adult age stage (Fig. 6.3). Early to Middle Jomon Izu specimens show similar kill-off pattern to that of mainland Kanto. Although there is the limitation of the small sample size, it seems that the kill-off pattern during the Late-Final Jomon on the Izu islands was different, with much higher survival rates at age stages II and III. Kill-off patterns of Hokkaido *Sus* samples are very different from those of Tohoku, suggesting that the slaughter concentrated on individuals between about 1 and 2 years of age.

AGE PROFILES BASED ON TOOTH ERUPTION AND WEAR

Figure 6.4 shows the age profile for *Sus* based on tooth eruption and wear for the Kanto region and Izu islands. In the Kanto region, teeth belonging to stage I (M_1 started to erupt–fully erupted) or II (M_2 started to erupt–fully erupted) are most abundant. This pattern is consistent from the Early to the Final Jomon period. The estimated age corresponding to the full eruption of M_2 is 16–18 months based on the data obtained from modern Japanese wild boar that were captured and raised at farms.

Age profiles of *Sus* specimens from the Yayoi Bronze Age (300 BC to 300 AD) and the Kodai period (after the 5th century AD) are shown in Fig. 6.5a–b for

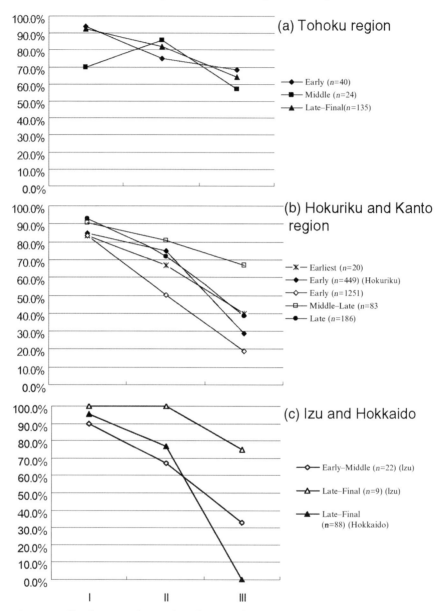

Fig. 6.3. Kill-off pattern for *Sus* based on epiphyseal fusion of limb bones. Elements used for epiphyseal fusion are, for stage I: distal scapula, acetabulum, distal humerus, proximal radius, proximal 2nd phalanx, distal calcaneum; for stage II: proximal 1st phalanx, distal metapodials, distal tibia, distal fibula, proximal calcaneum; for stage III: proximal humerus, distal radius, proximal and distal ulna, proximal and distal femur, proximal tibia, proximal fibula

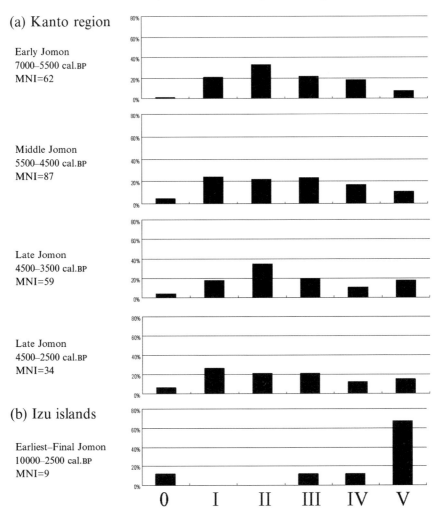

(a) Kanto region

Early Jomon
7000–5500 cal.BP
MNI=62

Middle Jomon
5500–4500 cal.BP
MNI=87

Late Jomon
4500–3500 cal.BP
MNI=59

Late Jomon
4500–2500 cal.BP
MNI=34

(b) Izu islands

Earliest–Final Jomon
10000–2500 cal.BP
MNI=9

0   I   II   III   IV   V

Fig. 6.4. Age profiles for *Sus* based on tooth eruption and wear. For Figs 6.4–6.5, only tooth rows still in the mandibles were used. The number of samples are expressed by MNI, with left and right mandibles matched to avoid double counting. The eruption stages are: I (M_1 started to erupt–fully erupted), II (M_2 started to erupt–fully erupted), III (M_2 worn), IV (M_3 erupted), V (M_3 erupted and worn to the last cusp)

comparison. The pattern for the Yayoi period is generally very similar to those from the Jomon period. In the Kodai period, however, stage III (M_2 worn) became more abundant, indicating a slightly later kill-off schedule.

Sus specimens from the Izu islands show quite different patterns (see Fig. 6.4). There appear to be more old animals among the samples, and

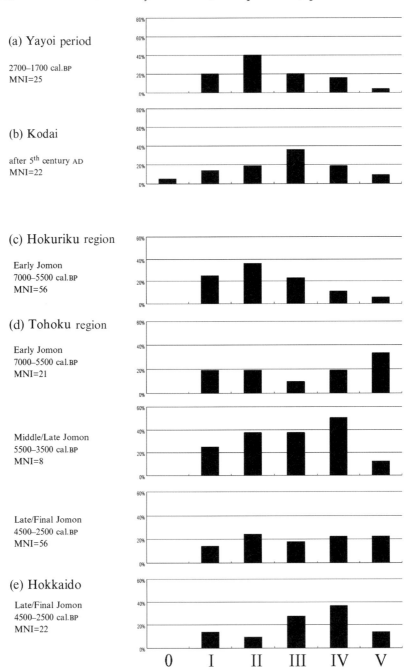

Fig. 6.5. Age profile for *Sus* based on tooth eruption and wear (see Fig. 6.4 for explanation)

teeth belonging to stage V (M_3 erupted and worn to the last cusp) are most abundant. Although the small sample size renders the pattern obscure, this result corresponds well with the epiphyseal fusion data. Age profiles of *Sus* specimens from Hokuriku (north central Japan), Tohoku, and Hokkaido, based on tooth eruption and wear, are compared in Fig. 6.5c–e. The age profile of *Sus* in Hokuriku shows a similar pattern to that of the Kanto region. In Tohoku, the proportions of stages IV and V are relatively higher, suggesting slaughter of *Sus* at older ages compared to Kanto. The results also correspond well with the slaughter patterns based on the epiphyseal fusion data, which also indicated a later kill-off schedule for the Tohoku specimens. In Hokkaido, which is outside the natural distribution of wild boar, the pattern is similar to that of contemporary Tohoku samples with the peak at stage IV.

REGIONAL VARIATION IN THE SIZE OF MODERN WILD BOAR IN JAPAN

The Japanese archipelago stretches some 3,000 km from north to south, resulting in considerable geographical variation in climate and vegetation. Since the habitat of Japanese wild boar ranges approximately from 31 to 41°N, the size of wild boar is also expected to vary between different geographical regions. As a basis for investigating the diachronic change in the size of archaeological *Sus* specimens, the regional size variation of wild boar should be examined, but the size of modern wild boar in Japan has not been studied systematically. Figure 6.6 shows the length of lower M_3 of modern wild boar from various regions in Japan. There is an east–west cline in the size of M_3, with the teeth being smaller in western Japan. The results suggest a considerable regional variation in the size of wild boar in Japan, which should be taken into account in any study of archaeological *Sus* remains.

THE SIZE OF ARCHAEOLOGICAL *SUS* SPECIMENS

Turning to the archaeological *Sus* specimens, the greatest length of lower M_3 of *Sus* from archaeological sites in the Kanto region and Izu islands are compared in Fig. 6.6. There is a gradual increase of the size of M_3 from the Earliest to the Late Jomon periods. The size of M_3 then decreases in the Final

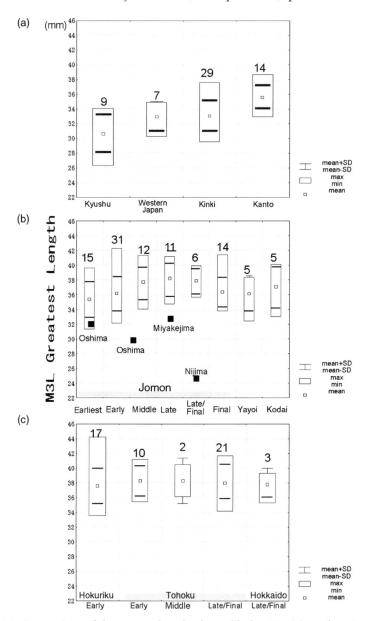

Fig. 6.6. Comparison of the greatest length of mandibular M_3: (a) modern Japanese wild boar populations from Kyushu and Honshu; (b) Jomon *Sus* samples from Kanto region; (c) Jomon *Sus* samples from Hokuriku, Tohoku, and Hokkaido

Jomon period and the Yayoi Bronze Age. The samples from the Izu islands are much smaller than those from the Kanto sites, except for a specimen from the site belonging to the Earliest Jomon period, which falls in the size range of the mainland samples.

In the Tohoku region, the size of the M_3 was consistent from the Early to the Final Jomon period (see Fig. 6.6). The size of M_3 is slightly larger in the Hokuriku and Tohoku regions than in the Kanto region in the Early Jomon period, especially when the mean value is compared. This result suggests that regional variation in size also existed during the Jomon period. Partly due to the size increase in the Kanto region, the Late–Final Jomon period specimens in the Kanto region are similar in size to those in the Tohoku region.

BODY SIZE OF ARCHAEOLOGICAL *SUS* SPECIMENS

In order to compare the postcranial measurements of *Sus* from archaeological sites from different periods and various geographical regions in Japan, we used the log ratio method (Uerpmann 1979; Meadow 1981, 1983, 1999). Measurements of a modern male wild boar from the Kanto region are used as the standard, which is the zero point on the x-axis of the graphs.

Figure 6.7 shows the log size index distribution of *Sus* from Jomon sites in the Kanto region (a) and Izu islands (b). The range of size distribution remains unchanged throughout the Jomon period, except for one small specimen in the Earliest Jomon period, which could be an unusual specimen or measurement error. The median values of LSI distributions suggest that the body size of *Sus* became slightly larger through the Jomon period, which corresponds well with the trend observed for the size of mandibular M_3. The postcranial measurements of *Sus* specimens from the Izu islands are much smaller than that from the Kanto region of the main island. This again corroborates the results obtained by the measurements of mandibular M_3. Almost all the *Sus* specimens from Izu islands are smaller than the standard animal, and there are a few samples smaller than the size range of the main island Jomon specimens.

Early Jomon period *Sus* samples from Hokuriku region derive from only one site (Fig. 6.7c). Notwithstanding this limitation, they are larger than those from the Kanto region in the same period, but similar in size to the *Sus* from the Tohoku region (Fig. 6.7d). In fact, the size range of *Sus* in the Kanto region became comparable to those in Hokuriku and Tohoku only in the Late–Final Jomon period, when the size reached its maximum.

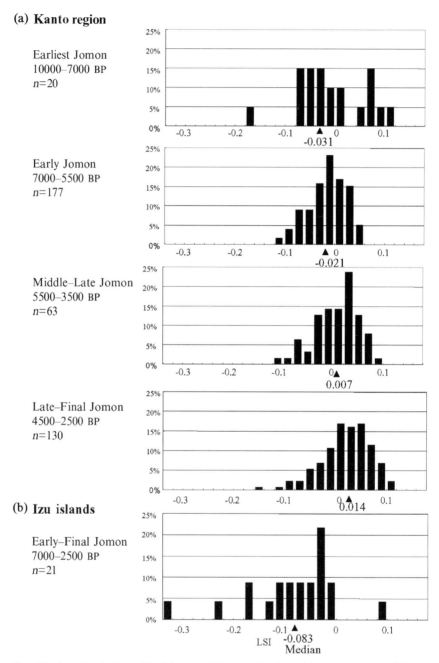

Fig. 6.7. Log size index of limb bones of Jomon *Sus* from (a) Kanto region, (b) Izu, (c) Hokuriku, and (d) Tohoku regions (*see across*)

(c) Hokuriku

Early Jomon
7000–5500 BP
n=436

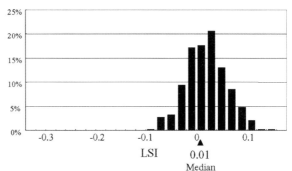

(d) Tohoku

Earliest–Early Jomon
10000–5500 BP
n=51

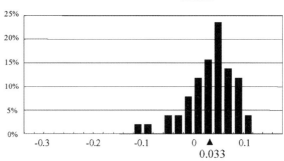

Early–Middle Jomon
7000–5500 BP
n=34

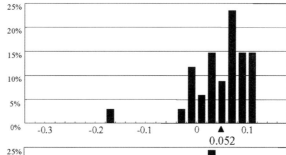

Late–Final Jomon
4500–2500 BP
n=131

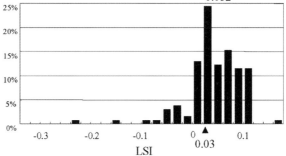

The size of *Sus* from archaeological sites in Tohoku changed little through the Jomon period. Again, these results are consistent with the trend observed in the size of mandibular M_3. Due to a few small specimens, however, the range of the log size index distribution is broader in the Late and Final Jomon periods. It is possible that this change indicates an increase of females in the sample. At present, however, we do not have enough data on sexual dimorphism of postcranial elements in Japanese wild boar to evaluate this slight shift in the size distribution.

Regional comparison of the archaeological *Sus* specimens is possible only for the Late Jomon period. Log size indices of postcranial measurements of *Sus* from Late Jomon sites from the Hokkaido, Tohoku, and Kanto regions are compared in Fig. 6.8. There are more larger specimens from Tohoku sites compared to contemporary specimens from Kanto sites. Although this suggests that there was a regional variation in the size of *Sus* in the past as well (with the populations in the north being slightly larger in size) the size ranges in the two regions are similar. It is noted that *Sus* from archaeological sites in Hokkaido, which outside the natural distribution of wild boar, are about the same size as those from the Tohoku region, or even larger.

DISCUSSION AND CONCLUSION

Based on the metrical analysis and comparison of kill-off patterns through time, we have no clear evidence so far of domestication of wild boar at the Jomon sites on Honshu. There was no significant change in the kill-off patterns of *Sus* in the Kanto or Tohoku region through time during the Jomon period. There might be regional differences in exploitation practices, because more adult animals are found in the assemblages from Tohoku. This preliminary observation, however, should be tested with additional data. Considering the differences in climate and topography of the two regions, hunting range, method, and season could be different.

A considerable geographical variation in the size of modern wild boar in Japan was found in our study. There appears to be a clear east–west cline in the size of the mandibular M_3. Regional variation in the size of *Sus* also existed in the archaeological specimens, with the population in the east and north-east being larger. This result is hardly surprising, given the considerable environmental differences between north-eastern and central Japan, in both climate and vegetation. Endo *et al.* (2000) report a certain degree of geographical variation in size among Japanese wild boar populations, although they pointed out that it does not strictly follow Bergmann's rule (Bergmann 1847).

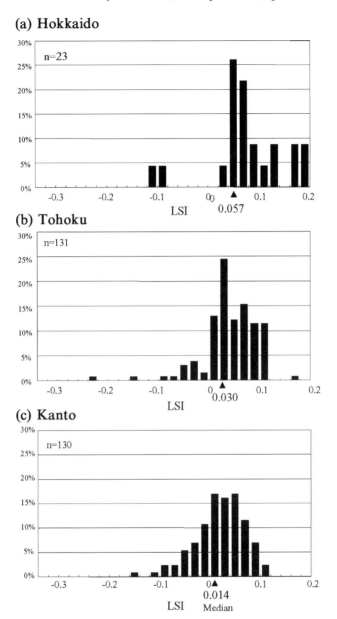

Fig. 6.8. Comparison of *Sus* log size index for the Late to Final Jomon periods (4500–2500 cal. BP) in Hokkaido, Tohoku, and Kanto regions

In order to assess the regional size variation of wild boar in the past, more measurement data of *Sus* from archaeological sites in different regions in Japan should be gathered for future study.

As for temporal changes in the size of *Sus* within a region, body size was either unchanged (in Tohoku) or became slightly larger (in Kanto) through the Jomon period. The increase in the body size is also reflected by the length of lower M_3 from Kanto sites. However, a careful assessment of the results is needed, because the size increase in Kanto might actually be related to the geographical variation of wild boar populations rather than representing a real size increase. Whereas our Early Jomon samples come from sites in western part of Kanto, the Middle to Final Jomon samples come from the north-eastern part of the region. Assuming from the east–west cline in size observed among modern wild boar populations, the body size of Jomon *Sus* populations in north-eastern Kanto would be expected to be larger than that in western Kanto. The slight size reduction of the Final Jomon *Sus* might partly be due to a deterioration of natural habitats caused by increasing human activities in the Kanto Region, but whether this change led to the beginnings of a domestication process is still debatable.

Although it is a commonly used osteometric tool for detecting domestication, the danger of employing size reduction has been pointed out by Zeder (2001). Based on the measurements of modern wild goats from different regions in Iran, she demonstrated the importance of regional and demographic factors in determining the size of animals. Our study also showed that the spatial variation in the size of wild boar populations should be carefully assessed as part of the investigation of the process of pig domestication in Japan, because an apparent diachronic change in size might actually be a result of geographical variation.

The results of our analysis of the kill-off patterns and size of *Sus* from Jomon sites on Honshu do not support the domestication of wild boar in the Jomon period, at least in the way that a domestic population was isolated from the wild population. Comparison of the kill-off patterns of a hunted population and a domestic population from Turkish sites showed that the pattern of the domestic pig population is characterized by relatively early kill-off (Hongo & Meadow 2000: fig. 4). The survival rate past the infant/juvenile age stage is much lower compared to that in the hunted population, and the proportion of fully adult individuals is also much smaller in a domestic population.

Although the kill-off patterns of *Sus* from Tohoku sites shows the late kill-off comparable to that of a hunted population, the data from the Hokuriku and Kanto sites show that *Sus* were culled mainly between the subadult and the adult age stage. Considering the high survival rate at epiphyseal fusion age stages I and II, however, it is unlikely that the *Sus* in Kanto and Hokuriku regions were under any kind of human control.

Therefore, the differences in the kill-off patterns between Tohoku and Kanto or Hokuriku regions are probably due to different hunting strategies. Relatively early kill-off could also be observed as a result of hunting, depending on the methods employed. In modern examples of wild boar hunting in Japan, it is known that young and inexperienced individuals less than 1 year old tend to be caught in the traps near human settlements. Older animals are mainly caught in the traps set deep in the mountain areas.

Wild boar easily adapt to the secondary environments around human settlements. Even recently, for example, some towns in Japan have had problems with wild boar that were being fed by people and became pests in towns, scavenging garbage and sometimes even attacking people in the streets to steal food from their hands. Also, wild boar piglets are often found, picked up, and raised by people in mountain villages in Japan—a practice that probably has a long history. These piglets are raised to be eaten later or are sometimes even kept for longer as a pets.

The appearance of clay 'pig' figurines and the burials of *Sus* together with humans found at some Middle Jomon and later period sites, however, suggest that the relationship between *Sus* and humans might have changed in the Middle Jomon period. Feeding of individual wild boar piglets might have become a common practice from the Middle Jomon period on. It is a matter of definition what exactly constitutes 'domestication', but in our opinion such a sporadic practice of keeping wild boar for only one generation should rather be regarded as delayed consumption rather than management or domestication, Such practice itself did not lead to full domestication, especially when wild boar were abundant and could easily be hunted. Taming of wild boar piglets, however, could have laid the foundation for the later adoption of domestic pigs during the Yayoi period. Genetic studies of *Sus* remains from the Yayoi period sites suggest that domestic pigs introduced from the continent were readily accepted at some sites while hunting of wild boar still continued at others (Morii *et al.* 2002).

The cases of the Izu islands and Hokkaido raise interesting questions about the introduction of wild boar outside of their natural distribution. According to the results of mtDNA analysis of Jomon *Sus* remains (Watanobe *et al.* 2004: 227), the *Sus* both from Hokkaido and the Izu islands had haplotypes closely related to those of Japanese wild boar in Honshu. Therefore, these *Sus* are likely to have been brought from Honshu to the islands by Jomon people. In contrast, the *Sus* remains from Jomon sites on Sado are found to be genetically unique to the island. Thus Jomon *Sus* found on Sado are likely to have belonged to a population that had been isolated since the Pleistocene and became extinct soon after the Jomon period, about 2,000 years ago (Watanobe *et al.* 2004: 226).

There are abundant ethnographic and historical examples in Japan of wild boar being brought to islands which lacked animal protein resources, and released to be hunted later. Recent examples of transportation of wild boar to islands are reported in Tsushima, Nagasaki Prefecture and Kamagarijima, Hiroshima Prefecture. Wild boar on the Tsushima islands were exterminated after considerable effort during the Edo period (17–19th century AD), because the residents of the island suffered starvation caused by intensive crop raiding by pigs. In recent years, however, wild boar have been reintroduced to the island by hunters. Taking advantage of the suitable habitat, the numbers of pigs on the island increased explosively. Kamagarijima is an island located off the shore of Hiroshima Prefecture where wild boar were not present naturally. In the 1980s, wild boar were introduced to the island, in order to use it as a natural cage for wild boar raised for their meat. However, by acquiring a new and suitable niche on the island, the animals reproduced rapidly and drove out the farmers by raiding crops. These wild boar also expanded their distribution to nearby islands a few kilometres away by swimming across the sea.

Examples of the transportation of *Sus* to islands have also been reported from the Mediterranean. *Sus*, *Ovis*, *Capra*, and *Bos* were introduced to the Early Neolithic site of Shillourokambos on Cyprus as early as 8300 cal. BC (Vigne & Buitenhuis 1999; Vigne *et al.* 2000*b*; Vigne 2003). This date is contemporary with, or preceding, the appearance of morphologically domestic forms of these ungulates at mainland sites. Therefore, it is argued that these animals were managed, or 'domesticated from the anthropological point of view' (Vigne 2003: 250) on the mainland before being brought to Cyprus. The issue is further complicated because species that were never domesticated (fallow deer and fox) were also transported to Cyprus. Based on the kill-off patterns and the size of the faunal remains from a later phase (7800–7500 cal. BC) at the Shillourokambos site, Vigne (2003) argued that pigs, sheep, and cattle were husbanded on the island, whereas feral populations of fallow deer and goats were hunted. Whether fallow deer was managed in some form or whether a wild herd was hunted is still debated (Davis 2003; Vigne 2003), which illustrates the difficulty in distinguishing a hunted assemblage from a managed one. Based on an imbalance in the sex ratio of fallow deer (greater number of females and young in the assemblage) at Khirokithia, another Neolithic site on Cyprus dated to the 7th millennium BC, Davis (2003: 265) suggested that fallow deer were also managed, by penning only the females near the site. An alternative interpretation for the same data was proposed by Vigne, who suggests that the imbalanced sex ratio is a result of the hunting of a wild herd consisting of females and young animals (Vigne 2003: 245).

The situation on the Mediterranean islands has some parallels with the case of the Jomon *Sus* on the Izu and Hokkaido islands in Japan. In the case of Izu (depite small sample size), the measurements of *Sus* from Ohshima island in the Earliest Jomon period falls within the smaller end of the size range of *Sus* from the Honshu sites, perhaps as a result of selection of animals which were easier to handle. The much smaller size and different kill-off patterns of the later Izu samples suggest that the *Sus* brought to the islands were not always immediately consumed, but were probably kept there for some generations. Whether or not these *Sus* brought to Izu were actually managed is still questionable. We do not think they were necessarily managed, as argued for the Cyprus case. It is not very difficult to capture wild boar, especially the immature individuals, put them on a boat and transport them to islands. As mentioned above, it is a common practice to transport and release wild animals on to islands to be hunted later (see also Horwitz *et al.* 2004). It is possible, however, that the introduced *Sus* were penned and fed in order to secure the meat supply on the island. Alternatively, they might equally well have been released or have escaped on to the islands. The apparent smaller size of the Jomon *Sus* from Izu could also be due to factors other than human influence, resulting from the genetic isolation on a small island or from the poorer vegetation of the islands.

Age profiles of Late–Final Jomon period Izu *Sus* suggest slaughter at older ages compared to the mainland. Especially, the absence of prime-age individuals as indicated by tooth eruption and wear suggests a very different exploitation practice of *Sus* on the Izu islands (see Fig. 6.4). Neither are the age profiles of Izu specimens are not comparable to the age profile of managed population.

The size and slaughter schedules of *Sus* from Hokkaido sites show different patterns from those at Izu sites. The size of Hokkaido specimens fall within the range of the mainland samples from Tohoku regions, or are even larger, when the measurements of postcranial bones are compared. The kill-off patterns based on epiphyseal fusion suggest that the majority of *Sus* were killed during subadult age stage, although the tooth data suggest an age profile rather similar to Tohoku specimens. There are a few possible reasons for the different patterns between Izu and Hokkaido samples. Introduction of *Sus* to Hokkaido was late compared to that to Izu, taking place mostly during the Late-Final Jomon periods. Also, since Hokkaido is much larger than the Izu islands, size diminution due to an 'island effect' might not be as extreme there. Perhaps the harsh winter environment in Hokkaido meant that introduced animals could not thrive, so the *Sus* population had to be continually replenished with new stock from the mainland. It has also been suggested that *Sus* were brought to Hokkaido alive primarily for ritual purposes (Nishimoto T. 1985). If so, prime age animals were brought to Hokkaido and kept for several months at most to be sacrificed. The larger size and slaughter peak at subadult age stage might support this theory.

The status of these island *Sus* populations in the Jomon period remains unclear, and the situation probably varied on different islands. We therefore need to carefully assess the degree of human influence on the breeding of these island *Sus* with more excavated data. On the other hand, the diminution of mandibular M_3 and body size in the Kanto region during the Final Jomon period might indeed be related to the beginning of more intense human intervention over the habitat of wild boar or the *Sus* population itself.

One of the effective means of detecting changes in human–*Sus* relations during the Jomon period might be the investigation of dietary changes of *Sus* using isotope analysis, such as the study already being undertaken by Minagawa *et al.* (2005) on Ryukyu wild boar. Our present data indicate that there were various exploitation strategies of wild boar in prehistoric Japan, including perhaps capturing and raising wild boar piglets which were also transported to islands. However, there is no evidence that *Sus* were managed over generations and reproduced in captivity on these islands, which is the essential factor leading to full domestication. The data at hand rather support the idea that domestic pigs were introduced to Japan in the Yayoi period. Possibly, future genetic analyses could add to the investigation and detection of the origin of introduced domestic pigs in Japan.

7

Wild boar and domestic pigs in Mesolithic and Neolithic southern Scandinavia

Peter Rowley-Conwy & Keith Dobney

INTRODUCTION

In Mesolithic and Neolithic southern Scandinavia, *Sus* is often the animal found most commonly on archaeological sites, and it undoubtedly formed a major part of the meat diet throughout the prehistoric period. Unfortunately, it is difficult to ascertain whether this meat comes from wild boar (*Sus scrofa*) or domestic pigs (*Sus scrofa* f. domestica), as archaeologists have only the bones to go on when seeking to determine the status of the animals they study. This contribution will examine bones from a series of sites, most in Denmark but some also in Sweden. Three main areas will be considered. First, Mesolithic animals will be discussed. These are universally regarded as wild boar, and the effects of the rising sea level and consequent fragmentation of their populations will be examined. Second, Danish Neolithic and later domestic animals will be discussed; these could either have been domesticated in Denmark from local wild boar, or could have been introduced from outside along with exotic agricultural items such as wheat or sheep. Third, we will consider Middle Neolithic animals from the Swedish island of Gotland in the Baltic Sea. Wild boar were almost certainly not present on Gotland during the Mesolithic, and the animals must therefore have been introduced by human agency. However, opinion is divided as to whether they were domestic pigs, wild boar introduced to found a hunted population, or a crossbred or feral population.

The sites to be examined are listed in Table 7.1. The various sites have been excavated at various times over the last century or so. Some were published shortly after being excavated, but others had to wait many years for publication. Excavation quality has certainly varied, but we believe this will probably not have exerted a major influence on the results we present. Our work is based on the mandibles, and these are large and robust. They are unlikely

Table 7.1. Sites mentioned in the present study.

Site	Site type	References
Early Mesolithic 9000–6400 BC		
Mullerup	Lakeside settlement	Sarauw (1904)
Holmegaard IV & VI	Lakeside settlement	Schilling (1999)
Lundby I	Lakeside settlement	Henriksen (1980)
Sværdborg	Lakeside settlement	Henriksen (1976)
Middle Mesolithic 6400–5400 BC		
Kongemose	Lakeside settlement	Jørgensen (1956)
Late Mesolithic 5400–3900 BC		
Norslund	Coastal settlement	Andersen & Malmros (1965)
Flynderhage	Shell midden	unpublished
Ringkloster	Lakeside settlement	Andersen (1975), (1998)
Agernæs	Coastal settlement	Richter & Noe-Nygaard (2003)
Sludegaard	Jaw cache in bog	Noe-Nygaard & Richter (1990)
Nivaa	Coastal settlement	Jensen (2001)
Bloksbjerg	Coastal settlement	Westerby (1927)
Middle Neolithic 3300–2500 BC		
Bundsø	Causewayed camp	Mathiassen (1939); Madsen (1988)
Troldebjerg	Causewayed camp	Winther (1935/38); Madsen (1988)
Ajvide	In graves on coastal settlements	Burenhult (2002)
Grausne		Österholm (1989)
Ire		Janzon (1974)
Late Bronze Age 1000–500 BC		
Voldtofte	Settlement	Berglund (1982)
Roman Iron Age AD 0–400		
Veileby	Settlement	Higham (1967*b*)

to be overlooked during even poor-quality excavations, and they survive better than many other parts of the skeleton. Samples are therefore unlikely to be biased either by recovery of preservation. In grouping sites by period, for example 'Early Mesolithic', we are certainly conflating sites of somewhat different ages. This is to some extent unavoidable, since not all the sites considered are equally well dated. It was felt preferable to group the sites into the main periods used by archaeologists, since these are both well-dated in themselves, and also calibrated against environmental change. Recent reviews of the Danish Mesolithic have been given by Grøn (1995) and Blankholm (1996) for the Early Mesolithic, by Johansson (2000) for the whole of the Mesolithic, and by Jensen (2001); the latter covers the Neolithic as well. The dates given for each period in Table 7.1 are the calibrated radiocarbon ages presented by Jensen (2001: 58).

MESOLITHIC WILD BOAR IN DENMARK

We start with the Early Mesolithic, and consider here five sites from four localities (Table 7.1). The Danish Early Mesolithic is a long period, but these sites, although not contemporaneous, cluster towards the middle and later part of the period; all probably fall into the period 8000–6400 BC. The landscape at this time was very different from today's (Fig. 7.1). Because the early postglacial sea level was lower, the outline of Denmark as we know it today had not yet appeared. Much of the southern North Sea bed was dry, and it would have been possible to walk dryshod from the sites considered here to the near-contemporary settlement of Star Carr (now near the east coast of England)—apart from crossing rivers such as the palaeo-Elbe. The Baltic sea existed in the form of a large freshwater lake (the Ancylus lake), which drained into the North Sea through two palaeochannels, known as the Dana and Svea rivers. Denmark thus formed a gently undulating and low-lying

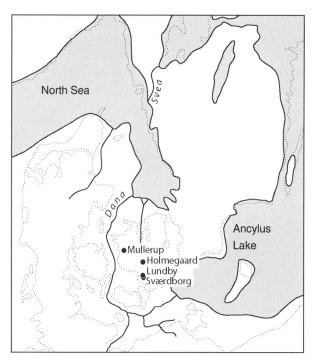

Fig. 7.1. Reconstruction of the landscape of the Danish Early Mesolithic showing sites from which *Sus* data derives

extension of the North European Plain, rather than the series of islands and waterways that characterizes the country today.

The sites to be examined all lie rather close together, on what is today the island of Zealand. Many typologically dated flinted scatters are known, but several have produced major faunal assemblages. These are all lakeside settlements, the bones being well preserved in peat deposits. The sites themselves are quite small, and some have the preserved floors of rather small huts. Most have been regarded as summer settlements, because they would probably have been flooded by winter rises in lake levels (e.g. Becker 1953; Andersen 1983; Grøn 1987). This has been supported by recent studies of wild boar tooth eruption (Rowley-Conwy 1993, 1999b). It remains unclear where the Early Mesolithic inhabitants were during the rest of the year. Perhaps most likely is that they wintered on the rivers or coasts that are now below sea level. Sites of the right date have been found by underwater archaeologists in the Sound (Larsson 1983; Fischer 1997a) and the Great Belt (Fischer 1997b), though whether these might be winter settlements cannot be determined. A few signs of marine exploitation are known: a grey seal mandible was found at Sværdborg I (Degerbøl 1933); a human skull found on the seabed in the Sound has been dated to late in the Early Mesolithic, and trace element analysis indicates a marine diet even though the contemporary sea shore was some way off (Tauber 1989).

The wild boar from these Early Mesolithic sites are uniformly large, among the largest we have encountered anywhere (Albarella *et al.* in press *a*). As an example, length and anterior breadth of M_3 are plotted in Fig. 7.3 below (measurements as defined by Payne & Bull 1988). They form a tight scatter, lengths varying between about 41 and 51 mm. Although the sites are close together (see Fig. 7.1), it is likely that these wild boar are typical of those over a wider area of the North European palaeo-plain. Rivers like the Dana or the palaeo-Elbe would be unlikely to act as barriers to movement because wild boar swim well and would be able to cross them with ease (Nowak 1999; Allen *et al.* 2001). Gene flow across the region would thus not be hindered.

Sea level rise during the Middle Mesolithic changed the regional geography. When the rising sea reached the -27 m submarine contour, it began to encroach rapidly into the present Danish waterways (Christensen 1995; Christensen *et al.* 1997); the even topography meant that the transgression was so fast that it would have been discernible within a human generation (Aaris-Sørensen 1988). The major new waterway was the Great Belt, 25 km across at its narrowest point, separating the islands of Fyn and Zealand. The Sound between Denmark and Sweden was also quite substantial, but the Little Belt between Jutland and Fyn was much narrower (Fig. 7.2). This led to the fragmentation of previously continuous species distributions, and in

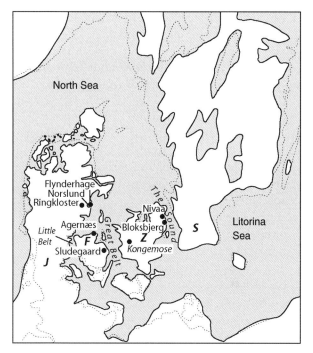

Fig. 7.2. Reconstruction of the landscape of the Danish Middle and Later Mesolithic showing sites from which *Sus* data derives. J = Jutland; F = Fyn; Z = Zealand; S = Sweden

some cases to local extinction. The aurochs, for example, became extinct on Zealand around 5000 BC, and in southern Sweden some 500 years later. A population persisted on Fyn until *c*.2500 BC; although this island is smaller than Zealand, it could presumably be replenished by some immigration across the Little Belt. Finally, the Jutland population became extinct around 500 BC (Aaris-Sørensen 1999). On Zealand, elk also became extinct, as did several species of carnivore (Aaris-Sørensen 1980). Hunting pressure exerted by humans was probably the major factor involved. The rising sea brought marine resources into these areas; human populations probably increased markedly, as did individual settlement size. This must have led to greatly increased levels of predation on the terrestrial fauna (Fischer & Malm 1997; Rowley-Conwy 1999*a*, 2001*a*).

Wild boar did not, however, become extinct on any of the islands. This was probably due to their comparatively greater reproductive rate. Instead of producing one or two offspring per year, wild boar can produce five or six piglets, or even more, per litter (Frädrich 1971; Oliver *et al.* 1993*a*). This means that there is a higher proportion of 'surplus' juveniles (Oliver *et al.*

1993*a*), which would be available for human predation. Some reports indicate that up to 30–50% of a wild boar population can be killed every year without long-term damage to the population (Haber 1961). Such levels of predation would prove disastrous for less fecund species, and this probably accounts for the various extinctions recorded on Zealand (Aaris-Sørensen 1980).

The effects of insularization can however be seen. Figure 7.3 plots dimensions of third molars (M_3) from Middle and Late Mesolithic sites on Zealand, as well as those from Jutland (including Fyn). A remarkable pattern emerges in the Late Mesolithic: the Zealand animals show a trend towards *narrower* M_3s compared to the Early Mesolithic, whereas the Jutland animals show a trend towards *broader* ones; length remains largely unchanged. The Middle Mesolithic sample from Kongemose is not, however, intermediate between the Early and Late samples from Zealand. These animals had *longer* M_3s proportional to their width, including two of the longest M_3s we have seen anywhere. These data are presented as separate histograms in Fig. 7.4. In terms of M_3 width, the Late Mesolithic Zealand specimens are clearly somewhat smaller than the rest. In terms of length, however, it is the Middle Mesolithic specimens that stand out as being larger than the others; the

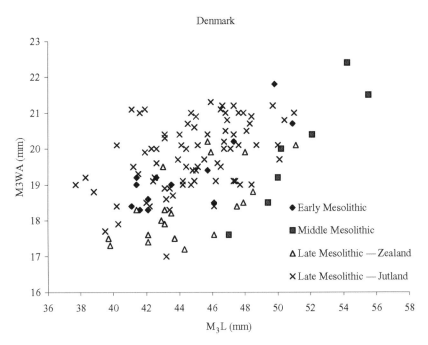

Fig. 7.3. Biometry of *Sus* permanent third molar (M_3)—width of the anterior cusp (M_3WA) against maximum length (M_3L)—from Mesolithic Denmark

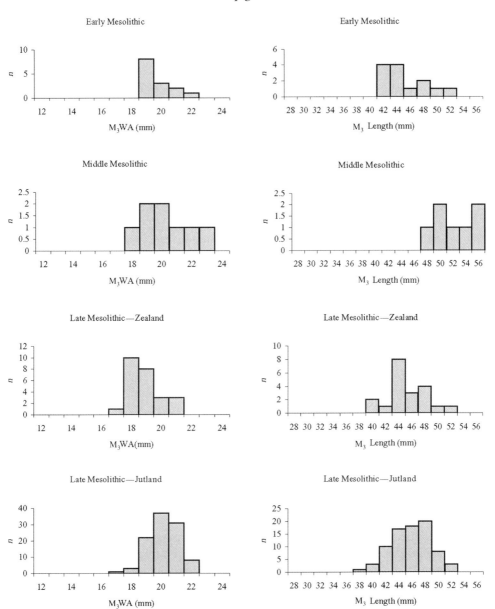

Fig. 7.4. Biometry of *Sus* permanent third molar (M₃)—width of the anterior cusp (M₃WA) against maximum length (M₃L)—from Mesolithic Denmark

Late Mesolithic Zealand animals, despite having narrower teeth, do not have shorter ones.

Samples are relatively small, particularly from Middle Mesolithic Konge-mose; but if we take them at face value the measurements imply that the Jutland and Zealand populations began differentiating almost as soon as the Great Belt became an effective barrier to gene flow. Differing intensities of human hunting may (as discussed above) have played an important selective role, although it is not clear why this should lead to wider M_3s on Jutland, and narrower ones on Zealand. If the Kongemose sample is indeed represen-tative of the Middle Mesolithic, it would suggest that selection on Zealand was initially towards *longer* teeth, which, however, did not increase in breadth; in the Late Mesolithic length reverted to the previous length dimensions, with breadth decreasing proportionally.

However selection may have acted, these results clearly show that it does not take long to have an effect. Christensen *et al.* (1997: 48) date the initial formation of the Great Belt to *c.*7000 BC, and it would be some little time after this that it had widened enough to become a genetic barrier. The Kongemose settlement is not very well dated; three ^{14}C ages fall between 6500 and 6000 BC, and there are some grounds to suspect that the settlement falls in the later part of this interval (Sørensen 1996: 91–3). The time interval from the isolation of Zealand to the Kongemose *Sus* assemblage is thus less than 1000 years. The Sound, between Zealand and Sweden, was formed at the same time as the Great Belt, but is much narrower; examination of Swedish Middle and Late Mesolithic wild boar could reveal whether it too formed a genetic barrier.

NEOLITHIC AND LATER *SUS* IN DENMARK

Sus mandibles from a series of Neolithic and later sites in Denmark have been examined (Table 7.1, Fig. 7.5). M_3 length and anterior breadth for these assemblages is plotted in Fig. 7.6, along with the entirety of the Mesolithic samples considered above. Almost all the Neolithic and later specimens are substantially smaller than the earlier ones. Over a century ago Herluf Winge concluded that this meant that the smaller animals were domesticated, his notional division in M_3 length being around 40 mm (Winge in Madsen *et al.* 1900: 158–60). In Fig. 7.6, the earlier and later scatters overlap at just about this point on the horizontal axis, suggesting that Winge was about right. The later scatter includes a few large outliers well above 40 mm in length. Since Winge's study, such Neolithic and later scatters have therefore

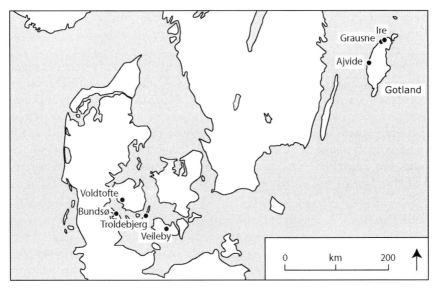

Fig. 7.5. Neolithic and later Denmark and Sweden, showing sites from which *Sus* data derives

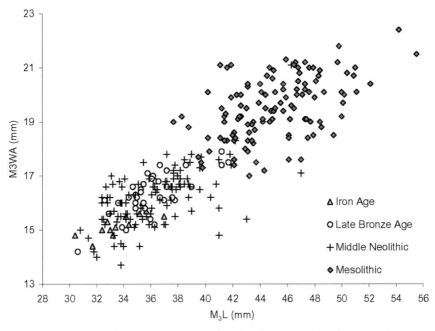

Fig. 7.6. Biometry of *Sus* permanent third molar (M_3)—width of the anterior cusp (M_3WA) against maximum length (M_3L)—from prehistoric Denmark

been interpreted as mostly comprising small domestic individuals, with a few large hunted wild boar (see for example Degerbøl 1939; Rowley-Conwy 2003).

The question to be addressed here is whether the domestic pigs of Neolithic and later Denmark are the descendants of local wild boar, and were locally domesticated within Denmark; or whether they are the descendants of populations domesticated elsewhere, and imported already domesticated. Winge did not really address this question, but one early worker did argue for indigenous domestication (Pira 1909: 373). Subsequently, work in southwest Asia identified ever-earlier agricultural communities in that region, and the date of pig domestication there was pushed back (e.g. Flannery 1983; Ervynck *et al.* 2001). This meant that there were domestic pigs elsewhere in western Eurasia that were contemporary with the Scandinavian

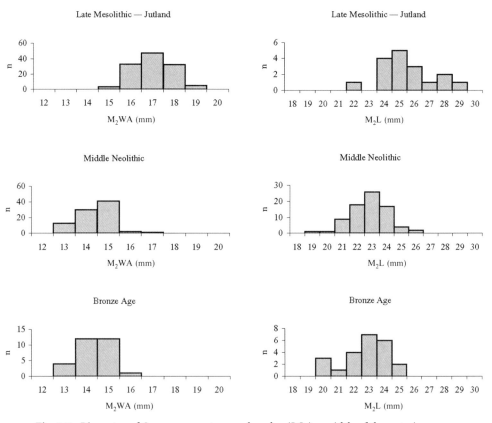

Fig. 7.7. Biometry of *Sus* permanent second molar (M_2)—width of the anterior cusp (M_2WA) against maximum length (M_2L)—from prehistoric Denmark

Mesolithic wild boar discussed above. Importation of domesticates as part of the 'Neolithic package' of domestic crops and animals was thus a reasonable possibility. In Europe as a whole, arguments have been advanced both for indigenous domestication and for importation (discussed by Albarella *et al.* 2006). One of us has recently argued that importation into Scandinavia may be more likely (Rowley-Conwy 2003). Figure 7.6 offers initial support for this position, because there is little overlap between the Mesolithic and later scatters: the Neolithic and Bronze Age populations are in fact of very similar size; the Neolithic is not metrically intermediate between the Mesolithic and Bronze Age. Change through time is thus in the form of a step rather than a trend. This pattern also emerges from a consideration of measurements of M_2, presented in histogram form in Fig. 7.7. Here too the Neolithic and Bronze Age animals are of very similar sizes, differing considerably from the Late Mesolithic wild boar.

This does not, however, prove that domestic pigs were imported into Denmark. There are two complicating factors which must be born in mind. First, the earliest domestic samples studied by us are of *Middle*, not Early, Neolithic date. The Late Mesolithic ends at *c*.3900 BC, and the Middle Neolithic samples date from around 3300–3000 BC. There is thus a chronological gap of some 700 years that is not represented in Figs 7.6 and 7.7. Could selection have acted so quickly to reduce the size of pigs? The size changes within the Mesolithic wild boar discussed above were minor in comparison (see Figs 7.3 and 7.4), but more intense selection might speed things up. Size reduction during the initial domestication process at the stratified site of Çayönü Tepesi in eastern Turkey was certainly more rapid (Ervynck *et al.* 2001), but local domestication in Denmark would imply an even more rapid size change. An argument in favour of local domestication would also have to account for the abrupt cessation of the selection for smaller pigs, since there was no further size reduction between the Middle Neolithic and the Late Bronze Age, a period of over 2000 years (and then its resumption in the Iron Age, when pigs again become smaller) (see Figs 7.6 and 7.7). Nevertheless, the recovery and metrical analysis of Early Neolithic material from Denmark remains a top priority; a substantial sample would help to resolve this issue.

The second complicating factor comes from a study of the DNA of modern domestic pigs and wild boar (Larson *et al.* 2005). Wild boar are relatively non-migratory, so their DNA is more geographically structured than that of some other species. European and Near Eastern wild boar show recognizable differences, and modern European domestic pigs carry the two *European* haplotypes, not the Near Eastern one. This must mean that wild boar were domesticated within Europe. It has been tentatively suggested on the basis of the modern DNA distributions that domestication occurred in central Europe rather than Scandinavia (Larson *et al.* 2005: 1619), but the complexities of DNA, both ancient and modern, are only beginning to be understood. It is not impossible that ongoing and future work may yet point to Scandinavia as a centre for domestication. There are at present no grounds to suggest it, but we can by no means rule it out.

A century of work has thus not resolved the issue of local domestication versus importation. At the moment, the balance of probabilities appears to be in favour of importation, but as stressed above this conclusion may change. Metrical analysis of a large sample of Early Neolithic pig mandibles would make a significant contribution to the debate, particularly if this were combined with the study of ancient DNA from the same specimens. Until such samples are available, however, the importation hypothesis remains likely, but unproven.

MIDDLE NEOLITHIC *SUS* ON GOTLAND

The island of Gotland lies in the Baltic Sea to the east of the Swedish mainland (see Fig. 7.5). Three Gotland assemblages are considered in the following, each comprising a group of jaws found interred with human remains. *Sus* are fairly common on settlement sites, but these are the only three graves from Gotland to contain such groups of jaws, others in the extensive cemeteries containing artefacts and bones of other kinds. The graves are no. 7 from Ire (Janzon 1974: 282–3, fig. 9), a grave from a test pit at Grausne (Österholm 1989: 151–6, figs 76 and 77), and no. 60 from Ajvide (Burenhult 2002: 114–15, fig. 105). Figure 7.8 shows Ire grave 7 during excavation. The jaws were evidently placed in the grave as a deliberately positioned cache of grave goods, and those from Grausne and Ajvide are similar. At Ire, there are 19 individual *Sus*, each represented by both the left and right halves of the mandible; at Grausne there are 46 half-mandibles from 34 different *Sus*; and at Ajvide there are 46 half-mandibles from 30 *Sus*.

The problems these assemblages present are more complex than those considered above. The Mesolithic and Neolithic of Denmark are associated with extensive evidence of hunting-gathering and agriculture respectively, so the wild and domestic status of the pig remains in the two periods has an economic context which is fairly well understood. The same cannot be said for the Gotland sites. Gotland falls within the area of southern Scandinavia that was occupied by the Funnel Beaker (TRB) Culture at the start of the Early Neolithic. This archaeological culture has traditionally been considered as the vehicle that took an agricultural economy into these regions, north to

Fig. 7.8. Inhumation from grave 7, Ire (Gotland) during excavation showing *Sus* mandibles cached at the feet of the human skeletons (after Janzon 1974). Photo G. Arwidsson. © Antikvarisk-Topografiska Arkivet, reproduced by permission

about the latitude of Stockholm. The Middle Neolithic is conventionally a period of agricultural *recession*, however, during which much of Sweden, including Gotland, saw a diminution or abandonment of farming and a re-adoption of full-time hunting and gathering. This occurred during the advance from the north-east of the Pitted Ware Culture; the Funnel Beaker Culture persisted in southernmost Sweden and throughout Denmark, and these areas remained agricultural. Troldebjerg and Bundsø (whose pigs were discussed above) belong to this culture and period (see for example Stenberger 1962; Malmer 2002; Österholm 1989 specifically for Gotland).

Some recent studies have concurred that agriculture did indeed spread far to the north in the Early Neolithic (Hallgren *et al.* 1997; Persson 1999). Various uncertainties about this economic scenario have recently been expressed, however, for example by Johansson (2003), who points out that agricultural evidence in the northern Funnel Beaker Culture regions remains modest, and by Strinnholm (2001), who argues that some agriculture continued in the Pitted Ware during the Middle Neolithic. Stable isotopes in human bones tend to support the traditional picture, however. The varying salinity of the Baltic Sea causes problems for such studies, but they appear to show an increase in terrestrial foods during the Early Neolithic, which would be consistent with agriculture replacing maritime hunting and fishing. This is followed by a reversion to a marine-based diet in the Middle Neolithic, consistent with a return to maritime hunting and fishing (Lidén 1995*b*; Lindquist & Possnert 1997). A recent major isotopic study of the Pitted Ware settlement and cemetery at Västerbjers, on the east coast of Gotland, has confirmed the importance of seal in the diet to such an extent that the author was moved to suggest that the people could be described as 'the Inuit of the Baltic' (Eriksson 2004: 154). In later periods a more terrestrial diet re-established itself as agriculture advanced again.

In such a problematic context it is not surprising that the status of the Middle Neolithic *Sus* on Gotland is contested. They could clearly be either wild, introduced to found a hunted population; or domestic (though perhaps crossed with wild boar), herded around the coastal settlements; or feral, the free descendants of Early Neolithic domestic pigs brought to the island. A point of major importance is that re-analysis of the deeply stratified site of Stora Förvar (on the islet of Stora Karlsö just off Gotland) has revealed very few *Sus* bones in its Mesolithic layers; and all those that have been dated are in fact of Neolithic age, and thus intrusive into the Mesolithic layers. Wild boar were thus *not* present on Gotland during the Mesolithic (Lindquist and Possnert 1997). The Middle Neolithic *Sus* in question are thus descendants of animals carried to the island by humans. It has been argued on this ground that the pigs were necessarily domestic (Jonsson 1986; Benecke 1990; Lindquist & Possnert 1997). However, wild animals can be introduced and released in order to found a population for hunting. Wild boar were apparently taken to Ireland during the Mesolithic for this purpose (McCormick 1999), and there are various other prehistoric examples involving other species in Europe and elsewhere (Rowley-Conwy 2004; see also Hongo *et al.* this volume). Thus the fact that Gotland is an island to which the animals were brought is not in itself sufficient reason to conclude that the pigs were domestic; this first line of evidence is inconclusive.

The second line of evidence is biometric. The large size of the Gotland *Sus* was noted by Ekman (1974), in his consideration of the material from Ire. Ekman was working before radiocarbon dating demonstrated the absence of Mesolithic *Sus*, so he assumed a long history of the species on the island. He expressed surprise (1974: 216) that insular dwarfing had not occurred, and subsequent work has shown that his surprise was not misplaced. A major study of wild boar across the Old World has shown that dwarfing occurs on islands the size of Gotland and larger, for example Corsica, Sardinia, and Okinawa and the other Ryukyu islands. Only when island size is as large as Taiwan or Sri Lanka does dwarfing not occur (Albarella *et al.* in press *a*).

Ekman's conclusion was that the Gotland animals were wild, since they were of similar size to mainland wild boar.

Writing a few years later, Jonsson (1986) suspected on geological and biogeographical grounds that the island had no native wild boar; the Middle Neolithic animals were thus introduced, and this led to his conclusion that they must be domestic (see above). To account for their large size, he suggested that cross-breeding with wild boar had occurred on the mainland; this would mean that some large mainland animals, for example those from the Neolithic site of Alvastra considered by Ekman to be wild boar, were in fact domestic. This conclusion was based on the assumption that the Gotland animals had to be domestic because they were transported. Rowley-Conwy & Storå (1997) suggested an alternative, namely that the animals were wild boar transplanted to found a hunted population.

Figure 7.9 plots M_3 length and breadth of the Gotland *Sus*, compared to the Mesolithic and Middle Neolithic specimens from Denmark already discussed. It is apparent that the animals are much larger than the Danish Neolithic domestic ones. Jonsson (1986) is clearly correct to argue that the transport of small domestic animals to Gotland cannot account for the metric data. The

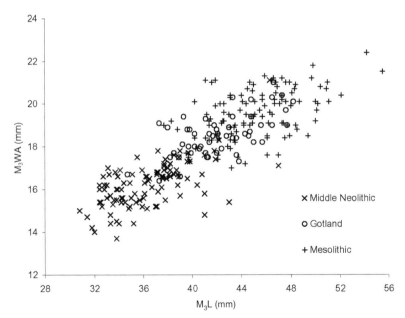

Fig. 7.9. Biometry of *Sus* permanent third molar (M_3)—width of the anterior cusp (M_3WA) against maximum length (M_3L)—comparing Gotland specimens to those from Mesolithic and Middle Neolithic Denmark

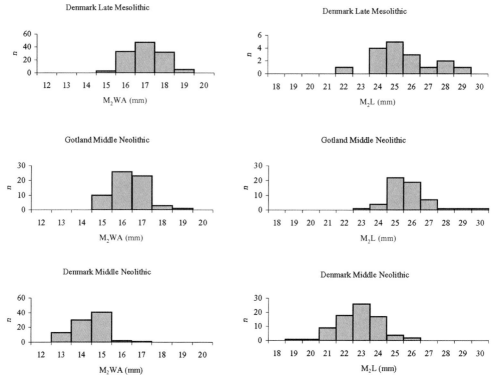

Fig. 7.10. Biometry of *Sus* permanent second molar (M_2)—width of the anterior cusp (M_2WA) against maximum length (M_2L)—comparing Gotland specimens to those from Mesolithic and Middle Neolithic Denmark

Gotland animals are not quite so large as the Danish Mesolithic specimens, although they overlap extensively. Although this could be consistent with a heavy admixture of wild genes, as Jonsson argues, it is also consistent with the introduction of pure wild boar to Gotland, which subsequently began to dwarf as noted above for islands of this size. Since we do not know how long the population had been present on Gotland before the assemblages considered here were formed, we cannot consider speed of dwarfing. Figure 7.10 plots M_2 length and breadth as histograms. In terms of length, the Gotland *Sus* align closely with the Danish Mesolithic. Their breadth, however, is rather reduced, though still much larger than the Danish Neolithic domestic animals. Such narrowing of teeth is exactly what occurred when Zealand was isolated in the Middle and Late Mesolithic (see above and Figs 7.3 and 7.4). In this respect the Gotland *Sus* conform to what we have already seen happen to wild boar when isolated; although in the case of Gotland, it happened only to M_2, not M_3.

The biometric discussion can be taken further. Tooth wear allows the mandibular wear stages of each jaw to be calculated, following the method of Grant (1982). Also recorded was the depth of the mandible between dP4 or P_4, and M_1: measurement 16b of von den Driesch (1976: Fig. 22b). Not surprisingly, there is a relationship between the two: mandible depth increases with age. This is plotted for the Gotland specimens in Fig. 7.11, compared to the Danish Mesolithic and Neolithic animals. The regression line for Gotland falls close to that for the Danish wild boar, whereas that for domestic pigs lies well below. The jaws of wild and domestic animals were evidently of different shapes, the domestic ones reflecting their smaller size. Figure 7.12 puts this in a wider context, bringing in wild boar from Germany and Poland, and a sample of feral pigs, measured by us, from northern Australia. The German and Polish wild boar group closely with the Danish ones, and the Gotland *Sus* fall in the middle of them. The Australian population has been feral for nearly 150 years, but has retained its domestic dimensions, falling very close to the Danish Neolithic ones. This appears to suggest that feralization does not result in the immediate reversion to wild boar characteristics in all respects.

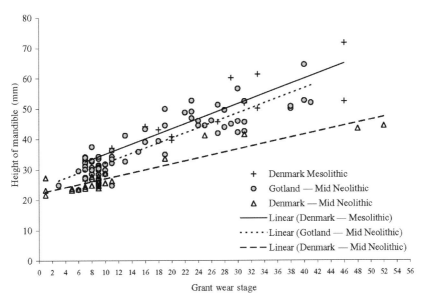

Fig. 7.11. Relationship between the height of the mandible in front of the M_1 (von den Driesch 1976: 58, measurement 16b) and individual mandible wear stages (after Grant 1982) of archaeological *Sus* specimens from Gotland and Denmark

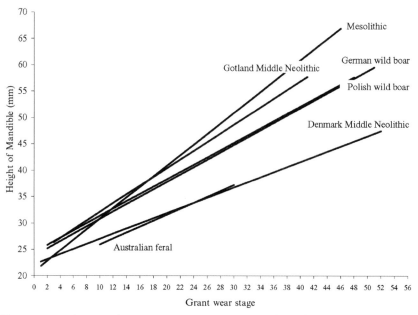

Fig. 7.12. As Fig. 7.11, but now comparing regression lines for both archaeological and modern wild boar comparative data sets

If this conclusion can be transferred to the Gotland animals (and more studies are needed before this can be assumed), it would suggest that the Gotland *Sus* were not the feral descendants of Early Neolithic domestic animals.

The conclusion from this biometric discussion is thus that there is nothing in these data that *requires* domestication to explain it; but domestication might perhaps remain a possibility *if* extensive or overwhelming wild admixture is argued—and *if* one assumes that transport demonstrates domesticity in the first place.

The pigs' foraging habits and diet provide the third line of evidence considered. If the animals were domestic, they would have spent time near the human settlements, and received or scavenged at least some of their food from their owners. Rowley-Conwy has questioned the niche a pig would occupy at a coastal hunter-gatherer settlement (Rowley-Conwy & Storå 1997: 124), but this has been answered by Masseti (this volume) who points out that much fish and marine mammal waste would be available for the pigs, citing recent examples from different parts of the world. The Gotland *Sus*, if domestic, might thus have subsisted in part on such marine offal. However, in her major study of Västerbjers, Eriksson examined the isotopes from eight *Sus* from that site and five more from Ire, and concluded that their diet was entirely terrestrial. This contrasts with the dogs, which were indubitably domestic, and which had a much higher marine component in their diet (Eriksson 2004:156). A smaller sample of *Sus* from Ajvide suggested the same (Lindquist & Possnert 1997). What has been reconstructed concerning the diet and foraging of the *Sus* does thus not support a domestic status.

A fourth line of evidence is provided by the study of linear enamel hypoplasia (LEH) in the teeth of the *Sus*. This is a growth defect in the tooth enamel. Each cusp grows from the tip downwards, being formed by a series of laminations. If growth is interrupted for any reason, the increment of laminations is temporarily halted, resulting in a hypoplasia event (Dobney and Ervynck 1998, 2000; Dobney *et al.* 2004, this volume). Enamel growth may be halted by developmental stress, which may have various causes. If *Sus* are born at the same time of year, and grow their teeth at consistent ages, hypoplasias occurring at consistent heights indicate stresses occurring throughout the population at similar ages. For example, M_1 forms very early in life, and consistently shows two peaks, interpreted as resulting from the stresses associated with birth, and with weaning, respectively. M_2 forms a little later, and a consistent peak of hypoplasias quite low on that tooth (= relatively late in crown formation) may result from the dietary stresses caused by the animals' first winter (Dobney *et al.* 2004: Fig. 4).

In general, it has been argued that wild boar show fewer LEHs than do domestic pigs, a pattern that recurs in both archaeological and recent animals (Dobney *et al.* 2004). LEH frequency is therefore plotted in Fig. 7.13. The four Mesolithic (assumed wild) boar samples have consistently low frequencies, but the individuals from Middle Neolithic Troldebjerg and Bundsø have higher frequencies. The Gotland *Sus* fall above even Troldebjerg and Bundsø, and on this measure are more similar to the domestic Neolithic pig assemblages from Denmark. The high frequencies of LEH are also similar to those of Neolithic domestic pigs reported from elsewhere in Europe, for example in France and Britain (Dobney *et al.* 2004: Fig. 6). However, the pattern is not completely consistent. In Denmark, Bronze Age Voldtofte has low frequencies of LEH similar to those of wild boar (Fig. 7.13) even though the pigs from this site were definitely domestic (see Figs 7.6 and 7.7). Nor do all wild boar populations have uniformly low frequencies: in Japan, *Sus* from the Jomon period are generally regarded by most to be hunted wild individuals, and yet have reported frequencies of LEH much higher than modern Japanese wild boar (Dobney *et al.* 2005: Fig. 3). The special conditions on a relatively small island such as Gotland might have led to wild populations being subject to more frequent physiological stress (e.g. increased population density and competition), perhaps the result of climatic or dietary stress, or of more frequent hunting and disturbance by the densely settled human population.

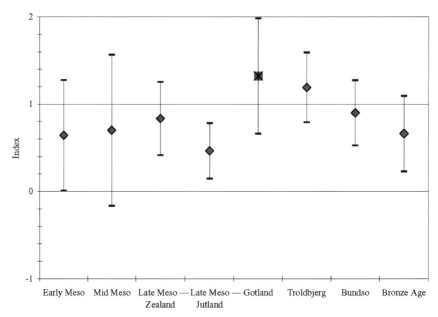

Fig. 7.13. Index comparing the average frequency of linear enamel hypoplasia (LEH) between all archaeological *Sus* specimens recorded

The distribution of LEHs on different teeth provides an alternative way of looking at these data. Figure 7.14 plots the Gotland data against the various archaeological wild boar populations from Denmark. The Gotland line is generally higher, reflecting the higher frequency of LEH previously discussed, but the overall outline is similar, M_3 generally having more LEHs than M_2. This would suggest that, for these animals, stress occurred more often during the second winter than the first. Figure 7.15 compares the Gotland pattern to those from the domestic pigs from Troldebjerg, Bundsø, and Voldtofte. Although frequencies are comparably high, the pattern is different: the domestic pigs have far more LEHs on M_2 than M_3, indicating greater stress frequency in the first winter. Thus in this respect, the Gotland samples tentatively align with the wild rather than the domestic animals. The major exception is Late Mesolithic Zealand, where LEHs on M_3 are relatively infrequent, and yet one might have expected this island environment to produce a pattern closer to that from Gotland.

Evidence from the Gotland *Sus* LEH patterns are thus rather contradictory and inconclusive. The high *frequency* of LEHs in the Gotland *Sus* suggests that they were domestic, but their *distribution* across the tooth row is closer to that

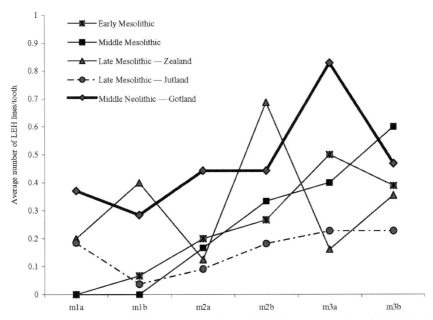

Fig. 7.14. Comparison of the average number of LEH lines per tooth and individual cusp between Mesolithic Danish and Neolithic Gotland *Sus* (for M_1 and M_2: a, anterior cusp; b, posterior cusp; for M_3: a, anterior cusp; b, central cusp)

found in ancient wild populations. Further work is needed before LEH can solve the Gotland problem for us.

A fifth line of evidence that has been discussed is the funerary nature of the Gotland samples, and the seasonality of the kill. Österholm (1989) points out that a human corpse is unlikely to remain unburied for more than a few days. Since the *Sus* jaws were buried in the same graves, the jaws of the requisite number of *Sus* must have been available: 19 in the case or Ire, 30 at Ajvide, and 34 at Grausne. The impossibility of guaranteeing the successful hunting of the requisite number suggests that the *Sus* were on hand and available for slaughter, that is to say, domestic (Österholm 1989). Examination of the ages at death of the animals, however, suggests an alternative, namely that the jaws were taken from animals killed at various times and cached or trophied. They were thus on hand—but as defleshed jaws, not live animals. This can be seen in Fig. 7.16. The three graves are plotted separately, compared to a sample from the settlement at Ajvide (from Rowley-Conwy & Storå 1997: fig. 5). Ages are probably fairly accurate but are not necessarily precise. The least accurate are animals approaching dental maturity, notionally aged

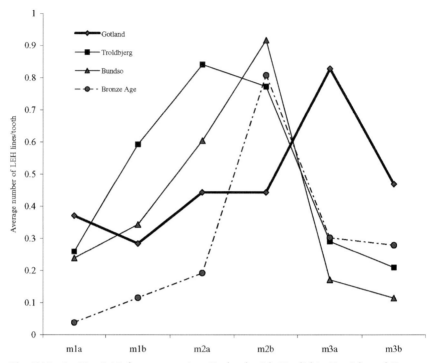

Fig. 7.15. As Fig. 7.14, but comparing Gotland with Neolithic Danish and Bronze Age *Sus*

around 25–7 months; jaws in this stage are therefore plotted, but do not contribute to the minimum killing periods.

The spread of ages within each grave makes it clear that the jaws do not result from a single mass kill. The animals were thus not slaughtered for the purposes of a feast, of the kind described by Sillitoe (this volume) or Rappaport (1968). The trophying of pig mandibles is also suggested by one other peculiarity of the jaws themselves: they are not usually broken up in the way that is commonly done on settlement sites, for the extraction of their marrow. Instead, a hole is usually cut in the side of the jaw, allowing the extraction of the marrow without the fragmentation of the mandible (Fig. 7.17). This unusual practice may result from a desire to exploit the marrow while leaving the jaw intact—presumably as a trophy and for subsequent use as grave goods. This caching of jaws for funerary use does not of course prove that the animals were wild; it merely means that they do not have to be domestic, and on hand for instant slaughter when required. The only other site discussed here where a similar pattern occurs is the Danish Mesolithic site of

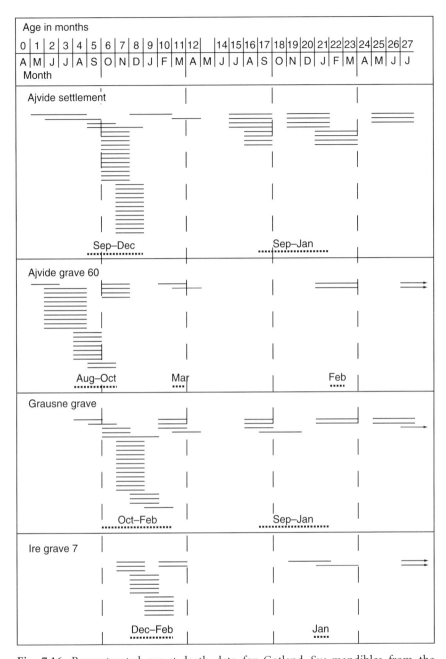

Fig. 7.16. Reconstructed age-at-death data for Gotland *Sus* mandibles from the settlement refuse of Ajvide compared to those found within three separate human graves from the sites of Ajvide, Grausne, and Ire (see Rowley-Conwy & Storå 1997: Fig. 5). The method of ageing has been described elsewhere (Rowley-Conwy 1993, 2001*b*; Rowley-Conwy & Storå 1997). Mean date of birth is assumed to be 1 April. Each line represents one *Sus* jaw (only one half-mandible from each individual is plotted). The minimum periods of killing are plotted below each; these are based on taking the innermost month of the jaws at each end of a concentration (omitting individual outliers)

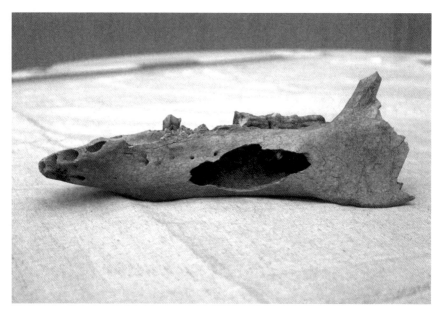

Fig. 7.17. Complete archaeological *Sus* half-mandible (possible trophy) from the site of Ajvide with a hole cut in the side of the jaw, allowing the extraction of the marrow without fragmentation (photo P. Rowley-Conwy)

Sludegaard, where jaws were recovered from a cache; these were of course wild boar, not domestic pigs (Noe-Nygaard & Richter 1990).

CONCLUSIONS

We have presented evidence above that indicates that Late Mesolithic wild boar populations began to diverge quite soon after being isolated from one another by the rising sea. Denmark is an area uniquely well placed in northern Europe for the speed of this change to be examined. Other areas such as Island South East Asia may in due time produce comparative data, and the various island groups into which pigs have been introduced such as Sardinia and Corsica, the Ryuku islands, and others, may also be relevant.

The evidence currently leans towards Neolithic domestic pigs in Denmark being imported from elsewhere, not locally domesticated; though for the reasons discussed, this conclusion is by no means certain. An Early Neolithic assemblage from Denmark or southern Sweden *might* resolve this.

The Gotland *Sus* remain among the most intractable. The multiple lines of evidence considered above do not permit a definite conclusion as to whether the Middle Neolithic *Sus* on that island were wild or domestic; but the biometrical discussion, as well as the distribution of LEH, tend to favour the hypothesis that they were wild. In any case, no strong argument supports the hypothesis that they were domestic. Our tentative conclusion at this stage is, therefore, that the Gotland populations are best considered wild, until further data or arguments are brought into play.

8

The economic role of *Sus* in early human fishing communities

Marco Masseti

INTRODUCTION

Recent archaeological excavations of the cave of Cyclops, located in the southern cliffs of the islet of Youra (northern Sporades, Greece) (Fig. 8.1) have provided evidence of continuous human activity from the Mesolithic Period (10000–6800 BC) up to the beginning of the Final Neolithic (4600/4500–3300/3200 BC). The results of the investigation of its Mesolithic stratigraphy lead to the assumption that the economy of the prehistoric local human community was based predominantly upon the exploitation of marine resources (Sampson 1996*a*, 1996*b*, 1998; Powell 2003). Archaeological evidence suggests that the island fishermen also exploited mammals, as indicated by the discovery of a huge assemblage of bones of *Sus scrofa* (Fig. 8.2), particularly numerous in the Lower Mesolithic levels, where they also displayed a larger size in comparison to those of the same species found in the Upper Mesolithic layers (Trantalidou 2003). Thus, beyond the marine resources, *Sus* appears to represent the wild animal most widely consumed by the local human community. The date of 7530 cal. BC–7100 cal. BC (8th millennium BC) was obtained for the oldest bones of these prehistoric ungulates, by radiocarbon analysis performed at the Beta Analytic Laboratory of Miami (USA) (Masseti 2002).

In the light of archaeozoological evidence, early human societies which based their subsistence mainly on marine resources also feature a certain association with pigs, which has been registered from other prehistoric European and Mediterranean archaeological contexts. In Italian coastal areas, for example, this can be observed in the reports from the II Mesolithic phase of the cave of Uzzo, in north-western Sicily (Tagliacozzo 1993), from the Early Neolithic–Chalcolithic layers of the Grotta del Genovese on the small island of Levanzo in the Egadi archipelago (Sicily) (Graziosi 1962;

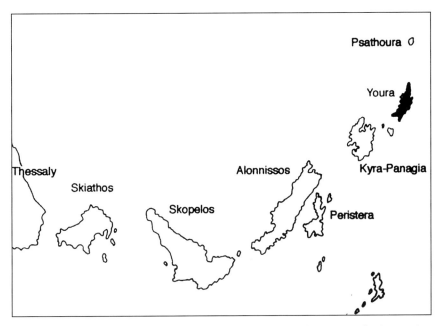

Fig. 8.1. Geographical location of the island of Youra, northern Sporades (Greece)

Fig. 8.2. Early human societies which based their subsistence mainly on marine resources also featuring a certain association with wild boars, *Sus scrofa*, have been recorded from several prehistoric European and Mediterranean archaeological contexts (photograph M. Masseti)

Cassoli & Tagliacozzo 1982), and possibly also from the proto-Mycenaean settlement (Middle–Late Bronze Age) of the islet of Vivara, in the Phlegraean archipelago (Gulf of Naples) (Marazzi 1998, 2001; Costantini & Costantini 2001; Pepe 2001). In northern Europe, the exploitation of pig resources has been found associated with several postglacial human settlements of the Baltic area, such as the Ertebølle Mesolithic culture of western Denmark (Rowley-Conwy 1984), of southern Sweden (Rowley-Conwy 1998), and of the Jutland peninsula (Rowley-Conwy 1994). But it is in particular off the shores of the eastern Scandinavian peninsula that the archaeological exploration of the Middle Neolithic contexts of the island of Gotland provided one of the most intriguing examples of the exploitation of pig resources within a prehistoric fishing community (Fig. 8.3). The Middle Neolithic levels of the coastal site of Ajvide yielded a wealth of archaeological material referred to the Pitted Ware culture (Österholm 1989). Its excavation has revealed an interesting archaeo-logical complex with different settlement areas, characterized by a marked dominance of osteological remains of fish and marine mammals. According to Rowley-Conwy & Storå (1997), such remains constitute more than 97% of the identified material. The most common mammals are represented by seals, followed through the stratigraphy by *Sus*, albeit with a slight tendency to a decrease of the species in the lower layers. According to NISP (number of

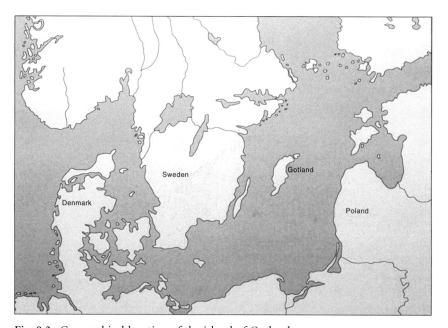

Fig. 8.3. Geographical location of the island of Gotland

identified specimens) counts, the ratio of pigs to seals is approximately 1:7 in layers 1 and 2, but 1:8 or 1:9 in layers 3–6. A marked dependency on marine proteins in the human diet has also been confirmed by the results of isotope studies of the human remains (Lidén 1995*a*; Lindquist & Possnert 1997).

Comparing the data available for the archaeological context represented by the Lower Mesolithic levels of Youra and that referred to the Pitted Ware of Gotland, my attention was drawn by an element which makes it possible to relate the two cultural events despite the great distance which separates them in both space and time: the undoubted importance of the role played by pigs within economic contexts markedly characterized by the exploitation of marine resources. What, notwithstanding the extreme differences between the two prehistoric human contexts here considered, can have led to such analogous importance being attributed to *Sus*? Why should pigs have represented the principal, if not the only, species of terrestrial macromammals exploited within this type of human community? What might have been the economic advantages, for the human community, of maintaining this species in such social conditions? And why did the fishermen of Mesolithic Youra and Middle Neolithic Gotland prefer *Sus scrofa* to other ungulates, despite the fact that other species were available in the surrounding natural environment? The cases in point provide the stimulus for a series of reflections on the biology and ecology of wild and domestic pigs, the advantages they might have represented for prehistoric human groups, and the possible economic role they may have played, considered within the broader framework of recently acquired archaeological and archaeozoological knowledge.

PIGS IN EARLY FISHING COMMUNITIES

The particularly ancient chronological dating (8th millennium BC) available for the oldest pigs of Youra would lead us to exclude the possibility that we are dealing with domestic animals, although archaeozoological investigation records that the process of swine domestication was already established in the Near East from the Middle Pre-Pottery Neolithic B (MPPNB) (cf. Schmidt *et al.* 1999; Peters *et al.* 2000). Thus, the evidence of human cultural control over these pigs could even be hypothesized, since they could have been imported on to the island from mainland areas, even located very far afield. The available archaeological documentation, based on still quite fragmentary evidence, would tend to indicate that the first relocations by sea in the Mediterranean basin were carried out by hunter-gatherers, in contexts of a Mesolithic type, probably as early as the 9th millennium BC (Jacobsen 1976;

Cherry 1979, 1981, 1990, 1992; Perlès 1979; Camps 1988; Simmons 1988, 1991; Renfrew & Aspinall 1990; Vigne & Desse-Berset 1995; Masseti 1998; Sampson 1998; Masseti & Darlas 1999). And the translocation of pigs in the Mediterranean islands is documented on Cyprus at least as far back as the local Pre-Pottery Neolithic, between the end of the 9th and the 8th millennium BC (Guilaine *et al.* 1996, 2000). The pigs of Middle Neolithic Gotland reveal a different scenario. In this case, the question about their presumed domesticity has already been discussed at great length by several authors, such as Ekman (1974), Jonsson (1986), Österholm (1989), Benecke (1990), Lindquist & Possnert (1997), and Rowley-Conwy & Storå (1997). Coming back, however, to the specific case of Youra we cannot exclude that wild boars could have lived naturally on the island, or in its immediate continental surroundings. It is still not absolutely clear whether Youra was in fact already an island during the Late Pleistocene and the Early Holocene (cf. Van Andel 1987; Cherry 1990; Patton 1996; Trantalidou 2003). Also, even if its highly specialized Mesolithic human economy argues for the fact that the separation from the nearby mainland was already established, wild boars could have reached the island, at different times, by swimming the narrow straits which may have separated it from the other northern Sporades and the nearest areas of the southern Balkan peninsula. In contrast, according to Rowley-Conwy & Storå (1997), the simple fact that Gotland was already an island means that pigs must have been introduced by man.

Modern scientific investigation considers wild boars as quite competent swimmers, although they cannot survive a crossing of more than a few miles of open sea. In eastern Asia, for example, it has been reported that bearded pigs, *Sus barbatus*, periodically cross the strait between the north-easternmost tip of Borneo to Sibutu and Tawi Tawi, the southernmost islands of the Sulu archipelago, in the south-west Philippines (Caldecott *et al.* 1993). And it is traditionally believed that, east of the Wallace line, the wild pigs of the islands of Sumbawa and Komodo could have extended their geographical range east of Java by swimming the narrow straits (Wallace 1869; Pfeffer 1968; Groves 1981, 1983). In this respect, a number of observations are also available for the Mediterranean basin. Off the delta of the river Ebro (Spain), adult specimens of *S. scrofa* are occasionally recorded swimming in the open sea, even at considerable distances from the mainland (M.A. Carretero pers. comm.). Von Wettstein (1942) reported that wild boars occasionally reached the island of Lefkada (Ionian archipelago, Greece) by swimming from the coast of Epirus opposite. It is also said that wild boars regularly reach the island of Samos (eastern Aegean sea) by swimming from the Anatolian coast opposite, where boars are still reputed as the commonest ungulates of the Samsundag range (Dilek Yarimadasi Milli Parki) (Masseti 2000). And, in the course of the present research, it was possible to report for the first time the occurrence of the species on the small Turkish islets of Cleopatra (Şehir Adalari), Değirmen Bükü, on the Seven Islands (Yediadalar) in the Gulf of Gökova, on the island of Yildiz in the gulf of Marmaris, the island of Domuz in the gulf of Fethiye, the island of Gemile opposite Olüdeniz, and the island of Geykova. All these islands are located very near to the south-western coast of Anatolia and wild boars have been often reported swimming across the narrow marine straits separating the islets from the continental shores. It seems that the few hundred metres which, in most cases, separate these islets from the opposite mainland do not represent any obstacle for the animals, which swim across to perpetrate night raids on the island crops.

COMMITTED OMNIVORES

As observed by Oliver (1984), swine are evidently tolerant of regional climatic conditions ranging from subarctic to tropical and, since they can nourish themselves on practically anything, they are also able to exploit a varied range of available habitats. Wild boars are in fact opportunistic feeders and committed omnivores, living mainly on a high-fibre, low-protein diet. As plant eaters they will browse fresh shoots and fruit, graze, and dig for tubers and rhizomes. They will also eat the faeces of other animals, prey on young and immobilized animals, and scavenge meat. There is an entire literature on the omnivorous feeding habits of wild boars and feral pigs (cf. Toschi 1965; Hoogerwerf 1970; MacFarland & Reeder 1977; Merton 1977; Thompson 1977; Wiewandt 1977; Wood & Barrett 1979; Pauwels 1980; Venero 1980; Clutton-Brock 1981; Juvik *et al.* 1981; Pavlov & Hone 1982; Oliver 1984; Serodio 1985; Spitz 1986; King 1990; Harrison & Bates 1991; Holden 1992; Oliver & Brisbin 1993; Oliver *et al.* 1993*a*; Massei & Genov 1995; Field *et al.* 2002). The consumption of invertebrate and small vertebrate prey may be a necessary component of the diet, since a study of free-ranging domestic pigs in Papua New Guinea revealed that animals fed *ad libitum* lost weight when denied earthworms (Rose & Williams 1983). Protein is in fact the most critical limiting factor in the nutrition of feral pigs; they require protein-rich foods, particularly during late pregnancy, lactation, and early growth (Giles 1980). Sows without a nitrogen intake of at least 15% may resorb fetuses (Pavlov 1980). Preliminary analyses on the stable isotope evidence of *Sus* diet from European and Near Eastern archaeo-logical sites suggest that pig diet became more carnivorous with progressive urbanization (Richards *et al.* 2002).

The scavenging tendency of boars has also been reported by several authors, such as Wodzicki (1950), Toschi (1965), Roberts (1968), Clutton-Brock (1981), Meads *et al.* (1984), King (1990), Field *et al.* (2002), Herrero & Fernández de Luco (2003), and others. Food which may be scavenged consists of the carcasses of animals which have died a natural death, the remains of prey left by carnivores, or offal and so forth around human settlements. As observed by van Lawick-Goodall (1970), the first problem for the scavenger is to find such food, which it may do by sight, hearing, or smell; the second, if the real killer is still finishing its meal, is to get there quickly before too many other scavenging competitors have arrived at the scene. Pigs do not, however, always scavenge meat. In the semi-arid region of Cuddie Springs, in eastern Australia, for example, Field *et al.* (2002) observed that carrion scavenging by pigs is particularly associated with drought following a long period of higher than average rainfall (Fig. 8.4). In other areas of peculiar trophic conditions, such as insular monsoon environments, it has also been possible to document the habit of wild pigs feeding on marine resources, even preying upon marine vertebrates and invertebrates.

Fig. 8.4. In the semi-arid region of Cuddle Spring, in eastern Australia, scavenging of carrion by feral pigs is particularly associated with drought following a long period of higher than average rainfall (photograph O. Brown)

EVENING SCENE IN KOMODO

In the evening, calm descends on the bay of Loho Liang, encircled by a broad ring of mountains in the Lesser Sunda sea (Indonesia). During the dry season, the sunset coincides with the lowering of the tide level along the indented coastline of Komodo (33,937 ha), a small volcanic islet located about 500 km off the eastern shore of Bali. This island is famous largely because it constitutes the last natural stronghold of the Komodo dragon, *Varanus komodoensis.* Wild pigs, too, occur on this island, reputed to have originated from specimens which could have colonized the island naturally (Groves 1983) (Fig. 8.5). They have been traditionally referred to the South East Asian subspecies *Sus scrofa vittatus.* Known as the banded pig, this is a rather variable taxon, with a distribution ranging from peninsular Malaysia to the islet of Peucang off western Java, and east of the Wallace line to Sumbawa and Komodo (Groves

Fig. 8.5. Adult female of the Komodo wild pig photographed in August 1984 at Banu Ungulung, located less than 3 km north-east of Loho Liang, the headquarters and visitor complex of the Komodo National Park. Banu Ungulung is the place where indigenous people used to feed goat carcasses to the Komodo dragons for the benefit of tourists. The swine were attracted there by the prospect of scavenging (photograph M. Masseti)

1981, 1983). Recent photographic evidence, however, seems to argue for the taxonomic identification of the wild suids of Komodo with a population of un-*vittatus*-like pigs, perhaps more closely related to the Sulawesi warty pig, *Sus celebensis* (C. Groves pers. comm.). This is a short-legged, short-eared species and of smaller size than all but the insular *S. scrofa*, with a natural distribution apparently limited to Sulawesi and a few other nearby islands (Groves 1983; Macdonald 1993). Beyond the Sulawesi island group, the species reveals a zoogeographically implausible distribution which suggests an active human role in its dispersal (Groves 1983, this volume). We cannot exclude the occurrence on Komodo of populations originated from *S. scrofa* × *S. celebensis* hybrids, such as other populations of wild pigs known from several islands east of the Wallace line (Groves 1983; Flannery 1990; Blouch 1995).

On Komodo, sunset is the time when the swine emerge from the monsoon jungle to snuffle around on the sandy seashore seeking out small fish, molluscs, and other marine titbits beached by the receding tide (Masseti 1984) (Fig. 8.6). In August 1984 I had the chance of observing this feeding habit of the wild pigs of Komodo, regularly every evening for eight consecutive days. According to Pfeffer (1957), the marine items preyed on by the animals include mudskippers

Fig. 8.6. On Komodo, sunset is the time when the wild pigs emerge from the monsoon jungle to snuffle around on the sandy seashore seeking out small fish, molluscs, and other marine titbits beached by the receding tide (photograph M. Masseti)

of the genus *Periopthalmus*, shrimps of the genus *Palaemonetes*, and crabs of the genera *Uca* and *Cenobites*. Again according to Pfeffer (1957), the boars of Komodo are phenotypically quite different from the feral pigs dispersed on the nearby islands of Flores and Rintja; the pig of Komodo is in fact '. . . long and lean, with greyish or pale brown skin sprinkled with a few short hairs, which give it a very unattractive naked look . . . many of the animals also have white spots on various parts of their bodies . . .'. Pfeffer (1957) attributed these phenotypic differences to the peculiar feeding habits of the swine of Komodo: 'These animals are, effectively, much more numerous than in Rintja and, moreover, the vegetable nourishment (fruits and tubers) is scarcer than in that island, so that we mostly saw the boars in the mangrove swamps where they nourished themselves on crustaceans and molluscs. This highly specialized diet has certainly had an influence on the physical appearance of our animal, and it may also play a role in the partial depigmentation observed in certain individuals.' This description effectively seems to coincide with that of the Sulawesi warty pigs which, according to Groves (1983), are very variable from black to red-brown to yellow in colour, even sometimes particoloured, depending on the hue and quantity of the saturated hairs. In any case, Pfeffer (1957) too made his observations on Komodo during the dry season, during the first two weeks of the month of July. Does any relation exist between this peculiar feeding habit of the Komodo pigs and seasonal conditions? Do they increase their consumption of marine animal resources as the availability of the edible vegetation decreases during the drought season? Can we predict this aspect of pig feeding activity in relation to explicit seasonal factors? Analogous feeding behaviour was also reported for wild pigs in mangrove areas of west Malaysia, where the items commonly consumed included molluscs, crabs, other arthropods, and even fish (Diong 1973; Oliver *et al.* 1993*b*).

Pigs on Komodo also frequent the areas where the dragons feed on carrion, where the swine are attracted by the prospect of scavenging. In the light of the above observations, we can assume that the diet of the pigs of Komodo must comprise a high level of animal proteins, albeit possibly limited to drought periods.

PIGS FOR WASTE DISPOSAL

The pigs' tendency to scavenge could have been an advantage for the human prehistoric communities, which may have exploited the pigs' capacity for refuse collection in the elimination of the organic waste produced by human activities. As we have already noted, a recent study on the stable isotope evidence of *Sus* diet from European and Near Eastern archaeological sites confirms the tendency towards an omnivorous diet with a high protein content in the case of pigs bred in close contact with anthropogenic environments (Richards *et al.* 2002). This peculiar attitude to scavenging, combined with the capacity to nourish itself on marine resources, would therefore have made the pig the ideal choice of ungulate for breeding within fishing communities which had to seasonally alternate the exploitation of suids and predation on marine resources. This combination may have favoured the choice of the pig over and above other ungulates in the recycling of waste, with the aim of breeding a domestic ungulate of large dimensions. This may explain why in many areas of developing countries, both in tropical Asia and in South America, domestic swine are still bred in a free-ranging state even within urban contexts. An analogous use of the ungulate has, for example, been recorded in several villages of the central Mexican plateau, such as that of San Juan Ajajalpan (Fournier 2003). In the humid lowland dwelling sites of the Chane river, in Bolivia, although some pigs are maintained on farms, the great majority are kept in the villages under a system described by Devendra & Fuller (1979) as small-scale subsistence production. This is a combination of scavenging pigs and backyard breeding systems described by Eusebio (1980): 'The pigs run free, scavenging for most of the year and their diet is supplemented by kitchen waste, maize and cassava' (Wilkins & Martinez 1983). In several areas of the Indian subcontinent, such as Agra and Calcutta, domestic pigs are also maintained in a kind of free-ranging condition.

Half wild and half domesticated, they move from open-air dumps to piles of refuse, snuffling around among rotten vegetable peelings, sheep bones, decomposing fruit and similar garbage, wallowing and snorting in the open drainage channels of towns and villages, rummaging unhesitatingly amidst the excrement and mud of the sewers in search of some titbit. They manage to eke out a fairly good living, judging by the size of the vast majority of these beasts . . . (Kapoor Sharma 2002, translation by MM).

In the light of all this, we cannot even exclude that this may have been precisely the role deputed to the species in several of the ancient cities of the Near East. In the early Mesopotamian site of Abu Salabikh (mid-3rd millennium BC), for example, archaeozoological evidence attests a high proportion of swine among the relative frequency of the domestic animals (Clutton-Brock & Burleigh 1978; Matthews *et al.* 1994). They were common, perhaps surprisingly so for this climate, and there were a few pig milk teeth with roots so far resorbed that they had probably been shed in life. According to Matthews *et al.* (1994), this suggests that the animals may have run free in the streets of the town. It seems fairly likely that pigs at Abu Salabikh were maintained under a system of small-scale subsistence production, by which the swine were allowed to derive their subsistence from the activity of scavenging, primarily expressed through the consumption of waste products. Even in modern India, the animals kept in such conditions '... are the refuse collectors' favourite animals, because by gobbling up the most disgusting waste they free the streets and gutters of rubbish, rendering their masters a dual service: in the first place because by eliminating the refuse they lighten their load, and secondly they free them of the burden of having to feed their animals.' (Kapoor Sharma 2002).

DISCUSSION AND CONCLUSIONS

As already observed, Rowley-Conwy & Storå (1997) argue that the Middle Neolithic Gotland pigs were probably wild, considering that it is otherwise hard to see what niche they would have filled since the rest of the economy was entirely based on wild resources. It seems clear that the question of whether these *Sus* were wild or domestic hinges on this identification of the niche they filled within the cultural framework of the Pitted Ware contexts; we have to understand what role they played in this prehistoric human economy. Did the pigs operate as refuse collectors, contributing to the elimination of the organic human waste produced, which was either deliberately given to them and/or scavenged on and around the settlement? Were the foodstuffs which they consumed and metabolized essentially made up of marine re-source waste? Could this have been one way of simplifying management problems, considering the human settlement and its surroundings as a sort of protected breeding area, which did not, however, prevent the pigs from also directly deriving their food supply from the carrying capacity of the local natural environment? Could an analogous role have also been played by the *Sus* of Mesolithic Youra? Effectively, we cannot exclude that in this case too the pigs may have been kept in similar conditions, enabling them to derive their nourishment from the carrying capacity of the natural insular environ-ment, integrating this with the leftovers of human meals, based predomin-antly on marine elements. The Mesolithic *Sus* of Youra may have operated as refuse collectors, cleaning up the human waste products and integrating their diet with the high-fibre vegetable food (grasses, acorns, berries, wild legumes, and roots) available in the natural environment of the island. Beyond this they may also have fed upon marine vertebrates and invertebrates, in line with the feeding habits observed in the wild pigs of Komodo. They could have in-dulged in the latter activity, scouting along the sandy shores of the limestone horst which surrounded the island below the cave of Cyclops, which would not yet have been below sea level in Mesolithic times (cf. Higgins & Higgins 1996).

But this does not help us to single out what economic role the pigs of Middle Neolithic Gotland filled, since the studies so far undertaken on these *Sus* do not suggest a marine diet (Lindquist & Possnert 1997; Rowley-Conwy & Storå 1997). The analysis of the stable isotope values tells us about the amount of marine protein in diets, where a $\delta^{13}C$ of 20‰ would mean 'no fish' and a $\delta^{13}C$ of 12‰ would imply 'all fish' (Tzedakis & Martlew 1999). According to Lindquist & Possnert (1997), although swine are omnivorous and could be expected to have consumed a lot of fish and sea mammal scraps on the dwelling sites of Pitted Ware Gotland, the Middle Neolithic *Sus* bones, varying in ‰^{13}C values between −22.1 and −20.5‰ on the PDB scale (named after a fossil octopus, *Belemnitella americana*, from the Pee Bee formation in South Carolina), do not reveal such marine $\delta^{13}C$ values. This probably shows that the Middle Neolithic pigs on Gotland were loosely herded in the acorn forests at some distance from the dwelling sites at the coastline, and seldom kept on such dwelling sites. It is even possible that the swine were so loosely herded in the forest that they lived more like wild boars than domestic pigs. Hence, despite the fact that *Sus* bones are often as abundant as seal bones in the faunal remains and swine is sometimes the most abundant species in the mammal remains, based on the $\delta^{13}C$ values in human, sea mammal, and swine bones, swine meat cannot have provided any important part of the human diet. In effect, again as observed by Lindquist & Possnert (1997), since human bones from the Pitted Ware culture graves and cultural layers of Gotland show up marine $\delta^{13}C$ values between −16.3 and −14.9‰ vs PDB and more, the most probable explanation is that fish provided the bulk of the human diet. However, this absence of consumption of non-marine items in the human diet raises several doubts that are still far from being explained. In the first place, this fact is in contrast with the high proportion of pig remains found in the Middle Neolithic dwelling sites. And secondly, it also runs counter to the seasonality of the killing of the boars, as observed by Rowley-Conwy & Storå (1997). Thus as things stand at present, the main question is no longer what the economic role filled by the swine of Middle Neolithic Gotland might have been, but why the remains of *Sus* are often as abundant as those of the seals, sometimes representing the preponderant species among the mammalian remains? What was the importance of these pigs for humans if they did not figure among the components of the human diet?

Let's for a moment suppose that the highly specialized economy of Middle Neolithic Gotland made an ultra-efficient use of the marine resources upon which it was based. This is to say that a minimal part of the carcasses of fishes and/or marine mammals, or possibly none at all, was left at disposal for consumption by the pigs. This would also mean that the production of waste remains was reduced to a minimum. We could assume that the Pitted Ware people of Gotland used every part of their marine prey, even eating the bone marrow and savouring the intestinal tissues of the digestive apparatus. In such conditions, very little would have remained at the disposal of the pigs, except for fish bones and sea shells which are inedible for the swine. Thus, since as already observed by Lindquist & Possnert (1997) the Pitted Ware pigs could have been raised on a free-range basis, did they supplement their diet by including human faeces? This is a way of simplifying management problems still adopted by several modern human cultures in various parts of the world. For example, according to Epstein (1971), nearly all the ethnic groups of pre-Nilotes, including the Berta, Gule, Gumuz, Ingessana, Koma, Mao, Masongo, and Meban, who are confined to the hill country between the White Nile and edge of the Ethiopian plateau, but excluding the pre-Nilotic Anuak, Shilluk, Barea, and Kunama, are reported to keep pigs. The pigs of these peoples are completely neglected and emaciated, having to find their own sustenance which consists of waste, human excrement, and any roots they may dig up. The Nepalese dwarf pigs too, a native breed, are rarely fed by their owners but have to eke out a miserable existence as roaming scavengers, competing with the pariah dogs for the refuse and excrement of the poor in the streets and outskirts of towns and villages (Epstein 1977). In Thailand too, Falvey (1981) reported that free-ranging pigs supplement their diet with many additional items, including human faeces. Nevertheless, the nutritional metabolism of the diet of an omnivorous animal, based on waste with a high content of animal proteins, demands a trophic balancing integrated through the continual utilization of vegetable resources, chiefly obtained through browsing on the typical plants of the polyphyte natural meadows (legumes and grasses), and also potentially supplemented by the consumption of marine plants and algae. Nor could it be based on a prevalent assumption of acorns, as supposed by Lindquist & Possnert (1997), because of the seasonal restriction on availability. Could Middle Neolithic Gotland pigs have based their diet mainly on human faeces, integrating this with the assumption of the high-fibre vegetable matter available in the insular environment and occasional scavenging and predation on either terrestrial or marine zoological organisms? This could not only explain the role they played in the Pitted Ware culture, but also justify the abundant quantity of boar osteological remains in the Middle Neolithic dwelling sites of Gotland. I should like to close this discussion by hazarding a final hypothesis regarding the δ^{13}C values in the swine bones of Gotland: could the metabolization of the human faeces on the part of the animals have failed to leave traces of the marine nourishment on which the human diet was based? Is it possible that the stable isotope values regarding this marine

nourishment were established at insignificant levels in the trophic metabolization which leads to the production of the faeces of the swine? And again,
can the non-marine δ^{13}C values of the pigs be in some manner set in relation
to the seasonality of predation of these same ungulates on the part of the
Middle Neolithic people of Gotland? It is to be hoped that future research will
provide a key contribution to the solution of these problems. In the meantime
the examples above have shown that pig populations played an important
part in the economy and society of ancient hunters, though the details of this
relation are still partly unknown.

9

An investigation into the transition from forest dwelling pigs to farm animals in medieval Flanders, Belgium

Anton Ervynck, An Lentacker, Gundula Müldner,
Mike Richards & Keith Dobney

INTRODUCTION

There is ample evidence to show that in medieval Europe, unlike today, pigs (*Sus scrofa* f. domestica) were herded in woodland (see for example ten Cate 1972; Laurans 1975; Mane 1997) (Fig. 9.1). For England, this statement has been contested (Rackham 1976, 1980, 1986), but a recent re-evaluation of the historical data indicates that pig husbandry traditions there were the same as in continental Europe (Wilson 2003). Nowadays, pigs have almost everywhere become farm animals, at best living outdoors in semi-confinement near farmhouses, or, at worst, being reared in intensive indoor units with very limited freedom of movement. At some point in time the animals thus made the transition from forest dwellers to farmyard inhabitants, a process that is hardly documented by historical data, or at least little investigated by historians. The aim of this chapter is to investigate whether the analysis of animal remains from archaeological sites can recognize this transition by identifying changes in the characteristics of diachronic pig populations, indicative of differing animal husbandry regimes.

Flanders (in present-day Belgium) was one of the most densely populated regions in medieval Europe, and as such, represents an appropriate case study area where the transition from forest to farmyard pigs can be explored. Historical data from Flanders confirm that deforestation was already very advanced towards the end of the High Medieval period (10th–12th centuries AD), so much so that reforestation campaigns were implemented (be it not always successfully) during Late Medieval times (13th–15th centuries AD)

Fig. 9.1. Pigs herded in the forest. Detail from the page for November in *Les Très Riches Heures du Duc de Berry* (the Book of Hours of the Duke of Berry), France, early 15th century (copyright Faksimile-Verlag, Luzern, 1984)

(Verhulst 1990; Tack *et al.* 1993; Tack & Hermy 1998). Deforestation, together with overhunting, resulted in the local extinction of wild woodland mammal species such as brown bear (*Ursus arctos*) in the 12th century, and wild boar (*Sus scrofa*) and red deer (*Cervus elaphus*) towards the end of the Middle Ages (Ervynck *et al.* 1999). In fact, in Flanders, virtually no parcel of land has been continuously under forest since medieval times, a phenomenon illustrated, for example, by the poverty of the carabid beetle fauna (an insect group with poor (re-)colonizing capacities) in present-day woodlands (Desender *et al.* 1999). Given the destruction of many natural habitats by human activity in medieval times, it was perhaps inevitable that Flemish pig herders had to seek an alternative to forest herding towards the end of the medieval period, or possibly even earlier. Since the Flemish medieval zooarchaeological record is an extensive one, a diachronic comparison of pig remains from medieval Flemish sites may reveal patterns that could be ascribed to this transition.

CHANGES IN PIG HUSBANDRY

The shift in living environment (from forest to farm) was an important step in the evolutionary history of the European domestic pig. Whereas, in the Near East, pigs must have been kept close to (and even on) settlements already in prehistory (Zeder 1991: 30–2, see also Grigson this volume), in north-western Europe they must have been primarily herded in forested environments from around 5000 BC (Benecke 1994). Thus, for the European pig, the Late Medieval shift towards breeding in confinement meant the final retreat from its natural environment. Without doubt, this must also have had consequences for animal welfare.

This significant change in the husbandry of the domestic pig is not only merely part of the evolutionary history of the species, but is also symptomatic of a change in the structure of medieval society. Pig herding in the forest was a characteristic part of the food economy of Europe's feudal period, more precisely of the food procurement strategy of a specific element of medieval feudal society, i.e. the nobility. During feudal times, society was subdivided into three orders: the clergy, the nobility, and the people. This system was accepted to be a divine construction and, as such, was unassailable. Since the use and ownership of the forest (as uncultivated land) was a noble privilege, pig-herding in woodland was a typical activity of the noble economy, one which linked the consumption of pork with power and prestige. In addition, in imitating the gastronomic ideals of the former Roman aristocrats (and attempting to acquire their grandeur), the meat of pigs was highly esteemed within a broader culinary context. Pork, being the product of animals bred only for meat production, became a symbol for plenty, a foodstuff ideal as the main component of gargantuan banquets, following the Germanic tradition of conspicuous dining on meat. Finally, wild boar also still represented one of the most dangerous hunted game, and hunting was closely associated with acts of male bravado and warlike prowess (Ervynck 2004). Thus, since domestic pig still resembled its wild conspecific (and both still inhabited the wild woodlands), a broader symbolic association existed in medieval society between wild boar and domestic pig.

Nowadays, these symbolic links have all but vanished. In north-western Europe, pork has generally become a meat product characterized by a poor culinary appreciation and low cost, with its canned form known as Spam (spicy ham) perhaps representing a gastronomic low point. This evolution is without doubt not only associated with the decline of the feudal nobility itself, but specifically with the fact that the rearing of pigs in confinement markedly lowered the quality of the meat. The animals ate organic refuse instead of foraging on woodland products, and the fact that they experienced less physical exercise resulted in lower blood circulation and less developed muscles, resulting in meat with a pale pink colour instead of being a deep purple. All this of course affected the texture and taste of the meat. As the result of a similar process, people in Belgium are now complaining about the quality of the wild boar meat served in restaurants, stating that it looks and tastes more and more like pork! The reason for this reputed loss in quality must, without doubt, reside in the practice of providing the wild boar, which live in enclosed forest parcels in the Ardennes, with supplementary food in fixed feeding stations. Consequently, the animals do not roam the forests any more. Instead, they wait patiently near the feeders the whole day, and no longer develop the muscular 'gamey' meat so characteristic of hunted animals.

SITES AND MATERIAL STUDIED

In order to explore whether the zooarchaeological record contains clear evidence of a major shift in pig husbandry during later medieval times, four archaeological sites have been selected from western and central present-day Flanders (Fig. 9.2). The sites were selected on the basis of the availability of large numbers of pig bones, and on their chronological and socio-cultural context. Two of the sites, Veurne and Ename, represent early castles dating back to High Medieval times; the other two, the castle of Londerzeel and the fishermen's village of Raversijde, date from the Late Medieval period. It was assumed that the former group would provide information about traditional pig-herding in Flemish forests, whereas the latter would bear evidence about the shift towards later pig-keeping in confinement. It should be noted that, in this context, the term 'Flanders' is used in its present-day geographical and political meaning (comprising the Dutch-speaking, northern part of Belgium). However, at the time of their occupation, the territory of two of the four sites selected did not come within the Flemish feudal borders (see further below).

The castle of Veurne developed from a circular fortification erected during the 10th–11th century as part of a line of defence works along the Flemish coast, and was certainly in the possession of the count of Flanders from the 11th century on (De Meulemeester 1979, 1980, 1981, 1982, 1990). The animal remains from the site, excavated by the Belgian National Service for

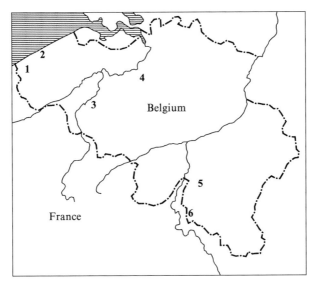

Fig. 9.2. Location of the sites in Belgium from which pig remains have been studied (1, Veurne; 2, Raversijde; 3, Ename; 4, Londerzeel; 5, Wellin; 6, Sugny)

Archaeology, have previously been studied by Maenhaut van Lemberge (1985) and Van Doorslaer (1985) and it has been shown that, during the 10th–11th century occupation, the bones from sheep and goats were the most frequent domestic meat-providing mammals (Fig. 9.3). Without doubt, this pattern can be explained by the location of the site on the border of the coastal area, at that time a dynamic landscape consisting of salty meadows, saltmarshes, mudflats, tidal gullies, and creeks (see Verhulst 1995). However, in comparison to two rural sites in the coastal area, pig remains ($n = 1837$) are more frequent at the castle than in the countryside. This can be explained by the privileged use of forested lands, most probably located towards the south of the site, on the hills of the Flemish Heuvelland (Ervynck & De Meulemeester 1996).

The castle of Ename, located in the valley of the river Schelde, was erected during the 10th century AD as the centre of a margraviate defending the western border of the Ottonian empire. During the 11th century, the fortification was already demolished when the count of Flanders invaded the area and incorporated Ename's territory into its possessions (Callebaut 1991). The site has previously been studied by the Belgian National Service for Archaeology and continued, first, by the Institute for the Archaeological Heritage of the Flemish Community, and now by the Flemish Heritage Institute. The excavated animal remains, dating from around 1000 AD (Callebaut *et al.*

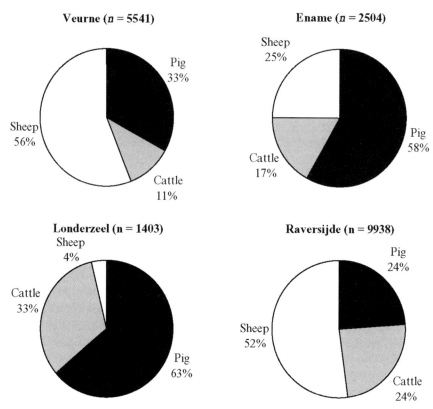

Fig. 9.3. Frequencies (based on NISP) of the main meat-providing domesticates at each site

2002)—and now in the process of re-analysis—demonstrate that pig-herding was extremely important for the meat supply of the castle (Van der Plaetsen 1991, $n = 1452$ for the pig remains) (Fig. 9.3). Historical sources confirm that forests were located within its territory, i.e. on the slopes of the hills commonly known in the area as the Flemish Ardennes (Tack *et al.* 1993).

During the Late Medieval period, the castle of Londerzeel belonged to the family of Vianden (present-day Luxemburg), who were for this part of their territory dependants of the duchy of Brabant. Excavations at the site, by the Institute for the Archaeological Heritage of the Flemish Community, recovered an archaeozoological assemblage dating from the 13th–14th centuries AD and characterized by a dominance of pig remains (Ervynck *et al.* 1994, $n = 892$) (Fig. 9.3). The ecological history of the area (Verhulst 1990) indicates that, during Late Medieval times, real forest was most probably no longer to be found in the vicinity of the castle.

The deserted fishermen's village of Raversijde was located west of Oostende, along the Flemish coast. Rescue excavations undertaken from 1992 to 1999 by the Institute for the Archaeological Heritage of the Flemish Community have mainly uncovered structural remains and refuse deposits dating from the 15th century AD, the final flourishing period of the settlement before it was deserted during the 16th century (Pieters 1997; Kightly *et al.* 2000). Preliminary archaeozoological analysis shows that pig was not especially common at the site (Fig. 9.3) ($n = 2380$, Bollen 1998; Ervynck & Lentacker unpubl. data), a pattern that can be linked to the local environment, i.e. coastal dunes and wet grasslands on clayey soil, with no forest cover. However, the fact that pig remains, including those from newborn or very young animals, were found at the site (and in meaningful numbers) indicates that some pig-breeding took place outside the forest confines during this period. It is probable that the pigs at Raversijde were kept in (semi-)confinement and were fed refuse from human consumption or even the leftovers collected after cleaning fishing nets or sorting the catch. In Flanders, this practice was still common in traditional fishermen's households until the middle of the 20th century (Lanszweert *pers. comm*).

For the purposes of comparison, data from two further sites will be included in the analysis. Both represent medieval noble sites located in the southern part of Belgium, i.e. in the forests of the Ardennes. The Early Medieval site of Wellin represents the centre of a large Carolingian domain (Evrard 1993, 1997). During excavation, a large context containing consumption refuse, dating from the 8th century AD, was found, with a clear dominance of pig remains among the large mammal bones (Wattiez 1984). General historical knowledge of the land use, occupation patterns, and evolution of the Belgian forests (Verhulst 1990), together with the actual ecological characteristics of the area, strongly indicates that primary woodland was amply present in the area, during Carolingian times. The castle of Sugny (Belgium) was erected towards the end of the 10th century AD and remained occupied until the end of the 11th century (Matthys 1991). Sugny is located in an area that is still wooded today. The animal remains recovered from the site once again were dominated by the remains of pig (Ervynck 1992; Ervynck & Woollett 2006).

METHODS

In order to reveal differences between the pig husbandry regimes at the sites mentioned, four approaches have been taken. First, the age-at-death profiles of the pig populations have been established as an evaluation of possible closer human interference with the Late Medieval pig populations, compared to the High Medieval ones. Second, stable isotope analysis of bone collagen, a now well-established technique of dietary reconstruction (for reviews see Katzenberg 2000; Mays 2000; Sealy 2001), was employed to investigate possible differences in diet between the earlier, forest-dwelling (and therefore probably mostly herbivorous) pigs and the later animals, who are likely to have been fed greater amounts of animal protein in the form of household scraps and waste, when kept in semi-confinement. Third, osteometric data were collected in order to investigate size changes in the animals, which could reflect different feeding regimes, or options taken when selecting animals for breeding. Finally, the 'living conditions' of pigs were assessed through the observation of a pathological condition generally related to undernourishment, or physiological stress occuring during development.

Age at death has been evaluated by recording the tooth eruption and wear stages of all mandibular molars, following the method of Grant (1982). The distributions of the molar wear stages (being the sums of the tooth wear stages) are presented using the running means or moving averages (see Ervynck 2005 for justification of this method). The transformation of the data into real age classes, and the evaluation of the possibility of a seasonal slaughtering pattern, was carried out following the line of reasoning outlined in Ervynck (1997, 2005). In all cases, more than 80 mandibles could be used within the analyses.

Stable isotopes ($\delta^{13}C$ and $\delta^{15}N$) of bone collagen were measured in the Department of Archaeological Sciences, University of Bradford. In addition to 20 samples of pigs (5 individuals from each site), samples of 20 cattle and 7 dogs were also analysed, in order to establish local isotopic baseline data for herbivores and carnivores for each of the 4 sites. All bone samples were prepared following a modified Longin method based on Brown *et al.* (1988) and described in detail in Müldner & Richards (2005). In short, the bone was demineralized in 0.5 mol/L HCl at $5°C$, rinsed to neutrality and gelatinized in a pH3 HCl solution at $70°C$ for 48 hours. After several filtering steps the purified 'collagen' was freeze-dried. Isotopic measurements were performed in duplicates on a Finnigan Delta Plus XL isotope ratio mass-spectrometer. Analytical error ($\pm 1\ \sigma$) was 0.2% or better for both $\delta^{13}C$ and $\delta^{15}N$.

For osteometric analysis, standard measurements of all permanent lower molars have been taken. These include maximum buccal–lingual breadth measurements of the mesial and distal cusps of the M_1 and M_2, and of the mesial and the central cusp of the M_3, as well as the maximum crown length of the M_1, M_2, and M_3. All breadth measurements were taken at the widest (lingual to buccal) part of the tooth crown. The mesiodistal length of the M_3

was measured at its maximum, near the base of the crown. Postcranial elements were measured following von den Driesch (1976). Because of the limited number of postcranial bones in each assemblage, the postcranial data have been combined using the log ratio technique (following the guidelines by Meadow 1999). These measurements include GLP of the scapula, Bd of the humerus, Bp of the radius, BPC of the ulna, Bd of the femur, and Bd of the tibia (for codes see von den Driesch 1976).

The observation of palaeopathological conditions has been limited to a developmental defect affecting tooth crown development, i.e. linear enamel hypoplasia (LEH). Given the young slaughtering ages for pigs, only patholo-gies that developed during the early stages of life (and that were not imme-diately lethal) could shed light upon the animals' living conditions. Given the abundance of pig dental material from each of the four sites, and the inter-pretational value of its analysis, the observation of LEH seemed an ideal approach within this context. The condition was identified and recorded using protocols devised by Dobney and Ervynck (1998) and further refined by Dobney *et al.* (2002). The data are presented and interpreted following Ervynck and Dobney (1999), Dobney and Ervynck (2000) and Dobney *et al.* (2004). An introduction to the nature and analysis of LEH can also be found in Dobney *et al.* (this volume).

RESULTS AND DISCUSSION

Age-at-death profiles

The distribution of the molar wear stages is given per site in Fig 9.4. The patterns observed can best be interpreted by comparison with the distribu-tions obtained within a previous study of medieval sites (Ervynck 1997), of which the graph for Wellin (Fig. 9.5) is probably the best example. For the four previously published sites, the peaks in the distribution have been consistently interpreted as the result of a seasonal slaughtering pattern in which there was a single breeding season, with birth always taking place around the same period within the year. In the case of Wellin there appears to have been a rather high proportion of perinatal deaths (Grant molar wear stages around 1), slaughtering just before the first winter (around stage 10), just before the second winter (around stage 19), and just before the third winter (around stage 28). Animals that died at later ages are grouped within the right 'tail' of the fourth (third winter) peak (see Ervynck 1997, 2005, for a justification of this interpretation). The two oldest sites in this study, Veurne

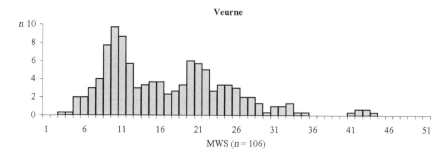

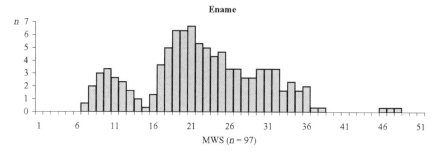

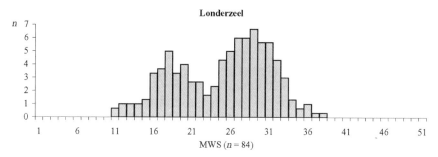

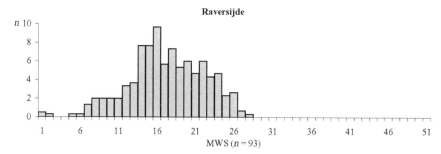

Fig. 9.4. Distribution of the pig mandibular molar wear stages (MWS *sensu* Grant 1982, using a three-class running mean) at each site

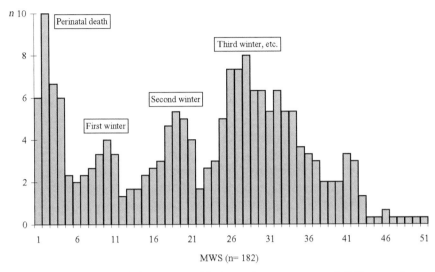

Fig. 9.5. Distribution of the pig mandibular molar wear stages (MWS *sensu* Grant 1982, using a three-class running mean) for the reference site of Wellin (data from Ervynck 1997)

and Ename, show peaks at the same locations along the distribution. At Veurne, there is a first winter peak around stage 10, a second winter peak around stage 20, but no third winter peak (indicating that all animals died rather young). At Ename, the first and second winter peaks occur around the same stages, but there is a third winter peak around stage 31 (corresponding with the one around stage 28 for Wellin). The distribution for Londerzeel (a site that was, in fact, already included in the original study of Ervynck 1997) shows a second winter peak around stage 18, a third winter peak around stage 29, but no first winter peak. Very young animals seem to have been absent from the slaughtered population.

At Raversijde, the animals were all slaughtered when relatively young but the distribution shows only one, broad peak. This peak does not coincide with the ones observed at the other sites and is located around stage 16. This would, following the earlier interpretations, indicate slaughtering occurring during summer. However, it is equally possible that we are dealing with animals with a broad reproductive season, or that produce more than one litter a year, and that are slaughtered when they reached a predetermined 'average' weight. In general, it remains clear that the slaughtering pattern at Raversijde differed fundamentally from that at the three other sites.

Stable isotope data (δ^{13}C and δ^{15}N)

The results of the isotopic measurements are presented in Table 9.1 and Fig. 9.6. 'Collagen' preservation was assessed by established quality indicators (DeNiro 1985; Ambrose 1990), and the bone was found to be generally well preserved. Two samples from Raversijde had to be excluded because they showed signs of diagenetic alteration. For interpretation of the results, the data set was subsequently augmented by 11 samples (5 pig and 6 cattle) from Ename and Raversijde which had been analysed earlier at the Royal Institute for Cultural Heritage (Brussels, Belgium) and have been published previously (Ervynck *et al.* 2003). The carbon and nitrogen data produced in Brussels and Bradford are in good agreement for the different sites and animal species. With some notable exceptions discussed below, the cattle from the four sites exhibit isotopic values that are typical for terrestrial herbivores in temperate C$_3$ ecosystems, whereas dogs are, as expected, enriched in δ^{15}N by several parts per thousand, indicating a diet high in animal protein (Schoeninger & DeNiro 1984; Kelly J.F. 2000). Interpreting the pig isotopic data in relation to the baseline values for herbivores and omnivores/carnivores for each site allows an interpretation of pig diet at the different locations.

Several of the cattle from Veurne display nitrogen values which are unusually high in comparison with other herbivore data from temperate Europe (van Klinken *et al.* 2000). Since it is unlikely (but not impossible) that they were fed significant amounts of animal protein, these values may best be explained by the consumption of plants with unusually enriched δ^{15}N ratios, e.g. as the result of manuring (Bol *et al.* 1998; Schwarcz *et al.* 1999). Possibly the data observed can also have been the result of different feeding practices within different husbandry strategies or regional differences in vegetation (see Heaton 1999; Bocherens 2000; van Klinken *et al.* 2000, and the references there). In any case, taking into account that the nitrogen isotopic baseline for herbivores at Veurne is relatively high, the five pigs can be divided into two groups. Three pigs plot in the same range as the cattle and seem therefore mostly herbivorous, but the two others, V-pig2 and V-pig3 (see Table 9.1), are much more enriched in ^{15}N and clearly had a significant amount of animal protein in their diet (Fig. 9.6).

Similar to the results from the site of Veurne, enriched δ^{15}N ratios for at least two of the cattle from Ename (E-cow3, E-cow4) suggest a comparatively high herbivore baseline for the site. The nitrogen values for the seven pigs all fall within the range of the cattle and suggest that like the cattle, they were predominantly fed a plant diet (Fig. 9.6). Minor differences in the δ^{13}C values

Table 9.1. Stable isotope measurements performed for this study at the University of Bradford. Additional data used (see text) are listed in Ervynck *et al.* (2003). Two samples excluded from the analysis (see text) are indicated by an asterisk.

Sample	Species	δ13C	δ15N	C:N	% Collagen
V-cow1	Cattle	−22.0	8.1	3.3	2.9
V-cow3	Cattle	−21.9	9.2	3.3	4.1
V-cow2	Cattle	−21.3	7.7	3.2	5.2
V-cow4	Cattle	−21.7	8.6	3.4	4.2
V-cow5	Cattle	−21.0	7.0	3.2	6.3
V-pig1	Pig	−21.2	8.6	3.4	5.8
V-pig2	Pig	−20.6	10.3	3.2	5.1
V-pig3	Pig	−21.2	12.0	3.2	3.5
V-pig4	Pig	−20.4	7.2	3.3	3.0
V-pig5	Pig	−20.7	6.8	3.4	4.5
E-cow1	Cattle	−22.2	6.4	3.3	2.1
E-cow2	Cattle	−22.6	7.6	3.3	2.1
E-cow3	Cattle	−22.3	9.6	3.2	1.6
E-cow4	Cattle	−22.1	8.6	3.2	1.6
E-cow5	Cattle	−22.5	5.7	3.3	2.9
E-dog1	Dog	−20.0	9.4	3.3	5.8
E-pig1	Pig	−20.7	5.7	3.4	2.0
E-pig2	Pig	−21.8	7.7	3.4	2.7
E-pig3	Pig	−21.1	6.9	3.2	5.2
E-pig4	Pig	−22.3	8.8	3.3	2.7
E-pig5	Pig	−22.1	8.6	3.2	4.8
L-cow1	Cattle	−22.7	6.3	3.5	0.6
L-cow2	Cattle	−22.1	6.2	3.3	4.4
L-cow3	Cattle	−22.3	6.3	3.3	3.5
L-cow4	Cattle	−22.4	7.2	3.3	3.2
L-cow5	Cattle	−22.0	5.9	3.3	4.3
L-dog1	Dog	−21.1	11.1	3.4	2.5
L-dog2	Dog	−20.4	10.7	3.3	2.8
L-pig1	Pig	−22.0	5.9	3.3	1.6
L-pig2	Pig	−21.4	6.2	3.3	1.9
L-pig3	Pig	−21.8	8.3	3.8	0.3
L-pig4	Pig	−21.2	8.7	3.3	1.5
L-pig5	Pig	−22.2	9.1	3.5	0.6
R-cow1*	Cattle	−21.5	6.2	3.7	0.3
R-cow2	Cattle	−21.8	6.2	3.2	2.7
R-cow3	Cattle	−22.0	7.0	3.2	4.5
R-cow4	Cattle	−21.9	7.5	3.2	2.2
R-cow5	Cattle	−22.6	6.0	3.6	0.9
R-dog1	Dog	−15.7	13.6	3.2	6.1
R-dog2	Dog	−18.3	12.5	3.2	5.5
R-dog3	Dog	−21.9	8.1	3.4	7.2
R-pig1	Pig	−20.1	9.4	3.4	1.8
R-pig2	Pig	−20.5	7.3	3.2	5.6
R-pig3	Pig	−20.8	9.2	3.2	6.3
R-pig4	Pig	−19.5	9.7	3.3	3.3
R-pig5*	Pig	−21.8	7.0	3.7	0.3

Abbreviations: E, Ename; L, Londerzeel; R, Raversijde; V, Veurne.

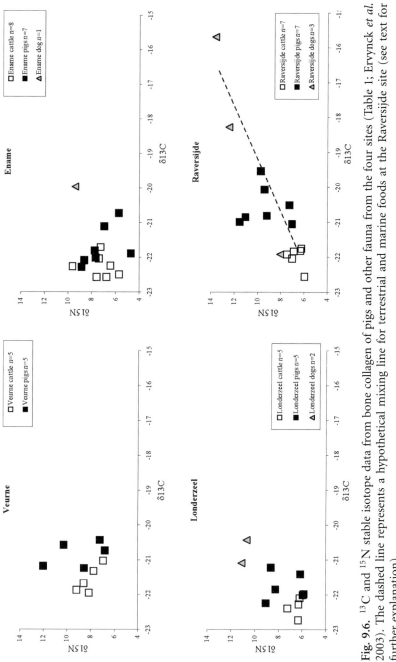

Fig. 9.6. ^{13}C and ^{15}N stable isotope data from bone collagen of pigs and other fauna from the four sites (Table 1; Ervynck *et al.* 2003). The dashed line represents a hypothetical mixing line for terrestrial and marine foods at the Raversijde site (see text for further explanation)

between the cattle and some of the pigs may relate to differences in the type of feed, or else different feeding locations (Tieszen 1991; Heaton 1999).

At Londerzeel, the cattle have δ^{15}N values much more similar to those found at other sites in temperate Holocene Europe. The pigs from this site can again be divided into two different groups: two of them (L-pig1 and L-pig2) plot with the herbivores, but the nitrogen values for the remaining three fall in between those of cattle and dogs and indicate that their diet was a combination of plant and animal protein (Fig. 9.6).

The cattle from Raversijde, like Londerzeel, have δ^{15}N values typical for temperate European cattle. The pigs from Raversijde appear to fall into three distinct groups: two of them (R-pig2, UtC9016, see Ervynck *et al.* 2003) are characterized as herbivorous by their relatively low δ^{15}N ratios. Three others (R-pig1, R-pig3, Rav-pig4) display enriched nitrogen values, but also plot along a hypothetical mixing line between the terrestrially feeding cattle and R-dog3 and the two remaining dogs which had an obvious marine component in their diet (Fig. 9.6). Although the pig δ^{13}C ratios are still well within the terrestrial range and it would normally be difficult to propose the input of marine protein from this data, the available animal reference values strongly suggest the consumption of some sea fish in a predominantly terrestrial 'mixed' diet of plant and animal protein (Richards & Hedges 1999). Marine food was almost certainly also part of the diet of the remaining two pigs (UtC9053 & UtC9057, see Ervynck *et al.* 2003). Their δ^{15}N ratios are much more enriched than those of the second group, however, and suggest that most of their diet was based on terrestrial animal protein rather than plant foods.

In summary, the stable isotope data reveal considerable variation in the diet of individual pigs at the four sites, although this may be exaggerated by the effects of sample-size and the isotopic variability of the local plants (as illustrated by the cattle values). The differences between the 'average diets' of cattle and pigs (Fig. 9.7) are most apparent at Raversijde, and can no doubt be attributed to the consumption of marine protein by the pigs, a resource that would hardly have been available to the animals at the inland sites. Overall, the isotopic results nevertheless suggest that the transition from herbivorous to omnivorous pigs was not perfectly clear-cut at a given point in time.

Osteometry

The measurements taken on the lower first molar (M_1) overlap between all four sites studied, with the data set from Raversijde possibly showing the highest values (Fig. 9.8). The data for the M_2 illustrate this pattern much more clearly, the scatter of the Raversijde pigs now being well separated from

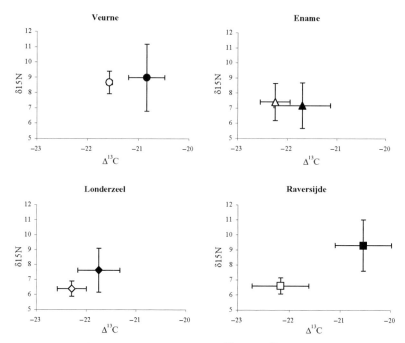

Fig. 9.7. Mean and standard deviation of the ^{13}C and ^{15}N stable isotope data from bone collagen of pig and cattle per site (solid symbols, pigs; open symbols, cattle) (for sample sizes see Fig. 9.6)

that of the other three sites, which show almost identical values (Fig. 9.8). In the case of the M_3, not enough measurements were available to perform the same analysis but a scatter plot (Fig. 9.8) again corroborates that the dental measurements from Veurne, Ename, and Londerzeel strongly overlap. Unfortunately, no data were available for M_3 from Raversijde because of the young age-at-death profile from that site. It should also be noted that a few rather large animals seem to be present within the Veurne and Ename material; these are possibly large males, (unrecognized) wild boar, or hybrids between wild boar and domestic pigs. Given their limited number, it is not likely, however, that the presence of these animals has seriously biased the analysis of the measurements taken on the M_1 and the M_2. The overall conclusion from the analysis of the dental measurements thus remains that the Raversijde animals are larger (in terms of their dentition) than the pigs from the three other sites.

The postcranial osteometry corroborates this conclusion. In a first approach, a log ratio analysis of six postcranial breadth measurements was made (Fig. 9.9a), using as a standard the 'average domestic pig' from the

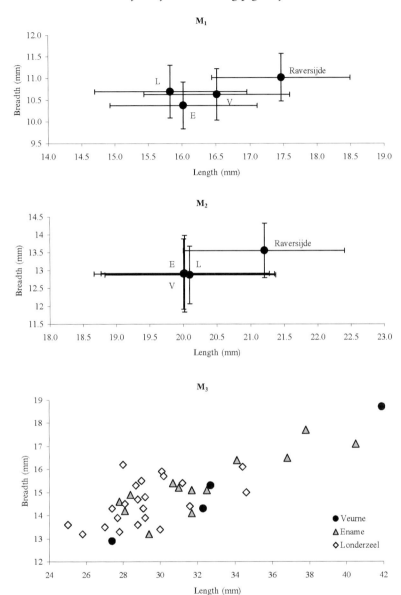

Fig. 9.8. Tooth dimensions of the three mandibular molars per site (M_1: $n = 94$ for Veurne (V), $n = 71$ for Ename (E), $n = 60$ for Londerzeel (L), $n = 66$ for Raversijde; M_2: $n = 43$ for Veurne (V), $n = 66$ for Ename (E), $n = 60$ for Londerzeel (L), $n = 51$ for Raversijde)

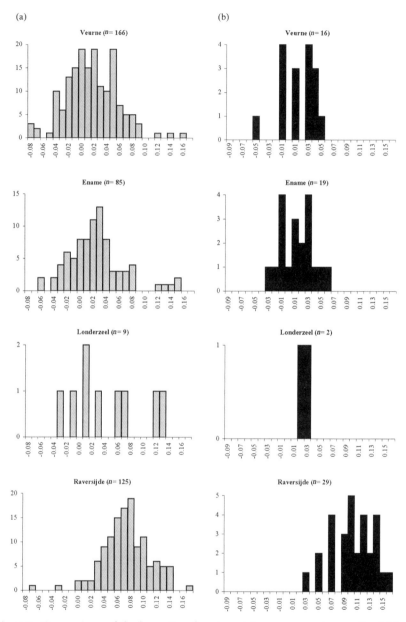

Fig. 9.9. Comparison of the log ratio of postcranial measurements per site: (a) log ratio of six postcranial breadths (see text); (b) log ratio of the astragalus

Table 9.2. Standard values used for the log ratio calculations combining six postcranial breadths (9th century pigs from Haithabu, data from Becker 1980: table 30).

Skeletal element	Measurement	Mean (mm)	Standard deviation	n
Scapula	GLP	33.8	2.0	855
Humerus	Bd	36.2	2.0	2341
Radius	Bp	27.8	1.9	127
Ulna	BPC	19.5	1.4	100
Femur	Bd	41.6	2.3	255
Tibia	Bd	27.0	1.5	1647

9th century trading settlement of Haithabu (Germany). The pig remains from this site were selected as a standard because of the (approximate) contemporaneity with the oldest sites from the Flemish data set, the geographical proximity of the study area, and the large number of measurements available from this site. The standard values used are listed in Table 9.2 (data from Becker 1980: table 30). The analysis shows that the sites of Veurne, Ename, and Londerzeel (although represented by a very small number of data) yielded pig remains that are roughly comparable to the Haithabu standard, but that the Raversijde animals have a more robust conformation. It should be noted that this conclusion is based on the evaluation of the average log ratios for each site but that, in each site, a few large animals were also present (Fig. 9.9a). Indeed, the possibility of the presence of wild boar remains (or their genetic input) has already been mentioned, but, again, this should not overtly bias the overall conclusion of the Raversijde pigs being more robust. Given the context of the site, and its surrounding landscape, it is certainly not possible that the high log ratio values for Raversijde can be explained by a dominance of wild boar bones among the *Sus* remains.

The previous log ratio analysis incorporated breadth measurements describing the relative robustness of the animals and but did not amalgamate different dimensions (for discussion, see Meadow 1999). Given the severe fragmentation of medieval pig material, length measurements were only available for the astragalus. Again, these data were compared with the average value of the Haithabu population (GLI: mean = 38.2, standard deviation = 2.1, $n = 1343$, data from Becker 1980: table 30), using the log ratio technique (Fig. 9.9b). The Raversijde sample again shows the highest values, suggesting that the animals from this site were not only more robust, but also taller, than the animals from the three other sites.

Palaeopathology: linear enamel hypoplasia

Information on the occurrence and frequency of linear enamel hypoplasia (LEH) for the sites of Ename, Londerzeel, Raversijde, Wellin, and Sugny has been gathered during previous research (Ervynck & Dobney 1999; Dobney *et al.* 2002). For the purpose of this analysis, LEH has also been recorded for the material from Veurne. In Fig. 9.10, the LEH frequency index is presented for all medieval sites, and compared with the index of Mesolithic and recent wild boar (data from Dobney *et al.* 2004) (see also Table 9.3). It seems logical that the values for the wild populations are lower than those for the domestic pigs, because, most probably, many of the options adopted within pig husbandry regimes (such as increasing the population density beyond the forest's carrying capacity, foraging in less productive environments, etc.) resulted in less favourable living conditions for the domestic herds, a pattern translated in higher levels of physiological stress and thus of LEH.

The differences in index values between the medieval sites are more difficult to explain, but the interpretation can begin from the assumption that the data for Wellin and Sugny represent populations living in essentially primary forest environments (since deforestation had not yet proceeded dramatically in the Ardennes during the High Middle Ages). If this is true, the index values suggest that the herds kept at the sites of Veurne and Londerzeel must have enjoyed comparably favourable living conditions, similar to those for wild boar. Alternatively, in the case of Londerzeel, it has been argued (Ervynck & Dobney 1999) that the pigs were most likely living in semi-confinement, and that, perhaps through an abundant food supply, they suffered less from physiological stress. However, given the dating of the site, such an explanation is less likely for Veurne. Regarding the index value for Ename, it has been argued (Ervynck & Dobney 1999) that the forest near that site probably

Table 9.3. Collections studied for the evaluation of linear enamel hypoplasia (see Figs 9.10, 9.11).

Collection	No. of M_1	No. of M_2	No. of M_3	Reference
Mesolithic wild boar	587	418	353	Dobney *et al.* (2004)
Wellin	115	121	137	Ervynck & Dobney (1999)
Sugny	61	62	37	Ervynck & Dobney (1999)
Veurne	53	33	12	This study
Ename	97	89	37	Ervynck & Dobney (1999)
Londerzeel	66	66	46	Ervynck & Dobney (1999)
Raversijde	75	69	4	Dobney *et al.* (2002)
Recent wild boar	249	240	173	Dobney *et al.* (2004)

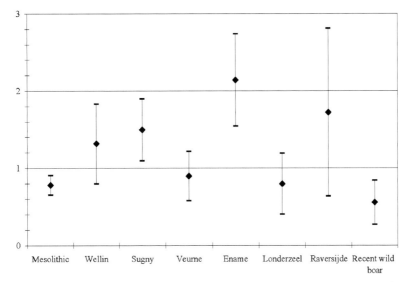

Fig. 9.10. Linear enamel hypoplasia index (*sensu* Ervynck & Dobney 1999) for all sites studied, compared with Mesolithic and recent north-west European wild boar (data from Dobney *et al.* 2004) (for sample sizes, see Table 9.2)

consisted mainly of young trees (the result of specific options within wood-land management), and thus did not provide good foraging opportunities for pigs (since young oak trees hardly produce any acorns). This interpretation is corroborated by historical data (Tack *et al.* 1993) and by the analysis of a 10th century pollen sample from the castle at Ename, showing a very low frequency of oak pollen (explained by the fact that young oak trees do not produce pollen).

The LEH index for Raversijde (Fig. 9.10) attains a high value but differs from the other data especially in its high standard deviation. In order to interpret this, it must be stressed that in the calculation of the index, per site, the relative frequencies of LEH on all teeth and cusps are taken into account by comparing them with the average frequency per tooth and cusp for all sites together (see Ervynck & Dobney 1999). This calculation, however, is only meaningful when the LEH frequency, per site, follows the same pattern along the tooth row. Figure 9.11 shows that this is indeed a valid assumption for all sites studied, except for Raversijde. That the teeth of the Raversijde pigs show a different pattern to the other sites (in particular an unusually high LEH frequency on the M_1), leads to the conclusion that there must have been a marked difference between the husbandry regime or living conditions of the Raversijde pigs compared with those of the other medieval pig populations.

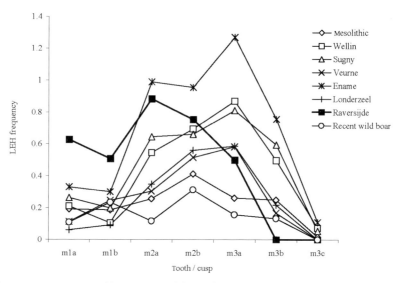

Fig. 9.11. Frequency of linear enamel hypoplasia (average number of lines observed per tooth and cusp) along the tooth row for each site (for sample sizes, see Table 9.2)

CONCLUSION

When the results presented are evaluated together, several conclusions can be drawn, although many possibilities remain open. Considering the question whether Late Medieval pigs were kept under a different husbandry regime compared to High Medieval animals, it seems clear that the Raversijde population varied in all aspects from the three other assemblages. The animals here are larger, show a different slaughtering profile and a different LEH pattern, and must have been fed on a diet that contained markedly more animal protein than was the case for herbivores from the same site. Most importantly, the average difference in diet between pigs and herbivores is more pronounced at Raversijde than at the other medieval sites. Since pigs were not rare at Raversijde, although the surrounding open landscape could not have provided ample feeding opportunities, it is more than likely that the pigs were living in semi-confinement. Structures related to such practices (such as styes) have not yet been found at the site but may have been located outside the excavation area (which covered part of the centre of the village) (Pieters, pers. comm.).

The interpretation of the status of the Late Medieval Londerzeel pigs is more problematic. The animals were not larger than High Medieval pigs, must have enjoyed a largely herbivorous diet and are characterized by a low LEH frequency. All this should point towards herding in well-forested environments. However, the historical context suggested that the area around the Late Medieval castle must have been heavily deforested. Even more puzzling is the fact that the frequency of pig remains is very high at the site and that the Londerzeel slaughtering profile differs from that of Veurne and Ename (and Wellin). Whether this combination of observations refers to pig-breeding in semi-confinement is impossible to prove, and perhaps other explanations must also be considered. For example, it cannot be ruled out that the noble family of Vianden imported pork from other parts of their territory (which included heavily forested areas in what is now southern Belgium and Luxemburg). In this context, it is interesting to note that the pig remains from the castle were completely dominated by cranial elements (Ervynck *et al.* 1994).

The two oldest collections, from Veurne and Ename, most probably represent the genuine forest-dwelling pigs of medieval times, and the two populations are indeed similar in most aspects. The only remarkable difference is the high LEH frequency at Ename, a pattern suggesting that pig-herding in the forests was then already threatened by other economic options in forest management, such as the preference for young trees in order to optimize wood production. Within this context, it is regrettable that no Late Medieval pig material is available from the Ename area.

Finally, through the approaches presented in this paper, only in the case of Raversijde could real differences between high and Late Medieval pigs be observed. This trend could possibly be related to the transition from forest dwelling pigs to farm animals. However, given the special geographic context of the site, it would be useful to extend future analysis by incorporating more Late Medieval pig remains from inland sites. This would certainly also help to interpret the patterns observed at Londerzeel. In a further step, material from medieval urban sites must also be taken into account.

Part C

Methodological Approaches

10

Age estimation of wild boar based on molariform mandibular tooth development and its application to seasonality at the Mesolithic site of Ringkloster, Denmark

Richard Carter & Ola Magnell

INTRODUCTION

Age estimation based on the dentition of animal remains is one of the most important methods used for analysis of the demography of past as well as contemporary animal populations by zooarchaeologists and wild game biologists (Wagenknecht 1967; Silver 1969; Morris 1972; Wilson *et al.* 1982). By constructing age profiles from faunal remains it is possible to study hunting of wild boar and pig husbandry in past societies (Higham 1967*a*; Rolett & Chiu 1994; Vigne *et al.* 2000*a*; Magnell 2005*a*). Age estimation can also be used for assessing seasonal occupation of settlements and slaughtering of pigs (Legge & Rowley-Conwy 1988; Rowley-Conwy 1993, 1998; Ervynck 1997). Several contributions to this volume provide good examples of how different aspects of the past relationship between humans and pigs can be understood from estimations of age.

Age estimations based on tooth development have several advantages over ageing methods based on tooth eruption and wear. Experiments with under-nourished pigs have shown that the tooth development is less affected by environmental factors than tooth eruption (McCance *et al.* 1961). A problem with age estimation of domestic animals based on tooth eruption is that the ages at eruption are known to vary between different breeds (Habermehl 1961; Silver 1969; Reiland 1978; Bull & Payne 1982). The rate of tooth wear is also variable between, and within, different populations as a result of several factors such as variation in tooth morphology, eruption, coarseness, and abrasives in the diet (Healy & Ludwig 1965; Grant 1978, 1982; Deniz & Payne 1982; Magnell 2005*b*). However, tooth development seems to vary less between different populations. In cattle, roe deer, and red deer no consistent differences between various breeds/populations or between males and females have been noted in tooth development (Brown *et al.* 1960: 27; Carter 2001*a*).

An advantage with age estimation based on tooth development is that the method considers several definable stages in the formation of all molariform teeth. Because the method is based on several characteristics in the dentition it is possible to give a very accurate assessment of dental maturity and the age of a specimen. In tooth eruption it can be a problem defining when a tooth has erupted and differentiating between gingival emergence, erupting through bones or coming into wear (Hillson 1986; O'Connor 2000). Age estimation based on tooth development can also be applied to loose teeth that are not fully formed and not too damaged. This makes the method suitable for application to assemblages of pigs, which often comprise large numbers of individual teeth.

Age estimation based on tooth development is a proven method for obtaining reliable ages from archaeological specimens. It has for a long time been a method for the ageing of human skeletal remains (Schour & Massler 1940; Liliequist & Lundberg 1971; Demirjian *et al.* 1973; Ubelaker 1989). Tooth development from radiographs has been studied in several species such as cattle, arctic fox, martens, fallow deer, red deer, beaver, and roe deer, but the method has rarely been applied to animal remains from archaeological sites (Brown *et al.* 1960; Kuehn & Berg 1981; Dix & Strickland 1986; Brown & Chapman 1991*a*, 1991*b*; Hartman 1992; Carter 1997).

Exceptions are studies of the seasonality of Mesolithic sites from northwest Europe based on mandibles of dentally immature red deer and roe deer by Carter (1997, 1998, 2001*a*, 2001*b*), and slaughtering of pigs from Polynesian prehistoric sites by Rolett and Chiu (1994). The latter study is based on tooth development data on the effects of undernutrition in the development of the skull, jaws and teeth in pigs (McCance *et al.* 1961). Since the aim of this important study by McCance *et al.* was not to develop a method of age estimation, it has limitations when applied to the ageing of pigs from archaeological sites. The sample size was relatively small and was based on modern breeds of pigs, which probably have faster dental development than primitive prehistoric breeds.

The need for precision in age estimations may vary depending on the aims of studies, but most often methods are used to assess the age of a specimen by creating age ranges as narrow and reliable as possible. This is especially important in studies aimed at identifying the seasonal killing of animals by humans. The development of mandibular molariform teeth in wild boar, from crypt formation to root completion, has been studied in order to increase the accuracy of age estimation in wild boar and primitive breeds of domestic pigs. Application of the method to animal remains from the Mesolithic site of Ringkloster, Denmark demonstrates how it can be used in the assessment of site seasonality. This method can also be used for constructing age profiles. Tooth development and its correlation with age are also of importance for the interpretation of linear enamel hypoplasia in archaeological samples of pigs (Dobney & Ervynck 2000).

MATERIALS

The study is based on radiographs of mandibles from 114 individuals of 1 to 48 months of age (Table 10.1). The sample consists of 56 mandibles from animals of known age; for the remainder only the kill dates are known. A total of 55 mandibles are from males, 47 from females, and 12 from wild boar of unknown sex. The age distribution of the sample is uneven, with most of the known age mandibles from animals aged 2, 6, 12, 18, and 24 months.

In order to get a sample large enough to cover all the tooth development stages, mandibles from different populations and collections have been studied. Most come from the Mammal Research Institute collection at Bialowieza, Poland. The known age mandibles are from wild boar ($n = 9$) and hybrids ($n = 26$). The latter came from enclosed areas near Bialowieza where breeding experiments between wild boar and domestic pig were conducted. Five mandibles of known age are from wild boar tagged as newborn piglets from Kampinos National Park outside Warsaw. Most of the mandibles of known kill date are from Bialowieza Primeval

Table 10.1. Origin and distribution of the sample in age groups. Bold indicates mandibles of known age.

	0–6 months	7–12 months	13–18 months	19–24 months	25–36 months	37–48 months	Totals
Enclosure - Poland	**1**	**3**	**2**	**2**	**1**		9
Hybrids - Poland	**7**	**9**	**5**	**2**	**2**	**1**	26
Tagged - Poland		**1**	**2**	**1**		**1**	5
Enclosure - Sweden		16					16
Wild - Poland	4	18	11	6	6	1	46
Wild - Sweden		4	4	2	2		12
Totals	12	51	24	13	11	3	114

Forest ($n = 30$), but also from other parts of Poland, such as Kampinos National Park ($n = 11$).

Mandibles of wild boar from north-east Scania, from the collections of the Department of Historical Osteology, Lund University, Sweden, are also included in the study. This part of the sample comprises mandibles of known age ($n = 16$) from farmed wild boar and mandibles of known kill date ($n = 12$) from hunted animals.

METHOD

Mandibular tooth development of the deciduous premolars (dP_2, dP_3, dP_4) and the molariform permanent teeth ($P_2, P_3, P_4, M_1, M_2, M_3$) was examined. All of the modern mandibles were radiographed with an X-ray machine used for intra-oral radiography. The right half-mandible was examined with the exception of a few specimens with damaged crypts where the left side was radiographed. Kodak Insight dental film (5×7 cm) was taped against the lingual side and the X-ray source was placed 20 cm from the buccal side of the mandible. Usually three overlapping radiographs were taken on each mandible in order to make it possible to study the complete molar row. The time for exposure varied between 0.16 and 0.62 s, depending on the age and quality of the mandible at standardized settings (Table 10.2). The archaeological specimens from Ringkloster were radiographed with different x-ray equipment and film. The settings used are also shown in Table 10.2.

It was more difficult to get high-quality radiographs of the mandibular dentition of wild boar older than 18 months than for other species, such as roe deer and red deer. This is probably because of the very compact and thick cortical bone in wild boar mandibles, especially surrounding the first and second molars.

Table 10.2. X-ray settings for modern and archaeological samples.

	Power (kV)	Amperage (mA)	Exposure time (secs.)	Film focus distance (cm)
Modern sample 0–12 months	63 kV	8	0,16–0,20	20
Modern sample 12–18 months	63 kV	8	0,32–0,40	20
Modern sample >18 months	63 kV	8	0,40–0,62	20
Archaeological sample–Ringkloster	60 kV	1.8	240	73

STAGES OF MOLARIFORM MANDIBULAR TOOTH
DEVELOPMENT IN WILD BOAR

Eight stages of development have been identified and defined for the molariform deciduous and permanent teeth of wild boar. The definitions of these stages differ slightly from that used for fallow, red, and roe deer by Brown and Chapman (1991*a*, 1991*b*) and Carter (1997, 2001*b*). This has been necessary because of the different morphology of pig teeth, but also in order to simplify and increase the objectivity in the identification of certain tooth developmental stages.

The rate of root formation varies slightly between roots on the same tooth. The most advanced stage is always scored. The mesial parts of the tooth develop slightly earlier than the distal parts. Additionally, the buccal roots of the molars are generally shorter than the lingual and therefore reach full root length earlier. In deciduous premolars it is important not to confuse the resorbing roots with those that are still developing. Deciduous premolars remain fully developed for only a very short period of time, as their roots resorb once the permanent tooth begins to develop below them.

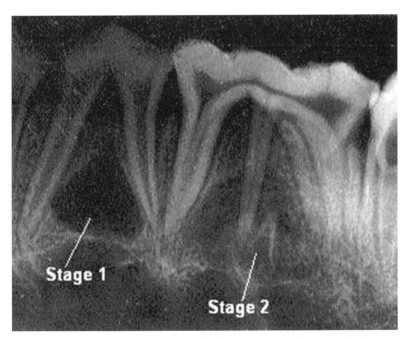

Fig. 10.1. Examples of stages 1 and 2 on developing P_3 and P_4 respectively

- *Stage 1:* A darkened area or crypt (on the radiograph) within which the tooth germ is beginning to develop and grow signifies stage 1. During early development the crypt gradually increases as mineral resorbing cells (osteoclasts) affect the surrounding bone. These darker areas are clearly visible against the surrounding bone on good-quality radiographs and in Fig. 10.1.

- *Stage 2:* At the bell stage of development, the first visible evidence of mineralization within the crypt marks stage 2 (see Fig. 10.1). The first evidence for this stage is usually a fine white line of mineralization outlining the mesial cusps of the premolars or molars.

- *Stage 3:* Mineralization continues until all the cusps are clearly outlined in stage 3. This can be clearly seen in Figs 10.2 and 10.3. The opacity of the cuspal outline is usually greater on the mesial cusps than those distally, reflecting higher levels of mineralization.

- *Stage 4:* Mineralization of the crown is complete at stage 4 when the start of root formation can be identified (Figs 10.4 and 10.5). This early evidence is indicated on the radiographs by a darkening at the mesial and/or distal ends of the tooth where the roots are beginning to form. Mineralization may be occurring at these points, but is too slight to be visible.

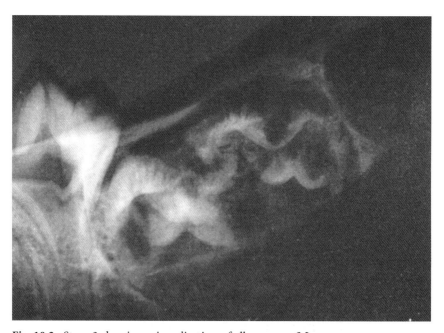

Fig. 10.2. Stage 3 showing mineralization of all cusps on M_1

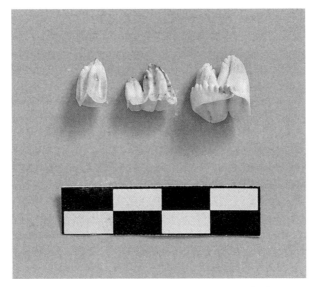

Fig. 10.3. Mineralization of the cusps (stage 3) of a loose M_3

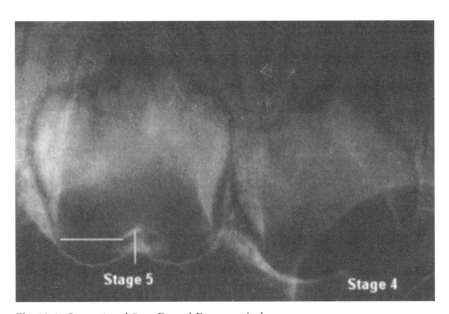

Fig. 10.4. Stages 4 and 5 on P_2 and P_3 respectively

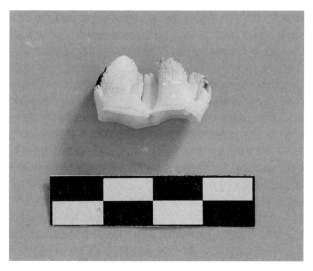

Fig. 10.5. Stage 4 on a loose M_2

- *Stage 5:* The process of tooth development continues with progressive stages of root formation. At stage 5, early root formation can be seen on radiographs as a fine white line of mineralization at the point where the mesial and distal roots meet at the crown base. The root is beyond the mere darkening described at Stage 4 (see Figs 10.4 and 10.8). The criterion for assessing this stage is that root length is equal or less than root width ($l \leq w$).

- *Stage 6:* The root continues to develop and grow reaching mid-root formation at stage 6 (see Figs 10.6 and 10.8). The criterion for assessing this stage is that root length is greater than minimum root width, but less than full length. A useful guide for determining when a molar root has achieved full length is that it approximately equals its own crown length measured at the occlusal surface. For premolars it is when root length is approximately one third longer than its own crown length.

- *Stage 7:* At this stage the root has attained full length, but the tip has not come to a point. At the root apex, where blood vessels and nerves pass through, an opening is clearly visible (see Fig. 10.7). This appears on radiographs as a flattened area. On loose teeth the walls surrounding the opening are very thin and easily broken. It is important to identify breakage (e.g. using a hand lens), as an earlier stage of development may be assigned.

- *Stage 8:* Finally full dental maturity occurs when the root apices appear to reach a point; the opening has become so small as to be invisible on the radiograph (see Figs 10.7 and 10.8). The mesial roots often reach stage 8 before the distal ones.

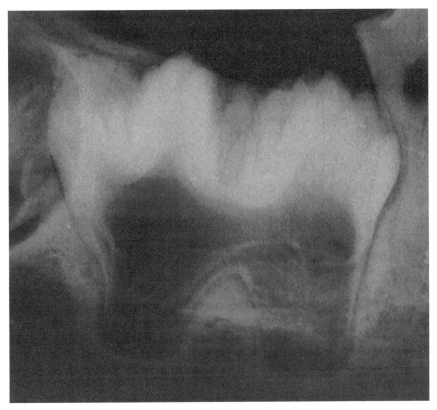

Fig. 10.6. M_2 at stage 6 showing that the root width is less than root length

CHRONOLOGY OF TOOTH DEVELOPMENT IN WILD BOAR

The development of the teeth starts *in utero*, and by birth the crown of the deciduous premolars and crypt of M_1 have formed (Tables 10.3 and 10.4). The earliest evidence of tooth formation, mineralization within the crypt (stage 2), for M_2, M_3, and P_2–P_4 is at 4, 7–12, and 5–12 months, respectively. Crown formation (stage 4) is complete for M_1 by 2 months, for M_2 at 7–8 months, and for M_3 at 12–18 months. For the premolars (P_2–P_4), crown formation is complete at 8–13 months. The ages at which the different tooth developmental stages form overlap on the premolars. However, development of P_2 is generally a few months delayed compared to the other premolars. Full root length and closure of the apex (stage 8) is observed on the roots of M_1 at 6 months of age, for M_2, and premolars by 18 months. The ages at root formation refer to the

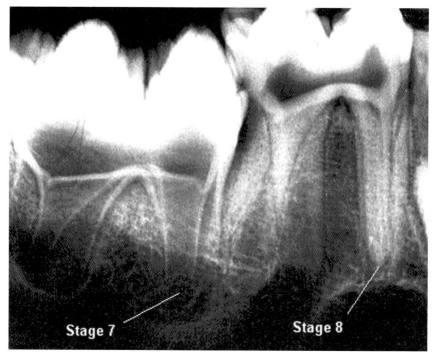

Fig. 10.7. M_1 and M_2 at stages 8 and 7 respectively

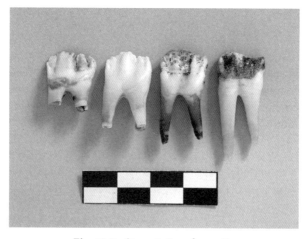

Fig. 10.8. Stage 5–8 on loose P_4

Table 10.3. Tooth development of molars in wild boar.

		1	2	3	4	5	6	7	8	
Mar	48									*2/2/2*
Feb	47									
Jan	46									
Dec	45									
Nov	44									
Oct	43									
Sep	42									
Aug	41									
Jul	40									
Jun	39									
May	38							*1*		*1/1*
Apr	37									
Mar	36							*4*		*4/4*
Feb	35									
Jan	34									
Dec	33									
Nov	32							*2*		*2/2*
Oct	31									
Sep	30							*1*		*1/1*
Aug	29									
Jul	28									
Jun	27									
May	26							*2*		*2/2*
Apr	25									
Mar	24						*6*	*3*		*9/9*
Feb	23									
Jan	22									
Dec	21						*4*			*4/4*
Nov	20									
Oct	19						*2*			*2/2*
Sep	18						*9*	*4*		*5/9*
Aug	17									
Jul	16					*3*		*2*		*1/3*
Jun	15									
May	14									
Apr	13				**6**		**3**	**3**		**6**
Mar	12		**8**	**12**	*2/1*	**15**	**5**	**1**		**22**
Feb	11									
Jan	10			**7**		**8**				**8**
Dec	9									
Nov	8			**12**		**12**				**12**
Oct	7	**7**		*1*		**8**		**3**		**5**
Sep	6	*1*		*4*				*2*		*2*
Aug	5	*1*		*2*				*2*		*2*
Jul	4			*2*		*2*				
Jun	3			*1*						
May	2				*3*					
Apr	1			*1*						
Mar	0	*1*								
		1	2	3	4	5	6	7	8	

Molar tooth development scores

Key: M₃ (1) M₂ (2) M₁ (3)

Age estimation of wild boar

Table 10.4. Tooth development of deciduous and permanent premolars in wild boar.

Month		(4)	(5)	(6)	(7)	(8)	1	2	3	4	5	6	7	8
Mar	48													2/2/2
Feb	47													
Jan	46													
Dec	45													
Nov	44													
Oct	43													
Sep	42													
Aug	41													
Jul	40													
Jun	39													
May	38													1/1/1
Apr	37													
Mar	36													4/4/4
Feb	35													
Jan	34													
Dec	33													
Nov	32													2/2/2
Oct	31													
Sep	30													1/1/1
Aug	29													
Jul	28													
Jun	27													
May	26													2/2/2
Apr	25													
Mar	24													9/9/9
Feb	23													
Jan	22													
Dec	21												4	4/4
Nov	20													
Oct	19											1	1/1	2/1
Sep	18											2	3/2	9/5/4
Aug	17													
Jul	16										1	1	2/3	1
Jun	15													
May	14													
Apr	13									1/5		6/5/1		
Mar	12						7	9/1		6/15		14/6	2	
Feb	11													
Jan	10						3	2		8/8/1				
Dec	9													
Nov	8							1		11/12	1			
Oct	7					(7/7/7)	1		8/7					
Sep	6					(3/3/3)	2/2		2/2					
Aug	5			(1)		(2/2)	1/2		1					
Jul	4			(2)		(2/2)								
Jun	3			(1/1)										
May	2	(2)		(1)	(2)	(3/1)								
Apr	1			(1/1)										
Mar	0	(1)	(1)											
Key:		P_4	P_3	P_2										

most developed root, which means that the completion of all roots occurs slightly later. Tooth development in wild boar is completed between 38 and 48 months, when the roots of M_3 are at full length and root apices have closed.

It has been observed that there are small variations in the ages of wild boar at different stages of tooth development; this can be explained by two factors. First, there is natural biological variation between individuals. Because of the overall small sample size for all tooth developmental stages it has been decided to use observed age ranges rather than calculating confidence intervals. Second, tooth development is a gradual, continuous process starting with the formation of the crypt and ending with the closing of the root apex. In order to create a practical ageing scheme we have divided the tooth development process into the eight easily defined stages described above. Within each stage there are likely to be specimens that are slightly less or more dentally developed than others resulting in age variations.

The slope of the linear regression of tooth development versus age was used as measurement to identify any sexual dimorphism or population differences in tooth development. No difference in the rate of tooth development between males and females is evident (Fig. 10.9).

The tooth development of the deciduous premolars and the first molar is similar in wild boar and in normal and undernourished modern breeds of

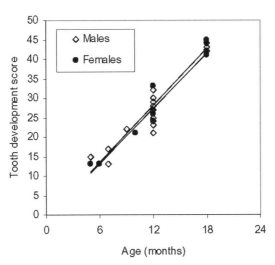

Fig. 10.9. Regression line and scatter plot of tooth development versus age for male and female wild boar

Table 10.5. Tooth development in wild boar compared with normal and undernourished domestic pig (McCance *et al.* 1961). Ages in months.

	Tooth formation begins (stage 2)			Crown formation complete (stage 4)			Root formation complete (stage 8)		
	Wild boar	Normal	Under-nourished	Wild boar	Normal	Under-nourished	Wild boar	Normal	Under-nourished
dP2	*in utero*	*in utero*	*in utero*	*in utero*	*in utero*	*in utero*	6	4–5	6–7
dP3	*in utero*	*in utero*	*in utero*	*in utero*	*in utero*	*in utero*	2–4	3	3
dP4	*in utero?*	*in utero*	*in utero*	*in utero*	*in utero*	*in utero*	2–4	3	3
M1	*in utero?*	*in utero*	*in utero*	2–4	2–3	2–3	6–7	7–8	13–14
M2	2–4	1–2	3	7–12	6–7	10–11	16–18	12–13	>15
M3	7–12	3–4	10–11	12–16	12–13	>15	38–48	>13	>15
P2	8–12	3–4	3	10–13	9–10	>15	18–21	12–13	>15
P3	6–7	1–2	3	8–12	7–8	13–14	18–19	12–13	>15
P4	5–7	1–2	3	10–13	7–8	13–14	16–18	12–13	>15

domestic pigs. In the premolars and second and third molars the tooth formation is delayed in wild boar by up to 6 months in comparison with normal domestic pigs (Table 10.5). This is in accordance with tooth eruption ages. Differences in eruption ages of the first molar are small between wild boar and domestic pig, but eruption of other molariform teeth and especially M₃ is generally later in wild boar (Bull & Payne 1982).

The greatest delay in tooth development occurs in undernourished domestic pigs. This comparison shows that tooth development of the deciduous premolars and first molar in wild boar can be used with confidence to age prehistoric primitive breeds of domestic pig. For the permanent premolars, and second and third molars, greater caution should be exercised.

NEW SEASONAL EVIDENCE AT RINGKLOSTER

The Late Mesolithic inland site of Ringkloster lies *c.*14 km from the coast in east central Jutland, Denmark and was located on an arm of a lake, Skanderborg Sø, which is now a peat bog. The site rested on firm ground and the adjacent lake was used as a midden for the settlement's refuse. It has been dated to the Middle and Late Ertebølle culture (4700–3990 BC). The site was excavated between 1969 and 1985, and the settlement has been described and interpreted by Andersen (1975, 1998). Møhl first reported on the animal bones (Andersen 1975), and subsequently a preliminary report was published by Rowley-Conwy (1998).

Site seasonality

The quantity and preservation of faunal remains from Ringkloster provides possibly some of the best seasonal evidence from any Mesolithic site in Europe (Rowley-Conwy 1998). This potential combined with its location, its large size (200 × 75 m), and the fact that it is one of the few excavated inland Ertebølle sites means that the Ringkloster assemblage is crucial for the understanding of this prehistoric culture.

An abundance of seasonal indicators invariably invites varying interpretations of site function and occupation. For example, there are many potential winter and spring indicators including wild boar tooth eruptions, newly born red and roe deer, and migratory bird bone evidence. It is also assumed that pine martens were killed in the winter when their pelts were of superior quality. Rowley-Conwy (1981, 1998) is of the opinion that during these months the site had a specific purpose, i.e. the intensive exploitation of wild boar, pine martens, and newborn red and roe deer. There are indications that the meatier parts of the wild boar and the skins of marten and deer were exported from the camp, possibly to a more permanent settlement situated at the coast. Rowley-Conwy (1998; *et al.* 2002) proposes that Ringkloster may well have been the scene of focused activity by more than one group from various coastal base camps. Andersen (1975, 1998) argues that the site was occupied in the autumn and early spring with movement to the east Jutland coast during the warmer months. He also points out that occupation throughout the year cannot be ruled out.

However, there is also evidence of human presence at Ringkloster during the summer. Møhl identified bones from juvenile red deer and wild boar killed during the summer months (Andersen 1975). Carter (2001*b*) has identified from tooth development that some juvenile red deer were killed in July or August. This evidence conflicts with the solely autumn/winter or winter/spring occupation proposed by Andersen (1998) and Rowley-Conwy (1998). From all the existing evidence, it is possible that Ringkloster was visited or occupied at all times of the year. The new pig evidence presented here will contribute to our knowledge and hopefully clarify when humans were at the site.

Materials and method

The excellent conditions for preservation at Ringkloster meant that a total of 53 juvenile specimens were suitable for examination and radiography at the Conservation Laboratories, University of Aarhus, Moesgård, Denmark.

Experience with modern and archaeological wild boar jaws from other sites indicated that higher power settings and exposure times were needed than for deer jaws. The X-ray equipment at Moesgård Museum was sufficiently powerful, and excellent images were obtained.

Tooth development from the radiographs was scored according to the method described above. The scores of the known age or known kill date specimens described and shown in Tables 10.3 and 10.4 were used to estimate the ages of the Ringkloster mandibles. A March birth date has been used to calculate the ages at death of the archaeological specimens.

The birth date of wild boar is known to vary, and sows may farrow at all seasons (Lauwerier 1983). However, reproduction studies of wild boar populations in Sweden and Germany have shown that 65% and 90% respectively are born between March and May; the median months are March and April, respectively (Briedermann 1990; Lemel 1999). From what is known of reproductive biology, climate, and environment during the Atlantic period, it is likely that the majority of wild boar were also born in spring. In areas with small seasonal changes in climate and vegetation, farrowing is less restricted to a specific period. But for southern Scandinavia, where there are marked seasonal differences, spring ensures the highest survival rates of piglets both today and during the Atlantic period.

There are two main reasons why sows farrow at other times of year. First, if piglets born during the spring die then the sows may come back into heat and produce a second litter later in the year (Tham 2001). It is likely that the same would have occurred during the Mesolithic. Second, it has been observed that wild boar may produce two litters at different times of the year when there is increased food availability (Lauwerier 1983; Durio *et al.* 1991). Little is known about the food abundance for wild boar during the Atlantic, but it is possible that more than one farrowing a year occurred when oak had mast years. However, this would only have happened every 6–9 years (Pucek *et al.* 1993).

Today in Sweden wild boar are supplied with fodder, thereby increasing the chance of survival for animals born outside the main farrowing season (Tham 2001). There is likely to have been less human interference during the Mesolithic, and it is therefore reasonable to assume that breeding was even more restricted to springtime. The fact that most wild boars are born during spring justifies the use of this species for estimating seasonality of archaeological sites, especially when seasonality estimates are derived from a reasonably sized sample rather than from single specimens. It is acknowledged that in a sample there may be some individuals born later in the year, but the vast majority of animals are likely to be born between March and May. Because of this possibility it is prudent to use other seasonal indicators, such as the bones of juvenile deer, to support estimations of seasonality from wild boar dentition.

Results and discussion (age interpretation and seasonal implications)

The estimated ages of 14 wild boar less than 12 months (piglets) and 39 between 12 and 36 months are shown in Figs 10.10 and 10.11. The estimated ages of 9 red deer and a single roe deer (Carter 2001*b*) have also been included in the diagrams. Combining the seasonal evidence from three species improves overall seasonal resolution at the site.

For piglets only, the maximum period of death is July to April and the minimum period is September to January. If the red and roe deer are included, then the periods extend from May to April and June to January, respectively. The maximum period now spans the whole year, but the minimum period is concentrated in the second half of the year.

For the older wild boar, age range estimations are generally larger (Fig. 10.11). But, if only specimens with higher ageing resolution are considered, then they

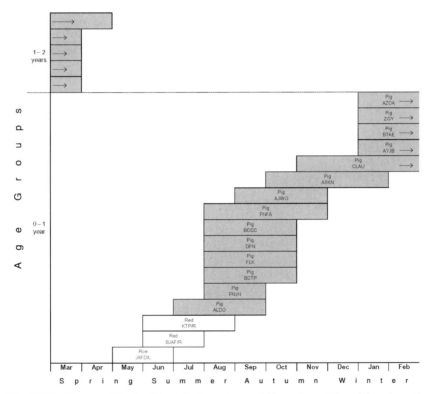

Fig. 10.10. Season of death of dentally immature wild boar ($n = 14$), red deer ($n = 3$), and roe deer ($n = 1$) aged 0–1 year from Ringkloster

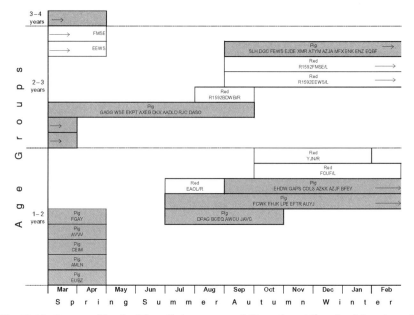

Fig. 10.11. Season of death of dentally immature wild boar ($n = 39$) and red deer ($n = 6$) aged 1–3 years from Ringkloster

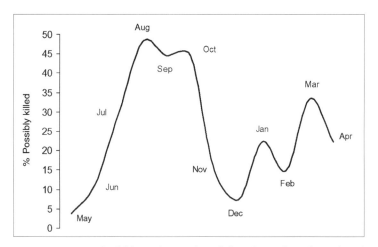

Fig. 10.12. Percentage of wild boar ($n = 22$), red deer ($n = 4$), and roe deer ($n = 1$) possibly killed for each month of the year that have age range estimations of 4 months or less and are under 24 months of age

appear to have been killed at various times of the year. If only wild boar, red deer, and roe deer under 24 months of age and with age range estimations of 4 months or less are considered, then killing is concentrated in summer and early autumn (Fig. 10.12). There is less evidence of killing during the winter and spring.

The body weight of wild boar varies considerable between different seasons. The mean body weight of boars aged 5 years from Germany increases 40 kg from late winter to late summer. The corresponding seasonal variation of body weight of sows aged 5 years is 20 kg (Briedermann 1990). By concentrating the hunting in late summer/early autumn when the animals are in prime condition, meat and fat yields would be greater than during the winter when they are at their leanest. This interpretation is based on the assumption that the seasonal hunting of juveniles is reflected in adults for whom body condition varies noticeable throughout the year.

Radiographs of wild boar mandibles showing various stages of tooth development and which are significant in assessing seasonality at the site have been reproduced in Figs 10.13–10.15. Reproductions will never be as clear as the original radiographs, but the different stages are visible.

These results conflict with an earlier study of the material by Rowley-Conwy (1998). Here a mean birth date in March has been assumed, whereas Rowley-Conwy bases his estimations on an April birth date. This makes age at death estimations one month earlier in our study than those of Rowley-Conwy. However, this does not explain such large discrepancies. The authors conclude that this is due to the application of different methods of age estimation.

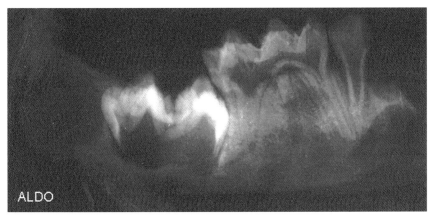

Fig. 10.13. Possibly the youngest specimen examined is ALDO. Although quite fragmented, M_1 is at stage 5, dP_4 and P_3 are at stage 1, and dP_4 and dP_3 at stages 8 and 7 respectively. From the modern tables this indicates death occurring between 4 and 6 months of age, i.e. during the summer months

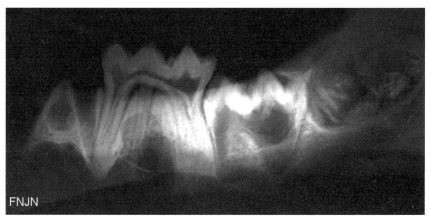

Fig. 10.14. Another good example is specimen FNJN. In this reproduction of the original radiograph the crown and root development are less clear, but there is no evidence of M_3, M_2 is at stage 2, M_1 at stage 6, P_4 and possibly P_3 at stage 1, and P_2 is missing. From the modern tables this indicates death occurring in August or September

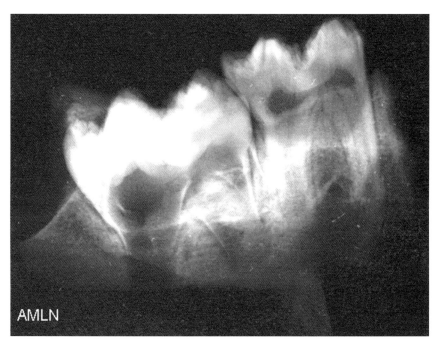

Fig. 10.15. A slightly older specimen AMLN. Here M_2 is at stage 6 whereas M_1 is at stage 8. The estimated age at death of this yearling pig is 12 or 13 months, and it was killed during spring

In this study age estimations are based on a fairly large sample of known age specimens. Tooth development is also known to vary less between different populations and to be less sensitive to environmental factors than tooth eruption and wear (Brown *et al.* 1960; McCance *et al.* 1961; Hillson 1986; Carter 2001*a*). As a result there is a high level of confidence in the age estimations from this study. The age estimations used by Rowley-Conwy (1998) are based on tooth eruption and wear according to a scheme developed by Higham (1967*b*). We are of the opinion that Rowley-Conwy's age ranges are too narrow given the inherent problems associated with tooth eruption and wear in wild boar. The ages at different stages of tooth eruption and wear given in Higham (1967*b*) are approximate. Using tooth eruption and wear in domestic pigs to age wild boar is unsuitable if the objective is to achieve the highest possible ageing resolution.

The eruption ages of domestic pig and wild boar are similar, but do differ. The second molar (M_2) erupts according to Higham (1967*b*) at 9–12 months, but the same tooth according to most populations of wild boar erupts at 12–14 months (Bull & Payne 1982; Genov *et al.* 1991*a*). According to Rowley-Conwy (1998) a large number of specimens were killed some time between January and April. However, if eruption ages of wild boar are used instead of domestic pigs then they may have been killed between April and June. In wild boar M_3 also erupts a few months later than in domestic pig. It is unreasonable to age specimens into 3 month intervals based solely on tooth wear due to variability within and between populations of wild boar and other animals (Grant 1978, 1982; Hillson 1986; Magnell 2005*b*).

CONCLUSION

There now appears to be sound evidence of summer human presence at the inland site of Ringkloster which conflicts with the purely autumn/winter or winter/spring occupation proposed by Andersen (1998) and Rowley-Conwy (1998). Taking into account both old and new evidence, favourable environmental conditions may have reduced mobility among Late Mesolithic groups to such an extent that they were able to operate from permanent inland base camps. A high proportion of animals killed during late summer/early autumn seem to indicate a seasonal intensification of hunting. This is at a time of the year when wild boars were in prime condition and hunters able to optimize yields.

11

A statistical method for dealing with isolated teeth: ageing pig teeth from Hagoshrim, Israel

Annat Haber

INTRODUCTION

Reconstructing kill-off patterns from faunal remains is an essential step in deciphering the association between humans and animals in ancient societies. Specifically, demographic patterns and trends are considered key parameters in studying the process of domestication as revealed in the archaeozoological record (Davis 1987; Clutton-Brock 1999; Reitz & Wing 1999). This is especially true in the case of pig domestication, where both archaeozoological and ethnoarchaeological evidence point to a prolonged process that has included, and still includes today, a wide diversity of associations between pigs and humans (Grigson 1982; Griffin 1998; Hongo & Meadow 1998; Lobban 1998; Redding & Rosenberg 1998; Rosman & Rubel 1989). Although several methods exist for the recording of tooth eruption and wear for the purpose of ageing teeth, these methods rarely include statistical means by which to compare the resulting kill-off patterns. A further complication, seldom addressed in the literature, is the use of isolated teeth. In this chapter I suggest a simple procedure to overcome these problems. This procedure is illustrated using data recorded for pig remains from Hagoshrim, a Neolithic site from Israel, and discuss its implications for the study of pig domestication in the southern Levant. However, this method is applicable to any mammalian assemblages where similar ageing methods are used.

Analysing kill-off patterns based on tooth eruption and wear usually involves the following stages (e.g. Hesse 1986, 2002; Rolett & Chiu 1994; Hongo & Meadow 1998; Ervynck *et al.* 2001; Horwitz 2001; Davis in press): (1) collecting the raw data by recording eruption and wear stages, most commonly (for pigs) based on the scheme provided by Grant (1982); (2) correlating the archaeozoological data with absolute ages from recent populations, based (for pigs) primarily on the works of Matschke (1967), Silver (1969), and Bull & Payne (1982); and (3) generating histograms or survivorship curves that summarize the raw data.

However, Grant's method and other common methods for generating survivorship curves produce information that does not lend itself easily to statistical testing. Furthermore, the method outlined by Grant (1982) is designed specifically for the analysis of half-mandibles, which are scarce in most archaeozoological assemblages. Published data from recent populations also refer to complete tooth rows, rendering them less useful for analysing isolated teeth. The tables provided by Higham (1967*a*), Matschke (1967), and Silver (1969) use eruption and wear stages of different teeth to recognize different age groups, leaving out some stages for most teeth, thus forcing the archaeozoologist to ignore many of the teeth in the assemblage and reduce the effective sample sizes. In order to include in the analysis as many loose teeth as possible, a correlation scheme is needed, that will provide a framework for grouping different tooth elements in various wear stages into age groups. The data recorded by Bull & Payne (1982) for Turkish wild boars allow some correlation between eruption and wear stages of teeth that were not given in the earlier publications, including maxillary teeth. Rolett & Chiu (1994: Table 4) provide an example for an explicit attempt to establish relationships between all eruption and wear stages of the three permanent molars, using the data from British archaeological sites analysed by Grant (1982), as well as their own observations on mandibles of modern and historical Marquesan pigs.

Rolett & Chiu (1994) also noticed the problem of biased representation of age groups, which is unique to the use of isolated teeth and is rarely addressed in the literature. Table 11.1 (their table 8) illustrates this complication: different age groups are represented by different numbers of elements simply due to the nature of tooth growth and replacement, thus the sub-adult age group would be biased towards a lower relative frequency than the young adult, and of course the immature and the mature adults would be the least abundant, even in an ideal case where no taphonomic factors are involved. It is easy to see how, in this case, a simple count of isolated teeth would artificially generate a distribution in which most individuals are supposedly killed as young adults, or, as postulated by Payne (1973) and widely cited ever since (cf. Munson 2000), at prime age when they just reached maturity and their growth rate became effectively zero. It is important to note that this is a different problem than the problem of independence of *fragments*: even if we accept the NISP assumptions and each fragment, or tooth for that matter, comes from a different individual, there is still the problem of representation of age groups, that is, how many *elements* are counted in each age group. The solution given by Rolett and Chiu (1994),

Table 11.1. Illustrating the problem of biased representation using pig molars from the Hanamiai site (TH1), Tahuata, Marquesas Islands: tooth eruption or wear stage versus age groups (reproduced with permission from Rolett & Chiu (1994)).

Age group Estimated age (in months)	immature < 5-8	subadult 5-8< <10-14	young adult 10-14< >18-26	mature adult > 18-26
M1 germ	5			
M1 a		9		
M1 b		5		
M1 c		5		
M1 d			1	
M1 e			3	
M1 f			1	
M2 germ		13		
M2 a		6		
M2 b			1	
M2 c			2	
M2 e				1
M3 germ			5	
M3 c				1
Total	5	38	13	2

also followed by Ervynck *et al.* (2001), was to use only non-overlapping tooth elements, which resulted in reducing sample size and losing data. In this study I employ a simple method, a two-dimensional X^2 test based on an intrinsic hypothesis that allows the analysis of both tooth rows and isolated teeth, regardless of their degree of completeness, and provides means for comparing kill-off patterns from different assemblages.

THE MATERIAL

The site of Hagoshrim is located in the Hula valley, northern Israel. Two seasons of excavation (1996 and 1997) were carried out by Nimrod Getzov of the Israel Antiquities Authority, and revealed a large site of about 80,000 m². The site includes three main strata (Getzov 1999: table 2). The oldest, Layer 6, was dated to the first half of the 8th millennium BP and identified as representing the Pre-Pottery Neolithic C culture. The following Layer 5, an equivalent of Jericho IX, was dated to the beginning of the 7th millennium BP. The youngest is Layer 4, dated to the second half of the 7th millennium BP, associated with the Wadi Raba culture. A total of 369 pig teeth, isolated and embedded, were recovered and counted in this study (Table 11.2).

Table 11.2. The three main layers of Hagoshrim, their chronological and cultural context, and the total number of pig teeth recovered and analysed in each layer. The dates are uncalibrated radiocarbon dates obtained for each layer.

Layer	Period	Culture	Sample size	Dates
Layer 6	Pre-Pottery Neolithic C		261	7562 ± 85 BP
				7735 ± 55 BP
Layer 5	Pottery Neolithic B	Jericho IX	58	6725 ± 120 BP
Layer 4	Late Neolithic / Early Chalcolithic	Wadi Raba	50	6505 ± 120 BP

THE METHOD

The eruption and wear stages were recorded based on Grant (1982) complemented by information from Bull & Payne (1982) and my own observations, using a collection of 21 adult wild pigs, males and females, curated in the Zoological Museum of Tel-Aviv University. Because the teeth were mostly isolated, absolute ages were needed to correlate between the various stages and combine them into five groups. The correlation scheme (Table 11.3) is based on Silver (1969) and Bull & Payne (1982), as well as on the recent collection. This also allowed the inclusion of upper teeth. Although Matschke (1967) and Bull & Payne (1982) reported differences between eruption and wear of lower and upper teeth, these differences proved negligible in this case, mainly because of the relatively low resolution defined for this study.

Table 11.3 summarizes the age group definitions and their correlations. It was decided to disregard M_1 and M_2 because there is a high degree of uncertainty in any attempt to distinguish between them when they are not embedded in the jaw. For Hagoshrim, sample sizes were large enough (especially once maxillary and deciduous teeth were included) to be able to ignore these elements and reduce the uncertainty. The fourth and third lower premolars were distinguished on morphological criteria; the fourth premolar is bulkier and its longitudinal recesses are deeper, rendering the occlusal surface more winding. Both loose and embedded teeth were counted in this study. Jaws with more than one tooth were counted once, based on one of the teeth. If the correlation scheme is correct, it should not matter which of the teeth is chosen. Obviously, the problem of biased representation appears here too: if we take into account the permanent premolars, the second age group (AG-2 in Table 11.3) is represented by six elements while the others are represented by four elements. Since AG-3 is the prime age, such a treatment would result in over-representation of young individuals.

Table 11.3. The five age groups used for pigs and their definitions based on eruption and wear of upper (\) and lower (/) dP$_3$, dP$_4$, P$_4$, and M$_3$ ('d', as in dP/3, refers to 'deciduous'). The small case letters in each cell correspond to Grant's (1982) stages.

	Age group (AG) with absolute ages in months				
	AG-1: 0-6	AG-2: 7-18	AG-3: 19-24	AG-4: 25-36	AG-5: older
dP/3	dentine invisible	dentine exposed			
dP\3	dentine invisible	dentine exposed			
dP/4	a–d, dentine invisible, or very small and isolated patches	e–j, dentine exposed			
dP\4	dentine invisible	dentine exposed			
P/4		a–c, dentine invisible	d–e, dentine exposed, but patchy	f, one patch of dentine, cusp still high	g–h, low cusp
P\4		a–c, dentine invisible	d–e, dentine exposed, but patchy	f, lingual patch of dentine appears, cusp still high	g–h, low cusp
M/3			a, root still open	b–c, dentine invisible or little patches and last cusp unerupted	d–k, big patches of dentine
M\3			root still open	dentine invisible and last cusp unerupted	big patches of dentine

By using the two-dimensional X^2 statistic, also known as the Pearson X^2, we bypass the problem of biased representation because the expected frequency of each cell is calculated on the basis of an intrinsic hypothesis that takes into account consistent differences in sample sizes (Sokal & Rohlf 1995). In other words, the relative differences are considered, rather than the absolute. In this case I compare the age structures of the three layers of Hagoshrim, Layers 6, 5, and 4, so the rows are assemblages (layers) and the columns are the age groups. The equation for calculating the X^2 statistic is:

$$X^2 = \sum [(O{-}E)^2 / E]$$

where O is the observed frequency of a specific cell and E is the expected frequency for the same cell, and the statistic is the sum of the relative deviations from expected. Note that the X^2 statistic is similar but not identical to the χ^2 distribution. The X^2 statistic is based on discrete values whereas the χ^2 distribution is based on continuous values, but it does result in an

Table 11.4. Pig mandibular and maxillary teeth assigned to age groups based on the definitions in Table 11.3. Totals (in bold font) give the age distributions for each of the three layers. The prime age, based on eruption of M/3, is AG-3 (in bold frame).

		AG-1: 0-6 m	AG-2: 7-18 m	AG-3: 19-24 m	AG-4: 25-36 m	AG-5: older	total
Layer 6	dP/3	0	1				1
	dP\3	0	1				1
	dP/4	0	6				6
	dP\4	0	2				2
	P/4		0	6	4	0	10
	P\4		3	2	2	1	8
	M/3			1	7	4	12
	M\3			4	4	2	10
	total	**0**	**13**	**13**	**17**	**7**	**50**
Layer 5	dP/3	0	5				5
	dP\3	1	6				7
	dP/4	0	4				4
	dP\4	0	0				0
	P/4		1	6	3	0	10
	P\4		2	4	3	0	9
	M/3			6	4	5	15
	M\3			3	2	3	8
	total	**1**	**18**	**19**	**12**	**8**	**58**
Layer 4	dP/3	7	15				22
	dP\3	3	13				16
	dP/4	18	31				49
	dP\4	4	24				28
	P/4		2	16	7	1	26
	P\4		5	19	14	5	43
	M/3			13	16	9	38
	M\3			12	17	10	39
	total	**32**	**90**	**60**	**54**	**25**	**261**

approximation to the continuous distribution, so the χ^2 distribution can be used for the significance test (Sokal & Rohlf 1995: 695).

The expected frequency is calculated by multiplying the row total by the column total and dividing it by the grand total (see Table 11.5 for an example). In other words, the expected frequency of each cell depends on the relative abundance of that layer among the three layers, and the relative abundance of that age group among all the age groups. If the two factors (dimensions) are affecting the cell count independently then this number should be the product of their effects (their relative abundances). Therefore, if a specific age group is consistently represented more than the others, it will be taken into account in the calculation of the expected frequencies, and the

Table 11.5. Observed and expected frequencies of each age group in each layer, based on the data in Table 11.4. The expected frequency, given in parenthesis, is calculated by multiplying the relative abundance of the layer and the age group. Thus, for example, the expected frequency of AG-1 in Layer 4 equals (261/369)*(33/369).

	ag-1	ag-2	ag-3	ag-4	ag-5	Total
Layer 6	0 (4.47)	13 (16.40)	13 (12.47)	17 (11.24)	7 (5.42)	50
Layer 5	1 (5.19)	18 (19.02)	19 (14.46)	12 (13.05)	8 (6.28)	58
Layer 4	32 (23.34)	90 (85.58)	60 (65.07)	54 (58.71)	25 (28.30)	261
Total	33	121	92	83	40	369

same for the layers. If the relative frequencies of the age groups in one layer change in a different manner than in another layer, it will add to the total deviations from the expected and will sum up to a significant X^2, indicating a dependence between the layers and the age groups.

It is important to note that this test does not evaluate whether the layers or the age groups occur at a given proportion, but only if they are manifested independently. Therefore, this test is highly relative and relies heavily on which assemblages are included and which are not. Thus, for example, in order to compare the southern Levant to the northern Levant it is advisable to acquire the raw data from all assemblages and re-analyse them in one test, rather than compare the results of the southern Levant analysis to those of the northern Levant analysis.

Results

The raw data are given in Table 11.4. Table 11.5 summarizes the observed and expected frequencies for each age group in each layer. A convenient way to examine these results visually is by plotting the standardized deviates (Fig. 11.1), which are calculated as the square root of the X^2 value of each cell retaining the original sign: (O–E) / $\sqrt{E}$. Thus, if a specific age group in a specific layer has a relative frequency which is higher than the expected value, it will have a positive value, and if it has a relatively lower frequency, it will have a negative value.

The overall X^2 is significant ($X^2 = 18.607$, df $= 8$, p $= 0.02$) (the age group distributions are thus dependent on the layers), indicating a change in kill-off patterns through time. Looking at the standardized deviates it is obvious that the change is mostly between Layers 5 and 4, at the end of the Pottery Neolithic, and involves mainly a shift towards a younger culling age. For comparison, age distributions were calculated based only on upper and lower deciduous fourth premolar and permanent third molar, and are shown in

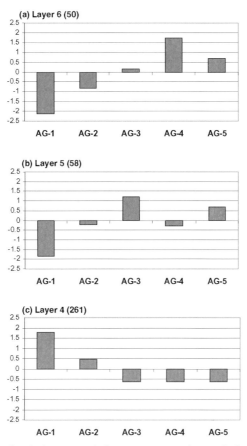

Fig. 11.1. Standardized deviates of the age groups for each layer. $X^2 = 18.607$, $df = 8$, $p = 0.02$. Based on data from Tables 11.4 and 11.5

Fig. 11.2. The same pattern emerges: Layer 4 is distinctly different from Layers 5 and 6 in the higher representation of the younger age groups.

Discussion

By comparing the three main assemblages of Hagoshrim, a significant pattern is revealed that allows the following conclusions. First, based on the kill-off patterns, no evidence is found for cultural control prior to the Wadi Raba period in the Late Neolithic. Combined with the morphometric analysis that was carried out in the more comprehensive study (Haber & Dayan 2004),

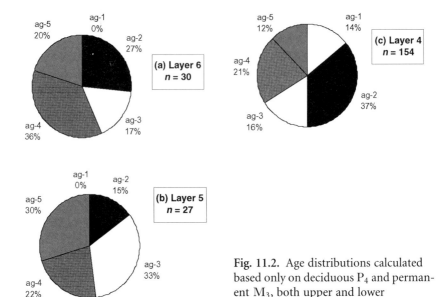

Fig. 11.2. Age distributions calculated based only on deciduous P_4 and permanent M_3, both upper and lower

there is a strong support for the assertion that complete domestication at the population level seems to have occurred at the same time as the changes in kill-off patterns. Thus, the change in kill-off patterns in the Late Neolithic is associated with the onset of domestication in the narrow sense of strict control over breeding, feeding, and protection.

The second conclusion is that domestication of pigs in Hagoshrim involves a shift towards a younger culling age. This specific trend in kill-off pattern has been associated with the domestication of sheep and goats for both theoretical and empirical reasons (e.g. Payne 1973; Kohler-Rollefson 1997; Zeder 1999; Munson 2000). Benecke (1993) and von den Driesch & Wodtke (1997) cautioned against using these arguments for pigs. Benecke (1993) found a high occurrence (75%) of young in populations that he considered to be morphometrically wild at Early Mesolithic to Late Neolithic sites from the Crimean peninsula, concluding that this pattern more likely reflects seasonal hunting rather than cultural control. Based mainly on Benecke (1993), von den Driesch & Wodtke (1997) discarded the high percentage of young pigs at 'Ain Ghazal as evidence for domestication. They also argued that the percentage of young pigs in wild populations would be naturally high (i.e. higher than the figure we are expecting in the case of sheep and goats), and that it would be easier to hunt the younger individuals than the older ones, arguably a more critical factor for pigs than for sheep and goats. However, the arguments of von den Driesch & Wodtke (1997) are less relevant when patterns are established and examined based on intrinsic comparisons rather than compared to extrinsic 'expected' hypotheses. Furthermore, the data presented by Benecke (1993) do not negate early stages of cultural control and strategies such as female breeding, as was suggested by Redding & Rosenberg (1998) for pigs at Hallan Çemi. A similar trend of increasing abundance of younger individuals was also found for pigs at Çayönü, which, like Hallan Çemi, is a Pre-Pottery Neolithic site in south-eastern Turkey (Hongo and Meadow 1998). The findings in Hagoshrim support the use of that trend as indication for domestication, or at least cultural control, especially when combined with other types of evidence.

CONCLUSION

The example discussed in this paper illustrates the importance of using appropriate statistical procedures. Mere counting of all isolated teeth where some age groups are artificially overrepresented in all assemblages could have obscured the changes that were found to occur between Layers 5 and 4 at Hagoshrim. Counting only non-overlapping elements would have resulted in smaller sample sizes that are more sensitive to statistical noise (random effects), and again would have obscured the meaningful patterns. By using the two-dimensional X^2 we were able to bypass the problem of biased representation, without reducing sample sizes, and at the same time compare the assemblages to find a statistically significant pattern. This is because the expected frequencies are based on an intrinsic hypothesis, the relative abundances of the two factors, rather than an extrinsic distribution that is based on various theoretical considerations. Indeed, this is a highly comparative method and it relies heavily on which assemblages are included and which are not. However, historical studies are comparative by definition, and although (most of the time) we cannot design experiments to test our hypotheses, we can design the appropriate comparisons and collect our data accordingly. Statistical methods such as the one presented here provide well-supported patterns through space and time which can serve as a basis for further exploration of various hypotheses.

12

Morphometric variation between populations of recent wild boar in Israel

Goggy Davidowitz & Liora Kolska Horwitz

INTRODUCTION

Today the wild boar (subspecies *Sus scrofa lybica* Gray, 1868) is the largest wild mammal found in Israel (Mendelssohn & Yom Tov 1999*a*). *Sus scrofa* has formed an integral part of the fauna of Israel since *c*.0.78 Mya, with the earliest skeletal remains derived from the Lower Palaeolithic site of Gesher Benot Ya'akov, Israel (Hooijer 1959; Geraads & Tchernov 1983). Remains of wild boar are commonly found in archaeological assemblages in this region (e.g. Davis 1982; Tchernov 1988), and according to 19th-century travellers, wild boar were abundant throughout Palestine, including the thickets of the Jordan river and the Dead Sea, and even extended into the arid regions of the northern Negev and Judean desert (Tristram 1866; Hart 1891; Bodenheimer 1958; Qumsiyeh 1996). However, during the period of the Mandate of Palestine (1923–48) the population size of wild boar was severely reduced by hunting, and as a consequence, their distribution was reduced to the Jordan valley, from the Hula Lake in the north to Sdom at the southern tip of the Dead Sea (Bodenheimer 1958; Mendelssohn & Yom-Tov 1999 a, 1999*b*) (Fig. 12.1). Since the creation of the State of Israel in 1948 they have been protected by legislation, which, coupled with the reduced numbers of predators, has resulted in a marked increase in their numbers. Nowadays, wild boar occupy most of their former habitats including the coastal region. The species has also been observed as far south as Nahal Besor in the northern Negev, but it has been proposed that these animals may represent hybrids of domestic pigs and wild boar (Mendelssohn & Yom-Tov 1999*b*).

Four main concentrations of wild boar can be identified in Israel today: the Upper Galilee (especially in the national park of Mount Meiron), the Hula Nature Reserve, the Golan Heights, and Sdom (Fig. 12.1). As shown in Table 12.1, these areas differ markedly in vegetation, altitude, and climate.

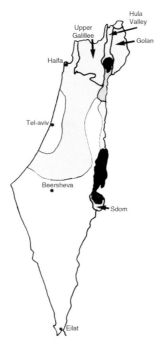

Fig. 12.1. Current distribution of *Sus scrofa lybica* in Israel and the West Bank (areas shaded in grey), and the location of the four populations studied here

A study of dental pathology in skeletal collections derived from these groups showed significant differences between the four areas (Horwitz & Davidowitz 1992). Specifically, the Sdom group was characterized by an unusually high frequency of hypodontia of the lower third incisor, indicative of inbreeding. Dental disease patterns (caries, periodontal disease, ante-mortem tooth loss) also differed between populations, although no attempt was made to differentiate between diet and possible age-related differences in the samples studied (Horwitz & Davidowitz 1992).

The current study was undertaken to investigate whether the four main populations of wild boar inhabiting Israel today differ in size, shape, or a combination of both. This distinction may facilitate an understanding of the source of variation in the wild boar populations of Israel. The approach we used consisted of morphometric analyses, comparing raw, log-transformed (see below), cranial and mandible measurements with the same measurements after they had size removed as a variable. The remaining variation of these size-free measurements is attributable to shape (see below). Additionally, we compared the raw and size-free data for juveniles,

Table 12.1. Habitats of four wild boar populations in Israel (based on data given in Orni and Efrat 1980).

Region	Vegetation type	Average altitude (m.a.s.l.)	Average annual rainfall (mm)	Mean annual daily temperature (°C)	Hottest annual temperature (°C)	Coldest annual temperature (°C)	Mean annual relative humidity (%)
Hula	Swamp with *Phragmites, Arundo, Typha, Juncus,* and *Platanus* spp.	73	550	20	27	11	57
Upper Galilee	Mediterranean maquis and forests with *Arbutus* and *Quercus* spp.	900	900	16	20	4	62
Golan Heights	Park forests *Quercus* spp. and herbaceous vegetation	1100	800	20	35	−0	57
Sdom	Semi-arid with salt marshes containing *Suaeda, Tamarix, Anthrocnemum,* and *Nitraria* spp.	−350	50	25	35	17	42

subadult and adult individuals. The purpose of this comparison was to reveal possible differences in growth patterns between populations.

Our working hypothesis was as follows. If population differentiation were due to size alone, differentiation would disappear after size correction. If population differentiation were due to shape alone, these differences would remain after factoring out size. If the differences between populations were due to both size and shape, then the shape component would be larger after correcting for size.

MATERIALS AND METHODS

The study populations

The samples examined in this study represent four main concentrations ('populations') of wild boar (Fig. 12.1, Table 12.1). The Sdom population numbers several dozen individuals (Mendelssohn & Yom-Tov 1999b). They occupy the thickets of the wet salines (Danin 1988) located at the southern tip of the Dead Sea and were observed in this locality in the mid 19th century (Tristram 1866). Beyond the salines, the environment is semi-arid. Today, this is a relict population and apparently isolated from the other wild boar in the country (Mendelssohn & Yom-Tov 1999a, 1999b). Mendelssohn *et al.* (1990) noted that, in the past, individuals in this population were smaller than those in the north (maximum body weight *c.*50 kg) but that they are now of similar size as a result of improved nutrition stemming from the availability of agricultural crops.

The Upper Galilee population is primarily derived from the Mount Meiron Nature Reserve and its environs. This encompasses one of the few surviving areas with indigenous Mediterranean oak maquis dominated by evergreen species (Danin 1988). In the 1970s the population of wild boar in the reserve numbered *c.*255 individuals (3.2 individuals per km^2 in an area of $80 \, km^2$) (Canaani 1972). However, given that some 4000 animals are hunted annually in Israel today (Mendelssohn & Yom-Tov 1999a), the size of this and other wild boar populations has undoubtedly risen considerably since then.

The Hula sample derives from the population that inhabits the swamp and reed thickets of the Hula Lake in the northern Jordan valley (Danin 1988). After a section of this swamp was drained for agriculture in the 1950s, some of the wild boar migrated westwards into Upper Galilee (Canaani 1976/1977). A survey carried out in the Hula Nature Reserve between 1969 and 1972 recorded the presence of at least 230 individuals (Canaani 1976/1977), but this is undoubtedly an underestimate of their numbers today.

The wild boar population inhabiting the basalt heights of the Golan in the north of the country is derived from the rocky, northern portion of the heights at an altitude of *c.*1000–1700 m.a.s.l. This region is characterized by high rainfall and snow cover in the winter, but is relatively poor in permanent water sources (Inbar 1987). The vegetation is characterized by remnants of oak woodlands, park-forest, and savannoid Mediterranean vegetation (Danin 1988). In the 19th century, large numbers of wild boar were observed in the Golan (Schumacher 1888), but their current number is unknown.

Bodenheimer (1953: 247) reported that Israeli wild boar more closely resemble the European form in size and strength than the gracile Egyptian type. The local wild boar are dimorphic, with mean adult body weight of 100.9 kg (range 73–150) for boars and 61.4 kg (range 53–82) for sows (Mendelssohn & Yom Tov 1999*a*). Females first give birth at 2 years of age but, given favourable nutrition or more intensive hunting pressure, can produce young as early as 1 year of age. Mating lasts from November to December, and sows give birth in March–April with litter sizes ranging from 3 to 8. Wild boar are omnivorous, feeding mainly at night on small vertebrates, insects, eggs, fruit, vegetables, tubers, roots, bark, seeds, nuts, and especially acorns (Qumsiyeh 1996; Mendelssohn & Yom Tov 1999*a*). Wild boar inflict enormous damage on agricultural crops in Israel (Israel Nature Reserves Authority 1985–86; Mendelssohn & Yom Tov 1999*a*), and licensed hunting is permitted in Israel on a seasonal basis from September through December.

Crania, mandibles and measurements

The crania and mandibles used in this study are of recent male and female wild boar held in the zoological collections of the Hebrew University of Jerusalem and Tel Aviv University (Table 12.2). The collections are made up of specimens that had been shot or found dead in different regions of Israel

Table 12.2. Sample sizes of crania and mandibles.

	Location	Juvenile	Sub-adult	Adult
Crania	Golan Heights	4	5	7
	Upper Galilee	14	9	6
	Hula	0	3	7
	Sdom	3	9	4
Mandibles	Golan Heights	6	3	6
	Upper Galilee	9	13	11
	Hula	2	2	9
	Sdom	0	6	6

over the past 40 years. We only used individuals derived from the four areas described above.

We aged the individuals using molar eruption and wear (Bull & Payne 1982; Matschke 1967): juveniles had only their first molar erupted and in wear (equivalent to Bull & Payne Group I, 7–11 months), subadults had their first and second molars erupted and in wear (equivalent to Bull & Payne Group II, 19–23 months), and adults had all three molars erupted and in wear (equivalent to Bull & Payne Group III, 31–35 months). Care was taken to include roughly equal proportions of males and females in all three age groups. Many of the skulls and mandibles were damaged; as a result we restricted the variables used to those present in all individuals. For the cranium, we used the standard pig metrics of von den Driesch (1976). These included 15 variables; 1a, 5, 7, 15, 19, 22, 23, 26, 29, 38, 40, 41, 43, 44, 45 as defined in Table 12.5. As our goal was to compare size and shape morphometrics, these variables included eight length variables, two height variables, and five breadth variables. For the mandibles we used the variables 1, 2, 5, 7a, 9, 9a, 11, 12, 13, 15, 16b, 16c, 17, 19 defined in Table 12.5. These included eight length, two breadth, and four height measurements.

Statistical analysis

Variables were log-transformed prior to all analyses. Differences among populations were determined by canonical variate analysis (SAS, PROC CANDISC) and significance between populations was determined from the *F*-statistics of the Mahalanobis distances between population centroids. To remove size from the variables, each variable was regressed on its first principal component (PC1) score (PROC PRINCOMP). The residuals from this regression were then used in a second size-free canonical variate analysis. In choosing the variables for this analysis, care was taken to ensure that PC1 for each age group was indeed a size vector, based on the loadings of the eigenvectors of PC1. PC1 was considered a size vector if all the loadings were of the same sign and had similar values. A comparison of the eigenvalues of the first canonical variate (CV1) before and after size correction indicated whether these differences were due to size or shape. These analyses were carried out separately for each age class and separately for the crania and the mandible (12 analyses in all). Samples sizes were too small to test males and females separately. All analyses were undertaken using SAS 6.12.

Results

The variables used are a combination of length, breadth, and height variables. Examination of the raw PC1 loadings (Tables 12.3 and 12.4) shows that PC1 was a size vector. PC1 of the raw juvenile mandible measurements included the highest degree of shape among all analyses. The removal of size changes PC1 from a size vector to a shape vector as intended. As a consequence, the percent variation described by PC1 dropped to about 30% of the variation explained before removal of size. After removal of size, the CV1 scores also change from a size to a shape vector (Tables 12.3 and 12.4). Removal of size decreased the amount of variation described by CV1 for the crania but had little effect on the amount of variation described by CV1 in the mandibles.

The first and second canonical variate biplots are shown in Figs 12.2 and 12.3. There does not appear to be any overall pattern of differentiation among populations. Generally, removal of size tends to eliminate most of the differences between populations. We note that although, statistically, the Galilee, Hula, and Sdom populations do not differ from each other in the adult mandibles (Fig. 12.3), the p-values of the pairwise Mahalanobis distances were only marginally non-significant ($0.06 > p < 0.07$) before removal of size. Population differentiation is much less pronounced once size is removed. At the adult stage, there are no significant differences between populations in skull shape and large overlaps between populations in the mandible. In the logged data, for all age groups, the Golan population is consistently the smallest. In the adult crania, the Golan population is the most distinct and closest to the Sdom population, and the Hula and Galilee populations are closest to each other.

Overall, there does not seem to be any predominant pattern in the CV1 or PC1 loadings with regard to their relative contributions to the patterns observed. One notable exception is in the adult cranium where the raw CV1 loadings show no pattern between the height, breadth, and length variables. Removal of size, however, results in positive values for all the length variables (most of these values are large) and negative values for the breadth and height variables. This indicates that with the eruption of M_3, the crania develop more in length relative to breadth and height. Thus, in the adults, cranial length develops on a different allometric trajectory from skull depth and skull breadth.

Discussion

Kusatman (1991) compared osteological measurements of Israeli wild boar from Upper Galilee and Hula with those from an East German population from Hakel and a small sample of Iranian wild boar. She reported that the animals from Israel were smaller than those from Turkey, Iraq, and Iran,

Table 12.3. First principal component and first canonical variate scores of log-transformed raw data and size-free data of the cranium (variables are defined in Table 12.5).

Variable	Dimension	Juvenile PC1 Raw	PC1 Size free	CV1 Raw	CV1 Size free	Sub-adult PC1 Raw	PC1 Size free	CV1 Raw	CV1 Size free	Adult PC1 Raw	PC1 Size free	CV1 Raw	CV1 Size free
1a	Length	0.2830	0.3758	0.4795	0.7556	0.3019	0.3981	0.3021	-0.1751	0.3007	0.3197	0.7607	0.8275
5	Length	0.2761	0.3603	0.4786	0.4060	0.2964	0.2415	0.4200	0.4380	0.2959	0.3105	0.6994	0.8944
7	Length	0.2827	0.3750	0.4775	0.7000	0.3024	0.4077	0.3470	-0.0002	0.3029	0.3701	0.7018	0.8751
15	Length	0.2825	0.3167	0.5492	0.1177	0.2854	0.2154	0.3643	-0.0986	0.2978	0.3318	0.6379	0.8440
19	Length	0.2800	-0.1451	0.5956	-0.2647	0.2870	0.1685	0.2245	-0.4422	0.2418	0.0687	0.4213	0.0793
22	Height	0.2481	0.2194	0.5020	-0.0307	0.2307	-0.2282	0.4228	-0.0591	0.1980	0.1045	0.5835	-0.5058
23	Length	0.2757	0.3288	0.4127	0.5349	0.2972	0.3894	0.3019	-0.0195	0.2491	0.1924	0.2410	0.0131
26	Length	0.2444	0.0604	0.5505	-0.1882	0.2764	0.0219	0.3351	0.1299	0.2521	0.2059	0.4868	0.9595
29	Length	0.1682	-0.1188	0.3025	-0.1007	0.1998	-0.2778	0.3573	0.1731	0.0772	-0.0667	0.3673	-0.6153
38	Width	0.2707	-0.3932	0.6419	-0.4304	0.2808	-0.2945	0.3162	-0.0789	0.2801	-0.2906	0.4454	-0.9068
40	Width	0.1731	-0.2607	0.2943	0.0852	0.1660	-0.1735	0.5080	0.5268	0.1950	-0.1457	0.3920	-0.1782
41	Width	0.2694	0.1162	0.4181	0.5053	0.2950	-0.1840	0.2923	0.1811	0.2930	-0.3173	0.5771	-0.5100
43	Width	0.2693	-0.1745	0.7074	-0.6677	0.0900	-0.1911	0.2674	0.2093	0.2471	-0.3496	0.4596	-0.8523
44	Width	0.2500	-0.1504	0.5038	-0.2014	0.1802	0.1847	-0.2683	-0.6107	0.2633	-0.2109	0.4581	-0.2962
45	Height	0.2629	-0.0614	0.5863	-0.0507	0.2765	0.1673	0.2638	-0.0943	0.2822	-0.2859	0.6059	-0.1001
% Variation		0.82	0.28	0.79	0.99	0.71	0.25	0.74	0.68	0.65	0.4	0.97	0.71

Table 12.4. First principal component and first canonical variate scores of log-transformed raw data and size-free data of the mandible (variables are defined in Table 12.5).

Variable	Dimension	Juvenile				Sub-adult				Adult			
		PC1 Raw	PC1 Size free	CV1 Raw	CV1 Size free	PC1 Raw	PC1 Size free	CV1 Raw	CV1 Size free	PC1 Raw	PC1 Size free	CV1 Raw	CV1 Size free
1	Length	0.3349	0.4874	0.1221	0.3856	0.3173	0.4099	0.1486	0.5246	0.2578	0.1181	0.0219	−0.0728
2	Length	0.3343	0.2784	0.2154	−0.3480	0.1406	0.4145	0.2157	0.6514	0.2989	0.1585	−0.0317	−0.0026
5	Length	0.3350	0.2992	0.1561	0.2585	0.3062	0.3113	0.2096	0.5021	0.3161	0.3978	−0.1136	0.2515
7b	Length	0.2053	−0.2554	0.4748	−0.4649	0.2626	−0.1330	−0.0516	−0.3461	0.2913	−0.4163	−0.1327	0.1970
9	Length	0.0479	−0.1657	−0.1483	0.1177	0.1450	−0.2037	−0.1010	−0.1089	0.1853	−0.1755	−0.0693	0.0512
9a	Length	−0.0539	−0.0160	−0.2612	−0.0162	0.1448	−0.3380	−0.2378	−0.4056	0.0746	−0.1042	−0.1039	0.0827
11	Length	0.2855	0.3823	0.0898	0.1308	0.2205	−0.0487	0.0122	−0.0512	0.2412	−0.1771	0.1267	−0.2308
12	Length	0.3307	0.1060	0.1072	0.4996	0.3038	0.3880	0.2934	0.6985	0.2984	−0.2473	−0.1891	0.3586
13	Height	0.3243	−0.0964	0.0854	0.5369	0.2964	−0.2594	−0.0809	−0.4233	0.2988	0.4481	−0.0776	0.1244
15	Height	0.0417	−0.2246	0.2356	−0.1804	0.2950	−0.2663	−0.1482	−0.4916	0.2938	0.4541	−0.0103	−0.0199
16b	Height	0.3319	−0.3477	0.2240	−0.2177	0.2981	0.0799	0.1983	0.2493	0.3198	−0.1425	−0.0173	−0.0528
16c	Height	0.3228	−0.3838	0.2707	−0.1836	0.3038	0.2913	0.2078	0.5513	0.2715	−0.2209	−0.1969	0.2867
17	Width	0.0287	0.1305	−0.8113	0.6682	0.1493	−0.0608	−0.4283	−0.3145	0.1534	−0.0807	0.6358	−0.7347
19	Width	0.3219	0.0071	0.2625	−0.3093	0.2763	0.0616	0.0057	−0.0047	0.3116	0.1117	0.0205	−0.1606
% Variation		0.62	0.27	0.99	0.97	0.69	0.25	0.46	0.49	0.64	0.24	0.49	0.54

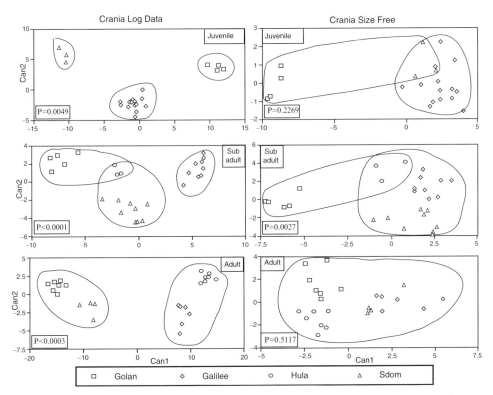

Fig. 12.2. Canonical variate biplots of the cranial measurements. CV1 is on the abscissa and CV2 on the ordinate. The raw variables (log-transformed) are in the left-hand panels and the size-free variables in the right-hand panels. The circles indicate populations that are significantly different ($P < 0.05$) based on the Mahalanobis distances of population centroids. The P-values are of a Wilks' lambda test of the hypothesis that all populations have the same mean

a finding that she attributed to geographical differences after Bergmann's law. Wild boar from Bulgaria (Genov *et al.* 1991*b*) and from Italy (Appollonio *et al.* 1988; Randi *et al.* 1989) also follow a geographic size cline with little variation in shape.

The four wild boar populations discussed here inhabit dramatically different ecological and climatic zones (see Table 12.1). In particular, Sdom is characterized by extremely arid conditions and consistently high temperatures. The Upper Galilee population inhabits a somewhat colder and much richer region, but the most extreme conditions are experienced by the Golan population where the climate exhibits the most variation between winter and summer temperatures (see Table 12.1).

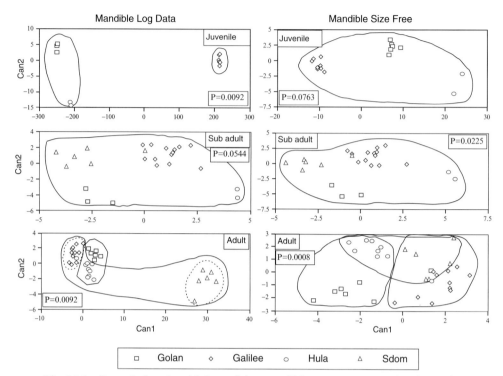

Fig. 12.3. Canonical variate biplots of the mandible measurements. CV1 is on the abscissa and CV2 on the ordinate. The raw variables (log-transformed) are in the left-hand panels and the size-free variables in the right-hand panels. The circles indicate populations that are significantly different ($P <0.05$) based on the Mahalanobis distances of population centroids. In the lower left panel the P-value of the pairwise Mahalanobis distances were only marginally non-significant ($0.06> P <0.07$) for Galilee and Sdom. The dotted circles indicate the population differentiation after relaxing the cut-off of α for estimating P

To differing extents, the four populations are also physically isolated from each other. This is particularly true of the Sdom population, which lies over 230 km from the closest Hula population (see Fig. 12.1). This is perhaps best illustrated by the high frequency of hypodontia in the Sdom wild boars compared to other populations. Despite their physical proximity to each other, altitudinal and climatic differences may have served to isolate wild boar populations in the Golan Heights from the populations of both Upper Galilee and Hula.

Although skull form and size do not provide the most accurate estimate of body size, we consider that they do provide an approximation and, in the

Table 12.5. Variables used in analysis.

Cranium

1a	Opisthocranion–prosthion
5	Premolars–prosthion
7	Basifacial axis; hormion–prosthion
15	Greatest length of the nasals; nasion–rhinion
19	Entorbitale–infraorbitale
22	Height of the lacrimal
23	Lateral length of the premaxilla; nasointermaxillare–prosthion
26	Length from the oral border of the alveolus of P1–aboral border of the alveolus of I3
29	Length of the premolar row; measured along the alveoli on the buccal side
38	Greatest breadth of the squamous part of the occipital bone
40	Least breadth of the parietal-least breadth between the temporal lines
41	Greatest frontal breadth-greatest breadth across the supraorbital processes; ectorbitale–ectorbitale
43	Zygomatic breadth = greatest breadth of skull; zygion–zygion
44	Greatest palatal breadth; measured across the outer borders of the alveoli
45	Height of the occipital region; basion–acrocranion

Mandible

1	Length from the angle: gonion caudale–infradentale
2	Length from the condyle: aboral border of the condyle process–infradentale
5	Length: gonion caudale–oral border of the alveolus of P_2
7a	Length of the cheek tooth row, M_3–P_2; measured along the alveoli on the buccal side
9	Length of the premolar row, P_1–P_4; measured along the alveoli on the buccal side
9a	Length of the premolar row, P_2–P_4; measured along the alveoli on the buccal side
11	Length; oral border of the alveolus of P_2–aboral border of the alveolus of I_3
12	Length of the median section of the body of mandible; from the mental prominence–infradentale
13	Aboral height of the vertical ramus; gonion ventrale–highest point of the condyle process
15	Oral height of the vertical ramus; gonion ventrale–coronion
16b	Height of the mandible in front of M_1; measured at right angles to the basal border
17	Breadth of the two halves across the alveoli of the canine teeth
19	Breadth of the two halves between the condyle processes; measured between the most lateral points of the two condyle processes

absence of postcranial body parts, can be used to estimate phenotypic differences. Our findings indicate that despite the different ecological zones inhabited, there were few statistically significant differences among the populations in the shape of the cranium or mandible. The closest resemblances were found between the Golan and Sdom populations on the one hand, and the Upper Galilee and Hula populations on the other. The latter may be due to migration of some boar from the Hula swamp to Upper Galilee after the draining of the Hula swamps in the 1950s (Canaani 1976/1977). However, this factor does not account for the similarity between the Sdom and Golan populations, which are both geographically and climatically the most distinct.

Our data do not support the hypothesis of a latitudinal gradient in body size (Bergmann's law) between the northern and southern wild boar populations. This may be attributed to the fact that they all represent relict populations derived from a much larger shared genetic pool. This explanation is less applicable to the wild pig populations from Upper Galilee and Hula, which appear to have shared a common gene pool since the migration of animals from the Hula in the 1950s. The population similarity evident in the two most distinct groups (Golan and Sdom) is most probably associated with their greater degree of isolation as well as marginal environmental conditions in their habitats. Both Sdom and Golan wild boar inhabit zones that experience higher annual average temperatures than Upper Galilee and Hula, as well as being relatively poor in water and vegetation.

CONCLUSION

The current study suggests that a combination of factors may account for size and shape variation in Israeli wild boars: geographic isolation (Davidowitz & Horwitz 1992), diet (Mendelssohn *et al.* 1990), and climate. A similar conclusion was reached by Endo *et al.* (2002) to account for variation in mandible shape and size of wild boar from Taiwan and Japan.

13

A dental microwear study of pig diet and management in Iron Age, Romano-British, Anglo-Scandinavian, and medieval contexts in England

Tom Wilkie, Ingrid Mainland, Umberto Albarella,
Keith Dobney & Peter Rowley-Conwy

INTRODUCTION

Insight into the diet of domestic animals in the archaeological record can elucidate diverse activities pertaining to ancient agricultural systems, including the utilization of the landscape by livestock and their herders (Bocherens *et al.* 2001; Bentley *et al.* 2003; Charles & Bogaard 2005), the impact of livestock farming on the environment (Amorosi *et al.* 1998; Witt *et al.* 2000; Mainland 2001), seasonality in husbandry practices (Akeret *et al.* 1999; Akeret & Rentzel 2001; Charles & Bogaard 2005), animal productivity (Amorosi *et al.* 1998) and the role of animals in society (Moens & Wetterstom 1988; Mainland & Halstead 2004). Research into the diet of domestic livestock has, however, largely focused on cattle, sheep, and goats (see for example all the references cited above) and it is only relatively recently that palaeodietary studies have begun to consider suid diet/nutrition and its potential value for elucidating the socio-economics of pig husbandry (e.g. Ervynck *et al.* this volume). This article presents one further such study: an analysis of dental microwear patterning in domestic pigs from selected Late Iron Age to medieval contexts in England, undertaken as part of a wider project into the potential application of dental microwear analysis to the question of pig diet and management in the prehistoric and historic past (Mainland *et al.* in prep.).

Dental microwear analysis, although still primarily used within palaeontology (Teaford 1994; Rose & Ungar 1998), is increasingly being applied in archaeology to reconstruct both human (Rose & Ungar 1998; Schmidt 2001) and animal diet (Beuls *et al.* 2000; Mainland & Halstead 2004). In common with many other palaeodietary techniques (e.g. Schwarcz & Schoeninger 1991), dental microwear will not identify the consumption of individual foodstuffs but rather reflects broad functional and/or dietary adaptations (Rose & Ungar 1998); for example, browsing vs grazing (Solounias & Hayek 1993), folivory vs frugivory (Teaford & Walker 1984), hard vs soft diet (Teaford & Oyen 1989). Preliminary studies in modern suid populations have indicated that one basic axis of variation in pig diet/management is potentially identifiable using dental microwear, namely the separation of indoor-reared/stall-fed and outdoor reared/rooting populations (Ward & Mainland 1999). Pigs reared outdoors and which are able to root within the soil for food are associated with striated enamel surfaces, a consequence of the ingestion of abrasive grit particles in soil; indoor-reared pigs, in contrast, have fewer striations, reflecting an absence of exogenous abrasive grit particles in the diet. Similar trends are noted in some rooting and non-rooting primates (Ungar & Teaford 1996; cf. Daegling & Grine 1999). This distinction is of interest, as very little is currently known about the organization and articulation within the landscape of pig husbandry in prehistory. In Europe, for example, extensive outdoor systems of pig husbandry, traditionally associated with woodland, are well documented in the recent past and historically (Trow-Smith 1957; Clutton-Brock 1981; Grigson 1982; Albarella *et al.* this volume), but, although such practices are widely assumed to have been important during earlier periods, there is little direct evidence for them in prehistoric contexts (Clutton-Brock 1981; Grigson 1982). Similarly, stall-fed pigs are known in the historical record for the Roman (White 1970) and medieval periods (Trow-Smith 1957) but archaeological evidence is once again sparse (Grigson 1982).

The primary aim of the research presented in this chapter is to assess the archaeological potential of Ward & Mainland's (1999) observations through the analysis of selected pig assemblages for which a range of management strategies were anticipated on contextual and historical grounds. Three archaeological sites were considered: Elms Farm, a semi-rural Late Iron Age/ Romano-British settlement in Essex (Johnstone & Albarella 2002) and two urban sites, both in York: 6–22 Coppergate (Anglo-Scandinavian) (O'Connor 1989) and 46–54 Fishergate (medieval) (O'Connor 1991). At Elms Farm, where livestock can assumed to have been produced locally (Johnstone & Albarella 2002: 31), pig husbandry was considered more likely to involve extensive outdoor systems, probably woodland pannage (see, e.g. Dobney & Ervynck 2000), whereas the Anglo-Scandinavian and medieval urban material might plausibly reflect stall-fed animals (e.g. O'Connor 1989: 183) or, perhaps even free-ranging urban pigs (e.g. Dyer 1998; Rixson 2000; Wiseman 2000).

MATERIAL AND METHODS

Material

A total of 32 mandibles were selected for study from the three archaeological sites considered; 10 of these were subsequently excluded because of damaged enamel surfaces or adhering dirt which could not be removed (Table 13.1). Inclusion was initially determined on contextual grounds, with sampling aiming for as small a chronological span as was feasible for each site. A further factor governing inclusion was the presence of a specific enamel wear facet in the mandibular M_2 (see below) which restricted analysis to individuals exhibiting Grant's (1982) wear stages a–e.

Coppergate is a well stratified urban site with evidence of occupation from the 1st to the 16th centuries AD (O'Connor 1989). The mandibles analysed ($n = 9$) date from the mid 9th to late 11th centuries AD and derive from organic-rich deposits associated with the tenement-like structures identified on the site (O'Connor 1989) (Table 13.1). The mandibles ($n = 5$) examined from Fishergate span the 13th to the 16th centuries AD (phase 6) and are associated with the occupation of the Gilbertine priory of St Andrew (O'Connor 1991; Kemp & Graves 1996). At Elms Farm, analysis was restricted to deposits dated to the Late Iron Age/Romano-British transition (mid 1st century BC to mid 1st century AD, $n = 5$) and to the Middle–Late Roman period (mid 2nd century to mid 4th century AD, $n = 3$) (Table 13.1). During these periods, the site was a sizable semi-rural settlement which has been tentatively interpreted as a small town (Atkinson & Preston 1998).

Methods

Analysis focused on facet 9 of the hypoconid (bucco-posterior cusp) in the mandibular M_2 (Fig. 13.1). This area of enamel, which represents a crushing facet, is widely employed for microwear research (Teaford 1994) and was used in this project to allow comparison with microwear trends in other species, in particular primates (Mainland *et al.* in prep). The lingual area of the facet was examined and was aligned parallel with the top of the scanning electron

Table 13.1. Tooth wear stage (after Grant 1982), enamel surface condition, and sex for the pig mandibular assemblages considered in this study.

Microwear reference number	Site	Context	Surface Damaged or Dirty?	Sex	Wear stage
1	Coppergate	8290	No	–	c
2	Coppergate	30352	Yes	–	c
3	Coppergate	29263	No	–	b/c
4	Coppergate	21925	Yes	F	c
5	Coppergate	13716	No	M	d
6	Coppergate	29263	No	–	b/c
7	Coppergate	19739	No	–	c/d
8	Coppergate	14184	No	–	c/d
9	Coppergate	8290	No	F	c/d
10	Coppergate	8290	No	M	c
11	Coppergate	30352	Yes	F	d
12	Coppergate	21925	Yes	–	a/b
13	Coppergate	14184	No	–	c/d
29	Elms Farm	13093	No	–	c/d
30	Elms Farm	4511	No	M	d
31	Elms Farm	6910	No	–	c
32	Elms Farm	6676	No	–	b/c
33	Elms Farm	5536	Yes	–	b/c
34	Elms Farm	5214	No	–	d/e
35	Elms Farm	20034	No	–	c/d
36	Elms Farm	11742	No	–	d/e
37	Elms Farm	4699	No	M	c
38	Elms Farm	4288	Yes	M	d/e
39	Fishergate	7035	Yes	F	d
40	Fishergate	10124	Yes	–	c/c
41	Fishergate	10130	No	–	c
42	Fishergate	3187	No	–	c
43	Fishergate	3240	Yes	–	d/e
44	Fishergate	3352	No	–	d
45	Fishergate	4234	No	–	c/d
46	Fishergate	2938	Yes	–	b
47	Fishergate	2507	No	F	c
48	Fishergate	5510	No	–	c
49	Fishergate	2162	Yes	–	b
50	Fishergate	4253	No	–	c
51	Fishergate	10004	Yes	–	b
52	Fishergate	10004	No	–	c
53	Fishergate	52731	Yes	–	–

microscope (SEM) screen to facilitate analysis of feature orientation. Standard microwear approaches were used to record and analyse microwear patterning: a single image of the enamel surface was captured at a magnification of 500× using a SEM and was recorded for microwear feature frequencies and

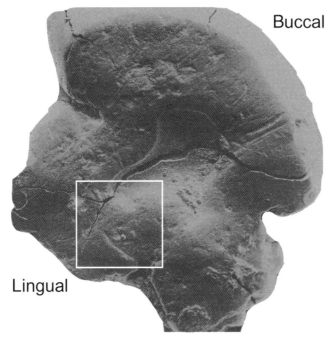

Fig. 13.1. A bucco-posterior cusp of a mandibular M_2 to illustrate sampling location (facet 9)

dimensions using Ungar's (1995) image analysis software for microwear analysis. Variables recorded were feature density, the ratio of pits to striations (expressed as a percentage of pits present out of all features), striation orientation, and the length and breath of striations and of pits. As is usual in microwear studies, features were classified into striations and pits using a length/breath ratio of 4:1. Pits are defined as features with a length/breath ratio of $<4:1$, striations those with a length/breath ratio of $> = 4:1$ (Teaford 1994). For the archaeological material, between group differences were assessed using descriptive statistics and the statistical significance of any differences identified using Mann–Whitney and ANOVA (Norušis 1990).

Modelling diet–microwear trends in suids

In dental microwear analysis, dietary reconstruction is reliant on analogy with known diet in modern populations (Mainland 2003*a*). Other than the pilot study undertaken on stall-fed and rooting pigs by Ward & Mainland (1999), very little work has been published on diet–microwear relationships in modern suids. Samples of modern free-ranging wild boar from the forests of north-east Germany ($n = 13$), forest-reared domestic pigs from Inverness ($n = 2$), and farm-reared wild boar kept in paddocks in Yorkshire and Northumberland ($n = 10$) were thus analysed to provide a modern comparative framework for the project. These include some of the rooting wild boar kept in paddocks examined in Ward & Mainland's (1999) original study ($n = 3$), but it was not possible to use their stall-fed individuals as the M_2 had not yet erupted in this group (see Mainland *et al.* in prep., for more detailed discussion of these populations and of microwear trends in modern suids). As the known-diet sample is small and limited in dietary breadth, interpretation was also based on trends documented in other species, specifically the various primate species studied by Teaford and co-researchers (Teaford 1994; Daegling & Grine 1999). Although there are differences in masticatory mechanics between suids and primates which are likely to have some impact on the kinds of microwear patterning evident in each species, there is enough consistency in microwear patterning across the mammalian orders (some with radically different dental/mandibular mechanisms) to allow some confidence in the use of general diet–microwear trends in this way: for example, grazing primates and grazing ruminants both exhibit a high frequency of striated features (Teaford 1994; Daegling & Grine 1999; Solounias *et al.* 2000; Mainland 2003*a*); soft-object feeding is associated with smaller pitted features in ruminants, primates, and chiroptera (Teaford & Oyen 1989; Strait 1993; Mainland 2003*b*).

RESULTS AND DISCUSSION

Pits are the dominant microwear feature identified in the pigs examined from Coppergate, Fishergate, and Elms Farm, with a mean relative frequency of pits in excess of 60% evident at each site (Table 13.2 and Figs 13.2–13.4). Despite this overall similarity, significant inter-site variation in microwear patterning was identified (Table 13.2). Pigs from Coppergate have a significantly higher relative frequency of pits, and microwear features at Fishergate tend to be larger than those at the other two sites—though significant differences are only recorded for striation breadth (Table 13.2).

To help interpret these trends, the Coppergate, Elms Farm, and Fishergate pigs were compared with modern forest-reared and paddocked pigs (Mainland *et al.* in prep.), and with modern folivorous, frugivorous (hard-object eating), grazing, and hypogeous (rooting) primates (Teaford 1994; Daegling & Grine 1999) (Table 13.3). Analysis focused on two variables, pit relative frequency and pit breadth, as these have been shown to be diagnostic of broad

Table 13.2. Summary table for pig microwear statistics from Coppergate, Elm's Farm, and Fishergate. *indicates significant differences between Coppergate and Fishergate (Mann–Whitney, $p < 0.05$); $\pm$ indicates significant differences between Coppergate and Elm's Farm (MannWhitney, $p < 0.05$); † indicates significant differences between Fishergate and Elm's Farm (Mann–Whitney, $p < 0.05$).

Variable	Site	n	Mean (um)	Standar. deviation	Minimum (um)	Maximum (um)
Pit length*	Coppergate	9	6.89	1.33	4.89	8.91
	Elm's Farm	8	7.24	2.01	5.29	11.37
	Fishergate	5	9.78	3.02	5.85	13.64
Pit breadth†	Coppergate	9	4.24	0.73	3.30	5.37
	Elm's Farm	8	3.89	1.06	2.31	6.03
	Fishergate	5	5.55	1.56	3.42	7.21
Striation length	Coppergate	9	23.53	8.79	9.28	32.00
	Elm's Farm	8	26.56	5.37	19.70	33.58
	Fishergate	5	30.52	4.94	25.81	37.49
Striation breadth†	Coppergate	9	3.06	0.79	1.83	4.07
	Elm's Farm	8	2.46	0.41	1.74	2.89
	Fishergate	5	3.86	1.19	2.44	5.30
% Pits* $\pm$	Coppergate	9	85.83	8.67	73.81	97.98
	Elm's Farm	8	60.82	14.79	35.48	77.37
	Fishergate	5	71.97	8.07	58.56	79.25
Defect frequency	Coppergate	9	94.55	24.60	58.00	137.00
	Elm's Farm	8	101.00	27.56	49.00	137.00
	Fishergate	5	90.60	18.94	64.00	111.00
Striation orientation*†	Coppergate	9	69.14	32.39	25.78	129.03
	Elm's Farm	8	68.24	26.09	36.42	101.94
	Fishergate	5	95.48	25.25	55.35	121.15

dietary adaptations in primates. Moreover, Ward & Mainland (1999) have argued for a relationship between pit frequency and level of rooting in suids. Folivorous and grazing primates are associated with few pits and smaller features; frugivores with a higher frequency of pits and with large features (Teaford 1994; Daegling & Grine 1999). These trends are attributed to the greater force required to comminute hard objects such as nuts in a frugivorous diet and to the consumption of fine abrasives such as opal phytoliths or exogenous dust particles for folivores/grazers (Teaford 1994; Rose & Ungar 1998; Daegling & Grine 1999). Teaford & Oyen (1989) have also suggested that a prevalence of small pits will reflect a soft-textured diet; here, microwear will form through an adhesion effect, with high levels of tooth–tooth contact effectively 'plucking' prisms from the enamel surface to create small pitted features. Primates, such as the Chacma baboon (*Papio ursinus*), which 'root' for food within soil exhibit wear comparable with hard-object feeders (Table 13.3), a pattern interpreted by Daegling & Grine (1999) as reflecting the

Fig. 13.2. A representative image of the microwear evident in the Coppergate pigs (top = lingual)

ingestion of mineral particles from soil along with food. In suids, variation in pit frequency seems also to reflect the level of exogenous grit ingested, though here rooting pigs are associated with a high frequency of striations and with smaller microwear features (Table 13.3) (Ward & Mainland 1999; Mainland *et al.* in prep). This apparent contradiction may reflect differences between primates and suids in masticatory mechanisms, rooting/foraging behaviours, or the kinds of abrasive encountered (Mainland *et al.* in prep.). An association between striations and mineral particles derived from dust, soil, etc. incidentally ingested along with food has, however, also been suggested for other primate species, including humans, as well as for various non-primates (Teaford & Lytle 1996; Ungar & Teaford 1996; Teaford *et al.* 2001; Silcox & Teaford 2002; Mainland 2003*b*).

Microwear in the three archaeological sites is clearly different from that evident in the modern pigs studied, both in terms of the relative frequency of pitted features and the overall size of pits represented, with more and slightly larger features indicated for the archaeological material (Figs 13.5 and 13.6; Table 13.3). A one-way ANOVA contrasting each of the individual archaeological sites and the modern pigs combined demonstrates a significant effect

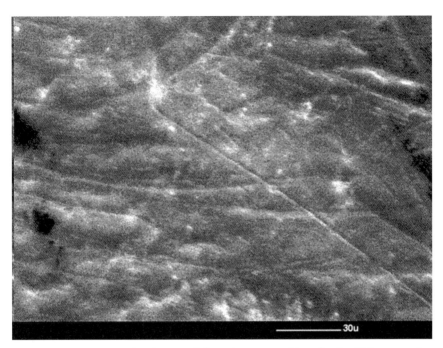

Fig. 13.3. A representative image of the microwear evident in the Fishergate pigs (top = lingual)

for both pit breadth and pit percentage ($p < 0.05$). Post-hoc tests indicate that this can be attributed to a significantly higher mean relative frequency (%) of pits for each archaeological site than in the combined modern pig populations, and to larger mean pit breadth in the Fishergate pigs (Scheffé post-hoc test, $p < 0.05$). All the modern pigs studied are derived from populations that are able to root for food, either in a 'natural' forest environment or in enclosed paddocks. The difference evident between the modern and archaeological samples, together with the overall emphasis on pits in the latter, which implies a diet lacking in abrasives such as exogenous grit or phytoliths, is thus considered indicative of husbandry practices whereby pigs had limited access to rooting or, perhaps, to phytolith-rich vegetation (though see Mainland 2003*b* for a critique of the role of phytoliths in microwear formation) in the period immediately before death, as microwear will reflect a short period, *c.*1–3 weeks before death. The prevalence of pits with an average breath of 3.89 and 4.24 *u*m at Coppergate and Elms Farms, respectively, which is roughly equivalent to prism diameter in pigs (*c.*4–5 *u*m) (Boyde 1969), is consistent with a soft-textured diet (Teaford & Oyen 1989). The tendency towards larger features at Fishergate may indicate the inclusion of larger abrasives in the diet

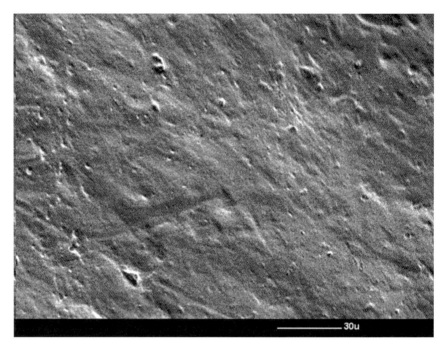

Fig. 13.4. A representative image of the microwear evident in the Elm's Farm pigs (top = lingual)

or of harder food items requiring greater occlusal force during comminution (Teaford 1994; Teaford & Oyen 1998; Daegling & Grine 1999). Nevertheless, as average pit breadth at Fishergate (5.5 *u*m) falls close to the size range for prism diameters in pigs, a soft-textured diet is again likely at this site.

CONCLUSIONS

Microwear patterns imply that pigs at Coppergate, Fishergate, and Elms Farm were fed on a soft-textured diet and had limited access to soil for rooting in the weeks immediately before slaughter. The patterning identified is consistent with stall-feeding on hard floors (Ward & Mainland 1999), though outdoor rearing on a high plane of nutrition cannot entirely be ruled out: Bolton (1954), for example, indicates that if grass in paddocks is kept short (and hence nutritious), outdoor-reared pigs tend not to root. Either way, the microwear evidence indicates a supplementation and/or careful control of pig diet at the three sites studied and is clearly not compatible with enclosed

Table 13.3. Selected microwear statistics for modern primates (after Daegling & Grine 1999) and suids.

Species	Diet/habitat	n	% pits	% pits sd	pb	pb sd
Cerocebus albigena	Frugivore	10	55.2	12.4	9.9	3.20
Cebus apella	Frugivore	10	45.1	16.2	8.4	1.50
Pongo pygmaeus	Frugivore	10	42.5	19.1	7.1	1.70
Frugivore mean	Frugivore	30	47.6	–	8.47	–
Papio ursinus	Rooting	10	43.3	11.6	10.72	4.13
Pan troglodytes	Mixed	10	24.2	14.2	6.9	2.60
Cebus nigrivattus	Mixed	10	16.2	8.6	8.6	1.80
Piliocolobus badius	Mixed	10	12.6	14	6.1	2.80
Cebus capucinus	Mixed	10	11.7	5.1	5.1	1.70
Mixed feeder mean	Mixed	40	16.18	–	6.68	–
Colobus guereza	Folivore	10	9.7	4.3	5.6	2.50
Aloutatta palliata	Folivore	10	9.7	18.6	9.2	6.60
Gorilla gorilla	Folivore	10	3.4	4	6	4.10
Folivore mean	Folivore	30	7.6	–	6.93	–
Theropithecus gelada	Grazer	n.s.	8.8	?	4.2	?
Sus domesticus	Forest Inverness	2	36.09	2.28	2.46	0.04
Sus scrofa	Forest Germany	11	18.31	15.35	3.56	2.21
Sus scrofa f. *domestica*	Rooting (paddock)	10	22.03	12.56	3.34	1.61

Abbreviations: n, sample size; %pits, mean relative frequency of pits (%) per group; pb, mean pit breadth per group; sd, standard deviation.

rooting pigs or with free-ranging forest-reared populations. O'Connor (1989) has suggested from the presence of fetal and neonatal pig bones that this species may have been kept in and around the tenement structures identified at Coppergate, and notes that 'for farrowing or fattening, the areas behind the Coppergate houses would have been amply spacious [for sows and their litters], with post and wattle fencing and hurdling being ideal for the construction of temporary pens as and where necessary' (O'Connor 1989: 183). The Fishergate individuals indicate that stall-fed pigs were also present at the priory of St Andrews in York during the medieval period. These may have derived from herds belonging to the priory as this establishment owned estates in York's hinterland (Kemp & Graves 1996: 57–60) and also had a small acreage of land in the priory precinct which seems to have been used for cultivation or other agricultural uses (Kemp & Graves 1996: 119). The rearing of pigs, including cereal-fed individuals, at medieval monastic establishments is attested historically (Harvey 1993: 52; Ayers *et al.* 2003). Unfortunately, because of its small size, the faunal assemblage from medieval Fishergate provides little additional evidence for specific patterns of pork consumption or of pig husbandry methods at the Gilbertine priory of St Andrews (O'Connor 1991; Bond & O'Connor 1999). The overall similarity between this

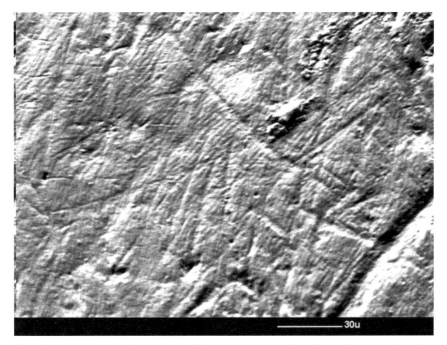

Fig. 13.5. A representative image of the microwear evident in modern rooting pigs (top = lingual)

faunal assemblage and those found elsewhere in the medieval city, however, has suggested to O'Connor (1991: 285; Bond & O'Connor 1999: 417) that the priory may have been using the city's markets for purchasing food. If so, microwear trends in the Fishergate pigs could provide some evidence for a more organized system of pig husbandry in which stall-fed pigs were reared specifically to supply the urban markets in medieval York. It would be unwise, however, to construct a market in stall-fed pigs from microwear patterns in five individuals at one (rather specialized) site; clearly further research on larger samples drawn from diverse contexts across York is required here to help elucidate pig husbandry and pork production in the medieval city.

The presence of stall-fed animals at Elms Farm was more unexpected, as extensively reared pigs had been anticipated for this site, given its mixed rural/urban status. In historic periods, however, the use of woodland pasture for pig herding was often seasonal, timed to coincide with the mast in autumn and early winter (Trow-Smith 1957; Harvey 1984; Campbell 2000). Outwith these periods, where it was more difficult to obtain adequate nutrition for pig herds in the forests, it is apparent that at least some populations were stall-fed

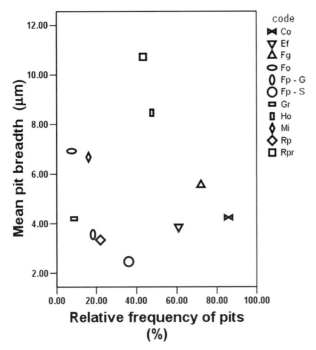

Fig. 13.6. A comparison of mean pit breadth and pit relative frequency in modern and archaeological suids and modern primates (see Table 13.3 for data values). Abbreviations: Rpr, rooting primates; Rp, rooting pigs; Mi, mixed feeder primates; Ho, frugivorous ('hard-object') primates; Gr, grazing primates; Fp-Inv, Inverness forest pigs; Fp-Gs, German forest pigs; Fo, folivorous primates; Fg, Fishergate; Ef, Elm's Farm; Co, Coppergate

around settlement sites (Trow-Smith 1957; Kelly F. 2000; Dyer 2003). If it can be assumed that husbandry practices in the Middle Ages will be reasonably representative of those in the Late Iron Age and Roman periods, two potential hypotheses can be stated for the microwear pattern at Elms Farm: (1) a large proportion of pigs were slaughtered outside the autumn/early winter season when most rooting would occur; (2) the Elms Farm pigs were not regularly subject to free-range pasture in the forest. The relatively small pig assemblage (see Johnstone & Albarella 2002) prevents a detailed analysis of seasonal kill-off patterns, difficult even in the best circumstances, based on ageing evidence. It is, however, unlikely that most slaughtering occurred in spring and summer, as these would be relatively mean periods for pig feeding, and therefore, the animals would have a tendency to loose weight. Ethnographic (Albarella *et al.* this volume) and historical (Harvey 1988) evidence indicates that the best slaughter season for pigs fattened in the forest is the winter, just before food resources (beech mast, chestnuts, acorns, etc) become scarce. It is, therefore, more likely that the microwear evidence reflects the semi-urban and nucleated nature of this site. Johnstone & Albarella (2002) have noted butchery patterns indicative of a specialist, organized processing of cattle carcasses which is more commonly associated with urban contexts in Roman Britain. This may indicate animal husbandry geared towards production for a 'market' or wider redistribution rather than subsistence farming. Perhaps this included fattened, stall-fed pigs.

Analysis of microwear patterns in domestic pigs from Coppergate, Elms Farm, and Fishergate has indicated the presence of stall-fed animals in semi-urban and urban contexts spanning the Late Iron Age/Romano-British to medieval periods and, moreover, has raised interesting questions with regards the economic focus of pig-rearing at Elms Farm and the supply of pork within medieval York. This first application of dental microwear analysis to archaeological pig assemblages thus clearly demonstrates that the technique is applicable within archaeology and that it has considerable potential for understanding pig husbandry and management in the (pre)historic past. To more fully explore the socio-economics of pig husbandry in the past using microwear (e.g. identifying evidence for seasonality in diet and management, for livestock fattening, for the 'special' treatment of particular individuals, for chronological change in diet, etc.), future analyses should now target large, well-preserved mandibular assemblages with, where possible, a restricted chronological range (see, e.g. Neolithic Arbon and Makriyalos, Mainland *et al*. in prep.). Further research on modern populations is, however, also critically important to document more fully the range of microwear patterning evident under different dietary regimes (e.g. browse, graze, frugivory, folivory, insectivory) and thus increase the dietary resolution possible.

14

The histopathology of fluorotic dental enamel in wild boar and domestic pigs

Horst Kierdorf & Uwe Kierdorf

INTRODUCTION

Studies into the behavioral ecology of wild boar and domestic pigs are promising, yet largely neglected, areas of archaeozoological research. Changes in both the diet and health of animals may reflect specific details about the possible scale and extent of human impact on hunted wild boar populations and domesticated pigs in the past. Histological and chemical 'signatures' of (for example) physiological stress, brought about by possible human influence, can often be recovered in the dental and skeletal tissues of *Sus*. However, a fuller interpretation of what the significance of these signatures might be can only be achieved if their aetiology is known, and that can only be done by studying these phenomena in modern extant populations.

One of the many aspects of the human–*Sus* relationship is the exposure of wild boar to contaminants from anthropogenic sources. An example of this is the pollution of wild boar habitats by fluoride from power plants and other emission sources, leading to the occurrence of characteristic dental changes, known as *dental fluorosis*, in the affected individuals of *Sus scrofa* (Fig. 14.1) (Kierdorf *et al.* 2000). However, dental fluorosis also occurs in wild and domestic mammals (and in humans) living in areas with increased environmental levels of fluoride from natural sources (Shupe *et al.* 1983; Cronin *et al.* 2000, 2003; Garrott *et al.* 2002; WHO 2002).

The macroscopic changes of dental fluorosis reflect a disturbance of the processes involved in enamel formation. Once the permanent dentition of an individual is fully formed, exposure to excess levels of fluoride will not lead to fluorotic enamel changes. Dental fluorosis can therefore be used as a highly sensitive indicator of excess fluoride exposure during the period of tooth formation in humans and other mammals (Fejerskov *et al.* 1988; DenBesten 1994; Boulton *et al.* 1999; Kierdorf & Kierdorf 1999; Kierdorf *et al.* 1999).

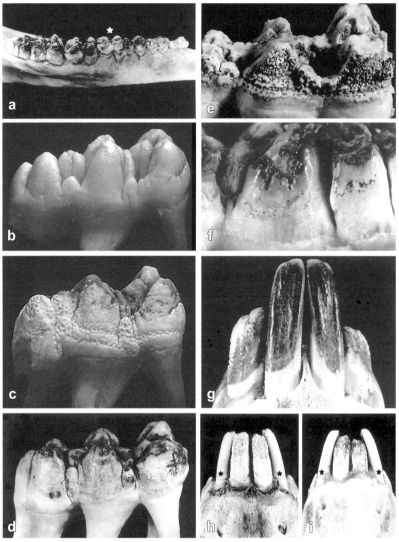

Fig. 14.1. Macroscopic views of fluorotic and non-fluorotic (b) teeth of wild boar and domestic pigs. (a) left P_2 to M_3 of fluorotic wild boar dentition, occluso-lingual view. Pronounced enamel opacity and discoloration in all teeth, with the M_1 (asterisk) being least affected. Note abnormal attrition of M_2 and hypoplastic defects of enamel in M_3; (b) non-fluorotic, right M_3 of a miniature pig with normal lustrous enamel, buccal view; (c) fluorotic right M_3 of a miniature pig showing enamel opacity and discoloration as well as pit-type enamel hypoplasia, buccal view; (d) fluorotic right M_3 of a wild boar showing enamel opacity and discoloration as well as an accentuation of the perikymatic pattern and enamel defects, buccal view; (e) fluorotic right M_3 of a wild boar showing severe pit-type enamel hypoplasia and increased wear, buccal view; (f) fluorotic right M_3 of a wild boar showing enamel staining and defects as well as an accentuated perikymatic pattern, lingual view; (g) I_1 and I_2 (partly erupted) of a fluorotic wild boar dentition. Blackish enamel staining and accentuation of the perikymatic pattern in I_1, and hypoplastic defects of enamel in I_2, labial view (h, i) fluorotic I_1 (partly erupted) of two wild boar showing severe enamel hypoplasia, whereas the enamel of the dI_2 (asterisks) is of a normal appearance, labial view.

Higher levels of fluoride also exert negative effects on the skeleton throughout the life of an individual, the pathological changes being known as *skeletal fluorosis* (WHO 2002). This crippling disability is a major human health problem in various regions of Africa, China, and the Indian subcontinent, where millions of people are affected (Finkelman *et al.* 1999; WHO 2002). The domestic pig has been sucessfully used as an experimental model for studying dental and skeletal fluorosis (Richards 1982).

This chapter reports the results of our studies on fluoride-induced pathological changes in dental enamel of wild boar from fluoride-polluted regions in central Europe (Kierdorf *et al.* 2000, 2005) and in miniature pigs experimentally exposed to increased levels of fluoride (Kierdorf *et al.* 2004).

STRUCTURE AND DEVELOPMENT OF DENTAL ENAMEL

Dental enamel is the most highly mineralized and, therefore, the hardest tissue of the mammalian body. Mature enamel consists of about 95–97% inorganic constituents by weight, the mineral being an impure hydroxyapatite. Unlike other mineralized tissues of the mammalian body (bone, calcified cartilage, dentine, cementum), dental enamel is a cell-free tissue. It is therefore incapable of repair or remodelling processes, and structural aberrations caused by disturbances during enamel formation remain as a permanent record in the tissue (Fejerskov & Thylstrup 1986; Hillson 1986, 1996; Schroeder 1992).

Dental enamel is formed by highly specialized ectodermal cells, the ameloblasts, which differentiate from the cells of the inner dental epithelium of the developing tooth and form a closely interconnected sheet of cells. Ameloblasts are long, columnar cells with a pronounced polar organization. Enamel formation by these cells can be broadly subdivided into a secretory and a maturation stage. During the secretory stage, a mineralized enamel matrix is formed whose mineral content increases gradually across the secretory stage (Smith 1998). Already during the secretory stage, the proteinaceous enamel matrix is processed and partially degraded by enzymes secreted along with the matrix. However, these processes are strongly intensified during the subsequent maturation stage (Hillson 1986, 1996; Warshawsky 1988; Sasaki *et al.* 1997; Smith 1998).

Each ameloblast possesses a cytoplasmic extension, the Tomes process, the proximal portion of which develops already in the pre-secretory cell and is present during the formation of a first layer of initial enamel that is deposited on the mantle dentine. Corresponding to the single flat secretory surface present in the early secretory ameloblast, the crystallites of the first-formed enamel layer are all oriented in parallel. With increasing secretory activity of the ameloblasts, their Tomes processes elongate and the distal or interdigitating portions of the processes become embedded in the secreted enamel matrix that itself forms a replica of the shape of the Tomes processes. When the layer of fully secretory ameloblasts is removed from the surface of forming enamel, a typical 'honeycomb' pattern becomes visible. This consists of holes, the so-called *Tomes process pits* that were previously occupied by the distal portions of the Tomes processes (Warshawsky *et al.* 1981; Warshawsky 1988; Boyde 1997).

The enamel produced by fully secretory ameloblasts shows a typical microstructure of prisms (rods) and interprismatic (inter-rod) enamel (Fig. 14.2a). The cells possess different secretory surfaces for the formation of enamel prisms (at the distal portion of the Tomes process) and interprismatic enamel (along the proximal portion of the Tomes process). The two secretory areas are arranged at a certain angle to each other and, in consequence, crystallite orientation varies between prisms and interprismatic enamel. Interprismatic enamel is secreted slightly ahead of the enamel prisms and forms the walls of the Tomes process pits. Therefore, each enamel prism is secreted into a pre-formed hole, and the shape and arrangement of the enamel prisms as well as the course followed by the prisms through the enamel layer are determined by the pattern of the interprismatic enamel. The ameloblast requires continuous high secretory activity to maintain this morphology. At the end of the secretory stage, the secretory activity of the ameloblasts gradually diminishes and, in consequence, a thin layer of final enamel is laid down by the ameloblasts whose distal Tomes processes have regressed and that possess a single, more or less flat secretory surface. Final enamel, like initial enamel, therefore lacks a prismatic structure but instead consists of crystallites that are all, oriented perpendicular to the enamel surface (Warshawsky *et al.* 1981; Warshawsky 1988; Sasaki *et al.* 1997).

The formation of enamel by ameloblasts is incremental, as reflected by the occurrence of incremental structures such as prism cross-striations and Retzius lines. Prism cross-striations are likely to be caused by a cyclical (circadian) variation in the rate of enamel matrix secretion, with the bulges representing periods of higher and the prism constrictions periods of lower secretory activity (Hillson 1996). Retzius lines mark a discontinuity in normal enamel microstructure. Where Retzius lines outcrop on to the enamel surface, *perikymata* are present at the enamel surface. Risnes (1990, 1998) observed discontinuities in enamel prisms and interprismatic enamel as well as periodic prism constrictions along staircase-type lines of Retzius. The prism constrictions were regarded as indicative of a physiologic periodic reduction in the diameter of the distal, prism-forming portion of the Tomes processes,

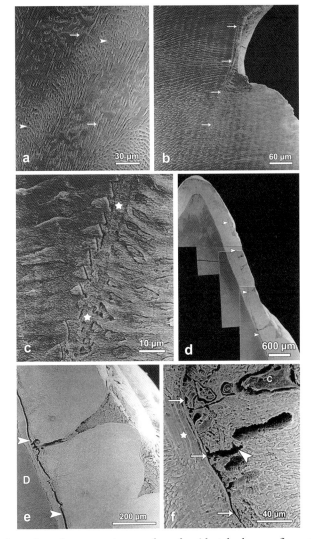

Fig. 14.2. Scanning electron micrographs of acid-etched, non-fluorotic (a) and fluorotic (b–f) enamel of wild boar and domestic pigs; the teeth were longitudinally sectioned in a bucco-lingual plane. (a) Sound enamel of a miniature pig M_3 showing normal enamel structure with prisms (arrows) and interprismatic enamel (arrowheads). (b) Fluorotic enamel of a miniature pig M_3. Note enhanced incremental line (arrows) underlying the base of a hypoplastic defect. (c) Discontinuity of enamel prisms and interprismatic enamel along the course of the enhanced incremental line indicated by arrows in b; asterisks indicate a zone of aprismatic enamel external to the enhanced incremental line. (d) Fluorotic P_2 of a wild boar showing an extended hypoplastic defect in its cuspal enamel as well as several pit-type hypoplastic defects that originate along a grossly accentuated incremental line (arrowheads). (e) Higher magnification of the hypoplastic enamel shown in d. A pit-type enamel defect (filled with mineralized deposits) originates at the incremental line that appears cleft-like (arrowheads). D: dentine. (f) Same specimen as e, internal hypoplastic defects of enamel (arrowhead) originate at the grossly enhanced incremental line (arrows). C: plug of cementum within a hypoplastic defect; asterisk indicates a zone of largely aprismatic enamel internal to the incremental line

reflecting a diminished rate of matrix secretion. The physiological causes underlying the formation of the Retzius lines, which in humans normally show a circaseptan periodicity, are not clear.

When the full thickness of enamel is attained at a certain location of the forming tooth crown, the ameloblasts proceed to the *post-secretory transition*, during which the cells perform a morphological and functional reorganization (Smith 1998). About 25% of the ameloblasts entering this transition process undergo cell death (*apoptosis*); the remainder progress to the maturation stage. During the maturation stage the enamel matrix is selectively degraded, matrix components and water are withdrawn from the tissue, and the mineral content of the tissue increases in steps by way of crystallite growth. Two morphologically distinct types of ameloblasts are present during the maturation stage: ruffle-ended and smooth-ended ameloblasts. There is evidence for a cyclic modulation of the individual ameloblast during enamel maturation—a repeated shift between the ruffle-ended and the smooth-ended morphology (Josephsen & Fejerskov 1977; Warshawsky 1988; Smith 1998).

STRUCTURAL ABERRATIONS OF FLUOROTIC DENTAL ENAMEL OF WILD BOAR AND DOMESTIC PIGS

Porcine fluorotic enamel shows a broad spectrum of structural aberrations (Kierdorf *et al.* 2000, 2004, 2005). Based on an understanding of the normal course of amelogenesis, these aberrations can be related to fluoride disturbance of the different processes involved in enamel formation. In what follows, we first describe the macroscopic alterations of fluorotic teeth of wild boar and domestic pigs. Then the histopathological changes ascribed to fluoride effects on the secretory and maturation stages of amelogenesis are presented, and finally the formation of coronal cementum in fluorotic teeth of wild boar will be discussed.

Macroscopic characteristics of fluorotic teeth in pigs

Normal, mature enamel is semitransparent and lustrous in appearance (Fig. 14.1b). In contrast, fluorotic teeth of wild boar and domestic pigs have dull and opaque enamel that often appears chalky (Fig. 14.1a, c, d). This condition of the enamel is already present on eruption of the teeth, which is evidence that it is of a developmental origin. Fluorotic teeth of wild boar and domestic pigs are furthermore characterized by a brownish to blackish staining of their enamel (Fig. 14.1a, d, f, g). This staining only develops, however, after the teeth have erupted into the oral cavity, thereby indicating that it is not a developmental phenomenon but occurs secondarily when the porous fluorotic enamel is exposed to the oral environment (Kierdorf *et al.* 2000, 2004). A further characteristic of the fluorotic teeth is their increased wear compared to normal teeth (Fig. 14.1a, e, f). The histopathological condition underlying the aforementioned alterations is a hypomineralization of the enamel (see below). As the degree of tooth wear is a function of time, the increased attrition of fluorotic teeth becomes progressively evident with advancing age of the animal. An additional prominent feature of fluorotic teeth of wild boar and domestic pigs is the presence of defects in the enamel surface. These defects vary considerably in size and shape, reaching from small, narrow pits to extended areas of missing enamel (Fig. 14.1c, e–i) (Kierdorf *et al.* 2000, 2004).

Enamel changes due to a disturbance of the secretory stage of amelogenesis

A typical feature of porcine fluorotic enamel, which can be visualized both by light microscopy and by scanning electron microscopy (SEM), is an accentuation of the incremental pattern in the tissue (Fig. 14.3a–c). In consequence, an enhancement of the perikymatic pattern is seen in the crowns of fluorotic teeth (Fig. 14.1d, f, g). The presence of incremental lines in the enamel reflects the rhythmic activity of the secretory ameloblasts. Apparently, increased exposure of the cells to fluoride leads to a pathological intensification of this rhythmic process. Often, individual, grossly accentuated incremental lines are present in fluorotic enamel (Figs 14.2b–f and 14.4). On microradiographs, these structures appear as broad lines of markedly reduced mineral content (Fig. 14.5a), and in the SEM they can be visualized as broad, sometimes cleft-like lines, that in the dried, acid-etched specimens appear devoid of enamel (Figs 14.2d–f and 14.4c–d). Frequently, the enamel located directly internal to these grossly accentuated incremental lines shows distinct morphological alterations, in that the normal prism/interprism structure is lost and replaced by a (largely) aprismatic structure (Fig. 14.2f) (Kierdorf *et al.* 2000). The presence of such layers of aprismatic enamel, the thickness of which can be quite variable, indicates a reduction of the distal, prism-forming portions of the Tomes processes of ameloblasts whose secretory activity has been impaired by a severe impact on the cells. The location of the grossly accentuated incremental line thus denotes the position of the surface of the

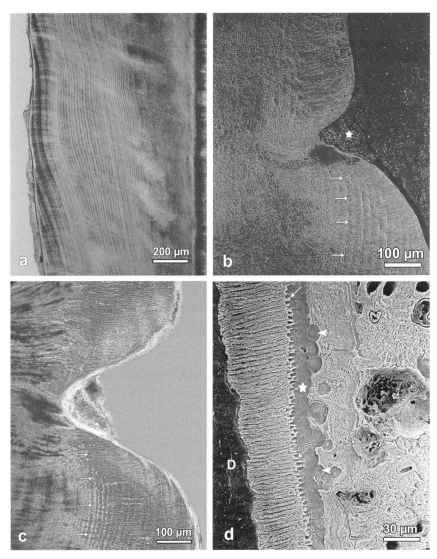

Fig. 14.3. Light and scanning electron micrographs of fluorotic enamel of wild boar (a, c, d) and a miniature pig (b); the teeth were longitudinally sectioned in a labio-lingual (incisors) or bucco-lingual (molars) plane. (a) Accentuated incremental pattern in the lingual enamel of a fluorotic I_1. Ground section; normal, transmitted light. (b) Pit-type hypoplastic defect in the enamel of an M_3 filled with mineralized deposit (asterisk). Note bending of incremental lines (arrows) corresponding to the outline of the pit. SEM; acid-etched specimen. (c) Pit-type hypoplastic defect in the enamel of a fluorotic I_1. Note bending of incremental lines (arrows) corresponding to the outline of the pit. Ground section; phase-contrast microscopy. (d) Densely structured aprismatic enamel (asterisk) intercalated between an inner zone of prismatic enamel and an outer enamel zone with disturbed microstructure. Note projections of interprismatic enamel (arrows) protruding from the prismatic enamel area into the aprismatic enamel and globular structures (arrowheads) located along the border with the outer enamel. Fluorotic I_1, D: dentine. SEM; acid-etched specimen

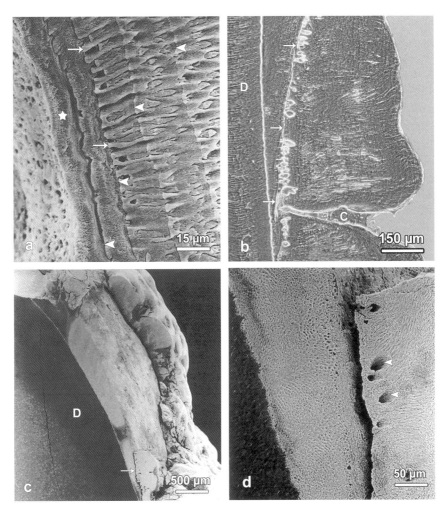

Fig. 14.4. Light and scanning electron micrographs of fluorotic enamel of a miniature pig (a) and wild boar (b–d); the teeth were longitudinally sectioned in a labio-lingual (incisor) or bucco-lingual (molars) plane. (a) Aprismatic (asterisk) and prismatic enamel underneath the base of a pit-type hypoplastic defect in the enamel of an M_3. Note that at the border with the aprismatic enamel, projections of interprismatic enamel (arrows) protrude above the level of the prisms; arrowheads: incremental lines. SEM; acid-etched specimen. (b) Pit-type hypoplastic defect partly filled with cellular cementum (C), in the buccal enamel of an M_2. A grossly accentuated incremental line (arrows) is located internal to this defect. Note numerous internal hypoplastic defects that also originate along this line. D: dentine. Ground section; phase-contrast microscopy. (c) Defect caused by post-eruptive loss of a large area of hypoplastic enamel along a cleft-like incremental line (arrow). D: dentine. SEM; acid-etched specimen. (d) Higher magnification of the cleft indicated by arrow in c. Arrowheads: internal hypoplastic defects. SEM; acid-etched specimen

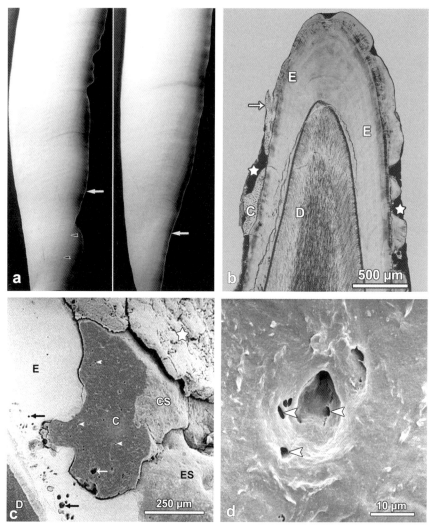

Fig. 14.5. Fluorotic enamel of pigs (a) and wild boar (b–d); the teeth were longitudinally sectioned in a labio-lingual (incisors) or bucco-lingual (molars) plane. (a) Microradiographs of fluorotic enamel of two M_3. Note subsurface hypomineralization beneath a thin outermost rim of higher mineral content (arrows) and presence of multiple accentuated incremental lines. Arrowheads: accentuated incremental line associated with a hypoplastic defect. (b) Presence of coronal cementum (C) covering hypoplastic enamel of a fluorotic I_1. Arrow: partly detached tongue of cementum, asterisks: post-eruptively acquired mineralized deposits, D: dentine, E: enamel. Ground section; normal, transmitted light. (c) Large hypoplastic defect filled with cementum (C) that contains numerous cementocyte lacunae (arrowheads) and larger cavities (white arrow) presumably representing vascular spaces. Asterisk: post-eruptively acquired mineralized deposits, black arrows: internal hypoplastic defects, CS: cementum surface, D: dentine, E: enamel, ES: enamel surface. Fluorotic I_1. SEM; acid-etched specimen. (d) Higher magnification of a cementocyte lacuna shown in c with openings of canaliculi (arrowheads). SEM; acid-etched specimen

enamel that was forming when the secretory ameloblasts stopped enamel formation, either permanently or temporarily.

The structural changes in the fluorotic enamel described above can be put in an order of increasing severity of secretory ameloblast dysfunction, ranging from an accentuation of the incremental pattern (ameloblasts still possess separate secretory regions for enamel prisms and interprismatic enamel), through a narrowing of the distance between incremental lines (indicating a reduced secretory rate that leads to a moderate reduction of enamel thickness in the affected crown area), or the occurrence of aprismatic enamel (reduction of the distal portion of the Tomes process in ameloblasts with markedly impaired secretory activity), to the presence of the broad, grossly accentuated incremental lines (complete cessation of secretory activity) (Kierdorf *et al.* 2000, 2004).

A conspicuous feature of fluorotic porcine enamel, which is often associated with the occurrence of the grossly accentuated incremental lines, is the presence of hypoplastic defects (Figs. 14.1c, e, g–i; 14.2b–f; 14.3b–c). The term *enamel hypoplasia* is used with slightly different meanings in the odontological literature (Hillson 1986; Goodman & Rose 1990; Schroeder 1991; FitzGerald & Saunders 2005). Here, this term will be used for a developmental defect of enamel (manifested as an area of missing enamel) caused by a disturbance of ameloblast function during the secretory stage of amelogenesis. If hypoplastic defects are present at the tooth surface, they can be referred to as *surface hypoplasia*; the term *internal hypoplasia* is used if the defects are located within the enamel layer and are thus only visible in a sectioned tooth (Kierdorf *et al.* 2005).

Both types of hypoplastic defects originate along grossly accentuated incremental lines (Fig. 14.4b). In the case of surface hypoplasia, the defects are often narrow (pit-type) and appear funnel-shaped on tooth sections. The presence of this type of hypoplasia denotes that in places groups of ameloblasts, which had stopped matrix production when exposed to a strong impact, never resumed their secretory activity. In sectioned teeth, surface hypoplasia can be distinguished from post-eruptive loss of surface enamel by the fact that the incremental lines show a distinct bending according to the outline of the hypoplastic defects (Fig. 14.3b, c). The internal hypoplastic defects appear as canal-like structures of varying length that do not open on to the enamel surface (Fig. 14.4b, d). They therefore apparently reflect an only temporary cessation of matrix secretion by groups of ameloblasts that eventually recovered and were able to resume matrix production. Since ameloblasts are closely interconnected, it may be speculated that groups of temporarily non-secretory ameloblasts had moved away from the enamel surface along with neighbouring secretorally active cells to which they were linked, leading to the formation of the canal-like internal hypoplastic defects (Figs 14.2f, 14.4d) (Kierdorf *et al.* 2000, 2005).

Pit-type hypoplastic defects in the enamel are a regular feature of fluorotic teeth of wild boar, and corresponding enamel defects could be induced experimentally in third molars (M_3) of miniature pigs administered a daily oral dose of 2 mg sodium fluoride per kilogram of body weight for 1 year along with their feed (Fig. 14.1c) (Kierdorf *et al.* 2000, 2004). Internal hypoplastic defects were not observed in the fluorotic enamel of these miniature pigs, and this type of developmental abnormality is therefore so far only known from fluorotic enamel of wild boar. It is not known why certain groups of ameloblasts stop matrix secretion for longer periods of time or completely, while neighbouring cells at the same stage of secretory activity are able to resume matrix formation quite early after an insult. The presence of a layer of aprismatic enamel external to a grossly accentuated incremental line denotes that it took some time for the ameloblasts to resume normal secretory activity and to re-establish a fully differentiated Tomes process (Fig. 14.2c).

In addition to the pit-type hypoplastic defects, more extended hypoplastic surface defects were also observed in fluorotic teeth of wild boar (Fig. 14.2d). These extended defects, which are sometimes also underlain by a grossly accentuated incremental line, result from an impairment of secretory activity in larger groups of ameloblasts. The enamel underlying such defects often shows a narrowing of the spacing between the incremental lines. The broad and severely hypomineralized incremental lines, whose presence goes along with a disruption of the normal enamel microstructure, represent zones of markedly reduced mechanical stability. Therefore, when exposed to mechanical stress during mastication, larger portions of surface enamel tend to flake off along these lines (Fig. 14.4c, d) (Kierdorf *et al.* 2000).

In severely fluorotic teeth of wild boar and domestic pigs, zones of aprismatic enamel with a very dense and homogenous structure were occasionally found (Kierdorf *et al.* 2000, 2004). In places, single or multiple globular or hemiglobular structures were discernible within these zones (Fig. 14.3d). Normal prismatic enamel was present internal to these zones, whereas the enamel external to the zones showed a disturbed structure. In longitudinally sectioned acid-etched teeth, the border of the dense enamel zones with the underlying prismatic enamel was characterized by projections of interprismatic enamel that protruded above the level of the prisms and reached into the aprismatic enamel zone (Fig. 14.3d, arrows). The development of the dense, sometimes globular areas of aprismatic enamel was hypothetically related to the formation of subameloblastic cysts, i.e. of cysts located between the detached layer of secretory ameloblasts and the surface of the forming enamel (Kierdorf *et al.* 2000, 2004). Because of the topography of the secretory surfaces of the Tomes process (described above), an abrupt detachment of the ameloblast layer from the enamel surface will result in the observed picture of projections of interprismatic enamel protruding above the level of the prisms. Projections of interprismatic enamel protruding into a zone of aprismatic enamel were occasionally also observed in superficial enamel underlying the base of hypoplastic surface defects (Fig. 14.4a). In these cases, the occurrence of this structural aberration is hypothetically attributed to a very rapid regression of the prism-forming portion of the Tomes process.

Enamel changes ascribed to a disturbance of the maturation stage of amelogenesis

The histopathological change underlying the characteristic opacity of fluorotic enamel is a subsurface hypomineralization and resulting increased porosity of different intensity (Aoba & Fejerskov 2002). Experimental studies in domestic pigs indicated that this hypomineralization can be induced if fluoride affects only the maturation stage of amelogenesis (Richards *et al.* 1986). From this it was concluded that the subsurface hypomineralization of fluorotic enamel can most likely be ascribed to a fluoride effect on enamel maturation.

On microradiographs, enamel hypomineralization is visible as zones of increased radiotranslucency of the tissue (Fig. 14.5a). A typical finding in unworn or slightly worn fluorotic teeth is the presence of a thin outermost surface rim of enamel with higher mineral content that covers the hypomineralized enamel (Fig. 14.5a). As demonstrated by Richards *et al.* (1992) in fluorotic human teeth, this thin, well-mineralized surface zone develops before tooth eruption and therefore does not represent post-eruptive mineral uptake by the porous fluorotic enamel.

How fluoride impairs enamel maturation is not fully understood. It appears, however, that inhibition of the enzymic degradation of enamel matrix proteins is of crucial importance (Whitford 1997; DenBesten 1999; Aoba & Fejerskov 2002). The resulting delay in protein removal is thought to impair crystallite growth in the tissue. In rodent incisors, a dose-dependent reduction in the frequency of modulation cycles of fluoride-exposed ameloblasts during enamel maturation, i.e. of alternation between the ruffle-ended and the smooth-ended ameloblast morphology, goes along with a marked reduction in protein removal from the tissue (DenBesten *et al.* 1985; Smith *et al.* 1993; DenBesten 1999). The reduced wear resistance of the hypomineralized enamel is the reason for the increased attrition of fluorotic teeth described above.

Formation of coronal cementum in fluorotic teeth of wild boar

In severely fluorotic teeth of wild boar, cellular cementum was occasionally found in hypoplastic defects of the enamel (Figs 14.4b, 14.5b–d) (Kierdorf *et al.* 2004). In some specimens, this tissue also covered larger areas of the tooth crown (Fig. 14.5b). Formation of this so-called *coronal cementum*, which is not normally present in wild boar teeth, indicates a premature breakdown of the enamel epithelium of the affected teeth before completion of amelogenesis. This is assumed to result in contact between mesenchymal cells of the dental follicle and the surface of the immature enamel, causing these cells to differentiate into cementoblasts. The presence of coronal cementum in the fluorotic wild boar teeth therefore denotes a severe fluoride-related effect on the integrity of the enamel organ.

CONCLUSION

Fluorotic enamel of wild boar and domestic pigs exhibits a spectrum of pathological alterations, demonstrating a negative impact of excess fluoride on the secretory and maturation stages of amelogenesis. Careful analysis of the changes in enamel microstructure and mineralization allows a reconstruction of the fluoride-induced changes on the cellular (ameloblast) level.

Enamel changes such as hypoplasia and hypomineralization can also be caused by factors other than excess fluoride exposure. Possible such factors are severe under-nutrition or infectious diseases during tooth formation. Wherever possible, the diagnosis of dental fluorosis should therefore, in addition to morphological observations, also be based on the determination of fluoride concentrations in bones and teeth.

Thus far, effects of excess fluoride exposure in wild boar have only been studied on the level of the individual, and no information on possible population effects is available. Such data is, however, available for wapiti from the Yellowstone National Park (USA), where an abbreviated age structure due to premature breakdown of the dentition was reported for a herd living in an area with high levels of fluoride from geothermal sources (Garrott *et al.* 2002). Further studies addressing the question of the population effects of excessive fluoride exposure in wild boar are therefore encouraged.

15

Economic and ecological reconstruction at the Classical site of Sagalassos, Turkey, using pig teeth

Sofie Vanpoucke, Bea De Cupere & Marc Waelkens

INTRODUCTION

Teeth are without doubt some of the most useful structures for zoological and archaeozoological research. Their complex crown morphology renders them extremely important in taxonomic determination, since subtle differences in shape and form can exist to species level. Of the various calcified tissues present in the mammalian body, tooth enamel is also the hardest and most stable. This is extremely important for the study of fossil remains, since teeth are very resilient to many taphonomic variables.

Teeth can provide many clues about an animal's past life. They are extremely conservative in their development and growth, which progresses in a relatively well-understood chronological sequence. As a result, crown development, and tooth eruption can provide some of the most useful archaeozoological evidence for the age at death of an individual. The mouth is also the place where the initial physical and chemical breakdown of food occurs; the teeth are the means of shearing, chopping, and mastication, and as such will be affected to varying degrees by any major changes in the physical and chemical make up of ingested food. Thus, normal progressive wear on the teeth at a macroscopic level also provides a useful and widely used methodology with which to estimate the relative age at death. Tooth development is also adversely affected by a wide range of physiological factors, which can leave a number of tell-tale 'footprints' in the dental tissues themselves. As a result, a permanent (and chronological) record of physiological stress can be routinely reconstructed from the study of ancient teeth. All of these approaches can be used to shed further light on aspects of animal husbandry regimes in the past.

Fig. 15.1. Location of the Sagalassos site in Turkey

This chapter deals with the pig remains excavated at Sagalassos, a Roman to Early Byzantine town in south-western Turkey. The ruins can be found approximately 7 km north of the village of Ağlasun in the province of Burdur, and 110 km to the north of Antalya (Fig. 15.1). The site lies on the southern slope of the western Taurus at an altitude of between 1450 and 1600 m a.s.l., and extends over 4 km² (Waelkens 1993). The cold and sub-humid Mediterranean climate in this region is characterized by short dry summers and cold wet winters, and the high precipitation level (with about 50% in the form of snow) has a positive effect on the numerous aquifers within the area around the town (Paulissen *et al.* 1993). The vegetation is now composed of scattered pines (e.g. *Pinus nigra*, *P. brutia*, and *Cedrus libani*) along with small bushes (e.g. *Quercus calliprinos*, *Q. coccifera*, and *Juniperus excelsa*), thorn-cushions (e.g. *Astragalus* sp.) and grasses. However, in antiquity the vegetation must have been more varied. Palynological evidence from the territory of Sagalassos indicates the presence of forests during the Middle Hellenistic to Late Imperial period with, among others, conifers and both evergreen and deciduous oak trees. Olive cultures were introduced, and an increase of walnut trees was also observed in the same period. Indeed, arboriculture and fruticulture must have reached their heyday in Imperial times (Vermoere *et al.* 2000).

The excavations at this ancient site have yielded an enormous amount of animal bones, which date from the 1st to the 7th century AD. The majority of this material can be classified as human consumption refuse and is dominated by the remains of domestic animals, i.e. sheep/goat, cattle, and pig (De Cupere 2001). Considering the importance of pig in the animal bone assemblage (around 20% during the whole period under study), research on the presence and nature of a developmental defect of tooth enamel (i.e. linear enamel hypoplasia—LEH) was instigated in order to obtain more information on pig-breeding and husbandry practices during the Roman–Early Byzantine period at Sagalassos. Further, some evidence for environmental conditions at the site might also be obtained.

Linear enamel hypoplasia is a deficiency in enamel thickness occurring during tooth crown formation. It is visible as depressions or lines on the tooth's surface, parallel with the cemento-enamel junction. As the ameloblasts, which secrete the enamel matrix, are very sensitive to physiological disruptions, the lines and depressions on the tooth's surface occur as a result of disruption in amelogenesis. Therefore, LEH is mostly caused by stress of infectious and nutritional nature (food availability and quality), or physiological stress (such as birth or weaning) (Goodman & Rose 1990; Ervynck & Dobney 1999; Dobney & Ervynck 2000). Tooth formation starts at the apex of the growing crown and proceeds down gradually to the cervical part of the crown. After this first stage of secretion, maturation of the enamel matrix takes place. As the formation of the tooth represents a clear chronological sequence, hypoplastic lines or depressions near the tip of the tooth were formed at a younger age than those at the cervix. Once the tooth is formed, the mature enamel becomes inert and cannot be remodelled (Skinner & Goodman 1992). A reconstruction of the chronological patterns of developmental stress during the tooth crown formation can be made by counting the lines and depressions and by measuring their position, after which these data are brought into relation with the known chronology for the formation and eruption of the individual teeth (see Table 15.1).

Previous research (Dobney & Ervynck 2000; Dobney *et al.* 2002) has shown that the frequency and chronology of LEH on modern and archaeological *Sus* molars shows clear (non-random) patterning. Patterns on the first molar (M_1) have been interpreted as indicating birth and weaning stress, whereas

Table 15.1. Ages of formation of the lower molars (summarized by Dobney & Ervynck 2000).

	Starts formation	Completely formed
M_1	*In utero*	3rd month of life
M_2	3rd month of life	10th–11th month of life
M_3	10th–11th month of life	21st–24th month of life

those on the M_2 and M_3 have been linked with nutritional stress during the animal's first and second winters respectively. Pigs attain their maximum meat and fat weight at the end of autumn, the most productive time for woodland foraging. Because of the scarcity and low quality of food in winter, and increased energy requirements, the pigs will lose weight during that season, thus being subjected to nutritional stress leading to LEH. Additional lines which can be observed on the molars are likely to be the result of other more random stress events.

In order to compare the occurrence of LEH between sites, an index is calculated, enabling the simultaneous evaluation of all observations on the different cusps of the three molars (Ervynck & Dobney 1999; Dobney *et al.* this volume). Given the fact that the occurrence of LEH will be related to food availability, the study of LEH can shed light on the environmental conditions in which a domestic animal population was kept.

MATERIALS AND METHODS

For this study, both mandibles and isolated teeth of pigs from Sagalassos were sampled. These originated from different areas excavated at the site during the years 1990–2003. The material was separated into three groups according to their date: period 1 from 1 AD until 300 AD, period 2 from 300 AD to 350 AD, and period 3 from 450 AD and 650 AD. Undated specimens are classified together with all the dated ones in the category of 'all periods'.

Initially, the slaughter age of pigs was established using the method of Grant (1982). This method evaluates the condition of the molar dentition, i.e. eruption and wear, known as *mandibular wear stages* (MWS) and gives relative age classes, ranging from 0 to 51. Some of these relative MWS can be roughly related to real ages, i.e. at the moment the molars erupt. Complete mandibles only ($n = 297$) have been used for the purpose of this study, in order not to bias the obtained MWS by estimation of a missing molar wear stage (see De Cupere 2001: 78–9).

A large number ($n = 1168$) of molar teeth from the lower jaw and isolated lower molar teeth were examined for LEH, according to the method of Dobney & Ervynck (1998) and Dobney *et al.* (2002). Each cusp of each molar tooth was subjected to a detailed inspection at its lingual surface. The use of oblique light helped in the observation of the lines or depressions, as did running a fingernail over the crown surface. Once the presence of LEH lines or depressions was established, their distance (height) from the cemento-enamel junction was measured along a perpendicular axis.

RESULTS AND DISCUSSION

Slaughter age of pigs

The frequency distributions of the MWS, for each chronological period considered, are given in Fig. 15.2. Some of these relative mandible wear stages can be related to real ages. It can be deduced from the raw data list that the M_1 erupts at MWS 3–4, the M_2 erupts around wear stages 9–13 and the M_3 around 18–28. The corresponding ages are approximately 6 months, 13 months, and 22 months (Silver 1969). Although many researchers use eruption ages based on 18th century breeds, Bull & Payne (1982) have shown that these data are probably unreliable and that eruption ages of wild boar or unimproved modern breeds are more suitable. Therefore, the upper limits of the ages given by Silver (1963) were taken here (see also Ervynck 1997).

The histograms of the MWS show some peaks, indicating that certain slaughter ages were preferred above others. In general, a first peak can be noticed at MWS 7 (between 6 and 13 months), followed by peaks at MWS 14 (more than 13 months), MWS 19 (about 22 months), MWS 23/24 (more than 22 months), and MWS 28/29 (more than 22 months). Assuming that the piglets are born in spring (March–April), the peak at MWS 7 (older than 6 months and younger than 13 months) can represent the slaughter of spring piglets before their first winter (W_1S). Similarly, the peak at MWS 19 can reflect the slaughter of spring piglets during their second winter at an age of about 22 months (W_2S), and a third peak at MWS 28/29 of animals during their third winter (W_3S) (cf. Ervynck 1997). However, more peaks are observed and these can possibly be explained by assuming that double farrowing was practised, with a spring litter and an autumn litter (September). These additional peaks at MWS 14 and 23/24 can represent the slaughter of autumn piglets during their second (W_2A) and third winter (W_3A) respectively, at an age of more than 13 months and more than 22 months (cf. Ervynck & Dobney 2002).

The peaks outlined above are represented in the histograms of all three periods. This seems to indicate that the practice of double farrowing was common in the region of Sagalassos during the whole time-span under study, i.e. from the 1st to the 7th century AD. However, some variation is noted among the three periods, e.g. during the last occupation period (450–650 AD) more than half of the animals were slaughtered before the age of 1 year, whereas during the period from 300–350 AD there is a larger proportion of those that were older than 1 year.

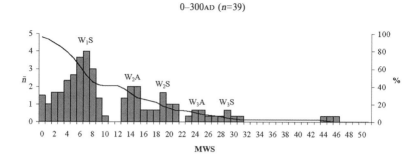

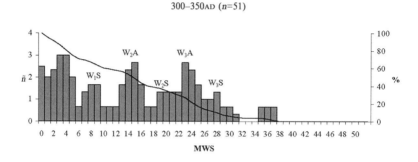

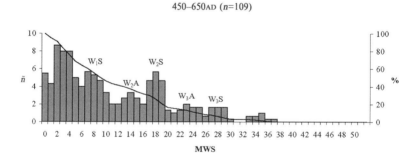

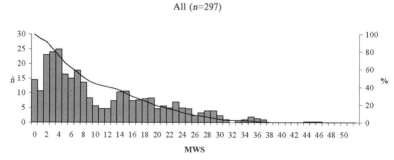

Fig. 15.2. Negative cumulative curve (%) and frequency distribution (calculated as running mean $\tilde{n}$) of the mandibular wear stages (MWS) of the three periods considered and of all material together (W_x: winter of x year; S: spring litter; A: autumn litter)

Linear enamel hypoplasia

Linear enamel hypoplasia was frequently observed on all three molars. The relative distributions of the height at which the lines and/or depressions occur are given in Figs 15.3–15.5 for the first (cusp a) and second cusp (cusp b). The third molar (M_3) is composed of three cusps, an anterior (a), a posterior (c), and a middle (b) cusp. The posterior cusp (cusp c) from M_3 is not illustrated here since very few observations of LEH were made at this part of the tooth. The largest number of observations was made on the second cusp.

When considering the first molar (Fig. 15.3), the majority of LEH defects are manifested as depressions, mostly on the second cusp of the tooth. Their distribution shows a clear peak on cusp b at the bottom of the crown. The distribution of the depressions on cusp a cannot easily be interpreted, since the number of observations ($n = 3$) is insufficient here. Lines, on the other hand, are located on both cusps at more varying heights. The distribution of LEH on the second molar (Fig. 15.4) shows a peak of depressions on the lower half of the tooth crown, for both cusp a and cusp b. The lines, again, occur at different heights on both cusps with even greater variability than on the first molar. The distribution pattern of the depressions and lines observed on the middle cusp of M_3 (cusp b) is quite similar, though less pronounced, compared to the second molar (Fig. 15.5). The posterior cusp (c) of M_3, however, shows a clear discrepancy with the two other cusps (see Fig. 15.7). This is undoubtedly linked with difficulties in observing the cemento-enamel junction. The latter is partially obscured by the ascending ramus of the mandible, hampering the observation and measurement of any LEH present. Observations on cusp c were thus eliminated from further analysis.

Depending on the age that the molars are formed (Table 15.1), the lines and depressions observed can be related to different chronological events (summarized by Dobney & Ervynck 2000). According to the time of formation of the lower molars, a time sequence from birth until ± 24 months of age can be examined. The hypotheses proposed by Dobney & Ervynck (2000) have been alluded to above, i.e. two lines or depressions on the M_1 related to birth and weaning and a depression on the M_2 related to nutritional stress during winter. These interpretations were tested here for the material from Sagalassos.

In the case of the first molar (M_1), the pig teeth from Sagalassos show only the lower LEH peak, at the bottom of the crown (proposed weaning line) (Fig. 15.3). The upper line or depression, related to birth, has until now not been observed on cusp b, and only two specimens may show this line on cusp a. Similar results have been observed at the medieval English site of Flixborough, where the absence of the birth line was possibly explained by the more severe wear of the occlusal and lateral surfaces of the teeth (Dobney *et al.* 2002: fig. 2). However, the absence of this line at Sagalassos cannot be the

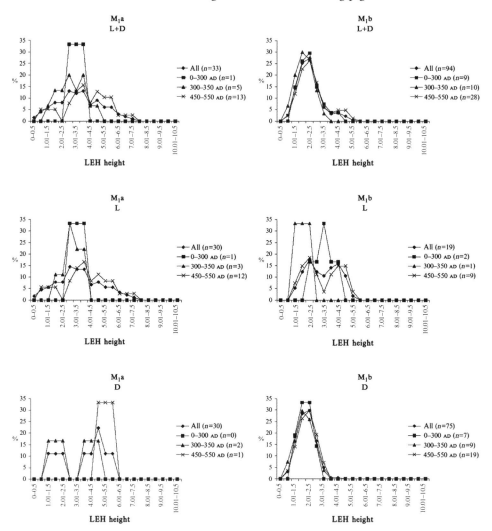

Fig. 15.3. Frequency distribution of the LEH height on the lower M_1 (L: lines; D: depressions; a: cusp a; b: cusp b)

result of the fact that the first molar shows advanced wear, since mandibles of young animals (i.e. with low molar wear stages of the M_1) were also involved in the study. It is possible that observations at a microscopic/histological level may nevertheless reveal these lines associated with birth. In the case of M_2 and M_3, the Sagalassos material clearly shows the peak at the bottom of the crown, which has been described as the reflection of nutritional stress during the first and the second winter respectively (Figs 15.4, 15.5).

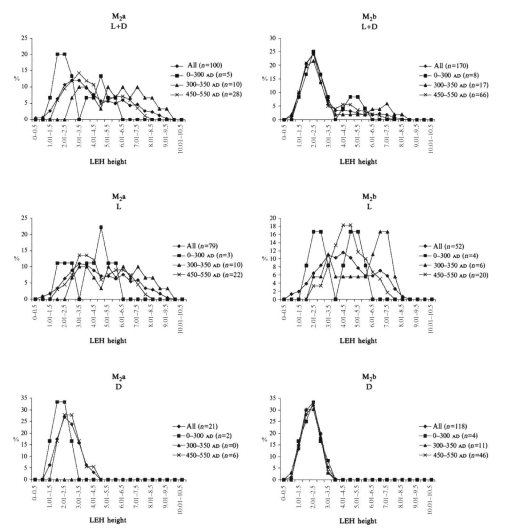

Fig. 15.4. Frequency distribution of the LEH height on the lower M_2 (L: lines; D: depressions; a: cusp a; b: cusp b)

Double farrowing?

The possibility of having two or even more litters a year depends widely, both in wild and domestic pig, on climate and food supply (Lauwerier 1983; Heptner *et al.* 1989: 67–8). Economic factors and human preference can also lead to the manipulation of the reproduction cycle of the domestic pig

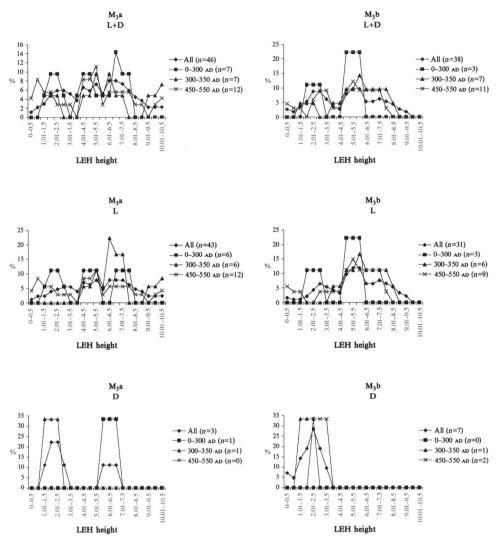

Fig. 15.5. Frequency distribution of the LEH height on the lower M₃ (L: lines; D: depressions; a: cusp a; b: cusp b)

(Lauwerier 1983). The advantages and disadvantages of one or two litters a year have been discussed by classical writers. Varro (1st century BC) describes a regime of two litters a year, adding that the piglets born in winter do not thrive well (*Res rusticae* II.4.13–14). Columella (1st century AD), on the other hand, gives information on two regimes. The first, which is in use in the (very) rural regions, produces one litter a year. The second regime, applied in the suburban districts where there is easy access to the city market, favours double-farrowing. The financial yield of the first litter can then be used to feed the second litter in winter (*De re rustica* VII.9.3–4) (White 1970: 318; Lauwerier 1983).

If the practice of double farrowing is applied, this should be visible through LEH patterns on the enamel of M_2 (Ervynck & Dobney 2002), since as described above, LEH can be used as an indicator of the pig's first winter. Piglets that are born in spring (April) are about 7 months when they enter their first winter. Considering the period of life when the M_2 is formed (Table 15.1) and, as the enamel grows from the top to the bottom, the LEH depression caused by food deficiency during this winter period should be found on the lower half of the crown. Piglets of a second litter, which are born in autumn, reach their first winter at a younger age. Hence, the tooth crown will not be as developed and, therefore, the depression caused by nutritional stress in winter should be visible on the upper half of the tooth crown. Thus, when the LEH on the second molar of both litters is compared, there will be a difference between the heights of the first winter line on M_2, and the distribution of these heights will show two peaks.

In this light, the presence of a single peak of depressions on the lower half of the crown of M_2 (Fig. 15.4), for the pigs of Sagalassos implies that they had only one litter a year. This appears to be in contrast to what is suggested by the distribution of the slaughtering ages based on the eruption and wear of the teeth previously outlined (Fig. 15.2). Of course, it must be remembered that several factors can cause variation in the MWS frequency distribution, e.g. unequal length of the MWS, variation in time of birth and slaughtering, individual variation of eruption and wear, variation of wear dependent on the available food, climatic conditions, etc. (Ervynck 1997). Nevertheless, a recent detailed re-examination of the system of recording tooth eruption and wear revealed that Grant's method was quite reliable for the pig mandibles (Ervynck 2005).

Double farrowing has, so far, nowhere been attested based on the macroscopic examination of LEH. As for Sagalassos, double farrowing (based on age at death data), has been suggested at medieval Sugny, Belgium (Ervynck 1997) and even established with a high degree of certainty at Roman Tienen, Belgium (Ervynck & Dobney 2002), but it was also impossible to find arguments for these practices at these sites based on LEH data (Ervynck & Dobney 2002).

Whether the practice of double farrowing can be attested by using LEH should thus be questioned. If the second litter is born only in late autumn (October–November), the M_2 of these piglets starts its formation by the end of the winter (at an age of 3 months, see Table 15.1). The harsh conditions of winter are almost over by the time that M_2 starts to develop. Further, one can assume that the piglets were given additional food. Considering their young age, they were perhaps taken better care of than the older individuals. Alternatively, a smaller amount of fodder is necessary to keep piglets in good condition than it is for their older mates. If nevertheless, these piglets are subjected to food shortage, can a depression during this early stage of tooth crown formation be visible on the tooth surface? At Sagalassos, about 48% of the M_2 (cusp b) was devoid of LEH (Fig. 7), and about 15% have lines only and no depressions. In order to evaluate whether the second-litter pigs are among these specimens, the individuals that show a wear stage interpreted as second-litter pigs (i.e. MWS 13–16 and 23–5) were controlled for the absence of any depression. In contrary to what was expected, several specimens with these wear stages did show a LEH depression, and even on the lower half of the crown of M_2—indicative for first-litter pigs. Although both methods (observation of LEH and Grant wear stages) seem to be reliable, their results are thus contradictory. One possible explanation could be that the peaks that are observed in the MWS histogram (Fig. 15.2) do not necessarily represent winter slaughter as proposed, but only regular intervals within the year (including wintertime) during which pigs were slaughtered. One can indeed assume that the supply of pig meat at a large town such as Sagalassos could not just be obtained by winter slaughter alone. Pigs were probably also slaughtered at other times of the year, e.g. slaughtering related to cultural or religious events, or depending on seasonal changes of the environmental or climatic conditions. Double farrowing may occasionally have occurred, but not in such a consistent manner that it would be reflected as separate peaks in the MWS histogram. In a similar way, the multiple peaks in the MWS histogram of medieval Sugny at Belgium, a castle in a sparsely inhabited and heavily forested region, where no agriculture was present and the consumption of meat was heavily dominated by pork (Ervynck 1997), may also reflect the slaughtering of pigs at different points in the year, instead of the winter slaughter only of pigs that were born twice a year.

Environmental conditions

The index of LEH was calculated for all pig molars from Sagalassos combined and compared with those calculated for other archaeological sites from southwest Asia and for recent wild boar from the same region (Fig. 15.6, with data from Dobney *et al.* this volume). It is clear that the occurrence of LEH at Sagalassos is not especially high: the mean index calculated for Sagalassos is

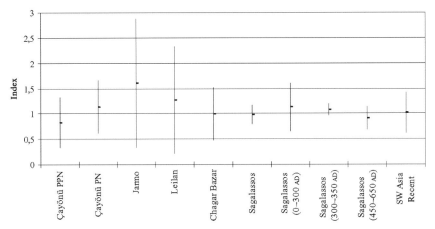

Fig. 15.6. Index comparing the average frequency of LEH of pig teeth from different south-west Asian sites and recent wild boars, calculated for all molars combined. The error bars represent mean plus and minus the standard deviation

similar to the one of the recent wild boars, but somewhat higher than the 'wild boars' from Pre-Pottery Neolithic Çayönü. On the other hand, the occurrence of LEH at Sagalassos is lower than at Jarmo and Leilan (for a description of these sites, see Dobney *et al.* this volume). As the presence of forest at the territory of Sagalassos during the Roman to Early Byzantine period has already been suggested by both palynological and archaeozoological analysis (Vermoere *et al.* 2000; De Cupere 2001), it is reasonable to assume that the pigs were herded in these woods. Their living conditions must have been good, with plenty of foraging opportunities, and the keeping of pigs under these conditions can probably be interpreted as a type of semi-natural husbandry.

If deforestation had taken place during this period, one can assume that this may have led to food shortages for the pigs, which in turn would have resulted in an increase of LEH. Considering the frequency of specimens affected with LEH lines or depressions at Sagalassos, no major changes through time were observed (Fig. 15.7). In addition, the index comparing the average frequency of LEH between the different periods, calculated for all molars combined, also shows little variation (Fig. 15.6). There is a tendency towards a small decrease of the average frequency through time, but the error bars around the averages per period overlap extensively. Therefore, it is probable that environmental conditions remained stable during the whole period under consideration. This is in agreement with earlier observations made on the composition of the livestock. The relative number of pig bones

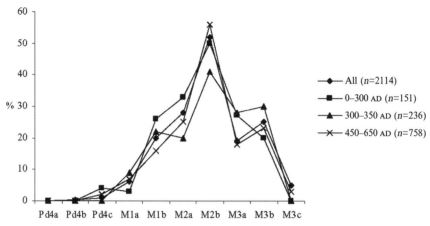

Fig. 15.7. Frequency of specimens affected by LEH (lines and depressions) calculated for each molar and cusp from the different periods

remained almost constant through time, indicating that changes in the natural environment, which may influence the keeping of pigs, did not take place (De Cupere 2001: 141, 174). The large-scale deforestation, which characterizes the environment nowadays, must have taken place during later periods.

CONCLUSION

Slaughter ages of pigs, reconstructed using the mandibular wear stages of the molars, suggest in the first instance that the practice of double farrowing may have been applied throughout the 1st–7th centuries AD at Sagalassos, with the assumption that pigs were slaughtered before or at the beginning of winter. Macroscopic examination of LEH, on the contrary, points towards one litter a year only and the combination of both results does indeed reject the hypothesis of double farrowing. Therefore, the peaks observed in the slaughter age distribution may instead reflect regular points in the year at which pigs were killed rather than a seasonal event.

The LEH index, calculated for all pig molars combined, indicated that the living conditions of the pigs at Sagalassos must have been good, with plenty of foraging opportunities. Considering the absence of large differences in the percentage of teeth affected with LEH, it is suggested that no major changes in the environment that affected pigs occurred from the 1st to the 7th century AD.

Part D

Ethnographic Studies

16

Ethnoarchaeology of pig husbandry in Sardinia and Corsica

Umberto Albarella, Filippo Manconi, Jean-Denis Vigne
& Peter Rowley-Conwy

INTRODUCTION

In this chapter we illustrate, with examples, present-day traditional practices of pig husbandry in Sardinia and Corsica. The approach to this work is ethnoarchaeological, which means that its main aim is to collect modern socio-economic data that can be useful for the interpretation of zooarchaeological remains of pigs and, more in general, for our understanding of the past (cf. Schiffer 1976: 31). The analysis of modern society as an aid to understanding the past has a long tradition in archaeology, and was particularly encouraged by the innovations in archaeological methods of the late 1960s and 1970s (e.g. Binford 1978; Gould 1980). The comparison between past and present is based on the concept of analogy (cf. Gould 1980: 29), which has been much discussed and criticized in the archaeological literature (Audouze 1992). Nevertheless, analogy remains a useful tool in archaeological interpretation as long as it is used cautiously and with an understanding of context (Hodder 1982). It can also be argued that archaeological interpretation is inevitably analogical as we cannot directly observe the past, and any attempt to improve our understanding of the past is based on comparative models, whether they are drawn from ethnographic observations or not.

The relation between people and animals represents a core factor in the functioning of past and modern societies. *Sus* hunting and husbandry in particular constitute very important activities in many different periods and areas of the world. There is a wealth of ethnographic studies on human–*Sus* relations in traditional societies, but this is mainly confined to the South Pacific (e.g. Rappaport 1968; Griffin 1998; Sillitoe 2003). Ethnoarchaeological studies of human–*Sus* relations are much rarer, though the work carried out by ethnographers has occasionally been used for archaeological interpretations (e.g. Nemeth 1998; Redding & Rosenberg 1998).

The geographic bias towards South East Asia, and New Guinea in particular, is understandable when we consider the abundance of wild and domestic pigs in those regions, and the great importance that they have for local economies and societies. Conversely, most of western Asia is dominated by Muslim cultures, where pig husbandry is not practised because of the prohibition of pork consumption (Simoons 1961). In Europe and the Mediterranean industrialized mass production of meat has almost completely replaced traditional systems of animal husbandry. Nevertheless, there are still a number of regions where traditional practices survive, but the potential of these areas for the investigation of patterns of animal husbandry of archaeological relevance has been somewhat neglected. A few ethnoarchaeological studies have focused on sheep and goat management (e.g. Lewthwaite 1984; de Lanfranchi 1991; Grant 1991) but pigs have by and large been overlooked (but see Fabre-Vassas 1994; Moreno García 2004).

Though traditional practices of pig husbandry are gradually disappearing in Europe and western Asia, they can still be observed in areas such as Armenia (pers. observations), Bulgaria (Genov 1999), Greece (pers. observations), Spain (Molenat & Casabianca 1979) and most remarkably in the western Mediterranean islands of Sardinia (Italy) and Corsica (France). Previous investigations of these islands have focused on zootechnical and veterinary aspects (cf. Molenat & Casabianca 1979; Texier *et al.* 1984), and this is the first time that an ethnoarchaeological study of traditional pig husbandry in Sardinia and Corsica, and perhaps in the rest of the Mediterranean, has been carried out. However, ethnographic parallels have been taken into account in works with a more general perspective, such as that by Vigne (1998), who has linked pig slaughter patterns found at a number of prehistoric and historic sites in the north-western Mediterranean with the ethnozoological data provided by Molenat & Casabianca (1979).

The idea of carrying out the research presented in this chapter first arose in 1986, when a visit to Ogliastra, in central-eastern Sardinia, made one of us (UA) aware of the peculiarly small size of the local breeds of pigs and the widespread free-range system of husbandry. Further visits and observations, together with the analysis of the existing literature and the local knowledge of two of us (FM and JDV), revealed that the phenomenon was widespread and dwarf pigs and extensive husbandry methods could be found throughout Sardinia as well as Corsica. The opportunity to undertake the work came, however, only in 2000 with the start of the project on the archaeology of pig domestication and husbandry, based at the University of Durham (UK) and funded by the Arts and Humanities Research Board and the Wellcome Trust.

AREA OF STUDY AND METHODS

The islands of Sardinia (Italy) and Corsica (France) are situated in the western Mediterranean, off the western shores of the Italian peninsula (Fig. 16.1). Both islands host thriving populations of wild boars, whose origins are hitherto unknown. The history and archaeology of these populations is discussed in detail in a separate paper (Albarella *et al.* 2006.), and it is here sufficient to say that no *Sus* (wild or domestic) were present on the islands before the 7th millennium BC (Vigne 1999). Wild boars are excellent swimmers (Nowak 1999) but, considering the fairly large distance of both islands from the continent, it is more likely that they were first brought across from the mainland by human colonists. It is unclear whether the earliest *Sus* that reached the islands were wild (cf. Groves 1989) or domestic (cf. Vigne 1988, 2002). If the latter is the case, as more recent archaeological evidence also seems to suggest (Costa 2004), modern animals must be regarded as descendents of domestic pigs that escaped human control and became feral.

Cross-breeding between wild (or feral) and domestic animals occurs regularly today, and must have occurred even more in the past, when free-range systems of pig-keeping were more or less the rule (cf. Manca dell'Arca 1780; della Marmora 1839). It is therefore not possible to regard wild and domestic populations as genetically distinct, and even their management is not clearly separable. As we will see in the rest of this chapter, there is a great diversity of management systems of pig populations on the two islands, ranging from the controlled hunting of wild animals to the intensive stock-breeding of improved domestic breeds.

Wild boars from Sardinia and Corsica are extremely small in comparison to other European animals (Fig. 16.2), a likely consequence of insular dwarfism, and a phenomenon observed for periods as early as the beginning of the Neolithic in Cyprus (Vigne *et al.* 2000*b*). The small size of these wild boar is reflected in the native domestic stock, which is also attested in the archaeological (cf. Vigne 1988; Manconi 2000) and historical literature (cf. Polybius XII, 3; Cetti 1774; della Marmora 1839, Forsyth Major 1883; Dehaut 1911). The miniature size of the pigs living in these islands undoubtedly affects husbandry and feeding strategies.

The work was carried out using two main methods: fieldwork (direct observation and photographic recording of pig activities, environment, and management), and interviewing of pig-breeders with the aid of a standard questionnaire. Conversations with the pig-breeders were tape-recorded and written notes were also taken. The two systems of recording were then checked against each other to minimize the possibility of misunderstandings, always possible in an area characterized by a multitude of local dialects.

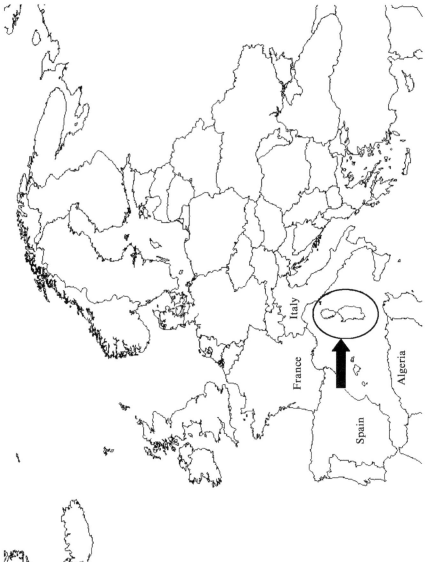

Fig. 16.1. Location of Sardinia and Corsica in relation to mainland Europe

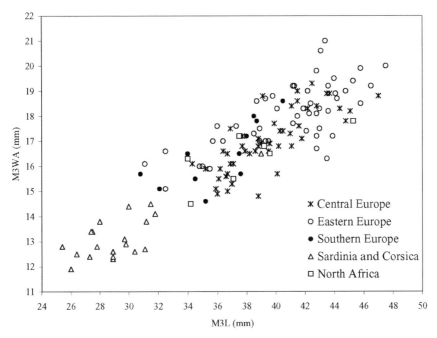

Fig. 16.2. Comparison of the size of the lower M₃ in Sardo-Corsican and other European wild boars

The survey is far from comprehensive and included only four main areas (Fig. 16.3): central eastern Sardinia (Ogliastra and Supramonte), northern Sardinia (Gallura), north-eastern Corsica (Castagniccia), and southern Corsica (Alta Rocca, area around Levie). The choice of the areas was partly dictated by deliberate selection and partly by logistics. Four breeders were interviewed in Gallura and four in the Alta Rocca (Levie area); none were interviewed in Ogliastra/Supramonte and Castagniccia, though many free-range pigs were observed in these areas. Sardinia and Corsica are mountainous islands, and the four areas discussed here are all characterized by a diverse terrain covered by a mix of woodland, Mediterranean maquis, and agricultural land. The Castagniccia area, in Corsica, is, as the name suggests, dominated by sweet chestnut woodland, ideal for pig pasture.

To understand the results of this work it is necessary to consider that, although traditional systems of husbandry are still practised in Sardinia and Corsica, both islands are now undergoing intense economic transformation. Traditional practices are disappearing rapidly as a result of the pressure to intensify productivity and keep pace with international economic forces. Pig husbandry is not immune from these changes, and in the two islands

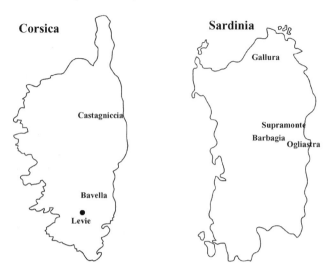

Fig. 16.3. Locations of the areas where observation of free-range pigs and conversations with pig breeders were carried out

a combination of tradition and innovation can be observed, although this occurs at a different level in different areas.

RESULTS

Observations

Observations of free-range pigs living in central-eastern Sardinia were undertaken in 1986, 1997, and 2002. The pigs living in this area are small, slim, and hairy and have a long and straight snout (Fig. 16.4). They are in many respects similar to wild boars, except for their hanging ears, variable colours, and occasional curly tails. Those observed are likely to belong to the traditional Sardinian breed, though its purity is questionable, as cross-breeding with imported animals is likely to have occurred. The 18th-century zoologist Cetti (1774: 87) described the domestic pig of Sardinia as having a straight and big tail, a body covered in bristles, which are straight on the back, and short, straight, bristly ears. A similar description is offered by Dehaut (1911) for the early 20th century. In the last few decades some of the characters of this traditional breed have been diluted through genetic introgression from continental pig breeds, but the Sardinian pig remains peculiar in its aspect and behaviour.

Fig. 16.4. A pig from of the traditional Sardinian breed from the region of Ogliastra (Sardinia) (photo UA 1986)

In this region pig herds are found in remote areas with a rather inhospitable terrain (Fig. 16.5). Even in June, not a rich season for woodland food resources, they seemed to live independently, feeding on short grass (Fig. 16.6) and possibly roots and worms. Despite a long search, no swineherd could be found in the vicinity. Conversations with local people led to the understanding that in the last 20 years traditional pig husbandry has been severely reduced and can only be observed in the most remote areas. Together with Barbagia (the area located just to the west, in the geographic centre of Sardinia) this is, however, the area where traditional practices and breeds are more likely to have survived.

The other area that we studied in Sardinia, the Gallura, is located in the far north of the island. Gallura maintains a certain cultural independence from the rest of the island, and seems to have been affected to a greater extent than central Sardinia by agricultural innovation and mechanization. Yet traditional practices survive in conjunction with more modern systems of husbandry, thus creating a fascinating stage of transition from the old to the new. In this area the introduction of allochthonous wild boars also seems to have been particularly intense (cf. Onida *et al.* 1995). The situation in this region can be best summarized through the analysis of the interviews with the pig breeders, discussed below.

Fig. 16.5. Typical landscape in Supramonte (Sardinia), where many free-range pigs were found in the woodland area (photo UA 2002)

Fig. 16.6. A young Sardinian pig from the area photographed in Fig. 16.5 tries to find some shade on a very hot day in June as it eats some poor and short grass (photo UA 2002)

In Corsica, one of the best-known areas for pig herding is the Castagniccia (Raichon *et al.* 1976; Molenat & Casabianca 1979). As is well known to people travelling in that area, roaming pigs can be found everywhere. Most pigs seem to live rather independently, pasturing along roads and in woodlands under little or no control. Pig types seem to be very variable, with many different coat colours represented and also different levels of improvement.

Fig. 16.7. Free-range pigs from Castagniccia (Corsica). Note the very straight snout (photo UA 2000)

Small pigs with very straight (wild boar type) snouts, are also found (Fig. 16.7). Though rich in pigs the Castagniccia is not, however, the best area to study traditional husbandry, as the pure original Corsican breed seems to have disappeared. Molenat & Casabianca (1979) have shown that the Castagniccia has been subject to a heavy introgression of the Large White breed, and tends to attract several pig types originating from across the island. The wealth of woodland products also causes seasonal movements, as some breeders periodically leave their pigs in the area to feed on sweet chestnuts (de Lanfranchi pers. comm.). This inevitably causes further cross-breeding and genetic contamination of the original domestic and wild populations (de Lanfranchi-Firroloni 1979).

The area where the traditional Corsican breed is more likely to be found is represented by the central part of the island where the main mountain watershed is located (cf. Molenat & Casabianca 1979: fig. 5). The Alta Rocca, where some of our pig breeders were interviewed, lies at the extreme south of this area, at the foothills of the Bavella mountains.

Interviews

The results of the interviews with the pig breeders of Sardinia and Corsica are summarized in Table 16.1, but some of the essential points will be highlighted in the rest of this section.

Table 16.1. Results of the interviews with pig breeders carried out in July 2002 by UA and FM.

Region	North Sardinia	North Sardinia	North Sardinia	North Sardinia	South Corsica	South Corsica	South Corsica	South Corsica
Locality	Scupetu	Perfugas	Limbara	Limbara	Levie	Mela	Orone and Incudine mountains	Levie
Breeder	Pala	Spezzigu	Carta	Alias	Ricci	Mattei	A.L.	Fondansaes
Herd	c.20 adult animals (but in the past up to 100); 2 males, the rest females	2 adult sows; sire borrowed	3 adults (1 male, 2 females) plus piglets	6 adults(1 male, 5 females), 8 piglets	1 male, 3 females, and c.10 piglets	5 adults (1 male, 4 females) and c.35 young animals kept for slaughter	c.50 animals (50% adults and 50% juveniles); male % varies between 25% and 50%	2 females for reproduction and about 10 young pigs for slaughter; male is borrowed for reproduction
Breed	Mixed	Mixed; but he used to have the traditional breed that was black and occasionally striped even when no cross-breeding with wild boars had occurred	Mixed	Mixed	Undefined breed of English origins	Unimproved traditional French breed	Enclosed: Belgian breed Pietrain and a few of the traditional Corsican breed; in the mountains: traditional Corsican breed, as other pigs would not survive in that environment	Traditional Corsican breed
Any wild boars?	Only in the past	No	No, but they live in the area	In the past	No	No	No	No
Any wild/ domestic crosses?	Yes, commonly, wild male × domestic female	Not in his case but he knows it is common	Yes, but when it happens they are slaughtered immediately because they do not grow enough	They often happen, but when the animals are kept free-range	Yes, but when it happens they are slaughtered immediately because they do not grow enough	Yes, but in such cases those animal that have straight ears are slaughtered immediately	Yes, but when it happens they are slaughtered immediately because they do not grow enough	Yes, but when it happens they are slaughtered immediately because they do not grow beyond 60–70 kg

Castration	All males are castrated, except those kept for reproduction	Most males are castrated, when no older than 1 month	Yes, from 3/4 months onwards	Most castrated when a few months old	In autumn at 3–4 months, but only those pigs that will be slaughtered young	In winter from a few months to 1 year of age	At 3 months, before weaning	Both males and females are castrated, generally at 2 months, but the females even at 3
Birth season	twice a year at any time	Any time of the year	Any time of the year	Even three times a year, at any time of the year	Twice a year, at any time of the year	Twice a year, any time of the year	Any time of the year	Twice a year at any time of the year
Where are the litters born?	In the sty, particularly in winter	In the past in a nest that the sow prepared before birth, but due to fox predation now mainly in sties	In the sty due to fox predation	In the sty to avoid fox predation	They are born in the sty, which they leave after a month, weaning occurs at 2 months	They are born in the wild and sometimes they are predated by foxes	In the sty due to fox predation	Generally in the sty to avoid fox predation
Purchase of animals	Boars for reproduction to avoid excessive inbreeding	No	Occasionally some piglets	Yes, to avoid inbreeding	Yes, to avoid inbreeding	Occasionally a boar	Occasionally boars to avoid inbreeding	Occasionally
Age at slaughter	Generally between 2 and 3 years	Piglets: 2–3 months (but nowadays at 25 days); males: 2–3 years; females: 4–5 years; castrates: less than 2 years	1–1.5 years, occasionally at 4–5 months	10–12 months	Males: c.3years; female: 3–4 years; castrates: 2–3 years	18 months	Those free in the mountains at 2 years, those which are enclosed at about 1 year as they eat better and grow faster	13–15 months
Slaughter season	Winter	Winter	Winter/spring	December–February	November–March	November (if it is cold) otherwise December	Winter	Late autumn, which is why the favourite birth season is in September

(Continued)

Table 16.1. (*Continued*)

	North Sardinia	North Sardinia	North Sardinia	North Sardinia	South Corsica	South Corsica	South Corsica	South Corsica
Region								
Locality Breeder	Scupetu Pala	Perfugas Spezzigu	Limbara Carta	Limbara Alias	Levie Ricci	Mela Mattei	Orone and Incudine mountains A.L.	Levie Fondansaes
Home range	30 ha, but in summer they tend to trespass	6 ha; they rarely go further because the area is enclosed by stone walls	A few hectares but the males tend to roam freely in a larger area	12 ha; they cannot trespass as the area is enclosed	50 ha	The larger ones in 50 ha, the smaller in 7 ha	Those in the mountains are totally free; the enclosed area is 1 ha	Completely free, the area is c.50 ha
Daily movements	In winter they go back to the sty for the night, in summer they stay outside	At night they find shelter in an abandoned building	At night they go back to the sty	In winter they go back to the sty for the night, in summer they stay outside	They go back to the sty at night but it is their choice as they are not closed in	They stay away also at night	Those enclosed spend the night in the sty but those living in the mountains find shelter in the bushes	They stay away also at night
Level of control	Generally they are totally free but they can be enclosed if they trespass or cause damage	Free, they only come back to feed	Free, they only come back to feed	They are free but come back in the evenings to feed	They tend to live near water sources, and only come back to feed	They are completely free	Those living in the mountains are totally free and independent, they are visited by the breeder only twice or three times a year	Completely free
Capture for slaughter	Attracted by food	Attracted by food	Attracted by food	They answer the call	They are shot with a rifle, in this way the quality of the meat is said to be better	They are driven to an enclosure	Attracted by food, even those in the mountains	They are attracted to an enclosure with food; shooting spoils the meat

Diet	Natural diet (acorns, grass, roots), supplemented with barley, maize, and corn	Natural diet supplemented with barley and in the past also chickpeas and broad beans	Natural diet integrated with barley, bran, and food scraps	Natural diet (grass, worms, pears, acorns) supplemented with barley, bran, bread, and foodscraps	Natural diet (acorns, chestnuts, roots, berries) with a small supplement of corn	In winter acorns and chestnuts, barley as a supplement	Those in the mountains have a fully natural diet; those enclosed eat acorns and chestnuts supplemented with corn and barley	For most of the year fully natural diet, with only a little supplementation to make sure that they can eventually be captured; in August corn and barley
Adult weight	c.200–250 kg	In the past 80–100 kg, now up to 150–200 kg	Max. 300 kg, but the traditional breed did not reach 150 kg	Generally 180–220 kg but they can reach 300 kg; the traditional breed could at the most reach 130 kg	90–120 kg when slaughtered, but they can reach 200 kg. Traditional breed max. 70 kg	Slaughtered at 90–120 kg, but they can reach 140–150 kg	In the mountains: max. 80 kg at 2 years (even if fed properly they would not grow to more than 90 kg); enclosed: max 200–20 kg at 2 years	Max. 120 kg, but if enclosed and well fed they can reach 150 kg
Losses	10 piglets disappeared in the previous year	Never, if they abandon the enclosed area they then come back	Never	Never	It happens	Occasionally in summer	They are occasionally stolen	It happens, but rarely
Agricultural damage	Occasionally, sometimes to vegetable gardens	Not in his area, but an iron wire is sometimes inserted in their snout to avoid the possibility of root-ing damage	It happens but not in his case	No, because the area is enclosed, but it could happen	No, due to iron wire inserted in the snout	No, due to iron wire inserted in the snout	No, due to iron wire inserted in the snout	No, due to iron wire inserted in the snout; then they graze like sheep
Products	Meat (also dried), lard, head	Just meat, for home use	Just meat	Just meat	Everything is used, bones are used to make jelly	All meat used to make ham and salami	Only meat	Meat used to make ham and salami; occasionally the piglets are sold alive

Herd

Most of the breeders interviewed kept only a relatively small number of animals (from 2 to 50), which is consistent with a non-communal, home-based system of husbandry. The proportion of adults and juveniles varied considerably, but the number of males was in some cases surprisingly high. However, two of the breeders—one from Sardinia and one from Corsica—had particularly small herds and borrowed their sires from other breeders.

Breeds

All breeders from northern Sardinia have genetically mixed animals, substantially more improved than the traditional Sardinian type. Yet even the heavier animals with pronouncedly foreshortened skulls (Fig. 16.8) seem to adapt well to a relatively independent life, in free-range conditions. Two of the Corsican breeders owned unimproved northern European breeds, whereas the others owned the traditional Corsican breed (Fig. 16.9). Of these two, particularly interesting is the case of a breeder from the village of Orone, near Levie, who has a double system of pig husbandry. Some animals, mainly imported but also including a handful of Corsican pigs, are kept enclosed in

Fig. 16.8. Pig from the Limbara area (Sardinia) belonging to the breeder Sebastiano Carta. Note the pronounced concavity of the snout and the heavy build, indicating that the animal belongs to an improved breed (photo UA 2002)

Fig. 16.9. Pig belonging to the traditional Corsican breed from Orone near Levie (Corsica) (photo UA 2002)

the vicinity of the village, whereas another small herd of pure Corsican animals is kept in the mountains at a substantial distance from the village.

Wild boars

Wild boars are traditionally hunted on both islands, but there are cases in which they are husbanded, though these will require enclosure, otherwise the animals would escape. In 1997 two of us (UA and FM) informally interviewed a wild boar breeder, who kept his animals in a pen built around a natural rock shelter at Monte Pulchiana, in northern Sardinia. It became clear that his activity was more like a hobby than a sustainable economic enterprise, and we were not surprised to hear in 2002 that his herd had eventually been disbanded. None of the eight interviewed breeders kept any wild boars, though two mentioned having owned some in the past. In general wild boars are not regarded as being very profitable, because of their extremely small size. All breeders agreed that interbreeding between wild boar and domestic pigs occurs, but the hybrids are invariably slaughtered immediately, as they do not grow sufficiently. Hybridization is therefore regarded as inevitable but undesirable. The perception of the problem may, however, have changed over time, as traditional domestic breeds were probably even smaller than they are today, that is before they became partly contaminated with allochthonous genes.

Castration

All breeders were consistent in claiming that castration is practised on all males (and in one case also females) not used for reproduction, and the practice is safe, with no casualties or infections ever recorded. The age of castration varied, ranging from 1 month to 1 year of age.

Litters

There is no specific birth season in Sardinia and Corsica, as pigs can be born at any time, though in Corsica a preference for the early autumn was mentioned. Most pigs, including those of the traditional Corsican breed, produce two litters per year, though one of the Sardinian breeders mentioned the possibility of treble farrowing. Most pigs, but not those kept in completely free-range conditions, give birth in a sty. This is mainly aimed at protecting the piglets from fox predation, a concern mentioned by all pig breeders.

Purchase

When small herds are kept, inbreeding is an issue and several breeders mentioned the need to buy the occasional animal to increase the genetic diversity of the herd.

Slaughter

The breeders unanimously agreed that the best slaughtering season is the winter, before the food shortage of woodland products. However, the age at slaughter seems to be extremely variable. In Sardinia it seems to be common practice to slaughter pigs when they are well into their third year, and females even when they are 4 or 5 years old. In Corsica pigs are generally killed at a younger age, when they are 1 or 2 years old. The age at slaughter is, however, connected with the speed of growth. For instance, the breeder from Orone kills his enclosed pigs at 1 year of age, whereas those living in the mountains, with their inferior diet and growth rate, are slaughtered when they are at least 2 years old. It is difficult to account for the reasons for the difference in kill-off patterns between the two islands, but it may relate somehow to the use of meat. In Corsica pig meat is almost entirely processed to make ham and salami (*charcuterie*), but in Sardinia there is a preference for fresh meat.

Movements

All Corsican breeders and one of the Sardinians keep at least one herd in completely free-range conditions, so that the animals can roam freely in an area up to 50 hectares; those enclosed live in areas ranging between 1 and 30 hectares. When trespass occurs the animals tend to go back and losses are rarely recorded. Males tend to roam in a larger area, and more movements occur in summer (presumably because less food is available, and this must be sought in a larger territory). Some of the free-range herds spend the day as well as the night in the scrub. Others, including all those that are enclosed, return to the sty for the night, particularly in winter. During the day the pigs tend to stay as close as possible to water sources.

Control

It is not possible to draw a clear distinction between free-range and enclosed pigs, as some of the latter (as in the case of the Sardinian breeder from Scupetu) live in an area that is almost as large as their maximum home-range. The labour involved is minimal as both free-range and enclosed pigs

Fig. 16.10. The Bavella mountains in Corsica, where pigs of the traditional breed survive with almost no support (photo UA 2000)

are sufficiently independent and need to be fed at most once a day. Castration and slaughter are the only other human activities involved. The two herds of the Corsican breeder from Orone represent the two extremes of the typical levels of control found in traditional husbandry. The herd kept near the village lives in small woodland of 1 hectare, while the other lives in rather impenetrable mountainous country (Fig. 16.10), and hardly requires any labour or control. This breeder only visits his pigs two or three times a year, but—remarkably—has no problems in making himself familiar to the animals, which immediately recognize his call. Only the small and sturdy traditional Corsican breed can live in the tough conditions occurring in the mountains; other pigs would die within weeks. This double system of husbandry practised by this breeder was already recognized by the geographer della Marmora (1839: 154) in early 19th century Sardinia. Della Marmora distinguishes the '*porco indomito*' (literally 'indomitable pig') from the '*porco manso*' (tame pig). About the former he writes that

e' tenuto in campagna, dove si nutre di radici, grani e di rettili per una parte dell'anno; poi ingrassa prodigiosamente quando ottobre gli offre abbondanti banchetti nelle foreste di querce dell'interno. Rientrato allora ... allo stato primitivo di natura, prende non solo le abitudini e l'aspetto dei cinghiali, con i quali si mescola di sovente, ma la sua carne acquista un gusto che si cercherebbe invano in quella dei porci allevati continuamente allo stato domestico (it is kept in the countryside where it feeds on roots, grains, and reptiles for part of the year; then it fattens prodigiously when in October it is offered abundant meals in the oak forests of the interior. Returned then... to its primitive natural state, not only does it assume the behaviour and appearance of wild boars, with which it often mixes, but its meat acquires a taste that would be sought in vain in pigs that are constantly kept in a domestic state).

Capture

For animals living in enclosed environments this is obviously not a problem, as they can easily be attracted by food or they just respond to the call of the swineherd. Those that are free-range also respond to the call for food but, being less tame, they may need to be driven into an enclosure. In Corsica we have seen several remains of stonewall enclosures that could have had such a function (Fig. 16.11). One of the Corsican breeders, however, shoots his animals. He claims that killing the pigs in this way makes the meat taste better. Another breeder, also working in the Alta Rocca, claimed exactly the opposite. In Levie in the 1980s, one of us (JDV) observed that some breeders trained dogs to catch and immobilize the pigs for slaughter, by biting their ears. This use may be related to the strategy adopted in this area to kill the pigs

Fig. 16.11. Abandoned enclosure in the Levie area (Corsica), which was probably used for pigs (photo UA 2000)

by piercing their heart, which causes an internal haemorrhage (Vigne & Marinval-Vigne 1992).

Diet

All pigs in Sardinia and Corsica are broadly self-sufficient in their procurement of food, particularly in late autumn and winter when they can rely on the products of the woodland—acorns and chestnuts. Outside this season the natural diet consists of grass, roots, berries, worms, and reptiles, to which is added feed provided by the swineherds mainly consisting of barley, corn, food scraps, and occasionally bran, maize, and legumes.

Weight

This of course depends on the breed; in relatively improved animals found in Sardinia it can reach as much as 300 kg. The maximum figures for the traditional breed range between 80 and 150 kg in Sardinia and 70 and 120 kg in Corsica. The Corsican pigs owned by one of the Levie breeders (Fondansaes) were said to be able to reach 150 kg if kept enclosed and well fed. The purity of this herd must, however, be questioned as this breeder claims to borrow a boar for reproduction from a colleague (Ricci), whom we also interviewed, and who has English pigs. The pigs kept by the Orone breeder in the Bavella Mountains are slaughtered at 80 kg, and apparently they cannot grow beyond 90 kg even if fed in the best possible conditions (cf. Quittet & Zert 1971). It therefore seems that the weight of the animals is determined by a combination of nutritional rates, environmental conditions, and genetics. The effect of the environment should not be underestimated, as dwarf pigs living in the Aegean island of Tilos were proved to be able to grow to a much greater weight when kept under controlled diet and conditions in an experimental agricultural station in Italy (Masseti 2002: 251).

Damage

Pigs can cause damage to crops and gardens by rooting, but this seems to be a relatively minor concern in Sardinia and Corsica; in some cases this is because the enclosed territory, however large, does not include any agricultural land. All Corsican breeders and one from Sardinia mentioned the insertion of an iron wire (but we have also seen rings) in the pig snout (Fig. 16.12) as an easy device to avoid rooting activity in pigs. One of the breeders from Levie mentioned that, once the iron has been applied, a pig 'grazes like a sheep'.

Fig. 16.12. Pig snout with the typical iron wire inserted to avoid rooting damage, from Bavella (Corsica) (photo UA 2000)

This practice was recorded in 16th century England (Wiseman 2000: 40) and probably still survives in areas where pigs can roam freely.

Products

Meat is by far the main product of the pig. In Corsica it is almost invariably processed to make *charcuterie*. Lard is also much used, and one of the breeders mentioned the use of bones to make jelly. Most of the meat is produced for family and private use, though the sale of the occasional piglet was mentioned by a breeder from Levie. The sale of *charcuterie* has significantly increased in Corsica with the development of tourist activities.

CONCLUSIONS

A great diversity of husbandry strategies is practised in Sardinia and Corsica. Many of these concern adaptation to specific climatic, environmental, and cultural conditions occurring on the two islands, and we should therefore be wary of using them as a model to apply to other societies, periods and parts of the world. Yet there are elements that provide useful insights into the type of challenges that pig breeders must have faced in a variety of situations in the past.

It is therefore worth highlighting what lessons we have learnt about traditional pig husbandry that may address archaeological questions. The first point to make is that zooarchaeologists may sometimes be too keen to make a clear distinction between the management of domestic and wild resources. This hardly seems to be applicable to all areas and situations. In Sardinia and Corsica not only is there a biological continuum between the two *Sus* forms, but also husbandry practices are geared towards a combined management of wild boar and domestic pigs, whose interbreeding is in some cases regarded as an opportunity, but more often as a nuisance.

There are several cases known in the archaeological literature in which it has been difficult to determine whether *Sus* had been hunted or reared. At the Turkish early Neolithic sites of Çayönü and Hallan Çemi, among the earliest to provide some evidence of impending pig domestication, there seems to be a gradual transition towards a domestic state that implies the occurrence of a number of other intermediate practices which cannot easily be classified as predation or husbandry (Hongo & Meadow 1988; Redding & Rosenberg 1988; Ervynck *et al.* 2001; Horwitz *et al.* 2004). These questions do not only apply to the onset of the domestication process, as similar dilemmas have also been raised concerning the status of early Neolithic *Sus* in France (Helmer 1992) and mid-Neolithic *Sus* in northern Italy (Jarman 1976; Rowley-Conwy 1997; Albarella, Tagliacozzo *et al.* 2006). To try solving the problem by introducing the possible existence of a third biological status placed somewhere in between the wild boar and the domestic pig would only mean moving from one simplistic explanation to another. Our study of modern Sardinian and Corsican pig husbandry indicates that the emphasis in our explanations must be on *management* rather than *biological status*, as the second is by and large the product of the first. In these two islands wild and domestic, local and imported, enclosed and free-range pigs all play a role in shaping a rather complex and dynamic economic system, which is difficult to place in predetermined categories.

Our study also draws attention to the difficulties related to attempts to assess seasonality from the study of *Sus* archaeological remains. In Sardinia and Corsica even the traditional fully unimproved breeds can give birth twice a year, and the litters can be born at virtually any time of the year, with the possible exception of the summer. This is probably a consequence of the mild Mediterranean climate that provides the opportunity for survival even to animals born at the beginning of the winter, and we must therefore be careful not to extend these conclusions to animals living in more rigid climatic conditions, where harsh winters can limit the flexibility of the birth season. Nevertheless, caution must be exercised when we assume spring births in view of the attempted detection of seasonal activities; in domestic pigs the picture can be more complex.

Slaughtering follows a more regular seasonal pattern, partly as a result of the seasonality of village activities, but also, as emphasized by Molenat & Casabianca (1979), as a consequence of the accumulation of fat occurring in the season of greatest food abundance (i.e. the autumn). This could explain why many archaeological kill-off profiles in the Mediterranean area show a clear seasonal pattern (Vigne 1998).

Much has been made of the potential incompatibility of free-range pig husbandry and agricultural activities, to the extent that this has been regarded as one of the issues affecting the shape of early farming societies (cf. Redding & Rosenberg 1998). The Corsican and Sardinian herders, whose pigs can roam as freely as is potentially possible for these animals, do not, however, perceive this as a major problem. One reason could be that both islands have a long tradition of greater reliance on livestock than on crops, which does not necessarily apply to other parts of the world. Yet it seems that a simple device, such as the use of an iron wire or ring in the pig's snout, makes these animals no more harmful to cultivated crops than sheep. It seems unlikely that early societies, even those which did not possess metals, could not think of similar strategies to avoid pig damage. It is certainly true that grazing—and not just rooting—can also cause damage, but if pigs could only graze they would be relieved of their specificity, as they could do no more damage than any other domestic livestock.

Finally, it is worth mentioning again that the two islands are currently undergoing a phase of rapid transition, which makes them ideal laboratories for the study of economic change. Much of the reasoning of modern Sardinian

Fig. 16.13. Small cattle of the traditional Corsican breed from Perfugas (Sardinia) (photo FM 2003)

and Corsican breeders echoes the questions and dilemmas of livestock pro-
ducers at the onset of the 16th and 17th centuries in central and northern
Europe (cf. Albarella & Davis 1996; Davis 1997; Davis & Beckett 1999).
Traditional practices and unimproved breeds are gradually disappearing, as
breeders face the increasing demands of market forces. This applies not only to
pigs but also to cattle, which in Sardinia and Corsica (Vigne 1988) are
characterized by a small and rather coarse breed that is becoming increasingly
rare (Fig. 16.13). The local unimproved breeds do not seem to be particularly
productive, but they have distinct advantages deriving from centuries of
adaptation to the local environment. They are sturdy, resilient and immune
to most local diseases and, as we have seen in the case of the 'indomitable' pigs
of the Bavella mountains, able to care for themselves. The main dilemma of the
Sardinian and Corsican breeders is whether to carry on with their low-impact,
environmentally sustainable, but also relatively unprofitable systems of husbandry, or to revert to more demanding, intensive but rapidly lucrative
practices. The latter choice could lead to the disappearance of endemic breeds,
traditional activities, and landscapes, and with them probably the whole
infrastructure of Sardinian and Corsican economy and proud independence
from international market forces. We can only wonder how many times
herders of the past must have faced similar dilemmas.

17

Traditional pig butchery by the Yali people of West Papua (Irian Jaya): an ethnographic and archaeozoological example

Jacqueline Studer & Daniel Pillonel

INTRODUCTION

Studies of traditional methods of animal slaughter, food preparation, and consumption offer archaeozoologists an excellent opportunity to study the link between human behaviour and the resulting bone assemblage. Numerous actualistic studies of butchery have been carried out by archaeologists using stone tools, often especially manufactured by the researchers (e.g. Schick & Toth 1993; Laroulandie 2000). In other instances, traditional butchery practices have been documented, but in most cases the artefacts used were metal. Examples come from the Nunamiut of Alaska (Binford 1981), the Bedouin herders of Israel (Klenck 1995), the Peul cattle herders of Mali (Chenal-Velardé 1996), the !Kung hunter-gatherers of Botswana (Yellen 1977), and semi-urban, urban and village communities from Algeria, France, and Sudan respectively (Chaix & Sidi Maamar 1992). Similarly, for a range of different communities, traditional food preparation and consumption practices have been documented and in many instances the resulting food residues examined (e.g. Brain 1969; Yellen 1977; Binford 1981; Gifford-Gonzalez 1989; Oliver J. 1993). In 1989, the opportunity was taken to document traditional butchery, cooking and consumption of a domestic pig by the Yali people of West Papua (or Irian Jaya). Since this community continues to use traditional artefacts made of stone and organic materials, it may offer a good analogue for the study of prehistoric butchery practices.

THE YALI

According to the most recent suvrey available, the Yali population comprises *c.*30,000 people (Silzer & Clouse 1991) who inhabit the eastern part of the well-known Baliem valley of west Papua. They primarily inhabit the Jayawi-jaya mountains of the central highlands at an altitude of between 1000 and 2000 m (Koch 1968: 85) although some Yali villages can be found at lower altitudes, down to 200 m, in the southern part of the distribution of the group (Boissière 1999: 55). Like many populations living in the mountainous regions of the island, the Yali are subsistence farmers who cultivate sweet potatoes, yam, taro, plantains, manioc, and sugarcane, and raise pigs, the latter serving a central function in their religious and social life (Koch 1968; Zöllner 1977; Boissière 1999). The men hunt small mammals and birds in the surrounding rainforests, while children and women complete their protein requirements by gathering invertebrates, fruits, mushrooms, and other plants.

The Yali village of Kosarek, where the authors stayed for 2 weeks in June 1989, had been evangelized 15 years before. Although occidental influence and (with special regard to our interest) the distribution of metal blades have influenced most of the islanders, the inhabitants of Kosarek continue to use their traditional tools, such as stone adzes, bamboo knives, and borers made with the half-mandible of rodents. During our 2 week stay, we only once observed a man using a metal axe.

BACKGROUND TO PAPUAN PIG MANAGEMENT

The particularly strong relationship between humans and domestic pigs living on the island of New Guinea has been the subject of a copious literature (e.g. Rappaport 1968; Koch 1968; Zöllner 1977; Boyd 1984; Kelly 1988, Sillitoe this volume). The following brief resume is not exhaustive but is based on selected readings which are relevant for the purpose of our research.

Women are responsible for taking care of the pigs. Young pigs are treated as pets and receive considerable attention, being carefully watched and fed. As soon as they are weaned, young pigs accompany their mistress to the culti-vated gardens (Malynicz 1970: 201). At first they are carried, but when they get a little older they are often led on a leash attached to their foreleg. Rappaport (1968: 58) and Dwyer (1996) indicate that a pig is considered old enough to look after itself and to follow its mistress in a dog-like fashion at about 4–5 months of age.

The pigs spend their day rooting in the forest and return home in the evening, when they are given their daily ration of garbage and tubers, mainly sweet potatoes. They have every opportunity to become feral, but almost all pigs return to the village. It also happens that some of the adult pigs are not fed but left to roam freely in the nearby forest until the owner needs them (Kelly 1988: 117; Boissière 1999: 64). In general, pigs are kept under the platform of the house or in a separate shed, but examples of pigs sharing the same quarters as humans are also documented (Michel 1983: 84).

Most of the time, pigs are kept in order to be consumed at festivities and ritual occasions, such as funerals, marriages, wars, and rain ceremonies. Pig feasts are large, communal gatherings where numerous animals are slaughtered and consumed (Rappaport 1968: 79–81; Heider 1970: 40; Koch 1968; Michel 1983: 76–80; Boyd 1984; Boissière 1999: 64). Not only do pigs and their consumption serve an important function in these rituals; they also play a crucial social, ritual, and mercantile role in exchange, and are a mirror of men's affluence.

It is clear that with regard to their pigs, the behaviour of the Papuan people is regulated by social and religious rules, and is strongly dependent on the ethnic origin of the group as well as the age and the sex of the people involved. This means that in the case of consumption of pig meat, prohibitions and obligations can vary not only between the different population groups, but also between valleys or even villages with an identical origin (Kelly 1988: 111).

DESCRIPTION OF THE BUTCHERY, COOKING, AND CONSUMPTION OF A PIG

One of the aims of our stay in the Yali village of Kosarek was to observe all stages of the preparation of a domestic pig, from its slaughter to its consumption, followed by collection and examination of the bone remains. This bone assemblage was then to be studied using conventional archaeozoological and taphonomic methods, in order to compare the activities documented with the resulting damage observed on the bones. The observations were classified into several categories, including presence/absence of bones or portions of them, and the identification of different types of modifications and their location on the bones.

Our 2-week stay in the village did not provide sufficient time to develop a strong relationship with the Yali. We tried to explain our research interest to them, and finally negotiated the purchase of a pig that two men would prepare in a traditional way, from butchery and cooking to consumption. This was the only way in which we would be allowed to collect the bones after the meal, a critical aspect of this study but one that was difficult to realize, as will be described below. It is clear that this event was totally artificial because it had no social or ritual context. However, as our focus was on the documentation of the traditional methods of butchery and consumption, the context was not our priority. Initially, there were two 'official' butchers, both men, but several friends who took part in the event soon assisted them. The slaughter was carried out with a bow and arrow, and bamboo knives and stone adzes were used for the butchery. The main steps of the butchery, cooking, and consumption process are described below.

Preparation

On 3 June 1989, at 8 a.m., the butchery began with the preparation of the fire for the wood pyre. The stones to be heated in the open fire and used as cook-stones inside the earth oven were already stocked in a hut. Handfuls of ferns were brought from the forest to sponge the blood and were later cooked with the meat (and eaten). The first butchery stage included all operations needed to obtain medium-sized pieces of the carcass, which could be put on the wood pyre in order to burn the hair off the carcass.

Slaughter

A subadult sow of about 18 months old had been attached to a pillar by its right forefoot. The owner (one of the two 'official' butchers) killed his pig with an arrow shot through the thorax (Fig. 17.1) (8.15 a.m.). The carcass was then deposited on a layer of leaves (banana and ferns) that would serve to contain the blood.

Ventral cuts using the bamboo knife

The carcass was laid on its left side. The butchery began by using a bamboo knife to make an incision of the skin under the right forelimb (Fig. 17.2a). To make the cut easier, the second butcher held the leg taut such that the skin was extended to a maximum (similar help was given for all incisions into the skin). The incision was then enlarged to the corner of the lips, crossing the ascending ramus of the right mandible (Fig. 17.2b). The butcher then made another incision under the right hindlimb (Fig. 17.2c), continuing this ventral cut until it joined the previous incision (Fig. 17.2d).

Fig. 17.1. Butchery and consumption of a sow by the Yali from Kosarek (photos by the authors). The pig is slaughtered with an arrow shot in the heart

Opening the thorax with a stone adze

The first use of the stone adze served to open the thorax. One butcher pounded several times on the exposed rib rack, from which the skin has previously been cleared away: it included the 1st right rib to about the 9th. The blade of the stone touched them perpendicular to their external face, approximately at the mid-point of their corpus. To stop the blood that began to run, a handful of ferns was put into the split and the two butchers raised the carcass and tilted it in order to pour the blood into a receptacle made of bark already lined with ferns (Fig. 17.2e). Taking up their bamboo knives again, they continued to skin the right flank. After repeating the same operation to preserve the blood, they deposited the carcass back on its right side. One of the butchers began to cut the skin, the fat, and the meat under the left forelimb to clear a portion of the first ribs. Still with the bamboo knife, the first ribs on the left side were isolated from each other by cutting the intercostal muscles at about their mid-point from the sternum. However, the ribs were still left attached to the sternum (Fig. 17.2f). Then, in a similar fashion to what had been done on the left side, a butcher took his stone adze and pounded the skinned thorax till the ribs broke (Fig. 17.2g). These blows fractured the ribs but without splitting the thorax. For this, each break was achieved by hand and it seems that one or two following ribs that were still intact were broken by finger pressure as well (Fig. 17.2h). More ferns were put inside the thorax to absorb the blood.

Fig. 17.2. Butchery and consumption of a sow by the Yali from Kosarek (continued, photos by the authors). (a) Initiation of butchery by an incision, with a bamboo knife, under the right forelimb. (b) Transverse incision across the ramus of the right mandible. (c) Incision under the right hindlimb while the legs are held in a fully extended position to facilitate cutting. (d) Ventral cut of the skin. (e) The two butchers tip the carcass in order to evacuate the blood into a bark receptacle. (f) Exposure and separation of left ribs using a bamboo knife. (g) Application of blows with a stone adze to the exposed ribs in order to open the thorax. (h) Breaking ribs by finger pressure

Extraction of the tongue and entrails

The tongue, including the internal organs of the thorax, was the first part of the body to be isolated. The butcher skinned the mandibles with a bamboo knife, removing the skin from the right side that had already been incised, and repeated this manipulation on the left side. The extraction of the tongue began from its oral extremity (Fig. 17.3a), with ventral cuts along the mandibles and further on through the throat as far as the abdomen, including the oesophagus. Finally, an adze blow at the abdominal level, above the stomach, sectioned this strip into a piece about 15 cm long, which looked like a tie.

Going back to the belly, one of the butchers checked carefully with his fingers around the liver, found the gallbladder, cut it out with his knife, and

Fig. 17.3. Butchery and consumption of a sow by the Yali from Kosarek (continued, photos by the authors). (a) Extraction of the tongue. (b) After having dismembered the two forelimbs with the bamboo knife, the butcher separated the rest of the carcass into two parts, applying blows to the trunk, in a caudal-ventral orientation, with the stone adze. (c) Separation of the hindlimbs by fracturing the pelvis on the ventral face with the stone adze

threw it away into the fire. The abdominal organs were not taken out at this moment but left inside the carcass as long as the upper part of the thorax was not dismembered.

Later, as the internal organs were all removed and the bladder extracted before being burned in the fire, one of the butchers asked an old woman passing by to go to the river to wash the intestines. The latter 'package' was deposited on banana leaves inside a narrow channel in the river. The membranes were separated by hand and bamboo knife under running water. The intestines were cut into segments about 1 m long and washed. The woman cleaned each section by turning it inside out along a stick, and washing them it. The stomach was also turned inside out and the internal membrane meticulously scraped.

Dividing the carcass

As already mentioned, the abdominal organs were still in place when the butcher split the anterior part of the carcass into pieces. He began to dismember the two forelegs. This operation was easily done by cutting the remaining skin that still attached the legs to the trunk with the bamboo knife. Moving on with his stone adze, the butcher applied several strong blows to the thoracic vertebrae to divide the rest of the carcass into two parts. He was standing behind the head, applying caudal–ventral blows relative to the trunk (Fig. 17.3b). The blows were aimed between the ribs, on the ventral part of the spine, at about the 6–8th thoracic vertebra. The final preparation at this stage was to place a large stone between the jaws of the pig, to keep the mouth open. It is not clear whether this was intended to facilitate cooking of the internal parts of the skull or whether it has some symbolic meaning.

The abdominal section was then prepared. First, the bladder was cut and burnt in the fire. The intestines were then extracted and given to the woman to be washed (see before). But when the butcher took his stone adze to dismember the hindlimbs, the liver and the kidneys were still inside the remaining carcass. He applied many heavy blows to the pelvis, mainly on the ventral face (Fig. 17.3c), and finished the operation by cutting the skin with the bamboo knife. Finally, the liver and the kidneys were extracted.

At this point, the preparation of the carcass for burning off the hair was complete, and the carcass, as shown above, had been divided into six pieces:

- the head, connected with the anterior part of the thorax: cranium, mandibles, vertebrae (from the atlas to the 6–8th thoracic vertebra), and adjacent ribs (dorsal part or complete)

- the posterior part of the trunk: vertebrae (from the 6–8th thoracic vertebra to the tail), part of the pelvis, sternum, and ribs (ventral fragments of some first ribs and from the 6–8th complete ribs, intact or broken)

- the four legs: the bones were complete except for the fragmented pelvis attached to the left and right hindlimbs respectively.

The remaining of the carcass consisted of the 'soft parts', i.e. compact internal organs (liver, spleen, kidneys), organs cut in sections (stomach, intestines) and the 'tie' (tongue and internal organs from the thorax still connected).

Burning on the wood pyre

The resulting six pieces of the carcass were roasted on the wood pyre directly over flames for a while, especially the skinned face (Fig. 17.4a). The skin of each piece was then scratched with a bamboo knife to remove all the hairs (Fig. 17.4b) and the nails were extracted and discarded as well. The fire was also used to slightly roast the intestines before depositing them in the earth oven (see below). Only one piece, an internal organ (probably the spleen, but this is not certain) was eaten at this time: the pig's owner roasted it on a stick and shared it, almost raw, with us. Among the vegetables only plantains were first grilled on the fire till the green skins became black before being cooked in the earth oven together with sweet potatoes, taro, and ferns.

Cooking (9.45–10.10 a.m.)

After the skin was cleaned in the fire, no more major butchery took place. Three men began to prepare the earth oven by digging a hole in the soil, 30 cm deep and 1 m across, next to the wood pyre. The following layers were observed in the earth oven (from the bottom upwards:): banana leaves, cook-stones, banana leaves, fresh ferns, pieces of pig meat surrounded by the internal organs surrounded on the external circle by the vegetables (ferns used during the butchery, sweet potatoes, taro, plantains), fresh ferns, banana leaves, cook-stones, banana leaves, cook-stones (Fig. 17.4c). To keep everything in position, bamboo leaves rapidly twisted together served as large bands to encircle the top of the mound. The six pieces of the carcass, as well as the internal organs, except the 'tie' which had disappeared in the meantime, were deposited in the oven and sprayed with the blood collected during the butchery. The stones were transported from the wood pyre to the earth-oven by grasping them with a split stick used like tweezers.

Fig. 17.4. Butchery and consumption of a sow by the Yali from Kosarek (continued, photos by the authors). (a) The six pieces of the carcass are roasted directly over flames. (b) The skin of each piece is scratched with a bamboo knife to remove all the hairs. (c) A final layer of cookstones covers the earth oven. (d) Man eating the snout of the pig; human gnawing marks were observed on the broken edge of the right zygoma. (e) Rib rack before being separated in smaller parts along the ribs

Consumption (10.10–11.30 a.m.)

Cooking inside the earth oven lasted 80 minutes. The vegetables and the meat were then taken out of the oven and the six pieces of the carcass were subdivided into smaller portions to enable all the people present, twelve men and about six children, to obtain something to eat. As there was suddenly a crowd of people it was difficult to follow all the events clearly, and we could only observe some of them in detail. In most cases, the people helped themselves by hand and simply took a bone or a piece of flesh from one of the larger pieces.

Concerning the head, the mandibles were easily dismembered by hand. The skin was still attached to the cranium, and a bamboo knife was used to separate it by means of a transverse incision above the snout. The cranium was separated into two pieces (we did not see this action, but it was documented on a slide showing a Yali holding a fragment of the cranium (Fig. 17.4d) (see below, 'Bone analysis'). A transverse blow with the adze to the top of the cranium created a hole which facilitated extraction of the brain.

The stone adze served as well to fragment the rib racks. We could follow only one such operation in detail: a large rib rack was cut by ventral blows along the vertebrae, isolating the corpus (Fig. 17.4e). It was then easy to prepare smaller portions by cutting the flesh between the ribs with the bamboo knife, isolating sections containing two or three ribs each.

The complete butchery process, from the slaughter that began at 8.15 a.m. till the distribution of the meat at 11.30 a.m., lasted 3 hours and 15 minutes.

COMMENTS ON THE YALI PIG BUTCHERY

Age of the pig

When we asked the Yali for a pig, we did not negotiate any characteristics of the animal, its age or weight, or its sex. The age of the sow (18 months) was based on assessment of tooth eruption and bone fusion (after Habermehl 1975) carried out in the laboratory in Geneva during the bone analyses. This seems to be the minimal age for the sexual maturity of a sow in the New Guinean lowlands (Malynicz 1970: 201; Dwyer 1996: 489). The pig that we received had not been fattened and was light enough to be rapidly prepared and cooked in the earth oven in only one layer.

Slaughter

We only witnessed this one slaughter of a pig by the Yali, but we were assured that the use of a bow was the standard practice in Kosarek. The arrowhead, a *minggin* type, is made of bamboo (Boissière 1999: 307–8). The Yali from the village of Holuwon, 80 km south-east of Kosarek, followed the same practice (Boissière 1999: 66), as well as the neighbouring group of the Dugum Dani from the Baliem valley (Heider 1970: 53 and personal observations of the authors). We assume that this manner of killing recalls hunting wild pig in the forest, and may represent a Central Highland tradition. Certainly it is not a common practice for the inhabitants of all the Highlands, as the Henga community of Papua New Guinea slaughter their pigs during communal feasts by smashing the skull with stones (Wiessner 2001: 131 uses the verb 'club', without more details). Another group from the Papua New Guinea Highlands, the Kalam, kill their pigs with a heavy stake: 'the domestic pigs are slaughtered by a series of blows with a heavy stake on the front of the skull, above the eyes, which considerably damages the cranium' (Bulmer 1976: 180). In a similar way, the Etoro from the Papuan Plateau hold the pig by the limbs and dispatch it with a blow to the head (Kelly 1988: 127). Another way of killing a pig is the practice of the Gogodala group, from the Lowlands of Papua New Guinea: 'an animal selected to be killed is chased about the village, sometimes for hours, pursued by man and boys armed with clubs and spears' (Baldwin 1982: 37).

Opening the thorax

An intact thorax is elastic, and it is not easy to open it through a longitudinal split on a body lying on the ground. In fact, it is much easier to cut the rib racks when there is solid support under the carcass (or, of course, if it is hanging up). But in this case, the Yali butcher inflicted as many blows as were necessary to break the ribs along the trunk. He wanted to free a ventral section, including the sternum, surrounded by a part of the ribs and left the rest of the thorax intact which would serve as container (especially for the blood).

Ribs broken by hand

The breaking of some of the ribs by finger pressure was only possible because the animal was a sub-adult sow. Even on this 18 month old animal, the first ribs were already too massive to be broken by hand.

Sequence of butchery stages

Because the body was lying on the ground during the butchery, one of the major problems was to contain the blood. This is probably why the butchers first prepared the carcass to extract the tongue and the internal organs of the thorax, before dismembering the legs (especially the forelimbs, which are easy to separate). In this way, the open carcass could be raised by its forelegs and the blood that had collected inside it could be poured into a receptacle. This operation was carried out several times. The intestines were also left attached to the carcass for as long as possible, thereby creating a natural container.

Division of the carcass and size of the pig

The carcass is usually divided relative to the size of the animal. In our case, the sow was small enough to be left intact without dismembering the long bones. By chance, at a distance of a two days' walk from the village of Kosarek, we saw another butchery carried out by the Yali but this time on a large wild boar hunted in the forest half an hour before. In this case, the butchery followed a similar pattern until the fire-cleaning of the skin. In the case of the wild pig, the long bones were partially dismembered with the bamboo knife so that the legs could be doubled up. This made it possible to avoid the need for an extremely large earth oven. The rib racks were also fragmented into many pieces using a metal axe, and the cranium was cut into three parts also with the axe. The volume of resulting meat was too large to be cooked in one layer in the earth oven. In consequence, the pieces were deposited in two layers separated by banana leaves and cook-stones. Unfortunately, unlike the domestic pig described here, we had no rights to collect the bones for study.

The absence of women

It is interesting to note that all the butchery was executed by men and watched by a crowd of men as well as some children. Even the consumption of the meat was a male business, but a woman was asked to wash the intestines. We have no idea if these practices can be considered as a true division of labour, a consequence of some strict (social or religious) rules, or just a coincidence. In the case of the Dugum Dani, Heider (1970: 54) mentions that the children were sent to the river to clean the intestines and that women sometimes participated in the butchery.

Comparisons with other Papuan groups

Except for descriptions of the way in which domestic pigs are killed, we found very few detailed descriptions of pig butchery with which to compare our observations. Bulmer (1976: 180) states that the Kalam jointed pigs prior to cooking, and that the pelvis was smashed with heavy stones to dismember the hindlimbs. Stones were used again to break the skull in order to extract the brain after cooking, but the mandibles were left intact. As far as we know, the most detailed description of butchery practice was published by Heider (1970: 52–5) for the Dugum Dani peoples who live close to the Yali. The Dugum Dani manner of butchering resembles that documented by us, but there are some small differences, which may characterize the two groups of people and their different traditions. However, it is important to note that we have recorded only one particular event, and that this occurred without a ritual context (although confirmed by another observation of wild boar butchery not detailed here). In contrast, Heider's summary is based on many observations of pigs that were prepared during ceremonies.

The Dugum Dani kill pigs with a bow and arrow. The ears and tails are cut off and taken into the houses. The carcass is then put, while still intact, on the fire and the hair scraped off with sticks. After this, the butchers begin the carcass preparation with two parallel cuts, one each on either side of the mouth down to the stomach and meeting at the anus. After the masseter muscles are sectioned with a knife, the mandibles are dismembered, with the bone being held in the hand; they are extracted by force and with great difficulty. The pelvis is broken with an adze blow to the pubic symphysis. Each side of the rib-rack is removed separately and usually in one piece, and the vertebral column is treated in the same manner. The cranium is opened with an adze blow to extract the brain (no more precise details are given by Heider). All pieces of the carcass, as well as the internal organs and the flesh, are cut into long strips and then cooked in an earth oven. Further damage to the long bones results from extraction of marrow, and the tusk was extracted from the mandibles using stones, which damaged the bones. Comparison with Yali butchery practices shows that they differ in the sequence of operations: by the Dani the mandible is dismembered and the brain extracted before cooking. In addition, in the initial stage of butchery by the Dani, two ventral cuts to the skin are made as opposed to only one by the Yali.

BONE ANALYSIS

As we requested, all participants deposited the pig bones at one place after the meal. These were then collected and cleaned by boiling in a pot with soap over a wood fire. This bone assemblage was brought back to the Natural History Museum in Geneva for study. The following section describes the skeletal element representation and the observed modifications to the bones as identified after visual inspection and examination using a binocular micro-scope (6×–18×). The location and nature of the damage is described in relation to the different stages of butchery and consumption.

Skeletal element representation

Figure 17.5 and Table 17.1 document the breakdown of skeletal elements recovered relative to the number in a complete pig skeleton. The cranium and mandibles were the only elements fully recovered (100%), followed by the metapodials, the long bones, and the ribs (94–89%); the least represented were the vertebrae and sesamoids (<50%). Although our ideal project was to study the complete skeleton, it transpired that numerous bones were missing. A humerus and half a pelvis were among the largest elements missing, suggesting that factors other than destruction of small bones during consumption were responsible.

Different reasons can be proposed to explain this disparate skeletal distri-bution. The most evident is that some parts of the carcass, containing one large bone or a range of smaller elements, may have been removed from the main consumption area to be eaten elsewhere. Although the adults complied

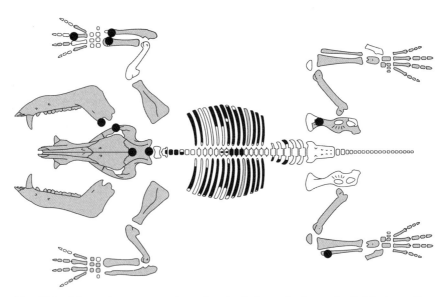

Fig. 17.5. Schematic representation of a pig skeleton (redrawn by F. Marteau after Helmer 1987: fig. 2) showing bones recovered (in grey) and skeletal elements with modifications (in black)

Table 17.1. Breakdown of skeleton elements from the Yali butchery and consumption event.

Skeletal elements	Bones	N observed	% N observed	Caused by
Cranium	1	1	100	
Mandibles	2	2	100	
Cervical vertebrae	7	3 (4)	44 (57)	Human dispersion
Thoracic vertebrae	14	3 (5)	21 (36)	Human dispersion
Lumbar vertebrae	5	0 (3)	0 (60)	Human dispersion
Sacral vertebrae	1	0	0	Human dispersion
Caudal vertebrae	20	0	0	Human dispersion or consumption
Ribs	28	25	89	Human dispersion
Girdles	4	3	75	Human dispersion
Long bones	14	13	93	Human dispersion
Patella	2	1	50	Human dispersion or consumption
Metapodials	16	15	94	Consumption
Tarsals/carpals	28	16	57	Consumption
Sesamoids	32	4	13	Collection and/or consumption
Phalanges	48	33	69	Consumption

N observed is the number of complete or almost complete bones ($<$ 2/3), ( ) is the number of bones including small fragments.

with our request to give us all the bones, we had more difficulties with the children who rapidly scattered with pieces of the pig in their hands. This manner of 'human dispersion' of the bones is the main factor responsible for the absence of skeletal elements (Table 17.1). Particularly the vertebrae, parts that were preferentially given to children, may have suffered this fate.

However, consumption damage, including human gnawing, and possibly spitting out or swallowing of small bones (complete elements or small parts of larger elements reduced during butchery) have also impacted the skeletal representation. Moreover, tiny bones such as sesamoids may have been lost during cleaning of the bone assemblage after the meal.

Primary butchery

Modifications to the bones have been divided according to four different activities: primary butchery, cooking, further division of the carcass for consumption, and damage resulting from consumption.

Three tools are associated with the initial butchery of the pig: bow and arrow, stone adze, and bamboo knife. It is interesting to note that despite the

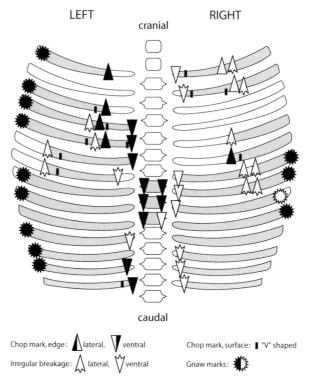

Fig. 17.6. Detail of modifications to the thorax showing chop marks, irregular fractures, and human gnaw marks (black triangle: orientation of the blow identified on the bone, white triangle: orientation of the blow documented only by the Yali butchery). The two parts of broken ribs could be re-assembled for the 4th and 5th left + 1st, 2nd, 7th, and 8th right ribs. Butchery: damages along the vertebrae were made by ventral blows and those on the mid-shaft of the ribs by lateral blows (cf. section on Yali butchery). During bone analysis, the determination of the fracturing agent (the stone adze) and the direction of the blow (ventral or lateral) was possible only in some cases (black triangles). In most of the cases, the fracture shows an irregular edge or, in the case of a true spiral mark (chop mark), the direction of the blow was not identifiable. Consumption: human gnaw marks affect the ventral end of the ribs and are characterized by ragged ends and shallow pits. The 9th right rib show an oblique edge which is not a clear gnaw mark

extensive use of the bamboo knife to remove limbs and sever flesh, no cut marks were found on any of the bones. The stone adze, however, caused major damage. This mainly affected the trunk and took the form of chop marks and breakage, which were caused by pounding the carcass with the adze in order to open the thorax (Figs 17.2g, 17.6). Chop marks associated with this action are typically found on the external face of the ribs at the mid-shaft region and are limited to the cranial part of the thoracic cage, including the first to the 7th (left side) and 8th (right side) ribs (Fig. 17.6). In cases where the bone was fractured, the broken end has an oblique edge and resembles a true spiral fracture typically found on fresh bone (Lyman 1994: 319) (39% out of an NISP of 18) or a saw-toothed profile (56% out of an NISP of 18). It is possible to distinguish the lateral orientation of the blow on six of the seven true spiral fractures. Other marks are V-shaped and represent lateral blows, which did not result in breakage of the bone (39% out of an NISP of 18); they are all found parallel and adjacent to a true spiral fracture.

It is interesting to note that on the six ribs with their two parts present, a true spiral was never observed on both sides of the fracture and was even absent in two cases, the 7th and 8th right ribs, which may have been broken by finger pressure only, as observed during the butchery (Fig. 17.2h). In addition, a direct fit of the bone fragments was impossible in only one case (8th right rib).

The pelvis was also fractured during this primary butchery with blows from the ventral side to dismember the hindlimbs. The right pelvis, which was broken into three pieces that could be joined, exhibited only one imprint resulting from the stone adze: a V-shaped mark on the ventral part of the ilium (Fig. 17.7a). All the pelvic fractures have a saw-toothed profile.

Cooking

For cooking, the pig carcass was initially divided into six pieces plus the internal organs. All these were placed on an open fire to remove the hair and for roasting. They were then placed in an earth oven with cook-stones. With the exception of the pelvis and the mid-shaft edge of the 8th right rib, we found no evidence of burning on the other skeletal elements or teeth. The pelvis has a carbonized area at the broken end of the neck of the ileum. The extent of the scorched zone is limited to the bone surface that was not covered by flesh, as shown by the straight edge of the burnt area (Fig. 17.7b). It is evident that this damage is a consequence of roasting the hindlimb over the flames, because the bone is completely blackened and the discoloration is not limited to a small area, which could have resulted from touching a cooking-stone.

As we observed numerous times, at the end of important ceremonies entailing the consumption of several pigs (Dani group), the bone remains were generally collected and burned in a large fire. This was of course not the case in our staged event.

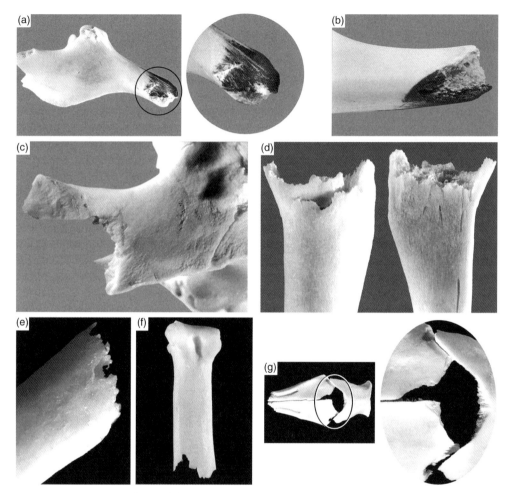

Fig. 17.7. Traces observed from the skeleton. (a) Chop mark on the right pelvis, ventral view: V-shaped mark on the ventral part of the cervix of the ileum (cf. Fig. 3c). (b) Burnt edge of the right pelvis, dorsal view: straight edge of the burnt area showing the limit of flesh protecting the bone from the flames (cf. Fig. 17.4a). (c) Human gnaw marks on the right zygoma: crashed edge and shallow pits (cf. Fig. 17.4d); one chop mark (V-shaped mark) is also recognizable. (d) Human gnaw marks on the distal end of the first left rib, lateral and medial view: ragged edge and cracks. (e) Human gnaw marks on the distal end of the first left rib: ragged edge and shallow pits. (f) Human gnaw marks on the right metacarpal III: ragged edge. (g) chop mark on the frontal bones: a unique transverse blow with the stone adze creates a hole that facilitates the extraction of the brain

Further division of the carcass for consumption

After cooking, the six pieces of the pig carcass (not counting the internal organs) were further subdivided for consumption. As people helped themselves to parts at random, this further division of the carcass was difficult to document. Some of this re-division was later reconstructed from the photographs we took. This is the case for the snout of the pig. In Fig. 17.4d, we can clearly see that this piece was fractured at the level of the zygoma: the right zygoma is broken but the break follows the natural sutures between the nasals and frontals, and the left maxilla and zygoma. Other divisions of elements intended for consumption can be deduced on the basis of the bone analysis, for example the dismemberment of the right leg from the foot, at the distal part of the radius and ulna (Fig. 17.5). This limb may have been crushed at the articulation between the radio-ulna and the carpals (maybe with a stone? or see below for an alternative hypothesis: gnawing).

The type of damage resulting during this further subdivision of the carcass into smaller packages of meat for consumption is manifested in chop marks visible on the ventral aspect of the ribs and vertebrae. As illustrated in Fig. 17.6, they affect the proximal part of the ribs and the lateral processes of the vertebrae with which they articulate. As this activity was carried out with the adze, the resulting bone modifications on the ribs resembled those resulting from primary butchery of the uncooked carcass as described above: V-shaped chop marks (10% of an NISP of 21), oblique edges (43% of an NISP of 21, including 24% with an identifiable ventral orientation) and sawtoothed profiles (29% of an NISP of 21). As we know that all ribs were separated from the vertebral column, it is interesting to note that 29% (9:21) were left intact. Of the small number of surviving vertebrae, the three centra of the thoracic vertebrae show tool impact marks on both lateral sides, and a ventral orientation for the blows can be identified on five of the six impacts. The lumbar vertebrae, represented only by four lateral processes, have suffered similar damage as shown by the orientation of the blows, all of them severed by a ventral blow.

Damage resulting from consumption

Several bones show typical gnaw marks, including pitting of the surface and a ragged end (Fig. 17.7c–e). As we know that no dogs were present during the butchery, all these toothmarks can be attributed to human gnawing. Clear gnaw marks were observed on the distal extremities of 12 ribs (Fig. 17.6) and on the broken end of the right zygoma which has a ragged edge, cracks, and shallow pits (Fig. 17.7c). The extent of damage to the ribs ranged from 2 mm to about 2 cm from the distal end: the extremities are crushed, cracks are visible, and small, shallow, rounded pits are also evident (Fig. 17.7d, e). As the distal ends of the ribs stay soft as long as the animal is growing, they can easily be chewed like the bones of a young chicken. On another rib, the distal end exhibits an oblique edge, which may be the consequence of human gnawing. Clearly identifiable human gnaw marks occur on 52% ($n = 12$) of the 23 distal ribs examined. This frequency increases to 57% when we include the oblique edge, gnaw damage that is less clear.

The same type of damage as observed on the distal ribs and right zygoma was observed on the broken diaphysis of the right metacarpal III, whose distal part is missing (Fig. 17.7f). This resemblance may confirm that the loss of the other elements of this forefoot was due to consumption. The phalanges are small, and the distal epiphysis of the metacarpals were unfused, so they could easily have been chewed. In the light of this interpretation, the crushing observed on the distal end of the radius and ulna of the same foot may also be attributable to human gnawing, even though clear pit marks are absent.

Unlike our study, where human gnawing damage was limited to the ribs, Brain (1969: 16) found that the Hottentots were capable of inflicting considerable damage to unfused limb bones with their teeth. In the latter case, both ends of the femur and the distal part of the metapodials suffered extensive damage from gnawing, and fifteen tail vertebrae were chewed and swallowed. In contrast, the phalanges, which were already fused, were undamaged. Surprisingly, the distal parts of the ribs were only slightly affected. A factor that may have contributed to the greater intensity of human gnawing damage in the Hottentot sample was the far longer time taken to consume the goat carcass: 2 days instead of 1 hour.

None of the bones resulting from the Yali butchery event exhibited evidence of marrow extraction, i.e. the breaking of long bones. Ethnography of the Dugum Dani from the Papuan Highlands (Heider 1970: 55) documents marrow extraction by smashing bones with rocks. Bulmer (1976: 180) notes that whether or not the Kalam of Papua New Guinea bother to smash long bones to extract the marrow depends on how much meat is available and on the hunger of those present. Thus, in the case of our study, the sufficient quantity of meat available for all present, the limited time taken for the meal, as well as the fact that we had requested that all bones be kept for us, may have contributed to the fact that the bones were not fractured for marrow. Although the bones were not broken, the cranium was fractured to extract the brain: a transverse blow created a hole in the frontal and left an oblique edge to the fracture (Fig. 17.7g).

CONCLUSIONS

The traditional pig butchery performed by the Yali from the village of Kosarek, in the Highlands of West Papua, offers an interesting ethnographic and archaeozoological case study. From the limited published literature examined by us, it is clear that Papuan Highlanders kill pigs in a variety of ways. However, the absence of comparable published data does not allow us to assess whether butchery and cooking of pigs follow different fashions as well. Among the Yali pig butchery was carried out using only two tools, a stone adze and bamboo knife, and this activity was restricted to males. It is important to note that the wild pig killed by Yali hunters in the neighbouring forest was butchered and cooked in the same manner as the domestic sow studied here, and the differences observed were only a consequence of the larger size of the wild animal.

With respect to the archaeozoology of this study, it was interesting to see that although we found bone damage in locations on the carcass that could clearly be related to specific butchery actions, much of the dismemberment of the carcass left no damage on the bones, for example cut marks from the bamboo knife. In some cases, the observed modification to the bones was not diagnostic of a specific butchery activity, while in others both the type of mark, its orientation, and its location enabled clear identification of its aetiology. We had not expected to find such clear evidence of human gnawing, which was especially common on the distal ribs. It may be that given more time, the frequency of this damage and number of bones affected would have increased. Bone survival was related to the dispersion of carcass elements by people and not just bone size or method of food preparation. It is suggested that all these factors need be taken into account when discussing bone taphonomy in archaeological contexts.

18

Pigs in the New Guinea Highlands: an ethnographic example

Paul Sillitoe

INTRODUCTION

Although archaeologists have long shown an interest in drawing on ethnographic parallels to further understanding of their findings (e.g. Orme 1981), anthropologists proved reluctant to engage in such endeavours for most of the 20th century. This was a reaction to the excesses of 19th century social evolutionary thinking that Europeans used in part to justify colonialism in various parts of the world, which they portrayed as an inevitable process as they, the 'fittest', encroached on the territories of 'savages'. We have gradually been moving towards a more constructive engagement with archaeologists, and it is in this spirit that I offer this contribution to this volume, and have cooperated with archaeologist colleagues on other projects (Shott & Sillitoe 2001; 2004 Sillitoe & Hardy 2003). Nonetheless it comes with the usual anthropological warning about the need to maintain a culturally relative frame of mind when reading this chapter with a view to illuminating any archaeological data.

There is no suggestion that the practices discussed here may be taken as somehow representative of any prehistoric population. Although those who live in a subsistence economy may offer more apt, better-scale comparisons with respect to pig-keeping than those who live in a market economy, the implication is not that they are stuck in the past. One cannot assume that such practices reflect those of ancient populations in Europe or elsewhere. They are unique cultural arrangements with their own histories. One of the most valuable lessons that we might draw from a consideration of ethnographic evidence is how enormously variable are human cultural formations, in this case in relation to pig management. In the Papua New Guinea Highlands it is

The data on pigs discussed in this chapter were published in *Managing Animals in New Guinea: preying the game in the Highlands* and I am grateful to Routledge for permission to use them again here.

with respect to socio-political exchange, which is developed in this region to extraordinary lengths (Sillitoe 1998), that we have to consider pig-keeping arrangements. The exchange focus conditions attitudes to pigs in ways that are unique, even surprising, for those of us accustomed to think in market terms. Furthermore, the data presented here should not be taken as typical of the Pacific region as they come from only one valley in the Highlands. The Melanesian region displays great cultural variety with regard to pig-keeping, as in other domains, and for a representative view one needs to consult a wide range of sources. The recent bibliographical review of Robin Hide (2003) is an excellent place to start such a appraisal, followed by some other ethnography (*e.g.* Vayda *et al.* 1961; Pospisil 1963: 203–18; Rappaport 1968; Hughes 1970: 272; Hide 1981; Boyd 1984, 1985; Kelly 1988; Dwyer 1993).

Highlanders are well known for their sizeable pig herds and colourful festivals at which they periodically slaughter large numbers of animals and distribute pork. The Wola of the Southern Highlands Province, the subject of this chapter, are no exception and, like people throughout Papua New Guinea, regularly transact pigs with one another. The exchange of these animals, with other wealth (including cash today and previously sea-shells and cosmetic oil), between defined categories of kin on specified social occasions, is a prominent feature of social life. As Lederman (1986: 16–17) elegantly puts it for those in the Mendi valley 'pigs are not simply good to eat; they are also a form of wealth and have value insofar as they are made to stand for social relationships. . . . Large pig herds are an artefact of sociopolitical relations that create high demand for pigs'. After the fashion of ethnographers elsewhere, I have investigated these activities while paying little attention to the logistics of pig-keeping (Sillitoe 1979). The transactions remain today a significant force for order in this fiercely egalitarian society with weak central government authority. Lawless 'rascal' activity is prevalent throughout the region. The government station at Nipa in the Nembi valley has some administrative offices, including nominally a police station, a high school, and a health centre, and several trade stores. Men who excel at exchange achieve locally positions of renown and influence, earning the appellative *ol howma*, approximating to bigmen elsewhere.

THE WOLA

The Wola occupy five valleys from the Mendi river in the east to the Augu in the west. The data discussed here come from the Nipa Basin Census Division, notably the Was valley in the west. The country is rugged, comprising sharp-crested mountain ridges. Watersheds and some valley areas are heavily forested, other settled parts are under regrowth, notably cane grassland. The Wola are swidden and fallow horticulturalists, their neat gardens dotted about valleys. Sweet potato is the staple, typically cultivated in composted mounds; other crops include bananas, taro, various cucurbits, and greens (Bourke *et al.* 1995; Sillitoe 1996). A marked gender division informs gardening activities, men undertaking the initial work of clearing and fencing and woman largely assuming responsibility for routine cultivation. Both humans and pigs depend on garden produce, pigs being fed largely on sweet potato.

People live in homesteads comprising nuclear or extended families, scattered along the sides of valleys, indistinctly grouped together on territories, to which kinship structures access to land (Sillitoe 1999), resulting in loosely constituted kin corporations. Wolaland is divided up into a large number of territories to which these kin groups, called *sem* 'families', claim rights collectively. Supernatural beliefs centred on ancestors' spirits causing sickness and death by 'eating' vital organs, other powers of sorcery and 'poison', and malevolent forest spirits. Sometimes people offered pigs to restrain these malicious supernatural powers. Today many people profess to be Christians and attend mission services. The region is described as peripheral in development terms, although the Highlands Highway runs through Wola territory. Cash crops are few. But with gas and oil finds the position may change, with exploitation of these in the near future.

The work involved in herding pigs follows the common Highlands pattern (Pospisil 1963; Rappaport 1968; Feacham 1973; Hide 1981; Boyd 1984). The daily routine is for a woman to release her pigs in the early morning to forage for the day in neighbouring fallow grassland and forest; except troublesome pigs, which she may keep penned up or tethered on a rope. Sometimes people put animals in harvested gardens to feed on any remaining tubers and other crops. They say that pigs forage for earthworms mainly, which are necessary for fattiness. In the late afternoon pigs are conditioned to return to the homestead. When they arrive they are fed their tuber ration (Fig. 18.1). They spend the night in stalls, traditionally built at the rear of women's houses, although today many are housed in adjacent lean-to shelters in response to admonitions that living with pigs is dirty and unhealthy. Some women regularly manage more pigs than others and are admired for their ability, earning the appellative of *ten howma* as a mark of their widely respected competence; as with men, this title carries no authority. The literal meaning of the term is 'woman communal-clearing', the *howma* clearing, or village green equivalent, being where many exchange events occur, often featuring pigs.

It should be noted that the free-ranging arrangement of the Wola differs from that found in some more densely populated Highlands regions

Fig. 18.1. Kwal feeding sweet potato tubers to her pigs in the late afternoon outside her house in the Was valley in the Southern Highlands Province of Papua New Guinea (copyright P. Sillitoe, University of Durham)

such as Chimbu where people more often tether or pen animals during the day (Hide 1981: 328) or some Enga who use river flats enclosed by steep banks (Feacham 1973: 27). The extent to which the recent avoidance of dwelling together with pigs reflects a Eurocentric reaction to living with 'dirty' animals on the one hand, or on the other hand represents sound health advice, I am unsure. After generations of living with pigs, one might have expected the Wola themselves to have discovered any dangers to their health (see Feacham 1973: 25, 1975 on environmental health hazards of pigs, notably to surface water supplies; Reay 1984: 71–2 on the effects of colonial interference on pig-keeping among the Kuma of the Western Highlands; and Watt *et al.* 1977: 23–31 for an example of extension advice about appropriate housing).

THE PIGS

A unique animal in behaviour, ecology, and cultural salience, the Wola word for pig is *showmay* or *taz*, among others. (The word for 'pig' changes between communities over short distances. In the Nembi valley, for instance, one hears

people speak of *maen* and in the Mendi valley *mok.*) Its zoological identity
has been disputed by taxonomists. The majority of writers identify the New
Guinea pig as *Sus scrofa* (Linnaeus 1758), the widespread 'common wild boar',
sometimes adding the subspecies name *papuensis* to differentiate it from its
European and Asian cousins (Baldwin 1978: 23, 1982: 41; Hughes 1970: 277,
citing Laurie & Hill 1954: 86). A few follow the suggestion that the subspecies
should be raised to a species designation and refer to *Sus papuensis*, the
'New Guinea pig' (Lesson & Garnot 1826). Yet others dispute this subspecies
identification, thinking that it should be *vittatus*, or the 'Indonesian banded pig'
(Jentink 1905, after Boie 1828). Following a thorough review of the evidence,
including a multivariate analysis of skull data, Groves (1981: 66, see also Groves
this volume) concludes that New Guinea pigs are hybrids of two species: *Sus
scrofa vittatus*, the 'banded pig' and *Sus celebensis*, the 'Sulawesi warty pig'
(other suggested scientific identifications have not found favour, such as *Sus
verrucosus* the 'warty pig', *Sus aruensis* the 'Aru pig', or *Sus niger* the 'black pig',
among others listed by Groves 1981: 66). This interpretation of the evidence
probably reflects the influence of human activities over the millennia on the
island's pig population, people bringing in animals from nearby Indonesia
and intervening in breeding behaviour. The population has not enjoyed the
reproductive isolation necessary for species evolution. The wild and domestic
pig populations remain today genetically continuous.

The Wola pig is a relatively short and stocky animal with an overall rounded
body outline, and 'heavy forequarters and light hindquarters' (Watt *et al.* 1977:
13). It has small, erect ears, and a long, heavy, wrinkled snout that ends in a
prominent and highly mobile fleshy disc. The tail is tufted and usually straight.
The animal has dark skin usually and conspicuous coat of coarse bristles which
can vary in colour from black through brown to white, sometimes patchy or
variably patterned, or striped in piglets. The bristles are prominent along the
spine, frequently standing erect in adults, running mane-like from between
the ears down the back and earning the animal the name of 'razorback pig'
(Vayda 1972: 905). When adult, pigs stand about 60 cm tall and may weigh
upwards of 75 kg. They are herd animals, although sometimes they fight.

The Wola distinguish between pigs according to their sex and size. Small
piglets of both sexes they call *hondba*, a term used for small animals generally.
An intact boar is a *tuw* (literally 'testicles'), and a male piglet may be specified
as a *tuw-hondba*. A hog or castrated male animal is a *saendapow*. A gilt or
female animal that has not littered is a *way*, and a female piglet may in turn be
designated a *way-hondba*. A sow is an *injiy* (literally 'mother'), again a term
used for other animals, including humans. A large mature animal with
prominent curling canine tusks is a *himalwaenk* (literally 'tooth-*waenk*'),
which people sometimes convey in speech with a bent fore finger hooked

into the cheek. If necessary people can use adjectives to specify the size of animals, such as *genk* 'small' and *onda* 'large', or appropriately qualified versions of these, such as *genkora* 'very small' or *ondasha* 'largish', and so on. In addition they classify pigs according to differences in appearance, largely coat colour plus one or two other features (Sillitoe 2003: 245–7).

The notion of a breed is a new one that has arrived with the introduction to the Southern Highlands of exotic breeds, notably Tamworths, Berkshires, and Large Blacks, by government agricultural officers (*didimans*) with a view to stock improvement and commercial production (Malynicz 1971: 72, 1973*a*: 20; Watt *et al.* 1977: 13–14; Devendra & Fuller 1979: 28–33; Eusebio 1980: 7–17). The Wola call these introduced pigs *susu* (from the Pidgin term *susu pik* 'milk pig', Malynicz 1973*a*: 17), and point out that they differ from indigenous pigs. They have large ears, short stubby snouts, shorter legs, and elongated, rounded body profiles. They have a soft muffled grunt compared to the loud squeals of indigenous pigs, and they are more sparsely bristled. People are impressed with the size to which these pigs can grow but few have ever owned one; some have never even seen one. They do not do well under local conditions; in the opinion of Malynicz (1973*a*: 20), a one-time Senior Veterinary Officer in Papua New Guinea, 'the main factors restricting growth are undernutrition of all nutrients'. The free-ranging local pig management regime soon results in cross-breeding between any exotic stock introduced into the region and local animals, giving rise to another new class of pig called *aumuw*. The appearance of these pigs varies, depending on the proportion of their genetic make-up originating from the foreign breed. They have larger ears than local pigs and less bristly coats with a less pronounced 'razorback' mane. In short, the local non-concept of breed reasserts itself, any introduced pigs being absorbed into the herd after a few generations without physical trace.

METHODOLOGY: PIG HERD SURVEYS

The data on pig demography discussed here come from a series of surveys conducted periodically over 24 years in two neighbouring *semonda* 'large family' communities in the Was valley, which have a combined population of between 300 and 400 persons (see Sillitoe 2003 for a full account). These data concern the herd in one geographical locality over time. The mobility of the Wola population has presented some problems in handling these longitudinal data. I have had to judge who was resident during any survey period. Some families maintain homesteads on other territories too, and I have included their pig herds if they had resided in the survey region sometime during the previous 12 months or so. Beyond this I have counted them as living elsewhere and discounted their herds (some of these families have subsequently moved back into the survey region, others have departed permanently). Regarding men who have migrated elsewhere to work (e.g. Mendi or Hagen), I have counted them in if their families have remained in the region. Or, if they have migrated *en famille*, I have treated them as families maintaining homesteads in two places and applied the 12-month rule (those who no longer maintain homes in the region and visit regularly I have discounted).

During each of the surveys all men in their late teens and older were asked a series of standard questions about the pigs in their herds at the time. The information for each survey was entered into a database for analysis, the results presented here. They supply a reasonably comprehensive longitudinal picture of pig herd demography. For comparative pig population census data see Hide (1981: 405–10) on the Sinasina, Feacham (1973: 28–9) on the Enga, Boyd (1984: 37–47) on the Awa, Kelly (1988: 132–43) and Dwyer (1990: 58–9) on the Etolo, and Dwyer (1993: 126–7) on a small Kubo population.

The data suggest that when herds are at their maximum extent they parallel the human population with one pig for every man, woman, and child, and fall to nearly 0.5 per capita at their lowest levels. The statistics on pigs per person for other regions show considerable variation too, probably reflecting to some extent widespread fluctuation in herd sizes over time. Malynicz (1976: 202) gives figures of 0.88–2.1 for communities in the Eastern and Western Highlands, Waddell (1972) 2.3 pigs per head and Feacham (1973: 29) 1.1–3.1 per head for the Enga, and Baldwin (1978: 23) quotes an upper figure of 2.5 for the Enga region, but Feil (1976: 445) reports considerably more at four pigs per person. Rappaport (1968) gives a range of 0.3–0.8 for the Jimi valley, Boyd (1984: 37) 0.55–0.7 for the Awa of the Eastern Highlands, and the Chimbu pig population according to Brookfield and Brown (1963: 59) is 'one grown pig per head: allowing for piglets, we might assume 1.5 adult pigs per head as maximum' (the Sinasina data of Hide (1981: 407) agree with these figures). Longhouse communities of the nearby Etolo on the Papuan plateau had between 0.52 and 1.39 pigs per person (Dwyer 1990: 58–9), and among the Anga there are 0.5 pigs per head (Bonnèmere & Lemonnier 1992: 140). For further statistics of pig populations in lowland and fringe highlands societies, see Dwyer (1993: 134) and Kelly (1988: 150, table 2).

The men surveyed were asked at the start how many pigs they owned. They were then asked for each of these animals to specify its sex and status (e.g. an *injiy* sow, *saendapow* hog, or whatever). Some of these assessments depend more than others on subjective judgements. There is no clear cut distinction between larger male piglets and sub-adult boars which have not serviced sows, and the same animal may be classed by some people as a *hondba* piglet and by others as a *tuw* boar. There is a similar blurred line between female piglets and gilts, although it is statistically less significant because there are large numbers of animals in both classes—unlike males, few of which remain intact for any time and are capable of servicing females. The classification of large hogs as *himalwaenk* tuskers is also liable to subjective variation; the point at which the canines are sufficiently large and curled to put an animal in this class is debatable (some people are given to exaggerating the status of their pigs).

Also recorded was the size of the beast according to one of seven descriptive classes: *onda ora* 'very large', *onda* 'large', *onda sha* 'largish', *genksha* 'smallish', *genk* 'small', *genkden* 'smaller' and *genk ora* 'very small' (newborn piglet). People can give reliable estimates using these comparative terms. Initially, I tried to survey all herds in the presence of the animals for enumeration purposes but this proved too difficult to arrange. Nonetheless I completed many questionnaires in view of the pigs of an evening as they returned home, and men's estimates accorded well with my own. For analytical purposes I amalgamated the first two size classes into a single 'large' category, the second pair into a 'medium' category, and the last three into a 'small' category.

The survey schedule also asked about local classification of the animal, usually by coat colour. Next I asked respondents how long they had owned the animal in question, in 'Christmas' years and moons. Again these data are somewhat subjective, being liable to memory error. But I was able to engage in limited cross-checking with earlier surveys for pigs owned over considerable time periods, memories becoming less reliable the longer the time. The list of questions included the name of the person responsible for herding the animal and her relation to the respondent. Finally, I took down details of how the person had obtained the pig (born to one of his sows, received in an exchange transaction such as a bridewealth or mortuary payment, through purchase, and so on), and for some pigs I was also able to note their subsequent disposal (slaughter, died of sickness, passed on in an exchange payment, and so on).

PIG DEVELOPMENT

According to the Wola, a sow is pregnant for three moons and litters during the fourth, called *hondba maeray* (lit. off-spring carries) (according to Hide 1981: 449, gestation for Highlands pigs is 114 days). A sow becomes restless at the time that she is due to farrow and may wander off, seeking a suitable nesting site. It is usual for sows to build a nest of vegetation,

Table 18.1. Pig litter statistics.

Total no. litters	Total no. piglets	Average size of litter	No. surviving piglets	Piglet death rate	Sow death rate	No. men questioned	No. never having litters	Average no. litters per man
321	1522	4.74	1189	22%	2.5%	77	12	4.2

often away in the forest or nearby in a clump of *Miscanthus* cane grass, in which to farrow and suckle their young. Sometimes women lose track of sows at this time and have to search for them. They do not interfere, but seek to lure the mother and her litter back to the homestead as soon as practicable with food. These practices are widespread throughout the Highlands (Malynicz 1970: 201) (the Sinasina are likewise careful not to disturb a sow that has recently farrowed: Hide 1981: 460). The number of piglets in a litter can vary from one to eight. The average is 4–5 (Table 18.1); this compares with Malynicz (1976: 204) who reports a range of 3.6–4.8, Hide (1981: 460) who reports the mean Sinasina litter as 4.8 (for 23 litters), Boyd (1984: 42) who records 4.1 (for 15 litters) for the Awa, Kelly (1988: 136) who records 5.6 (for 9 litters) for the Etolo, and Pospisil (1963: 203) who reports the average Kapauku litter as 6 piglets (for 8 litters). These figures are low compared to litter rates elsewhere in the tropics, particularly commercial ones (Devendra & Fuller 1979: 47, give figures from 4.3 to 14).

The mortality rate is high, with nearly one-quarter of piglets dying, and sometimes, disastrously, farrowing sows also die (2.5% according to these data), which deters some people from breeding. The piglet mortality rate in Kapauku herds is similar, at 27% (Pospisil 1963: 207), in Sinasina herds it is higher with 42% of piglets dying and a thumping 37% of sows (Hide 1981: 453, 462). Eastern Highlands data suggest piglet mortality rates of 38–47% (Malynicz 1976: 204), and on the Papuan plateau, where the pig herding system is more extensive with domestic animals foraging in the forest alongside wild ones, 56% of young pigs die and 5% of sows (Kelly 1988: 137, 140). The number of litters that men have is low. A survey of a sample of men, asking them for details of all the litters that they could recall in their herds, revealed an average of 4.2 litters per man. The numbers understandably increase with age (Table 18.2), the data suggesting that men have on average two litters a decade. This translates into a mean total for men of a dozen litters throughout the course of their lives, some men having fewer than this and others more; the maximum number was a man with 3 wives who had managed 27 litters between them (16 was the maximum number of litters managed by any woman). Even allowing for memory failure, particularly for

Table 18.2. Pig litters according to men's ages (difference significant (av. litters): $\chi^2 = 15.50$ (d.f. $= 5, a = 0.05$)).

Age	No. men	No. litters	Average no. litters per man	Total no. piglets	No. piglets surviving	No. sows lost
<20 yrs	7	3	0.4	12	6	
20–29 yrs	26	54	2.1	278	208	1
30–39 yrs	21	94	4.5	411	311	
40–49 yrs	17	108	6.4	522	406	7
50–59 yrs	4	48	12	240	204	
>60 yrs	2	13	6.5	58	54	

older men, these statistics are low and illustrate peoples' somewhat reluctant attitudes to pig production. They suggest a particularly low reproduction rate, below those reported elsewhere, such as 27% of Awa sows farrowing in a year (Boyd 1984: 42), 28% of Maring sows (Rappaport 1968: 70) and 32% of Asaro sows (Malynicz 1976: 207). The Wola people say that some sows make better mothers than others, with higher piglet survival rates and larger litters. People may breed more than average from such sows and hang on to them until their fertility declines, whereas they dispose more readily of others. The interval between litters is long, for the relatively few sows that breed more than once.

The principal concern of pig-keepers is to promote the rapid and healthy growth of their animals. According to the Wola the rate at which pigs grow varies, as does the final size they reach when fully grown—the same as human beings, they point out. Some piglets grow rapidly at first but develop more slowly in adolscence, others are slow starters but race away when adolescent, and so on. Some animals remain *dimb* 'diminutive' all their lives, and these runts never seem to grow beyond the size others reach during adolescence. Others develop into large *himalwaenk* 'tuskers' with rolls of fat on their bodies, particularly *saendapow* hogs that not only grow faster than females but also on the whole attain larger sizes when adult. The sexual dimorphism is marked if a female litters, sows losing weight and condition—the Sinasina data show reproducing sows losing 0.2 kg per month (Hide 1981: 474). It can take them sometime to regain their weight, which further deters people from arranging for them to breed (Malynicz 1976: 208 notes the Chimbu prevent breeding to ensure sows grow).

The variation in development makes it difficult to specify growth rates and adult size of animals. Sows may have their first litter at about 2 years when sub-adult (Sinasina pigs do not breed until they are 18–24 months old, Hide 1981: 452). They attain their final size at about 6 years (this rate of development compares with that reported by Malynicz (1976: table III) for Eastern

Highlands herds). Pigs range in size and weight from small piglets, which at
2 months measure some 45 cm from tip of snout to base of tail and weigh in at
about 3–4 kg, to large males, which measure some 1.4 m long and can weigh
up to 130 kg. These weights are estimated from girth measurements, using
Hide's (1981: 647) valuable conversion table (Dwyer 1993: 125 has an equation to estimate pig weights). According to Malynicz (1970: 201), 1 year old
pigs average 22.7 kg and grow at 1.8 kg per month, a finding that Hide's (1981:
473) data confirm, Sinasina pigs putting on 1.6 kg per month average in their
first year, although their growth rates vary considerably from 0.9 to 2.2 kg per
month. These growth rates are considerably less than those achieved by exotic
breeds under commercial conditions, which may have a selective advantage,
for as Malynicz (1973*a*: 17) comments 'It is interesting to speculate that the
low growth potential of native pigs is a fitness characteristic which may
increase their survival rate under conditions of nutritional stress'. Even
when housed and fed under the same regime as commercial pigs they grow
more slowly, putting on weight at only 0.47 of the rate of Berkshires and
Tamworths (Malynicz 1973*b*: 25, table 2). 'The indigenous pig is significantly
slower growing, has a lower food consumption, a worse feed conversion ratio,
and smaller eye muscle and back fat dimensions at an equivalent slaughter
age' (Malynicz 1973*b*: 24). The natural lifespan of a pig people say is 12–16
years, although few live this long, except for exceptionally good breeding sows
that persons may be reluctant to slaughter.

   Nobody has ever suggested to me that one might take a sow that has grown
rapidly into a large adult and cross it with a boar that is growing quickly to
breed a litter of fast-growing offspring with the potential to achieve heavy
adult weights. When I try to discuss the idea of selection (see Dwyer 1996),
someone usually points out that the piglets in any litter vary in their rates of
development and adult size. There are dominant ones which may grow
quickly into large animals and there are runts which fail to develop to any
serious adult size, regardless of parentage. Furthermore, breeding with juvenile boars makes it difficult to select a sire according to growth potential with
any certainty, because overall growth rate and final size are difficult to hazard,
particularly as castration impacts noticeably on these traits.

PIG HERD DEMOGRAPHY

The average size of a man's herd is 4.3 animals, ranging in surveys from 1 to
27 pigs. The average number of animals in a woman's charge is lower at
3.3 animals, ranging from 1 to 16 pigs. Men call on unmarried and widowed

Table 18.3. Average numbers of pigs owned.

	Large pigs	Medium pigs	Small pigs
Men	1.1	1.6	1.6
Women	0.9	1.2	1.2

relatives to assist their wives with pig-herding. If we take all men in the samples, including those with no pigs, the average size of men's herds falls close to that of women's at 3.4 animals (these statistics come from 679 sample men, 540 of whom controlled a total of 2298 pigs, and 487 sample women herding a total of 1594 pigs). The composition of these average herds according to size of pigs is given in Table 18.3. The statistics compare with those reported elsewhere; Brookfield & Brown (1963: 58–9) for example report an average of 2–4.5 animals a family among the Chimbu, and Hide (1981: 319) gives an average 3.5 pigs per household for the nearby Sinasina.

These averages conceal the fluctuation that occurs in pig herds. They are in a state of constant flux, not only as animals are born or die or the occasional one runs wild, but also as their owners give and receive them in exchanges with one another and intermittently slaughter beasts. Figure 18.2 gives some indication of the fluctuation that occurs in pig numbers. A population can fall by some 50% on occasion or, conversely, double in size on others. The graph marks the principal events responsible for the falls in numbers, which were large communal pig kills (see Sillitoe 1979 for ethnographic details) and a severe drought. The fluctuation is to expected given the numerous reports from across the Highlands of festivals at which people kill large numbers of pigs. Others have documented similar population movements elsewhere (see

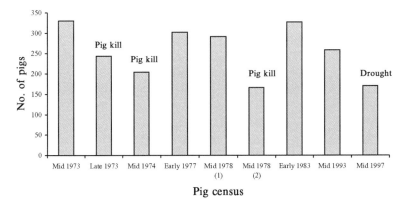

Fig. 18.2. Pig populations

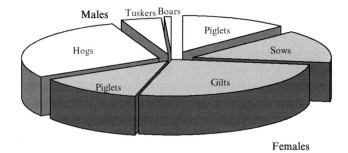

Fig. 18.3. Mean composition of pig herds according to pig classes

Hide 1981: 405–18 for a sophisticated reconstruction of herd recovery following festival slaughters among the Sinasina). The drought induced fall might also have been expected given the periodic occurrence of devastating shortfalls in food supply across the region (see Sillitoe 1996: 73–102 on the occurrence and consequences of these in the Wola region), although the magnitude is salutory, paralleling a pig kill.

A look at the mean composition of herds, according to the gender and age status of animals (*injiy* sows, *way* gilts, *saendapow* hogs and so on), reveals that *way* gilts predominate among females and *saendapow* hogs among male animals (Fig. 18.3). The number of piglets of either sex are approximately equal, and similar to the number of *injiy* sows in a herd. The data indicate that although the composition of the herd varies over time, the structure remains broadly constant regarding the proportion of different class animals. Gilts predominate among females and hogs among male animals whatever the size and structure of the herd (Table 18.4). It is the proportion of piglets to adult

Table 18.4. Pig census data according to pig classes.

Class	Wola Term	Mid 1973	Late 1973	Mid 1974	Early 1977	Mid 1978 (1)	Mid 1978 (2)	Early 1983	Mid 1993	Mid 1997	Mean
Females:											
Sows	*injiy*	38	24	18	68	58	18	64	33	20	37.9
Gilts	*way*	85	60	48	75	77	55	70	78	62	67.8
Piglets	*hondba way*	42	38	40	27	33	31	40	30	3	31.6
Males:											
Hogs	*sandapow*	96	73	54	82	85	32	82	72	75	72.3
Tusker hogs	*himalwaenk*	26	12	5	15	14	2	13	10	9	11.8
Boars	*tuw*	3	1	1	1	4	3	2	1	1	1.9
Piglets	*hondba tuw*	40	36	38	34	25	25	56	35		32.1
TOTALS		330	244	204	302	296	166	327	259	170	255.3

pigs that shows the most marked variation, which to be expected given the periodic mass culls that characterize pig herd management.

The Wola, similar to people throughout the Highlands, arrange large pig kills called *showmay tok liy* (literally 'pig pole kill') at intervals of every few years. These large communal events are a highlight of their transaction-dominated lives, at which many people collect for a massive exchange of pork (see Sillitoe 1979: 256–76 for details; also Ryan 1961, and Lederman 1986: 174–212). Men kill pigs with heavy wooden clubs fashioned for the purpose (Sillitoe 1988: 70–2), hitting animals several times across the bridge of the snout. They singe off their bristles over fires and butcher them following a standard procedure that involves removing a strip of belly pork, breaking open the rib cage to remove internal organs and peeling the chest flesh away to give two sides of pork, each with a front and rear leg attached (see Fig. 18.4). They invariably cook pork in earth ovens with tender young tree-fern fronds, distributing the cooked meat to relatives and friends. There is no indication in the data, nor has any person ever suggested to me, that there is any correlation between pig kill events and ritual and warfare, as argued for the Maring by Rappaport (1968) in his oft-cited work, in which he postulates a homeostatic ecological relationship between pig killing, demography, and human protein demands. Neither is there any evidence of regular 'pig cycles'; Lederman (1986:176) also questions their existence in the Mendi valley. Others have also thoroughly criticized Rappaport's argument and the data on which it depends (Friedman 1974, 1979; McArthur 1974, 1977; Bergmann 1975; Wagner 1977; Hide 1981: 549–62), although the author tried gamely, if vainly, to defend it (Kelly & Rappaport 1975; Rappaport 1977, 1984; see also Vayda & McCay 1977, Rappaport's model deriving substantially from ideas put forward in Vayda *et al.* 1961). Rappaport's subsequent intellectual interests served to distance him from neofunctional ecology (Biersack 1999; Rappaport 1999), although his cybernetic model of behaviour has proved attractive to many and has featured in many accounts of human ecology (e.g. Shantzis & Behrens 1973; Morren 1977; Bayliss-Smith 1982: 25–36).

After a pig kill, the proportion of *hondba* piglets in the herd goes up by some 10%, from around one-quarter of the herd to one-third (Table 18.5). Of the adult animals, it is the number of *injiy* sows that shows the largest proportional change, at 7%, suggesting that pig kills mark the culling of large numbers of aging sows from a herd. The percentage of *himalwaenk* tuskers killed is also predictably large, although the numbers of animals involved is fewer. None of these changes in herd composition is statistically significant. The proportion of *way* gilts and *saendapow* hogs remains similar at around one-quarter of the herd, although the numbers of animals slaughtered is large. These findings are similar to those reported elsewhere—at a Sinasina pig

Fig. 18.4. Preparing pig carcasses for cooking at a large pig kill (*showmay tok liy*) in the Papua New Guinea Highlands (copyright P. Sillitoe, University of Durham)

Table 18.5. Composition of normal pig herd and after pig kill according to pig classes (no significant difference: $\chi^2 = 4.47$ (d.f. $= 6, a = 0.05$)).

| | Normal Herd | | After Pig Kill | |
	Mean	Percent	Mean	Percent
Females				
Sows	52.2	17.2	20.0	9.8
Gilts	77.0	25.4	54.3	26.5
Piglets	34.4	11.4	36.3	17.8
Males				
Hogs	83.4	27.5	53.0	25.9
Tusker hogs	15.6	5.2	6.3	3.1
Boars	2.2	0.7	1.6	0.8
Piglets	38.0	16.6	33.0	16.1

festival people 'killed almost equal numbers of males and females thus showing no tendency to keep females for breeding' (Hide 1981: 486).

The evidence suggests that a prolonged food shortage, whether for a drought or some other reason, not only reduces the size of a herd as after a pig kill but also impacts on its structure in a different way to a pig kill, and potentially adversely for the recovery of the herd. A review of pig populations according to the size of animals (*onda* and *onda ora* large and so on, which predictably parallels the gender–age discriminations and reduces us to three classes), shows the difference graphically (Fig. 18.5, Table 18.6). After pig kills, the number of large animals in a herd declines noticeably. This to be expected, people killing many mature animals carrying a lot of fat and meat for distribution. During a

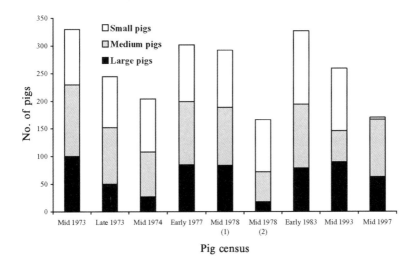

Fig. 18.5. Pig populations by size classes

Table 18.6. Pig census data according to size of pigs.

Pig Size Classes	Wola Term		Mid 1973	Late 1973	Mid 1974	Early 1977	Mid 1978(1)	Mid 1978(2)	Early 1983	Mid 1993	Mid 1997	Mean
Large	*onda ora & onda*	F	52	25	13	51	48	12	58	60	26	38.3
		M	48	25	14	34	40	6	21	30	37	28.3
Medium	*onda sha & genk sha*	F	61	49	43	65	61	38	60	24	56	50.8
		M	69	53	38	49	44	16	55	32	48	44.9
Small	*genk. genkden & genkora*	F	52	48	50	52	59	54	56	57	3	47.9
		M	48	44	46	51	44	40	77	56		45.1
TOTALS			330	244	204	302	296	166	327	259	170	255.3

drought, such as the El Niño induced event of 1997 when the reversal of Pacific currents affected rainfall patterns, the reverse happens and the number of small pigs in a herd declines dramatically. When a food shortage occurs people reduce the rations fed to pigs, even stop feeding them altogether, as they come into direct competition for the limited food available (humans eating small and sub-standard tubers usually fed to pigs). Small animals, particularly piglets, are the first to weaken and die as sows dry up.

All pigs lose condition and weight in a severe famine, and many may eventually die. People deny that they systematically kill pigs singly in these times, although in times of food shortage people may decide to stage a pig kill to reduce the burden (the 1974 kill was prompted in part by such a shortage). This is contrary to the suggestion that pigs may serve as a food store, buffering people against lean times, and that large pig kills serve to take the pressure off when herds burgeon in extended good times (Vayda *et al.* 1961; Vayda 1972; see Rappaport (1968: 64–8) for an extended critique of this argument). One of the Sinasina pig populations closely documented by Hide (1981: 417) also evidenced an 'oddly top-heavy structure' with few young pigs, which the author argues was the result of people stopping pig breeding to allow sows to fatten up for a festival slaughter. 'The major husbandry goal prior to a festival is the production of large pigs for slaughter. Continuation of normal reproduction, implying numbers of small animals and thin sows, and the deflection of fodder for their growth to sizes still well below that sought, would hinder the achievement of this goal'. He had no evidence of piglets dying in large numbers, although his fieldwork coincided with the large 1972 pan-Highlands drought. The Awa pig population reported by Boyd (1984: 38, 41) also had a top-heavy structure at one point, which he attributes to low natural rates of reproduction due to falling numbers of feral boars in the adjacent forest that people rely on to inseminate sows.

Pig herds are slow to recover after a stressful natural event such as a drought, whereas after a pig kill, there are many small pigs to bring along and replace the large ones slaughtered (Table 18.6). After pig kills almost one-half the herd is made up of piglets, whereas normally they make up somewhere around one-third of the herd and in famine considerably less. The proportions of medium-sized pigs remains comparable in herds at normal times and after pig kills, at 34% and 39% respectively, but they increase in famine to over 60%. The proportions of large pigs are the reverse of the piglet pattern, increasing from 15% following a pig kill to 29% under normal conditions and 37% during a drought. All of these variations are statistically significant with high residual values (Table 18.7). The standard demographic

Table 18.7. Mean composition of normal pig herd, after pig kill, and in famine according to size classes (difference significant: $\chi^2 = 60.13$ (d.f. $= 6, a = 0.05$)).

Pig size classes	Sex	Normal Herd		After Pig Kill		Famine	
		Mean	Percent	Mean	Percent	Mean	Percent
Large	F	53.8	17.8	16.7	8.1	26	15.3
	M	34.6	11.4	15.0	7.3	37	21.8
Medium	F	54.2	17.9	43.3	21.2	56	32.9
	M	49.8	16.4	35.7	17.4	48	28.2
Small	F	55.2	18.2	50.7	24.8	3	1.8
	M	55.2	18.2	43.3	21.2	0	0.0
TOTALS		302.8	100.0	204.7	100.0	170	100.0

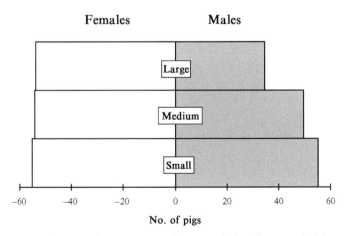

Fig. 18.6. Mean demographic structure of pig population (between kills)

Pigs in the New Guinea Highlands

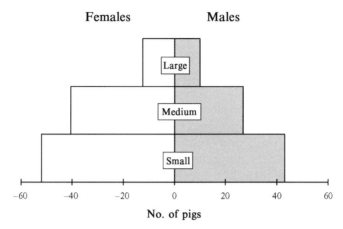

Fig. 18.7. Mean demographic structure of pig population (after kills)

bar graphs show the situation in normal times and following pig kills (Figs 18.6, 18.7). For comparative demographic pyramids of Sinasina pig herds, see Hide (1981: 415–16), of Awa herds see Boyd (1984: 38), and of herds in the Eastern and Western Highlands see Malynicz (1976: 203). During the interval between pig kills, herds develop an atypical demographic structure which reflects the Wola practice of keeping adult pigs alive for long periods of time once they reach maturity and not, as in commercial farming, killing them for sale and consumption. Instead of the usual demographic pyramid we have a rectangle, with some tendency towards a pyramid on the male side, reflecting the readiness of people to slaughter these animals in preference to breeding females when a pig is required between kills, for example at a funeral feast (a trend noted by Boyd (1984: 40) too among the Awa; see also Malynicz (1976: 203) whose graph of a Kerowagi pig population evidences a similar structure). Immediately after a pig kill the population structure more closely approximates to a pyramid, particularly on the male side; the difference with the female side again reflecting breeding concerns, people keeping more medium sized females to serve as the sows of the immediate future.

PIG MOVEMENTS

It is not only at pig kills that people dispose of animals. The composition of the herd in any region constantly changes as people dispose of animals in various other ways. During an 18-month period, when I attempted to

Table 18.8. Source and disposal of pigs during 18-month period. (sources: 1) bridegroom exchange (*hogol*), 2) bridewealth (*injiykab*), 3) caught as wild piglet, 4) compensation for shot pig, 5) crop harvest payment, 6) debt repayment (*saen*), 7) foster pig (*maha*), 8) garden clearing payment, 9) gift, 10) inherited, 11) litter, 12) mortuary exchange (*ol tobway/ol bay*), 13) mourning exchange (*gwat*), 14) pig herding payment (*hentiya*), 15) purchase (*showmay hesay*), 16) reimbursement exchange(*haypuw*), 17) reparation exchange (*showmay enjay*), 18) side of pork payment, 19) sire payment (*tuwshiy*), 20) swapped).

SOURCE	1	2	3	4	5	6	7	8	9	10	11	12	13	14	15	16	17	18	19	20	TOT
DISPOSAL																					
Bridegroom exchange (*hogol*)		7			1	2						1									11
Bridewealth exchange (*injiykab*)						3	3		1		8	3	1		3				1	1	24
Compensation payment									1												1
Crop harvest payment											1										1
Debt repayment (*saen*)											1										1
Foster pig (*maha*)					1						15	1			2	1					20
Foster disputed & reclaimed		1					3				5	1									10
Funeral feast (*hombera*)		1					3		1	2	1	1									9
Garden clearing payment											1										1
Gift (*ponay*)											15										15
Inherited													1		1						2
Killed & eaten by family							1				2										3
Killed & pork sold		1					2				2				2						7
Killed by other's sow, sold carcass												1									1
Lost at cards	1																				1
Mission feast						1	4				3	1							1		10
Mortuary exchange (*ol tobway/olbay*)		4		1		1	1		2		4		1			1					15

(*Continued*)

Table 18.8. (*Continued*)

SOURCE	1	2	3	4	5	6	7	8	9	10	11	12	13	14	15	16	17	18	19	20	TOT
DISPOSAL																					
Mourning exchange (*gwat*)					1	1	1				4	1	1		1						9
Pig herding payment (*hentiya*)					1									1	1						2
Ran wild & shot for funeral feast												1									1
Reimbursement exchange (*haypuw*)		1																			1
Remained in herd	3	10			1	3	51	1	3		32	6	4	1	14	1	1	4	1		136
Reparation exchange (*komb*)						1	1			1	1										3
Shot damaging garden, pork sold												1						1			2
Sick & family ate	1					1	3		1		26	1			1						34
Sick & pork sold		2	1																		3
Sick & buried pork, feared infection											5		1								6
Sire payment											5										5
Sold								1			12				3		1				17
Swapped				1								1			1						3
Unknown							1			2	6	1						1			11
TOTALS	5	27	1	2	4	11	74	2	9	5	150	20	9	2	29	3	2	6	3	1	365

keep track of pig movements in the herds of the two neighbouring *semonda* 'large-families' (Table 18.8), the turnover rate was 55% (i.e. people still had in their herds 45% of the pigs they had at the beginning of the survey period). The total number of animals involved was 525, and of these 229 were disposed of at some time during the 18 months and 223 were acquired during that period; 28% of these latter acquisitions were both acquired and disposed of during this period (i.e. they were not owned at either the beginning or end of the survey but passed through the herds). Note that Table 18.7 documents only the source and disposal of the pigs in herds at the start of the survey, plus those animals acquired and disposed of during the survey period, a total of 365 pigs (it excludes those acquired during the 18 months and still in the herds at the end of this time). The data on herd composition at the start and end of the survey period is comprehensive, but it is probable that I failed to document all the animals that passed through the herds during this period (see Boyd 1984: 40–7, for comparable data on an Awa community's herd over a 12 month period). A pig kill occurred within 1 month of the end of the survey and the turnover rate shot up to 86% (only 14% of the pigs in the herds at the start of the survey remained). And the percentage of animals acquired during the period and subsequently disposed of also increased to 44%, reflecting again the dramatic impact pig kills have on herd composition.

Other data on how long pigs have been in herds evidence a predictable decline over time, in line with these findings for 18 months. During an interval of 3 years between two surveys, over which time pig kills occurred, the number of pigs remaining in herds throughout was 11%, and after an interval of 4.5 years, again with pig kills intervening, it was down to 2%. Other data, on the time for which people had owned the pigs in their herds (Table 18.9) (compare to Table 6.1 in Lederman (1986: 204) on time pigs were owned in Mendi valley) give a further indication of the rate at which their composition changes. There is a predictable steady decline with time: some 45% of animals remain in peoples' herds for 1 year or less; 23% for 1–2 years; 14% for 2–3 years; and then 9%, 6%, and 2% for the next 3 years respectively. It is of interest to consider how people dispose of pigs, other than slaughtering them in large kills, and in what proportions (Table 18.8, Fig. 18.8) (compare to Dwyer (1993: 130–2) who gives details of how the Kubo disposed of pigs over a 15 month period). The largest proportion, at 18%, change hands at socio-political exchange events (bridewealths, mortuary transactions, etc.). The pie graph indicates the considerable number of animals lost to sickness at 12%, either dying or slaughtered when ill. A fair number of pigs, some 9%, people foster with others, in a customary arrangement where the recipient pays the giver when he in turn disposes of the animal. People slaughter a

Table 18.9. Time pigs owned.

Months	Total	Percent
<1	36	3.7
1–2	40	4.2
2–3	55	5.7
3–4	72	7.5
4–5	100	10.4
5–6	33	3.4
6–7	49	5.1
7–8	14	1.4
8–9	17	1.8
9–10	4	0.4
10–11	11	1.1
11–12	4	0.4
12–18	136	14.0
18–24	84	8.7
24–30	76	7.9
30–36	63	6.5
36–48	83	8.6
48–60	57	5.9
60–72	18	1.9
>72	14	1.4
Totals	966	100

similar proportion, frequently in small feasts such as those that occur at funerals following interment. They sold 5%, and dispersed a further 3% in various payments, including assistance with tasks and debt repayments. A final 6% were disposed of in various other contexts, as gifts, inheritance, and so on.

The other side to pig movements is reflected in the source of animals in herds (Table 18.8, Fig. 18.9) (compare to Hide's (1981: 510, fig. 8.10) bar graphs of Sinasina pig acquisitions). These fall into fewer classes. The largest number of pigs in herds at 41% are 'home raised', coming from litters of sows

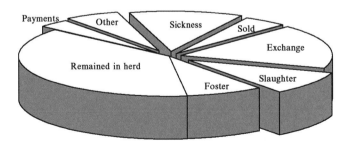

Fig. 18.8. Disposal of pigs from herds ($n = 354$)

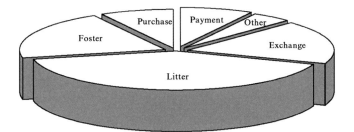

Fig. 18.9. Source of pigs in herds ($n = 365$)

owned. A considerable proportion of animals are foster pigs received from others, amounting to some 20% of herds. Exchange transactions are the next most common source of animals, these comprising 18% of herds. Next are animals purchased from others at 8% and, comprising a similar percentage, animals received in payment for services rendered and debt repayments. The final 5% come from miscellaneous other sources, including gifts and inheritance. There is no evidence that people prefer to trade for females to increase breeding stock, as Meggitt (1958: 288) suggests for the Enga. The reverse is equally plausible, men seeking males that fatten up more quickly and reach larger final weights. According to the data presented here, 55% of animals purchased in trade were male and 45% female ($n = 136$ animals).

Comparative ethnography suggests that herds elsewhere comprise animals from a similar range of sources. The Awa of the Eastern Highlands, living at lower altitudes, obtain a larger percentage by capturing feral piglets, and they rely on locally farrowed piglets considerably more, these comprising 69% of their herds (Boyd 1984: 29–34, 38–9). The herds of the Sinasina have similar origins (Hide 1981: 433–44): one community's herd comprised 51% home-produced animals, but another had considerably fewer home-produced animals with 44% coming from trade and 31% in gifts. Hide interprets the difference in terms of pig festival cycles (after the work of Vayda *et al.* (1961) and Rappaport (1968)), resulting in a system with conscious long-term planning of pig production:

Trade plays a major part in rebuilding pig populations at the beginning of the cycle... As the proportion of pigs produced increases from under one quarter to over one half... the proportion traded decreases to level off at about one quarter, apparently remaining stable for the rest of the cycle. The interesting feature of the second half of the cycle is the suggested increase in the proportion of pigs acquired by gift exchange at the expense of produced pigs (1981: 442).

The author attributes this difference to men restricting reproduction later in the cycle to ensure herds of large animals for slaughter at festival time: 'a co-ordinated cycle of pig management culminating in a pig population

composed mainly of large animals...implying the restriction, at some stage
of the cycle, of reproduction' (1981: 540). This interpretation sits uneasily
with Wola practices. Wola pig kills are less predictable events, and the chaotic
way in which they schedule them—requiring that a community first agrees
that one is due and then featuring considerable wrangling as men strive to
reach a consensus over timing—would make such planning difficult (Sillitoe
1979, see also Rappaport 1968: 158–9, on consensus formation among the
Maring, and Lederman 1986: 187–212, on the political dimension to timing
of pig kills). Here people rely more on exchange opportunities and trade to
build up their herds with large animals before a kill.

There is probably an element of truth in the argument that pig kills effect
some control over porcine demography, and reduce the number of large animals
when the burden of their care is inordinately heavily (as Rappaport 1968: 160–5
graphically argues for the Maring, where pigs destroy unacceptable numbers of
gardens). But among the Wola these stresses appear to be a relatively short-term
phenomenon exacerbated, if not precipitated, by the promise of a forthcoming
pig kill! When the community-wide consensus is that the time for a pig kill
approaches, the event taking place maybe in a year or so's time, men seek to
augment their herds with large beasts to slaughter. Lederman (1986: 204–5)
observed the same behaviour in the Mendi valley, putting the case lucidly 'people
get a substantial number of the pigs they kill at the eleventh hour...this is not
the result of production constraints; it is a systematic social pattern generated by
the rules of exchange and is one of the meaningful 'points' or goals of Festival
activity' (the increase in receipts of pigs through exchange observed by Hide
(1981) among the Sinasina, discussed previously, may reflect something similar). At a large *sa* pig kill in the Was valley, for example, men had obtained one-
third of the 135 animals they slaughtered in only the previous 12 months. Some
18 months before the kill 34% of herds came from 'home produced' litters and

Table 18.10. Source of pigs in herds pre- and post-pig kill (difference significant:
$\chi^2 = 61.93$ (d.f. $= 15$, $= 0.05$)) (some of the totals in this table exceed the census
counts because they include the herds of men living elsewhere in other communities
who chose to come and take part in the pig kill).

Source	Pre-Kill		Immediately Before Kill		Immediately After Kill		Post-Kill	
	No.	%	No.	%	No.	%	No.	%
litter	104	34	96	31	74	42	199	52
foster	76	25	89	28	48	27	62	16
exchange	63	21	69	22	28	16	51	13
purchase	29	10	25	8	8	4	20	5
payment	20	7	22	7	11	6	43	11
other	10	3	13	4	9	5	9	3

31% from exchange and trade, and immediately before the kill these percentages had changed little to 31% and 30% respectively, the difference made up largely by foster pigs (Table 18.10). Immediately after the kill the proportion of 'home produced' animals in herds increased to 42% and those obtained in exchange and trade fell to 20%, as a result of men slaughtering a larger proportion of animals obtained in these transactional contexts than acquired in other ways. Some 2 years or so after another pig kill in the same *sa* sequence 'home produced' litter pigs dominated, comprising 52% of herds, an increase largely at the expense of foster pigs, the proportion of animals obtained through exchange and trade was nearly constant at 18% of herds. High residual values, pre-kill for exchange and purchase and post-kill for litters, confirm these trends statistically. The *sa* pig kills were part of a large exchange cycle that was highly fashionable in the 1970s and 1980s and swept through the region, but is no longer to be in vogue (Sillitoe 1979; Lederman 1986).

In short, the logic driving pig kills is not so much demographic and nutritional as transactional. Herds may swell just before a pig kill, particularly with larger animals, and crash immediately afterwards, but the evidence suggests that they soon return to 'normal' levels. One explanation is that pig kills draw on a wider region than the community staging the event, with some movement of large pigs resulting in a 'buffering' effect. After a natural calamity, on the other hand, such as an extended drought, herds recover more slowly because all the communities in a region are affected, unlike pig kills that deplete the herd in only one locality at a time; this exacerbates the demographic effect of losing many young pigs. Pig kills are the apotheosis of socio-political exchange. Although people are reluctant to dispose of highly valued pigs piecemeal in small events, they willingly slaughter them at large events to which hundreds of people come. These are truly grand occasions, celebrations of the exchange ethic, at which pork passes between thousands of hands as people repeatedly carve it up, meat sometimes passing between two, three, or more individuals before consumption.

The demands of exchange critically inform people's approach to pig management. They wish to handle many animals in large numbers of transactions, and slaughter several at periodic large pig kills and distribute large amounts of pork and fat. We might assume that these demands would translate into a desire to breed many animals. The requirements of exchange intervene in other ways, modifying any urge to breed pigs. The ready castration of young boars, many of them before they reach sexual maturity, reflects attitudes to breeding, with only two or three animals in any locality at any time able to service sows. Men with male piglets are more interested in turning them into rapidly growing and docile *saendapow* hogs than in selecting breeding stock. Regarding *way* gilts and *injiy* sows, we might assume that keeping these as large adults is less wasteful in energetic terms than herding fully grown *saendapow* hogs, because they will produce litters. Nevertheless, many of these female animals are as unproductive as their large male equivalents because people are often reluctant to allow them to breed. When sows farrow they lose condition and weight, which dramatically reduces their value, and they can take many months to feed up again. A large fat pig now is more desirable for someone with his eye on current exchange commitments, and inclined to pay little attention to production issues, than a skinny sow and litter of piglets which will take years to grow into valuable beasts. The impact of this cultural logic is evident on pig herd demography.

Part E

Pigs in Ritual and Art

19

Wild boar hunting in the Eastern Mediterranean from the 2nd to the 1st millennium BC

Anne-Sophie Dalix & Emmanuelle Vila

INTRODUCTION

Recent studies of the archaeozoological material from the site of Ras Shamra-Ugarit (Fig. 19.1) and of related textual sources have been added to the archaeological data; these studies demonstrate in an unexpected manner the importance which the wild boar held on this site during the Late Bronze Age. Is this importance characteristic of Ugarit or of the Late Bronze Age? This question encouraged us to look for traces of wild boars and wild boar hunting in the osteological, iconographic, and textual data for this period in neighbouring regions. This study represents the first stage in research which is intended to be carried out in more detail. Thus here we will only propose avenues for reflection.

THE WILD BOAR AT THE CITY OF UGARIT

General presentation of Ugarit

The site of Ras Shamra on the Syrian coast corresponds to the ancient city-state of Ugarit, the flourishing capital of a small coastal kingdom. Its key geographical situation and its port rendered it a point of contact between Mesopotamia and the Mediterranean world. The city prospered in the Late Bronze Age before being destroyed by the 'sea people' in about 1180 BC. The 'sea people' and the 'people from the North' are known exclusively from Egyptian sources (Ramsès III, Medinet Abu). They are considered to be the destroyers of almost all the

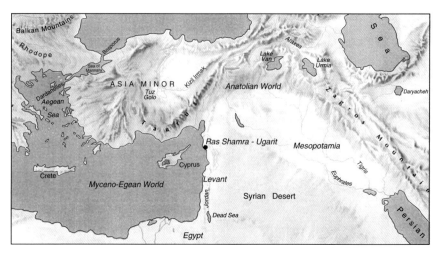

Fig. 19.1. Location of the Ras Shamra-Ugarit site

Levantine cities of the coast at that period. The excavations of the port (Minet-el-Beida), the royal palace, the sanctuaries, and the residential quarters have produced many objects which are evidence of relations with Egypt, Cyprus, and Anatolia, as well as exceptional archives (2nd millennium BC)—numerous economic, administrative, literary, and mythological texts on clay tablets. Ugarit was an important commercial crossroads (Yon 1997).

Osteological information

The archaeozoological study carried out on nearly 7000 bone remains reveals a food economy based on the breeding of cattle, sheep, and goats (Vila in press *c*). Evidence of pig rearing was not found. Hunting was not a common activity, being concentrated mainly on deer and sometimes wild boar. Although its domestic equivalent the pig was not bred at Ugarit, the wild boar was hunted and consumed on the site: 22 remains, some with butchering marks, provide the evidence (Vila & Dalix 2004).

Iconographic information

The wild boar is not only present in the faunal remains, but is also represented on archaeological objects found at Ugarit. It is represented in two forms: a 'realist' form on weapons, and a more imaginary, 'metaphorical' form, on rhytons.

Two weapons carry representations of wild boars. One is the head of a boar on the wider end of a spear blade (Schaeffer 1939: fig. 104, pl. XXII), the other is the forequarters of a boar on the heel of an axe, accompanied by two lions who spit out the blade (Schaeffer 1939: fig. 100–3, pl. XXII). The heel of the axe is also decorated with floral and geometric motifs in filigree. Also notable is an axe from Choga Zambil in southern Iran which has the same iconographic register as that of Ugarit, but with a different fabrication; the heel is decorated with a boar couchant and a big cat which spits out the blade. The axe was discovered in a temple and carries an inscription in the name of a king (Ghirshman 1966: pl. LXXXIII). To our knowledge there are no other parallels. At Choga Zambil there are also a number of boar figurines. The archaeological contexts of the two discoveries at Ugarit, hunting arms apparently not used for the hunt, are distinctive. The axe was discovered in a temple called 'Hurrian' which could correspond to the palace chapel (Callot 1986). The spear is from a deposit of bronze objects discovered near what is called the house of the 'grand priest' on the acropolis.

Rhytons are recipients related to the pouring of liquids, and are usually attributed a religious function. Five rhytons represent the head of an animal with an open mouth and an elongated muzzle ending in a kind of snout which is sometimes emphasized with black paint (Schaeffer 1949: figs 92–3; Courtois 1978: fig. 40). On some of these examples, the background decoration evokes the floral motifs on the heel of the axe. These animals have horns, and have often been interpreted as goats. However, François Poplin's commentary on one of these rhytons is particularly convincing (Poplin 2000: 6). He considers that in mental imagery 'the boar is a horned beast who has his horns in his mouth' and states that on this object 'they would have left the mouth for the place which they have on beasts with conventional horns, particularly goats'. We have proposed that these could be metaphorical representations of wild boars. All these objects—rhytons, axe and spear—thus appear to belong to the realm of religious practices (Figs 19.2, 19.3, after Vila & Dalix 2004).

Epigraphic information

The wild boar also appears in a text written in Ugaritic (the local language) initially entitled 'the hunts of Baal'. In the metaphorical form of creatures qualified as 'voracious', it plays the role of protagonist at the side of the god Baal in a combat between them. Following a recent study, a certain number of elements have led us to identify the creatures as wild boars and to reinterpret the text as a boar hunt undertaken by Baal with a spear and a bow (Dalix 2006). The association with Baal, above all a divinity of fertility and fecundity

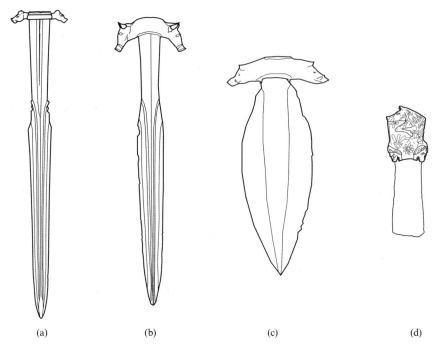

Fig. 19.2. Representations of wild boar on arms: (a) spear from Ras Shamra (after Schaeffer 1939: fig. 104); (b) spear from the Borowski collection (after Heim 1983: Plate 10); (c) spear from Sarkisla (after Bittel 1987: fig. 2a–b); (d) axe from Ras Shamra (after Schaeffer 1939: fig. 101)

(Yon 1985: 189), as a hunter is new and raises a certain number of questions. Moreover, the text differs from the mythological texts known at Ugarit. It is composed of two parts, the hunt and a libation ritual, and then it presents the 'voracious ones' who are not mentioned in the lists of divinities. The cycle of Baal consists of a series of texts where Baal confronts three adversaries: Yam (the Sea), Mot (Death), and the 'voracious ones'. The first two texts are mythological, concerning the intervention of known gods. The third text differs from the mythological ones because it presents a ritual at the end, and because the 'voracious ones' are unknown in the list of divinities. It may be asked how these creatures were able to enter into the realm of the divine to become adversaries worthy of the god Baal.

At this stage of the study, we emphasize the concordance of the sources:

- The wild boar appears at Ugarit as both a species which is hunted and consumed on the site, as a decorative motif on hunting arms, and as an element of the magical and religious bestiary.

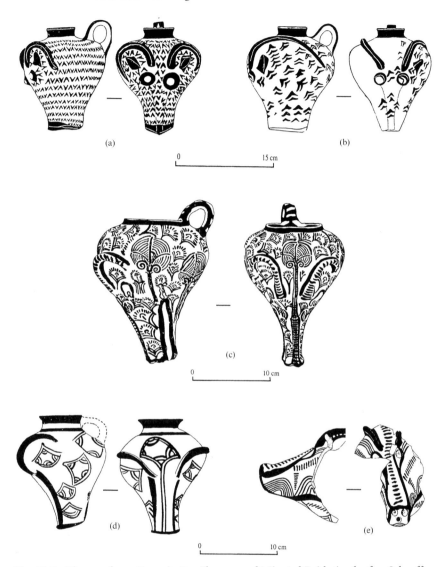

Fig. 19.3. Rhytons from Ougarit: Ras Shamra and Minet el Beida (a–d, after Schaeffer 1939: figs 92–3; e, after Courtois 1978: fig. 40)

- The context of discovery of the arms relates to the palace and thus to the king, or to a building which is closely related to the temple of Baal.
- The text confirms the relation of the wild boar with the god Baal. Two activities are described, the hunt and the ritual of libation. These imply the use of objects which have been found in the excavations: arms and rhytons.

The question now is whether these elements are peculiar to the site of Ugarit, or can similar aspects be found on other sites of the Late Bronze Age? Can we attempt to find the origin of this mental image of the wild boar at Ugarit? It must not be forgotten that Ugarit is located at the centre of several possible areas of influence: the Levant, Egypt to the south, Mesopotamia to the east, the Mycenean–Aegean world to the west, and Anatolia to the north. These contacts are evident in the material culture of the site.

In what follows, a preliminary analysis of the available data is presented. The data will be briefly assessed from the point of view of archaeozoology, iconography, and textual sources. Of course, we have to take into account the difficulty of separation of wild boar and domestic pig bones in the archaeological fauna samples in some geographical areas. The identification is easier in the Near East than in Anatolia, for instance.

THE WILD BOAR IN THE REGIONS NEIGHBOURING UGARIT

The natural distribution area of the wild boar is vast. It extends from Europe to Japan, taking in India and North Africa. The species can live in relatively varied biotopes thanks to its territorial mobility and omnivorous diet. Wild boar consume anything edible: fruits, roots, invertebrates, small vertebrates, and even carrion. They prefer forested regions and wooded cover and do not penetrate arid regions as they need to drink regularly and to have access to marshes and muddy areas in order to roll. In circumstances of drought and vegetation decline, they venture into cultivated zones and cause damage to crops. All of the Mediterranean region, including the Levantine coast, the Greek islands, and Turkey (Fig. 19.1) offers forested spaces favourable to wild boar. The animals also like the shrubby and wooded banks of the great Near Eastern and Egyptian river valleys of the Euphrates, the Tigris, and the Nile.

The Levant

In relation to the Levantine coast in the Late Bronze Age, the data on the wild boar assembled at Ugarit is so far unique. The species is rarely found in faunal studies, having appeared only at Kamid el-Loz (Bökönyi 1990), at Tell Afis (Wilkens 2000), and at Tel Dothan in a special context, a molar in a tomb (Lev-Tov & Maher 2001). Moreover, there is no mention of the wild boar in any preserved epigraphic source, and as an iconographical motif it is understated. Only one representation of a wild boar on a spear, from the Borowsky collection, presents close similarities to that of Ugarit. Unfortunately, its provenance is unknown, but it is probably contemporary and of Levantine origin (Heim 1983: Pl. 10). Besides this, one other representation of a wild boar is known, although of a later period (9th–7th c. BC). It is painted on a vessel from Horvat Teman in the southern Levant (Beck 2002: Fig. 4). The presence of the wild boar is thus exceptional on Levantine sites contemporary to Ugarit (Vila & Dalix 2004) (see also Parayre 2000, for a general study about the wild boar in the ancient Near East).

Egypt

In the Late Bronze Age, the kingdom of Egypt dominated the Levant, and Ugarit in particular, up to the battle of Kadesh (19th dynasty, 1282 BC). The archaeological sites from which faunal remains have been studied are rare, and the wild boar, to our knowledge, has not been identified (Boessneck 1988*a*: 76–7). Moreover, to our knowledge confirmed representations of wild boars in the Late Bronze Age do not exist in Egypt. In contrast, pigs appear in their domesticated form in everyday scenes (Lobban 1998). Representations of boars/pigs exist in mythological scenes with the god Seth (Newberry 1928; Lobban 1998: figs 6, 7). In *Book of the Dead*, Seth is described as appearing as a black pig who blesses Horus with a look (Barguet 1967: Chapter 112, 148–9). The black pig (could this be an evocation of the wild boar?) is in this context the emblem of the god, who appears not to be part of the Egyptian canonical pantheon. It may be noted that Baal was long present in Egyptian onomastics, where he was assimilated with Seth, an enemy of Osiris who like Baal is the divine guarantor of political power. In the final analysis, except for this possible identification, the wild boar is absent from the Egyptian world. The other references in the texts also concern pigs, herds of pigs related to the temple, or the pig, or parts of its body, as entries into medicinal recipes (Newberry 1928; Heck & Westendorf 1984: 763).

Mesopotamia

In Mesopotamia, which comprises northern Syria as well as Iraq, the wild boar is very rarely noted in faunal studies. Two remains were found at El Quitar on the Euphrates (Buitenhuis 1988: 169) but the species is absent at Tell Bderi on the Khabur (Becker 1988). Late Bronze Age representations are also extremely rare and it is sometimes difficult to determine whether they are pigs or wild boars. The wild boar appears at Nuzi in a religious context in the form of an enamelled terracotta head which had probably been applied to a wall in a 15th century BC temple dedicated to the goddess Ishtar. The other representations from the Mesopotamian world do not seem to be clearly related to religious contexts or to votive objects at that period. It may be noted that at Larsa in Iraq at the beginning of the 2nd millennium BC, the figurine of an animal was made probably representing a pig (Anonymous 2001: fig. 165). Recipients from Tell Rimah in Syria, 'pigpots', also represent pigs (Postgate & Oates 1997: Pl. 19, figs 1189, 1190). At Babylon in Iraq, a wild boar in combat with a lion is represented on an engraved pottery fragment (Anonymous 1992). The combat of the lion and the wild boar is a theme also observed on a Mesopotamian cylinder seal dated stylistically to the 13th century (Mayer-Opificius 1986: fig. 6) (about the wild boar in Mesopotamia, see also Parayre 2000: 155–8). In the epigraphic data, references to wild boars are anecdotal. In the royal archives at Puzrish-Dagan in southern Mesopotamia there is a reference to wild boars with other wild animals at celebrations in the presence of the king but there is no element which endows them with any particular importance (Lion & Michel 2001: 51). A tablet from Mari in Syria also refers to the presence of young wild boars and stags in the palace and other documents mention that they were bred in the royal reserves like other wild species (Lion 2001: 51).

The Mycenean–Aegean world

Our investigation relates to the oriental part of this geo-historical area. Possible contacts between Ugarit and the occidental part are not so clear as with Cyprus. Nevertheless, we have also made some observations on Crete. Hunting was omnipresent in the Mycenean–Aegean world, particularly in textual and iconographical data. There are many studies on this topic (cf. Hamilakis 2003). For our particular focus about the Levant and specially Ugarit, we need not examine all archaeological facts from the Greek mainland.

The island of Cyprus had close contacts with Ugarit, seen clearly in the material from that site. But faunal studies do not seem to present any evidence for wild boar hunting in the Late Bronze Age. At the sites of Hala Sultan Tekke (Ekman 1977) and Agios Dimitrios (Croft 1989), there are no bone remains attributed to the wild boar. However, it may be noted, with reservation, that at Enkomi there was an intentional burial of three wild boars, a female and two young, of which the skeletons were found in a Late Bronze Age house (Karageorghis 1969: 514–15). The wild boar is present in the iconography, although we cannot attribute any religious connotation. At Kition, a painted vase shows two running boars, so-called 'flying boar' (Late Bronze Age Mycenean IIIc, Karageorghis *et al.* 1981: pl. II–17, pl. X, 27). At Myrtou, a bronze tripod (Late Bronze Age) is decorated with animal registers, in one of which is a wild boar confronting a dog (Karageorghis 1968: Pl. XXII3). It is only in a later repertoire on a painted vessel (7th c. BC) that we may observe a complex scene with a wild boar and a hunter armed with a spear, presided over by a figure seated in a chariot (Karageorghis & Des Gagniers 1974; Buchholz 2000: fig. 6c).

In Crete too, wild boar remains are rare in the Late Bronze Age. A few bones were identified at Prinias (13th–6th centuries BC, Wilkens 1996), but are absent at Malia (Late Minoan) (Helmer & Vila 1997, and study in progress), at Ayia Triada (Late Minoan, Wilkens 1996) and at Eleutherna (in the early levels, 1500 BC, Nobis 1999). They are also absent on later sites such as Vronda and Kastro (1050–700 BC, Klippel & Snyder 1991), as well as Knossos (Geometric period, Jarman 1973). An evidence of the appearance of the boars is the decoration of the helmets found in the tombs of warriors which in most cases depict wild males, because they are enormous (Morris 1990). The Linear B texts offer no support, as the animals which appear on the lists of the archives are only domestic pigs. There is no reference to wild boars (Raulwing 1992). However, there are several examples of a wild boar motif on arms and on a rhyton. First, a bronze dagger blade from Lasithi which is quite early (19th–18th century BC) is engraved with the scene of a wild boar hunt: the hunter is armed with a spear or lance (Higgins 1967: 43, figs. 36–7). The incisions were probably filled with gold, a technique known by Syrian craftsmen. This is the only Cretan prototype of sword blades found in the tombs at Mycenae (Higgins 1967: 43). A lance point found at Anemosphilia and dated to the 18th–17th century BC is decorated with a somewhat hybrid boar head incised on the blade (Sakellarakis & Sapouna-Sakellarakis 1997: 598, fig. 622). At Gournia (Late Minoan I) a rhyton with the head of a boar/pig was found (Zervos 1956: fig. 580). A wild boar appears in a fresco in the palace at Knossos (Kaiser 1976: T. 27) as well as in a relief at Palaikastros (Kaiser 1976: fig. 21a), but in these two cases their context, alone or associated with personages or animals, is unknown because of the poor preservation of the materials. A fragmentary figurine of a boar was also found at Lakkos, dated simply to the Bronze Age (Sakellarakis & Sapouna-Sakellarakis 1997: 529, fig. 529). These objects probably had a votive function, although this is not confirmed, but they are completely different stylistically from those of Ugarit. A representation of a wild boar also exists in a special context dated to about 1400 BC. In a cave at Vernopheto (Kato Pervolakia) is a fresco which presents a scene related to fishing and hunting, in the centre of which a female figure interpreted as a goddess raises her arms. The wild boar in the register of animals appears to be wounded (Rutkowsji 1986: 63, fig. 71).

Thus, from an iconographic point of view, the representation of the wild boar on Crete relates to the hunt and to the natural world (except for the rhyton of Gournia), as it appears on hunting arms and in hunting scenes. This tallies with other representations in the Aegean zone where the wild boar figures in hunting scenes, particularly on the famous fresco of Tiryns. In the Peloponnese, in the Late Bronze Age, the wild boar is found in hunting scenes, for example on seals where the hunter is always armed with a spear (Laffineur 1992: pl. XXVIc). This is also the motif on the fresco at Tiryns where the wild boar is chased by dogs and wounded by a lance or sword; the human hand holding it is discernible (Rodenwaldt 1976: fig. 55, pl. XIII). Apparently it does not appear as decoration on arms. A rhyton with a boar's head was found at Ayios Konstantinos, but it is probably a domestic pig's head (Konsolaki-Yannopoulou 2001: pl. LXVIIIb–d; Hamilakis & Konsolaki 2004). The rhyton is associated with a large number of bone remains of young pigs in the sanctuary (Room A).

The Anatolian world

In Anatolia, the wild boar is rarely present in the faunal material studied. For the Late Bronze Age, at Lidar Hüyük, some 50 bone remains were identified as wild boar (0.5% of the total number of faunal remains, Kussinger 1988) and at Sirkeli Höyük, one bone only (0.2% of the total number of faunal remains, Vogler 1997). For the same period, at Alishar Hüyük (Vogel 1952), Bogazköy (Patterson 1937), and Gordion (Zeder & Arter 1994), no remains of wild boar were identified. At Kaman-Kalahöyük, wild boar remains have not been identified with certainty (Hongo 1998).

In the second millennium BC, the wild boar is represented in monumental Hittite art, on one of the steles of the palace façade at Alaça Hüyük (14th century BC), confronting a hunter who is drawing his bow (Macqueen 1975: photo 57). It is also represented at Tell Halaf (Neo-Hittite, 8th century BC), in present-day Syria, on one of the numerous basalt steles which decorate the exterior walls of a temple and a small palace (Moortgat 1955: pl. 58a). The wild boar is also represented on objects, some of which were found in religious contexts. These are rhytons which are stylistically different from each other; the whole body of the boar is represented as at Kultepe-Kanis (13th century BC, Özgüç 1998: figs 2, 4). Certain other vessels presented by Özgüç are open to question. Moreover, Özgüç discusses the relation between the god Ushmu and the wild boar based on representations on cylinder seals from Kultepe (Özgüç 1965: pl. 7, 19–21). In our opinion, it is difficult to specifically identify the animal which is the attribute of the two-faced god on these cylinder seals. The head only is represented at Alaça Hüyük (Kosay & Akok 1966: 166, pl. 25, k–l), Alalakh (Wooley 1955: 239, AT 38/147), and Bogazköy (Klengel & Klengel 1970: fig. 54). At Alalakh, the representation evokes that of the rhytons of Ras Shamra. The tusks are ideally dispropor-tionate and seem to emerge from the mouth. In this case, our interpretation of this special object is subject to caution but is founded on our hypothesis of the mental representations of animals. At Bogazköy the wild boar takes on different forms, the rhyton in the form of a boar head (1st half of the 1st millennium BC?) previously mentioned, some figurines, and a decoration in relief on a fragmentary recipient (Parzinger & Sanz 1992: figs 138–41). The latter, on which a wild boar wounded frontally by a spear appears, was discovered in the sanctuary zone at Hattusa (2nd mill. BC, Parzinger & Sanz 1992: figs. 66–76). To this list of objects having a possibly votive connotation may be added a spear decorated with two boar heads, discovered at Sarkisla (Bittel 1987: 21–31, fig. 2a–b). It is a remarkable thematic parallel to the spear of Ugarit, although its fabrication as well as the form of its blade are different.

From the point of view of epigraphic data, the site of Bogazköy, besides the archaeological objects, also produced texts in which the wild boar is men-tioned. It appears either as a real animal, or as a symbol, in the lists of wild animals which in all probability were dedicated to the royal palace or to religious purposes (Neu 1974: 15, 31–3). In the cycle of the Ki-Lam festival, the wild boar is mentioned three times among the zoomorphic figurines,

Also to be noted among wild boar representations is the decoration of a bronze bowl from Kinik Kastamonu, dated to the 13th century BC, which depicts a hunter armed with a spear confronting a wild boar (Emre & Çinaroglu 1993: fig. 23). This scene appears in the lower register of the bowl which presents confronting animals—lions and bulls, lion and lion, man with spear and stag—altogether different from the upper register which is a representation of hunting stags and ibexes with bow and arrow. Here the appearance of the wild boar occurs in a symbolic scene which does not correspond to an allegory of the hunt but rather to wild nature, to the confrontation of animal forces in which humans also play a role. The icono-graphic motif of the wild boar is very ancient in Anatolia. It appears in the Neolithic at Gobekli Hüyük, in relief on a pillar, and as a sculpted statue. At Catal Hüyük, it figures in a hunting fresco (Klengel & Klengel 1970: 21) and a boar head decorates the handle of a flint knife. Morever, at Catal, the wild boar mandibles inserted into the walls of a room decorated with bucrania indicate that they had a votive character. Thus, Anatolia is the geographic zone where we find the most iconographic manifestations of the wild boar in the form of objects with religious character: rhytons, figurines, spear. Moreover, some are similar typologically to those of Ugarit.

'animals of the gods', (twice in silver, once in lapis lazuli) carried during ceremonial processions (Singer 1983: 92–3, Kbo X 23 V). The wild boar is the only animal which appears several times in different materials. It is also associated, as a silver figurine, with the god Habandali (Singer 1983: 95–7). The mention of a boar/pig, as a rhyton, is found in a fragment of text which describes the king performing a libation to the god protector of the lance with a silver recipient in the form of a pig (Haas 1994: 537). The content of these texts also reveals that the lance has an important votive value and a strong religious connotation, and that there exists an association of the axe and the lance in the Hittite rites. The Hittite laws prescribed the extreme penalty of death for the theft of a bronze lance at the palace gate (Singer 1983: 58, 82, 84, 90, 91; Haas 1994: 203). The bronze lance also belonged to the royal funerary ritual (Haas 1994: 203). The lance and the axe are two of the ritual objects used in religious ceremonies (Haas 1994: 201–2, 762–3, 768). On one of the chariots of the procession of Ki-Lam stand statuettes of the king of the mountain with their lances (Haas 1994: 751). Axe and lance appear sometimes in the same ritual, and were even exchanged during the Ki-Lam celebrations, the king exchanging a lance for an axe (Singer 1984: 16–22; Haas 1994: 204, 753).

The archaeological evidence for this association is rare; although axes, lances, and spears are found on many sites, they are undecorated 'everyday' objects. Representations of animals on these arms are very rare. This association of votive hunting weapons, the spear and the axe, is found on two sites, Sarkisla and Ugarit. These two types of objects were not discovered in the same contexts; however, their simultaneous presence on these sites could not be a coincidence. At Sarkisla, only the spear is decorated with boar heads; the axe carries various zoomorphic motifs but no boar. At Ugarit the boar is present on both types of weapon. In the course of our research, we noted the extreme rarity of decorated spearheads. We discovered four: one with felines at Alalakh, and three with wild boar protomes, from Ras Shamra, the Borowsky collection and Sarkisla (Emre & Cinaroglu 1993: 690–1). These lance points with animal protomes recall the representation of the 'Sword God', in relief on a large scale on the cliffs of the sacred site of Yazilikahya (Bittel 1987).

CONCLUSION

To judge from the scattered osteological data from the regions studied, the wild boar makes a marginal appearance in the archaeological fauna. Hunting the wild boar was clearly not undertaken to meet the vital needs in meat resources of the local populations. One may question the reasons for such hunting activity when evidence of it is found on a site. From the iconographic point of view, the wild boar is encountered only in the Mycenean–Aegean and Hittite worlds, as has been demonstrated. In general, in the iconographic repertoire of the ancient Near East, the species occupies an insignificant place in terms of frequency, in contrast to bulls, lions, and goats. The case of the bull is particularly clear; it is found in a more or less stereotyped form either as a decorative motif or as a wild or domesticated animal integrated into more complex scenes which can include the gods. This ambivalence probably reflects an ambivalence in its conceptual value: the bull can have a value which is religious, such as an emblematic animal of the storm god, or profane. But as we have seen, the wild boar usually appears on objects with specialized functions—hunting weapons and rhytons—as well as in hunting scenes. It never seems to be used as a simple decorative motif.

In the Mycenean–Aegean world, the theme of the wild boar and wild boar hunting is expressed from the Late Bronze Age onwards in a relatively secular manner, which will later become quite clear in the Classical period, as seen in the texts and iconography. The hunt thus brings together the moral values of an individual in actions where courage must be shown: confrontation of the hunter with the wild animal, preparation for war, and passage to adulthood (Schnapp 1979).

In the Hittite and Neo-hittite worlds of the of the 2nd and 1st millennia BC respectively, the wild boar and wild boar hunting come under a different theme, which is related to the religious sphere. It is represented in a repetitive manner on religious objects, which demonstrates that its image is used in a communal perspective. It is cited in the texts among the 'animals of the gods', but there is no indication that it was considered to be the emblem of a god. The other illustrations of the wild boar related to the hunt—decorations of hunting arms, scenes on recipients and orthostats—either by context or by function, are also related to religion. But what link can be established between these two statements? As a religious object did it enter into preventive rituals, preparatory for the hunt? If we consider the wild boar to be representative of natural forces which are dangerous and deadly, we can then envisage the development of a particular cultural conception. Hunting the wild boar necessitates the elaboration of a ritual context which implies the use of votive arms and rhytons (Collins 2002*a*: 250; Collins 2002*b*: 314), as at Ugarit. But this interpretation does not find an echo in the official religious texts of the Hittites.

This similarity between the Ugaritian and Hittite kingdoms is probably related to a common ideological current. Moreover, it must not be forgotten that it is found in large urban centres, Ugarit, Alalakh, Bogazköy, Alaça Hüyük, where the hunt is no longer an ordinary activity of which the techniques are part of ordinary knowledge. The disappearance of the economic necessity of hunting as well as the rise of an urban way of life meant that the city-dwellers were distanced from wild nature, which was no longer a familiar universe, and could be viewed as hostile. Hunting became an act which required the elaboration of a preventive ritual.

In conclusion, although the motif of the wild boar and the indications concerning the existence of rites related to wild boar hunting are found in the great Hittite centres, they do not seem to be linked explicitly to royal power. The originality of the capital of Ugarit lies in the concordance between the osteological, iconographic and epigraphic data. The text entitled 'the hunts of the god Baal' is an exceptional document and possesses elements which back up the thesis of the gravity and the ritualization of wild boar hunting. So far there is no parallel in ancient Near Eastern literature. It is important to emphasize that the conception of this ritualized hunting occurs in the framework of a great urban centre, whose emblematic figures are represented by Baal and his terrestrial manifestation, the king. Baal was both the defender of living species, particularly humans, and guarantor of the cyclic rhythms of nature. In this role he fights against Mot (Death) to safeguard the generations, and against Yam (the Sea, a natural force with destructive power) to protect sailors. We may ask whether the struggle against the wild boar is not a complementary part of the role of Baal as protector, this time of farmers and hunters. This hypothesis would explain why the wild boar is named in a metaphorical form. Entering by means of this metaphor into the 'semi-divine' sphere and thus an adversary worthy of Baal, the wild boar would symbolize the chthonic forces which menace the natural cycle of fertility. An Indo-European influence in this conception of the wild boar cannot be excluded (cf. Wyatt 1981). This literary motif would move beyond the geographic framework of the kingdom of Ugarit and the chronological framework of the Late Bronze Age to reappear some seven centuries later in a somewhat modified form in the legends of Adonis. Nothing confirms that this literary motif originates at Ugarit itself, but as Ribichini (1981) has shown, the Adonis legends draw from oriental tradition, particularly the Levantine.

20

The pig in medieval iconography

Sarah Phillips

INTRODUCTION

Representations of the pig can be found in a wide variety of visual material worldwide, and throughout time. The term 'pig' is used here as a general term to cover all domestic and wild forms of *Sus scrofa* (where relevant and possible precise distinction between these forms will be specified). The images that exist, vary in terms of the form or shape of the pig, the representation of its characteristic features according to sex (male–boar vs female–sow), form (domestic or wild), age (adult pig or piglet), or physical characteristics (i.e. snout, tusks, tail, trotters, hair and hide coloration, razorback, and bristles). A visual appreciation of different living forms can be found in works such as Burnie (2001) or Buczacki (2002). This chapter is concerned with the creation and use of visual images of the pig. It offers a selection of materials dating in range from the medieval to the early modern period and will cite selected examples to represent continuity or change in the use of images where appropriate. The materials providing representations of the pig include (but are not exclusive to) illuminated manuscripts, prints and posters, engravings and drawings on either parchment or paper, canvas paintings, stained and painted glass, wood carvings, embroidery and textiles, stonework, moulded or cast metal, ceramic wares, and figurines. Exclusive porcine works discussing this iconography include those by Foster (1977), Ryba (1983), Brochier (1988), Bonera (1991), and Lawson (1995). In addition to depictions of pigs, functional and decorative and artistic uses were also found for the inedible body parts of real pigs such as the tusks appearing in visual cultural materials reflecting the precious value of the animal by some people. The main approach of this paper is thematic in order to emphasize how visual representations of the pig have had associations with filth, shame, lust, fantasy, care and consumption, inspiration, and human identity.

A FILTHY BEAST

Many assumptions have been made about the relative importance of the sources of inspiration drawn upon for the creation of particular images or motifs in the surviving media, and the availability of these to their creators (for a discussion on the practice of artistic transmission during the Middle Ages, see Scheller 1995). One very much exploited and misunderstood source for the medieval period has been various 'books of beasts' known as bestiaries. The most comprehensive discussion on the use and consumption of bestiaries can be found in Baxter (1998), though for further clarification on the nature and content of these books, reference can be made to Cronin (1941), McCulloch (1962), Henderson (1982), Clark & McMunn (1989), George & Yapp (1991), and Brown (2000).

The bestiary was a type of book presenting a number of real and fabulous creatures to its medieval audience. A considerable number of bestiaries have survived throughout Europe. In England alone, up to 50 Latin bestiaries are known (Baxter 1998: 147–8) dating from the 12th to the 15th centuries. Although we do not know what attitudes were held toward the bestiaries by people in the medieval period, a number of modern-day authors have suggested that they were used as a means of demonstrating and communicating moral or religious instruction, particularly by the ecclesiastical sectors of society. Monks, for example, could use the books as a means of training, in order to improve behaviour, since the creatures presented often had characteristics associated with human traits. It is possible that bestiaries could also have been used as a means to influence perception and attitude, by portraying and representing the behaviours of people, with good/positive and bad/negative associations through animal characters such as the pig. Recent research by Baxter (1998) has made an attempt to pinpoint the patronage and circulation of the first and second families of bestiaries (see McCulloch 1962, for an outline of these families and references to pigs in particular manuscripts). This aspect is important if the consumption and content of bestiaries are to be appreciated. Estimates of their availability, both geographically and chronologically, provide clues that can be used to indicate how they might have been originally used, i.e. as practical and active texts from which to teach moral instruction by monks or as highly decorative books kept as possessions in order to demonstrate wealth and status.

The text of the bestiaries was frequently accompanied by colourful pictures or miniatures of the creatures featured, such as those of the 'Boar' and 'Sow with piglets' from an English bestiary known as MS Bodley 764 (*c*.1240–60)

Fig. 20.1. Bestiary boar in MS Bodley 764, fol. 38v. (copyright the Bodleian Library, University of Oxford, UK)

Fig. 20.2. Bestiary sow and piglets in MS Bodley 764, fol. 37v. (copyright the Bodleian Library, University of Oxford, UK)

(Figs 20.1, 20.2). Other examples can be found in White (1984) and Mermier (1992). The descriptions offered to accompany this text are similar to those found in other European bestiaries of the period. The pig was described negatively, as a filthy beast because 'it sucks up filth, wallows in mud, and smears itself with slime' (Barber 1992: 84). The sow (the female) was said to signify 'sinners, the unclean and heretics', the 'luxurious liver' and a creature that 'thinks on carnal things' (Barber 1992: 84–6). In contrast, the boar (the male), was regarded more positively, and said to signify the 'fierceness of the rulers of this world' and 'in the spiritual sense the boar means the devil because of its fierceness and strength' Barber (1992: 87). The enraged boar was therefore a dangerous beast to be feared, just like other kinds of members of human society. Carroll (1976: 94, 117) offers a summary of Elizabethan non-religious prose, where the creature is used symbolically, supporting its 'foaming ferocity', drawing upon sources such as Topsell's *Histoire of Foure-Footed Beastes* (South 1981), and its 'brutishness' from Pliny's *Natural History*.

Medieval handbooks on hunting have referred to the sport and extreme hazards of hunting the ferocious boar, with its tusks that could gore to death both dogs and humans (Thiebaux (1968–9: 281). One example of a 'hunting book' is that of Edward, 2nd Duke of York, dating from the 15th century, which suggests 'there is neither a lion noe leopard that slayeth a man at one stroke as a boar doth . . . a proud beast and fearce and perilous' (Baillie-Grohman & Baillie-Grohman 1909: 46–53).

A BODY OF SHAME

The pig (usually the sow) has been a creature regarded with contempt, and used as a means of transmitting shame upon its human associates, in other media for centuries. European 'defamatory' or 'shaming' pictures are one example of this, and these have been in existence from at least the late 13th century. Although no samples from England or France have been found (this is not to say they were not used or did not exist at the time), similarly offensive and humiliating pictures from Germany, known as *Schandbilder*, have survived. *Schandbilder* were painted or drawn on large sheets of paper, and are thought to have been displayed in public places such as the church, town hall, and shops (as well as less reputable places such as brothels), similar to the 'Wanted' posters of the American West. These pictures are numerous, and portray debtors demeaned through being shown engaged in activities involving the anus of female animals, whether a sow, mare, she-ass, or bitch. Explanatory threatening and insulting letters have been found accompanying the drawings and so supporting their function. They were very much part of the visual culture of the period, being used as an effective means of shaming the individuals or groups who were the subject of complaint. The threat of the public display of these drawings or posters is believed to have been enough to encourage reparation (by a debtor). One example of the pig being used visually to shame is a depiction of Herzog Johann von Bayern-Holland illustrated as a painted manuscript in the Hessisches Staatsarchiv, Marburg, Germany (*c.*1420) (reproduced in Jones 2002: 38–9, pl. 5), representing the trouble-maker lifting up a pig/sow's tail with one hand and holding a seal with the other. The humiliation of being seen to touch the anus of another animal (perhaps one held in social contempt), of coming into contact with its dung, and of stuffing an honourable family seal (or now, by association, a dishonourable or even worthless one) up the animal's rectum, was obviously not the best form of publicity.

A second example related to the *Schandbild* is the woodcut of the *Judensau* (Jews' sow), illustrated in Fig. 20.3. This image is similar to the bestiary image of a sow shown in Fig. 20.2, yet is more unisex in that the creature also has the tusks of a boar, and instead of little piglets there are people suckling milk from the sow (see also the discussion in Sillar & Meyler 1961: 24). At least six of the seven small people are also depicted wearing a pointed hat, which is a further

Fig. 20.3. The *Judensau* or Jews' sow,
*c.*1470, late 15th century (N 45 411
Judensau woodcut, copyright
Historisches Museum Frankfurt am
Main, Germany)

marker that they are intended to be understood as Jews. Hassig (1999: 75)
discusses how medieval sumptuary laws were forced upon the Jews, and that
this involved them being visually distinguished by the wearing of both the
'Jew badge' and a 'pointed hat' (*pileum cornutum*). The *Judensau* as a motif is
thought to offer a generic insult aimed at an entire community (for further
discussion concerning the *Judensau* see Shachar 1974, and more recently
Fabre-Vassas 1997: 97).

It was observed that Jews avoided not only eating pigs but even touching
them, as sexual relations between a Jew and a Christian were equated with
bestiality and punishable by death (Hassig 1999: 74). Bestiality (sexual practice
between humans and animals) was prohibited, and this was based upon Jewish
law (and ultimately included the Jews themselves) (for further discussion see
Kisch 1943: 109, 124; Kearney 1991: 163; and for the extreme insult of
buggering of animals: Jones 2002: 84). The fact that one of the human figures
is mounted backwards is also significant. This orientation has been regarded as
a further symbol of the intent to degrade and humiliate humans, and parallels
for such representations relating to the Jews have been found within other
documents, dating from the 15th to the 18th century (Mellinkoff 1973: 172).

A LUSTY ANIMAL

Not all uses of the pig were necessarily related to religious belief or contexts.
Filth and shame could also come from being related to a creature associated
with sexuality and lust, in a society where it was felt that the existence of non-
procreative marital sex should preferably be concealed. Many images in the
Middle Ages can be linked with morality, or a lack of it, as *exempla* or
instructional stories that were used to teach a moral lesson. They were a
reminder of piety in an age where the temptation of sins of the flesh were
a social concern (for examples of exempla see Scheller 1995, and for exempla

in manuscripts see Randall 1957). They served also to emphasize humour and merrymaking in human nature (Katzenellenbogen 1939; Jones 1989, 1991, 2002; Grössinger 1997, 2002; Brown 2000).

The 'Flemish' tradition of the anthologization of pictorialized proverbs and folly can be found represented in a wide variety of material from tapestries to paintings, such as the variety of proverbs extant in the painting by Bruegel the Elder of 1557, 'Netherlandish Proverbs' (Jones 2002: 38–9, Plate 6). 'Anger riding the boar' is one porcine proverbial example of the seven deadly sins, as illustrated on a misericord from Norwich Cathedral (Sillar & Meyler 1961: 16–17, fig. 14.1). Images such as these illustrate a variety of scenes from real life, including visual representations of pigs in a variety of situations both real and perhaps more fantastic or unusual. This point can also be picked up in Sillar & Meyler (1961: 24).

Fontana (1993) highlights that the sow has been long associated with fertility throughout the ancient world on account of the large size of her litters, numerous mammary glands, and demonstration of maternal care, but cites the New Testament where Christ 'drives unclean spirits into the Gadarene swine, symbolizing the need for men and women to triumph over their lower natures' (Fontana 1993: 93). It is possible that the sow with her many piglets was an expression of reproductive and sexual excess, and thus we find images of the pig offering associations of a more sexual as opposed to reproductive significance.

The pig and the prostitute may have been placed into a related mental category by certain people within the medieval period on account of their common association with lust and lechery, and, further, in that they were creatures perceived to threaten morality (see also the discussion of the swine used as a symbol within the literature of Chaucer, Rowland 1971: 77ff.). Pigs obviously needed to be constrained from wandering the city streets for the protection of people, and it was in order to achieve this that laws were made for their control in England. Goldberg (1999: 172–3) cites an ordinance from York, dating to 1301 AD, which equates the treatment and punishment of pigs with that of prostitutes if caught within the city (see also Prestwich 1976). A pig had its trotters cut off if caught transgressing (thus preventing it wandering the streets ever again), whereas the prostitute would have the door and roof timbers of the building in which she was lodging removed, thus depriving her of a shelter or home and discouraging her accommodation and further trade within the city. It is possible that some of the images we see depicting pigs and female humans echo this lustful link. Perhaps the association has been carried as late as the painting on canvas by Félicien Rops, a 19th century artist from Namur, Belgium, which depicts pigs in association each with a naked female. Other authors make an analogy between the prostitute and the nun, and in France the word 'abbesse' was used for the leaseholder of a public brothel (see Rossiaud 1984: 4–5). Hieronymus Bosch's work, 'Garden of Earthly Delights' (*c*.1505–10), is one painted example which depicts a pig dressed like a mother superior embracing a naked man. This imagery has been said to allude to the practice of wills being made under pressure in favour of monasteries (Benton 1992: 104). However, it seems that dressing pigs up as humans might not have been that unusual. As late as the 18th century, pigs were still being considered in human terms, by being dressed in human clothing, tried in courts of law as criminals, and executed like humans by hanging following charges of murder (Caras 2001: 115). Hanging was a punishment in England, for crimes such as partially eating and killing children (13th–17th centuries). One example of such a murder was that of a 6 month old baby, Agnes Perone, in Oxford in 1392: 'Witnesses said that a sow ate off the head of the said Agnes, even to the nose, and so she died, and the sow was arrested' (Rowland 1971: 75).

A CREATURE OF FANTASY

The 'Topsy Turvy World' or the 'World Turned Upside Down' (Jones 2002: 160) is regarded as a place where role reversals in human/animal relationships can be found (Benton 2004: 69). This is a land where 'the bull milks the woman, the hares roast the huntsman, the ox slaughters the butcher...the mice hang the cat, the geese hang the fox...the priest ploughs while the peasant celebrates mass' (Jones 2002: 147). Similarly, the 'Land of Cockaigne' is the joyous literary Utopia equivalent to the 'Topsy Turvy World' in medieval England (Pleij 2001). It represented a paradise for vice, lechery, sin, or a world characterizing life's realities. In Cockaigne 'pigs, for example, trot up ready-roasted, the carving knife already lodged in their sides, spitted geese fly about advertising themselves, and ready-roasted larks fly into the mouth!' (Jones 2002: 144). In some cases, unusual images for the period can be attributed to the representation of such a parallel reality. These constructs are fantastical places where the impossible becomes possible, e.g. a land where pigs do indeed fly, as illustrated by the image of a winged pig balancing on an orb, dating to the 1530s (Fig. 20.4). Kearney's (1991: 35) work on swine symbolism discusses the conceptual image of a winged pig further, suggesting it can be traced back to the work of the Roman writer Claudius Aelianus (Aelian) who reported that a winged 'sow' actually had lived on the island of Klazomenae in the Aegean sea (Book XII: 38). Although this was not necessarily a reality, the idea that such a creature might have been

Fig. 20.4. Winged pig on a world-orb, woodcut sheet of Cornelis Anthonisz, 1538–48 (image RP-P-BI-134, copyright Rijksmuseum, Amsterdam, the Netherlands)

thought to be real is supported by the finding of a winged 'boar' appearing in part on coinage of Clazomenae, and further by a winged and tailed pig on a Carian stater of Ialysus, Rhodes, dating back as early as the 5th century BC (Sillar & Meyler 1961: 109, pl. 5.1).

Other types of unusual images, unlikely to have been observed from real life but representing animals used as human characters (perhaps in order to mock), can be widely found, for example, in the numbers of pig musicians such as the bagpiping or harping pig, the fiddle-playing pig, and the whistle-blowing or singing pig (Sillar & Meyler 1961: 25–7; Kearney 1991: 261; Benton 2004: 79–83). Jones (2002: 155) suggests that 'animal musicians' were common characters in medieval *drôleries*. The animal musician theme is therefore frequently depicted in a number of ecclesiastical contexts, including roof bosses, gargoyles, lead badges, stained glass (Fig. 20.5), misericords (the carving underneath the seat ledge within the choir stalls of medieval colleges, churches, and cathedrals: Fig. 20.6), binding stamps,

Fig. 20.5. Image of a boar musician from stained glass roundel, Waddesdon Manor, Waddesdon, Buckinghamshire, *c*.1375–1425 (copyright EM 13/76 from the Rothschild Collection, National Trust, UK)

Fig. 20.6. Detail of a pig musician from Durham Castle misericord (photo by the author, taken with permission of Durham Castle archaeologist)

books of hours or manuscripts, and also, frequently, contemporary continental stallwork in France, Spain, Switzerland, and Germany (Jones 2002). 'Animal instruments' or instruments made with animals can also be found as images, e.g. the bagpipe, or rather animal-bagpipe, being a pig, dog, or cat and being played by another animal such as an ape or human. This is unlikely to have been a reality, though the fact that bones of pigs have been utilized to make musical instruments certainly is. Lawson (1995) cites the finding of perforated pig metapodial bones from bone-working waste and general refuse from Saxon, medieval, and postmedieval contexts. These have been interpreted as a type of sound-making device (as opposed to previous interpretations as toggles or bobbins) and so possibly were made as musical toys. This is further supported by ethnographic parallels and excavated finds with sound-making associations from sites in Scandinavia and eastern Europe. Others can be found in France, Germany, Netherlands, Spain, and Switzerland (Lawson 1995). Nevertheless, we have no real evidence to clarify why the image of the pig musician was used, other than modern common speculation of the parallels made with the sound made by the animal and compared with the sound or tone of the bagpipe instrument being played (Druce 1934: 6).

Some believe these representations to have a moralistic purpose, such as Jones (2002: 269) who indicates that the bagpipe could have been regarded as a phallic symbol, and Caras (2001: 112) who suggests that the image of a bagpiping pig in German sculpture represented lust. Others, however, suggest a satirical reason. We have contemporary literary references to the harping sow in English nonsense verse from the late 15th century. Jones (2002: 58–9) cites a late 15th century manuscript, discussed by Wright & Halliwell (1841), which allots animals to an instrument that alliterates with its name, for example the fox fiddled, the lark plays the lute, and the turbot plays the trumpet; the alliteration works for each animal except for the sow (perhaps a hog?) who plays the harp. In addition to the musical themes identified such as pigs dancing or playing musical instruments, other types of pig representations exist as a contrast, on wood carvings within the choir stalls and misericords. There are at least 25 varied scenes of pigs, boars, sows, and/or piglets occuring within England, Scotland, and Ireland alone (Remnant 1969–99; Jones 2002). The scenes carved reveal naturalistic scenes with more realistic images such as pigs shown with their litter, boar, sow and piglets fighting or attacking other animals, boar hunts, pigs being driven into forests, pigs being fed or eating acorns or nuts under trees, pigs being held by the ear, pigs being roasted or stored as food by humans, and even pigs being saddled and ridden.

CARE AND CONSUMPTION

During the Middle Ages, the months and seasonal labours and activities were commonly represented in manuscripts, books of hours and psalters, such as the 14th century *Luttrell Psalter*. A number of these feature the pig, and show humans preparing food for these creatures in order to fatten them up (knocking down mast, i.e. acorns or beech nuts), as well as possibly depicting humans killing pigs during the late autumn months for feasting and consumption over the winter. This is also seen in medieval stained glass roundels for the month of November from the Church of All Saints, Dewsbury, West Yorkshire (*c.*1335–50 AD) (Ayre 2002: 146), and Bilton Church, Rugby, Warwickshire, dating from the 14th century (Sillar & Meyler 1961: pl. VIII). Each roundel depicts a single person (bearded in the former and hooded in the latter) swinging an axe over his head and standing next to a pig. Images such as these indicate the consistent importance of the animal to the human for consumption during the various seasons of the year, and attempts by humans to look after these creatures through collecting food for them. The month of November was the common month for slaughtering the beast, and was known as *Slachtmonat* (in Old High, Middle High, and Early New High German, though the word is still in use today). The fact that the pig was a valued animal adds further support to its regular appearance within ecclesiastical contexts, where swineherds (the guardian of the pig) were afforded their own patron saint (St Anthony), and this association can be found as a more general image in medieval stained glass scenes. However, the preparation and eating of pigs is not so frequently depicted in all the various types of media compared with others such as in manuscrips (Salisbury 1994), nor was this a practice consistent among all people around the world. Within orthodox Judaism and Islam, the pig is not eaten.

The belief that the pig and its flesh were dirty, diseased, and perhaps poisonous, could have been developed from observing the symptoms of medical conditions we know today as trichinosis, tapeworm, and fever. These might have been prevalent in a time where standards of food hygiene were poor and refrigeration had yet to develop, and this would mean that the pig could have been realistically linked to the onset of illness and even provoked the fear of death among those who ate the animals' flesh, except for the pig itself, of which the gluttonous nature meant that it that did not even spare eating its own young (Aelian, Book X: 16) nor refrain from eating corpses. Aelian therefore viewed the swine as a creature of sheer gluttony as a result of this observation. If people believed that a pig had the ability to cause harm after its death, this would make the pig an inspirational animal for those wishing to inflict insult upon others, and this concept has permeated even relatively modern cultural beliefs.

When Muslim mutineers were seriously challenging imperial Great Britain in India, the rumour was spread that the bodies of Muslim warriors slain in battle would be gathered up by the British troops and sewn inside freshly obtained pigskins. These would-be warriors of heaven would thus spend eternity wrapped in filth, corruption and shame (Caras 2001: 113).

Handoo (1990) offers further discussion on cultural attitudes to animals and birds.

AN IMAGE OF IDENTITY

The pig has been a creature used to reflect identity, and so there are many representations of pigs' or boars' heads in family heraldic emblems (for a list see Sillar & Meyler 1961: 175). Caras (2001: 114) suggests King Arthur had the head of a boar on his shield because it might have equated with the boar's courage, valour, or power. The boar was also used by the royal House of York from 1461 to 1485, whose insignia displayed a white boar *passant argent* [a beast walking, silver]. The link of the prominent family of the royal house of York to the boar can be found in York's Anglo-Saxon name of 'Eoforwic' or 'boar farm'. The last York family king, Richard III, even had it sewn on to badges for his wardrobe, as well as featuring it on the *sinister* [left-hand] side of his *cognisance* [distinguishing badge] (though this has now been lost to five white lions in the modern coat of arms for the city, Kearney 1991: 305). The English royal coat of arms has displayed a variety of creatures such as the lion, swan, bull, hart, yale, and dragon according to the families occupying the throne at that time (Whittick 1960: 29). The emblematic image of the boar might therefore have become more popular in commercial contexts in this period in honour of the king. An example is the White Boar Inn in Leicester, where Richard III is reputed to have spent his last night before his death in the battle of Bosworth Field. However, Sillar & Meyler (1961: 136) suggest that, after this period, it is possible that the white boars were cancelled out by some who had them repainted 'true blue' to represent the boar of the Earl of Oxford who helped the new king, Henry VII, reach the throne.

Whittick (1960: 109) indicates that, as time progressed, differentiation and distinctiveness had to increase to account for the growing number of the same class of establishments within a limited area, and this meant that many commonly understood symbols lost their function in symbolizing the goods or services sold, and many were inconsistently combined. An essay written in 1710 supporting the regulation of signs emphasizes this, where the streets were 'filled with blue boars, black swans and red lions; not to mention flying pigs and hogs in armour'. Thus, although the image of a pig was perhaps once used to convey loyalty or an association with particular goods or services sold (shop and inn signs in an age of illiteracy), the use of the boar and understanding of the pig became less consistent, at times confusing, and even caused misunderstanding among the people of its own time. It is for this reason that establishing an iconographic reading or symbolic value for an image of a pig, or the representation of a pig in combination with other things, becomes increasingly difficult to justify throughout time. It is true that some representations of animals such as the pig can be linked to heraldic and symbolic devices, either in its naturalistic or more stylistic form, but this does not mean that every representation made has such an association, or was intended to inspire such a complex or meaningful cognitive response. Nevertheless, generalistic interpretations have been made and expressed by various authors about the symbolic value of the pig, e.g. Evans (1896), Collins (1913), Druce (1934), Whittick (1960), Sillar & Meyer (1961), Cirlot (1962), Thiebaux (1968–9), Fontana (1993), and Caras (2001). Cirlot's dictionary of symbols (1962: 30) suggests a simplistic symbolic significance of the boar as a creature associated with ambivalence, intrepidity (citing a Spanish source), and licentiousness (drawing on a French source). However, a positive, distinctive, and sacred association was also stressed in the way the animal was regarded by Babylonian and Semitic cultures, and from Celtic and Gallic legends. In contrast, Fontana (1993) identifies the use of the pig in the Buddhist 'wheel of life'. This displays three delusions at its centre, which are thought to keep humans away from Nirvana and revolving on the wheel of life. These delusions are embodied in the form of animals, and include the red cock, the green snake, and the black pig, these animals symbolizing lust, hatred, and ignorance respectively. Positive links are cited to the civilizations of Egypt and Greece, the Celts, North Americans, and Hindus, and negative associations to the Buddhist, Judaic, and Christian faiths (Fontana 1993: 56, 78).

CONCLUSION

The pig is an intelligent animal that inspires all kinds of emotions in various people. Without doubt, it was regarded highly by certain social groups, not the least for its economic value, but also for its visual currency. It was therefore used by a variety of people for a wide range of purposes depending upon their attitudes to the pig, and their beliefs in what the creature represented to them, either practically or symbolically. This difference can be identified from the surviving representations. It is impossible to attribute a single meaning for all representations of *Sus*, and those suggested will vary according to the sources consulted. It is clear that animals and birds were an important and significant source of inspiration in the medieval world, hence the vast range of representations and decorative motifs utilized in the period. Creatures were used in place of humans to express their behaviour and traits, and we find them used as characters in fables, in stories of lives the saints, and yet others within manuscripts and poems (Carroll, 1976; Cohen, 1994: 60–1; Salisbury, 1996: 49). Their body parts were also used to treat various forms of human sickness (see Sheldon 1977, for further discussion on the medical uses of animals). Unfortunately, this meant that pigs were the subject of cruelty, humiliation, and shame, as if they were humans.

The lifetime of a pig representation could have been extensive, and could have had multiple meanings and associations, linked to the changing human spectrum of those experiencing environmental, social, religious, political, economic, and industrial activity. The only certainty is that the pig was chosen by humans as a creature to be represented on a variety of materials (ranging from the more traditional aristocratic and religious forms of art and artefacts to those of popular and folk art), from the earliest times that humans created images (Klingender 1971; Benton 1992, 1997, 2004). It is difficult to confirm who made the decision to represent a particular creature, such as the pig, in what material, location, and context, and the relative degree of influence a patron, sponsor, or craftsperson held in the creation, detailing, and positioning of an image. Some of these clearly might have been imitated or copied from other sources, with or without their original meaning. No single textual or visual source can be regarded as a generalistic reflection of all peoples' knowledge, understanding, and attitude toward *Sus* in the medieval period.

The number of surviving representations does not necessarily have any relationship to the frequency with which the species occurred in that period either (see the discussion on birds by Ticehurst 1923: 29). Therefore, frequency of representation of pigs is not necessarily linked to the real frequency of pig occurrence, nor of real observation, and further, the phenomenon of representation is a difficult signifier to use in assessing the social popularity of the creature or its importance (see Gunnthorsdottir 2001). Nevertheless, we can try to expose the infinitely complex possibilities, and utilize imagery to trace the appearance of pigs as represented through time (Wiseman 2000: 6). At times, the pig seems rather a negative character and has been used to parallel undesirable qualities in humans in terms of its (supposed) filthy, unclean, and gluttonous nature. However, it is not certain whether the moralistic parallel of this beast was shared by the rest of the population, and as such we have no reason to believe that people paid any attention to the written media. What is true is that 'no animal on earth is more unjustly treated than the pig: abused, mocked, insulted, vilified, exploited, and, in the end, slaughtered' (Bonera 1991: 6).

Glossary

Aetiology: The causes of diseases or pathologies

Allele: Any one of a number of DNA sequences occupying a given locus (position) on a chromosome, most often used to refer to DNA sequences that code for a specific gene. Each gene can appear in many forms, i.e. many alleles

Allochthonous: Of animals, from another region; hence imported, introduced, or translocated (cf. **autochthonous**)

Allopatric: With a different geographical distribution, occupying different areas or regions (cf. **sympatric**)

Ameloblast: Cell that secretes enamel proteins which eventually mineralize to form the dental enamel of the tooth crown

Amelogenesis: The actual formation of dental enamel, which occurs in two stages: the secretory stage and the maturation stage

Amino acid: A basic chemical molecule, coded for by a series of three base pairs of DNA. Amino acids constitute the building blocks of proteins

Artiodactyla: The mammalian order which originally contained just the even-toed or cloven-hoofed mammals (as opposed to the Perissodactyla or odd-toed mammals such as horses), but which is now broadened to include other groups (see Chapter 1)

Autochthonous: Of animals, native or indigenous to a particular region under discussion (cf. **allochthonous**)

Bergmann's law: The principal that, all other things being equal, animals in a warmer environment will tend to be smaller than animals of the same species in a colder environment

Bestiary: A medieval book depicting animals, real or fabulous, and giving details of their natural history and/or associated mythology

Bone collagen: A protein which is the main organic structural component of bone

Cementoblast: Cell that produces cementum, the hard tissue that covers the tooth roots (cf. **cementum**)

Cemento-enamel junction: The physical junction between the tooth enamel and root cementum as observed on the external portion of the tooth crown

Cementum: The hard tissue that covers the tooth roots (cf. **cementoblast**)

Chalcolithic (or Copper Age): The period transitional between the Neolithic and Bronze Ages, when copper was in use alongside stone

Chromosome: Generally, a long, continuous piece of DNA on which rest genes, regulatory elements, and other intervening nucleotide sequences (cf. **nucleotide**)

Crypt: The cavity in the mandibular or maxillar bone within which a tooth is initially formed, prior to eruption

Dentine: The mineralized dental tissue between the tooth enamel or cementum and the pulp cavity of the tooth

Diachronic: Of different date. Diachronic changes are changes through time

Dimorphism: The characteristic of showing two clearly different forms (sexual: see **sexual dimorphism**)

Diploid: Cells that contain two copies of each chromosome (one set of chromosomes from each parent) are known as diploid cells

DNA: Deoxyribonucleic acid (usually in the form of a double helix) is found in all living cells and contains the genetic instructions for all cellular life forms

Domestic: In one definition, a group of animals isolated from their wild relatives by human action, so that selective breeding by humans may alter the genetic characteristics of the group (other definitions exist). Not synonymous with the taming of an individual

Enamel: The highly mineralized dental tissue that forms the outer (white) surface of the tooth crown

Epiphyseal fusion: Growing bones consist of three main components: (1) the epiphysis (the separate articular ends), (2) the diaphysis (ends of the long bone; age ossifies and finally closes the separate growing shaft), and (3) the metaphyses (zone of growing cartilage) which separates and joins the two. Epiphyseal fusion occurs around skeletal maturity, when the cartilage ossifies and joins the separate growing components

Epiphysis: The separate growing (usually articular) end of a long bone

Ethnoarchaeology: The study of the behaviour and/or material culture of contemporary societies, specifically to provide insights that may help archaeologists interpret the material remains they find

F_1/F_2 generation: The F_1 generation refers to the first generation of progeny in a breeding experiment from a controlled cross. The F_2 generation is the hybrid offspring of F_1 parents

Farrowing: Of pigs, the yearly occurrence of giving birth. Double farrowing thus refers to the production of two litters of offspring in one year

Feral: Animals living in the wild with no human control, but whose ancestors escaped from human control; the behaviourally wild descendants of formerly domestic animals

Fertile Crescent: A term first coined by archaeologist J. H. Breasted of the University of Chicago to broadly define a region in the Middle East where early agriculture and civilization began. This region includes ancient Egypt, the Levant, and Mesopotamia

Folivore: An animal that eats mainly leaves

Frugivore: An animal that eats mainly fruit

Funnel Beaker Culture (or TRB):   The earliest Neolithic culture of the southern Baltic coasts, Denmark, and southern Sweden as far north as the latitude of Stockholm. This group introduced agriculture to these regions. Named after the culture's characteristic ceramic form

Gamete: The specialized germ cells (usually sperm and eggs) that come together during fertilization in sexually reproducing organisms

Gene: The fundamental units of heredity in living organisms, coded by genetic material (usually DNA). Genes control the development, appearance, and behaviour of the organism

Genotype: The genetic constitution of an individual organism

Gilt: A young female pig

Germplasm: A term often used synonymously with DNA, to describe the genetic resources of an organism

Haploid (or monoploid): A cell with half the full number of chromosomes

Hematopoiesis: The formation of blood cellular components

Heterozygous: The condition, in a diploid or polyploid organism, of possessing at least two different alleles of the same gene (cf. **diploid, polyploid, homozygous**)

Histology: The microscopic study of the structure and morphology of thinly sectioned tissue

Holocene: A geological epoch covering the last 12,000 years (see **Pleistocene**)

Homozygous: The condition, in a diploid or polyploid organism, of possessing no more than one identical allele of the same gene (cf. **diploid, polyploid, heterozygous**)

Hydroxyapatite: A calcium mineral which is the main non-organic component of teeth and bones

Hypodontia: Having fewer than the standard number of teeth

Hypogeous: In this context, refers to animals that root for food in the subsoil

Interprismatic enamel: Enamel with a homogeneous appearance that occurs between the enamel prisms—the main structural components of dental enamel

Isohyet: A line drawn on a map indicating points of equal precipitation

Jomon: A long period within Japanese prehistory, which nominally runs from *c.* 13000 to 2500 years BP. The term (in Japanese) refers to the 'corded' decoration of the distinctive pottery style which defined it

Linnaean taxonomy: The hierarchical system of classification of species into genera, genera into tribes, and so on into higher-level groupings such as family and order; devised by Carolus Linnaeus, an 18th century Swedish naturalist. It is (with modifications) still the fundamental system of biological classification

Locus: The position on a chromosome where a gene, or some other sequence, is located (see **microsatellites**)

Meiosis: The process that divides one diploid cell into four haploid cells in eukaryotes in order to create gametes (see **diploid, haploid, gamete**)

Mendel: Gregor Johann Mendel (1822–1884) is often referred to as the 'father of genetics' for his study of the inheritance of traits in pea plants. Mendel demonstrated that trait inheritance follows particular laws, which were later named after him

Mesolithic: The period of European prehistory falling between the end of the Upper Palaeolithic, coterminous with the last glacial period, and the appearance of the agricultural **Neolithic** (q.v.); thus, hunter-gatherer societies of Holocene age

Mesopotamia: Literally the land 'between rivers', referring to the region broadly defined by the basins of the rivers Tigris and Euphrates in the Middle East, and including modern-day Iraq, eastern Syria, and south-eastern Turkey

Microsatellites: Polymorphic loci present in nuclear DNA that consist of repeating units of 1–4 base pairs in length (see **locus**)

Misericord: A fold-up seat in the choir of a church, often with an elaborately carved lower surface visible only when the seat is turned up

Missense mutation: A type of point mutation in which a single nucleotide is changed resulting in a changed amino acid. This type of change can, but does not necessarily render the resulting protein non-functional

Monogenic: Pertaining to a single gene

Monotypic: Of a genus, one that contains only a single species

Mutation: Changes to the genetic material (usually DNA or RNA), usually caused by copying errors during cell division or by exposure to radiation

Neolithic: Across most of the Old World, the prehistoric period characterized by the first appearance of farming, but in north-eastern and eastern Europe also applied to the latest hunter-gatherer cultures characterized by the presence of pottery

Nomadism: A human subsistence strategy involving large-scale movement around the landscape and the absence of permanent settlements

Nucleotide: The structural units of DNA and RNA

Osteochondrosis: A pathological condition associated with living bone characterized by interruption of the blood supply (in particular to the epiphysis), followed by localized bone necrosis (death), and possibly later regrowth

Pastoralism: A mobile form of farming principally involving the tending of domestic animals

Perikymata: Incremental lines visible on the enamel surface which are the result of a discontinuity in normal enamel microstructure (cf. **Retzius lines**)

Phenotype: The set of observable characteristics of an individual such as its size, proportions, colour, etc., produced by the interaction of its genetic makeup or **genotype** (q.v.) and the effects of the environment

Phytolith: A mineralized microscopic body (usually silica) found in the tissues of plants and thought to aid the structural stability of leaves and stalks

Phylogeny: The origin and evolution of a group of organisms

Pitted Ware Culture: The Middle Neolithic culture of the central and southern Baltic, and most of southern Sweden, occupied parts of the area formerly of the **Funnel Beaker Culture** (q.v.). Despite being termed 'Neolithic', regarded by many as a largely hunter-gatherer culture. Named from the pitted pottery that characterizes the culture

Pleistocene: A geological epoch which runs from 1.8 million to 12,000 years BP

Polymorphism: Generally, the possession of multiple possible states for a single property, though in genetics it means possessing multiple alleles or differences at single nucleotide positions

Polyploid: Cells that contain more than two copies of each of their chromosomes

Primate: Any species which falls within the taxonomic order of Primates, which includes lemurs, monkeys, and apes (the latter including humans)

Prokaryotes: Organisms without a cell nucleus or any other membrane-bound organelles, and in most cases unicellular

Retzius lines: Incremental discontinuities which occur during normal dental enamel growth and are only visible histologically (cf. perikymata)

Rhyton: A ceramic drinking cup, probably with a religious meaning

RNA (ribonucleic acid): A nucleic acid consisting of nucleotide monomers which is involved in the translation of genes into proteins

Scavenging: The practice of free-range domestic animals finding their food for themselves on and around human settlements. Such food may include waste from butchery or fishing as well as cultivation; therefore particularly appropriate for omnivorous animals such as pigs

Sexual dimorphism: The manifestation of differences in size, morphology, or any other characteristic between the sexes

Soma: The entire body of an organism, exclusive of the germ cells

Stable isotope: Varieties of atoms that are not radioactive. The most common ones used in archaeology for dietary and migration studies are isotopes of carbon, nitrogen, and oxygen

Swidden horticulture: The practice of clearing a temporary field and burning the cut vegetation, planting in the ash, and then clearing a new field after two or three years' cultivation. Such regimes often involve sporadic movement of the people's settlement as well

Sympatric: With the same geographical distribution, occupying the same area or region (cf. **allopatric**)

Taphonomy: Formally defined in palaeontology as the transition from the biosphere to the lithosphere, i.e. the process of fossilization. In zooarchaeology the term covers the various processes through which animal remains go before they become incorporated in archaeological deposits; such as butchery, processing for consumption, cooking and eating, discard, destruction by dogs and other scavengers, and also chemical or erosional destruction while buried

Tomes process: The projection on the distal portion of **ameloblasts** (q.v.), which secretes the enamel matrix

Translocation: The movement by humans of a group of animals to a region the animals did not previously occupy, such as an island. Usually such animals are domestic, but wild individuals may also be translocated in order to establish new populations for hunting

TRB Culture: See **Funnel Beaker Culture**

Ungulata: A classification originally containing the hoofed mammals including both the **artiodactyla** (q.v.) and the perissodactyla, but now broadened to include other groups (see Chapter 1)

Yayoi: An archaeological period in Japan which runs from about 2,500 to 1,700 years BP. It is named after the region of Tokyo where excavations first uncovered artefacts associated with this period, and is generally thought to represent the arrival in Japan of farmers from the Korean peninsula (who cultivated rice and kept domesticated pigs)

Zoogeography: The study of the geographic distribution of animal species

References

Aaris-Sørensen K. (1980). Depauperation of the mammalian fauna of the island of Zealand during the Atlantic period. *Videnskabelige Meddelelser fra Dansk Naturhistorisk Forening* 142, 131–8.

—— (1988). *Danmarks Forhistoriske Dyreverden*. Copenhagen: Gyldendal.

—— (1999). The Holocene history of the Scandinavian aurochs (*Bos primigenius* Bojanus, 1827). In: Weniger G.-C. (ed.), *Archäologie und Biologie des Auerochsen* (Wissenschaftliche Schriften des Neanderthal Museums 1), 49–57. Mettman: Neanderthal Museum.

Abe M. (1981). Faunal remains from Higashinara site. *Higashinara Excavation Report* II, 121–3 [in Japanese].

Adams R.M. (1962). Agriculture and urban life in early south-western Iran. *Science* 136, 109–22.

—— (1981). *Heartland of Cities*. Chicago: University of Chicago Press.

Aelian (Claudius Aelianus) (1972). *On The Characteristics of Animals* (English translation by A.F. Scholfield, 1972). London: Loeb Classical Library.

Akeret O. & Rentzel P. (2001). Micromorphology and plant macrofossil analysis of cattle dung from the Neolithic lake shore settlement of Arbon Bleiche 3. *Geoarchaeology* 16, 687–700.

—— Haas J.N., Leuzinger U. & Jacomet S. (1999). Plant macrofossils and pollen in goat/sheep faeces from the Neolithic lake-shore settlement from Arbon Bleiche 3, Switzerland. *The Holocene* 9, 175–82.

Albarella U. & Davis S. (1996). Mammals and birds from Launceston Castle, Cornwall: decline in status and the rise of agriculture. *Circaea* 12(1), 1–156.

—— Davis S., Detry C. & Rowley-Conwy P. (2005). Pigs of the 'Far West': the biometry of *Sus* from archaeological sites in Portugal. *Anthropozoologica* 40(2), 27–54.

—— Dobney K. & Rowley-Conwy P. (2006). The domestication of the pig (*Sus scrofa*): new challenges and approaches. In: Zeder M.A., Bradley D.G., Emshwiller, E. & Smith B.D. (eds), *Documenting Domestication: New Genetic and Archaeological Paradigms*, 209–27. Berkeley, CA: University of California Press.

—— & Serjeantson S. (2002). A passion for pork: meat consumption at the British late Neolithic site of Durrington Walls. In: Miracle P. & Milner N. (eds), *Consuming Passions and Patterns Of Consumption*, 33–49. Cambridge: McDonald Institute.

Albarella U. & Serjeantson S. (in press a). Size and shape of the Eurasian wild boar (*Sus Scrofa*), with a view to the reconstruction of its Holocene history. *Mammal Review*.

Albarella U., Tagliacozzo A., Dobney K. & Rowley-Conwy P. (2006). Pig hunting and husbandry in prehistoric Italy: a contribution to the domestication debate. *Proceedings of the Prehistoric Society* 72, 193–227.

——Manconi F., Rowley-Conwy P. & Vigne J.-D. (2006). Pigs of Corsica and Sardinia: a biometrical re-evaluation of their status and history. In: Tecchiati U. & Sala B. (eds), *Studi archeozoologici in onore di Alfredo Riedel*, 285–302. Bolzano: Province of Bolzano.

Allen M.S., Matisoo-Smith E. & Horsburgh A. (2001). Pacific 'babes': issues in the origins and dispersal of Pacific pigs and the potential of mitochondrial DNA analysis. *International Journal of Osteoarchaeology* 11, 4–13.

Alves E., Ovilo C., Rodriguez M.C. & Silio L. (2003). Mitochondrial DNA sequence variation and phylogenetic relationships among Iberian pigs and other domestic and wild pig populations. *Animal Genetics* 34(5), 319–24.

Amberger G. (1987). Tierknochenfunde vom Tell Abqa/Iraq. *Acta Praehistorica et Archaeologica* 19, 111–29.

Ambrose S.H. (1990). Preparation and characterization of bone and tooth collagen for stable carbon and nitrogen isotope analysis. *Journal of Archaeological Science* 17, 431–51.

Amorosi T., Buckland P.C., Edwards K.J., Mainland I.L., McGovern T.H., Sadler J.P. & Skidmore P. (1998). They did not live by grass alone: the politics and palaeoecology of animal fodder in the North Atlantic region. *Environmental Archaeology* 1, 41–54.

Andersen K. (1983). *Stenalderbebyggelsen i den Vestsjællandske Åmose*. Copenhagen: Fredningsstyrelsen.

Andersen S.H. (1975). Ringkloster: en jysk inlandsboplands med Ertebøllekultur (with English summary). *KUML* 1973–74, 11–108.

——(1998). Ringkloster. Ertebølle trappers and wild boar hunters in eastern Jutland. A survey. *Journal of Danish Archaeology* 12, 13–59.

——& Malmros C. (1965). Norslund. En kystboplads fra ældre stenalder. *KUML* 1965, 35–114.

Andersson L., Haley C.S., Ellegren H., Knott S.A., Johansson M., Andersson K. *et al.* (1994). Genetic mapping of quantitative trait loci for growth and fatness in pigs. *Science* 263, 1771–4.

Andersson-Eklund L., Marklund L., Lundstrom K., Haley C.S., Andersson K. *et al.* (1998). Mapping quantitative trait loci for carcass and meat quality traits in a wild boar × Large White intercross. *Journal of Animal Science* 76, 694–700.

——Uhlhorn H., Lundeheim N., Dalin G. & Andersson L. (2000). Mapping quantitative trait loci for principal components of bone measurements and osteochondrosis scores in a wild boar × Large White intercross. *Genetical Research* 75, 223–30.

Anezaki T. (2002). Study of *Sus* mandibles excavated from the Torihama Shell Midden: investigating a possible domestication. *Bulletin of Torihama Shell Midden* 3, 1–10 [in Japanese].

—— (2003). Changes in dental size of prehistoric pig populations in Japan. *Zooarchaeology Society of Japan* 20, 23–39.

—— Toizumi T., Eda M. & Uzawa K. (in press). Haneo, the faunal analysis of an Early Jomon wet site. In: Croes D.R. & Coles B. (eds), *Wet Sites Connections. Linking Indigenous Histories, Archaeology, and the Public.*

Angress S. (1959). Mammal remains from Horvat Beter (Beersheba). *'Atiqot* 2, 53–71.

Anonymous (1992). *Das vorderasiatische Museum Berlin, ad. Staatliche Museum Berlin.* Mainz: Philipp von Zabern.

—— (2001). *La Mésopotamie entre le Tigre et l'Euphrate, catalogue d'exposition, 2001.* Taipei: Musée national d'Histoire.

Aoba T. & Fejerskov O. (2002). Dental fluorosis: chemistry and biology. *Critical Reviews in Oral Biology & Medicine* 13, 155–70.

Apollonio M., Randi E. & Toso S. (1988). The systematics of the wild boar (*Sus scrofa* L.) in Italy. *Bollettino di Zoologia* 3, 213–21.

Arnon I. (1972). *Crop Production in Dry Regions.* London: Leonard Hill.

Atkinson M. & Preston S. (1998). The Late Iron Age and Roman settlement at Elms Farm, Heybridge, Essex, excavations 1993–1995: an interim report. *Britannia* XXIX, 85–110.

Audouze F. (ed.). (1992). *Ethnoarchéologie: justification, problèmes, limites. Actes des 12ᵉ rencontres internationales d'archéologie et d'histoire d'Antibes.* Juan-les-Pins: Éditions APDCA.

Aurenche O., Cauvin J., Cauvin M.-C., Copeland L., Hours F. & Sanlaville P. (1981). Chronologie et organisation de l'espace dans le Proche Orient de 12000 à 5600 avant J.C. In: Sanlaville P. & Cauvin J. (eds), *Préhistoire du Levant*, 571–601. Paris: Éditions du CNRS.

Ayers K., Ingrem C., Light J., Locker A., Mulville J. & Serjeantson D. (2003). Mammal, bird and fish remains and oysters. In: Hardy A., Dodd A., & Keevill G.D. (eds), *Aelfric's Abbey: Excavations at Eynsham Abbey, Oxfordshire, 1989–1992* (Thames Valley Landscape Volume 16), 341–2. Oxford: Oxford Archaeology.

—— (2002). *Medieval Figurative Roundels.* (Corpus Vitrearum Medii Aevi. Summary Catalog 6). Oxford: Oxford University Press.

Baillie-Grohman W.A. & F.N. (eds) (1909). *The Master of Game By Edward, Second Duke of York: The Oldest English Book on Hunting.* London: Chatto & Windus.

Baldwin J.A. (1978). Pig rearing versus pig breeding in New Guinea. *Anthropological Journal of Canada* 16, 23–7.

—— (1982). Pig rearing and the domestication process in New Guinea and the Torres Straits region. *National Geographic Society Research Reports* 14, 31–43.

Banning E.B., Rahimi D. & Siggers J. (1994). The Late Neolithic of the southern Levant: hiatus, settlement shift or observer bias? The perspective from Wadi Ziqlab. *Paléorient* 20(2), 151–64.

Barber R. (1992). *Bestiary.* Woodbridge: Boydell Press.

Barguet P. (1967). *Le livre des morts des anciens Egyptiens.* Paris: Éditions du Cerf.

BARTOSIEWICZ L. (1998). Interim report on the Bronze Age animal bones from Arslantepe (Malatya, Anatolia). In: Buitenhuis H., Bartosiewicz L. & Choyke A.M. (eds), *Archaeozoology of the Near East III* (ARC-Publicaties 18), 221–32. Groningen: Centre for Archaeological Research & Consultancy.

BATE D.M.A. (1938). Animal remains from the Megiddo Tombs. *University of Chicago Oriental Institute Publication* 32, 205–13.

BAXTER R. (1998). *Bestiaries and Their Users in the Middle Ages.* Stroud: Sutton Publishing.

BAYLISS-SMITH T. (1982). *The Ecology of Agricultural Systems.* Cambridge: Cambridge University Press.

BECK P. (2002). The drawings from Horvat Teman. In: Beck P. (ed.), *Imagery and Representation, Studies in the Art and Iconography of Ancient Palestine: Collected Articles*, 94–170. Tel Aviv: Emery and Claire Yass publications in Archaeology.

BECKER C. (1980). *Untersuchungen an Skelettresten von Haus- und Wildschweinen aus Haithabu* (Berichte über die Ausgrabungen in Haithabu 15). Neumünster: Karl Wachholtz.

—— (1988). Die Tierknochen vom Tell Bdèri 1985. *Damaszener Mitteilungen* 3, 379–86.

BECKER C.J. (1953). Die Maglemosekultur in Dänemark. Neue Funde und Ergebnisse. In: Vogt E. (ed.), *Actes de la IIIe Session, Zurich 1950*, 180–3. Zurich: Congrès International des Sciences Préhistoriques et Protohistoriques.

BEECHEY C.V., CATTANACH B.M., BLAKE A. & PETERS J. (2005). *Mouse Imprinting Data and References.* Harwell, Oxfordshire: MRC Mammalian Genetics Unit. <*http://www.mgu.har.mrc.ac.uk/research/imprinting/index.html*>.

BELLWOOD P. (1996). The origins and spread of agriculture in the Indo-Pacific region: gradualism and diffusion or revolution and colonization? In: Harris D.R. (ed.), *The Origins and Spread of Agriculture and Pastoralism in Eurasia*, 465–98. London: UCL Press.

BENECKE N. (1990). Pig domestication in Sweden during the Middle Neolithic—some new archaeozoological data. *Benbiten* 3(3), 1–4.

—— (1993). The exploitation of *Sus scrofa* (Linne, 1758) on the Crimean Peninsula and in southern Scandinavia in the Early and Middle Holocene, two regions, two strategies. In: Desse J. & Audoin-Rouzeau F. (eds), *Exploitation des animaux sauvages a travers le temps*, 233–45. Juan-les-Pins: Éditions APDCA.

—— (1994). *Der Mensch und seine Haustiere. Die Geschichte einer jahrtausendealten Beziehung.* Stuttgart: Theiss.

BENTLEY R.A., KRAUSE R., PRICE T.D. & KAUFMANN B. (2003). Human mobility at the early Neolithic settlement of Vaihingen, Germany: evidence from strontium isotope analysis. *Archaeometry* 45, 471–86.

BENTON J.R. (1992). *The Medieval Menagerie: Animals in the Art of the Middle Ages.* New York: Abbeville Press.

—— (1997). *Holy Terrors.* New York: Abbeville Press.

—— (2004). *Medieval Mischief. Wit and Humour in the Art of the Middle Ages.* Stroud: Sutton Publishing.

BERGLUND J. (1982). Kirkebjerget—a Late Bronze Age settlement at Voldtofte, southwest Funen. *Journal of Danish Archaeology* 1, 51–63.

BERGMANN C. (1847). Über die Verthältnisse der Wärmeökonomie der Tiere zu ihrer Grösse. *Göttinger Studien* 3, 595–708.

BERGMANN F. (1975). On the inadequacies of functionalism. *Michigan Discussions in Anthropology* 1(1), 2–23.

BEULS I., DE CUPERE B., VAN MELE P., VERMOERE M. & WAELKENS M. (2000). Present-day traditional ovicaprine herding as a reconstructional aid for understanding herding at Roman Sagalassos. In: Mashkour M., Choyke A.M., Buitenhuis H. & Poplin F. (eds), *Archaeozoology of the Near East IV* (ARC-Publicaties 32), 216–23. Groningen: Centre for Archaeological Research & Consultancy.

BIERSACK A. (1999). Introduction: from the 'new ecology' to the new ecologies. *American Anthropologist* 101(1), 5–18.

BIGELOW L. (2000). Zooarchaelogical investigations of economic organization and ethnicity at Late Chalcolithic Hacinebi: a preliminary report. *Paléorient* 25(1), 83–9.

BIGNON O., BAYLAC M., VIGNE J-D. & EISENMANN V. (2005). Geometric morphometrics and the population diversity of Late Glacial horses in Western Europe (*Equus caballus arcelini*): phylogeographic and anthropological implications. *Journal of Archaeological Science* 32, 375–91.

BINFORD L.R. (1978). *Nunamiut Archaeology.* New York: Academic Press.

—— (1981). *Bones. Ancient Men and Modern Myths.* New York: Academic Press.

BINTLIFF J.L. & VAN ZEIST W. (eds) (1982). *Palaeoclimates, Palaeoenvironments and Human Communities in the Eastern Mediterranean in Prehistory* (BAR International Series 133). Oxford: British Archaeological Reports.

BITTEL K. (1987). Der Schwertgott in Yazilikaya. *Anadolu (Anatolia)* XXI 1978–80, 21–31.

BLANKHOLM H.P. (1996). *On the Track of a Prehistoric Economy. Maglemosian Subsistence in Early Postglacial South Scandinavia.* Aarhus: University Press.

BLOUCH R.A. (1995). Conservation and research priorities for threatened suids of south and southeast Asia. *Ibex Journal of Mountain Ecology* 3, 21–5.

BLYTH E. (1851). Report on the Mammalia and more remarkable species of birds inhabiting Ceylon. *Journal of the Asiatic Society Bengal* 20(2), 153–85.

BOARD OF EDUCATION, MIYAGI PREFECTURE (1986a). Tagara shell midden. *Site Report of Cultural Heritage of Miyagi Prefecure* 111, 183–515 [in Japanese].

—— (1986b). *Site Report of Cultural Heritage of Miyagi Prefecure* 119, 4–15 [in Japanese].

BOCHERENS H. (2000). Preservation of isotopic signals (^{13}C,^{15}N) in Pleistocene mammals. In: Ambrose S.H. & Katzenberg M.A. (eds), *Biogeochemical Approaches to Palaeodietary Analysis,* 65–88. New York: Kluwer Academic–Plenum.

—— MASHKOUR M., BILLIOU D., PELLÉ E. & MARIOTTI A. (2001). A new approach for studying prehistoric managements in arid areas: intra-tooth isotopic analyses of archaeological Caprine from Iran. *Compte Rendu de l'Académie des Sciences. Paris, Série II* 332, 67–74.

BODENHEIMER F.S. (1953). *Animal Life in the Land of Israel.* Tel Aviv: Dvir [in Hebrew].

BODENHEIMER F.S. (1958). The present taxonomic status of the terrestrial mammals of Palestine. *Bulletin of the Research Council of Israel* B, 165–90.

BOESSNECK J. (1987). Tierknochenfunde vom Uch Tepe. *Acta Praehistorica et Archaeologica* 19, 131–63.

BOESSNECK J. (1988*a*). *Die Tierwelt des Alten Ägypten*. München: Verlag C.H. Beck.

—— (1988*b*). Tierknochenfunde vom Tell Chuera / Nordost Syria. In: Moortgat-Correns U. (ed.), *Tell Chuera in Nordost-Syrien: vorläufige Berichte über die neunte und zehnte Grabungskampagne 1982 und 1983* (Schriften der Max Freiherr von Oppenheim-Stiftung 13–14), 79–98. Berlin: Gebr. Mann.

—— (1992). Besprechung der Tierknochen- und Molluskenreste von Hassek Höyük. *Naturwissenschaftliche Untersuchungen und lithische Industrie. 1st Forschung* 38, 58–74.

—— (1993). Tierknochen. In: Böck B. *et al.* (eds), *Uruk (Warka) 1989* (Baghdader Mitteilungen 24), 86–96. Berlin: Deutsches Archäoloisches Institut. Abteilung Baghdad.

—— & KOKABI M. (1981). Tierknochenfunde. In: Orthmann W. (ed.), *Halawa 1977–1979*, 89–104. Bonn: Dr. Rudolf Habelt .

—— & VON DEN DRIESCH A. (1975). Tierknochenfunde vom Korucutepe bei Elazig in Ostanatolien. In: van Loon M.N. (ed.), *Korucutepe I: Studies in Ancient Civilisation*, 1–216. Amsterdam: North Holland.

—— &——(1989). Die Faunenreste vom Tell Halawa am Assad-See Nordsyrien (Drittes und Anfang zweites Jahtausend v. Chr). In: Orthmann W. (ed.), *Halawa 1980–1986.* (Saarbrücker Beiträge zur Altertumskunde 52), 113–52. Bonn: Dr. Rudolf Habelt .

—— —— & STEGER U. (1984). Tierknochenfunde des Ausgrabungen der Deutschen Archäologischen Instituts Baghdad in Uruk-Warka, Iraq. *Baghdader Mitteilungen* 15, 149–89.

—— —— & ZIEGLER R. (1993). Die Faunenreste. In: Wilhelm G. & Zaccagnini C. (eds), Tell Karrana 3. *Baghdader Forschungen* 15, 233–6.

BOISSIÈRE M. (1999). *Ethnobiologie et rapports à l'environnement des Yali d'Irian Jaya (Indonésie).* Thèse, Université de Montpellier II.

BÖKÖNYI S. (1973). Tell Taya (1968–69): animal bones. *Iraq* 35, 184–5.

—— (1974). *History of Domestic Mammals in Central and Eastern Europe*. Budapest: Akademiai Kiado.

—— (1976). Development of early stock rearing in the Near East. *Nature* 264(5581), 19–23.

—— (1977). *Animal Remains from the Kermanshar Valley* (BAR International Series 34). Oxford: British Archaeological Reports.

—— (1983). Late Chalcolithic and Early Bronze I animal remains from Arslantepe (Malatya), Turkey: a preliminary report. *Origini, Preistoria e Protostoria de la Civilita Antiche* 12(II), 581–98.

—— (1990). *Kamid el-Loz 12. Tierhaltung und Jagd* (Saarbrücker Beiträge zur Altertumskunde 42). Bonn: Dr. Rudolf Habelt.

—— & FLANNERY K.V. (1969). Faunal remains from Sakheri Sughir. In: Wright H.T. (ed.), *The Administration of Rural Production in an Early Mesopotamian Town*

(Anthropological Papers, Museum of Anthropology, University of Michigan 38), 143–9. Ann Arbor: University of Michigan.

BOL R., WILSON J.M., SHIEL R.S., PETZKE K.J., WATSON A. & COCKBURN J. (1998). Effects of long-term fertilizer and manure treatments on the distribution and ^{15}N natural abundance of amino acids in the Palace Leas Meadow Hay Plots: a preliminary study. In: Stankiewicz B.A. & van Bergen P.F. (eds), *Nitrogen-Containing Macromolecules in the Bio- and Geosphere*, 309–20. Washington, DC: American Chemical Society.

BOLLEN A. (1998). *Archeozoölogisch onderzoek van laat-middeleeuwse contexten uit Raversijde.* Master's thesis, University of Gent, Belgium.

BOLTON K. (1954). *Outdoor Pig-keeping.* Ipswich: Pig Publications.

BOND J.M. & O'CONNOR T. (1999). *Bones from the Medieval Deposits at 16–22 Coppergate and Other Sites in York* (The Archaeology of York 15(5)) York: Council for British Archaeology.

BONERA F. (1991). *Pigs: Art, Legend, History.* Boston: Bulfinch Press.

BONNÈMERE P & LEMONNIER P. (1992). Terre et échanges chez les Anga. *Études Rurales* 127–8, 133–58.

BOULTON I.C., COOKE J.A. & JOHNSON M.S. (1999). Lesion scoring in field vole teeth: application to the biological monitoring of environmental fluoride contamination. *Environmental Monitoring and Assessment* 55, 409–22.

BOURKE R.M., ALLEN B.J., HIDE R.L., FRITSCH D., GRAN R., HOBSBAWN P. *et al.* (1995). *Southern Highlands Province: Text, Summaries, Maps, Code Lists and Village Identification* (Agricultural Systems of Papua New Guinea Working Paper 11). Canberra: Human Geography Department, Australian National University.

BOURKE S.J. (1997*a*). The 'Pre-Ghassulian' sequence at Teleilat Ghassul: Sydney University Excavations 1975–95. In: Gebel H.G.K., Kafafi Z. & Rollefson G.O. (eds), *The Prehistory of Jordan II: Perspectives from 1997* (Studies in early Near Eastern Production, Subsistence and Environment 4), 395–417. Berlin: Ex Oriente.

—— (1997*b*). The urbanisation process in the south Jordan Valley: renewed excavations at Teleilat Ghassul 1994–1995. In: *Studies in the History and Archaeology of Jordan* 6, 249–59. Amman: Department of Antiquities.

BOYD D.J. (1984). The production and management of pigs: husbandry options and demographic patterns in an Eastern Highlands herd. *Oceania* 55, 27–49.

—— (1985). 'We must follow the Fore': Pig husbandry itensification and ritual diffusion among the Irakia Awa, Papua New Guinea. *American Ethnologist* 12, 119–36.

BOYDE A. (1969). Correlation of ameloblast size with enamel prism pattern: use of scanning electron microscope to make surface area measurements. *Zeitschrift für Zellforschung und Mikroskopische Anatomie* 93, 583–93.

—— (1997). Microstructure of enamel. In: Chadwick D. & Cardew G. (eds), *Dental enamel* (Ciba Foundation Symposium 205), 18–31. Chichester: Wiley.

BRAEMER F. & ÉCHALLIER J.-C. (1995). Le marge désertique en Syrie du Sud au IIIe millénaire. Éléments d'appréciation de l'évolution du milieu. In: van der Leeuw S. (ed.), *L'homme et la dégradation de l'environnement*, 345–56. Juan-les-Pins: Editions APDCA.

BRAIN C.K. (1969). The contribution of Namib desert Hottentots to an understanding of Australopithecine bone accumulations. *Scientific Papers of the Namib Desert Research Station* 39, 13–22.

BRAUN A., GROVES C.P., GRUBB P., YANG Q. & XIA L. (2001). Catalogue of the Musée Heude collection of mammal skulls. *Acta Zootaxonomia Sinica* 26, 608–60.

BRIEDERMANN L. (1990). *Schwarzwild.* Berlin: VEB Deutscher Landwirtschartverlag.

BROCHIER J.-J. (1988). *Anthologie Du Sanglier.* Paris: Hatier.

BROOKFIELD H.C. & BROWN P. (1963). *Struggle for Land: Agriculture and Group Territories Among the Chimbu of the New Guinea Highlands.* Melbourne: Oxford University Press.

BROTHWELL D. (2001). Iodine and bones: a contribution to theoretical zooarchaeology. In: Buitenhuis H. & Prummel W. (eds), *Animals and Man in the Past. Essays in Honour of Dr. A. T.Clason, Emeritus Professor of Archaeology, Rijksuniversiteit Groningen, the Netherlands* (ARC-Publicatie 41), Groningen: .ARC.

BROWN C. (2000). Bestiary lessons on pride and lust. In: Hassig, D. (ed.), *The Mark of The Beast.* London: Routledge.

BROWN T.A., NELSON D.E., VOGEL J.S. & SOUTHON J.R. (1988). Improved collagen extraction by modified Longin method. *Radiocarbon* 30, 171–7.

BROWN W.A.B & CHAPMAN N.G. (1991*a*). Age assessment of fallow deer (*Dama dama*): from a scoring scheme based on radiographs of developing permanent molariform teeth. *Journal of Zoology* 224, 367–79.

—— —— (1991*b*). Age assessment of Red Deer (*Cervus elaphus*): from a scoring scheme based on radiographs of developing permanent molariform teeth. *Journal of Zoology* 225, 85–97.

—— CHRISTOFFERSON P.V., MASSLER M. & WEISS M.B. (1960). Postnatal tooth development in cattle. *American Journal of Veterinary Research* 21, 7–34.

BRUFORD M.W., BRADLEY D.G. & LUIKART G. (2003). DNA markers reveal the complexity of livestock domestication. *Nature Review Genetics* 4(11), 900–10.

BUCHHOLZ H.G. (2000). Kyprische Bildkunst zwischen 1100 und 500 v.Chr.. In: Uehlinger C. (ed.), *Image as Media* (Orbis Biblicus et Orientalis 175), 215–66. Fribourg: University Press.

BUCZACKI S. (2002). *Fauna Britannica.* London: Hamlyn.

BUITENHUIS H. (1983). The animal remains from Tell Sweyhat, Syria. *Palaeohistoria* 25, 131–44.

—— (1985). Preliminary report on the faunal remains of Hayaz Hüyük from the 1979–1983 seasons. *Anatolica* 12, 61–74.

—— (1988). *Archeözoologisch Onderzoek Langs de Midden-Eufraat.* Ph.D. Thesis, Rijksuniversiteit Groningen, Nederland.

BULL G. & PAYNE P. (1982). Tooth eruption and epiphysial fusion in pigs and wild boar. In: Wilson B., Grigson C. & Payne S. (eds), *Ageing and Sexing Animal Bones from Archaeological Sites* (BAR British Series 109), 55–71. Oxford: British Archaeological Reports.

BULMER R. (1976). Selectivity in hunting and in disposal of animal bone by the Kalam of the New Guinea Highlands. In: de Sieveking G., Longworth I.H. & Wilson K.E. (eds), *Problems in Economic and Social Archaeology*, 169–86. London: Duckworth.

BURENHULT G. (2002). The grave-field at Ajvide. In: Burenhult G. (ed.), *Remote Sensing, Vol 2. Applied Techniques for the Study of Cultural Resources and the Localization, Identifcation and Documentation of Subsurface Prehistoric Remains in Swedish Archaeology* (Theses and Papers in North European Archaeology 13b), 31–167. Stockholm: Institute of Archaeology, University of Stockholm.

BURNIE D. (2001). *Animal*. London: Dorling Kindersley.

BUTZER K.W. (1978). The late prehistoric environmental history of the Near East. In: Brice W.C. (ed.), *The Environmental History of the Near and Middle East since the Last Ice Age*, 5–12. New York: Academic Press.

CALDECOTT J.O., BLOUCH R.A. & MACDONALD A.A. (1993). The bearded pig (*Sus barbatus*). In: Oliver W.L.R. (ed.), *Pigs, Peccari, and Hippos*, 136–45. Gland: International Union for the Conservation of Nature and Natural Resources. Species Survival Commission.

CALLEBAUT D. (1991). Castrum, Portus und Abtei von Ename. In: Böhme H.W. (ed.), *Burgen der Salierzeit. Teil 1. In den nördlichen Landschaften des Reiches* (Römisch-Germanisches Zentralmuseum Monographien 25), 291–309. Sigmaringen: Jan Thorbecke Verlag.

——DE GROOTE K., ERVYNCK A. & VAN STRYDONCK M. (2002). Was het nu '70 of '80? Radiokoolstofdateringen voor het castrum te Ename (Oudenaarde, prov. Oost-Vlaanderen). *Archeologie in Vlaanderen* VI, 231–41.

CALLOT O. (1986). Communication: La région nord du Palais d'Ougarit. *Comptes Rendus de l'Académie des Inscriptions et des Belles-Lettres* 1986 (novembre–décembre), 735–55.

CAMPBELL B. (2000). *English Seigniorial Agriculture, 1250–1450*. Cambridge: Cambridge University Press.

CAMPS G. (1988). *Préhistoire d'un île*. Paris: Editions Errance.

CANAANI G. (1972). *The ecology and behaviour of the wild pig in the region of Mount Meiron*. Master's thesis, Tel Aviv University [in Hebrew].

——(1976/1977). Wild boars in Galilee. *Land and Nature* 2, 68–71 [in Hebrew].

CARAS R.A. (2001). *A Perfect Harmony. The Intertwining Lives of Animals and Humans throughout History*. Purdue, West Lafayette, IN: Purdue University Press.

CARROLL W.M. (1976). *Animal Conventions in English Renaissance Non-Religious Prose (1550–1600)*. Westport, CT: Greenwood Press.

CARTER R.J. (1997). Age estimation of roe deer (*Capreolus capreolus*) mandibles from Mesolithic site of Star Carr, Yorkshire, based on radiographs of mandibular tooth development. *Journal of Zoology* 241, 495–502.

——(1998). Reassessment of seasonality at the Early Mesolithic site of Star Carr, Yorkshire based on radiographs of mandibular tooth development in red deer (*Cervus elaphus*). *Journal of Archaeological Science* 25, 851–6.

——(2001a). *Human subsistence and seasonality in mesolithic northwest europe based on studies of mandibular bone and dentition in red deer (Cervus elaphus) and roe deer (Capreolus capreolus)*. Ph.D. thesis, University of London.

CARTER R.J. (2001*b*). Dental indicators of seasonal human presence at the Danish Boreal sites of Holmegaard I, IV and V and Mullerup and the Atlantic sites of Tybrind Vig and Ringkloster. *The Holocene* 11, 359–65.

CASSOLI P.F. & TAGLIACOZZO A. (1982). La fauna della Grotta di Cala dei Genovesi a Levanzo. *Rivista de Scienze Preistoriche* XXX–VII, 48–58.

CETTI F. (1774). *Quadrupedi, Uccelli, Anfibi e Pesci di Sardegna*. Anastati reprint. Cagliari: GIA Editrice.

CHAIX L. & SIDI MAAMAR H. (1992). Voir et comparer la découpe des animaux en contexte rituel: limites et perspectives d'une ethnoarchéozoologie. In: Audouze F. (ed.), *Ethnoarchéologie: Justification, problèmes, limites. XIIe Rencontres internationales d'Archéologie et d'Histoire d'Antibes*, 268–91. Juan-les-Pins: Éditions APDCA.

CHARLES M. & BOGAARD A. (2005). Identifying livestock diet from charred plant remains: a Neolithic case study from southern Turkmenistan. In: Davies J., Fabiš M., Mainland I., Richards M. & Thomas R. (eds), *Diet and Health in Past Animal Populations. Current Research and Future Directions*, 93–103. Oxford: Oxbow Books.

CHEN H. & LEIBENGUTH F. (1995). Restriction patterns of mitochondrial DNA in European wild boar and German Landrace. *Comparative Biochemistry and Physiology* 110B, 725–8.

CHENAL-VELARDÉ I. (1996). Etude taphonomique, observations ethnologiques et interprétations archéologiques: essai sur les techniques de boucherie à Hamdallahi (Mali, XIXe siècle). *AnthropoZoologica* 23, 85–95.

CHERRY J.F. (1979). Four problems in Cycladic prehistory. In: Davis J.L. & Cherry J.F. (eds), *Papers in Cycladic Prehistory* (UCLA Institute of Archaeology, Monograph 14), 22–47. Los Angeles: UCLA.

—— (1981). Pattern and process in the earliest colonisation of the Mediterranean islands. *Proceedings of the Prehistoric Society* 47, 41–68.

—— (1990). The first colonization of the Mediterranean islands: a review on recent research. *Journal of Mediterranean Archaeology* 3, 145–221.

—— (1992). Palaeolithic Sardinians? Some questions of evidence and method. In: Tykot R.H. & Andrews T.K. (eds), *Sardinia in the Mediterranean: A Footprint in the Sea*, 43–56. Sheffield: Sheffield Academic Press.

CHILDE V.G. (1958). *The Prehistory of European Society*. Harmondsworth: Penguin.

CHRISTENSEN C. (1995). The littorina transgressions in Denmark. In: Fischer A. (ed.), *Man and Sea in the Mesolithic* (Oxbow Monograph 53), 15–22. Oxford: Oxbow Books.

—— FISCHER A. & MATHIASSEN, D.R. (1997). The great sea rise in the Storebælt. In: Pedersen L., Fischer A. & Aaby B. (eds), *The Danish Storebælt since the Ice Age*, 45–54. Copenhagen: A/S Storebælt Fixed Link.

CIRLOT J.E. (1962). *A Dictionary of Symbols*. London: Routledge & Kegan Paul.

CLARK W.B. & MCMUNN M.T. (1989). *Beasts and Birds of the Middle Ages: The Bestiary and Its Legacy*. Philadelphia: University of Pennsylvania Press.

CLUTTON-BROCK J. (1979). The mammalian remains from the Jericho Tell. *Proceedings of the Prehistoric Society* 45, 135–57.

—— (1981). *Domesticated animals from early times*. London: William Heinemann & British Museum (Natural History).

—— (1999). *A Natural History of Domesticated Mammals*. Cambridge: Cambridge University Press.

—— & BURLEIGH R. (1978). The animals remains from Abu Salabikh: preliminary report. *Iraq* 40(2), 89–100.

COHEN E. (1994). Animals in medieval perceptions. The image of the ubiquitous other. In: Manning A. & Serpell J. (eds), *Animals and Human Society. Changing Perspectives*, 59–80. London: Routledge.

COLLINS A.H. (1913). *Symbolism of Animals and Birds Represented in English Church Architecture*. London: Pitman.

COLLINS B.J. (2002*a*). Animals in Hittite literature. In: Collins B.J. (ed.), *A History of the Animal World in the Ancient Near East*, 237–50. Leiden: E.J. Brill.

—— (2002*b*). Animals in the religion of ancient Anatolia. In: Collins B.J. (ed.), *A History of the Animal World in the Ancient Near East*, 309–34. Leiden: E.J. Brill.

COLYER F. (1936). *Variations and Diseases of the Teeth of Animals*. London: John Bale, Sons & Danielson.

COSTA L.J. (2004). *Corse préhistorique*. Paris: Errance.

COSTANTINI L. & COSTANTINI L.B. (2001). I resti vegetali carbonizzati di Vivara. In: Pepe C. (ed.), *La ricerca archeologica a Vivara e le attività dei laboratori dell'Istituto Universitario Suor Orsola Benincasa*, 83–6. Napoli: Istituto Universitario Suor Orsola Benincasa.

COURTOIS J. (1978). Corpus céramique de Ras Shamra—Ugarit, niveaux historiques d'Ugarit, Bronze Moyen et Bronze Récent. In: Schaeffer C.F.A. (ed.), *Ugaritica VII. Mission de Ras Shamra XVIII*, 191–370. Paris: Paul Geuthner.

CROFT P. (1989). Animal bones. In: Todd I.A. *et al.* (eds), *Kalavasos-Ayios Dhimitrios II, Vasilikos Valley Project 3* (Studies of Mediterranean Archaeology LXXI (3)), 70–2. Göteborg: Paul Amstroms Förlag.

CRONIN G.J. (1941). The bestiary and the medieval mind. *Modern Language Quarterly* 2, 191–8.

CRONIN S.J., MANOHARAN V., HEDLEY M.J. & LOGANATHAN P. (2000). Fluoride: a review of its fate, bioavailability, and risks of fluorosis in grazed-pasture systems in New Zealand. *New Zealand Journal of Agricultural Research* 43, 295–321.

—— NEALL V.E., LECOINTRE J.A., HEDLEY M.J. & LOGANATHAN P. (2003). Environmental hazards of fluoride in volcanic ash: a case study from Ruapehu volcano, New Zealand. *Journal of Volcanology and Geothermal Research* 121, 271–91.

CUCCHI T., ORTH A., AUFFRAY J.-C., RENAUD S., FABRE L., CATALAN J., HADJISTERKOTIS E. *et al.* (2006). A new endemic species of the subgenus *Mus* (Rodentia, Mammalia) on the island of Cyprus. *Zootaxa* 1241, 1–36.

DAEGLING D.J. & GRINE F.E. (1999). Terrestrial foraging and dental microwear in *Papio ursinus*. *Primates* 40, 559–72.

DALIX A.-S. (2006). Baäl et les sangliers dans CAT 1.12. *Historiae* 3, 35–68.

DANIN A. (1988). Flora and vegetation of Israel and adjacent areas. In: Yom-Tov Y. & Tchernov E. (eds), *The Zoogeography of Israel*, 129–57. Dordrecht: Dr. W. Junk Publishers.

DARWIN C. (1859). *On the Origin of Species by Means of Natural Selection or the Preservation of Favoured Races in the Struggle for Life.* London: John Murray.

—— (1868). *The Variation of Animals and Plants Under Domestication.* London: John Murray.

DAVIS S. (1976). Mammal bones from the Early Bronze Age city of Arad, northern Negev, Israel: some implications concerning human exploitation. *Journal of Archaeological Science* 3, 153–64.

—— (1982). Climatic change and the advent of domestication: the succession of ruminant artiodactyls in the late Pleistocene-Holocene in the Israel region. *Paleorient* 8, 5–15.

—— (1984). The advent of milk and wool production in western Iran: some speculations. In: Clutton-Brock J. & Grigson C. (eds), *Animals and Archaeology: 3. Early Herders and their Flocks* (BAR International Series 202), 265–78. Oxford: British Archaeological Reports.

—— (1987). *The Archaeology of Animals.* London: Routledge.

—— (1988). The mammal bones from Tel Yarmuth. In: de Miroschedji P. *et al.* (eds), *Yarmouth I, Rapport sur les trios campagnes de fouilles à Tel Yarmouth (Israel), 1980–1982*, 143–9. Paris: ADPF, Editions Recherche sur les Civilisations.

—— (1997). The agricultural revolution in England: some zoo-archaeological evidence. *AnthropoZoologica* 25–6, 413–28.

—— (2003). The zooarchaeology of Khirokitia (Neolithic Cyprus) including a view from the mainland. In: Guilaine J. & Le Brun A. (eds), Le Néolithique de Chypre. *Bulletin de Correspondance Hellénique. Supplément* 43, 253–68.

—— in press. The animal bones from Nahal-zehora I and II. In: Gopher A. (ed.), *Archaeological Investigations at Nahal Zehora: Villages of the Pottery Neolithic in the Menashe Hills, Israel.* Tel-Aviv: Institute of Archaeology, Tel-Aviv University.

——& BECKETT J. (1999). Animal husbandry and agricultural improvement: the archaeological evidence from animal bones and teeth. *Rural History* 10(1), 1–17.

DECHERT B. (1995). Faunal remains from Hirbet-ez Zeraqon. In: Buitenhuis H. & Uerpmann H.-P. (eds), *Archaeozoology of the Near East II*, 79–87. Leiden: Backhuys.

DE CUPERE B. (2001). *Animals at Ancient Sagalassos. Evidence of the Faunal Remains* (Studies in Eastern Mediterranean Archaeology IV). Turnhout: Brepols.

DEGERBØL M. (1933). *Danmarks Pattedyr i Fortiden i Sammenligning med recente Former* (Videnskabelige Meddelelser fra Dansk Naturhistorisk Forening 96). Copenhagen: C.A. Reitzel.

—— (1939). Dyreknogler. *Aarbøger for Nordisk Oldkyndighed og Historie* 1939, 85–198.

DEHAUT E.G. (1911). Les suidés. In: Dehaut E.G. (ed.), *Matériaux pour servir à l'histoire zoologique et paléontologique des îles de Corse et de Sardaigne*, 60–8. Paris: G. Steinheil.

DE LANFRANCHI F. (1991). Relations entre l'espace pastoral en Corse et le répartition del sites préhistoriques. In: Maggi R., Nisbet R. & Barker G. (eds), *Archeologia della pastorizia nell'Europa meridionale I* (Rivista di Studi Liguri LVI 1–4), 123–35. Bordighera: Instituto Internazionale di Studi Liguri, presso Museo Bicknell.

DE LANFRANCHI-FIRROLONI J. (1979). Le porc dans l'élevage traditionnel. *Cahier du Centre d'Etudes et de Recherche du Musée de Lévie* 1, 1–12.

DELLA MARMORA A. (1839). *Viaggio in Sardegna. La geografia fisica e umana. Vol. I.* Nuoro: Editrice Archivio Fotografico Sardo.

DE MEULEMEESTER J. (1979). De circulaire versterking en de Warandemotte te Veurne. *Conspectus* MCMLXXVIII, *Archaeologia Belgica* 213, 152–6.

—— (1980). De circulaire versterking te Veurne. *Conspectus* MCMLXXIX, *Archaeologia Belgica* 223, 109–13.

—— (1981). De Warande-motte te Veurne. *Conspectus* MCMLXXX, *Archaeologia Belgica* 238, 72–5.

—— (1982). De grafelijke motte te Veurne. *Conspectus* MCMLXXXI, *Archaeologia Belgica* 247, 117–21.

—— (1990). Les castra carolingiens comme élément de développement urbain: quelques suggestions archéo-topographiques. *Château Gaillard. Etudes de Castellologie médiévale* XIV, 95–119.

DEMIRJIAN A., GOLDSTEIN H. & TANNER J.M. (1973). A new system of dental assessment. *Human Biology* 45, 211–28.

DE MIROSCHEDJI P., SADEQ M., FALTINGS D., BOULEZ V., NAGGHAR-MOLINER L., SYKES N. & TENGBERG M. (2001). Les fouilles de Tell es-Sakan (Gaza): nouvelles données sur les contacts Egypto-Cananéens au Ive–IIIe millénaires. *Paléorient* 27(2), 75–104.

DENBESTEN P.K. (1994). Dental fluorosis: its use as a biomarker. *Advances in Dental Research* 8, 105–10.

—— (1999). Mechanism and timing of fluoride effects on developing enamel. *Journal of Public Health Dentistry* 59, 247–51.

—— CRENSHAW M.A. & WILSON M.H. (1985). Changes in the fluoride-induced modulation of maturation stage ameloblasts of rats. *Journal of Dental Research* 64, 1365–70.

DENIRO M.J. (1985). Postmortem preservation and alteration of *in vivo* bone collagen isotope ratios in relation to palaeodietary reconstruction. *Nature* 317, 806–9.

DENIZ E. & PAYNE S. (1982). Eruption and wear in the mandibular dentition as a guide to ageing Turkish Angora goats. In: Wilson B., Grigson C. & Payne S. (eds), *Ageing and Sexing Animal Bones from Archaeological Sites* (BAR British Series 109), 155–205. Oxford: British Archaeological Reports.

DEPARTMENT OF ARCHAEOLOGY, NATIONAL MUSEUM OF CHINESE HISTORY *et al.* (ED.) (2001). *The Dongguan Site in Gucheng, Yuanqu.* Beijing: Science Press.

DESENDER K., ERVYNCK A. & TACK G. (1999). Beetle diversity and historical ecology of woodlands in Flanders. *Belgian Journal of Zoology* 129(1), 139–56.

DESSE J. (1988). The animal bone remains. In: Dollfuss G. *et al.* (eds), Abu Hamid, an early fourth millennium site in the Jordan Valley. In: Garrard A. & Gebel H.G. (eds), *The Prehistory of Jordan: The State of Research in 1986* (BAR International Series 396), 595–7. Oxford: British Archaeological Reports.

DEVENDRA C. & FULLER M.F. (1979). *Pig Production in the Tropics.* Oxford: Oxford University Press (Oxford Tropical Handbooks).

DEVER W.G. (1989). The collapse of the urban early Bronze Age in Palestine—towards a systemic analysis. In: de Miroschedji P. (ed.), *L'urbanisation de la Palestine a l'age du Bronze Ancien* (BAR International Series 527 (ii)), 225–46. Oxford: British Archaeological Reports.

DEVER W.G. (1992). Pastoralism and the end of the Urban Early Bronze Age in Palestine. In: Bar-Yoef O. & Khazanov A. (eds), *Pastoralism in the Levant, Archaeological Materials in Anthropological Perspectives* (Monographs in World Archaeology 10), 83–92. Madison, WI: Prehistory Press.

—— (1995). Social structure in the Early Bronze Age IV period in Palestine. In: Levy T.E. (ed.), *The Archaeology of Society in the Holy Land*, 282–96. Leicester: Leicester University Press.

DIENER P. & ROBKIN E. (1978). Ecology and evolution and the search for cultural origins: The question of Islamic pig prohibition. *Current Anthropology* 19, 493–540.

DIONG C.H. (1973). Studies of the Malayan wild pig in Perak and Johore. *Malayan Nature Journal* 26, 120–51.

DIX M.L. & STRICKLAND M.J. (1986). Use of radiographs to classify martens by sex and age. *Wildlife Society Bulletin* 14, 275–9.

DOBNEY K., ANEZAKI T., HONGO H., MATSUI A., YAMAZAKI K., ERVYNCK A. *et al.* (2005). The transition from wild boar to domestic pig as illustrated by dental enamel defects (LEH): a Japanese case study including the site of Torihama. *Torihama Shell Midden Papers* 4–5, 51–78.

—— & ERVYNCK A. (1998). A protocol for recording enamel hypoplasia on archaeological pig teeth. *International Journal of Osteoarchaeology* 8(4), 263–74.

—— —— (2000). Interpreting developmental stress in archaeological pigs: the chronology of linear enamel hypoplasia. *Journal of Archaeological Science* 27(7), 597–607.

—— —— ALBARELLA U. & ROWLEY-CONWY P. (2004). The chronology and frequency of a stress marker (linear enamel hypoplasia) in recent and archaeological populations of *Sus scrofa* in north-west Europe, and the effects of early domestication. *Journal of Zoology* 264, 197–208.

—— —— & LA FERLA B. (2002). Assessment and further development of the recording and interpretation of linear enamel hypoplasia in archaeological pig populations. *Environmental Archaeology* 7, 35–46.

—— JAQUES D. & VAN NEER W. (2003). Diet, economy and status: evidence from the animal bones. In: Matthews R. (ed.), *Excavations at Tell Brak vol. 4. Exploring a Regional Centre in Upper Mesopotamia, 1994–1996*, 417–30. Cambridge: McDonald Institute & British School of Archaeology in Iraq.

DRUCE G.C. (1934). The sow and pigs: a study in metaphor. *Archaeologia Cantiana* 46, 1–6.

DUCOS P. (1968*a*). *L'origine des animaux domestiques en Palestine.* Bordeaux: Publications de l'Institut de Préhistoire de l'Université de Bordeaux.

—— (1968*b*). La faune de Selenkahiyé. *Annales Archeologiques arabes Syriennes* 18, 33–4.

—— (1991). La faune de Tell Turlu (Turquie) et les animaux domestiques dans la culture de Halaf. *Akkadia* 72, 1–19.

—— (1993). Proto-élevage et élevage au Levant sud au VIIe millénaire B.C.: les données de la Damascène. *Paléorient* 19(1), 153–73.

—— GALLO ORSI U., MACCHI E. & PERRONE A. (1991). Monthly birth distribution and structure of an alpine population of wild boar (*Sus scrofa*) in north-west Italy. In: Spitz F., Janeau G., Gonzalez G. & Aulagnier S. (eds), *Ongulés/Ungulates 91. Proceedings of the International Symposium Ongulés/Ungulates 91*, 395–7. Paris: Société Française pour l'Etude et la Protection des Mammifères & Institut de Recherche sur les Grands Mammifères.

DWYER P.D. (1990). *The Pigs That Ate the Garden: A Human Ecology from Papua New Guinea*. Ann Arbor, MI: Michigan University Press.

—— (1993). The production and disposal of pigs by Kubo people of Papua New Guinea. *Memoirs of the Queensland Museum* 33, 123–42.

—— (1996). Boars, barrows and breeders: the reproductive status of domestic pig populations in mainland New Guinea. *Journal of Anthropological Research* 52, 481–500.

DYER C.C. (1998). *Standards of Living in the Later Middle Ages: Social Change in England c. 1200–1520* (2nd edn.) Cambridge: Cambridge University Press.

—— (2003). *Making a Living in the Middle Ages: The People of Britain 850–1520*. London: Penguin Books.

EDFORS-LILJA I., ELLEGREN H., WINTERO A.K., RUOHONEN-LEHTO M., FREDHOLM M., GUSTAFSSON U. *et al.* (1993). A large linkage group on pig chromosome 7 including the MHC class I, class II (*DQB*), and class III (*TNFB*) genes. *Immunogenetics* 38, 363–66.

—— GUSTAFSSON U., DUVAL-IFLAH Y., ELLERGREN H., JOHANSSON M., JUNEJA R.K. *et al.* (1995). The porcine intestinal receptor for *Escherichia coli* K88ab, K88ac: regional localization on chromosome 13 and influence of IgG response to the K88 antigen. *Animal Genetics* 26, 237–42.

—— WATTRANG E., MARKLUND L., MOLLER M., ANDERSSON-EKLUND L., ANDERSSON L. & FOSSUM C. (1998). Mapping quantitative trait loci for immune capacity in the pig. *Journal of Immunology* 161, 829–35.

EKMAN J. (1974). Djurbensmaterialet från stenålderslokalen Ire, Hangvar sn, Gotland. In: Janzon G. (ed.), *Gotlands Mellanneolitiska Gravar* (Acta Universitatis Stockholmiensis, Studies in North-European Archaeology 6), 212–46. Stockholm: Almqvist & Wiksell.

—— (1977). Animal bones from a Late Bronze Age settlement at Hala Sultan Tekke, Cyprus. In: Äström P. *et al.* (eds), *Hala Sultan Tekke 3* (Studies of Mediterranean Archaeology XLV (3)), 166–76. Göteborg: Paul Amstroms Förlag.

EMRE K & ÇINAROGLU A. (1993). A group of metal Hittite vessels from Kinik-Kastomonu. In: Mellink M.J., Porada E., Özgüç T. (eds), *Aspects of Art and Iconography: Anatolia and its Neighbors*, 675–713. Ankara: Türk Tarih Kurumu Basimevi.

ENDO H. (1971). *The Origin of the Domestic Animals of Africa. Volume II*. New York: Africana.

—— (1977). *Domestic Animals of Nepal*. New York: Holmes & Meier.

Endo H. & Bichard M. (1984). Pigs. In: Mason I.L. (ed), *Evolution of Domesticated Animals*, 145–62. London: Longman.

——Hayashi Y., Sasaki M., Kurosawa Y., Tanaka K.& Yamazaki K. (2000). Geographical variation of mandible size and shape in the Japanese wild pig (*Sus scrofa leucomystax*). *Journal of Veterinary Medical Science* 62(8), 815–20.

Endo H., Kurohmmaru M. & Hayashi Y. (1994). An osteometrical study of the cranium and mandible of Ryukyu wild pig in Iriomote Island. *Journal of Veterinary Medical Science* 56(5), 855–60.

—— Kurohmaru M., Hayashi Y., Ohsako S., Matsumoto M., Nishinakagawa H. *et al.* (1998*b*). Multivariate analysis of mandible in the Ryukyu wild pig (*Sus scrofa riukiuanus*). *Journal of Veterinary Medical Science* 60(6), 731–3.

——Maeda S., Yamagiwa D., Kurohmaru M., Hayashi Y., Hattori S. *et al.* (1998*a*). Geographical variation of mandible size and shape in the Ryukyu wild pig (*Sus scrofa riukiuanus*). *Journal of Veterinary Medical Science* 60(1), 57–61.

—— —— Yamazaki K., Motokawa M., Pei J.-C.K., Lin L.-K. *et al.* (2002). Geographical variation of mandible size and shape in the wild pig (*Sus scrofa*) from Taiwan and Japan. *Zoological Studies* 41(4), 452–60.

Eriksson G. (2004). Part-time farmers or hard-core sealers? Västerbjers studied by means of stable isotope analysis. *Journal of Anthropological Archaeology* 23, 135–62.

Ervynck A. (1992). Medieval castles as top-predators of the feudal system: an archaeozoological approach. *Château Gaillard. Etudes de Castellologie médiévale* XV, 151–9.

—— (1997). Detailed recording of tooth wear (Grant, 1982) as an evaluation of the seasonal slaughtering of pigs? Examples from Medieval sites in Belgium. *Archaeofauna* 6, 67–79.

—— (2004). *Orant, pugnant, laborant.* The diet of the three orders in the feudal society of medieval north-western Europe. In: O' Day S.J., Van Neer W. & Ervynck A. (eds), *Behaviour Behind Bones. The Zooarchaeology of Ritual, Religion, Status and Identity*, 215–23. Oxford: Oxbow Books.

—— (2005). Detecting seasonal slaughtering of domestic mammals: inferences from the detailed recording of tooth eruption and wear. *Environmental Archaeology* 10(2), 153–69.

—— & De Meulemeester J. (1996). La viande dans l'alimentation seigneuriale et la variété des terroirs: l'exemple des Pays-Bas méridionaux. In: Colardelle M. (ed.), *L'homme et la nature au Moyen Age. Paléoenvironnement et sociétés occidentales*, 36–41. Paris: Editions Errance.

—— & Dobney K. (1999). Lining up on the M$_1$: a tooth defect as a bio-indicator for environment and husbandry in ancient pigs. *Environmental Archaeology* 4, 1–8.

—— —— Hongo H. & Meadow R. (2001). Born free? New evidence for the status of *Sus scrofa* at Neolithic Çayönü Tepesi (Southeastern Anatolia, Turkey). *Paléorient* 27(2), 47–73.

—— & —— (2002). A pig for all seasons? Approaches to the assessment of second farrowing in archaeological pig populations. *Archaeofauna* 11, 7–22.

——Van Neer W. & Van der Plaetsen P. (1994). Dierlijke resten. In: Ervynck A. (ed.), *'De Burcht' te Londerzeel. Bewoningsgeschiedenis van een motte en een bakstenen kasteel* (Archeologie in Vlaanderen Monografie I), 99–170. Zellik: Instituut voor het Archeologisch Patrimonium.

―――― & Lᴇɴᴛᴀᴄᴋᴇʀ A. (1999). Introduction and extinction of wild animal species in historical times: the evidence from Belgium. In: Benecke N. (ed.), *The Holocene History of the European Vertebrate fauna. Modern Aspects of Research* (Archäologie in Eurasien 6), 399–407. Berlin: Deutsches Archäologisches Institut, Eurasien-abteilung.

―― Vᴀɴ Sᴛʀʏᴅᴏɴᴄᴋ M. & Bᴏᴜᴅɪɴ M. (2003). Dieetreconstructie en herkomstbepaling op basis van de analyse van de stabiele isotopen ^{13}C en ^{15}N uit dierlijk en menselijk skeletmateriaal: een eerste verkennend onderzoek op middeleeuwse vondsten uit Vlaanderen. *Archeologie in Vlaanderen* VII, 131–40.

―― & Wᴏᴏʟʟᴇᴛᴛ J. (2006). Top-predator or survivor? The castle of Sugny (Belgium), as seen through its animal remains. In: De Meulemeester J. (ed.), *Mélanges d'archéologie médiévale. Liber amicorum en hommage à André Matthys*, 78–89. Namur: Ministère de la Région Wallonne, Marolaga.

Eꜱꜱᴇ D.L. (1991). *Subsistence, Trade and Social Change in Early Bronze Age Palestine* (Studies in Oriental History 50). Chicago: Oriental Institute, University of Chicago.

Eᴜꜱᴇʙɪᴏ J.A. (1980). *Pig Production in the Tropics* (Intermediate Tropical Agriculture Series). Harlow: Longman.

Eᴠᴀɴꜱ E.P. (1896). *Animal Symbolism in Ecclesiastical Architecture*. London: William Heinemann.

Eᴠʀᴀʀᴅ M. (1993). L'archéologie du haut moyen âge en Calestienne. *De la Meuse à l'Ardenne* 16, 229–45.

―― (1997). Wellin. La nécropole mérovingienne et l'habitat carolingien. In: Corbiau M.-H. (ed.), *Le patrimoine archéologique de Wallonie*, 433–6. Namur: Division du Patrimoine.

Fᴀʙʀᴇ-Vᴀꜱꜱᴀꜱ C. (1994). *La bête singulière. Les juifs, les chrétiens et le cochon*. Paris: Gallimard.

―― (1997). *The Singular Beast. Jews, Christians, & the Pig*. New York: Columbia University Press.

Fᴀʟᴠᴇʏ L. (1981). Research on native pigs in Thailand. *World Animal Review* 38, 16–22.

Fᴇᴀᴄʜᴀᴍ R.G.A. (1973). The Raiapu Enga pig herd. *Mankind* 9(1), 25–31.

―― (1975). Pigs, people and pollution: interactions between men and environment in the Highlands of New Guinea. *South Pacific Bulletin* 25(3), 41–5.

Fᴇɪʟ D.K. (1976). People, pigs and punishment. *Australian Natural History* 18(12), 444–7.

Fᴇᴊᴇʀꜱᴋᴏᴠ O. & Tʜʏʟꜱᴛʀᴜᴘ A. (1986). Dental enamel. In: Mjör I.A. & Fejerskov O. (eds), *Human Oral Embryology and Histology*, 50–89. Copenhagen: Munksgaard.

―― Mᴀɴᴊɪ F., Bᴀᴇʟᴜᴍ V. & Møʟʟᴇʀ I.J. (1988). *Dental Fluorosis—A Handbook for Health Workers*. Copenhagen: Munksgaard.

Fᴇɴɢʜᴀᴏ Aʀᴄʜᴀᴇᴏʟᴏɢʏ Tᴇᴀᴍ. (2000). The Institute of Archaeology, Chinese Academy of Social Sciences Excavation at Fengxi in 1997. *Kaogu Xuebao* 2, 199–256.

Fɪᴇʟᴅ J., Bʀᴏᴡɴ O. & Lᴇᴛɴɪᴄ M. (2002). Seasonal and other variation in the effects of scavengers on experimental faunal assemblages. In: Albarella U., Dobney K., Huntley J. & Rowley-Conwy P. (eds), *Abstracts of the ICAZ Durham Conference, University of Durham*, 50. Durham: ICAZ.

Fɪɴᴋᴇʟᴍᴀɴ R.B., Bᴇʟᴋɪɴ H.E., Zʜᴇɴɢ B. (1999). Health impacts of domestic coal use in China. *Proceedings of the National Academy of Sciences of the USA* 96, 3427–31.

FINNEGAN M. (1979). Faunal remains from Bab edh-Dhra and Numeira. In: Rast W.E. & Schaub R.T. (eds), The southeastern Dead Sea plain expedition: an interim report of the 1977 season. *Annual of the American Schools of Oriental Research* 46, 177–80.

FISCHER A. (1997*a*). *Marinearkæologiske forundersøgelser forud for etablering af en fast Øresundsforbindelse.* Copenhagen: Miljø- og Energiministeriet, Skov- og Naturstyrelsen.

—— (1997*b*). People and the sea—settlement and fishing along the mesolithic coasts. In: Pedersen L., Fischer A. & Aaby B. (eds), *The Danish Storebælt since the Ice Age*, 63–77. Copenhagen: A/S Storebælt Fixed Link.

—— & MALM T. (1997). The settlement in the submerged forest in Musholm Bay. In: Pedersen L., Fischer A. & Aaby B. (eds), *The Danish Storebælt since the Ice Age*, 78–86. Copenhagen: A/S Storebælt Fixed Link.

FISCHER P.M. (1997). Tall Abu al-Kraraz: occupation throughout the ages. The faunal and botanical evidence. In: Zaghoul M. *et al.* (eds), *Studies in the History and Archaeology of Jordan*, 159–65. Amman: Department of Antiquities.

FITZGERALD C.M. & SAUNDERS S.R. (2005). Test of histological methods of determining chronology of accentuated striae of deciduous teeth. *American Journal of Physical Anthropology* 127, 277–90.

FLANNERY K.V. (1983). Early pig domestication in the fertile crescent: a retrospective look. In: Young T.C., Smith P.E.L. & Mortensen P. (eds), *The Hilly Flanks. Essays on the Prehistory of Southwestern Asia* (Studies in Ancient Oriental Civilization 36), 163–88. Chicago: Oriental Institute, University of Chicago.

—— & CORNWALL I.W. (1969). The fauna from Ras al Amiya, Iraq: a comparison with the Deh Luran Plain sequence. In: Hole F., Flannery K.V. & Neely J.A. (eds), *Prehistory and Human Ecology of the Deh Luran Plain* (Memoirs of the Museum of Anthropology, University of Michigan 1), 435–8. Ann Arbor, MI: Ann Arbor: Museum of Anthropology, University of Michigan.

—— & WRIGHT H.T. (1966). Faunal remains from the 'hut sounding' at Eridu, Iraq. *Sumer* 22, 61–3.

FLANNERY T.F. (1990). *Mammals of New Guinea.* Carina, Queensland: Robert Brown & Associates.

FONTANA D. (1993). *The Secret Language of Symbols. A Visual Key to Symbols and their Meaning.* London: Pavilion Books.

FORSYTH MAJOR C.J. (1883). Studien zur Geschichte des Wildschweine (gen. *Sus*). *Zoologischer Anzeiger* 6, 295–300.

FOSTER J. (1977). A boar figurine from Guilden Morden, Cambridgeshire. *Medieval Archaeology* 21, 166–7.

FOURNIER D. (2003). Quel recupero meticoloso. *Slow* 39, 6–13.

FRÄDRICH H. (1971). A comparison of behaviour in the Suidae. In: Geist V. & Walther F. (eds), *The Behaviour of Ungulates and its Relation to Management*, 133–43. Morges, Switzerland: International Union for Conservation of Nature and Natural Resources.

FRANGIPANE M. & SIRACUSANO G. (1998). Changes in subsistence strategies in East Anatolia during the 4th and 3rd millennium BC. In: Anreiter P. *et al.* (eds), *Man and* the Animal World: Studies in Archaeozoology, Archaeology, Anthropology and Palaeo-linguistics, in Memoriam Sándor Bökönyi*, 237–46. Budapest: Archaeolingua Kiadó.

FRIEDMAN J. (1974). Marxism, structuralism and vulgar materialism. *Man* 9, 444–69.

—— (1979). Hegelian ecology: between Rousseau and the world spirit. In: Burnham P. & Ellen R.F. (eds), *Social and Ecological Systems*, 253–70. London: Academic Press.

GANJI M.H. (1968). Climate. In: Fisher W.B. (ed.), *Cambridge History of Iran I. The Land of Iran*, 212–49. Cambridge: Cambridge University Press.

GARROTT R.A., EBERHARDT L.L., OTTON J.K., WHITE P.J. & CHAFFEE M.A. (2002). A geochemical trophic cascade in Yellowstone's geothermal environments. *Ecosystems* 5, 659–66.

GAUTIER A. (1977). Sondage dans le Tell d'Apamée (1974). Etude des restes osseux animaux. *Bulletin de la Societé Royale Belge Anthropologie et Préhistoire* 88, 77–93.

GENOV P.V. (1999). A review of the cranial characteristics of the wild boar (*Sus scrofa* Linnaeus 1758), with systematic conclusions. *Mammal Review* 29(4), 205–38.

—— MASSEI G., BARBALOVA Z. & KOSTOVA V. (1991a). Aging wild boar (*Sus scrofa* L.) by teeth. In: Spitz F., Janeau G., Gonzalez G. & Aulagnier S. (eds), *Ongulés/Ungulates 91. Proceedings of the International Symposium Ongulés/Ungulates 91*, 399–402. Paris: Société Française pour l'Etude et la Protection des Mammifères & Institut de Recherche sur les Grands Mammifères.

—— NIKOLOV H., MASSEI G. & GERASIMOV S. (1991b). Craniometrical analysis of Bulgarian wild boar (*Sus scrofa*) populations. *Journal of Zoology* 225, 309–25.

GEORGE W. & YAPP B. (1991). *The Naming of the Beasts: Natural History in the Medieval Bestiary*. London: Duckworth.

GERAADS D. & TCHERNOV E. (1983). Femurs humains du Pleistocene moyen de Gesher Benot Ya'acov (Israel). *L'Anthropologie* 87,138–41.

GETZOV N. (1999). Hagoshrim. *Hadashot Arkheologiyot: Excavations and Surveys in Israel* 110, 2–3.

GHIRSHMAN R. (1966). *Tchoga Zanbil (Dur Untash), vol. I, La ziggurat, Mission de Susiane* (Mémoires de la Délégation Archéologique en Iran. Mission de Susiane). Paris: P. Geuthner.

GIFFORD-GONZALEZ D. (1989). Ethnographic analogues for interpreting modified bones: some cases from East Africa. In: Bonnichsen R. & Sorg M.H. (eds), *Bone modification*, 179–246., College Station, TX: Texas A&M University Press.

GILES J.R. (1980). *The ecology of feral pigs in western New South Wales*. Ph.D. thesis, University of Sydney.

GIUFFRA E., EVANS G., TÖRNSTEN A., WALES R., DAY A., LOOFT H. *et al.* (1999). The Belt mutation in pigs is an allele at the Dominant white (*I/KIT*) locus. *Mammalian Genome* 10, 1132–6.

—— KIJAS J.M.H., AMARGER V., CARLBORG O., JEON J.T. & ANDERSSON L. (2000). The origin of the domestic pig: independent domestication and subsequent introgression. *Genetics* 154(4), 1785–91.

—— TÖRSTEN A., MARKLUND S., BONGCAM-RUDLOFF E., CHARDON P. *et al.* (2002). A large duplication associated with Dominant White color in pigs originated by homologous recombination between LINE elements flanking KIT. *Mammalian Genome* 13, 569–77.

GOLDBERG P. & ROSEN A. (1987). Early Holocene paleoenvironments of Israel. In: Levy T.E. (ed.), *Shiqmim I* (BAR International Series 356), 23–33. Oxford: British Archaeological Reports.

GOLDBERG P.J.P. (1999). Pigs and prostitutes: streetwalking in comparative perspective. In: Lewis, K.J., Menuge N.J. & Phillips K.M. (eds), *Young Medieval Women*, 172–93. Stroud: Sutton Publishing.

GONGORA J., PELTONIEMI O.A.T., TAMMEN I., RAADSMA H. & MORAN C. (2003). Analyses of possible domestic pig contribution in two populations of Finnish farmed wild boar. *Acta Agriculturae Scandinavica Section A . Animal Science* 53, 161–5.

GOODMAN A.H. & ROSE J.C. (1990). Assessment of systemic physiological perturbations from dental enamel hypoplasias and associated histological structures. *Yearbook of Physical Anthropology* 33, 59–110.

——BROOKE-THOMAS R., SWEDLAND A.C. & ARMELAGOS G.J. (1988). Biocultural perspectives on stress in prehistoric, historical and contemporary population research. *Yearbook of Physical Anthropology* 31, 169–202.

GOULD R.A. (1980). *Living Archaeology*. Cambridge: Cambridge University Press.

GRANT A. (1978). Variation in dental attrition in mammals and its relevance to age estimation. In: Brothwell D.R., Thomas,K.D. & Clutton-Brock J. (eds), *Research Problems in Zooarchaeology*, 103–6. London: Institute of Archaeology.

——(1982). The use of tooth wear as a guide to the age of domestic ungulates. In: Wilson B., Grigson C. & Payne S. (eds), *Ageing and Sexing Animal Bones from Archaeological Sites* (BAR British Series 109), 91–108. Oxford: British Archaeological Reports.

——(1991). Ethnoarchaeological studies: animals. In: Barker G. & Grant A., Ancient and modern pastoralism in central Italy: an interdisciplinary study in the Cicolano Mountains. *Papers of the British School at Rome* LIX, 72–8.

GRAZIOSI P. (1962). *Levanzo. Pitture e incisioni*. Firenze: Sansoni Editore.

GREENFIELD H.J. (2002). Preliminary report on the faunal remains from the Early Bronze Age site of Titris Höyük. In: Buitenhuis H., Choyke A.M., Mashkour M. & Al-Shiyab A.H. (eds), *Archaeozoology of the Near East V* (ARC-Publicaties 32), 251–60. Groningen: Centre for Archaeological Research & Consultancy.

GRIFFIN P.B. (1998). An ethnographic view of the pig in selected traditional Southeast Asian societies. *MASCA Research Papers in Science and Archaeology* 15, 27–37.

GRIGSON C. (1982). Porridge and pannage: pig husbandry in Neolithic England. In: Limbrey S. & Bell M. (eds), *Archaeological Aspects of Woodland Ecology* (BAR International Series 146), 297–314. Oxford: British Archaeological Reports.

——(1984a). Preliminary report on the mammal bones from Neolithic Qatif, site Y3, on the Sinai coastal plain (excavations of 1979, 1980 and 1983). Unpublished report.

——(1984b). Preliminary report on the mammal bones from Chalcolithic Qatif, site Y2 (including Ya), on the Sinai coastal plain (excavations of 1979, 1980 and 1983). Unpublished report.

—— (1987). Shiqmim: pastoralism and other aspects of animal management in the Chalcolithic of the Northern Negev. In: Levy T.E. (ed.), *Shiqmim I* (BAR International Series 356), 219–41 & 535–46. Oxford: British Archaeological Reports.

—— (1989). Size and sex—morphometric evidence for the domestication of cattle in the Near East. In: Milles A., Williams D. & Gardner N. (eds), *The Beginnings of Agriculture* (BAR International Series 496), 77–109. Oxford: British Archaeological Reports.

—— (1993). The mammalian remains from the Chalcolithic site of Horvat Beter; excavations of 1982. *'Atiqot* 12, 28–31.

—— (1995*a*). Cattle keepers of the northern Negev: animal remains from the Chalcolithic site of Grar. In: Gilead I. (ed.), *Grar, a Chalcolithic Site in the Northern Negev*, 377–452. Beersheva: Ben-Gurion University of the Negev Press.

—— (1995*b*). Plough and pasture in the early economy of the Southern Levant. In: Levy T.E. (ed.), *The Archaeology of Society in the Holy Land*, 245–68 & 573–6. Leicester: Leicester University Press.

—— (1997). Mammalian remains. In: Levy T.E., Alon D., Smith P., Yekutieli Y., Rowan Y., Goldberg P. *et al.* (eds), Egyptian-Canaanite Interaction at Nahal Tillah, Israel (ca. 4500–3000 BCE): an interim report on the 1994–1995 excavations. *Bulletin of the American Schools of Oriental Research* 307, 24–5.

—— (2003). Animal husbandry in the Late Neolithic and Chalcolithic at Arjoune: the secondary products revolution revisited. In: Parr P.J. (ed.), *Excavations at Arjoune, Syria* (BAR International Series 1134), 187–240. Oxford: Archaeopress.

—— (2006). Farming? Feasting? Herding? Large mammals from the Chalcolithic of Gilat. In: Alon D. & Levy T.E. (eds), *Archaeology, Anthropology and Cult: The Sanctuary at Gilat, Israel*. London: Equinox.

—— (in press). The animal bones from Shiqmim. In: Levy T.E., Rowan Y.M. & Burton M.M. (eds), *Desert Chiefdom: Dimensions of Subterranean Settlement and Society in Israel's Negev Desert (c.4500–3600 BC) Based on New Data from Shiqmim*. London: Equinox.

GRØN O. (1987). Seasonal variation in Maglemosian group size and structure: a new model. *Current Anthropology* 28, 303–27.

—— (1995). *The Maglemose Culture* (BAR International Series 616). Oxford: Tempus Reparatum.

GRÖSSINGER C. (1997). *The World Upside Down*. London: Harvey Miller.

—— (2002). *Humour and Folly in Secular and Profane Prints of Northern Europe, 1430–1540*. London: Harvey Miller.

GROVES C. (1981). *Ancestors for the Pigs: Taxonomy and Phylogeny of the Genus Sus* (Technical Bulletin 3). Canberra: Australian National University, Department of Prehistory, Research School of Pacific Studies.

—— (1983). Pigs east of the Wallace Line. *Journal de la Société des Océanistes* 77(34), 105–19.

—— (1989). Feral mammals of the Mediterranean islands: documents of early domestication. In: Clutton-Brock J. (ed.), *The Walking Larder. Patterns of Domestication, Pastoralism, and Predation*, 46–58. London: Unwin Hyman.

GROVES C. (1997). Taxonomy of wild pigs (*Sus*) of the Philippines. *Zoological Journal of the Linnean Society* 120, 163–91.

——— (2001). Taxonomy of wild pigs of Southeast Asia. *Asian Wild Pig News* 1(1), 3–4.

GRUBB P. (1993*a*). Order Artiodactyla. In: Wilson D.E. & Reeder D.M. (eds), *Mammal Species of the World: a Taxonomic and Geographic Reference*, 377–414. Washington, DC: Smithsonian Institution Press.

——— (1993*b*). The Afrotropical Suids *Phacochoerus, Hylochoerus* and *Potamochoerus*: taxonomy and distribution. In: Oliver W.L.R. (ed.), *Pigs, Peccaries, and Hippos: Status Survey and Conservation Action Plan*, 66–75. Gland: International Union for the Conservation of Nature and Natural Resources. Species Survival Commission.

——— & GROVES C.P. (1993). The Neotropical Tayassuids: taxonomy and description. In: Oliver W.L.R. (ed.), *Pigs, Peccaries, and Hippos: Status Survey and Conservation Action Plan*, 5–7. Gland: International Union for the Conservation of Nature and Natural Resources. Species Survival Commission.

GUILAINE J., BRIOIS F., COULAROU J., VIGNE J.-D. & CARRÈRE I. (1996). Shillourokambos et les debuts du Neolithique à Chypre. *Espacio, Tiempo y Forma, Serie I, Prehistoria y Arquelogia* 9, 159–71.

——— ——— VIGNE J.-D. & CARRÈRE I. (2000). Découverte d'un Néolithique précéramique ancien chypriote (fin 9°, début 8° millénaires cal. BC), apparenté au PPNB ancien/moyen du Levant nord. *Comptes Rendus de l'Académie des Sciences, Paris. Sciences de la Terre et des Planets* 330, 75–82.

GUNNTHORSDOTTIR A. (2001). Physical attractiveness of an animal species as a decision factor for its preservation. *Anthrozoos* 14, 204–15.

HAAK W., FORSTER P., BRAMANTI B., MATSUMURA S., BRANDT G., TANZER M. *et al.* (2005). Ancient DNA from the first European farmers in 7500-year-old Neolithic sites. *Science* 310(5750), 964–5.

HAAS W. (1994). *Geschichte der Hethitischen Religion*. Leiden: E.J.Brill.

HABER A. (1961). Le sanglier en Pologne. In: Bourlière F. (ed.), *Ecology and Management of Wild Grazing Animals in Temperate Zones*, 74–6. Morges: International Union for Conservation of Nature and Natural Resources.

HABER A. & DAYAN T. (2004). Analyzing the process of domestication: Hagoshrim as a case study. *Journal of Archaeological Science* 31, 1587–601.

HABERMEHL K.-H. (1961). *Die Alterbestimmung bei Haustieren, Pelztieren und beim Jagdbaren Wild*. Berlin: Paul Parey.

——— (1975). *Die Altersbestimmung bei Haus- und Labortieren*. Berlin: Paul Parey.

HABU J. (2001). *Subsistence-Settlement Systems and Intersite Variability in the Moroiso Phase of the Early Jomon Period of Japan* (Archaeological Series 14). Ann Arbor, MI: International Monographs in Prehistory.

HALLGREN F., DJERW U., GEIERSTAM M. & STEINEKE M. (1997). Skogsmossen, an early neolithic settlement site and sacrificial fen in the northern borderland of the Funnel-beaker culture. *Tor* 29, 49–111.

HAMILAKIS Y. (2003). The sacred geography of hunting: wild animals, social power and gender in early farming societies. In: Kotjabopoulou E., Hamilakis Y., Halstead

P., Gamble G. & Elefanti P. (eds), *Zooarchaeology in Greece. Recent Advances* (British School of Athens Studies 9), 239–47. London: The British School at Athens.

—— & Konsolaki E. (2004). Pigs for the Gods: burnt animals sacrifices as embodied rituals at Mycenean sanctuary. *Oxford Journal of Archaeology* 23(2), 135–51.

Handoo J. (1990). Cultural attitudes to birds and animals in folklore. In: Willis R. (ed.), *Signifying Animals: Human Meaning in the Natural World*, 37–42. London: Routledge.

Hanotte O., Tawah C.L., Bradley D.G., Okomo M., Verjee Y., Ochieng J. & Rege J.E.O. (2000). Geographic distribution and frequency of a taurine *Bos taurus* and an indicine *Bos indicus* Y specific allele amongst sub-Saharan African cattle breeds. *Molecular Ecology* 9(4), 387–96.

Harlan J.R. (1982). The garden of the Lord: a plausible reconstruction of natural resources of southern Jordan in Early Bronze Age. *Paléorient* 8(1), 71–8.

Harrington F.A. (1977). *A Guide to the Mammals of Iran*. Tehran: Department of the Environment.

Harris M. (1974). *Cows, Pigs, Wars and Witches*. New York: Random House.

Harrison D.L. (1968). *The Mammals of Arabia. Volume II. Carnivora, Artiodactyla, Hyracoidea*. London: Ernest Benn.

—— & Bates P.J.J. (1991). *The Mammals of Arabia* (2nd edn.). London: Harrison Zoological Museum.

Hart H.C. (1891). *Some Account of the Flora and Fauna of Sinai, Petra and Wadv 'Arabah*. London: Palestine Exploration Fund.

Hartman G. (1992). Age determination of live beaver by dental X-ray. *Wildlife Society Bulletin* 20, 216–20.

Harvey B. (1993). *Living and Dying in England 1100–1540: The Monastic Experience*. Oxford: Clarendon Press.

Harvey P.D.A. (1984). *The Peasant Land Market in Medieval England*. Oxford: Clarendon Press.

Harvey S. (1988). Domesday England. In: Hallam H.E. (ed.), *The Agrarian History of England and Wales: Volume II 1042–1350*, 45–138. Cambridge: Cambridge University Press.

Hassanin A. & Douzery E.J.P. (2003). Molecular and morphological phylogenies of Ruminantia and the alternative position of the Moschidae. *Systematic Biology* 52, 206–28.

Hassig D. (1999). Sex in the bestiaries. In: Hassig D. (ed.), *The Mark of the Beast*. New York: Routledge.

Hatt H.T. (1959). *The Mammals of Iraq* (Miscellaneous Publication of the Museum of Zoology, University of Michigan 106). Ann Arbor, MI: University of Michigan.

Healy W.B. & Ludwig T.G. (1965). Wear of sheep's teeth. I. The role of ingested soil. *New Zealand Journal of Agricultural Research* 8, 737–52.

Heaton T.H.E. (1999). Spatial, species, and temporal variations in the $\delta^{13}C/\delta^{12}C$ ratios of C_3 plants: implications for palaeodiet studies. *Journal of Archaeological Science* 26, 637–49.

Heck W. & Westendorf W. (1984). Schwein. In: *Lexikon der Ägyptologie*, 762–4. Wiesbaden: Harrassowitz.

HEIDER K.G. (1970). *The Dugum Dani. A Papuan Culture in the Highlands of West New Guinea.* Chicago: Aldine.

HEIM S.M. (1983). *Echelles vers le ciel. Notre héritage judéo-chrétien, 5000 av. J.-C.—500 ap. J.-C.* Toronto: Hunter Rose.

HEISE-PAVLOV P.M. & HEISE-PAVLOV S.R. (2003). Feral pigs in tropical lowland rainforest of northeastern Australia: ecology, zoonoses and management. *Wildlife Biology* 9(1), 21–7.

HELGEN K.M. (2003). Major mammalian clades: a review under consideration of molecular and palaeontological evidence. *Mammalian Biology* 68, 1–15.

HELLWING S. (1988–89). Animal bones from Tel Tsaf. *Tel Aviv* 15–16, 47–51.

—— & GOPHNA R. (1984). The animal remains from the Early and Middle Bronze Ages at Tel Aphek and Tel Dalit: a comparative study. *Tel Aviv* 11, 48–59.

HELMER D. (1987). *Fiches descriptives pour les relevés d'ensembles osseux animaux* (Fiches d'ostéologie animales pour l'archéologie, série B, mammifères, 1). Juan-les-Pins: Éditions APDCA.

——(1992). *La domestication des animaux par les hommes préhistoriques.* Paris: Masson.

—— & VILA E. (1997). Les mammifères terrestres. In: *Malia et la Crète de l'Âge du Bronze, Grèce, aux origines du monde égée. Dossiers d'Archéologie* 222, 72–3.

HENAN PROVINCIAL INSTITUTE OF CULTURAL RELICS AND ARCHAEOLOGY (ed.) (1999). *Wuyang Jiahu.* Beijing: Science Press.

HENDERSON A.C. (1982). Medieval beasts and modern cages: the making of meaning in fables and bestiaries. *Publications of the Modern Language Association of America* 97, 40–9.

HENRIKSEN B.B. (1976). *Sværdborg I, Excavations 1943–44.* Copenhagen: Akademisk Forlag.

—— (1980). *Lundby-Holmen. Pladser af Maglemose-Type i Sydsjælland (with English summary)* (Nordiske Fortidsminder B6). Copenhagen: Det Kongelige Nordiske Oldskriftselskab.

HEPTNER V.G., NASIMOVICH A.A. & BANNIKOV A.G. (1989). *Mammals of the Soviet Union. Volume I. Ungulates.* Leiden, New York: E.J. Brill.

HERRERO J. & FERNÁNDEZ DE LUCO D. (2003). Wild boars (*Sus scrofa* L.) in Uruguay: scavengers or predators? *Mammalia* 67(4), 485–92.

HERRING S.W. (1972). The role of canine morphology in the evolutionary divergence of pigs and peccaries. *Journal of Mammalogy* 53, 500–12.

HESSE B. (1986). Animal use at Tel Mikne-Ekron in the Bronze Age and Iron Age. *Bulletin of the American School of Oriental Research* 264, 17–27.

——(1990). Pig lovers and pig haters: patterns of Palestinian pork production. *Journal of Ethnobiology* 10(2), 195–225.

——(2002). Between the revolutions: animal use at Sha'ar Hagolan during the Yarmukian. In: Garfinkel Y. & Miller M.A. (eds), *Sha'ar Hagolan 1: Neolithic Art in Context,* 247–56. Oxford: Oxbow Books.

HIDE R.L. (1981). *Aspects of pig production and use in colonial Sinasina, Papua New Guinea.* Ph.D. thesis, Columbia University.

—— (2003). *Pig husbandry in New Guinea: a Literature Review and Bibliography.* Canberra: Australian Centre for International Agricultural Research.

HIGGINS M. & HIGGINS R. (1996). *A Geological Companion to Greece and the Aegean.* London: Duckworth.

HIGGINS R. (1967). *Minoan and Mycenaean Art.* London: Thames & Hudson.

HIGGS E.S. & JARMAN M.R. (1969). The origins of agriculture: a reconsideration. *Antiquity* 43, 31–41.

HIGHAM C.F.W. (1967*a*). Stock rearing as a cultural factor in prehistoric Europe. *Proceedings of the Prehistoric Society* 33, 84–106.

—— (1967*b*). The economy of Iron Age Veileby (Denmark). *Acta Archaeologica* 38, 222–41.

HILLSON S. (1986). *Teeth.* Cambridge: Cambridge University Press.

—— (1996). *Dental Anthropology.* Cambridge: Cambridge University Press.

HILZHEIMER L. (1941). *Animal Remains from Tell Asmar* (Studies in Ancient Oriental Civilization 20). Chicago: Oriental Institute, University of Chicago.

HO S.Y.W. & LARSON G. (2006). Molecular clocks: 'When times are a-changin'. *Trends in Genetics* 22, 79–83.

HODDER I. (1982). *The Present Past. An Introduction to Anthropology for Archaeologists.* London: Batsford.

HOLDEN P. (1992). *Wild Pig in Australia.* Kienthurst, Australia: Kangaroo Press.

HOLE F. (1999). Economic implications of possible storage structures at Tell Ziyadeh, NE Syria. *Journal of Field Archaeology* 26, 267–83.

——FLANNERY K.V. & NEELY J.A. (1969). *Prehistory and Human Ecology of the Deh Luran Plain* (Memoirs of the Museum of Anthropology, University of Michigan 1). Ann Arbor. MI: University of Michigan.

HONE J. & O'GRADY J. (1980). *Feral Pigs and their Control.* Sydney: New South Wales Department of Agriculture.

HONGO H. (1998). Patterns of animal husbandry in central anatolian in the second and first millenia BC: Faunal remans from Kaman-Kalehöyük, Turkey. In: Buitenhuis H., Bartosiewicz L. & Choyke A.M. (eds), *Archaeozoology of the Near East III* (ARC-Publication 18), 255–75. Groningen: Centre for Archaeological Research & Consultancy.

—— ISHIGURO N., WATANOBE T., SHIGEHARA N., ANEZAKI T., LONG V.T. *et al.* (2002). Variation in mitochondrial DNA of Vietnamese pigs: relationships with Asian domestic pigs and Ryukyu wild boars. *Zoological Science* 19, 1329–35).

——& MEADOW R.H. (1998). Pig exploitation at Neolithic Çayönü Tepesi (Southeastern Anatolia). *MASCA Research Papers in Science and Archaeology* 15, 77–98.

—— & —— (2000). Faunal remains from Prepottery Neolithic levels at Çayönü, southeastern Turkey: a preliminary report focusing on pigs (*Sus* sp.). In: Mashkour M., Choyke A.M., Buitenhuis H. & Poplin F. (eds), *Archaeozoology of the Near East IV* (ARC-Publicaties 32), 121–40. Groningen: Centre for Archaeological Research & Consultancy.

HOOGERWERF A. (1970). *Udjong Kulon. The Land of the Last Javan Rhinoceros.* Leiden: E.J. Brill.

HOOIJER D.A. (1959). Fossil mammals from Jisr Banat Yaqub, south of Lake Huleh, Israel. *Bulletin of the Research Council of Israel* 8G, 177–99.

HORWITZ L.K. (1985). The En Shadud faunal remains. In: Braun E. (ed.), *En Shadud. Salvage Excavations at a Farming Community in the Jezreel Valley. Israel* (BAR International Series 249), 168–77. Oxford: British Archaeological Reports.

HORWITZ L.K. (1987). Animal remains from the Pottery Neolithic levels at Tel Dan. *Mitekufat Haeven, Journal of the Israel Prehistoric Society* 20, 114–18.

—— (1988). Bone remains from Neve Yam, a pottery Neolithic site off the Carmel coast. *Mitekufat Haeven, Journal of the Israel Prehistoric Society* 21, 99–108.

—— (1989a). Diachronic changes in rural husbandry practices in Bronze Age settlements from the Refaim Valley, Israel. *Palestine Exploration Journal* 121, 44–54.

—— (1989b). Sedentism in the Early Bronze IV: a faunal perspective. *Bulletin of the American Schools of Oriental Research* 275, 15–25.

—— (1990). Animal bones from the site of Horvat Hor: a Chalcolithic cave-dwelling. *Mitekufat Haeven, Journal of the Israel Prehistoric Society* 23, 153–61.

—— (1996). The faunal remains from Me'ona. *'Atiqot* 28, 37–9.

—— (1997). Faunal remains. In: Braun E. (ed.), *Yiftah'el: Salvage and Rescue Excavations at a Prehistoric Village in Lower Galilee, Israel* (Israel Antiquities Authority Reports 2), 155–72. Jerusalem: Israel Antiquities Authority.

—— (1999). The fauna. In: Golani A. & Van den Brink E.C.M.(eds), Salvage excavations at the Early Bronze Age 1A settlement at Azor. *'Atiqot* 38, 33–9.

—— (2001). The mammalian fauna. In: Eisenberg E., Gopher A., Greenberg R. *et al.* (eds), *Tel Te'o: A Neolithic, Chalcolithic, and Early Bronze Age Site in the Hula Valley* (Israel Antiquities Authority Report 13), 171–94. Jerusalem: Israel Antiquities Authority.

—— (2002a). Fauna from five submerged pottery Neolithic sites off the Carmel Coast. *Mitekufat Haeven, Journal of the Israel Prehistoric Society* 32, 147–74.

—— (2002b). Mammals. In: Garfinkel Y. *et al.* (eds), Ziqim, a Pottery Neolithic site in the southern coastal plain of Israel: a final report. *Mitekufat Haeven, Journal of the Israel Prehistoric Society* 32, 122–7.

—— (2002c). Fauna from the Wadi Rabah site of Abu Zureiq. *Israel Exploration Journal* 52, 167–78.

—— (2007). Animal remains from the Late Chalcolithic–Early Bronze Age dwelling and burial caves at Shoham (North), Lod Valley. *'Antiqot* 55.

—— & DAVIDOWITZ G. (1992). Dental pathology of wild pigs (*Sus scrofa*) from Israel. *Israel Journal of Zoology* 38, 111–23.

—— HELLWING S. & TCHERNOV E. (1996). Patterns of animal exploitation at Early Bronze Age Tel Dalit. In: Gophna R. (ed.), *Excavations at Tel Dalit*, 193–216. Tel Aviv: Ramot.

—— & TCHERNOV E. (1989). Animal exploitation in the Early Bronze Age of the Southern Levant: an overview. In: de Miroschedji P. (ed.), *L'urbanisation de la Palestine a l'age du Bronze Ancien* (BAR International Series, 527 (ii)), 279–96. Oxford: British Archaeological Reports.

—— —— (1998). Diachronic and synchronic changes in patterns of animal exploitation during the Neolithic of the Southern Levant. In: Anreiter P. *et al.* (eds), *Man and the Animal World: Studies in Archaeozoology, Archaeology, Anthropology and Palaeolinguistics, in Memoriam Sándor Bökönyi*, 307–18. Budapest: Archaeolingua Kiadó.

————— Hongo H. (2004). The domestic status of the Early Neolithic fauna of Cyprus: a view from the mainland. In: Peltenburg E. & Wasse A. (eds), *Neolithic Revolution: New Perspectives on Southwest Asia in Light of Recent Discoveries on Cyprus* (Levant Supplementary Series 1), 35–48. Oxford: Oxbow Books.

————— Mienis H.K., Hakker-Orion D. & Bar-Yosef-Mayer D.E. (2002). The archaeozoology of three Early Bronze Age sites in Nahal Besor, north-western Negev. In: Van den Brink E.C.M & Yannai E. (eds), *In Quest of Ancient Settlements and Landscapes. A Volume in Honour of Ram Gophna*, 107–34. Tel Aviv: Ramot.

Hours F., Aurenche O., Cauvin J., Cauvin M.-C., Copeland L. & Sanlaville P. (1994). *Atlas des sites du Proche Orient (14000–5700 BP)*. Paris: Maison de l'Orient méditerranéen.

Hudson M.J. (1999). *Ruins of Identity: Ethnogenesis in the Japanese Islands*. Honolulu: University of Hawai'i Press.

Hughes I. (1970). Pigs, sago and limestone: the adaptive use of natural enclosures and planted sago in pig management. *Mankind* 7, 272–8.

Ijzereef G.F. (1977–78). Summary of paleontological results from Selenkahiye, Syria. *Annals Archéologiques Arabes Syriennes* 1977, 27–8.

Imamura K. (1996). *Prehistoric Japan: New Perspectives on Insular East Asia*. Honolulu: University of Hawai'i Press.

Inaba M. (1983). Sika deer and wild boar remains from Torihama Shell Midden. In: *Site Report of Torihama Shell Midden Excavation in 1981–1982*, 65–81. Board of Education, Fukui Prefecture, Wakasa Historical Museum [in Japanese].

—— (1987). The Golan—geographic aspects. *Ariel* 50–1, 11–15 [in Hebrew].

Ingold T. (1974). On reindeer and men. *Man*, 9, 523–38.

Institute of Archaeology, Chinese Academy of Social Sciences *et al.* (eds) (2001). *The Yuchisi Site in Mengcheng*. Beijing: Science Press.

—— (eds.) (2003). *Zengpiyan—a Prehistoric Site in Guilin* (Archaeological Monograph Series Type D 69). Beijing: The Cultural Relics Publishing House.

Inukai T. (1960). Wild boar in Hokkaido: an ethnological view. *Hoppo Bunka Kenkyu* 15, 1–6 [in Japanese].

Israel Nature Reserves Authority (1985–86). Agricultural damage at Neot Hakikar. Unpublished report [in Hebrew].

Jackson I.J. (1994). Molecular and developmental genetics of mouse coat color. *Annual Review of Genetics* 28, 189–217.

Jacobsen T.W. (1976). 17.000 anni di preistoria greca. *Le Scienze* 98, 68–81.

Jansen T., Forster P., Levine M.A., Oelke H., Hurles M., Renfrew C. *et al.* (2002). Mitochondrial DNA and the origins of the domestic horse. *Proceedings of the National Academy of Sciences of the USA* 99(16), 10905–10.

Janzon G.O. (1974). *Gotlands Mellanneolitiska Gravar* (Acta Universitatis Stockholmiensis, Studies in North-European Archaeology 6). Stockholm: Almqvist & Wiksell.

Jarman M.R. (1973). Preliminary report on the animal bones. In: Coldstream J.N. (ed.), *Knossos, the Sanctuary of Demeter* (British School of Archaeology at Athens. Supplementary volume 8), 177–9. London: Thames & Hudson.

Jarman M.R. (1974). The fauna and economy of Tel Eli. *Mitekufat Haeven, Journal of the Israel Prehistoric Society* 12, 50–70.

—— (1976). Prehistoric economic development in sub-Alpine Italy. In: Sieveking G.d.G., Longworth I.H. & Wilson K.E. (eds), *Problems in Economic and Social Archaeology*, 375–99. London: Duckworth.

Jensen J. (2001). *Danmarks Oldtid. Stenalder 13,000–2,000 f. Kr.* Copenhagen: Gyldendal.

Jensen O.L. (2001). Kongemose- og Ertebøllekultur ved den fossile Nivåfjord. In: Jensen O.L., Sørensen S.A. & Hansen K.M. (eds), *Danmarks Jægerstenalder—Status og Perspektiver*, 115–29. Hørsholm: Hørsholm Egns Museum.

Jentink F.A. (1905). *Sus*-studies in the Leyden Museum. *Notes from the Leyden Museum* 26, 155–95.

Jeon J.-T., Carlborg Ö., Törnsten A., Giuffra E., Amarger V., Chardon P. et al. (1999). A paternally expressed QTL affecting skeletal and cardiac muscle mass in pigs maps to the IGF2 locus. *Nature Genetics* 21, 157–8.

Johansson A.D. (2000). *Ældre Stenalder i Norden*. Copenhagen: Sammenslutningen af Danske Amatørarkæologer.

Johansson M., Ellegren H., Marklund L., Gustavsson U., Ringmar-Cederberg E. et al. (1992). The gene for dominant white color in the pig is closely linked to *ALB* and *PDGFRA* on chromosome 8. *Genomics* 14, 965–9.

Johansson Moller M., Chaudhary R., Hellmen E., Hoyheim B., Chowdhary B. & Andersson L. (1996). Pigs with the dominant white coat color phenotype carry a duplication of the *KIT* gene encoding the mast/stem cell growth factor receptor. *Mammalian Genome* 7, 822–30.

Johansson P. (2003). *The Lure of Origins. An Inquiry into Human-Environmental Relations, focused on the 'Neolithization' of Sweden* (Coast to Coast book 8). Uppsala: Uppsala University, Department of Archaeology and Ancient History.

Johnstone C. & Albarella U. (2002). *The Late Iron Age and Romano-British Mammal and Bird Bone Assemblage from Elms Farm, Heybridge, Essex* (Centre for Archaeology Report 45/2002). Portsmouth: English Heritage.

Jones G.F. (1998). Genetic aspects of domestication, common breeds and their origin. In: Rothschild M.F. & Ruvinsky A. (eds), *The Genetics of the Pig*, 17–50. Wallingford: CAB International.

Jones M. (ed.) (1989). *The Depiction of Proverbs in Late Medieval Art*. Strasbourg: Universite des Sciences Humaines, Departement d'Etudes allemandes.

—— (1991). Folklore motifs in late medieval art III: erotic animal imagery. *Folklore* 102, 2.

—— (2002). *The Secret Middle Ages*. Stroud: Sutton Publishing.

Jonsson L. (1986). From wild boar to domestic pig—a reassessment of Neolithic swine of northwestern Europe. *Striae* 24, 125–9.

Jørgensen S. (1956). Kongemosen—endnu en Åmose-boplads fra ældre stenalder. *KUML* 1956, 23–40.

JOSEPHSEN K. & FEJERSKOV O. (1977). Ameloblast modulation in the maturation zone of the rat incisor enamel organ: a light and electron microscopic study. *Journal of Anatomy* 124, 45–70.

JOSHI M.B., ROUT P.K., MANDAL A.K., TYLER-SMITH C., SINGH L. & THANGARAJ K. (2004). Phylogeography and origin of Indian domestic goats. *Molecular Biology and Evolution* 21(3), 454–62.

JOSIEN T. (1955). La faune Chalcolithique des gisements palestiniens de Bir es-Safadi et Bir abou Matar. *Israel Exploration Journal* 5, 246–56.

JUVIK J.O., ANDRIANARIVO A.J. & BLAND C.P. (1981). The ecology and status of *Geochelone yniphora*: a critically endangered tortoise in northwestern Madagascar. *Biological Conservation* 19, 297–316.

KAISER B. (1976). *Untersuchungen zum minoischen Relief.* Bonn: Dr Rudolf Habelt.

KANEKO H. (1983). Faunal remains from Kadota shell midden at the verification excavation of locality. In: *Kadota Shell Midden*, 69–74. Board of Education of Okayama Prefecture [in Japanese].

——(1987). Vertebrate faunal remains and artifacts made of bones, antlers, and canines found from Kurawa Site in Hachijyo Island. In: Hachijyo Town Board of Education (ed.), *Hachijyo Town Kurawa Site, Tokyo Prefecture*, 87–103 [in Japanese].

KAPOOR SHARMA R. (2002). Un maiale fra i rifiuti. *Slow* 26, 44–9.

KARAGEORGHIS V. (1968). *Mycenaean Art from Cyprus.* Nicosia: Department of Antiquities.

——(1969). Chronique des fouilles et découvertes archéologiques à Chypre en 1968 (pl.X). *Bulletin de Correspondance Hellénique* 93, 431–569.

——BIKAI P.M., COLDSTREAM J.N., JOHNSTON A.W., ROBERTSON M. & JEHASSE L. (1981). *Excavations at Kition IV, The Non-Cypriote Pottery.* Nicosia: Department of Antiquities.

——& DES GAGNIERS J. (1974). *La céramique chypriote de style figuré: âge du Fer (1050–500 av. J.-C.).* Rome: Consiglio Nazionale delle Ricerche, Istituto per gli Studi Micenei ed Egeo-Anatolici.

KASAHARA Y. (1981). Identification of plant seeds from the Torihama shell midden, with special reference to the seeds of egoma and/or shiso mint and tar-like samples. In: Board of Education of Fukui Prefecture (ed.), *Torihama Shell Midden: Preliminary Report of the 1980 Fiscal Year Excavation: The Excavation of an Early Jomon Wet Site, Vol. 2*, 65–87 [in Japanese].

KATO S. (1980). Animal keeping by Jomon people, in particular on the problem of wild pigs. *Rekishi Koron* 54, 45–50 [in Japanese].

KATZENBERG M.A. (2000). Stable isotope analysis: a tool for studying past diet, demography and life history. In: Katzenberg, M.A. & Saunders S.R. (eds), *The biological anthropology of the human skeleton*, 305–27. New York: Wiley.

KATZENELLENBOGEN A. (1939). *Allegories of the Virtues and Vices in Medieval Art.* London: Warburg Institute.

KAWAMURA Y. (1991). Quaternary mammalian faunas in the Japanese Islands. *Quaternary Research* 30, 213–20.

KEARNEY M. (1991). *The Role of the Swine Symbolism in Medieval Culture.* Lewiston: Edward Mellen.

KELLY F. (2000). *Early Irish Farming: a Study Based on the Law-texts of the 7th and 8th Centuries AD.* Dublin: Dublin Institute for Advanced Studies.

KELLY J.F. (2000). Stable isotopes of carbon and nitrogen in the study of avian and mammalian trophic ecology. *Canadian Journal of Zoology* 78, 1–27.

KELLY R.C. (1988). Etoro suidology: a reassessment of the pig's role in the prehistory and comparative ethnology of New Guinea. In: Weiner J.F. (ed.), *Mountain Papuans: Historical and Comparative Perspectives from New Guinea Fringe Highlands Societies,* 111–86. Ann Arbor, MI: Michigan University Press.

——— & RAPPAPORT R. (1975). Function, generality, and explanatory power: a commentary and response to Bergmann's arguments. *Michigan Discussions in Anthropology* 1(1), 24–44.

KEMP R.L. & GRAVES C.P. (1996). *The Church and Gilbertine Priory of St Andrew, Fishergate* (The Archaeology of York 11(2)). York: Council for British Archaeology.

KERJE S., LIND J., SCHÜTZ K., JENSEN P. & ANDERSSON L. (2003). Melanocortin 1-receptor (MC1R) mutations are associated with plumage colour in chicken. *Animal Genetics* 34, 241–8.

KIERDORF U. & KIERDORF H. (1999). Dental fluorosis in wild deer: its use as a biomarker of increased fluoride exposure. *Environmental Monitoring and Assessment* 57, 265–75.

KIERDORF H., KIERDORF U. & SEDLACEK F. (1999). Monitoring regional fluoride pollution in the Saxonian Ore mountains (Germany) using the biomarker dental fluorosis in roe deer (*Capreolus capreolus* L.). *Science of the total Environment* 232, 159–68.

——— ——— RICHARDS A. & SEDLACEK F. (2000). Disturbed enamel formation in wild boars (*Sus scrofa* L.) from fluoride polluted areas in Central Europe. *Anatomical Record* 259, 12–24.

——— ——— ——— & JOSEPHSEN K. (2004). Fluoride-induced alterations of enamel structure: an experimental study in the miniature pig. *Anatomy and Embryology* 207, 463–74.

——— ——— & WITZEL C. (2005). Deposition of cellular cementum onto hypoplastic enamel of fluorotic teeth in wild boars (*Sus scrofa* L.). *Anatomy and Embryology* 209, 281–6.

KIGHTLY C., PIETERS M., TYS D. & ERVYNCK A. (2000). *Walraversijde 1465.* Brugge: Provincie West-Vlaanderen & Instituut voor het Archeologisch Patrimonium.

KIJAS J.M.H. & ANDERSSON L. (2001). A phylogenetic study of the origin of the domestic pig estimated from the near-complete mtDNA genome. *Journal of Molecular Evolution* 52(3), 302–8.

——— MOLLER M., PLASTOW G. & ANDERSSON L. (2001). A frameshift mutation in MC1R and a high frequency of somatic reversions cause black spotting in pigs. *Genetics* 158, 779–85.

——— WALES R., TÖRNSTEN A., CHARDON P., MOLLER M. & ANDERSSON L. (1998). Melanocortin receptor 1 (MC1R) mutations and coat color in pigs. *Genetics* 150, 1177–85.

Kim K.-I., Lee J.-H., Li K., Zhang Y.-P., Lee S.-S., Gongora J. & Moran C. (2002). Phylogenetic relationships of Asian and European pig breeds determined by mitochondrial DNA D-loop sequence polymorphism. *Animal Genetics* 33, 19–25.

King C.M. (ed.) (1990). *The Handbook of New Zealand Mammals*. Auckland: Oxford University Press.

Kisch G. (1943). The Jewish execution in medieval Germany. *Historia Judaica* 5.

Klenck J.D. (1995). Bedouin animal sacrifice practices: case study in Israel. *MASCA Research Papers in Science and Archaeology* 12, 57–72.

Klengel E. & Klengel H. (1970). *Die Hethiter: Geschichte und Umwelt: eine Kulturgeschichte Kleinasiens von Çatal Hüyük bis zu Alexander dem Grossen Wien.* Munich: A. Schroll.

Klingender F.D. (1971). *Animals in Art and Thought.* London: Routledge & Kegan Paul.

Klippel W.E. & Snyder L.M. (1991). Dark-Age fauna from Kavousi, Crete, the Vertebrates from the 1987 and 1988 excavations. *Hesperia* 60, 179–86.

Klungland H., Vage D.I., Gomez-Raya L., Adalsteinsson S. & Lien S. (1995). The role of melanocyte-stimulating hormone (MSH) receptor in bovine coat color determination. *Mammalian Genome* 6, 636–9.

Knott S.A., Marklund L., Haley C.S., Andersson K., Davies W., Ellegren H., *et al.* (1998). Multiple marker mapping of quantitative trait loci in a cross between outbred wild boar and large white pigs. *Genetics* 149, 1069–80.

Koch K.-F. (1968). Marriage in Jalémo. *Oceania* 39(2), 85–109.

Kohler I. (1981). Animal remains. In: Helms S. (ed.), *Jawa. Lost City of the Black Desert*, 249–52. London: Methuen.

Kohler-Rollefson I. (1997). Proto-elevage, pathologies and pastoralism: a postmortem of the process of goat domestication. In: Gebel H.G.K., Kafafi Z. & Rollefson G.O. (eds), *The Prehistory of Jordan II* (Studies in early Near Eastern Production, Subsistence and Environment 4), 557–66. Berlin: Ex Oriente.

Konsolaki-Yannopoulou E. (2001). New evidence for the practice of libation in the Aegean bronze age. In: Laffineur R. & Hägg R. (eds), *POTNIA. Deities and Religion in the Aegean Bronze Age* (AEGAEUM 22), 213–25. Liège & Austin: Université de Liége & University of Texas.

Kosay H.Z. & Akok M. (1966). *Ausgrabungen von Alaca Höyük.* Ankara: Türk Tarih Kurumu.

Kuehn D.W. & Berg W.E. (1981). Use of radiographs to identify age-classes of fisher. *Journal of Wildlife Management* 45, 1009–10.

Kumar S., Tamura K., Jakobsen I.B. & Nei M. (2001). MEGA2: molecular evolutionary genetics analysis software. *Bioinformatics* 17, 1244–5.

Kuşatman B. (1991). *The origins of pig domestication with particular reference to the Near East.* Ph.D. thesis, University College London.

Kussinger S. (1988). *Tierknochenfunde vom Lidar Höyük in Südostanatolien (Grabungen 1979–86),* Inaugural Dissertation, Institüt für Palaeoanatomie, Domestikationsforschung und Geschichte der Tiermedizin, Munich.

Laffer J.P. (1983). The faunal remains from Banahilk. In: Braidwood L.S. Braidwood R.J., Howe B., Reed C.A. & Watson P.J. (eds), *Prehistoric Archaeology along the*

Zagros Flanks (University of Chicago Oriental Institute Publication 105), 629–47. Chicago: Oriental Institute, University of Chicago.

LAFFINEUR R. (1992). Iconography as evidence of social and political status in mycenaean Greece. In: Laffineur R. & Crowley J.L. (eds), *Aegean Bronze Age Iconography: Shaping a Methodology* (AEGAEUM 8), 105–12. Liège: & Austin: Université de Liége & University of Texas.

LAI S.-J., LIU Y.-P., LIU Y.-X., LI X.-W. & YAO Y.-G. (2006). Genetic diversity and origin of Chinese cattle revealed by mtDNA D-loop sequence variation. *Molecular Phylogenetics & Evolution* 38(1), :146–54.

LAN H. & SHI L. (1993). The origin and genetic differentiation of native breeds of pigs in Southwest China: an approach from mitochondrial DNA polymorphism. *Biochemical Genetics* 31, 51–60.

LAROULANDIE V. (2000). *Taphonomie et archéozoologie des oiseaux en grotte: applications aux sites paléolithiques du Bois-Ragot (vienne), de Combe Saunière (Dordogne) et de la Vache (Ariège)*. Thèse, Université de Bordeaux I.

LARSON G., DOBNEY K., ALBARELLA U., FANG M., MATISOO-SMITH E., ROBINS J. *et al.* (2005). Worldwide phylogeography of wild boar reveals multiple centres of pig domestication. *Science* 307, 1618–21.

—— CUCCI T., FUJITA M., MATISOO-SMITH E., ROBINS J., ANDERSON A. *et al.* (2007). Phylogeny and ancient DNA of *Sus* provides insights into Neolithic expansion in Island Southeast Asia and Oceania. *Proceedings of the National Academy of Sciences USA* 104, 4834–9.

LARSSON L. (1983). Mesolithic settlement on the sea floor in the Strait of Öresund. In: Masters P.M. & Flemming N.C. (eds), *Quaternary Coastlines and Marine Archaeology*, 283–301. New York: Academic Press.

LAURANS R. (1975). L'élevage du porc à l'époque médiévale. In: Pujol R. (ed.), *L'homme et l'animal. Premier colloque d'ethnozoologie*, 523–34. Paris: Institut International d'Ethnosciences.

LAURIE E.M.O. & HILL J.E. (1954). *List of Land Mammals of New Guinea, Celebes and Adjacent Islands 1758–1952*. London: British Museum.

LAUWERIER R.C.G.M. (1983). Pigs, piglets and determining the season of slaughtering. *Journal of Archaeological Science* 10, 483–8.

LAWRENCE B. (1980). Evidences of animal domestication at Çayönü. In: Çambel H. & Braidwood R.J. (eds), *Istanbul ve Chicago Üniversiteleri Karma Projesi Güneydoğu Anadolu Tarihöncesi Araştir malari* I / *The Joint Istanbul-Chicago Universities Prehistoric Research in Southeastern Anatolia* I, 285–308. Istanbul: Istanbul Üniversitesi Edebiyat Fakültesi Yayinlari.

LAWSON G. (1995). *Pig Metapodial Toggles and Buzz-discs* (Finds Research Group 700–1700, Vol. Datasheet 18). <*http://www.frg700-1700.org.uk/sheet.html*>

LEDERMAN R. (1986). *What Gifts Engender: Social Relations and Politics in Mendi, Highland Papua New Guinea*. Cambridge: Cambridge University Press.

LEE J. & SEYMOUR S. (2003). Feral pigs in Australia: a successful invasion. In: *Pigs and Humans*. Conference abstracts of the workshop held at Walworth Castle (UK), 26–28 September 2002.

LEGGE A.J. & ROWLEY-CONWY P. (1988). *Star Carr Revisited—A Re-analysis of the Large Mammals.* London: Birkbeck College.

LEMEL J. (1999). *Populationstillväxt, dynamik och spridning hos vildsvinet, Sus scrofa, i mellersta Sverige. Slutrapport.* Uppsala: Forskningsavdelningen, Svenska jägareförbundet.

LERNAU H. (1978). Faunal remains, strata III-I. In: Amiran R. (ed.), *Early Arad,* 83–113. Jerusalem: Israel Exploration Society.

LESSON R.-P. & GARNOT P. (1826). Mammifères nouveaux ou peu connus, décrits et figurés dans l'Atlas zoologique du Voyage autour du Monde de la Corvette la Coquille. *Bulletin des Sciences Naturelles et Géologie Paris* 1826, 95–6.

LEV-TOV J. (2000). Late prehistoric faunal remains from new excavations at Tel Ali (northern Israel). In: Mashkour M., Choyke A.M., Buitenhuis H. & Poplin F. (eds), *Archaeozoology of the Near East IV* (ARC-Publicaties 32), 208–15. Groningen: Centre for Archaeological Research & Consultancy.

—— & MAHER E. (2001). Food in Late Bronze age funerary offerings: faunal evidence from Tomb 1 at Tell Dothan. *Palestine Exploration Quarterly* 133, 91–110.

LEWTHWAITE J. (1984). The art of corse herding: archaeological insights from recent pastoral practices on west Mediterranean islands. In: Clutton-Brock J. & Grigson C. (eds), *Animals and Archaeology 3: early herders and their flocks* (BAR International Series 202), 25–37. Oxford: British Archaeological Reports.

LIDÉN K. (1995a). A dietary perspective on Swedish hunter gatherer and Neolithic populations. An analysis of stable isotopes and trace elements. In: Lidén K. (ed.), *Prehistoric Diet Transitions* (Theses and Papers in Scientific Archaeology 1). Stockholm: Archaeological Research Laboratory, University of Stockholm.

—— (1995b). *Prehistoric Diet Transitions* (Theses and Papers in Scientific Archaeology 1). Stockholm: Archaeological Research Laboratory, University of Stockholm.

LILIEQUIST B. & LUNDBERG M. (1971). Skeletal and tooth development. *Acta Radiologica* 11, 97–112.

LINDQUIST C. & POSSNERT G. (1997). The subsistence economy and diet at Jakobs/Ajvide and Stora Förvar, Eksta parish and other prehistoric dwelling and burial sites on Gotland in long term perspective. In: Burenhult G. (ed.), *Remote Sensing, Vol 1. Applied Techniques for the Study of Cultural Resources and the Localization, Identifcation and Documentation of Subsurface Prehistoric Remains in Swedish Archaeology* (Theses and Papers in North European Archaeology 13a), 29–90. Stockholm: Institute of Archaeology, University of Stockholm.

LINNAEUS C. (1758). *Systema Naturae.* Stockholm: Laurentius Salvius.

LION B. & MICHEL C. (2001). Porcs. In: Joannes F. (ed.), *Dictionnaire de la civilisation mésopotamienne,* 670–1. Paris: Robert Laffont.

LOBBAN R.A. (1998). Pigs in Ancient Egypt. *MASCA Research Papers in Science and Archaeology* 15, 137–48.

LOYET M.A. (2000). Preliminary report on the Tell Kurdu faunal remains (1999). *Anatolica* 26, 78–80 & 93.

LYMAN R.L. (1994). *Vertebrate Taphonomy* (Cambridge Manuals in Archaeology). Cambridge: Cambridge University Press.

MACDONALD A.A. (1993). The Sulawesi warty pig (*Sus celebensis*). In: Oliver W.L.R. (ed.), *Pigs, Peccari, and Hippos*, 155–60. Gland,: International Union for the Conservation of Nature and Natural Resources. Species Survival Commission.

MACFARLAND C.G. & REEDER W.G. (1977). Breeding rearing and restocking of giant tortoises (*Geochelone elephantopus*) in the Galapagos islands. In: Martin R.D. (ed.), *Breeding Endangered Species in Captivity*, 33–7. London: Academic Press.

MACQUEEN J.-G. (1975). *The Hittites and their Contemporaries in Asia Minor*. Southampton: Thames & Hudson.

MADSEN A.P., MÜLLER S., NEERGAARD C., PETERSEN C.G.J., ROSTRUP E., STEENSTRUP K.J.V. & WINGE H. (1900). *Affaldsdynger fra Stenalderen i Danmark*. Copenhagen: C.A. Reitzel.

MADSEN T. (1988). Causewayed enclosures in South Scandinavia. In: Burgess C., Topping P., Mordant C. & Maddison M. (eds), *Enclosures and Defences in the Neolithic of Western Europe* (BAR International Series 403), 301–36. Oxford: British Archaeological Reports.

MAENHAUT VAN LEMBERGE V. (1985). *De Warandemotte te Veurne: site catchment en voornaamste grote huisdieren (varken, rund)*. Master's thesis, University of Gent, Belgium.

MAGNELL O. (2004). The body size of wild boar during the Mesolithic in southern Scandinavia. *Acta Theriologica*, 49(1), 113–30.

——(2005*a*). Harvesting wild boar—a study of prey choice by hunters during the Mesolithic in South Scandinavia by analysis of age and sex structures in faunal remains. *Archaeofauna* 14, 27–41.

——(2005*b*). Tooth wear in wild boar (*Sus scrofa*). In: Ruscillo D. (ed.), *Recent Advances in Ageing and Sexing Animal Bones*, 189–203. Oxford: Oxbow Books.

MAINLAND I.L. (2001). The potential of dental microwear for exploring seasonal aspects of sheep husbandry and management in Norse Greenland. *Archaeozoologia* 11, 79–100.

——(2003*a*). Dental microwear in modern Greek ovicaprids: identifying microwear signatures associated with a diet of leafy-hay. In: Kotjabopoulou E., Hamilakis Y., Halstead P., Gamble C. & Elefanti P. (eds), *Zooarchaeology in Greece: Recent Advances* (British School of Athens Studies 9), 945–50. London: The British School at Athens.

——(2003*b*). Dental microwear in grazing and browsing Gotland sheep (*Ovis aries*) and its implications for dietary reconstruction. *Journal of Archaeological Science* 30, 1513–27.

——& HALSTEAD P. (2004). The diet and management of domestic sheep and goats at Neolithic Makriyalos. In: Davies J., Fabis M., Mainland I., Richards R. & Thomas R. (eds), *Diet and Health in Past Animal Populations*, 104–12. Oxford: Oxbow Books.

——WILKIE T., ALBARELLA U., DOBNEY K. & ROWLEY-CONWY P. (in preparation). *Molar Microwear in Wild Boar and Domestic Pig and its Potential for Palaeodietary Reconstruction*.

MAIRS L.D. (1994). Animal bones from the 1992 field season: preliminary report. In: Bourke S.J. *et al.* (eds), Preliminary Report of the University of Sydney's fourteenth season of excavations at Pella (Tabaqat Fahl) in 1992. *Annual of the Department of Antiquities of Jordan* 38, 121–6.

—— (1995). Report on the faunal remains from al-Ghassūl. In: Bourke S.J. *et al.* (eds), A first season of renewed excavation by the University of Sydney at Telaylāt al-Ghassūl. *Annual of the Department of Antiquities of Jordan* 39, 58–60.

—— (1998). Archaeozoological report (1994–1995). In: Bourke S.J. *et al.* (eds), Preliminary Report of the University of Sydney's sixteenth and seventeenth seasons of excavation at Pella (Tabaqat Fahl) in 1994–1995. *Annual of the Department of Antiquities of Jordan* 42, 201–5.

—— (2000). Archaeozoological report. In: Bourke S.J. *et al.* (eds), A second and third season of renewed excavation by the University of Sydney at Telaylāt al-Ghassūl (1995–1997). *Annual of the Department of Antiquities of Jordan* 44, 201–5.

MALLOWAN M.E.L. (1946). Excavations in the Balikh Valley, 1938. *Iraq* 8, 111–59.

MALMER M. (2002). *The Neolithic of South Sweden. TRB, GRK and STR.* Stockholm: Kungl. Vitterhets Historie och Antikvitets Akademien.

MALYNICZ G.L. (1970). Pig keeping by the subsistence agriculturalist of the New Guinea Highlands. *Search* 1(5), 201–4.

—— (1971). Research on pig production. *Harvest* 1(2), 71–3.

—— (1973*a*). The productivity of exotic and indigenous pigs under village conditions. Parts 1 & 2. *Papua and New Guinea Agricultural Journal* 24(1), 16–22.

—— (1973*b*). Growth and carcass measurements of indgenous and exotic pigs raised in two housing systems in Papua New Guinea. *Papua and New Guinea Agricultural Journal* 24(1), 23–5.

—— (1976). A demographic analysis of Highlands village pig production. In: Enyi B.A.C. & Varghese T. (eds), *Agriculture in the Tropics (10th Waigani Seminar Proceedings)*, 201–9. Port Moresby: University of Papua New Guinea.

MANCA DELL'ARCA A. (1780). *Agricoltura di Sardegna.* Napoli: Vincenzo Orsino.

MANCONI F. (2000). La fauna dell'Età del Ferro degli scavi 1988 e 1990 del Nuraghe S. Imbenia di Alghero (Sassari). In: *Atti del 2° Convegno Nazionale di Archeozoologia, Asti, 14–16 Novembre 1997*, 267–77. Forli: Abaco edizioni.

MANE P. (1997). 'Toujours pourceaux paitront glands' ou l'élevage du porc à travers l'iconographie médiévale. In: Kubkorá J., Klápště J., Ježek M., Meduna P. *et al.* (eds), *Život v archeologii středověku (Life in the archaeology of the middle ages)*, 439–50. Praha: Arceologicky ústav AV ČR.

MANNEN H., KOHNO M., NAGATA Y., TSUJI S., BRADLEY D.G., YEO J.S. *et al.* (2004). Independent mitochondrial origin and historical genetic differentiation in North Eastern Asian cattle. *Molecular Phylogenetics and Evolution* 32(2), 539–44.

MARAZZI M. (1998). Micenei a Vivara o Micenei di Vivara? Nuove scoperte e nuove ipotesi sulla composizione di una comunità marinara protostorica. In: Marazzi M. & Moccheggiani Carpano C. (eds), *Vivara. Un'isola al centro della storia*, 73–85. Napoli: Altrastampa Edizioni.

—— (2001). Dieta alimentare e movimenti di 'beni organici' a Vivara: una ricerca fra fisica e biochimica. In: Pepe C. (ed.), *La ricerca archeologica a Vivara e le attività dei laboratori dell'Istituto Universitario Suor Orsola Benincasa*, 93–4. Napoli: Istituto Universitario Suor Orsola Benincasa.

MARIANI P., MOLLER M.J., HOYHEIM B., MARKLUND L., DAVIES W., ELLEGREN H. & ANDERSSON L. (1996). The extension coat color locus and the loci for blood group O and tyrosine aminotransferase are on pig chromosome 6. *Journal of Heredity* 87, 272–6.

MARKLUND L., MOLLER M.J., SANDBERG K. & ANDERSSON L. (1996). A missense mutation in the gene for melanocyte-stimulating hormone receptor (*MC1R*) is associated with the chestnut coat color in horses. *Mammalian Genome* 7, 895–9.

MARKLUND S., KIJAS J., RODRIGUEZ-MARTINEZ H., RONNSTRAND L., FUNA K., MOLLER M. *et al.* (1998). Molecular basis for the dominant white phenotype in the domestic pig. *Genome Research* 8, 826–33.

MASSEI G. & GENOV P. (1995). Preliminary analyses of food availability and habitat use by the wild boar in a Mediterranean area. *Ibex. Journal of Mountain Ecology* 3, 168–70.

MASSETI M. (1984). Sulle orme di Salgari. Komodo l'isola dei draghi. *La Città* V 281, 20.

—— (1998). Holocene endemic and anthropochorous wild mammals of the Mediterranean islands. *AnthropoZoologica* 28, 3–20.

—— (2000). Wild cats (Mammalia, Carnivora) of Anatolia, with some observations on the former and present occurrence of leopards in south-eastern Turkey and on the Greek island of Samos. *Biogeographia* 21, 607–18.

—— (2002). *Uomini e (non solo) topi. Gli animali domestici e la fauna antropocora.* Firenze: Firenze University Press.

—— & DARLAS A. (1999). Pre-Neolithic man and other mammals on the Eastern Mediterranean islands. *Arkeos* 5, 189–204.

MATHIASSEN T. (1939). Bundsø, en yngre stenalders boplads på Als. *Aarbøger for Nordiske Oldkyndighed og Historie* 1939, 1–55.

MATSCHKE G.H. (1967). Ageing European wild hogs by dentition. *Journal of Wildlife Management* 31, 109–13.

MATSUI A. (1986). Faunal analysis of Kamei site. In: *Kamei Site*, 423–484. Board of Education of Osaka Prefecture and Osaka Cultural Propeties Center [in Japanese].

—— (1995). Faunal remains from Harunotsuji Site (Takamoto Point). In: *Excavation report of Ashibe Town Cultural Properties*, 85–91 [in Japanese].

—— & MARUYAMA M. (2003). Faunal remains from Shinpo Site (Node-Seihou portion). In: *Site report at Node-Seihou portion 1*, 157–82. Board of Education, Kobe City [in Japanese].

—— & MIYAJI A. (2000). Faunal remans from Tshuboi Daifuku Site. *Bulletin of Museum, Archaeological Institute of Kashihara, Nara Prefecture* 75, 194–205.

MATSUMOTO T. (1979). Ryokuto (Mung Bean). In: Fukui Prefecture Board of Education (ed.), *The Torihama Shell Midden: The Excavation of an Early Jomon Wet Site, Vol. 1*, 162–3 [in Japanese].

MATTHEWS W., POSTGATE J.N., PAYNE S., CHARLES M.P. & DOBNEY K. (1994). The imprint of living in an Early Mesopotamian city: questions and answers. In:

Luff R. & Rowley-Conwy P. (eds), *Whither Environmental Archaeology?* (Oxbow Monograph 38), 171–212. Oxford: Oxbow Books.

MATTHYS A. (1991). Les fortifications du 11e siècle entre Lesse et Semois. In: Böhme H.W. (ed.), *Burgen der Salierzeit. I. In den Nördlichen Landschaften des Reiches* (Römisch-Germanisches Zentralmuseum Monographien 25), 225–80. Sigmaringen: Jan Thorbecke Verlag.

MAYER-OPIFICIUS R. (1986). Bemerkungen zur Mittelassyrischen Glytik des 13. und 12. Jhdts. v. Chr.. In: Kelly-Buccellati M. (ed.), *Inside through Images* (Bibliotheca Mesopotamica 21), 161–9. Malibu: Undena Publications.

MAYS S. (2000). New directions in the analysis of stable isotopes in excavated bones and teeth. In: Cox M. & Mays S. (eds), *Human Osteology: In Archaeology and Forensic Science*, 425–38. London: Greenwich Medical Media.

McARDLE J. (1975–77). A numerical (computerized) method for quantifying zooarcheological comparisons. *Paléorient* 3, 181–90.

McARTHUR M. (1974). Pigs for the ancestors. A review article. *Oceania* 45(2), 87–123.

—— (1977). Nutritional research in Melanesia: a second look at the Tsembaga. In: Bayliss-Smith T.P. & Feacham R.G. (eds), *Subsistence and Survival: Rural Ecology in the Pacific*, 91–128. London: Academic Press.

McCANCE R.A., FORD E.H.R. & BROWN W.A.B. (1961). Severe undernutrition in growing and adult animals. 7. Development of the skull, jaws and teeth in pigs. *British Journal of Nutrition* 15, 213–24.

McCORMICK F. (1999). Early evidence for wild animals in Ireland. In: Benecke N. (ed.), *The Holocene History of the European Vertebrate Fauna: Modern Aspects of Research* (Archäologie in Eurasien 6), 355–72. Berlin: Deutsches Archäologisches Institut, Eurasien-abteilung.

McCULLOCH F. (1962). *Medieval Latin and French Bestiaries*. Chapel Hill, NC: University of North Carolina Press.

McMAHON A., TUNCA O. & BAGDO A.-M. (2001). New excavations at Chagar Bazar, 1999–2000. *Iraq* 63, 201–22.

MEADOW R.H. (1981). Early animal domestication in South Asia: a first report of the faunal remains from Mehrgarh, Pakistan. In: Härtel H. (ed.), *South Asian Archaeology 1979*, 143–79. Berlin: Dietrich Reimer Verlag.

—— (1983). The vertebrate remains from Hasanlu Period X at Hajji Firuz. In: Voigt M.M. (ed.), *Hasanlu Excavation Reports 1: Hajji Firuz Tepe, Iran* (Philadelphia Museum Monograph 50), 369–422. Philadelphia: University Museum, University of Pennsylvania.

—— (1999). The use of size index scaling techniques for research on archaeozoological collections from the Middle East. In: Becker C., Manhart H., Peters J. & Schibler J. (eds), *Historia Animalium ex Ossibus. Beiträge zur Paläoanatomie, Archäologie, Ägyptologie, Ethnologie und Geschichte der Tiermedizin. Festschrift für Angela von den Driesch* (Internationale Archäologie. Studia honoraria 8), 285–300. Rahden, Westfalen: Verlag Marie Leidorf.

MEADS M.J., WALKER K.J. & ELLIOTT G.P. (1984). Status, conservation and management of the land snails of the genus *Powelliphanta* (Mollusca, Pulmonata). *New Zealand Journal of Zoology* 11, 277–306.

MEGGITT M.J. (1958). The Enga of the New Guinea Highlands: some preliminary observations. *Oceania* 28(4), 253–330.

MEIJAARD E. & GROVES C. (2002). Upgrading three subspecies of babirusa (*Babyrousa* sp.) to full species level. *Asian Wild Pig News* 2(2), 33–9.

MELLINKOFF R. (1973). 'Riding backwards'. *Viator* 4, 135–76.

MENDELSSOHN H. & YOM-TOV Y. (1999a). *Fauna Palaestina—Mammalia of Israel.* Jerusalem: The Israel Academy of Sciences and Humanities.

—— & —— (1999b). A report of birds and mammals which have increased their distribution and abundance in Israel due to human activity. *Israel Journal of Zoology* 45, 35–47.

—— —— & CANAANI G. (1990). Suidae. In: Mendelssohn H. & Yom-Tov Y. (eds), *Plants and Animals of the Land of Israel Vol. 7,* 245–52. Tel Aviv: Ministry of Defence [in Hebrew].

MERMIER G.R. (ED.) (1992). *A Medieval Book of Beasts: Pierre de Beauvais' Bestiary.* Lewiston, Queenston & Lampeter: The Edwin Mellen Press.

MERPERT N. & MUNCHAEV R.M. (1973). Early agricultural settlements in the Sinjar Plain, northern Iraq. *Iraq* 35, 93–113.

MERTON D.V. (1977). Controlling introduced predators and competitors on islands. In: Temple S.A. (ed.), *Endangered Birds—Management Techniques for Preserving Threatened Species,* 121–2. Madison, WI: University of Wisconsin Press.

METZGER M. (1983). Faunal remains at Tell el Hayyat. *Annual of the Department of Antiquities of Jordan* 27, 98–9.

MICHEL T. (1983). *Interdependenz von Wirtschaft und Umwelt in der Eipo-Kultur von Moknerkon. Bedingungen für Produktion und reproduktion bei einer Dorfschaft im zentralen Bergland von Irian Jaya (West-Neuguinea), Indonesien* (Mensch, Kultur und Umwelt im zentralen Bergland von West-Neuguinea 11). Berlin: Dietrich Reimer Verlag.

MILLER N.F. (1997). Farming and herding along the Euphrates: environmental constraint and cultural choice (fourth to second millennium B.C.). *MASCA Research Papers in Science and Archaeology* 14, 123–32.

MILLER R. (1990). Hogs and hygiene. *Journal of Egyptian Archaeology* 76, 125–40.

MINAGAWA M., MATSUI A. & ISHIGURO N. (2005). Carbon and nitrogen isotope analyses for prehistoric *Sus scrofa* bone collagen to discriminate prehistoric boar domestication and inter-islands pig trading across the East China Sea. *Chemical Geology* 218, 91–102.

MOENS M.F. & WETTERSTROM W. (1988). The agricultural economy of an old kingdom town in Egypt's west delta: insights from the plant remains. *Journal of Near Eastern Studies* 47, 159–73.

MOHR E. (1960). *Wilde Schweine* (Neue Brehm-Bücherei 247). Wittenberg-Lutherstadt: Ziemsen Verlag.

MOLENAT M. & CASABIANCA F. (1979). *Contribution à la maîtrise de l'elevage porcin extensif en Corse* (Bulletin Technique du Departement de Genetique Animale 32). Jouy-en-Josas: Institut National de la Recherche Agronomique.

MÖLLERS F. (2004). The free little pigs. *Wildlife Magazine* 22(9), 56–62.

MOORTGAT A. (1955). Die Bildwerke, in M. F. von der Oppenheim, *Tel Halaf III, Die Bildwerke*. Berlin.

MORENO GARCÍA M. (2004). Hunting practices and consumption patterns in rural communities in the Rif mountains (Morocco)—some ethno-zoological notes. In: O'Day S.J., Van Neer W. & Ervynck E. (eds), *Behaviour Behind Bones. The Zooarchaeology of Ritual, Religion, Status and Identity*, 327–34. Oxford: Oxbow Books.

MORII Y., ISHIGURO N., WATANOBE T., NAKANO M., HONGO H., MATSUI A., NISHIMOTO T. (2002). Ancient DNA reveals genetic lineage of *Sus scrofa* among archaeological sites in Japan. *Anthropological Science* 110(3), 313–28.

MORREN G.E.B. (1977). From hunting to herding: pigs and the control of energy in montane New Guinea. In: Bayliss-Smith T.P. & Feacham R.G. (eds), *Subsistence and Survival: Rural Ecology in the Pacific*, 273–315. London: Academic Press.

MORRIS C.E. (1990). In pursuit of the white tusked boar. Aspects of hunting in Mycenaean society. In: Hägg R. & Nordquist G.C. (eds), *Celebrations of Death and Divinity in the Bronze Age Argolid* (Acta Instituti Atheniensis Regni Suediae XL), 149–63. Stockholm: Paul Astroms Forlag.

MORRIS P.A. (1972). A review of mammalian age determination methods. *Mammal Review* 2, 69–104.

MOUNT L.E. (1968). *The Climatic Physiology of the Pig*. London: Edward Arnold.

MOUSE GENOME INFORMATICS (n.d.). *Mouse Genome Database*. Bar Harbor, ME: The Jackson Laboratory. <*http://www.informatics.jax.org/searches/accession_report. cgi?id=MGI:96677*>

MUDAR K. (1982). Early Dynastic III animal utilization in Lagash: a report on the fauna of Tell al-Hiba. *Journal of Near Eastern Studies* 41, 23–34.

MÜLDNER G. & RICHARDS M. (2005). Fast or feast: reconstructing diet in later medieval England by stable isotope analysis. *Journal of Archaeological Science* 32, 39–48.

MUNSON P.J. (2000). Age correlated differential destruction of bones and its effect on archaeological mortality profiles of domestic sheep and goats. *Journal of Archaeological Science* 27, 391–407.

NAORA N. (1935). Mammal remains excavated from the shell middens. *Dolmen* 4–7, 31–6.

—— (1937*a*). On pigs in prehistoric Japan. *Jinruigaku Zasshi* 52(8), 286–96 [in Japanese].

—— (1937*b*). Study of pigs in the Japanese prehistory. *Anthropological Science* 52(8), 286–96.

—— (1938*a*). Molar teeth excavated from Kohama-hama site in the Yayoi Period, on Miyake Island. *Jinruigaku Zasshi* 53–2, 28–30 [in Japanese].

—— (1938*b*). Pig molar excavated from Kohama-hama Site, Miyake Island, Yayoi period. *Anthropological Science* 53, 68–70.

NEEV D. & EMERY K.O. (1967). The Dead Sea. *Bulletin of the Geological Survey of Israel* 41.

NELSON S. (ed.) (1998*a*). *Ancestors for the Pigs: Pigs in Prehistory* (MASCA Research Papers in Science and Archaeology 15), Philadelphia: University of Pennsylvania Museum of Archaeology and Anthropology.

—— (1998*b*). Pigs in the Hongshan culture. In: Nelson S.M. (ed.), *Ancestors for the Pigs. Pigs in Prehistory* (MASCA Research Papers in Science and Archaeology 15), 99–107. Philadelphia: University of Pennsylvania Museum of Archaeology and Anthropology.

NEMETH D.J. (1998). Privy-pigs in prehistory? A Korean analog for Neolithic Chinese subsistence practices. *MASCA Research Papers in Science and Archaeology* 15, 11–26.

NEU E. (1974). *Der Anitta-Text* (Studien zu den Bogazköy-Texten 18). Wiesbaden: Otto Harrassowitz.

NEWBERRY P.E. (1928). The pig and the cult-animal of Set. *Journal of Egyptian Archaeology* 14, 211–25.

NEZER C., MOREAU L., BROUWERS B., COPPIETERS W., DETILLEUX J., HANSET R. *et al.* (1999). An imprinted QTL with major effect on muscle mass and fat deposition maps to the IGF2 locus in pigs. *Nature Genetics* 21, 155–6.

NISHIMOTO N. & ANEZAKI T. (1998). Faunal remains from Shimobayasi Nishida Site. In: *Shimobayashi Nishida Site*, 167–70. Board of Education, Fukuoka Prefecture [in Japanese].

—— —— (1999*a*). Faunal analysis of Ikego site No.1-A. In: *Site Report of Ikego Sites 1-A*, 287–309. Board of Cultural Heritage of Kanagawa Prefecture [in Japanese].

—— —— (1999*b*). Faunal analysis of Ikego site No.1-A East. In: *Site Report of Ikego Sites IX*, 287–309. Board of Cultural Heritage of Kanagawa Prefecture [in Japanese].

—— —— (1999*c*). Mammal remains from Ikego sites. In: *Site Report of Ikego Sites IX*, 409–39. Board of Cultural Heritage of Kanagawa Prefecture [in Japanese].

—— —— & OTA A. (2003). Faunal analysis of Shimo-ota Shell midden. In: Sounan Cultural Heritage Center (ed.), *Site Report of Shimo-ota Shell Midden*, 269–91 [in Japanese].

NISHIMOTO T. (1985). On wild pigs in Hokkaido in the Jomon Period. *Kodai Tansou* II, 137–52 [in Japanese].

—— (1989). Faunal remains from Shimogori-kuwanae site. In: Oita Prefectural Board of Education (ed.), *Site Report of Shimogori-kuwanae Site*, 48–61 [in Japanese].

—— (1991*a*). Pigs from Yayoi period. *Bulletin of the National Museum of Japanese History* 36, 175–94 [in Japanese].

—— (1991*b*). Hunting of deer and pig during the Jomon period. *Kodai* 91, 114–32 [in Japanese].

—— (1994). Domesticated pigs in the Early Agriculture Period in Japan. *ArchæoZoologia* VI (2), 57–70.

—— (2003). Domestication of pigs in the Jomon period. *Bulletin of the National Museum of Japanese History* 108, 1–16 [in Japanese].

NISHINO M. (1999). The large shell midden and productive activity in the middle Jomon. *Bulletin of Cultural Properties Centre of Chiba Prefecture* 19, 135–50 [in Japanese].

NOBIS G. (1999). Archäozoologische Studien an Tierresten aus Eleutherna auf Kreta—Grabungen 1994–1997. *Tier und Museum* 6(3–4), 49–67.

Noe-Nygaard N. & Richter J. (1990). Seventeen wild boar mandibles from Sludegårds Sømose—offal or sacrifice?. In: Robinson D.E. (ed.), *Experimantation and Reconstruction in Environmental Archaeology* (Symposia for Environmental Archaeology 9), 175–89. Oxford: Oxbow Books.

Nokariya I. (1990). Vertebrate remains from Kusakari shell midden site. *Bulletin of Cultural Properties Centre of Chiba Prefecture* 171, 198–216 [in Japanese].

Norušis M.J. (1990). *SPSS/PC+ Advanced Statistics 4.0.* Chicago: SPSS Inc.

Nowak R.M. (1999). *Walker's Mammals of the World. Volume II.* Baltimore, MD: The John Hopkins University Press.

Oates J. (1973). The background and development of early farming communities in Mesopotamia and the Zagros. *Proceedings of the Prehistoric Society* 39, 147–81.

O'Connor T. (1989). *Bones from Anglo-Scandinavian Levels at 16–22 Coppergate* (The Archaeology of York 15(3)). York: Council of British Archaeology.

—— (1991). *Bones from 46–54 Fishergate* (The Archaeology of York 15(4)). York: Council of British Archaeology.

—— (2000). *The Archaeology of Animal Bones.* Stroud: Sutton Publishing.

Okomura N., Kurosawa Y., Kobayashi E., Watanobe R., Ishiguro N., Yasue H. & Mitsuhashi T. (2001). Genetic relationship amongst the major non-coding regions of mitochondrial DNAs in wild boars and several breeds of domesticated pigs. *Animal Genetics* 32, 139–47.

Oliver J. (1993). Carcass processing by the Hadza: bone breakage from butchery to consumption. In: Hudson J. (ed.), *From Bones to Behavior: Ethnoarchaeological and Experimental Contributions to the Interpretation of Faunal Remains* (Center for Archaeological Investigations. Occasional Paper 21), 200–27. Carbondale, IL: Southern Illinois University.

Oliver W.L.R. (1984). Introduced and feral pigs. In: *Feral Mammals—Problems and Potential.* Workshop on Feral Mammals organized by the Caprinae Specialist Group of the Species Survival Commission at the IIIrd International Theriological Conference, Helsinki, August 1982, 87–126. Gland: International Union for the Conservation of Nature and Natural Resources. Species Survival Commission.

—— (ed.) (1993). *Pigs, Peccaries and Hippos.* Gland: International Union for the Conservation of Nature and Natural Resources. Species Survival Commission.

—— & Brisbin I.L. (1993). Introduced and feral pigs: problems; policy, and priorities. In: Oliver W.L.R. (ed.), *Pigs, Peccari, and Hippos,* 179–91. Gland: International Union for the Conservation of Nature and Natural Resources. Species Survival Commission.

—————— & Takahashi S. (1993*a*). The Eurasian wild pig (*Sus scrofa*). In: Oliver W.L.R. (ed.), *Pigs, Peccari, and Hippos,* 112–21. Gland: International Union for the Conservation of Nature and Natural Resources. Species Survival Commission.

—— Groves C.P., Cor C.R. & Blouch R.A. (1993*b*). Origins of domestication and pig culture. In: Oliver W.L.R. (ed.), *Pigs, Peccari, and Hippos,* 171–79. Gland: International Union for the Conservation of Nature and Natural Resources. Species Survival Commission.

OMIM (ONLINE MENDELIAN INHERITANCE IN MAN) (n.d. *a*). *V-KIT Hardy-Zucker-man 4 feline sarcoma viral oncogene homolog; KIT*. Baltimore, MD: Johns Hopkins University. <*http://www.ncbi.nlm.nih.gov/entrez/dispomim.cgi?id=164920*>.

—— (n.d. *b*). Melanocortin 1 receptor; MC1R. Baltimore, MD: Johns Hopkins University. <*http://www.ncbi.nlm.nih.gov/entrez/dispomim.cgi?id=155555*>.

ONIDA P., GARAU F. & COSSU S. (1995). Damages caused to crops by wild boars (*S. scrofa meridionalis*) in Sardinia (Italy). *Ibex* 3, 230–5.

ONO K. & NOGARI I. (1982). Mammal and bird remains. In: *New Town in the South-east Portion of Chiba 10. Kokanza Shell Midden*, 203–17. Cultural Properties Centre of Chiba [in Japanese].

ONO M. (1984). On the problem of boar keeping during the Jomon period. In: Local History Research Association (ed.), *Kofu Bonchi: Sono Rekishi to Chiikisei*, 47–76. Tokyo: Yuzankaku [in Japanese].

ORME B. (1981). *Anthropology for Archaeologists*. London: Duckworth.

ÖSTERHOLM I. (1989). *Bosättningsmönstret på Gotland under Stenåldern* (Theses and Papers in Archaeology 4). Stockholm: Institute of Archaeology, University of Stockholm.

OTA Y., MATSUSHIMA Y. & MORIWAKI H. (1982). Notes on the Holocene sea-level study in Japan: on the basis of the 'Atlas of Holocene Sea-Level Records in Japan'. *Quaternary Research* 29(1), 31–48 [in Japanese].

ÖZGÜÇ N. (1965). *The Anatolian Group of Cylinder Seal Impressions from Kültepe*. Ankara: Türk Tarih Kurumu Basimevi.

ÖZGÜÇ T. (1998). Boar-shaped cult vessels and funeral objects at Kanis. *Altorienta-lische Forschungen* 25(2), 247–56.

PARAYRE D. (2000). Les suidés dans le monde Syro-Mésopotamien aux époques historiques. *Topoi. Orient-Occident. Supplement* 2, 141–206.

PARZINGER H. & SANZ R. (1992). *Die Oberstadt von Hattusa, hethitische Keramik aus dem Zentralen Tempelviertel*. Berlin: Gebr. Mann Verlag.

PATTERSON B. (1937). Animal remains. In: von der Osten H.H. (ed.), *The Alishar Hüyük Seasons of 1930–1932* (Oriental Institute Publications 30), 294–309. Chicago: University of Chicago Press.

PATTON M. (1996). *Islands in Time*. London: Routledge.

PAULISSEN E., POESEN J., GOVERS G. & DE PLOEY J. (1993). The physical environment at Sagalassos (Western Taurus, Turkey). A reconnaissance survey. In: Waelkens M. & Poblome J. (eds), *Sagalassos II. Report on the Third Excavation Campaign of 1992* (Acta Archaeologica Lovaniensa Monographiae 6), 229–47. Leuven: Leuven University Press.

PAUWELS W. (1980). *Study of Sus scrofa vittatus, its ecology and behavior in Ujong Kulon Nature Reserve, Java, Indonesia*. Ph.D. thesis, University of Basel.

PAVLOV P.N. (1980). *The diet and ecology of the feral pig (Sus scrofa) at Girilambone, New South Wales*. Ph.D. thesis, Monash University, Melbourne.

—— & HONE J. (1982). The behaviour of feral pigs, *Sus scrofa*, in flocks of lambing ewes. *Australian Wildlife Research* 9, 101–9.

PAYNE S. (1973). Kill-off patterns in sheep and goats: mandibles from Asvan Kale. *Anatolian Studies* 23, 281–303.

—— (1988). Animal bones from Tell Rubeidheh. In: Killick R.G. (ed.), *Tell Rubeidheh, an Uruk Village in the Jebel Hamrin* (Iraq Archaeological Reports 2), 98–135. Warminster: Aris & Phillips.

—— & BULL G. (1988). Components of variation in measurements of pig bones and teeth, and the use of measurements to distinguish wild from domestic pig remains. *ArchæoZoologia* 2, 27–65.

PEPE C. (2001). Un itinerario di ricerca e di didattica nel Laboratorio di Bioarcheologia: le faune. In: Pepe C. (ed.), *La ricerca archeologica a Vivara e le attività dei laboratori dell'Istituto Universitario Suor Orsola Benincasa*, 89–91. Napoli: Istituto Universitario Suor Orsola Benincasa.

PERLÈS C. (1979). Des navigateurs méditerranéens il y a 10,000 ans. *La Recherche* 96, 82–3.

PERSSON P. (1999). *Neolitikums Början. Undersøkningar kring Jordbrukets Introduction i Nordeuropa* (Coast to Coast book 1, GOTARC B 11). Uppsala & Gothenburg: Departments of Archaeology.

PETERS J., HELMER D., VON DEN DRIESCH A. & SEGUI S. (2000). Early animal husbandry in the Northern Levant. *Paléorient* 25(2), 27–48.

—— VON DEN DRIESCH A. & HELMER D. (2005). The upper Euphrates–Tigris basin: cradle of agro-pastoralism?. In: Vigne J.-D., Peters J. & Helmer D. (eds), *The First Steps of Animal Domestication: New Archaeozoological Approaches*, 99–124. Oxford: Oxbow Books.

PFEFFER P. (1957). Notes sur le peuplement mammalien des iles de Florès. Komodo et Rintja (petites isles de La Sonde). *Mammalia* 21(4), 405–19.

—— (1968). *Asia, A Natural History*. New York: Chanticleer Press Edition.

PIELBERG G., OLSSON C., SYVÄNEN A.-C. & ANDERSSON L. (2002). Unexpectedly high allelic diversity at the *KIT* locus causing dominant white color in the domestic pig. *Genetics* 160, 305–11.

—— DAY A.E., PLASTOW G.S. & ANDERSSON L. (2003). A sensitive method for detecting variation in copy numbers of duplicated genes. *Genome Research* 13, 2171–7.

PIETERS M. (1997). Raversijde: a late medieval fishermen's village along the Flemish coast of Belgium, province of West-Flanders, municipality of Ostend. In: De Boe G. & Verhaeghe F. (eds), *Rural Settlements in Medieval Europe. Papers of the 'Medieval Europe Brugge 1997' Conference. Volume 6* (I.A.P. Rapporten 6), 169–77. Zellik: Institute for the Archaeological Heritage of the Flemish Community.

PIRA A. (1909). Studien zur Geschichte der Schweinerassen, inbesondere derjenigen Schwedens. *Zoologischen Jahrbüchern. Supplement* 10(2), 233–426.

PLEIJ H. (2001). *Dreaming of Cockaigne. Medieval Fantasies of the Perfect Life*. New York: Columbia University Press.

PLINY (PLINIUS). *Natural History* (English translations by H. Rackham (I–V and X), W.H.S. Jones (VI–VIII) & D.E. Eichholz (X)). London: Loeb Classical Library.

POCOCK R.I. (1934). Animal remains. In: Woolley C.L. (Ed.), *Ur Excavations: Publications of the Joint Expedition of the British Museum and of the Museum of the University of Pennsylvania to Mesopotamia. Vol. 2: The Royal Cemetery: A Report on the Predynastic and Sargonid Graves Excavated Between 1926 and 1931*, 409–10. London: British Museum.

Polybius (210–125 bc) *Histoire* (French translation by D. Roussel, 1970). Brussels: Gallimard.

Poplin F. (2000). De la corne à l'ivoire. In: Béal J.-C. & Goyon J.-C. (eds), *Des ivoires et des cornes dans les mondes anciens (Orient-Occident)*, 1–10. Lyon: Université Lumière Lyon 2.

Porter V. (1993). *Pigs. A Handbook to the Breeds of the World.* Mountfield: Helm Information.

Pospisil L. (1963). *Kapauku Papuan Economy* (Yale University Publications in Anthropology 67). New Haven, CT: Yale University Press.

Postgate D.C. & Oates J. (1997). *The Excavations at Tell Rimah. The Pottery* (British School of Archaeology. Archaeological reports 4). Warminster: Aris and Phillips.

Postgate N. (1992). *Early Mesopotamia.* London: Routledge.

Poulain T. (1978). Étude de la faune, de quelques restes humains et de coquillages provenant to Ras Shamra (sondages 1955 a 1960). In: Schaeffer C.F.-A. (ed.), *Ugaritica VII*, 161–80. Paris: Mission Archéologique de Ras Shamra.

Powell J. (2003). Fishing in the Mesolithic and Neolithic—the cave of Cyclops, Youra. In: Kotiabopoulou E., Hamilakis Y., Halstead P., Gamble C. & Elefanti P. (eds), *Zooarchaeology in Greece. Recent Advances* (British School at Athens Studies 9), 75–84. London: The British School at Athens.

Prag K. (1985). Ancient and modern pastoral migration in the Levant. *Levant* 17, 81–8.

Préhistoire du Levant (1981). Paris: Éditions du CNRS.

Prestwich M. (1976). *York Civic Ordinances, 1301* (Borthwick Papers 49). York: Borthwick Institute, University of York.

Pucek Z., Jedrzejewski W., Jedrzejewska B. & Pucek M. (1993). Rodent population dynamics in a primeval deciduous forest (Bialowieza National Park) in relation to weather, seed crop, and predation. *Acta Theriologica* 38, 199–232.

Quittet E. & Zert P. (1971). *Races porcines en France* (2nd edn.). Paris: la Maison Rustique.

Qumsiyeh M.B. (1996). *Mammals of The Holy Land.* Lubbock, TX: Texas Tech University Press.

Rackham O. (1976). *Trees and Woodland in the British Landscape. The Complete History of Britain's Trees, Woods and Hedgerows.* London: J.M. Dent.

—— (1980). *Ancient Woodland: Its History, Vegetation and Uses in England.* London: Edward Arnold.

—— (1986). *The History of the Countryside. The Classic History of Britain's Landscape, Flora, and Fauna.* London: J.M. Dent.

Raichon C., de Verneuil B. & Molénat M. (1976). L'élevage du porc en Castagniccia. *Ethnozootechnie* 16, 68–74.

Randall L.M. (1957). Exempla as a source of Gothic marginal illumination. *Art Bulletin* 39, 97–107.

Randi E., Apollonio M. & Toso S. (1989). The systematics of some Italian populations of wild boar (*Sus scrofa*): a craniometric and electrophoretic analysis. *Zeitschrift für Saugertierkunde* 54, 40–56.

RAPPAPORT R. (1968). *Pigs for the Ancestors. Ritual in the Ecology of a New Guinea People.* New Haven, CT: Yale University Press.

——(1977). Ecology, adaptation and the ills of functionalism (being, among other things, a response to J. Friedman). *Michigan Discussions in Anthropology* 2, 138–90.

——(1984). Epilogue. In: Rappaport R. (ed.), *Pigs for the Ancestors: Ritual in the Ecology of a New Guinea People* (2nd enlarged edn.), 299–479. New Haven, CT: Yale University Press.

——(1999). *Ritual and Religion in the Making of Humanity.* Cambridge: Cambridge University Press.

RAULWING P. (1992). Die Haustierhaltung in Pylos/Messenien am Ende des 2. Jahrtausends v. Chr. nach den Aussagen der frühgriechischen Linear B-Tafeln. *Tier und Museum* 3, 48–61.

REAY M. (1984). A high pig culture of the New Guinea highlands. *Canberra Anthropology* 7, 71–7.

REDDING R. (1981). The faunal remains. In: Wright H.T. (ed.), *An Early Town on the Deh Luran Plain: Excavations at Tepe Farukhabad* (Memoirs of the Museum of Anthropology, University of Michigan 13), 233–61. Ann Arbor, MI: Museum of Anthropology, University of Michigan.

——(2005). Breaking the mold: A consideration of variation in the evolution of animal domestication. In: Vigne J.-D., Peters J. & Helmer D. (eds), *The First Steps of Animal Domestication: New Archaeozoological Approaches*, 41–9. Oxford: Oxbow Books.

——& ROSENBERG M. (1998). Ancestral pigs: a New (Guinea) model for pig domestication in the Middle East. *MASCA Research Papers in Science and Archaeology* 15, 65–76.

REILAND S. (1978). Growth and skeletal development of the pig. *Acta Radiologica. Supplement* 358, 15–22.

REITZ E.J. & WING E.S. (1999). *Zooarchaeology.* Cambridge: Cambridge University Press.

REMNANT G.L. (1969–99). *A Catalogue of Misericords in Great Britain.* Oxford: Clarendon Press.

RENFREW C. & ASPINALL A.A. (1990). Aegean obsidian and Franchthi Cave. In: Perlès C. (ed.), *Les Industries Lithiques Tailées de Franchthi (Argolide, Grèce). Tome 2: Les industries lithiques du Mésolithique et du Néolithique initial*, 257–70. Bloomington, IN: Indiana University Press.

RIBICHINI S. (1981). *Adonis. Aspetti orientali di un mito greco* (Studi Semitici 55 = Pubblicazioni del Centro di Studio per la Civiltà Fenicia e Punica 22). Roma: CNR, Istituto per la civiltà Fenicia e Punica 'Sabatino Moscati'.

RICHARDS A. (1982). *The pig as an experimental model for studying fluorosis.* Ph.D. thesis, Royal Dental College, Aarhus, Denmark.

——KRAGSTRUP J., JOSEPHSEN K. & FEJERSKOV O. (1986). Dental fluorosis developed in post-secretory enamel. *Journal of Dental Research* 65, 1406–9.

——LIKIMANI S., BAELUM V. & FEJERSKOV O. (1992). Fluoride concentrations in unerupted fluorotic human enamel. *Caries Research* 26, 328–32.

RICHARDS M. & HEDGES R.E.M. (1999). Stable isotope evidence for similarities in the types of marine foods used by late mesolithic humans at sites along the Atlantic coast of Europe. *Journal of Archaeological Science* 26, 717–22.

—— DOBNEY K., ALBARELLA U., FULLER B., PEARSON J., MÜLDNER G. *et al.* (2002). Stable isotope evidence of *Sus* diets from European and Near Eastern archaeological sites. In: Albarella U., Dobney K., Huntley J. & Rowley-Conwy P. (eds), *Abstract of the ICAZ Durham Conference, University of Durham*, 108. Durham: ICAZ.

RICHTER J. & NOE-NYGAARD, N. (2003). A late Mesolithic hunting station at Agernæs, Fyn, Denmark. *Acta Archaeologica* 74, 1–64.

RISNES S. (1990). Structural characteristics of staircase-type Retzius lines in human dental enamel analyzed by scanning electron microscopy. *Anatomical Record* 226, 135–46.

—— (1998). Growth tracks in dental enamel. *Journal of Human Evolution* 35, 331–50.

RIXSON D. (2000). *The History of Meat Trading*. Nottingham: Nottingham University Press.

ROBBINS L.S., NADEAU J.H., JOHNSON K.R., KELLY M.A., ROSELLI-REHFUSS L., BAACK E. *et al.* (1993). Pigmentation phenotypes of variant extension locus alleles result from point mutations that alter MSH receptor function. *Cell* 72, 827–34.

ROBERTS G. (1968). *Game Animals in New Zealand*. Wellington: AH & AW Reed.

RODENWALDT G. (1976). *Die Fresken des Palastes. Tiryns, Die Ergebnisse der Ausgrabungen des Instituts II*. Mainz: Philipp von Zabern.

ROLETT B.V. & CHIU M.-Y. (1994). Age estimation of prehistoric pigs (*Sus scrofa*) by molar eruption and attrition. *Journal of Archaeological Science* 21, 377–86.

ROSE C.J. & WILLIAMS W.T. (1983). Ingestion of earthworms, *Pontoscolex corethrurus*, by village pigs, *Sus scrofa papuensis*, in the highlands of Papua New Guinea. *Applied Animal Ethology* 11, 131–9.

ROSE J.C. & UNGAR P.S (1998). Gross dental wear and dental microwear in historical perspective. In: Alt K.W., Rösing F.W. & Teschler-Nicola M. (eds), *Dental Anthropology*, 349–86. Vienna: Springer-Verlag.

ROSEN A. (1997). Environmental change and human adaptational failure at the end of the Early Bronze Age in the southern Levant. In: Dalfes H.N., Kukla G. & Weiss H. (eds), *Third Millennium BC Climate Change and Old World Collapse*, 25–37. Berlin: Springer-Verlag.

—— (2006). *Civilizing Climate: Adapting to Climate Change in the Ancient Near East, from Foraging Societies to Empires*. Lanham, MD: Altamira Press.

ROSMAN A. & RUBEL P.G. (1989). Stalking the wild pig: hunting and horticulture in Papua New Guinea. In: Kent S. (ed.), *Farmers as Hunters—Implications of Sedentism*, 28–36. Cambridge: Cambridge University Press.

ROSSIAUD J. (1984). *Medieval Prostitution*. Oxford: Blackwell.

ROWLAND B. (1971). *Blind Beasts: Chaucer's Animal World*. Kent, OH: Kent State University Press.

ROWLEY-CONWY P. (1981). Mesolithic Danish bacon: permanent and temporary sites in the Danish Mesolithic. In: Sheridan A. & Bailey G. (eds), *Environmental Archaeology. Towards an Integration of Ecological and Social Approaches* (BAR International Series 96), 51–5. Oxford: British Archaeological Reports.

—— (1984). The laziness of the short-distance hunter: the origins of agriculture in western Denmark. *Journal of Anthropological Archaeology* 3, 300–24.

—— (1993). Season and reason: the cases for a regional interpretation of Mesolithic settlement patterns. In: Peterkin G.L., Bricker H. & Mellars P (eds), *Hunting and Animal Exploitation in the Later Palaeolithic and Mesolithic of Eurasia* (Archaeological Papers of the American Anthropological Association 4), 178–88. Chicago: American Anthropological Association.

—— (1994). Meat, furs and skins: Mesolithic animal bones from Ringkloster, a seasonal hunting camp in Jutland. *Journal of Danish Archaeology* 12, 87–98.

—— (1997). The animal bones from Arene Candide. Final report. In: Maggi R. (ed.), *Arene Candide: Functional and Environmental Assessment of the Holocene Sequence* (Memorie dell'Istituto Italiano di Paleontologia Umana. New series 5), 153–277. Rome: Ministero per i Beni Culturali e Ambientali.

—— (1998). Cemeteries, seasonality and complexity in the Ertebølle of southern Scandinavia. In: Zvelebil M., Domanska L. & Dennell R. (eds), *Harvesting the Sea, Farming the Forest. The Emergence of Neolithic Societies in the Baltic Region* (Sheffield Archaeological Monographs 10), 193–202. Sheffield: Sheffield Academic Press.

—— (1999*a*). Economic prehistory in southern Scandinavia. In: Coles J., Bewley R.M. & Mellars P. (eds), *World Prehistory. Studies in Memory of Grahame Clark* (Proceedings of the British Academy 99), 125–59. Oxford: Oxford University Press.

—— (1999*b*). East is east and west is west but pigs go on forever: domestication from the Baltic to the Sea of Japan. In: Anderson S. (ed.), *Current and Recent Research in Osteoarchaeology* (2), 35–40. Oxford: Oxbow Books.

—— (2001*a*). Time, change and the archaeology of hunter-gatherers: how original is the 'original affluent society'? In: Panter-Brick C., Layton R.H. & Rowley-Conwy P. (eds), *Hunter-Gatherers. An Interdisciplinary Perspective* (Biosocial Society Symposium Series 13), 39–72. Cambridge: Cambridge University Press.

—— (2001*b*). Determination of season of death in European wild boar *(Sus scrofa ferus)*: a preliminary study. In: Millard A.R. (ed), *Archaeological Sciences 1997. Proceedings of the Conference held at the University of Durham, 2–4 September 1997* (BAR International Series 939), 133–139. Oxford: Archaeopress.

—— (2003). Early domestic animals in Europe: imported or locally domesticated?. In: Ammerman A. & Biagi P. (eds), *The Widening Harvest. The Neolithic Transition in Europe: Looking Forward, Looking Back* (Colloquia and Conference Papers 6), 99–117. Boston: Archaeological Institute of America.

—— (2004). How the west was lost. A reconsideration of agricultural origins in Britain, Ireland and southern Scandinavia. *Current Anthropology* 45 supplement, 83–113.

—— Halstead P & Collins P. (2002). Derivation and application of a food utility index (FUI) for European wild boar *(Sus scrofa* L.). *Environmental Archaeology. The Journal of Human Palaeoecology* 7, 77–87.

—— & Storå J. (1997). Pitted Ware seals and pigs from Ajvide, Gotland: methods of study and first results. In: Burenhult G. (ed.), *Remote Sensing, Vol 1. Applied Techniques for the Study of Cultural Resources and the Localization, Identifcation and Documentation of Subsurface Prehistoric Remains in Swedish Archaeology* (Theses and Papers in North European Archaeology 13a), 113–127. Stockholm: Institute of Archaeology, University of Stockholm.

RUBEL P.G. & ROSMAN A. (1978). *Your Own Pigs You May not Eat: A Comparative Study of New Guinea Societies.* Canberra: Australian National University Press.

RUTKOWSJI B. (1986). *The Cult Places of the Aegean.* New Haven, CT: Yale University Press.

RYAN D. (1961). *Gift exchange in the Mendi valley.* Ph.D. thesis, Sydney University.

RYBA M. (1983). *Pig Art.* New York: Quill.

SAKELLARAKIS Y. & SAPOUNA-SAKELLARAKIS E. (1997). *Archanes, Minoan Crete in A New Light II.* Athens: Ammos Publications, Aleni Nakou Foundation.

SALISBURY J.E. (1994). *The Beast Within: Animals in the Middle Ages.* New York: Routledge.

—— (1996). *Human Animals of Medieval Fables.* In: Flores N.C. (ed.), *Animals in the Middle Ages.* London: Routledge.

SAMPSON A. (1996*a*). Excavations at the Cave of Cyclops on Youra, Alonnessos. In: Alram-Stern E. (ed.), *Die Ägäische Frühzeit. 2. Serie. 1. Band, das Neolithikum in Griechenland mit Ausnahme von Kreta and Zypern,* 507–17. Wien: Verlag der Österreichen Akademie der Wissenschaften.

—— (1996*b*). The Cyclops cave at Youra Alonnissos. In: Papathanassopoulos G.A. (ed.), *Neolithic Culture in Greece,* 58–9. Athens: N.P. Goulandris Foundation.

—— (1998). The Neolithic and Mesolithic occupation of the cave of Cyclops, Youra, Alonnessos, Greece. *The Annual of the British School at Athens* 93, 1–22.

SARAUW G. (1904). En stenalders Boplads i Maglemose ved Mullerup. *Aarbøger for Nordisk Oldkyndighed og Historie* 1903, 148–315.

SARNAT H. & MOSS S.J. (1985). Diagnosis of enamel defects. *NewYork State Dental Journal* 51(2), 103–6.

SASAKI T., TAKAGI M. & YANAGISAWA T. (1997). Structure and function of secretory ameloblasts in enamel formation. In: Chadwick D. & Cardew G. (eds), *Dental Enamel* (Ciba Foundation Symposium 205), 32–50. Chichester: Wiley.

SAUER C.O. (1952). *Agricultural Origins and Dispersals.* Washington, DC: American Geographical Society.

SAVOLAINEN P., ZHANG Y.P., LUO J., LUNDEBERG J. & LEITNER T. (2002). Genetic evidence for an East Asian origin of domestic dogs. *Science* 298(5598), 1610–13.

SCHAEFFER C.F.A. (1939). Une hache d'arme mitannienne de Ras Shamra. *Ugaritica* I, 107–25.

—— (1949). Corpus céramique de Ras Shamra, 1ère partie. *Ugaritica* II, 131–300.

SCHÄFFER J. & BOESSNECK J. (1988). Bericht über die Tierreste aus der halafzeitlichen Çavi Tarlasi (Nisibin/Osttürkei). *Istanbuler Mitteilungen* 38, 37–62.

SCHELLER R.W. (1995). *Exemplum. Model-Book Drawings and the Practice of Artistic Transmission in the Middle Ages (ca. 900-ca. 1470).* Amsterdam: Amsterdam University Press.

SCHICK K.D. & TOTH N. (1993). *Making Silent Stones Speak: Human Evolution and the Dawn of Technology.* New-York: Simon and Schuster.

SCHIFFER M. (1976). *Behavioural Archaeology.* New York: Academic Press.

SCHILLING H. (1999). *Maglemosekulturens Bosættelse i Holmegårds Mose.* Ph.D. thesis, University of Copenhagen.

SCHMIDT C.W. (2001). Dental microwear evidence for a dietary shift from two non-maize reliant prehistoric populations from Indiana. *American Journal of Physical Anthropology* 114, 139–45.

SCHMIDT K., VON DEN DRIESCH A., PETERS J. & HELMER D. (1999). Frühe Tier-und menschenbilder vom Göbekli Tepe—Kampagnen 1995–98. Ein kommentierter Katalog der Grossplastik und der Reliefs. *Istanbuler Mitteilungen* 49, 5–21.

SCHNAPP A. (1979). Images et programmes. Les figurations archaïques de la chasse et du banquet. *Revue Archéologique* 2, 195–218.

SCHOENINGER M. & DENIRO M. (1984). Nitrogen and carbon isotopic composition of bone collagen from marine and terrestrial animals. *Geochimica et Cosmochimica Acta* 48, 625–39.

SCHOUR I. & MASSLER M. (1940). Studies in tooth development: the growth pattern of human teeth. II. *Journal of American Dentist Association* 27, 1918–31.

SCHROEDER H.E. (1991). *Pathobiologie oraler Strukturen* (2nd edn.). Basel: Karger.

—— (1992). *Orale Strukturbiologie* (4th edn.). Stuttgart: Thieme.

SCHUMACHER G. (1888). *The Jaulan.* London: Richard Bentley.

SCHWARCZ H. & SCHOENINGER M. (1991). Stable isotope analyses in human nutritional ecology. *Yearbook of Physical Anthropology* 34, 283–321.

—— DUPRAS T.L. & FAIRGRIEVE S.I. (1999). ^{15}N enrichment in the Sahara: in search of a global relationship. *Journal of Archaeological Science* 26, 629–36.

SEALY J. (2001). Body tissue chemistry and palaeodiet. In: Brothwell D.R. & Pollard A.M. (eds), *Handbook of Archaeological Sciences*, 269–79. Chichester: Wiley.

SERODIO H.H. (1985). *Alguns estudos da biologia do jabali (Sus scrofa L., 1758), em Portugal.* Lisboa: Relatorio de Estagio. Universidade Classica de Lisboa, Facultade de Ciencias.

SHACHAR I. (1974). *The Judensau: A Medieval Anti-Jewish Motif and Its History.* London: Warburg Institute.

SHANTZIS S.B. & BEHRENS W.W. (1973). Population control mechanisms in a primitive agricultural society. In: Meadows D.L. & Meadows D.H. (eds), *Towards Global Equilibrium*, 257–88. Cambridge, MA: Wright-Allen Press.

SHELDON S.E. (1977). The eagle: bird of magic and medicine in a Middle English translation of Kyranides. *Tulane Studies in English* 22, 1–20.

SHIGEHARA N., HONGO H. & AMITANI K. (1991). Mammal fauna remains from the Torihama Shell Midden in the research of 1985. *Bulletin of the National Museum of Japanese History* 29, 329–42 [in Japanese].

SHOTT M. & SILLITOE P. (2001). The mortality of things: correlates of use life in Wola material culture using age-at-census data. *Journal of Archaeological Method & Theory* 8(3), 269–302.

—— —— (2004). Modeling use-life distributions in archaeology using New Guinea Wola ethnographic data. *American Antiquity* 69(2), 339–55.

SHUPE J.L., PETERSON H.B. & LEONE N.C. (eds) (1983). *Fluorides—Effects on Vegetation, Animals and Humans.* Salt Lake City, UT: Paragon Press.

SILCOX M. & TEAFORD M.F. (2002). The diet of worms: an analysis of mole dental microwear and its relevance to dietary inference in fossil mammals. *Journal of Mammology* 83, 804–14.

SILLAR F.C. & MEYLER R.M. (1961). *The Symbolic Pig: An Anthology of Pigs in Literature and Art.* Edinburgh: Oliver & Boyd.

SILLITOE P. (1979). *Give and Take: Exchange in Wola Society.* Canberra: Australian National University Press.

—— (1988). *Made in Niugini: Technology in the Highlands of Papua New Guinea.* London: British Museum Publications.

—— (1996). *A Place Against Time: Land and Environment in the Papua New Guinea Highlands.* Amsterdam: Harwood Academic.

—— (1998). *An Introduction to the Anthropology of Melanesia: Culture and Tradition.* Cambridge: Cambridge University Press.

—— (1999). Beating the boundaries: land tenure and identity in the Papua New Guinea Highlands. *Journal of Anthropological Research* 55(3), 331–60.

—— (2003). *Managing Animals in New Guinea. Preying the Game in the Highlands.* London: Routledge.

—— & HARDY K. (2003). Living lithics: ethnoarchaeology in Highland Papua New Guinea. *Antiquity* 77(297), 555–66.

SILVER I.A. (1969). The ageing of domestic animals. In: Brothwell E. & Higgs E. (eds), *Science in Archaeology*, 283–302. London: Thames & Hudson.

SILZER P.J. & CLOUSE H.H. (QUOTED BY BOISSIÈRE 1999) (1991). Index of Irian Jaya language (*Irian: Bulletin of Irian Jaya*). Jayapura.

SIMMONS A.H. (1988). Extinct pygmy hippopotamus and early man in Cyprus. *Nature* 333, 554–7.

—— (1991). Humans, island colonization and Pleistocene extinctions in the Mediterranean: the view from Akrotiri *Aetokremnos*, Cyprus. *Antiquity* 249, 857–69.

SIMOONS F.J. (1961). *Eat Not This Flesh. Food Avoidances from Prehistory to the Present.* Madison, WI: University of Wisconsin Press.

—— (1994). *Eat Not This Flesh* (2nd edn.). Wisconsin, MI: University of Wisconsin Press.

SIMPSON G.G. (1945). The principles of classification and a classification of mammals. *Bulletin of the American Museum of Natural History* 85, 1–350.

SINGER I. (1983). *The Hittite KI.LAM festival, T. 1.* Wiesbaden: Harrassowitz.

—— (1984). *The Hittite KI.LAM festival, T. 2.* Wiesbaden: Harrassowitz.

SKINNER M. & GOODMAN A.H. (1992). Anthropological uses of developmental defects of enamel. In: Saunders S.R. & Katzenberg M.A. (eds), *Skeletal Biology of Past Peoples: Research Methods*, 153–74. New York: Wiley-Liss.

SMITH C. (2000). A grumphie in the sty: an archaeological view of pigs in Scotland, from the earliest domestication to the agricultural revolution. *Proceedings of the Society of Antiquaries of Scotland* 130, 705–24.

SMITH C.E. (1998). Cellular and chemical events during enamel maturation. *Critical Reviews in Oral Biology & Medicine* 9, 128–61.

——Nanci A. & Denbesten P.K. (1993). Effects of chronic fluoride exposure on morphometric parameters defining the stages of amelogenesis and ameloblast modulation in rat incisors. *Anatomical Record* 237, 243–58.

Sokal, R. & Rohlf F.J. (1995). *Biometry.* New York: W. H. Freeman.

Solounias N. & Hayek L.A.C. (1993). New methods of tooth microwear analysis and application to dietary determination of two extinct ungulates. *Journal of Zoology* 229, 421–45.

——Scott McGraw W., Hayek L. & Wedelin L. (2000). The paleodiet of the giraffid. In: Vbra E.S. & Schaller G.B. (eds), *Antelopes, Deer and Relatives*, 84–95. New Haven, CT: Yale University Press.

Sørensen S.A. (1996). *Kongemosekulturen i Sydskandinavien.* Jægerspris: Egnsmuseet Færgegården.

South M. (ed.) (1981). *Topsell's Histories of Beasts.* Chicago: Nelson-Hall.

Spitz F. (1986). Current state of knowledge of wild boar biology. *Pig News & Information*, 7(2), 171–5.

Stahl U. (1989). *Tierknochenfunde vom Hassek Höyük (Südostanatolien).* Inaugural-Dissertation, Ludwig-Maximilians Universität, Munich.

Stampfli H.R. (1983). The fauna of Jarmo with notes on the animal bones from Matarrah, the 'Amuq and Karim Shahir. In: Braidwood L.S., Braidwood R.J., Howe B., Reed C.A. & Watson P.J. (eds), *Prehistoric Archaeology along the Zagros Flanks* (Oriental Institute Publications 105), 431–83. Chicago: Oriental Institute, University of Chicago.

Stanley H.F., Kadwell M. & Wheeler J. C. (1994). Molecular evolution of the family Camelidae—a mitochondrial DNA study. *Proceedings of the Royal Society of London Series B. Biological Sciences* 256(1345), 1–6.

Stenberger M. (1962). *Sweden* (Ancient Peoples and Places 30). London: Thames & Hudson.

Stolba A. & Wood-Gush D (1989). The behaviour of pigs in a semi-natural environment. *Animal Production* 48, 419–25.

Strait S. (1993). Molar microwear in extant small-bodies faunivorous mammals: an analysis of feature density and pit frequency. *American Journal of Physical Anthropology* 92, 63–79.

Strinnholm A. (2001). *Bland Säljägare och Fårfarmere. Struktur och Forändring i Västsveriges Mellanneolitikum* (Coast to Coast book 4). Uppsala: Uppsala University, Department of Archaeology and Ancient History.

Sugaya M. & Toizumi T. (1998). An extensive Jomon cemetery with the human, a dog and pigs, Shimo-ota shell mound, Mobara City, Chiba Pre. *Zoo-archaeology* 11, 69–74 [in Japanese with English summary].

Sultana S., Mannen H. & Tsuji S. (2003). Mitochondrial DNA diversity of Pakistani goats. *Animal Genetics* 34(6), 417–21.

Swine Genome Sequencing Consortium (n.d.) <*http://www.piggenome.org/*>

Tack G. & Hermy M. (1998). Historical ecology of woodlands in Flanders. In: Kirkby K.J. & Watkins C. (eds), *The Ecological History of European Forests*, 283–92. Wallingford: CAB International.

TACK G. & HERMY M. VAN DEN BREMT P. & HERMY M. (1993). *Bossen van Vlaanderen. Een historische ecologie.* Leuven: Davidsfonds.

TAGLIACOZZO A. (1993). Archeozoologia della Grotta dell'Uzzo, Sicilia. Ministreo per i Beni culturali e ambientali, Soprintendenza Speciale al Museo Nazionale Preistorico Etnografico 'Luigi Pigorini'. *Bullettino di Paletnologia Italiana* 84, 1–278.

TAUBER H. (1989). Danske arkæologiske C-14 dateringer. *Arkaeologiske Udgravninger i Danmark* 1988–1989, 210–28.

TCHERNOV E. (1988). The paleobiological history of the southern Levant. In: Yom-Tov Y & Tchernov E. (eds), *The Zoogeography of Israel*, 159–250. Dordrecht: Dr. W. Junk.

TEAFORD M.F. (1994). Dental microwear and dental function. *Evolutionary Anthropology* 17, 17–30.

TEAFORD M.F., LARSEN C.S., PASTOR R. & NOBLE V. (2001). Pits and scratches. Microscopic evidence of tooth use and masticatory behavior in La Florida. In: Larsen C.S. (ed.), *Bioarchaeology of La Florida: Human Biology in the Northern Frontier New Spain*, 82–112. Gainesville, FL: University Press of Florida.

—— & LYTLE J.D. (1996). Diet-induced changes in the rates of human tooth microwear: a case study involving stone-ground maize. *American Journal of Physical Anthropology* 100, 143–7.

—— & OYEN O.J. (1989). Differences in the rate of molar wear between monkeys raised on different diets. *Journal of Dental Research* 68, 1513–18.

—— & WALKER A. (1984). Quantitative differences in dental microwear between primate species with different diets and a comment on the presumed diet of *Sivapithecus. American Journal of Physical Anthropology* 64, 191–200.

TEN CATE C.L. (1972). *Wan god mast gift ... Bilder aus der Geschichte der Schweinezucht im Walde.* Wageningen: Centre for Agricultural Publishing and Documentation.

TEXIER C., LUQUET M., BOUBY A., MOLENAT M., HOERTER J. & SALLIOT G. (1984). Inventaire des quatre dernières races locales porcines continentales. *Journées Recherche Porcine en France* 16, 495–506.

THAM M. (2001). *Vildsvin—beteende och jakt.* Stockholm: Bilda Förlag.

THENIUS E. (1979). *Die Evolution der Säugetiere.* Stuttgart: Gustav Fischer Verlag.

THIEBAUX M. (1968–9). The mouth of the boar as a symbol in medieval literature. *Romance Philology* 22, 281–99.

THOMPSON R.C. & MALLOWAN M.E.L. (1933). The British Museum excavations at Nineveh. *Liverpool Annals of Archaeology* 20, 71–186.

THOMPSON R.L. (1977). Feral hogs on national wildlife refuges. In: Wood G.W. (ed.), *Research and Management of Wild Hog Populations*, 11–15. Georgetown, SC: The Belle W. Baruch Forest Science Institute of Clemson University.

TICEHURST N.F. (1923). Some British birds in the fourteenth century. *British Birds* 17, 29–35.

TIESZEN L.L. (1991). Natural variations in the carbon isotope values of plants: implications for archaeology, ecology, and palaeoecology. *Journal of Archaeological Science* 18, 227–48.

TOHOKU HISTORY MUSEUM (1986). *Satohama Shell Midden IV* (Tohoku History Museum 15). Tohoku.

—— (1987). *Satohama Shell Midden X* (Tohoku History Museum 43). Tohoku.

Toizumi T., Anezaki T., Eda M. & Uzawa K. (2003). Faunal analysis of the Haneo shell midden. In: *Site Report of Haneo Shell Midden*, 298–352. Kanagawa: Tamagawa Cultural Research Institute [in Japanese].

Toschi A. (ed.) (1965). *Fauna d'Italia. Mammalia. Lagomorpha, Rodentia, Carnivora, Ungulata, Cetacea.* Bologna: Edizioni Calderini.

Trantalidou K. (2003). Faunal remains from the earliest strata of the Cave of Cyclope. Youra. In: Galanidou N. & Perlès C. (eds), *The Greek Mesolithic: problems and perspectives* (British School at Athens Studies 10), 143–72. London: The British School at Athens.

Tristram H.B. (1865). *The Land of Israel.* London: Society for Promoting Christian Knowledge.

—— (1866). Report on the mammals of Palestine. *Proceedings of the Zoological Society of London* 36, 84–93.

Trow-Smith R.A. (1957). *History of British Livestock Husbandry to 1700.* London: Routledge & Kegan Paul.

Troy C.S., MacHugh D.E., Bailey J.F., Magee D.A., Loftus R.T., Cunningham P. et al. (2001). Genetic evidence for Near-Eastern origins of European cattle. *Nature* 410(6832), 1088–91.

Tzedakis Y. & Martlew H. (eds) (1999). *Minoans and Myceneans. Flavours of Their Time.* Athens: Greek Ministry of Culture–National Archaeological Museum.

Ubelaker D.H. (1989). The estimation of age at death from immature human bone. In: Iscan M.Y. (ed.), *Age Markers in the Human Skeleton*, 55–70. Springfield, IL: Charles C. Thomas.

Uerpmann H.-P. (1979). *Probleme der Neolithisierung des Mittelmeerraums.* (Tübinger Atlas des vodern Orients, Reihe B 28). Wiesbaden: Dr. Ludwig Reichert.

—— (1986). Halafian equid remains from Shams ed-Din Tannira in northern Syria. In: Meadow R.H. & Uerpmann H.-P. (eds), *Equids in the Ancient World* (Beihefte zum Tübinger Atlas des Vorderen Orients. Reihe A (Naturwissenschaften) 19(1)), 246–65. Wiesbaden: Dr. Ludwig Reichert.

Umemoto K. & Moriwaki T. (1983). Identification of Leguminosae from a Jomon site: mung beans excavated from the Torihama shell midden. In: Board of Education of Fukui Prefecture (ed.), *The Torihama Shell Midden: Preliminary Report of the 1983 Fiscal Year Excavation and Results of Analyses: The Excavation of an Early Jomon Wet Site, Vol. 4,* 42–26 [in Japanese].

Ungar P.S. (1995). *Microwear Image Analysis Software.* Version 2.2.

—— & Teaford M.F. (1996). Preliminary examination of non-occlusal dental microwear in anthropoids: implications for the study of fossil primates. *American Journal of Physical Anthropology* 100, 101–13.

Van Andel T.J. (1987). The landscape. Part I. In: Van Andel T.J. & Sutton S.B. (eds), *Landscape and People of the Franchthi Region. Excavations at Franchthi Cave, Greece. Fasc. 2,* 3–62. Bloomington, IN: Indiana University Press.

Van der Plaetsen P. (1991). Die Tierknochen aus dem *castrum* von Ename. In: Böhme H.W. (ed.), *Burgen der Salierzeit. Teil 1. In den nördlichen Landschaften des Reiches*

(Römisch-Germanisches Zentralmuseum Monographien 25), 309. Sigmaringen: Jan Thorbecke Verlag.

VAN DOORSLAER H. (1985). *Archeozoölogie van de Warandemotte te Veurne.* Master's thesis, University of Gent, Belgium.

VAN KLINKEN G.J., RICHARDS M. & HEDGES R.E.M. (2000). An overview of causes for stable isotopic variations in past European human populations: environmental, ecophysiological, and cultural effects. In: Ambrose S.H. & Katzenberg M.A. (eds), *Biogeochemical Approaches to Palaeodietary Analysis*, 39–63. New York: Kluwer Academic & Plenum Publishers.

VAN LAERE A.S., NGUYEN M., BRAUNSCHWEIG M., NEZER C., COLLETTE C., MOREAU L. *et al.* (2003). Positional identification of a regulatory mutation in IGF2 causing a major QTL effect on muscle growth in the pig. *Nature* 425, 832–6.

VAN LAWICK-GOODALL H. &. J. (1970). *Innocent Killers.* London: Collins.

VAN ZEIST W. & BOTTEMA S. (1982). Vegetational history of the eastern Mediterranean and the Near East during the last 20,000 years. In: Bintliff J.L. & Van Zeist W. (eds), *Palaeoclimates, Palaeoenvironments and Human Communities in the Eastern Mediterranean in Later Prehistory* (BAR International Series 133), 277–321. Oxford: British Archaeological Reports.

VAYDA A.P. (1972). Pigs. In: *Encyclopaedia of Papua and New Guinea*, 905–8. Melbourne: Melbourne University Press.

—— LEEDS A. & SMITH D.B. (1961). The place of pigs in Melanesian subsistence. In: *Proceedings of the 1961 Annual Spring Meeting of the American Ethnological Society*, 69–77. Seattle, WA: University of Washington Press.

—— & MCCAY B.J. (1977). Problems in the identification of environmental problems. In: Bayliss-Smith T.P. & Feacham R.G. (eds), *Subsistence and Survival: Rural Ecology in the Pacific*, 411–18. London: Academic Press.

VENERO J.L. (1980). Alimentacion invernal del jabali (*Sus scrofa baeticus* Thomas) en el Parque nacional de Doñana (España). In: *Actas II Reunion Iberoamericana de Conservacion y Zoologia de Vertebrados. Caceres, 1982*, 35–8.

VERHULST A. (1990). *Précis d'histoire rurale de la Belgique.* Brussels: Vrije Universiteit Brussel.

—— (1995). *Landschap en landbouw in middeleeuws Vlaanderen.* Brussels: Gemeentekrediet.

VERMOERE M., SMETS E., WAELKENS M., VANHAVERBEKE H. & VANHECKE L. (2000). Late Holocene environmental change and the record of human impact at Gravgaz near Sagalassos, southwest Turkey. *Journal of Archaeological Science* 27, 571–95.

VIGNE J.-D. (1988). *Les Mammifères post-glaciaires de Corse* (Étude archéozoologique. Supplément à Gallia-Préhistoire 26). Paris: Éditions du CNRS.

—— (1998). Faciès culturels et sous-système technique de l'acquisition des ressources animales. Application au Néolithique ancien méditerranéen. In: d'Anna A. & Binder D. (eds), *Production et identité culturelle* (Actes du colloque d'Antibes, novembre 1996), 27–45. Antibes: Éditions APDCA.

—— (1999). The large 'true' Mediterranean islands as a model for the Holocene human impact on the European vertebrate fauna? Recent data and new reflections. In: Benecke N. (ed.), *The Holocene History of the European Vertebrate Fauna. Modern Aspects of Research* (Archäologie in Eurasien 6), 295–322. Berlin: Deutsches Archäologisches Institut, Eurasien-abteilung.

—— (2002). Instabilité des premières élevages néolithiques: l'apport de la documentation insulaire méditerranéenne. In: *Manières de faire … manières de voir. De l'objet à l'interprétation* (*IXe rencontres culturelles interdisciplinaires du Musée de l'Alta Rocca à Levie, 21–22 juillet 2001*), 77–84. Ajaccio: Alain Piazzola éd.

—— (2003). Unstable status of early domestic ungulates in the Near East: The example of Shillourokambos (Cyprus, IX–VIIIth Millennia Cal. B.C.). In: Guilaine J. & Le Brun A. (eds), Le Néolithique de Chypre. *Bulletin de Correspondance Hellénique. Supplément* 43, 239–51.

—— Bridault A., Horard-Herbin M.-P., Pellé E., Fiquet P & Mashkour M. (2000*a*). Wild boar—age at death estimates: the relevance of new modern data for archaeological skeletal material. 2. Shaft growth in length and breadth. Archaeological application. *Ibex. Journal of Mountain Ecology* 5, 19–27.

—— & Buitenhuis H. (with collaboration of Davis S.) (1999). Les premiers pas de la domestication animale à l'Ouest de l'Euphrate: Chypre et l'Anatolie centrale. *Paléorient* 25(2), 49–62.

—— Carrère I., Saliège J.-F., Person A., Bocherens H., Guilaine J. & Briois F. (2000*b*). Predomestic cattle, sheep, goat and pig during the late 9th and the 8th millenniun cal. bc on Cyprus: preliminary results of Shillourokambos (Perkklisha, Limassol). In: Mashkour M., Choyke A.M., Buitenhuis H. & Poplin F. (eds), *Archaeozoology of the Near East IV* (ARC-Publicaties 32), 52–75. Groningen: Centre for Archaeological Research & Consultancy.

—— & Desse-Berset N. (1995). The exploitation of animal resources in the Mediterranean Islands during the Pre-Neolithic: the example of Corsica. In: Fischer A. (ed.), *Man and Sea in the Mesolithic*, 309–18. Oxford: Oxbow Books.

—— & Marinval-Vigne M.-C. (1992). A propos de la mise à mort sans effusion de sang: l'abattage du porc en Corse du sud. *AnthropoZoologica* 14–15, 73–5.

Vila E. (1995). Analyse de la faune des secteurs nord et sud du Steinbau I (Tel Chuera, Syrie, Troisième millénaire av. J.-C.. In: Orthmann, W. (ed), *Ausgrabungen in Tell Chuera in Nordost Syrien I. Vorbericht über die Grabungskampagnen 1986 bis 1992*, 267–79. Saarbrücken: Saarbrücker Druckerei.

—— (1997). Comparaison des vestiges osseux animaux du gisement ossifère et des habitats à Khirbet-el-Umbashi (Syrie): différences et similitudes. *AnthropoZoologica* 25–26, 777–83.

—— (1998*a*). *L'exploitation des animaux aux IVe et IIIe millénaires avant J.-C.* (Monograph du CRA 21) Paris: Éditions du CNRS.

—— (1998*b*). Interpreting the faunal remains of El Kowm 2—Caracol (IVth Millennium BC, Syria). In: Buitenhuis H., Bartosiewicz L. & Choyke A. M. (eds), *Archaeozoology of the Near East III* (ARC-Publicaties 18), 120–9. Groningen: Centre for Archaeological Research & Consultancy.

VILA E. (2005). Analyse archéozoologique de la faune de Tell Shiuk Fawqani. In Bachelot E. & Falese M. (eds), *Tell Shiuk Fawqani 1966–1998*. History of the Ancient Near East Monographs VI, vol. 2, 1080–1108. Padua.

—— (in press *a*). *Une occupation villageoise sur le Khabour: analyse de la faune de Mulla Mutar.*

—— (in press *b*). *Étude de la faune de Kutan.*

—— (in press *c*). L'économie alimentaire carnée et le 'monde animal' à Ras Shamra: analyse préliminaire des restes osseux de mammifères. In: Calvet Y. & Yon M. (eds), *Actes de la table ronde Ras Shamra—Ougarit.* Lyon: Travaux de la Maison de l'Orient.

VILA E. & DALIX A.-S. (2004). Alimentation et idéologie: la place du sanglier et du porc à l'Age du Bronze sur la côte levantine. *AnthropoZoologica* 39(1), 219–36.

VOGEL R. (1952). Reste von Jagd-und Haustieren. In: Bittel K. & Naumann R. (eds), *Bogazköy-Hattusa I*, 128–53. Stuttgart: W. Kohlhammer Verlag.

VOGLER U. (1997). *Faunenhistorische Untersuchungen am Sirkeli Höyük/Adana, Türkei (4.1. Jahrtausend v. Chr.)*, Inaugural Dissertation, Institüt für Palaeoanatomie, Domestikationsforschung und Geschichte der Tiermedizin, Munich.

VON DEN DRIESCH A. (1976). *A Guide to the Measurement of Animal Bones from Archaeological Sites* (Peabody Museum Bulletin 1). Cambridge, MA: Peabody Museum of Archaeology and Ethnology.

—— (1993). Faunal remains from Habuba Kabira in Syria. In: Buitenhuis H. & Clason A.T. (eds), *Archaeozoology of the Near East*, 52–9. Leiden: Universal Book Services.

—— & WODTKE U. (1997). The fauna of 'Ain Ghazal, a major PPN and early PN settlement in central Jordan. In: Gebel H.G.K., Kafafi Z. & Rollefson G.O. (eds), *The Prehistory of Jordan II* (Studies in early Near Eastern Production, Subsistence and Environment 4), 511–56. Berlin: Ex Oriente.

VON WETTSTEIN O. (1942). Die Säugerwelt der Ägäis, nebst einer Revision des Rassenkreises von *Erinaceus europaeus. Annales Naturhistorisches Museum Wien* 52, 245–78.

WADDELL E. (1972). *The mound builders: agricultural practices, environment, and society in the Central Highlands of New Guinea* (American Ethnological Society Monograph 53). Seattle, WA: University of Washington Press.

WADDELL P.J., OKADA N. & HASEGAWA M. (1999). Towards resolving the interordinal relationships of placental mammals. *Systematic Biology* 48, 1–5.

WAELKENS M. (1993). Sagalassos. History and archaeology. In: Waelkens M. (ed.), *Sagalassos I. First General Report on the Survey (1986–1989) and Excavations (1990–1991)* (Acta Archaeologica Lovaniensia Monographiae 5), 37–81. Leuven: Leuven University Press.

WAGENKNECHT E. (1967). *Die Altersbestimmung des erlegten Wildes*. Berlin: VEB Deutscher Landwirtschart Verlag.

WAGNER R. (1977). Scientific and indigenous Papuan conceptualisations of the innate: a semiotic critique of the ecological perspective. In: Bayliss-Smith T.P. & Feacham R.G. (eds), *Subsistence and Survival: Rural Ecology in the Pacific*, 385–410. London: Academic Press.

WALLACE A.R. (1869). *The Malay Archipelago: The Land of Orang-utan, and the Bird of Paradise. A Narrative of Travel, with Studies of Man and Nature.* New York: Harper & Brothers.

WAPNISH P. & HESSE B. (1991). Faunal remains from Tel Dan: perspectives on animal production at a village, urban and ritual center. *ArchæoZoologia* 4(2), 9–86.

WARD J. & MAINLAND I.L. (1999). Microwear in modern rooting and stall-fed pigs: the potential of dental microwear analysis for exploring pig diet and management in the past. *Environmental Archaeology* 4, 25–32.

WARMAN S.M. (2005). Two novel methods for the study of dental morphological variation in *Sus scrofa*, in order to identify seperate breeding groups within archaeological assemblages. In Vigne J.-D., Helmer D. & Peters J. (eds), *The First Steps of Animal Domestication*, 61–78. Oxford: Oxbow Books.

WARSHAWSKY H. (1988). The teeth. In: Weiss L. (ed.), *Cell and Tissue Biology* (6th ed.), 597–640. Baltimore: Urban & Schwarzenberg.

—— JOSEPHSEN K., THYLSTRUP A. & FEJERSKOV O. (1981). The development of enamel structure in rat incisors as compared to the teeth of monkey and man. *Anatomical Record* 200, 371–99.

WATANOBE T., HAYASHI Y., OGASAWARA N. & TOMOITO T. (1985). Polymorphism of mitochondrial DNA in pigs based on restriction endonuclease cleavage patterns. *Biochemical Genetics* 23, 105–13.

—— ISHIGURO N., NAKANO M., MATSUI A., HONGO H., YAMAZAKI K. & TAKAHASHI O. (2004). Prehistoric Sado island populations of *Sus scrofa* distinguished from contemporary Japanese wild boar by ancient mitochondrial DNA. *Zoological Science* 21, 219–28.

—— —— —— TAKAMIYA H., MATSUI A. & HONGO H. (2002). Prehistoric introduction of domestic pigs onto the Okinawa Islands: ancient mitochondrial DNA evidence. *Journal of Molecular Evolution* 55, 222–31.

—— ISHIGURO N., OKAMURA N., NAKANO M., MATSUI A., HONGO H. & USHIRO H. (2001). Ancient mitochondrial DNA reveals the origin of *Sus scrofa* from Rebun Island, Japan. *Journal of Molecular Evolution* 52, 281–9.

—— —— KIMURA J., YASUDA Y., SAITOU N., TOMITA T. & OGASAWARA N. (1986). Pig mitochondrial DNA: polymorphism, restriction map orientation, and sequence data. *Biochemical Genetics* 24, 385–96.

WATSON J.P.N. (1980). The vertebrate fauna from Arpachiyah. *Iraq* 42, 152–3.

WATSON, L. (2005). *The Whole Hog. Exploring the Extraordinary Potential of Pigs.* London: Profile Books.

WATT I.R., McKILLOP R.F., PENSON P.J. & ROBINSON N.A. (1977). *Pigs* (Rural Development Series Handbook 5). Port Moresby: Department of Primary Industry.

WATTENMAKER P. & STEIN G. (1984). An archaeological study of pastoral production in the Karababa Basin of the Turkish Lower Euphrates Valley. Unpublished paper read at ASOR Annual Meeting, Chicago, 1984.

—— —— (1986). Early pastoral production in southeast Anatolia: faunal remains from Kurban Höyuk and Gritille Höyük. *Anatolica* 13, 90–6.

WATTIEZ R. (1984). *Archeozoölogie van een vroegmiddeleeuws site te Wellin (provincie Luxemburg)*. Master's thesis, University of Gent, Belgium.

WEBER J.A. (1997). Faunal remains from Tell es-Sweyhat and Tell Hajji Ibrahim. *MASCA Research Papers in Science and Archaeology* 14, 133–67.

—— (2001). A preliminary assessment of Akkadian and post-Akkadian animal exploitation at Tell Brak. In: Oates D., Oates J. & McDonald H. (eds), *Excavations at Tell Brak. Vol. 2: Nagar in the Third Millennium*, 345–50. London: British School of Archaeology in Iraq.

WEBLEY D. (1969). A note on the pedology of Teleilat Ghassoul. *Levant* 1, 22–3.

WEISS H. (1997). Evidence for Mid-Holocene environmental change in the western Kharbur drainage, northeastern Syria. In: Dalfes H.N., Kukla G. & Weiss H. (eds), *Third Millennium BC Climate Change and Old World Collapse*, 711–23. Berlin: Springer-Verlag.

WEISS H. COURTY H.-A., WETTERSTROM W., SENIOR L., MEADOW R., GUICHARD F. & CURNOW A. (1993). The genesis and collapse of third millennium north Mesopotamian civilization. *Science* 261, 995–1004.

WESTERBY E. (1927). *Stenalderbopladser ved Klampenborg. Nogle Bidrag til Studiet af den Mesolitiske Periode*. Copenhagen: C.A. Reitzel.

WHEELER PIRES-FERREIRA J. (1997). Tepe Tulai: faunal remains from an early campsite in Khuzistan, Iran. Paléorient 3, 275–80.

WHITCHER S.E., GRIGSON C. & LEVY T.E. (1998). Recent faunal analysis at Shiqmim, Israel: a preliminary analysis of the 1993 assemblage. In: Buitenhuis H., Bartosiewicz L. & Choyke A. M. (eds), *Archaeozoology of the Near East III* (ARC-Publicaties 18), 102–14. Groningen: Centre for Archaeological Research & Consultancy.

WHITE K.D. (1970). *Roman Farming*. London: Thames & Hudson.

WHITE T.H. (1984). *The Book of Beasts*. New York: Dover.

WHITFORD G.M. (1997). Determinants and mechanisms of enamel fluorosis. In: Chadwick D. & Cardew G. (eds), *Dental Enamel* (Ciba Foundation Symposium 205), 226–45. Chichester: Wiley.

WHITTICK A. (1960). *Symbols, Signs and their Meaning*. London: Leonard Hill.

WHO (2002) *Fluorides* (Environmental Health Criteria 227). Geneva: World Health Organization.

WIESSNER P. (2001). Brewing change: Enga feasts in an historical perspective (Papua, New Guinea). In: Hayden B. & Dietler M. (eds), *The Archaeological Importance of Feasting*, 115–43. Washington, DC: Smithsonian Institution Press.

WIEWANDT T.A. (1977). Pigs. In: *Unit Plan for the Management of Mona Island Forest Reserve*, 182–212. San Juan: Forestry Task Force, Puerto Rico Department of Natural Resources.

WILKENS B. (1996). Faunal remains from Italian excavations on Crete. In: Reese D.S. (ed.), *Pleistocene and Holocene Fauna of Crete and Its First Settlers* (Monographs in World Archaeology 28), 241–61. Madison, WI: Prehistory Press.

—— (2000). Faunal remains from Tell Afis (Syria). In: Mashkour M., Choyke A.M., Buitenhuis H. & Poplin F. (eds), *Archaeozoology of the Near East IV* (ARC-Publicatie 32), 29–39. Groningen: Centre for Archaeological Research & Consultancy.

WILKINS J.V. & MARTINEZ L. (1983). Bolivia. An investigation of sow productivity in humid lowland villages. *World Animal* 47, 15–18.

WILSON B., GRIGSON C. & PAYNE S. (1982). *Ageing and Sexing Animal Bones from Archaeological Sites* (BAR British Series 109). Oxford: British Archaeological Reports.

WILSON D.M. (2003). *Resources, roles, and conflict: active resource management in the Anglo-Norman kingdom.* Master's thesis, Department of History, University of Houston.

WINTHER J. (1935–8). *Troldebjerg* (main volume and supplement). Rudkøbing: privately published.

WISEMAN J. (2000). *The Pig. A British History.* London: Duckworth.

WITT G.B., BERGHAMMER L.J., BEETON R.J.S. & MOLL E.J. (2000). Retrospective monitoring of rangeland vegetation: ecohistory from deposits of sheep dung associated with shearing sheds. *Australian Ecology* 25, 260–7.

WODZICKI K.A. (1950). Introduced mammals of New Zealand: an ecological and economic survey. *New Zealand Department of Scientific and Industrial Research Bulletin* 98.

WOOD G.W. & BARRETT R.M. (1979). Status of wild pigs in the United States. *Wildife Society Bulletin* 7, 237–46.

WOOLEY S.L. (1955). *Alalakh, an account of the Excavations at Tell Atchana in the Hatay, 1937–1949.* Oxford: Society of Antiquaries of London.

WRIGHT H. (1969). *The Administration of Rural Production in an Early Mesopotamian Town* (Anthropological Papers, Museum of Anthropology, University of Michigan 38). Ann Arbor, MI: University of Michigan.

—— MILLER N. & REDDING R. (1980). Time and process in an Uruk rural centre. In: Barrelet M.T. (ed.), *L'Archéologie de l'Iraq du debut de l'Epoche Neolithique avant notre Ère* (Colloques International du CNRS 580), 265–82. Paris: Éditions du CNRS.

WRIGHT T. & HALLIWELL J.O. (1841). *Reliquia Antiquae I. Early English Poetry, Ballards, and Popular Literature of the Middle Ages.* London: The Percy Society.

WYATT N. (1981). Ba'al's boars. *Ugarit Forschungen* 19, 391–8.

YAMAZAKI K. (1997). Faunal remains from Aikoshima shell midden. *Report of Cultural Properties of Iwaki City* 47(2), 1–92 [in Japanese].

—— TAKAHASHI O., SUGAWARA H., ISHIGURO N. & ENDO H. (2005). Wild boar remains from the Neolithic (Jomon Period) sites on the Izu islands and in Hokkaido, Japan. In: Vigne J.-D., Peters J. & Helmer D. (eds), *The First Steps of Animal Domestication, Proceedings of the 9th ICAZ Conference, Durham 2002*, 160–76. Oxford: Oxbow Books.

YELLEN J. (1977). Cultural patterning in faunal remains: evidence from the !Kung Bushmen. In: Ingersoll D., Yellen J. & MacDonald W. (eds), *Experimental Archaeology*, 271–331. New York: Columbia University Press.

YON M. (1985). Baal et le roi. In: Huot J.L., Yon M. & Calvet Y. (eds), *De l'Indus aux Balkans: recueil à la mémoire de Jean Deshayes*, 177–90. Paris: Éditions Recherches sur les Civilisations.

—— (1997). *La Cité d'Ougarit sur le Tell de Ras Shamra* (Guides archéologiques de l'IFAPO 2). Paris: IFAPO.

YONEDA M., SUZUKI R., SHIBATA Y., MORITA M., SUKEGAWA T., SHIGEHARA N. & AKAZAWA T. (2004). Isotopic evidence of inland-water fishing by a Jomon population excavated from the Boji site, Nagano, Japan. *Journal of Archaeological Science* 31, 97–107.

YUAN J. (2001). The problem of the origin of domestic animals in the Chinese Neolithic. *Wenwu* 2001(5), 51–8 [in Chinese].

—— & FLAD R.K. (2002). Pig domestication in ancient China. *Antiquity* 76 (293), 724–32.

—— & TANG J. (2000). A study of the animal bones from the Huanyuanzhuang site north of the Huanshui River in Anyang City, Henan. *Kaogu* 11, 75–81.

ZEDER M.A. (1990). Animal exploitation at Tell Halif. In: Seger J.D. *et al.* (eds), Bronze Age settlements at Tell Halif: phase II excavations, 1983–1987. *Bulletin American Schools Oriental Research. Supplement* 26, 1–32.

—— (1991). *Feeding Cities: Specialized Animal Economy in the Ancient Near East* (Smithsonian Series in Archaeological Inquiry). Washington, DC: Smithsonian Institution.

—— (1994). After the revolution: post-Neolithic subsistence in Northern Mesopotamia. *American Anthropologist* 96, 97–126.

—— (1995). The role of pigs in Middle Eastern subsistence: a view from the southern Levant. In: Seger J. (ed.), *Retrieving the Past: Essays on Archaeological Research and Methodology in Honour of Gus van Beek*, 297–312. Winona Lake, IN: Eisenbrauns.

—— (1998*a*). Regional patterns of animal exploitation in the Khabur basin, 7000 to 1500 BC. In: Anreiter P., Bartosiewicz L., Jerem E. & Meid W. (eds), *Man and the Animal World: Studies in Archaeozoology, Archaeology, Anthropology and Palaeolinguistics, In Memoriam Sándor Bökönyi*, 569–80. Budapest: Archaeolingua Kiadó.

—— (1998*b*). Pigs and emergent complexity in the Near East. In: Nelson S.M. (ed.), *Ancestors for the Pigs. Pigs in Prehistory* (MASCA Research Papers in Science and Archaeology 15), 109–22. Philadelphia: University of Pennsylvania Museum of Archaeology and Anthropology.

—— (1999). Animal domestication in the Zagros: a review of the past and current research. *Paleorient* 25(2), 11–25.

—— (2001). A metrical analysis of a collection of modern goats (*Capra hircus aegargus* and *C. h.* hircus) from Iran and Iraq: Implications for the study of caprine domestication. *Journal of Archaeological Science* 28(1), 61–79.

—— (2003). Food provisioning in urban societies, a view from Northern Mesopotamia. In: Smith M.L. (ed.), *The Social Construction of Ancient Cities*, 156–83. Washington, DC: Smithsonian Books.

—— & ARTER S.R. (1994). Changing patterns of animal utilization at ancient Gordion. *Paléorient* 20(2), 105–18.

ZERVOS C. (1956). *L'art de la Crète néolithique et minoéenne.* Paris: Éditions Cahiers d'Art.

ZOHARY M. (1962). *Plant Life of Palestine.* New York: Ronald Press.

—— (1973). *Geobotanical Foundations of the Middle East.* Stuttgart: Gustav Fischer.

ZÖLLNER S. (1977). *Lebensbaum und Schweinekult. Die Religion der Jali im Bergland von Irian-Jaya (West-New-Guinea).* Darmstadt: Theologischen Verlag Rolf Brockhaus.

ZVELEBIL M. (1995). Hunting, gathering, or husbandry? Management of food resources by the late mesolithic communities of temperate Europe. *MASCA Research Papers in Science and Archaeology. Supplement* 12, 79–104.